WOMEN in FILM

An International Guide

WOMEN in FILM

An International Guide

Edited by   Annette Kuhn
with   Susannah Radstone

Fawcett Columbine ·
New York

A Fawcett Columbine Book
Published by Ballantine Books

Library of Congress Catalog Card Number: 89-92613

ISBN: 0-449-90575-6

Grateful acknowledgment is made to the following individuals or archives for
providing photographs for use on the cover (counterclockwise beginning with top
photo in left hand column):

Bhumika—National Film Archive, London, England; Dorothy Arzner—Photofest,
New York, NY; *Den Muso*—Souleymane Cissé; Marlene Dietrich—Swedish Film
Institute, Stockholm, Sweden; Susan Seidelman—Photofest, New York, NY; *Diary
for My Children*—Artificial Eye Film Company Ltd, London, England; Agnes
Varda—Photofest, New York, NY; Ida Lupino—Photofest, New York, NY;
Olivia—Circles: Womens Film and Video Distribution, London, England; Lina
Wertmuller—Photofest, New York, NY; Esther Ralston—Photofest, New York,
NY; Jean Harlow—The Hulton Picture Company, London, England; Agnes
Varda—Photofest, New York, NY; Gillian Armstrong—Photofest, New York,
NY

Cover design by William Geller

Manufactured in the United States of America

First American Edition: January 1991
10 9 8 7 6 5 4 3 2 1

CONTENTS

Preface and acknowledgements   vii

The contributors   xi

Women in Film: An International Guide   I

Answers to trivia boxes   438

Index of films directed, written or produced by women   440

General index   465

PREFACE *and* ACKNOWLEDGEMENTS

Women in Film: An International Guide is the outcome of several years' effort by a substantial number of people. Work began in earnest on the project, which was first conceived in 1986, early in 1988. Around six hundred entries written by seventy-nine contributors – writers, scholars, film critics, filmmakers – from many countries were commissioned and written throughout 1988 and most of 1989.

As a work of reference, the *Guide* ranges over the entire spectrum of cinema – both historically and geographically – in terms of personalities and film movements. It also deals with ideas and concepts in film theory and criticism, and includes explanations of 'technical' terms and jargon in regular use in critical writing on film, with the aim of making specialist writing in these areas (and perhaps even some of the entries in the *Guide*!) more accessible to the 'lay' cinemagoer. This commitment to accessibility and comprehensiveness is combined with a particular approach to the content of the *Guide* – one shaped by feminist perspectives. None of the many, and often very useful, cinema reference books currently available offers this distinctive mix of viewpoint and coverage.

No single-volume reference book can realistically hope fully to cover an entire subject area, however; and decisions on what to include in the *Guide* have been guided consciously throughout by its feminist commitment. Editorial choices have consequently been made in relation to the overall objectives of bringing to the fore contributions by women – inadequately acknowledged, unfortunately, in existing reference books in the field – to the history and development of cinema; and of shedding fresh light on the accepted film canon. Far from making the *Guide* a work of purely sectional interest, this approach, we hope, will provoke debates and incite curiosity about cinema – its past, its present, and its future – not just among women and feminists, but among filmgoers of other genders and persuasions, too.

Within an overall editorial program shaped by these objectives, contributors to the *Guide* were invited to write entries on specified topics. For some of these topics – the majority of national cinemas, most especially – contributors decided upon their own entry headings, though always within editorially predefined parameters as to overall coverage and constraints on entry length. Thus while the *Guide*'s authority as a work of reference owes everything to its contributors' expertise, final responsibility for what is included here (and, of course, for what is excluded) lies with its editors.

Among the areas most exhaustively covered in the *Guide* are the various national cinemas – virtually all of the world's cinemas are discussed, though not every country has its own separate entry. In the West, cinema is often equated with Hollywood: and while acknowledging the fascination of Hollywood and the cultural dominance of the US film industry, the *Guide* seeks to encourage users to consider these within an international framework.

Just as comprehensively covered as national cinemas, however, are women directors of the past. Nevertheless it has been impossible to discuss all of the many women directors at work today, nor many of the numerous women who have ever worked in the world's film industries in other capacities; though coverage in both these areas is nonetheless more extensive than in other cinema reference books. We have been highly selective where actresses and male directors, especially those working in Hollywood, are concerned – on the grounds that such personalities are well documented elsewhere. Where a decision has been made to include a male director or an actress, this is on the grounds of his or her significance in feminist debates on cinema, or more generally of the interest his or her work holds for women.

Each contributor was urged, whilst bearing in mind the *Guide*'s overall objectives, to approach her particular topics in her own way. It would have been inappropriate, especially with such a wide coverage of cultures and national cinemas, to impose any single view or editorial 'line' on writers. The result is a purposefully intended diversity, a multiplicity of voices that we very much hope combines in a melodic chorus.

One of the outcomes – at once both cheering and a little daunting – of our project is that it has brought to light numerous gaps in knowledge about the world's cinemas, and many inadequacies in our own critical and theoretical approaches to them, as well some rather promising and as yet unexplored areas of filmmaking practice. While this state of affairs obviously might have to do in some measure with the editors' cultural backgrounds and education, it is also (and much more significantly) connected with the larger limitations of western approaches to film criticism and the writing of film history. Some of the *Guide*'s absences and shortcomings are more excusable than others: all of them, we hope, will prompt new research and fresh approaches to film theory and criticism, as well as lively discussion in kitchens and seminar rooms.

In the tradition of the reference book, entries in the *Guide* are arranged alphabetically; and contributors are credited at the end of each entry by their initials (a key to contributors' initials, together with brief biographical details, follows this introduction). Most of the entries include a suggestion for further reading material about the topic or personality covered, and wherever possible reference is made to material published in English and in print at the time of writing. (Readers finding difficulty obtaining material through bookshops are advised to inquire at a local college or public library.)

Every entry on a personality carries basic biographical information in addition to a discussion of the individual's work in cinema. Entries on filmmakers include filmographies: for women filmmakers (with a handful of exceptions – usually where films have been lost or are unattributable for some other reason) filmographies are always complete. For male filmmakers details of whose work are readily available in other publications, filmographies are usually selective. For non-English-language films, original release titles are given at least once per entry, together, where appropriate, with English and/or US release titles.

The majority of entries incorporate references across to other entries in the *Guide*. Where such crossreferences are given within the main body of the entry, they appear in small capitals; and additional crossreferences are sometimes to be found at the end of an entry. Crossreferencing has been designed to allow readers to follow arguments, historical developments, and connections across widely dispersed entries. While some crossreferences will be primarily informative – as when a contributor uses a theoretical concept which is explained elsewhere in the *Guide* – or are aimed at providing a map of a topic by reference to other entries in the same subject area, others may lead the reader along unexpected avenues and byways. The entry on Louise BROOKS, for example, can lead to FEMINIST INDEPENDENT FILM, via WEIMAR CINEMA and MELODRAMA: the same entry could equally well be the starting point for any number of other intriguing trails. . . .

Women in Film: An International Guide aims to be informative, refreshing, and provocative: to be an authoritative source of information on aspects of film history, criticism, and theory not covered in other cinema reference books; while at the same time offering the reader hours of pleasurable exploration and enhancing her or his enjoyment of films.

The editors acknowledge with gratitude the assistance and support of many friends and colleagues in the production of *Women in Film: An International Guide*. For their help in making contact with contributors, our thanks to Tuike Alitalo, Rosa Bosch, Julianne Burton, Richard Dyer, Brian Horrocks, Keyan Tomaselli, and Ginette Vincendeau. For supplying illustrations, thanks are due to Artificial Eye, Cinema of Women, Circles, the National Film Archive, and to many of the contributors. For production assistance, thanks are due to Claudia Brusdeylins, Patrizia Niedzwiecki, and Ulrike Sieglohr for their work on translations; to Samantha Cook, who undertook calmly, cheerfully and with immense efficiency the daunting task of checking all the entries for accuracy and consistency; and to Susan Critchlow for her very professional typing of a substantial portion of the manuscript.

Philippa Brewster's contribution to the project has been immeasurable. From her came the original idea for the *Guide*, and her input into its planning and overall design has been more than considerable. Throughout its production she has provided indispensable support in various forms, not the least among which being editorial suggestions on many contributions, and devising of trivia questions and answers. Finally, we must thank all of our contributors for their enthusiasm, for the expert knowledge and thorough research that have gone into each and every entry, and for the patience with which they have borne the project's many vicissitudes.

THE CONTRIBUTORS

AB   Annette Brauerhoch, West German film scholar and critic; an editor of *Frauen und Film*, Europe's only feminist film journal.

AF   Annette Foerster, Netherlands-based freelance journalist and film publicist specializing in women's cinema; co-organizer of the International Gay and Lesbian Film Festival Holland, 1986.

AG   Alison Gumbley, Film Studies graduate of the University of East Anglia; currently coordinator of the Norwich Women's Film Weekend and an organizer of the Birmingham Film and Television Festival.

AH   Ann Hardy, a video director who also writes and lectures in film theory at Victoria University, Wellington, New Zealand.

AKo   Anu Koivunen, student of film at the University of Turku; currently completing a doctoral thesis on Finnish women's films of the 1930s and 1940s.

AKu   Annette Kuhn, editor of the present volume and lecturer in Film and TV Studies at the University of Glasgow; has published widely on film theory, feminism and representation, and cinema history.

ALi   Amanda Lipman, former editor of the London listings magazine *City Limits*; writer and broadcaster on film.

ALo   Ana López, assistant professor of Communication at Tulane University, New Orleans; extensive publications on Latin American film include *The New Latin American Cinema*.

AM   Angela Martin, freelance film and video editor, teacher and writer; compiler of the British Film Institute dossier *African Films*, and contributor to TV programs on African and Arab cinemas.

ASW   Astrid Soederbergh Widding, lecturer in Cinema Arts at the University of Stockholm.

AW   Andrea Weiss, US writer and filmmaker currently living in London; co-director of *International Sweethearts of Rhythm*, and author of *Vampires and Violets: Lesbianism in the Cinema*.

BC   Barbara Creed, lecturer in Film at La Trobe University, Melbourne; has published widely in the area of feminist film theory, and is currently writing a book on women in the horror film.

BE   Barbara Einhorn, specialist on the situation of women, women's literature, and women's organizations in Eastern Europe, with particular reference to East Germany.

BF   Brigitte Filion, graduate of Concordia University's (Montreal) Cinema Department; currently studying at the Sorbonne in Paris.

BKQ   Barbara Koenig Quart, author of *Women Directors: The Emergence of a New Cinema*, and of articles and reviews for US journals *The Nation, Ms,* and *Film Quarterly*.

BR   Behjat Rezaei, Iranian writer and film critic based in London, whose work has appeared in *Teheran Moussavvare, Spare Rib, Asian Times,* and other publications.

CB   Charlotte Brunsdon, lecturer in Film Studies at the University of Warwick, and editor of the collection *Films for Women*.

CF   Carol Flinn, assistant professor of English at the University of Florida in Gainesville, whose essays on feminist theory, film sound and music have been published in *Wide Angle, Screen,* and other journals.

CG   Christine Gledhill, London-based freelance writer and lecturer, mother of two sons, and editor of *Home Is Where the Heart Is: Studies in Melodrama and the Woman's Film*.

CH-N   Carmen Huaco-Nuzum, PhD candidate in the Department of History of Consciousness, University of California, Santa Cruz, researching systems of representation and the image of the latina in Mexican film.

CM   Caroline Merz, co-founder of the Norwich Women's Film Weekend; author of *After the Vote*, a history of the Townswomen's Guild movement.

CS   Cherry Smyth, London-based freelance writer and community video worker, currently editing a book on the representation of women in cinema.

DJY   Denise J Youngblood, professor of Soviet History at the University of Vermont, specializing in popular cinema and the cultural politics of the Soviet film industry.

EAK   E Ann Kaplan, Director of the Humanities Institute in the State University of New York at Stony Brook; author of *Women and Film: Both Sides of the Camera*.

ER   Esther Ronay, born in Hungary, an independent filmmaker active in the women and film movement in Britain since the early 1970s; member of the London Women's Film Group from 1970 to 1976, and now a film editor, film tutor, and TV director.

ES   Ella Shohat, assistant professor of Cinema Studies at the City University of New York; author of *Israeli Cinema: East/West and the Politics of Representation*.

EY   Esther Yau, PhD candidate at the University of California, Los Angeles, whose writings have been published in *Film Quarterly* and *Discourse*.

FC   Felicity Collins, lecturer in Film Theory and Criticism at Melbourne University Institute of Education, who has published extensively on independent and feminist film, and on Australian film institutions.

FF   Freda Freiberg, lecturer in Cinema Studies in the Visual Arts Department at Monash University, Melbourne, whose publications include *Women in Mizoguchi Films*, and *Don't Shoot Darling: Women's Independent Filmmaking in Australia*.

GB   Giuliana Bruno, Italian film theorist and critic currently teaching at Bard College, New York; co-editor of *Off Screen: Women and Film in Italy*.

GS   Gillian Swanson, lecturer in Film, Media, and Women's Studies at Griffith University, Queensland, and a corresponding editor for *Screen*.

GV   Ginette Vincendeau, lecturer in Film Studies at the University of Warwick and member of the editorial board of *Screen*; co-editor of *French Film: Texts and Contexts*, and currently working on a book on French cinema in the 1930s.

HP-C   Hsiung-ping Chiao, Taiwan-based film critic for the *China Times Express* and author of four books on Taiwan, Hong Kong, and Hollywood films.

HS   Heiny Srour, Lebanese-born scriptwriter and filmmaker now working in London; formerly film critic specializing in Arab and Third World cinemas.

IK   Irene Kotlarz, Director of the Bristol Animation Festival and freelance consultant, programmer, and lecturer on animation.

JaS   Janet Staiger, associate professor teaching Critical and Cultural Studies at the University of Texas, Austin; co-author of *The Classical Hollywood Cinema: Film Style and Mode of Production to 1960*.

JBo   Jacqueline Bobo, assistant professor of Radio, Television and Motion Pictures at the University of North Carolina, Chapel Hill, who has written on black women's reception of the film *The Color Purple*.

JBu   Julianne Burton, professor of Latin American Literature and Film at the University of California, Santa Cruz; editor of *Cinema and Social Change in Latin America* and *The Social Documentary in Latin America*.

JcS   Jackie Stacey, lecturer in the Sociology Department at Lancaster University, is completing a PhD on the construction and reception of female stars in Hollywood in the 1940s and 1950s.

JG   June Givanni, program advisor at the British Film Institute, specializing in black films; coordinator of Third Eye: London's Festival of Third World Cinema (1983); and organizer of the Greater London Council's anti-racist film program (1984–5).

JK   Julia Knight, freelance writer working in the independent film and video sector in Britain; currently writing a book on West German women filmmakers.

JL   Jacqueline Levitin, filmmaker and film critic, teaches at Concordia University in Montreal and at Simon Fraser University, Vancouver; films include *Pas fou comme on le pense (Not Crazy Like You Think)*.

JRo   Jane Root, London-based series producer of Channel Four Television's weekly program *The Media Show*; author of *Pictures of Women* and *Open the Box*.

JRy   Janet Ryland, Deputy Head of the School of Media, Arts, Design at Solihull College of Technology; research interests include feminist art practice.

JSh   Judith Shulevitz, writer and critic based in New York; studied film at Yale University and the University of Paris III, and writes for the *New York Times Book Review*, *Social Policy*, and other magazines.

JT   Janet Thumim, London-based teacher of art history and film studies, currently writing a book on women in popular cinema.

JYY   Joanne Y Yamada, a Communication specialist at the John A Burns Medical School at the University of Hawaii, writes regularly on cinema for the *Hawaii Herald* and has curated two Japanese film series for the Honolulu Academy of Arts.

KA   Kay Armatage, filmmaker, senior programmer for the Toronto Festival of Festivals, and assistant professor at the University of Toronto, where she is Chair of Women's Studies and teaches Cinema Studies.

KL-J   Kally Lloyd-Jones, formerly a classical dancer, studied Film and TV at Glasgow University, and is now working on a book on dance and film.

LF   Lilie Ferrari, London-based freelance writer and researcher specializing in film and television aimed at female audiences; currently co-editing a book on teaching popular music.

LR   Lorna Rasmussen, a filmmaker and teacher working with the US independent distribution cooperative New Day Films.

LS   Lesley Stern, lecturer in Film and Theater at the University of New South Wales; has written widely on feminism and cinema.

MBH   Mary Beth Haralovich, professor of Film History at the University of Arizona; research interests include the social history of the Hollywood film.

ME   Maria Enzensberger, lecturer in Film Studies at Staffordshire Polytechnic, contributor to *Screen*, and editor/translator of volume III of Sergei Eisenstein's *Selected Writings*.

MKe   Marjorie Keller, professor in the Department of Art, University of Rhode Island, and filmmaker whose work includes *Misconception*, *Daughters of Chaos*, and *The Answering Furrow*.

MKo   Maaret Koskinen, lecturer in the Department of Theater and Cinema Studies, Stockholm University, and film critic for the Swedish national newspaper *Dagensnyheter*.

MMc   Marsha McCreadie, author of *Women on Film: The Critical Eye*, is daily film reviewer for the *Arizona Republic*, and has contributed to *American Film*, *Literature/Film Quarterly*, *Films in Review*, and *Film Comment*.

MMo   Meaghan Morris, full-time writer who worked for several years as a film critic for the *Sydney Morning Herald* and the *Australian Financial Review*; author of *The Pirate's Fiancee: Feminism, Reading, Postmodernism*.

NT   Nissa Torrents, born in Barcelona, is lecturer in Latin American Film and Narrative at University College, London, and has published extensively on art, film, and literature.

PB   Philippa Brewster, former editor of the Cinema list at Routledge & Kegan Paul; co-founder and editorial director of the feminist imprint Pandora Press.

PC   Pam Cook, associate editor of the *Monthly Film Bulletin* at the British Film Institute; editor and co-writer of *The Cinema Book*.

PW   Patricia White, distribution coordinator at Women Make Movies, the feminist film distributor based in New York City.

RB   Rosa Bosch, deputy head of programming of the National Film Theatre/London Film Festival.

RET   Ruth Elizabeth Tomaselli, based at the Contemporary Cultural Studies Unit at the University of Natal, Durban, has co-edited two books on the media and one on ethnographic film.

RT   Rosie Thomas, lecturer in Film Theory at Harrow College of Higher Education, has researched and written widely on Indian popular cinema.

SB   Sarah Butterfield, a British-born photographer and filmmaker now living in Montreal, has recently completed *Intérieur nuit/Working Nights* for the National Film Board of Canada.

SHa   Sylvia Harvey, lecturer in Film and Cultural History at Sheffield City Polytechnic; author of *May '68 and Film Culture*, and of articles on independent cinema and documentary film.

SHi   Sumiko Higashi, professor of History and Film at the State University of New York, Brockport; author of *Virgins, Vamps and Flappers: The American Silent Movie Heroine*.

SM   Stephanie McBride, lecturer in Film and Media Studies at Dublin City University; formerly Education Officer at the Irish Film Institute.

SP   Sylvia Paskin, London-based writer, researcher, and lecturer on literature, the media, and feminism; regular reviewer for the *Monthly Film Bulletin* and co-editor of two poetry anthologies.

SR   Susannah Radstone, assistant editor of the present volume, lecturer in Film, English and Cultural Studies at the University of Keele, and editor of *Sweet Dreams: Sexuality, Gender and Popular Culture*.

TA   Tuike Alitalo, journalist and film critic; vice-president of the Finnish Society for Film Studies.

TP   Tessa Perkins, senior lecturer in Communication Studies at Sheffield City Polytechnic; author of articles on stereotypes, Doris Day, and *Supergirl*.

TS   Tytti Soila, lecturer in the Department of Theater and Cinema Studies at Stockholm University.

US   Ulrike Sieglohr, lecturer in Film Studies in various institutions in London; currently researching postwar European art cinema.

VR   Veronika Rall, PhD candidate in History of Consciousness at the University of California, Santa Cruz; author of articles in *Frauen and Film* and *Beitrage fuer Film- und Fernsehwissenschaft*.

WJA   Wendy Jill Annecke, teacher of mathematics and English as a second language, MA student, single parent, and member of the South African women's pro-democracy organization, Black Sash.

ZB   Zuzana Blueh, Czech-born and now London-based freelance journalist, translator, and broadcaster; contributor to *Index on Censorship*, *New York Review of Books*, *Stern*, and other publications.

ZP   Zuzana Pick, associate professor of Film Studies at Carleton University, Ottawa, was born in Czechoslovakia and grew up in Colombia; editor of *Latin American Filmmakers and the Third Cinema*.

WOMEN IN FILM
An International Guide

ABORIGINAL FILM AND VIDEO

Aborigines have figured prominently in the cinema of AUSTRALIA since its beginnings – but they have figured as subjects of, and performers in, films made by white filmmakers. It is only recently that they have gained access to the means of production in independent film and video and thus acquired a voice in and some control over their own representation.

White anthropologists, missionaries and adventurers made numerous ETHNOGRAPHIC FILMS about aboriginal communities in the first half of the twentieth century; and exhibited them without regard for aboriginal law, which restricts the viewing of ceremonies and people according to rigorous guidelines. In the third quarter of the century, a number of more respectful films on aboriginal culture were made by documentary filmmakers employed by government film units, but only in the late 1970s did aborigines actually collaborate with white independent filmmakers, who were sympathetic to the cause of aboriginal land rights and connected with the politically radical Sydney Filmmakers Co-operative in the production of films on aboriginal issues. Aboriginal matriarch Essie Coffey narrated and co-directed *My Survival as an Aboriginal* in 1979, while the entire Borroloola community was involved in creative decision-making on the production of *Two Laws* (1981), a four-part DOCUMENTARY dealing with the struggles of the community through direct testimonies and dramatic reenactments of past and present conflicts with the white authorities. These two documentaries are notable not just for the involvement of aboriginal individuals or communities in production, but also for the inclusion of the aboriginal woman's voice, a voice largely absent from the documentaries of male anthropologists and filmmakers. This was a result of the participation of radical women directors (Martha Ansara and Carolyn Strachan, respectively) who established close relations with the black women in the communities they were filming.

As a result of political lobbying, aboriginal individuals and communities gained increased access to the media in the 1980s. Individual women have recently begun to produce, write and direct short films and videos which represent aboriginal women with strength, pride and humor. Tracey Moffatt's *Nice Coloured Girls* (1987) is notable for its bold confident tone and playful experimenting with film form. Lorraine Mafi-Williams's *Eelemani: The Story of Leo and Leva* (1988) is a more conventional combination of documentary and drama, narrated compellingly and humorously by aboriginal storyteller and elder Millie Boyd. A network of aboriginal communities, linked through the Central Australian Aboriginal Media Association (CAAMA), now produces audio and video programs and distributes them throughout Central Australia, thus ensuring continuity of their languages and cultures and representation of their views. CAAMA has formed a company, Imparja, which secured the Remote Commercial Television Satellite license for broadcast to the whole of Central Australia. The noncommercial national television networks ABC and SBS have also recently introduced magazine programs on aboriginal issues with aboriginal presenters.

As yet, there has been no feature film

My Survival as an Aboriginal, by Essie Coffey

wholly produced and directed by aboriginal people, and the feature film industry continues to represent them as noble savages, jokesters or pathetic victims. The two most popular features amongst aboriginal audiences are *Jedda* (Chauvel, 1955) which, despite its patronizing narration, invests the tribal aboriginal male protagonist with phallic power and dramatizes the failure of white society to 'civilize' aboriginal woman; and *Wrong Side of the Road* (Lander, 1981), an episodic road movie centering on the lives and performances of two aboriginal rock groups, No Fixed Address and Us Mob.

Michael Leigh, 'Curiouser and Curiouser', in *Back of Beyond: Discovering Australian Film and Television*, ed. Scott Murray (Sydney: Australian Film Commission, 1988)

See also: MAORI FILM; NATIVE AMERICAN FILM; NATIVE CANADIAN FILM   FF

ABREU, GILDA DE (1904–79)

BRAZILIAN filmmaker Gilda de Abreu was a remarkable person. A singer of operetta and popular song, she was also a songwriter and actress who went into scriptwriting, directing and producing, founding her own production and distribution company, Pro Arte, in 1951. She directed *O ebrio* (1946), one of Brazil's most popular films ever, and her later melodrama *Coração de madre* (1951) was also a great hit. It was not easy to command respect in the 1940s film sets but Gilda de Abreu, dressed in trousers, managed with great success to break into a man's world.

O ebrio/The Drunkard (1946); *Coração de madre/A Mother's Heart* (1951)

Elice Munerato and Maria Elena Darcy de Oliveira, 'When Women Film', in *Brazilian Cinema*, ed. Randal Johnson and Robert Stam (Rutherford, NJ: Fairleigh Dickinson University Press, 1982)
                                        NT

ACTING

Acting styles vary enormously historically and culturally. What is regarded as 'good' acting in one culture or at one time can seem stilted or excessive in another.

In the West acting styles have moved progressively toward naturalism, and away from more formal approaches to PERFORMANCE characteristic of theatrical acting at the beginning of the century. While in SILENT CINEMA highly stylized performances were encouraged, the advent of SOUND and the development of increasingly sophisticated EDITING and MISE-EN-SCENE made such performances appear excessive – though developments in film technology should be seen as enabling such changes rather than necessitating them. The move to naturalistic acting in western cinema was associated with the emphasis on fully rounded characters which characterizes CLASSICAL HOLLYWOOD CINEMA. In the USA, Lee Strasberg's Actors' Studio trained large numbers of American film actors in the 'Method' – a quintessentially naturalistic acting style which emphasizes emotionality. Consequently, male performances (such as those by Marlon Brando and James Dean) became 'feminized,' placing a question mark over the place of female performers in American films of the fifties and early sixties. British film actors have been far less influenced by the Method, and British acting styles still seem more formal than American. There is evidence of ethnocentrism among western critics, who often fail to acknowledge the legitimacy of cultural differences in acting styles: INDIA's popular cinema, for example, has been dismissed because of its non-naturalistic acting.

Acting is one of the few professions in which women have been able to succeed, though even here discrimination exists in terms of both the range and the types of roles available. It is, however, worth noting that – until recently at least – male film STARS were much more likely than female stars to be discussed in terms of their acting ability. This is probably an extension of the view of man as active and woman as spectacle: passive object of the LOOK rather than initiator of action.

'Acting', special issue of *Screen*, vol. 26, no. 5 (1985)   TP

ADVERTISING

The exchange value of female SEXUALITY has long been central to film advertising practices and the film industry has been well aware of the role of advertising in mediating representations of women. This link has been most fully exploited in Hollywood, where in the heyday of the HOLLYWOOD STUDIO SYSTEM film advertising was governed by an Advertising Code, similar to the PRODUCTION CODE which oversaw the content of films. Written in 1930, the Advertising Code was not widely enforced until 1933 when, in response to public criticism, an Advertising Advisory Council was created to approve all aspects of advertising campaigns prior to their release. A full range of Hollywood film advertising can be found in pressbooks, forerunners to today's smaller presskits. Prepared by the studios for distribution to exhibitors for use in advertising and promoting films, pressbooks could have a dozen or more oversized pages offering stories about the film's production and stars to plant in newspapers, ballyhoo exploitation ideas, information on the promotion of tie-ins, and art mattes for newspaper advertising. Considered historically, pressbooks show changes in the way female sexuality has been used to advertise films. After 1933 the Advertising Advisory Council required that film advertising tone down its use of female sexuality, with the result that women were represented as more wholesome (more fully clad and less overtly sexual) than previously. With World War II and the wide popularity of 'candid-camera' magazines in the 1940s, the exploitation of female sexuality returned through the display of the female figure in the pinup.

Still photography is central to film advertising, forming the basis of poster art and publicity. Each Hollywood studio had its ranks of still photographers, some of whom, like George Hurrell, became quite famous for glamor photography. 1940s discussions in *International Photographer*, the still photographers' professional journal, show the centrality

Gold Diggers of 1933 **lobby display**

of female sexuality in the design and conception of still photography. Categories of stills included: poster (designed to illustrate or sell), portrait (formally posed), glamor (an abstraction of sex or beauty), sex art (sex interest is dominant, but appears casual and natural), home art (illustrates way of life), leg art (satisfies interest in model's figure). Advice to photographers on instructing their models was directed at the attainment of an idealized feminine body: 'sit flat' (weight on buttocks for illusion of more slender hips), 'palms up' (feminine hands), 'arch the back' (breasts are lifted), 'on your toes' (lengthen legs and improve ankle line). When asked why the standard procedure in Hollywood advertising was to take cheesecake photographs of STARS and starlets, one publicist commented: 'Because girls sold, that's why, and they still do.' Yet feminist critical and historical perspectives show that film advertising partici-

pates in the construction and distribution of a female sexuality which is neither 'natural' nor unchanging, but very much related to the film industry and the wider society.

Mary Beth Haralovich, 'Film Advertising, the Film Industry and the Pin-up: The Industry's Accommodations to Social Forces in the 1940s', *Current Research in Film, Volume I*, ed. Bruce Austin (Norwood, NJ: Ablex, 1985)

See also: CONSUMERISM; FANDOM; FASHION; FILM CRITICISM   MBH

AFRICA

A continent of many peoples with distinct identities, languages, cultures and a rich and civilized history plundered by European colonialism, Africa had been definitively carved up by England, France, Belgium and Portugal by 1900. Frontiers were laid down which split peoples as effectively as the Berlin Wall: millions of Africans had already been snatched and sold into slavery and thousands more would be forced into foreign armies, fighting each other in wars that did not concern them. By 1900, too, the last of the great warriors against colonialism had been quashed. By the end of World War II, however, not only was there renewed determination to win Africa back, but changes in world trade and production patterns meant that the cost of maintaining the colonies was no longer profitable to Europe. In the years around 1960 most of the territories below the Sahara and above South Africa (known as Black Africa) were shed; but not before their continued economic dependence on Europe and their self-definition as 'nation states' had been ensured. International trading, patterns of agriculture, means of transport and communication, even education, were all determined by – and for the benefit of – Europe.

This brief but traumatic moment in Africa's history is the soil in which her cinema tried to grow, and even today women are virtually invisible behind the camera: Thérèse Sita-Bella, a Cameroonian journalist, has made nothing since *Tam-tam à Paris* (1963); Sarah MALDOROR is a Guadeloupian living in France who made only a few films in Africa. Aside from these, and one or two newcomers, Safi FAYE remains the principal African woman filmmaker. However, African filmmakers in general have had a greater struggle to work than those in almost any other part of the world. The environment in which African cinema has grown has not been a healthy one. From early days, for example, films were shown in the colonies for a mixture of educational and entertainment purposes, mainly by missionaries and colonial officers (a film for Rhodesia [Zimbabwe] showed young girls how to become good maids, for example); and of course ETHNOGRAPHIC FILMS were also made by Europeans. As commercial distribution and exhibition circuits grew up in Europe, these were extended to create audiences for European films in Africa. In 1946 the Motion Picture Export Association of America (MPEAA) was formed with a view to colonizing the world's screens; and after the African independences were established major US companies like WARNER BROS and MGM formed a single company to distribute their films in anglophone Africa. The (British) Colonial Film Unit was by this time defunct; but Belgian, French and Portuguese companies continued to operate in the former colonies of those countries.

It was against this backdrop that the first films by African filmmakers were made. Ousmane SEMBENE's black-and-white short *Borom Sarret* caused an excited ruffle at the 1963 Tours Festival: the emergence of a new filmmaker and the birth of a new cinema were loudly proclaimed. By the time the first Tunisian Journées Cinématographique de Carthage (JCC) was launched in 1966 for African and Arab films, Senegal had produced a further nine films; Mustapha Alassane of Niger had made seven; four other francophone countries had produced eight films between them; and South African Lionel Ngakane had made two (albeit in London). In 1968 Upper Volta (Burkina Faso) launched the Festival Panafricain du Cinéma de Ouagadougou (FESPACO) and in 1970 the Fédération Panafricain des Cinéastes (FEPACI) was set up. More films appeared, though the principal anglophone ones were made in West Africa – beginning with Sam Aryety's *No Tears for Ananse* (Ghana, 1968); and Nigeria's Ola Balogun, who has had one of the most prolific of all African film careers. Other anglophone countries tended to produce documentary shorts for information, education and – more recently – television.

The leaning of one set of countries to documentaries and the other to fiction features and shorts is related to the colonial experience. Many francophone African students studied filmmaking as an art form in France, and a considerable number of their films (even into the eighties) were financed by the pre-production sale of noncommercial rights to, and the provision of post-production facilities by, the Ministère de la Coopération in Paris. The Agence de Coopération Culturelle et Technique also makes production possible through various funds and a money prize for best script. No such arrangements on either level existed in England: students tended to be funded for training at either the British Council's Film Unit (cut in 1980) or the news film agency, Visnews (both in London), returning to work in the various ministries at home or – as and when it was set up – in television. There are exceptions to this 'rule': Ousmane Sembene and Souleymane CISSE studied in Moscow; from the late seventies a few students from various African countries studied in Poland or Czechoslovakia; Kwaw Ansah (Ghana) and Haile Gerima (Ethiopia) studied in the USA.

Production funding has, on occasion, come from Czechoslovakia, and one or two early Tanzanian films were made

5

with help from Sweden. The German television company ZDF has financed some African films and CHANNEL FOUR TELEVISION in Britain has begun to do so. Otherwise films are financed precariously by bank loans, grants, family and friends. Because in almost every country the amount of production is very small, there is virtually no production structure. In any case, however films may be financed, in the marketplace of distribution and exhibition they are left to sink or swim, so that very few have any chance of recouping their costs. Until quite recently distribution and exhibition circuits in Africa were still controlled from Paris, London, Geneva and New York. Box office profits, untaxed, were taken out of the countries in which films had been made; and there was consequently no income to plow

> Who is Countess Bathory and what is she to women's cinema?

back into production. Equally, there was no interest on the part of distributors and exhibitors in dealing with African-produced films. Very early on, however, FEPACI made demands for state support of cinema and for a different relationship with the foreign 'majors': attempts began to be made in 1970 to nationalize the importation of films, but in response the majors threatened to blank the screens. Compromise solutions were eventually reached: for example, Upper Volta's tax on box office receipts allowed two feature films to be made and a new cinema to be built, but control essentially remained in the hands of foreigners. Only Algeria and Guinea-Conakry maintained a position of no compromise over the control of film importation.

In the early eighties an interstate agreement between fourteen francophone countries was made for cooperative distribution and production arrangements. One or two films have been made under the auspices of CIPROFILM, but the Consortium Inter-africain de Distribution Cinématographique (CIDC) suffered severely from both the strength of foreign companies and the weakness of governments' political will. Many contribution obligations were not met; in addition the fifty or so African films taken into distribution by CIDC have met with hostility on the part of the still foreign and very commercially oriented cinema owners. In 1982, new proposals around filmmakers' original demands were made: state control but, alongside it, positive encouragement of private investment and various initiatives to aid and finance production, distribution and exhibition.

For the time being, and despite the fact that when films have been shown in commercial cinemas at home they have played to packed houses, the main exhibition outlet remains European and American art houses, FILM FESTIVALS and cultural events or film study courses. FEPACI's inaugural manifesto called for a 'responsible, free and committed cinema' in which filmmakers would be 'creative artisans at the service of their people': but filmmakers continue to be, in effect, guerrillas in a war of cultural independence – hence, also, the thematic concerns of many African films.

There is a tendency to shoot on location using natural light, nonprofessional actors and a local language. The incorporation of local events and ceremonies is common. It is rare to find central protagonists on the model of CLASSICAL HOLLYWOOD CINEMA: the major concern is with issues, so that characters express the collective psyche and people's relationships to and within society, rather than psychological motivation and personal conflict. For this reason, certain consistent thematic concerns have surfaced over the years in socially motivated films. Many deal with the history of, and resistance to, colonization: *Emitai* (Ousmane Sembene, Senegal, 1972); *Sambizanga* (Sarah Maldoror, Angola, 1972); *Cry Freedom* (Ola Balogun, Nigeria, 1981); *Sarraounia* (Med Hondo, Burkina

Faso/France, 1986). The use of religion as a weapon of colonialism is treated in *The Chapel* (Jean-Michel Tchissoukou, Congo, 1980) and *Ceddo* (Ousmane Sembene, Senegal, 1977).

The relationship between Africans and Europe since independence is played out in many different ways: in terms of conflicting cultural identity (*Boubou-cravate* [Daniel Kamwa, Cameroon, 1973]); being a foreigner (*Concerto pour un exil* [Désiré Ecaré, Ivory Coast, 1968]; *Les Princes noirs de St Germain-des-Prés* [Ben Diogaye Beye, Senegal, 1975]; *Les Bicots-nègres, vos voisins / Your Neighbours the Niggers* [Med Hondo, Mauritania/France, 1973]); wanting to leave for Europe (*Touki-Bouki* [Djibril Mambety Diop, Senegal, 1973]).

Africa's power relations *vis-à-vis* the West also inform many films dealing with post-independence corruption: *FVVA/Woman, Villa, Car, Money* (Mustapha Alassane, Niger, 1972); *Xala/The Curse* (Ousmane Sembene, Senegal, 1974); *Money Power* (Ola Balogun, Nigeria, 1982–4). Corruption is equally behind the political ineffectiveness of governments over agricultural policy (*Fad Jal* [Safi Faye, Senegal, 1979]) or fishing (*Geti Tey* [Samba Felix Ndiaye, Senegal, 1978] is a rare film dealing with this topic). Underlying many films is the dichotomy between new and imposed ways of conducting society and the traditional ways. In *Tiyabu Biru* (Moussa Yoro Bathily, Senegal, 1978) young boys of the village cannot undergo their initiation ceremony because the price of the necessary cattle has been raised above villagers' means; in *L'Exile/The Exile* (Oumarou Ganda, Niger, 1980), a major theme is the fact that at one time a person's word was matched by actions, while now politicians can promise anything and not deliver.

Medicine is frequently a site of conflict between the established and the new (*Le Médecin de Gafiré/The Doctor of Gafiré* [Mustapha Diop, Niger, 1983]); but conflict is also played out in terms of religion (as in early films by Oumarou Ganda)

and the move from village to town (*Le prix de la liberté* [Jean-Pierre Dikongue-Pipa, Cameroon, 1978]; *Abusuan* [Henri Duparc, Ivory Coast, 1972]; *Paweogo* [Kollo Sanou, Burkina Faso, 1983]) and back to the village (*Le Retour/The Return* [Ignace-Solo Randrasana, Madagascar, 1973]; *Yam Daabo/The Choice* [Idrissa Ouedraogo, Burkina Faso, 1987]).

Several films are set in precolonial times and make no reference to them: *La Rançon d'une alliance/The Price of Alliance* (Sebastian Kamba, Congo, 1973); *Samba le grand* (Mustapha Alassane, Niger, 1978); *Wend Kuni/Gift of God* (Gaston Kabore, Burkina Faso, 1972); *Yeelen/The Light* (Souleymane Cissé, Mali, 1987); and, from Ethiopian filmmaker Haile Gerima, the hauntingly poetic *Mirt Sost Shi Amit/Harvest 3000 Years* (1976). Like many African filmmakers, Gerima takes as one of his themes the condition of women. His young peasant girl sees her future mapped out in the pain on her mother's and grandmother's faces.

One of the most common themes concerning women has to do with arranged marriages and the bride-price: a young girl is forced by her parents to marry an older man because he can pay more for her than the younger man she really loves (*Muna Moto/The Other Man's Child* [Jean-Pierre Dikongue-Pipa, Cameroon, 1976]). The same theme appears in *Le Wazzou polygame* (Oumarou Ganda, Niger, 1970), a film about the morality of polygamy – later to be the subject of Ousmane Sembene's *Xala* and Ben Diogaye Beye's *Seye Seyeti/One Man, Several Women* (Senegal, 1980). In *Djeli* (Kramo Lancine Fadika, Ivory Coast, 1981) two young people are forbidden to marry by their elders because they come from different castes, and in *Love Brewed in the African Pot* (Kwaw Ansah, Ghana, 1981) the young couple do marry, but external interference eventually sends the wife insane. Désiré Ecaré has perhaps gone further than any other filmmaker in dealing with the situation of women in his film *Visages de femmes/Faces of Women* (Ivory Coast, 1985), which tells the stories of three different women.

Amongst the few films by women are those by CARIBBEAN-born Sarah Maldoror: *Monangambeee* (1969) and *Sambizanga* (1972), both for Angola. In 1989 the CRETEIL Film Festival programed short films by Leonie Yangba Zowe of the Central African Republic (*Yangba-Bola* and *Lengue*, both 1985) and Flora M'Mbugu-Schelling of Tanzania. There are now undoubtedly more African women attending film schools and gaining experience 'on the job': some of these should eventually emerge as filmmakers in their own right, and not simply remain in support roles. But for the present Safi Faye remains the principal African woman filmmaker.

Ferid Boughedir, *Le cinéma africain de A à Z* (Brussels: OCIC, 1987)

See also: ALGERIA; EGYPT; HONDO, MED; MOROCCO; SOUTH AFRICA; TUNISIA   AM

AHRNE, MARIANNE (1940–   )

A SWEDISH film director, actress and author, Marianne Ahrne had acquired an interesting set of experiences before entering the Stockholm Film School at the age of twenty-seven: she had run away to Paris, paddled down the Mississippi on a ferry, and trained horses in Denmark. She had also taken her BA at the University of Lund in 1966, majoring in Foreign Languages. During her studies in Lund, Ahrne acted at the Student Theater. She later continued her acting career in France at Théâtre des Carmes in Avignon, and in Denmark at the famous experimental theater Odinteatret. She began her film career as a documentary filmmaker and editor, working for Swedish television and for RAI in Italy. Many of her early documentaries were made in France, including one of her most important productions, made in collaboration with Simone de Beauvoir, *Promenade in the Land of the Aged* (1974).

Marianne Ahrne has on several occasions dissociated herself from 'women's cinema,' protesting against the tendency to categorize all films made by women according to the gender of their director. The themes of her films, however, are often treated from a woman's point of view. *Abortion Problems in France* (1971) and *Divorce Problems in Italy* (1971) are the titles of two of her early documentaries. Her feature films tend to focus on young women struggling with problems of identity and communication.

Balladen om Therese/The Ballad of Therese (1970); *Illusionernas Natt/Palace of Illusions* (1970); *Ferai* (1970); *Få mig att skratta/Make Me Laugh* (1971); *Abortproblem i Frankrike/Abortion Problems in France* (1971); *Skilsmässoproblem i italien/Divorce Problems in Italy* (1971); *Den sista riddarvampyren/The Last Knight Vampire* (1972); *Storstadsvampyrer/Big City Vampires* (1972); *Camargue, det forlorade landet/Camargue – the Lost Country* (1972); *Drakar, drümmar och en flicka från verkligheten/Dragons, Dreams – and a Girl from Reality* (1974); *Promenad i de gamlas land/Promenade in the Land of the Aged* (1974); *Fem dagar in Falköping/Five Days in Falköping* (1975); *Långt borta och nära/Near and Far Away* (1976); *Frihetens murar/Roots of Grief* (1978); *På liv och död/A Matter of Life and Death* (1986)   TS

AKERMAN, CHANTAL (1950–   )

BELGIAN filmmaker Chantal Akerman became famous with *Jeanne Dielman, 23 Quai du Commerce, 1080 Bruxelles* (1976). A divorcee (Delphine Seyrig) lives alone with her son. She keeps house and in the afternoon entertains men for money. She kills the third man who visits because he gives her physical pleasure and so disturbs her routine. The organization of this film is very special: in showing in real time domestic chores like peeling potatoes and washing up, the scenes do not so much function on an informative level as reveal the awful life led by the woman. Although Akerman does not want to call herself a feminist, this film may be regarded as a classic example of feminist film language.

Chantal Akerman's *J'ai faim, j'ai soif*

Between 1974 and 1988 Akerman wrote and directed seven feature films. She also made several video documentaries, including *Un jour Pina a demandé* (1983), about Pina Bausch's Wupperthaler Tanztheater, and *Letters Home* (1986), based on a stage play about Sylvia Plath. In her first film, *Je tu il elle* (1974), Akerman herself played the leading part, that of a young woman who cannot see the difference between I (je), you (tu), he (il), and she (elle). For a while she shuts herself up in an empty room, visits a female friend to go to bed with her, and is eventually given a lift by a lorry driver – all this in order to approach the extremes of lust and pain. The scene in which the two women make love consists of three long static shots: its duration rules out any possibility of voyeurism, since we see only the lust and the violence of this love, and it is an uncomfortable experience.

Akerman likes to draw attention to the mother–daughter relationship on which all her films are based. This relationship structures, in a very penetrating manner, *News from Home* (1976) and *Les rendezvous d'Anna* (1978). In *News from Home* images of nearly empty and very similar-looking streets in New York are combined with the filmmaker's own voice, reading aloud letters written by her mother to her absent daughter. The words always say the same, nothing and everything; the letters are never answered – but the droning voice reveals that the daughter has completely assimilated them. In *Les rendezvous d'Anna*, an attractive woman traveler – a filmmaker – loiters around in stations and hotels, the universe of homeless persons. Apart from some chance meetings, she spends a day and a night with her mother in a hotel. In *Toute une nuit* (1982), solitude takes on physical shape: through a sultry night in Brussels, several bodies are looking for each other. Some of them manage to find one other, others do not. In *L'homme à la valise* (1984), Akerman again plays the leading

Akerman's *News from Home*

part. For want of inner peace, the protagonist is unable to work. She becomes obsessed with the man who has a room in the same apartment. The merciless camera and ironic stream of consciousness put the woman's compulsive behavior in perspective. Chantal Akerman's latest film to date is the musical *The Golden Eighties* (1986), which was a box office success in both Belgium and France.

Saute ma ville (1968); *L'enfant aimé* (1971); *Hotel Monterey, La chambre* (1972); *Hanging out-Yonkers* (1973); *Jeanne Dielman, 23 Quai du Commerce, 1080 Bruxelles* (1974); *News from Home* (1976); *Les rendezvous d'Anna* (1978); *Toute une nuit, Hôtel des acacias* (1982); *Un jour Pina a demandé* (1983); *L'homme à la valise/The Man with the Suitcase, J'ai faim, j'ai soif* (1984); *Family Business, Une lettre de cinéaste* (1985); *The Golden Eighties* (1986)

Angela Martin, 'Chantal Akerman's Films: a Dossier', *Feminist Review*, no. 3 (1979)   AF

ALGERIA

Born of the War of Liberation against France, cinema blossomed after Algeria's independence in 1962. About a decade later, Mohamed Lakhdar-Hamina won the Palme d'Or in Cannes for *Sinin El Jamr/Chronicle of the Years of Embers* (1975). ONCIC, the state monopoly for importation, production and distribution of films, together with the state television RTA, has fostered a wealth of talent. The director of ONCIC, Ahmed Rachedi, made *L'aube des Damnés* (1965), a classic of anti-imperialist cinema, with archive footage – but proved less inspired in super-productions. In the first decade of its independence Algeria, the country of the 'one million martyrs,' cried its wounds. The praiseworthy *Rih El Awras/The Wind of the Aures* (M Lakhdar Hamina, 1966) was awarded the first feature prize in Cannes, and *Al Tariq/The Road* (Slim Riad, 1968) launched Algerian cinema internationally. In most of the films of this period, Algerian women, whose imprisonment, torture and death had made headlines in real life, were a mere backdrop. There were some exceptions: the documentary *Elles/The Women* (1970) by Ahmed Lallem looks at a society 'made by men and for men'; and the lyrical and moving feature *Noua* (Abdelaziz Tolby, 1972) blends a lucid analysis of the independence struggle with a realistic portrayal of women and their bold role. It is the starving women of the Algerian peasantry, suffering from the rapist excursions of the son of the Algerian feudalist allied to the French settlers, who start the armed struggle.

Nationalization of the oil industry and land reform led to a new type of cinema: Cinema Djidid was bent on analyzing the contradictions of Algerian society. The debate on women became livelier than in other ARAB CINEMAS. *Al Fahham/The Coalburner* (Mohamed Bouamari, 1972) is representative of this new cinema: a coalburner is put out of work by the arrival of the gas industry, and his wife goes to the factory leading social resistance. Her husband dreams of 'facing the venerable representatives of social hypocrisy and throwing at their face the veil of his wife.' The oppression of women is dealt with in other films by Bouamari (*The Heritage* [1975], and in more hermetic tone *First Steps* [1979]); and is also the theme of other Algerian films (*Riah Al Janoub/South Wind* [Slim Riad, 1975]; *Vent de sable/Sand Winds* [Lakhdar Hamina, 1982]); and also *Leila and the Others* (1978) and *Houria* (1986), both by Sid Ali Mazif, who made one of the most socially aware and underrated films of the first period of Algerian cinema, *Sueur noire/Black Sweat* (1972), which is about the struggle of the miners during the war of independence. On the predicament of men, prisoners of their masculinity, *Omar Gatlato* (Merzak Allouache, 1976) – literally Omar-his-virility-killed-him – was a great success in its depiction of a second generation of Algerians living in overcrowded houses, tired of empty government slogans, chewing over past heroic days.

In recent years, Algerian cinema has been restructured. More freedom is now given to private capital. A new wind is blowing. *Les folles années du twist/The Mad Years of the Twist* (Mahmoud Zemmouri, 1983) irreverently depicts the sacrifices of the glorious forefathers. The fine *Kissat Lika/The Story of an Encounter* (Ibrahim Tsaki, 1983) deals with the problem of equality and noncommunication: in this film, dialogue takes place only between equals; two deaf-mute adolescents, an American girl and an Algerian boy, love each other but cannot communicate with their money-chasing parents. The misfortune of women affects all Algerian society in *Al Kalaat/The Citadel* (Mohamed Chouik, 1988): the hero, a man too sensitive for his macho culture, is married off by his polygamous father to a shop-window dummy. Since the debut in 1978 of the talented Assia DJEBAR, the only woman filmmaker in Algeria, Algerian history has also undergone review by male filmmakers. Recently, Hadji Rahim made *Barberousse*, about the French colonial prison of the same name, showing only male prisoners. But in the real Barberousse, heroines of the War of Liberation were also jailed and tortured. In reply, Hassan Bouabdallah and Ali Mouzaoui hastily made a documentary, *Barberousse Akhawati/Barberousse, My Sisters* (1986), interviewing these heroines, who found the feature film insulting and inaccurate.

Hala Salmane, *Algerian Cinema* (London: British Film Institute, 1976)

See also: AFRICA   HS

ALTENLOH, EMILIE (1888–1985)

Emilie Altenloh was raised in an upper-class family in Voerde, GERMANY, and studied Business and Law in Heidelberg. She earned a doctorate in 1913 with a dissertation on the sociology of cinema, published in 1914 under the title *Zur Soziologie des Kino. Die Kino-Unternehmung und die soziale Schicht ihrer Besucher*. Altenloh's book, the first scholarly publication on cinema in Germany, goes far beyond empirical analyses of film production and the filmgoing public. It also considers, historically, the origins of cinema and raises questions concerning the aesthetic specificity of film. Focusing on problems of cinematic reception, Altenloh not only stresses class differences and the varying occupational ranks of the viewing public, but also devotes a great deal of attention to gender specificities and to the female spectator, largely ignored by contemporary male-centered theories. In this sense, Altenloh may be regarded as the initiator of the concept of the female gaze. She points out connections: cinema is understood as a network consisting of film as medium, its conditions of production and distribution and its consumers, as well as various forms and locations of reception.

In her later years, Emilie Altenloh no longer pursued her work on cinema, but worked as director of a provincial welfare agency in Schleswig-Holstein, serving briefly as a Parliamentarian in the German Reichstag, and after World War II as a Senator in Hamburg.   *VR*

ALTMAN, ROBERT (1925–)

While Altman's work is often bracketed with NEW HOLLYWOOD CINEMA, his style is so diverse that it is difficult to find characteristics common to his films; though his best-known works feature large casts, multiple plots, a European influence and a preoccupation with national identity. His career began in television, where he directed episodes for various shows. In 1963 he formed Lion's Gate Films with Ray Wagner, but it was not until *That Cold Day in the Park* (1969) that Altman came to the attention of Hollywood. *M*A*S*H* (1970) signaled the start of a series of great episodic spectacles, and also of his 'community' approach to filmmaking. Actors were encouraged to develop close relationships, participating in script changes and developments on the set. *M*A*S*H* was followed by the offbeat *Brewster McCloud* (1970), a portrayal of a series of bizarre events similar in concept to *The Long Goodbye* (1973) and *Nashville* (1975).

Nashville is generally seen as the high point of Altman's career, and his most controversial film. It tells the story of twenty-four different characters through a MUSICAL which expresses the director's preoccupation with the cultural and national identity of America. Other Altman films include *Buffalo Bill and the Indians* (1976), *Three Women* (1977) and *A Wedding* (1978). *Three Women* in some ways prefigures Altman's later *Come Back to the Five and Dime, Jimmy Dean, Jimmy Dean* (1982) in that it centers entirely on the emotions of women. The President of Twentieth Century-Fox, Alan Ladd Jr, offered, in light of the then current fashion for 'women's films,' to finance the film, but Altman saw this as 'no different from the thinking that produced black exploitation films like *Superfly*.' The film was poorly received by critics, and closed after a few weeks at a loss. The release of *Popeye* (1980) again showed Altman concerning himself with Americanness; Popeye appears in the quaint town of Sweethaven – a microcosm of conservative America – and disrupts it by his defiant nonconformity: 'I yam wot I yam.'

In 1981 Altman announced the end of his career as a commercial filmmaker and sold off his share in Lion's Gate Films; but in 1982 he reemerged to direct *Come Back to the Five and Dime, Jimmy Dean, Jimmy Dean*, an adaptation of a stage play by Ed Graczyk which Altman had directed on Broadway. As with his earlier films, poor critical response contrasted with the warmth with which the film was received by audiences. It tells the story of a reunion of six female members of a James Dean fan club at a dime store in Texas. Through conversations, jokes and arguments, in the present and in flashbacks, each woman reveals secrets concealed for twenty years.

Gerard Plecki, *Robert Altman* (Boston: Twayne Publishers, 1985)   *LF*

AMARAL, SUZANA (1933–)

BRAZILIAN director Suzana Amaral began filmmaking late in life. Her first documentaries were on art subjects and her first short, *A Project for Thought and Speech* (1980), on a didactic theme, dealt with 'women's issues.' She worked for television and in 1985 directed her first feature, *A hora dele estrela/The Hour of the Star*. Well received at home, the film collected major prizes in film festivals. Based on a novel by Clarice Lispector, the film upsets many STEREOTYPES in its presentation of the female protagonist, who is neither beautiful nor middle-class. An anti-heroine, starved of affection and respect, she wanders through life looking for an image she can adopt and adapt.

Amaral's films include *Semana de 22/The Week of 1922* (1971); *Coleçao de marfil/Ivory Collection* (1972); *Projeto pensamiento e linguajen/A Project for Thought and Speech* (1980); *São Paolo de todos nos/Our São Paolo* (1981); *A hora dele estrela* (1985)

NT

AMAZONS

Literally meaning women warriors, this term is commonly used figuratively to describe strong women who struggle to resist patriarchal definitions and modes of behavior, and who attempt either to break down gender boundaries or to explore woman-centered ways of living. For most feminists the term carries strongly positive overtones, reassuring us that women have always struggled against patriarchy. In cinema, which particular characters or actors we see as amazons is likely to be a rather personal choice, though amazons will tend to come from a particular range of role types (TOMBOYS, CAREER WOMEN, PHALLIC WOMEN, FEMMES FATALES, for example). In popular cinema, though, amazons as fictional characters rarely remain amazons for the duration of the film. In awarding them that status, therefore, we are generally identifying an element of the character or STAR image – often reading against the grain of the text, refusing to accept the ending of the film in which the HEROINE is 'put back in her place.'

Examples of amazons in Hollywood cinema include Rosalind Russell in *His Girl Friday* (Howard Hawks, Columbia, 1939); Katharine HEPBURN in *Christopher Strong* (Dorothy Arzner, RKO, 1933) and *Adam's Rib* (George Cukor, MGM, 1949); Greta GARBO in *Queen Christina* (Rouben Mamoulian, MGM, 1933); Joan CRAWFORD in *Johnny Guitar* (Nicholas Ray, Republic, 1954) and in the first half of *Mildred Pierce* (Michael Curtiz, Warner Bros., 1945); and Eve Arden all the way through the same film; Jane Fonda for her political commitment and courage in the 1960s and 1970s and for parts of *Klute* (Alan J Pakula, 1971), *Julia* (Fred Zinnemann, 1977) and *Nine to Five* (Colin Higgins, 1980); Mae WEST for putting men in their place in all her films; Maureen O'Hara for doing it angrily in *Dance, Girl, Dance* (Dorothy Arzner, RKO, 1940). Outside Hollywood, amazons are literally women warriors in KUNG FU films; and FEMINIST INDEPENDENT FILM has created its own amazons, like the heroines of Marleen GORRIS's *A Question of Silence* (1981).

Charlotte Brunsdon (ed.), *Films for Women* (London: British Film Institute, 1986)

TP

ANIMATION

A form of filmmaking in which images are produced frame by frame and movement is created through projection, animated film shares many visual conventions of EDITING and MISE-EN-SCÈNE with live-action cinema. The means of producing individual images may vary: paper cutouts, puppets, objects such as beads or sand moved under the camera between frames; alternatively, an illusion of natural movement may be produced from hundreds and thousands of individual drawings; or the animator may even draw or scratch images directly onto the film itself, without using a camera at all.

Women have often been at the creative and experimental forefront of animation – Lotte REINIGER designing her own multiplane camera for her silhouette animations in GERMANY in the 1920s, Caroline LEAF in CANADA delicately manipulating sand and paint under her camera, Lillian Schwarz in the USA pioneering computer animation. In the mainstream commercial industry, however, women have been, and still are, much less visible – with a few notable exceptions such as Joy BATCHELOR of Halas and Batchelor, BRITAIN's largest animation studio throughout the 1940s and 1950s; or Annabel Jankel who, with her partner Rocky Morton, launched the modern animated music video, and invented 'Max Headroom'; or Diane Jackson, director of *The Snowman* (1982).

The predominant form of animation, developed under the HOLLYWOOD STUDIO SYSTEM, is the cartoon. Characters are painted on separate transparent sheets of acetate layered onto a painted background, in a process known as the 'cel' technique. Very expensive, this process lends itself to an elaborate division of labor, with separate roles such as director, key animator, 'inbetweener', background artist and many more. The division of labor, perfected – though not invented – by the Walt Disney studio, has been both hierarchical and gender based: when recruiting a new workforce to staff his burgeoning studio in the 1930s, Disney advertised for male art school graduates to become animators. As is clear from a documentary [about its own operation] made by the studio in 1941 following a major strike (released as part of the feature *The Reluctant Dragon* (Alfred L Werker, Disney, 1941)), women occupy administrative roles or less creative grades such as color mixing and paint and trace. The color mixer ensures that shades of paint used throughout a production match perfectly. Requiring a skilled eye for color comparable to that required, say, by a picture restorer, this has nevertheless been an underrated grade. Paint and tracers, as the name suggests, transfer the animators' drawings from paper to cel and color them. These traditional roles still exist – though some women, such as the American Tissa David, or in Britain Spud Houston and Alison DE VERE, have succeeded in becoming directors or key animators.

Certain GENRE conventions which accompanied the development of the cartoon – animal characters, screwball comedy, fairytales, violence and the chase – were defined in relation to Hollywood features. Technical and stylistic conventions enabled a large mobile workforce to produce films high in production values which looked as if they were from the hand of a single artist. Characters were designed on model sheets in advance by the character department, and would be based on simple shapes, proportions and character traits.

Most of the best-known cartoon characters were developed in the 1930s and 1940s, and were anthropomorphized male animals. They reflect the dominant views of the time regarding gender, SEXUALITY and ethnicity, complete with the anxieties of their creators. Porky Pig, in *Porky's Romance* (Frank Tashlin, Warner Bros., 1937), has premarital nightmares of Petunia Pig's uncontrollable fecundity and insatiability. Pepe le Pew, a French Don Juan skunk (supposedly based on Charles Boyer), tirelessly pursues a reluctant cat from one film to another. The joke is based on genre differences displacing gender difference – the cat has a stripe down its back and accidentally looks like a skunk. In *For Scentimental Reasons* (Chuck Jones, Warner Bros., 1949), as the cat frantically flees its pongy pursuer, Pepe pauses in a moment of self-doubt to ask the audience: 'Do I [really] offend?'. Bugs Bunny, though in many ways one of the boys, often slips into the 'feminine' role of flirt and tease, even sometimes kissing his hunter/pursuer Elmer Fudd on the lips. The hunt often turns to sexual pursuit, as Bugs anarchically crossdresses in films such as *What's Opera Doc?* (Chuck Jones, Warner Bros., 1957).

The Hollywood cartoon portrays 'otherness' in the form of physical and behavioral STEREOTYPES. The male character – Bugs, Mickey Mouse, Daffy Duck – represents the norm. Female counterparts have eyelashes, bows, high heels, and sometimes a humanized hourglass figure. In addition, classic cartoon movement makes everything squash, stretch and bounce – resulting in a plethora of wiggly hips and bouncing bosoms, the most recent example being Jessica Rabbit in *Who Framed Roger Rabbit?* (Robert Zemeckis, 1988). Jessica is a descendant of Frank Tashlin's Hata Mari, a spy-pigeon in wartime propaganda cartoons, and of the showgirl in a series of fairy-tale spoofs by Tex Avery, such as *Red Hot Riding Hood* (MGM, 1943). Both were fetishized glamor girls whose cartoons were used for encouraging lusty heterosexuality among the US troops during World War II.

The Avery films also contain the figure of Grandma, who in *Red Hot Riding Hood* owns a Manhattan nightclub and has a taste for city wolves. She is among the few spunky female characters of the American animated cartoon: others are Betty Boop and Olive Oyl, produced by the New York-based Fleischer studios. While it is hard to recuperate Betty Boop for feminism, in her early, pre-PRODUCTION CODE days she had an encouragingly disruptive effect not only on the men in her films, but also on Hollywood's censors. Olive Oyl, in films such as *A Dream Walking* (Max Fleischer, 1934), took care of herself and often outsmarted Popeye and Bluto. *Olive for President* (Max Fleischer, 1937) even fantasizes her as the president of the USA.

Many women animators have rejected the mainstream industry whether for political or artistic reasons, from experimentalists Claire Parker and Mary Ellen BUTE in the 1930s and Faith Hubley in the 1950s to Susan Pitt, Sally Cruikshank and Jane Aaron working today. A specifically feminist challenge to mainstream animation began in the early 1970s. Women had to choose whether to retain the cartoon form as a humorous way of getting the message across or to opt for a more avant-garde approach. Some women have tried to subvert the conventions of the cartoon, producing an anarchic array of inflatable men and male strippers in films such as *Second Class Mail* (Alison Snowden, 1984) and *Girls' Night Out* (Joanna Quinn, 1986). Monique Renault, a French feminist now working in the NETHERLANDS, makes feminist cartoons on subjects like women in the Catholic church, women at work, and PORNOGRAPHY.

Other feminists have rejected the cartoon for a variety of reasons. In the West, animators like Vera NEUBAUER have rejected the cartoon tradition as too tied to conventions of sexist stereotyping and of naturalistic movement which denies the reality of animation as film produced frame by frame. In INDIA animators like Nina Sabnani, who works on very low budgets at the National Institute of Design in Ahmedabad, are developing forms of representation for Indian audiences which reject western influences and reflect the interaction of the traditional and the modern in Indian culture. *Shub Vivah* (Sabnani, 1984) is a government information film against dowry, its representational style being based on traditional paintings made by the women of Madubani for their own dowries.

Roger Noake, *Animation* (London: MacDonald, 1988)

See also: LANCTOT, MICHELINE; LEEDS ANIMATION WORKSHOP; MACSKASSY, KATALIN   IK

ANTI-APARTHEID FILM AND VIDEO

In SOUTH AFRICA noncommercial films and videos have been used by the national resistance movement to document the injustices and inhumanity of apartheid policies and to begin rerecording the country's history. While prior to the 1980s struggles around gender oppression tended to be subordinated to the struggle for national liberation, there is now growing awareness of the need to bring gender into the political arena and to develop appropriate concepts of women's empowerment and liberation. Consequently, the history of women in the struggle and the place of women in society is the focus of several propaganda DOCUMENTARIES, three of which warrant particular attention.

In *Awake from Mourning* (Chris Austin, 1981), four women explain the Maggie Magaba Trust, established in 1979 for 'the development of women in general,

> What is gynesis? And who coined this new theoretical term?

for their dignity and their self-respect.' The Trust's inspiration was a 'spirit of self-help amongst women.' Various self-help projects financed or supported by the Trust are visited: sewing cooperatives, a training center, educational projects and vegetable gardens which supply the ingredients for local soup depots. Survival rather than feminist consciousness is the theme. 'Black' women speak for themselves about their alienation from their families and work; about the impossibility of trying to maintain a family life through the experience of forced removal and the tedium which comes from working in a factory: 'For fifteen years I top-stitched collars on shirts.' 'The oneness of womanhood' stressed throughout the film is not necessarily an expression of nascent feminism, however. The cooperation of women is not a goal in itself, but rather a way of overcoming economic and political oppression. *Tsiamelo/A Place of Goodness* (Betty Wolpert, 1984) can be seen as a sequel to *Awake from Mourning*. Ellen Kuzwayo and Blanche Tsimatisima trace the history of their family over four generations of self-reliance up to the

time of their forced removal from their family farm, Tsiamelo. *You Have Struck a Rock* (Debora May and Georgina Karvells, 1981) focuses on the protest of 'black' women against carrying 'passes' – compulsory identity documents used to enforce the state's segregationist policy. The indifference of 'black' men to the repression of 'black' women is addressed. Lilian Ngoyi, Helen Joseph, Dora Tamana, Frances Baard and others tell their stories, which are illustrated with archival footage.

Other South African anti-apartheid films and videos include: *Last Grave at Dimbasa* (Nana Mahomo, 1973); *Last Supper in Hortsley Street* (Lindi Wilson, 1984), a moving reconstruction of the last family forced to leave the 'coloured' township of Cape Town, District Six, when it was de-proclaimed and rezoned as a 'white' area; *Mayfair* (Tony Bensusan, Brian Tilley, Paul Weinberg and Wendy Schwegman, 1984); *Now We Have No Land* (Hennie Serfontein, 1985); *The Ribbon* (Harriet Gavshon, 1987)

WJA/RET

ANTONIONI, MICHELANGELO (1912–)

A film director working in ITALY, Antonioni has given attention to female character construction and has placed women centrally, and with a nonobjectifying gaze, in his narratives. His 1950 feature debut, *Cronaca di un amore*, chronicles a love affair involving class difference. Female screenwriter Suso CECCHI D'AMICO co-wrote with Antonioni *I vinti/The Vanquished* (1952), *La signora senza camelie/Camille without Camellias* (1953) and *Le amiche/The Girl Friends* (1955), an elaborate cinematic choreography of relations among women. Antonioni's mature work includes: *L'avventura* (1959); *La notte* (1960); *L'eclisse/The Eclipse* (1962) and *Il deserto rosso/Red Desert* (1964). Actress Monica Vitti is a strong presence in all of these films, representing intelligent women who inquire about issues of identity and (dis-) placement in the world. Often shot in

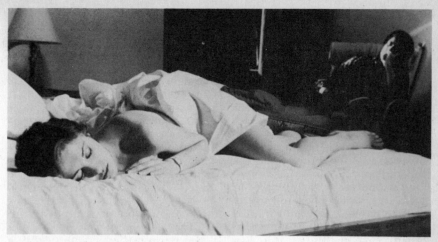

Antonioni's *Identificazione di una donna*

moments of silence or interior monologue, Vitti circulates in a cinematic world of existential malaise, characterized by *temps morts*, moments of nonaction dispersed in a nonlinear, nontraditional narrative with open endings. Extreme attention to the spatial aesthetic of MISE-EN-SCENE and the architecture of composition result in strikingly graphic, distinct shots. Antonioni's more recent films include *Professione: reporter/The Passenger* (1975), and *Identificazioni di una donna/Identification of a Woman* (1982). In the realm of Italian male directors, Antonioni's inquiry into identity parallels Pier Paolo Pasolini's more controversial, less easily accountable contribution to the understanding of this broad issue which is so relevant for feminism.

Antonioni's films include: *Cronaca di un amore/Story of a Love Affair* (1950); *I vinti/The Vanquished* (1952); *La signora senza camelie/Camille without Camellias* (1953); *Le amiche/The Girl Friends* (1955); *L'avventura/The Adventure* (1959); *La notte/The night* (1960); *L'eclisse/The Eclipse* (1962); *Il deserto rosso/Red Desert* (1964); *Professione: reporter/The Passenger* (1975); *Identificazioni di una donna/Identification of a Woman* (1982)

Seymour Chatman, *Antonioni or, The Surface of The World* (Los Angeles: University of California Press, 1985) GB

ARAB CINEMAS

The term Arab cinemas refers to the socially and aesthetically significant cinemas which have appeared in some of the twenty-two Arab countries officially forming the Arab League. Ascribing nationality to Arab films is difficult. Economic and/or political censorship have forced a number of filmmakers to leave their own countries and work in other Arab countries and now, increasingly, in Europe; nevertheless, Arab film production can usefully be examined country by country. Arab cinema has been dominated since the twenties by EGYPT with its wealth of studios, experienced directors, technicians, film stars, singers and belly-dancers. Egypt's mostly shallow commercial productions, imitating the worst of Hollywood, were imitated in turn by neighboring countries in the Middle East. With the arrival of Nasser in 1952, political, economic and social considerations surfaced and with them authorial voices. But it was the decolonization of the Arab countries of Northern Africa in the sixties, the shattering defeat of June 1967 and the emergence of the Palestinian Resistance Movement which triggered the birth of true NATIONAL CINEMAS. On the whole, while Arab male directors challenged the international patriarchal order (imperialism), Arab women challenged it both internationally and at home: this in turn was a positive influence on some of the more conscious male filmmakers.

In the sixties the film market was already divided and the new Arab cinemas, unable to cover costs in local markets, could not become fully fledged film industries. A number of filmmakers emigrated to the West, driven out of their countries by political or economic censorship. Some of these directors look today for 'international' solutions: through the use of English, international film stars, international subjects, exoticism at the expense of original film style and genuine interest in their people's cause.

Often in films made by men artistic excellence is combined with sexist images of women. The two best films to come from the Arab World, *El Mumia/ The Night of Counting the Years* (1970), by the Egyptian Shadi Abdelsalam – and *Les baliseurs du désert/Searchers in the Desert* (1984) by TUNISIA's Naceur Khemir – are both concerned with a glorious past and project equally traditional images of women as mothers, prostitutes or FEMMES FATALES. A similar process is observable in some of the best anti-imperalist films, such as *Al Makhdou-Oun/The Cheated* (Toufic Saleh, 1972), about PALESTINE. On the other hand, had it not been for their lack of artistic merit conventional Egyptian films of the sixties would have become feminist classics. Directors who portrayed women's predicament with sympathy rarely went beyond pitying them. A combination of aesthetic innovation and nonsexist images came only with the emergence of Arab women's self-expression, when the modern Arab woman appeared on the screen not as a sex-object, a heart, a reproduction instrument or a victim of social or political events, but as a citizen of her society, reflecting as an autonomous subject on the problems of her time: history, politics, economics, religion – subjects hitherto reserved to men. Of hundreds of male directors only a few dozen have achieved quality, but most of the dozen or so contemporary Arab female directors have made films of artistic merit. However, artistic quality has come at the cost of considerable pain even for male directors: Shadi Abdelsalam struggled in vain for seventeen years after his internationally acclaimed first and only feature film, and died before making another.

The emergence of women filmmakers in new cinemas came with the fall of patriarchal idols following June 1967. A challenge to traditional values, including patriarchy, followed. These women often expressed themselves in documentaries (Attiat El Abnoudi, Selma Baccar), while features range from straightforward commercial cinema (Ines Deghidi, Nadia Hamza, Nadia Salem) through mainstream ART CINEMA (Joceline Saab and Nejia Ben Mabrouk) to innovation (Assia DJEBAR and Heiny SROUR). Some women directors have encountered immense obstacles: Egyptian Attiat El Abnoudi sweated two years to achieve her first ten-minute short. A number have faced lawsuits from producers who confiscated their films. Joceline Saab of LEBANON, who does not consider herself a feminist, spoke of having felt 'taken hostage.' Nejia Ben Mabrouk spoke of having been 'raped' as a woman in her right of self-expression. Nevertheless, the emergence of quality films made by women proves their urge for self-expression, their unpreparedness to capitulate to a man's world, and their obligation to negotiate for power.

Heiny Srour, 'L'image de la femme dans le cinéma arabe de fiction', *Image et Son*, no. 318 (1977)

See also: ALGERIA; HONDO, MED; IRAN; IRAQ; KUWAIT; MOROCCO

HS

ARBEITERFILM

Arbeiterfilm, or 'worker film,' was the name given to a type of filmmaking in WEST GERMANY during the period 1967–77. Frequently co-financed, and in some cases co-produced, by the Cologne television station *Westdeutscher Rundfunk* (WDR), the *Arbeiterfilm* focuses on the lives and experiences of the contemporary German working classes. Hailed as progressive, the GENRE – often a thought-provoking combination of DOCUMENTARY and feature-film modes of address – explores workers' struggles for dignity and economic survival at the workplace, and aims to bring about a change of political consciousness in the viewer. According to British film theorists Richard Collins and Vincent Porter, the first 'true' example of the genre is *Rote Fahnen sieht man besser/Red Flags Can Be Seen Better*, made by Rolf Schuebel and Theo Gallehr in 1971, which deals with the closure of a factory from the employees' point of view. Whilst male directors, such as Christian Ziewer and R W FASSBINDER, are well known for their worker films, women filmmakers have also made substantial contributions to the genre.

Helma SANDERS-BRAHMS, for example, made *Der Angestellte/The White-Collar Worker* (1971), about a systems analyst who develops plans for rationalization, to which he himself falls victim, and *Shirins Hochzeit/Shirin's Wedding* (1975) focusing on a young Turkish woman. Marianne Luedcke also made three films in collaboration with Ingo Kratisch which fall within the genre: *Die Wollands/The Wolland Family* (1972), about a welder; *Lohn und Liebe/Wages and Love* (1973), dealing with the struggle for sexual equality in the workplace; and *Familienglueck/Wedded Bliss* (1975), looking at how social factors affect private life. Moreover, the concerns of the later *Arbeiterfilm* were prefigured in many ways by the personalized documentaries of another woman filmmaker, Erika Runge. As early as 1968 Runge made *Warum ist Frau B. gluecklich?/Why is Mrs B. Happy?*, examining the life of a miner's widow; in 1970 she followed this with *Ich heisse Erwin und bin 17 Jahre/My Name is Erwin and I'm 17* (1970), a portrait of a young apprentice.

Richard Collins and Vincent Porter, *WDR and the Arbeiterfilm: Fassbinder, Ziewer and others* (London: British Film Institute, 1981)   JK

ARGENTINA

The part women have been able to play in the development of cinema in Argentina has been minimal – though paradoxically, María Luisa BEMBERG is one of the few contemporary Argentine directors whose films are regularly distributed internationally, and executive producer Lita STANTIC has succeeded in building up a solid body of work since the 1970s.

As in most of LATIN AMERICA, a group of European immigrants was responsible for the first film screening in Argentina – in Buenos Aires in July 1896. These immigrants invested first in foreign films and projection equipment and spaces for theatrical exhibition, and only later in production technology and studio facilities. Although by 1908–9 local distributors were also producing short features and documentaries, there was no consistent national production until World War I curtailed the influx of European film imports.

However, it was the coming of SOUND that defined the Argentine industry and propelled it to prominence in Latin America: the schism in the international film market produced by the sudden untranslatability of Hollywood cinema opened a space for Argentine films throughout Latin America. While other national industries – in MEXICO and BRAZIL, for example – withered when confronted with the challenge of sound technology, Argentine production flourished, basically because it transformed the tango into a vehicle for cinematic expansion. Although Carlos Gardel, tango's premier star, was whisked off to Joinville, Paris, in 1931 to make films for PARAMOUNT, a new breed of Argentine producers and male and female tango stars quickly took his place. Angel Mentasti, for instance, nicknamed the 'czar of the Argentine cinema,' founded Argentina Sono Films and cast his first production, *Tango!* (1933), with every well-known tango orchestra and singer. The film was so successful that its 'review' formula (minimal script/maximum music) was consecrated in dozens of subsequent Sono Film features, and tango-melodramas – especially those starring popular singer-actress Lamarque LIBERTAD – became enormously popular among female audiences. Meanwhile, the pioneers of Argentine radio founded a rival company, Lumiton, and built extensive studios in the style of the Hollywood majors. Annual feature production between 1932 and 1942 increased from two to fifty-six films, a record that would never be bettered.

The industry continued for several years to exploit the links between the cinema and the tango tradition until, having exhausted its public, it began to seek more middle-class audiences with sophisticated and urbane productions. For example, male director Francisco Mugica specialized in *aqua con azúcar* comedies, the Argentine equivalent of ITALY's 'white telephone' films. The most interesting male directors, however, were linked to a REALIST cinematic strain: Mario Soffici explored the poverty of the countryside in his *Prisioneros de la tierra/Prisoners of the Land* (1939), while Leopoldo Torres Rios focused on urban problems in his *La vuelta al nido/Return to the Nest* (1938). The prosperity of the Argentine industry lasted less than a dozen years, however, and after World War II Mexico became dominant in the Latin American market. The national industry's decline was due to aesthetic as well as economic problems. A wartime export embargo by the USA had cut off Argentina's access to celluloid and crippled production. After the war, the industry sought international status by underplaying the national characteristics that had originally promoted its success (the *lufardo* slang of inner-city Buenos Aires, the tango-melodrama, the urban melodrama), but the Strindberg, Tolstoy, and Ibsen adaptations that took their place did not generate much popular interest.

Once production declined, it became apparent that the Argentine studios were, and always had been, dependent upon distributors and exhibitors, sectors closely affiliated with foreign concerns uninterested in developing the NATIONAL CINEMA. Furthermore, Juan Perón's government, though based on state protectionism, had no policy for the development of the national film industry. Some protectionist measures were implemented in the mid to late 1940s, with screen quotas and a limit on imports, but these were mere palliatives that did not address the deeper contradictions of the system. Perón's protectionist measures were not successful, but their sudden abolition by the military government that deposed him in 1955 gave the *coup de grâce* to an already weakened industry and essentially ended studio-system production in Argentina. After a postwar peak of fifty-six films in 1950, the annual number of productions declined steadily and reached a low of fifteen films in 1957. New protectionist measures were put into effect in 1957, but the impetus for the 'New' Argentine cinema of the late 1950s and early 1960s arose not from changes in the commercial sector but from a transformation in the relationship between filmmakers and the cinema.

With an emphasis on AUTHORSHIP promoted by the popular European cinema and by the collaborative work of Leopoldo TORRE-NILSSON and Beatriz GUIDO, the general sociocultural renovation of the 1960s led to the emergence of the NUEVA OLA movement and to the establishment by Fernando BIRRI of a school devoted to nonindustrial filmmaking with a different vision of the national cinema. Furthermore, the spirit of pan-Latin American solidarity typical of Latin American filmmaking of the 1960s was also evident in the work of clandestine filmmakers who took up cinema, on the margins of a still struggling commercial industry, as an active agent for political change at a time of great turbulence in Argentine politics. The best-known of these groups was the pro-Perón *Grupo Cine Liberación* (Fernando Solanas, Octavio Getino, and Gerardo Vallejo). Their film *La hora de los hornos/The Hour of the Furnaces* (1968–9) remains one of the most significant achievements of international political filmmaking and their manifesto, 'Towards a Third Cinema,' a crucial document for the development of the New Latin American Cinema.

When a Perónist (Campora) assumed the presidency in 1973, the political euphoria of the period reinvigorated all filmmaking, even in the weak commercial sector, and production (fifty-four films in fourteen months) and cinema attendances (40 per cent increase) grew dramatically. However, political pressures and terrorist activities soon escalated and filmmakers of all persuasions went into exile to avoid being 'disappeared' by paramilitary squads. After 1976 – when a military coup deposed Isabel Perón – cinema activities came to an almost complete standstill: only sixteen films were produced in 1976 and seventeen in 1977. The military junta that ruled Argentina until 1983 imposed a regime of terror and censorship that curtailed the development of the national cinema. However, sweeping changes were made following the election of Raúl Alfonsín to the presidency: filmmaker Manuel Antín was named director of the Instituto Nacional de Cinematografía and promised to restore production to thirty films per year, censorship was abolished, and the film critic Jorge Miguel Couselo was appointed head of the film classification board. Although production levels for 1986 and 1987 were not as high as anticipated, and the industry continued to struggle with inflation and decreasing

Who was sacked from the staff of US magazine McCalls for making rude remarks in reviewing The Sound of Music?

theatrical audiences, the success of films like *La historia oficial /The Official Story* (US)/*The Official Version* (GB) (Luis Puenzo, 1986), *Tangos: El exilio de gardel/ Tangos: The Exile of Gardel* (Fernando Solanas, 1986) and *Miss Mary* (María Luisa Bemberg, 1986) bodes well for the future of the Argentine cinema.

John King and Nissa Torrents (eds), *The Garden of Forking Paths: Argentine Cinema* (London: British Film Institute, 1987)

ALo

ARMSTRONG, GILLIAN (1950–)

Gillian Armstrong has been promoted as one of the big five, along with Peter Weir, Fred Schepisi, Bruce Beresford and George Miller, in AUSTRALIA's grab for marketable auteurs to promote official culture abroad during the 1970s. She started her film career at Melbourne's film school, Swinburne, before graduating to the interim program of the Australian Film and Television School in 1974. She directed a number of shorts including *One Hundred a Day* (1973), *Satdee Night* (1973), *The Singer and the Dancer* (1976), and a documentary series tracing the lives of three working-class Adelaide women over fourteen years (*Smokes and Lollies* [1975], *14's Good, 18's Better* [1980], *Bingo, Bridesmaids and Braces* (1988]). Armstrong's move into features with *My Brilliant Career* (1979) signaled a return to narrative features by women directors after a forty-six-year absence. The film draws on Australian woman novelist Miles Franklin's novel of the same title, promoting women in major production roles – Margaret Fink as producer and Eleanor Witcombe as screenwriter, for example. Armstrong is one of the few women filmmakers to refer back to the bush heroines of Australia's silent cinema, following the archival work of Joan Long, whose Film Australia documentaries *The Pictures That Moved* (1969) and *The Passionate Industry* (1973), along with Hilary Furlong's *Don't Call Me Girlie* (1985), constitute attempts by second-wave feminism to make links with early Australian film history. Armstrong's subsequent features have continued to focus on the experiences of women, and *Mrs Soffel* (1984) constituted her encounter with the big-budget Hollywood machine before she returned to Australia to direct *High Tide* (1987). The stylistic inventiveness of her early narratives has not been evident in the conventionality and softcore focus on women in her features, with the possible exception of *Starstruck* (1982), a musical comedy described by critics Susan Dermody and Elizabeth Jacka as a celebration of 'ocker' (working-class Australian) matriarchy.

The Roof Needs Mowing (1971); *One Hundred a Day* (1973); *Satdee Night* (1973); *Gretel* (1973); *Smokes and Lollies* (1975); *The Singer and the Dancer* (1976); *My Brilliant Career* (1979); *14's Good, 18's Better* (1980); *Starstruck* (1982); *Not Just a Pretty Face* (1983); *Mrs Soffel* (1984); *High Tide* (1987); *Bingo, Bridesmaids and Braces* (1988)

Susan Dermody and Elizabeth Jacka, *The Screening of Australia: Anatomy of a National Cinema*, Volume 2 (Sydney: Currency Press, 1988)   FC

ART CINEMA

Feminist film culture has tended to adopt an ambivalent attitude toward the group of cinemas which can be collectively described as 'art cinema'; a term which was only a shorthand come-on, but which has recently found a theoretical underpinning. Distinguished primarily by a desire to define itself against narrative-led American GENRE cinema, art cinema is composed of a number of different film movements including Italian NEO-REALISM, Argentina's NUEVA OLA, the French NEW WAVE, and NEW GERMAN CINEMA. All however, share certain characteristics. They are 'directors' cinemas,' grounded in a belief that AUTHORSHIP is the primary key to understanding a film. Alongside an interest in REALISM (contemporary settings, 'real' locations, 'real' social issues) there is a stress on visual style, often emphasized through expressionist techniques (dream-sequences, flashbacks, colored filters, freeze frames). Characters tend to assume greater importance than 'plot,' and are developed through a 'psychological realism' which stresses their subjective view of events.

The realism of art cinema is also sexual in content. As writers of film advertisements well know, 'European' and 'artistic' have become code words for graphic representations of sex. Born in the era when the PRODUCTION CODE strictly limited portrayals of sex in American films, European art cinema continued to capitalize on its risqué reputation long after these restrictions disappeared.

In its early years, art cinema's combination of realism, expressivity and EROTICISM seemed to mark a startling leap forward in the filmic status of women. Art cinema's stars were earthy, sensual and beautiful in an unconventional and apparently uncontrived manner. Characters played by stars like Silvana Mangano in *Riso amaro/Bitter Rice* (Giuseppe De Santis, 1948), Jeanne Moreau in *Jules et Jim* (François Truffaut, 1961) and Jean Seberg in Jean-Luc GODARD's *A bout de souffle/Breathless* (1959) were free spirits, liberated from the constraints of narrative and of bourgeois morality in a way impossible to imagine in Hollywood. But as FEMINIST FILM THEORY evolved, it began to stress art cinema's habitual representation of women as passive childlike objects; poetic mysteries to be desired but never ultimately understood by a male protagonist who is often quite explicitly an alter ego for a male director. *Une Femme est une femme/A Woman is A Woman* (Jean-Luc Godard, 1961); *Et Dieu créa la femme/And God Created Woman* (Roger Vadim, 1956); *Une Femme mariée/ A Married Woman* (Jean-Luc Godard, 1964): the titles are significant: woman's function in these films is that of unknowable essence.

By the mid 1970s, this view of womanhood was made all the more uncomfortable by the growth of a new erotic subgenre of art cinema. Represented at its most extreme by films such as Liliana CAVANI's *Il portiere di notte/ The Night Porter* (1974) and *Ultima tango a Parigi/Last Tango in Paris* (Bernardo Bertolucci, 1972), this form of art cinema became a topic of hot debate by feminists, many of whom saw its explicitness as unnecessary and inevitably exploitive. More complex discussion grew around another group of films which grew out of art cinema: the political COUNTER-CINEMA practiced by directors like Jean-Luc Godard in films such as *Weekend* (1968). Here the conventions of art cinema were challenged, but the place of women changed little.

Despite the powerful influence of female STARS on art cinema, comparatively few women have become known as art cinema directors. The films of Margerite DURAS, Agnes VARDA and Nelly Kaplan do, however, provide an interesting counterpoint to art cinema's central themes, employing the same drifting, sexualized female characters but placing their own, rather than a male observer's, subjectivity at center stage.

By the end of the seventies, however, the government-sponsored financial resources available in several European countries as a bulwark against increasing penetration by American cinema were being used by a number of avowedly feminist directors. The sexual exoticism of art cinema was used by some to investigate themes of female sexuality and, occasionally, lesbianism. At the same time others, such as Margarethe von TROTTA, Helma SANDERS-BRAHMS and Marleen GORRIS, attempted the hitherto largely ignored task of setting their psychologically complex HEROINES in specific political and social contexts. The aesthetic influence of art cinema can also be seen in some FEMINIST INDEPENDENT FILM: Chantal AKERMAN, for instance, uses many themes familiar from traditional art cinema, but reworks them in a highly structured formal manner.

David Bordwell, 'Art Cinema as a Mode of Film Practice', *Film Criticism*, vol. 4, no. 1 (1979)

See also: ANTONIONI, MICHELANGELO; BERGMAN, INGMAR   JRo

ART DIRECTION

In the early 1910s, three-dimensional sets began to replace horizontal painted backdrops in US film productions. Set construction contributed to the appearance of reality and to the possibility of actors playing scenes in greater depth. By the mid 1910s, an art director oversaw set design. By the 1920s and the rise of the HOLLYWOOD STUDIO SYSTEM, the role of art direction in film production grew increasingly important and complex. With the need for continuity and efficiency in feature film production, art direction extended beyond set design to influence all aspects of MISE-EN-SCENE: COSTUMES, props and character movement within the set, as well as cinematography (the effects of LIGHTING and lenses) and SPECIAL EFFECTS (inserting mountain views through windows). Art direction ensures the coherence of a film's overall design by making all visual elements compatible with the film's period (realistic contemporary life, historical epics) or GENRE (FILM NOIR claustrophia, SCIENCE FICTION futurism, and so on). Central to art direction is the process of interpreting the script so that the dramatic interest of the story, and character traits and their conflicts, are clearly understood. In *The Best Years of Our Lives* (William Wyler, Goldwyn, 1946) women resocialize men returning from World War II. That Fred (Dana

Andrews) is correct in choosing Peggy (Teresa Wright) as a wife instead of Marie (Virginia Mayo) is confirmed through the film's art direction, which produced mise-en-scène contrasting the class and the 'womanly' qualities of the two women. *All That Heaven Allows* (Douglas Sirk, Universal, 1954) underscores Cary's (Jane Wyman) struggle for self-realization by contrasting, at the visual level, oppressive suburban living with the alternative lifestyle offered to Cary by her lover Ron (Rock Hudson). In MUSICALS such as *Gold Diggers of 1933* (Busby Berkeley, Warner Bros., 1933) and *Gentlemen Prefer Blondes* (Howard Hawks, Twentieth Century-Fox, 1953) art direction is designed to emphasize the spectacle of women's bodies.

Leon Barsacq, *Caligari's Cabinet and Other Grand Illusions: A History of Film Design*, trans. Michael Bullock (New York: New American Library, 1978)
MBH

ARZNER, DOROTHY (1906–79)

The only woman to produce a body of work as a film director in the heyday of the HOLLYWOOD STUDIO SYSTEM in the 1930s and 1940s, Arzner began her career in film production as an editor, an

:::
Her films include Duet for Cannibals *and* Brother Carl, *but she is best known for another talent. Who is she?*
:::

area in which women were sometimes able to get work in Hollywood, particularly during the era of SILENT CINEMA: among her projects as a film editor was the Rudolph Valentino vehicle *Blood and Sand* (Fred Niblo, 1922), on which she also did some direction. In 1927 Arzner was offered her first solo directorial opportunity, by her employer PARAMOUNT, on *Fashions for Women*. In 1932 she left Paramount to go freelance, and subsequently directed films at RKO, COLUMBIA and MGM. After *First Comes*

Courage, starring Merle Oberon (1943) Arzner went into retirement, and until her death lived in California, occasionally working on writing, teaching and small directing projects. Dorothy Arzner was 'rediscovered' in the 1970s by feminist film critics Karyn Kay and Gerald Peary in the USA, and Claire JOHNSTON and Pam Cook in Britain. Arzner's work was subjected to reevaluation in the light of its nascent, if necessarily constrained, feminism. Two of her films in particular have attracted contemporary critical attention: *Dance, Girl, Dance*, in which dancer Judy (Maureen O'Hara) turns on an audience of men ogling her performance and berates them for their voyeurism; and *Christopher Strong*, starring Katharine HEPBURN, whose fictional exploits as pioneering aviator are said to be based on the real-life activities of Amy Johnson.

Fashions for Women (Paramount, 1927); *Ten Modern Commandments* (Paramount, 1927); *Get Your Man* (Paramount, 1927); *Manhattan Cocktail* (Paramount, 1928); *The Wild Party* (Paramount, 1929); *Sarah and Son* (Paramount, 1930); *Anybody's Woman* (Paramount, 1930); *Paramount on Parade* (Paramount, 1930); *Honor Among Lovers* (Paramount, 1931); *Working Girls* (Paramount, 1931); *Merrily We Go To Hell* (Paramount, 1932); *Christopher Strong* (RKO, 1933); *Nana* (MGM, 1934); *Craig's Wife* (Columbia, 1936); *The Bride Wore Red* (MGM, 1937); *Dance, Girl, Dance* (RKO, 1940); *First Comes Courage* (Columbia, 1943)

Claire Johnston (ed.), *Dorothy Arzner: Towards a Feminist Cinema* (London: British Film Institute, 1975)   *EAK*

ASANOVA, DINARA (1942–85)

A leading SOVIET director from Kirghizia, Asanova joined the Lenfilm studio in 1974. She directed nine feature films, usually focusing on the problems of adolescents. Her films were often sharply critical of Soviet social conditions and contemporary problems, but apparently never met with the ire of the censors. Asanova's films were extremely popular and widely seen in the USSR, and although her work is virtually unknown in the West she must be considered one of the most successful Soviet directors of the mid seventies and early eighties.

Among her notable pictures are: *Ne bolit golova u diatla* (about a first romance, with the prosaic world of adults used as counterpoint); the prizewinning *Kliuch bez prava peredachi* (1977, concerning the problems of high-school students); and her penultimate, *Patsany* (1983, a story of juvenile delinquents originally made for television). A hallmark of Asanova's work was her use of both professional and nonprofessional actors for verisimilitude.

Rudolfino (1970); *Ne bolit golova u diatla/ Woodpeckers Don't Get Headaches* (1975); *Kliuch bez prava peredachi/The Restricted Key* (1977); *Beda/Misfortune* (1978); *Zhena ushla/My Wife Has Left* (1980); *Nikudyshnaia/Good-for-Nothing* (1980); *Chto ty vybral/Which Would You Choose?* (1981); *Patsany/Young Toughs* (1983); *Milyi, dorogoi, liubimyi, edinstvennyi/ Dear, Dearest, Beloved, Only One* (1984)
DJY

AUDIENCE AND SPECTATOR

These two terms have taken on increasing importance in the study of cinema in recent years. Both indicate an emphasis on reception and consumption as an important aspect of understanding how meanings are produced by films, while each suggests a rather different approach to analyzing the relationship between viewers and films. 'Spectator' is a term associated with a mode of analysis focusing on the subject positions constructed by the film, and belongs to PSYCHOANALYTIC FILM THEORY. 'Audience,' on the other hand, refers to the actual people in the cinema and is associated with a more sociological or CULTURAL STUDIES approach to the visual media, especially TELEVISION and VIDEO.

However, the distinction is problematic and the relationship between the two terms is the source of much debate.

The difference can best be understood in terms of historical developments in FILM THEORY. 'Spectatorship' was put on the agenda, largely by FEMINIST FILM THEORY, as part of a more general reevaluation of CLASSICAL HOLLYWOOD CINEMA in the mid 1970s. 'Spectator' is a theoretical construct used to refer to the positions produced by a film through which the viewer is invited to follow its narrative and visual progression. Often 'spectator' is used interchangeably with 'textual position.'

Filmmaker and theorist Laura MULVEY's psychoanalytic critique of the visual pleasures offered by Hollywood fiction film produced widespread debate about the relationship between gender and spectatorship in a patriarchal culture. In her now classic 1975 article 'Visual Pleasure and Narrative Cinema,' Mulvey suggests that the construction of the spectator in Hollywood films is inevitably 'masculine.' Through an analysis of voyeuristic and fetishistic forms of visual PLEASURE in Hollywood films such as *Vertigo* (Alfred Hitchcock, Paramount, 1958) and *Morocco* (Josef von Sternberg, Paramount, 1930) Mulvey condemns the pleasures of spectatorship typically produced by popular cinema in the West. The film TEXT's construction of gendered spectator positions (masculine and feminine positions) has been considered in later work, in which Mulvey herself, as well as other feminist theorists, have developed a less pessimistic approach to popular film. This involves considering the female spectator's pleasure in narrative film (rather than merely her objectification by the male LOOK) by seeking moments of disruptive and transgressive FEMININITY.

In the 1980s feminist work on popular culture has been moving away from a preoccupation with film texts and toward a concern with the social contexts of their consumption. Feminist critics emphasize the process of consumption as

25

an active practice of negotiation and interaction of text, spectator and context, developing analyses which no longer see women in terms of how they are positioned by the mechanisms of patriarchal film, but increasingly ask questions about how women in the audience might actively make sense of (and take pleasure in) popular films. An example of this approach can be seen in the study of GENRES specifically aimed at female markets, where the importance of women as audiences is stressed: this allows for a consideration of the relationship between production and consumption of films: genres such as MELODRAMA, ROMANCE and the WOMAN'S PICTURE have all been looked at in this context. Some studies continue to emphasize psychoanalytic questions, being concerned with how certain films offer particular desires, identifications and pleasures to the female spectator. Others look at the development of 'women's genres' in a social and historical context.

Along with this interest in audiences and their contexts comes an increasing emphasis on the social identities, as opposed to the individual psyches, which construct audiences prior to the viewing of a film. Social identities – such as race, class and SEXUALITY, as well as gender – may produce different readings of the same film, depending on the different social knowledges and experiences of audience members. The homogeneous category of 'female spectator,' therefore, can be questioned and seen to be mediated to some extent by other social identities. This indicates a shift toward a more 'empirical' interest in social audiences and in particular viewing contexts. As yet, however, work on cinema audiences has not been developed as far as it has been in other areas of media and cultural studies. The question of spectatorship and audience has also been crucial to INDEPENDENT CINEMA. FEMINIST INDEPENDENT FILM has often been concerned with making processes of spectatorship visible in order to challenge the voyeurism of popular cinema. Feminist films like Marleen GORRIS's *A Question of Silence* (1981) have attempted to address a female spectator. There has also been considerable debate amongst feminist filmmakers about appropriate strategies for oppositional cinema – which audiences to address, whether to aim for a broad appeal and rework popular and recognizable genres, or whether to go for more challenging approaches to filmmaking which will tend to appeal to more limited audiences. Making films for particular audiences, whilst at the same time retaining control over distribution and exhibition, have been important strategies of independent feminist cinema.

Lorraine Gamman and Margaret Marshment, *The Female Gaze: Women as Viewers of Popular Culture* (London: Women's Press, 1988)

See also: BLACK WOMEN AND FILM THEORY; CONSUMERISM; FANDOM; FEMINIST DISTRIBUTION; FEMINIST EXHIBITION   JcS

AUDRY, JACQUELINE (1908–77)

Born in FRANCE, film director Audry once described her work as 'a defence of Woman as a human being but also in terms of her femininity.' Audry went through the classic channels of continuity work and assistantship to (among others) Jean Delannoy and Max OPHULS, before directing her first short, *Les Chevaux du Vercors*, in 1943. Aesthetically, her films belong to the French 'tradition of quality' of the 1940s and 1950s attacked by NEW WAVE critics. This term refers to well-made studio films, tasteful literary adaptations and period reconstructions, with an emphasis on sophisticated dialogue and florid acting.

What sets Audry apart from mainstream French quality cinema, however, is her choice of subject matter. Though, like many of her contemporaries, she kept returning to glamorous belle époque settings, her COLETTE adap-

Marina de Berg and Edwige Feuillère in Jacqueline Audry's *Olivia*

tations (*Gigi* (1948), *Minne* (1950), *Mitsou* (1956)), that of Victor Marguerite's *La Garçonne* (1956), or the portrayal of lesbian relationships in *Olivia* (1951), her most celebrated film, show her consistent interest in transgressive women figures. Even though the subversiveness of these HEROINES may ultimately be limited by conventional narratives and the titillating potential of the subjects, these women are never treated as perverse curiosities. Besides, Audry's focus on women alone is exceptional in French cinema, traditionally centered on male characters. Although several of her films were box office successes, she suffered a series of setbacks in her career (her version of *Gigi* was originally released without her name) and the fact that she managed to make eighteen features is in itself remarkable.

Les Chevaux du Vercors (short, 1943); *Les Malheurs de Sophie* (1944); *Gigi* (1948); *Sombre dimanche* (1948); *Minne ou l'ingénue libertine/Minne* (1950); *Olivia/Pit of Loneliness* (1951); *La Caraque blonde* (1952); *Huis-clos* (1954); *Mitsou* (1956); *La Garçonne* (1956); *L'École des cocottes, C'est la faute d'Adam* (1957); *Le Secret du cheva-* *lier d'Éon* (1959); *Les Petits Matins* (1961); *Cadavres en vacances* (1961); *Cours de bonheur conjugal* (1964); *Fruits amers* (1966); *Le Lys de mer* (1969); *Un grand Amour de Balzac* (1972)

Michèle Levieux, 'Jacqueline Audry', *La Revue du cinéma*, no. 396 (1984)   GV

AUSTRALIA

Film production in Australia reached a precocious peak in 1911. From 1906, with the advent of Australia's first feature, *The Story of the Kelly Gang* (Charles Tait), theatrical troupes and film production companies were regularly producing features which established the recurring themes and motifs of an unselfconsciously national cinema. The most popular films drew on stories of convicts, the gold rushes, bushrangers and outback life. Films based on British and American GENRES, especially COMEDY and MELODRAMA, were prolific but less successful. The bush heroine/squatter's daughter emerged as the dominant female type, independent and knowledgable, a spirited mate and loyal partner, in the indigenous genres exemp-

Serious Undertakings, by Helen Grace

lified in the silent period by *A Girl of the Bush* (Franklyn Barrett, 1921) and in the sound period by *The Squatter's Daughter* (Ken G Hall, 1933). Her double was often the sophisticated city girl or the girl from the bush seduced by the city slicker.

DOCUMENTARY and religious excursions into filmmaking occurred as early as 1896, culminating in the Salvation Army's spectacular *Soldiers of the Cross* (Joseph Perry, Herbert Booth), a mixed-media lecture presented in 1900. In 1901 Walter Baldwin Spencer, on a scientific expedition to Central Australia, shot the first of the six thousand or more ETHNOGRAPHIC FILMS that have been produced in Australia on aborigines. Documentary filmmaking has been described as the backbone of the industry, persisting from the first actuality films of the 1890s, through the Commonwealth Film Unit/Film Australia, to the Documentary Fellowships of the 1980s.

The major stumbling block for a continuity of features production was put in place as early as 1912, when Australasian Films and Union Theatres established joint control over the exhibition and distribution trade. A number of entrepreneurs – including Raymond Longford and Lottie LYELL, Franklyn Barrett, John Gavin and Beaumont Smith – continued to make films into the 1920s. However, the lack of outlets for independently produced films put local production into a decline from which it did not recover until the 1970s. In 1927–8, a royal commission into the industry recommended the imposition of a quota to ensure the exhibition of Australian films; but this proved impossible to enforce. By 1930 American distribution agents had broken the monopoly of Australasian Films, and Hoyts (partly owned by Fox since 1930) had transformed exhibition into a duopoly which remained in force until the late sixties when a third national chain, Village Theatres, was established. The control of DISTRIBUTION and EXHIBITION by American interests is the most significant feature of the Australian film industry.

The introduction of sound and highly capitalized studio production brought about the deathknell of women's widespread behind-the-camera participation in SILENT CINEMA, exemplified by the shortlived careers of the McDONAGH SISTERS, Paulette, Isobel and Phyllis, who managed to make four features between 1926 and 1933. In 1932, Stuart Doyle of Greater Union Theatres (formerly Australasian-Union) established Cinesound, Australia's most successful studio, run by Ken G Hall on the model of the HOLLYWOOD STUDIO SYSTEM. It produced a string of commercial successes (including Hall's *On Our Selection*, 1932) until feature production came to a standstill in 1940 with World War II. Charles and Elsa CHAUVEL, with the backing of Universal's Australian agent Hercules McIntyre, dominated feature production during and after the war, with *Forty Thousand Horsemen* (1940), *The Rats of Tobruk* (1944), *Sons of Matthew* (1949) and *Jedda* (1955).

In 1970 the virtually defunct feature film industry finally attracted sustained government subsidies with the setting up of the Australian Film Development Corporation; and a preoccupation with questions of national identity then emerged as the touchstone of a selfconsciously NATIONAL CINEMA. Audiences flocked to the early sex comedies (*Alvin Purple* [Tim Burstall, 1973]) but it was not until the release of Peter Weir's *Picnic At Hanging Rock* in 1975 that critics and the funding bodies – the Australian Film Commission (AFC) and the State Film Corporations – found the distinctively Australian qualities they needed to sustain the dominant rhetoric of cultural nationalism. *Picnic At Hanging Rock* was the first of a genre of picturesque period films capable of showcasing a nostalgic Australianness to the world. Landscape and light became the focus of critical acclaim for an inoffensive series of films whose audiences were falling away in droves by 1979 when Gillian ARMSTRONG's *My Brilliant Career* won the

genre one of its many reprieves. The worthiness of the genre was rivaled only by a number of mostly low-budget social realist films (for example *The Promised Woman* [Tom Cowan, 1975], *Mouth to Mouth* [John Duigan, 1978], *Fran* [Glenda Hambly, 1984]), whose focus on contemporary urban issues provided a welcome relief from the nostalgia of the costume dramas. With the introduction of tax concessions for film investments and profits in 1981, purely commercial films with little or no interest in questions of national identity or contemporary Australian life attracted large amounts of tax avoidance business and, for the most part, disappeared into video markets.

The blockbuster successes of Kennedy Miller's *Mad Max* cycle (1979–85) and Paul Hogan's *Crocodile Dundee* films (1986 and 1987) were exceptions to the rule that tax avoidance films were no more commercially successful than their more culturally respectable counterparts. Somewhere between the two poles of cultural worthiness and commercial product lie buried a number of hard-to-classify films which have been labeled Australian gothic or eccentric. These films (including the seminal *Shirley Thompson versus the Aliens* (Jim Sharman, 1972), *The Cars That Ate Paris* (Peter Weir, 1974), *Pure S* (Bert Deling, 1976), *Journey Among Women* (Tom Cowan, 1977)) proffer much more oblique and challenging notions of Australianness, displaying allegiances to underground film and trash culture.

The revival of the feature film industry in the 1970s brought about a split between industry and culture that has animated the rhetoric supporting nonfeature filmmaking for the last two decades. AVANT-GARDE, political and 'social issues' filmmaking converged in the transformation of the Ubu Film Group's distribution service into the Sydney Filmmakers Co-operative in the late sixties. The setting up of the Experimental Film Fund (EFF) in 1970 provided a unique opportunity for

29

the encouragement of a diversity of approaches to the film medium. However, the fund quickly developed its own aesthetic which encouraged safely innovative filmmaking devoted to social issues, the mastery of conventional narrative codes and the acquisition of credentials or craft skills. The EFF was absorbed into the AFC as the Creative Development Branch in 1978. A number of mostly Melbourne-based filmmakers have continued to work in an avowedly avant-garde mode, chiefly Arthur and Corinne CANTRILL, Nigel Buesst, Paul Winkler, Jonas Balsaitis, Dirk de Bruyn, Michael Lee and John Dunkley-Smith.

Feminist filmmaking, which emerged as part of the women's liberation movement in the early seventies, has been closely tied to the Sydney Filmmakers Co-operative and REEL WOMEN in Melbourne, and has been administered through the AFC by the WOMEN'S FILM FUND. The 1980s have been a decade of diversification, which has left overtly

feminist filmmaking in a vacuum. A number of women have produced or directed features (*Silver City* [Sophia Turkiewicz, 1984], *Malcolm* [Nadia Tass, 1986], *Two Friends* [Jane Campion, 1986], *High Tide* [Gillian Armstrong, 1987], *Australian Dream* [Jackie McKimmie, 1987], *Bachelor Girl* [Rivka Hartman, 1987], *Pieta* [Monique Schwarz, 1987], *The Pursuit of Happiness* [Martha Ansara, 1987], *Tenderhooks* [Mary Callaghan, 1988], *Celia* [Ann Turner, 1988]) and some younger women have found their way into filmmaking via the extremely cineliterate super-8mm scenes in Sydney and Melbourne (Catherine Lowing, Anne Marie Crawford, Jayne Stevenson, Virginia Hilyard, Barbara Campbell, Maj Green) or through video (Jill Scott).

The decision to fund films directly through the Film Finance Corporation set up in 1988, rather than through tax subsidies, marks a new phase for Australian film. Much of the nationalist rhetoric

Tracy Moffatt directing *Nice Coloured Girls*

which has mediated the film industry/ film culture split since the sixties has been declared dead in the wake of widespread disenchantment generated by two decades of predominantly middlebrow filmmaking. The underlying agenda of revitalizing a nineteenth-century myth of national identity has muffled other voices attempting to articulate, in documentary or shorts, aspects of Australianness based on class, race, gender, and ethnic differences (*My Survival As An Aboriginal* [Essie Coffey, 1979], *Two Laws* [Borroloola Aboriginal Community, Carolyn Strachan and Alessandro Cavadini, 1981], *Greetings From Wollongong* [Mary Callaghan, 1982], *Serious Undertakings* [Helen Grace, 1982], *For Love or Money* [Megan McMurchy and Jeni Thornley, 1983], *The Drover's Wife* [Sue Brooks, 1985], *Nice Coloured Girls* [Tracey Moffatt, 1987], *Ten Years After . . . Ten Years Older* [Anna Kannava, 1987], or voices attempting to engage with issues more obliquely concerned with, or antithetical to, questions of identity (*Ocean Ocean* [Kieran Finnane, 1987], *Passionless Moments* [Jane Campion, 1984], *Salt, Saliva, Sperm and Sweat* [Philip Brophy, 1988]).

Albert Moran and Tom O'Regan (eds), *An Australian Film Reader* (Sydney: Currency Press, 1985)

See also: ABORIGINAL FILM AND VIDEO; LAWSON, SYLVIA; SYDNEY WOMEN'S FILM GROUP   FC

AUTEUR, AUTEUR THEORY *see* AUTHORSHIP

AUTHORSHIP

The 'auteur theory' of the 1960s was initially a polemic for serious critical discussion of Hollywood films, previously dismissed as unworthy objects of criticism. The 'great tradition' in literature is a tradition of great 'authors,' who as unique individuals guarantee the originality of their work through its expression of a personal vision. Authorship thus defines and protects 'literature' against mass-produced fiction with its reliance on syndicated writing, genres, conventions, formulae and mass audiences.

These features, however, are exactly the hallmarks of mainstream entertainment cinemas, which constitute a massive collective, industrial enterprise. Thus while the notion of director as 'auteur' has always been more readily accepted in ART CINEMA and AVANT-GARDE FILM, critical acceptance as authors of directors working within the HOLLYWOOD STUDIO SYSTEM did not take place without a struggle. In this context, criticism focused on the possibilities of directorial control over film contents by means of such elements as visual style or MISE-EN-SCENE, which may escape the influence of the studio. One after another, Hollywood directors were identified as artists, expressing a personal vision which it was the film critic's job to analyze and make available to educated readers.

These discoveries, not surprisingly, failed to include the very few women who had managed to become directors, and an early task of FEMINIST FILM THEORY was to recover their work. However, within the broader sphere of FILM THEORY, GENRE criticism, ideological analysis and STRUCTURALISM had exposed the individualist and romantic ideology at work in the auteur theory. In the monographs on film directors that flowered in the sixties and early seventies, feminists can now read a reiterated male angst about the romantic hero faced with a post-industrial world and the disturbance of gender relations threatened by the women's movement.

Feminist work on women directors has never been able to assume in such an unproblematic way that the language of cinema could express a personal vision. In particular, images of women are understood as expressions of male desires or anxieties. Given the IDEOLOGY embedded in film language – and indeed in the notion of FEMININITY – the presence of a woman director cannot guarantee a feminist – nor even a 'feminine' – film. Moreover, collectivity as against individualism is a valued element in feminist practice. Rather than authentic personal vision, feminist auteur studies look for signs of struggle with cinematic codes and cultural conventions; for a female 'voice' or perspective that speaks from and to the contradictions of women's lives and the way we are represented.

Pam Cook, 'Authorship and Cinema', in *The Cinema Book*, ed. Pam Cook (London: British Film Institute, 1985)   CG

AVANT-GARDE FILM

The avant-garde film, which came into existence in Paris during the 1920s in the Dadaist and Surrealist milieu, has been a form accessible to women filmmakers from its very beginning. Women were among the first to respond to Jean Cocteau's challenge to take up a camera, just as a writer might pick up a pen. Germaine DULAC in the 1920s and 1930s, Maya DEREN in the 1940s, Marie MENKEN in the 1950s and Carolee SCHNEEMANN in the sixties, all paved the way for women to choose film as a medium for personal expression and aesthetic inquiry. The field is indebted to Dulac and Deren also for their founding theories of avant-garde film: both were rigorous and prolific writers in defense of their vocation.

The 1960s saw a blossoming of this heterodox field, with filmmakers using available and inexpensive 8mm and 16mm film equipment and stock. The works produced have been divided by critic P Adams Sitney into the following categories: trance, lyrical, mythopoeic, absolute animation, graphic, picaresque, and structural; and by film theorist Annette Michelson into formalist and radical divisions as well. The works of Marie Menken, for example, are primarily lyrical and diaristic: her film *Notebook* (1962), which inaugurated the diary form as viable aesthetic enterprise in film, is acknowledged by Stan Brakhage and Jonas Mekas (two major American

figures in the genre) as a key influence on their own work. Carolee Schneemann extended the form by loop printing and reediting highly charged personal material into a coherent and visible structure in her films. Throughout the 1970s, women within the US and Canadian avant gardes centered their enterprise mainly in the personal film, while the European avant garde concentrated its efforts on the material analysis of cinema. The 1980s have seen a growth in films made with 'appropriated' images – commercial, industrial, and scientific film reedited in order to critique their latent content.

Since the 1960s there have also arisen numerous showcases for avant-garde films (and latterly VIDEOS) as well as DISTRIBUTION cooperatives. New York, San Francisco, London, and to a lesser extent Paris, Hamburg, and Cologne became centers for the making, viewing, and dissemination of INDEPENDENT CINEMA. A utopian sixties-style egalitarianism has permitted women's participation as makers, teachers, and administrators of cooperatives and showcases to a degree unusual in more established institutions.

The rise of feminism and its revaluation of the 'personal as political,' together with an increasing number of departments in art schools and universities devoted to the avant garde, have fostered a resurgence – and a transformation – of work in the field which continues into the 1990s. The films of Yvonne RAINER and Chantal AKERMAN reintroduce issues of NARRATIVE whilst also exploring images and roles of women in cinema: their work has formed a bridge between the avant-garde and mainstream cinemas. Highly structured but potently imagistic works by Abigail CHILD, Nina FONOROFF and others have extended the work begun in the 1960s by Carolee Schneemann and her male counterparts, Stan Brakhage, Michael Snow and Peter Kubelka, responding to the debates within feminism and at the same time asserting their personal, often eccentric, visions. However, despite some overlapping of categories, the avant-garde film distinguishes itself from other non-mainstream cinema practices (DOCUMENTARY, COUNTERCINEMA, FEMINIST INDEPENDENT FILM, and so on) by its commitment to the notion of the filmmaker as sole consciousness behind, and inventor of, the form specific to each film.

P Adams Sitney, *Visionary Film: The American Avant Garde 1943–1978* (New York: Oxford University Press, 1979)

See also: BUTE, MARY ELLEN; CANTRILL, CORINNE AND ARTHUR; CLARKE, SHIRLEY; DURAS, MARGUERITE; EPSTEIN, MARIE; EXPORT, VALIE; FRIEDRICH, SU; GRUBEN, PATRICIA; HAMMER, BARBARA; HD; HEIN, BIRGIT; IDEMITSU, MAKO; NEUBAUER, VERA; NICHOLSON, ANNABEL; REINIGER, LOTTE; RHODES, LIS; WIELAND, JOYCE   *MKe*

AZMI, SHABANA (1948–)

Launched in INDIA's 'parallel cinema' with Shyam Benegal's first feature *Ankur/The Seedling* (1974), a film about feudal corruption and the exploitation of women, Shabana quickly became known as an intelligent, accomplished and versatile actress. The range of her abilities is remarkable: on the one hand she has proved herself with brilliant performances in the work of all the major Indian art cinema directors: Shyam Benegal (notably *Ankur*, *Nishant/Night's End* [1975], *Junoon* [1978] and *Mandi* [1983]), Mrinal Sen (*Khandhar/The Ruins* [1984]), Satyajit Ray (*Shatranj ke Khilari/The Chess Players* [1977]), and she has won several national prizes and a growing international recognition, particularly after her role in John Schlesinger's *Madame Sousatzka* (1988). On the other hand she has, from the earliest days of her career, achieved star status through her many box office successes in the mainstream cinema and is the only actress to cross the art/mainstream cinema divide with such skill and apparent ease. Azmi, along with Smita PATIL, has been crucial in broadening the range of strong sympathetic central female roles in contemporary Indian cinema, and in the mid 1980s was a key actress for the emergent 'middle cinema.'

Her family had broad cultural, intellectual and political interests: her mother was a well-known theater actress and her father an eminent Urdu poet actively involved in Communist Party affairs. Shabana was brought up in Bombay and, following a first degree in psychology, took the Film and Television Institute of India acting course. In the eighties she has become increasingly involved in political campaigning, lending her star status to a number of causes, from support for the celebrated Shah Banu divorce case (contesting Muslim personal law which refuses women rights to alimony) to a tour of northern India to help to calm Hindu–Muslim friction. She has also embarrassed the Indian government on a number of issues, from making public accusations of their collusion in the murder of Delhi street theater activist Safdar Hashmi to undertaking a hunger strike to draw attention to the plight of Bombay's pavement dwellers. She is married to the scriptwriter and poet Javed Akhtar and lives in Bombay. *RT*

BACALL, LAUREN (1924–)

Known to many as the 'female Humphrey Bogart,' Hollywood STAR Bacall, the strong-minded, seductive heroine of *To Have and Have Not* (Howard Hawks, Warner Bros., 1945), became a new kind of pinup, for women and men. Betty Perske was born in New York and trained at the American Academy of Dramatic Arts, but had more success initially as a model than as an actress. When her face appeared on the cover of *Harper's Bazaar* in 1943, director Howard HAWKS offered her a contract and turned her into his protegee. 'I wanted to create a woman who seemed even tougher than Bogart. So I created the image of Lauren Bacall and she'll have to live with it for the rest of her life,' he said later. But by teaming Bacall with Bogart for *To Have and Have Not*, Hawks became the unconscious and then unwilling catalyst in one of the most famous real-life/onscreen love affairs. The success story was repeated with the same team the following year in *The Big Sleep* (Howard Hawks, Warner Bros., 1946) and later with *Dark Passage* (Delmer Daves, Warner Bros., 1947) and *Key Largo* (John Huston, Warner Bros., 1948).

As a Jewish girl from a modest background (which must, ironically, have rankled with the antisemitic Hawks), Bacall embodied a classless and independent, though not career-oriented, woman. *To Have and Have Not* launched her as a cross between a carefree girl and a sophisticated woman whose creation, the twinklingly ironic come-hither 'look,' was, she explained later, only a device to stop herself shaking. Ending up with Bogart after a movie's worth of flirtation and testing each other may be seen, given her assured performances, not as giving in but as shared success. Bacall's image was guaranteed an extra dimension by her political involvement as one of the leaders of the Committee for the Fifth Amendment, founded in the face of postwar McCarthyism.

After her marriage to Bogart, there were long gaps in her film career. Many of her films were flimsy, though others, like *The Cobweb* (Vincente Minnelli, MGM, 1955) and *Written on the Wind* (Douglas Sirk, Universal, 1956) succeeded as great MELODRAMAs in which she gave sterling performances, if not with the warmth of her earlier work. Since then Bacall has become, on stage and screen, a celebrity *grande dame* – as her appearance in several Agatha Christie movies would appear to confirm.

Lauren Bacall, *By Myself* (London: Jonathan Cape, 1979)   ALi

BANI ETEMAAD, RAKHSHAN (1953–)

Bani Etemaad is an unorthodox film director in post-revolutionary IRAN. She studied cinema at the Teheran University of Dramatic Arts and subsequently worked as assistant director and production manager. In 1981 she was offered a seat in the directors' room of Iranian television. There she made a number of DOCUMENTARIES examining the chronic economic sickness the Islamic regime inherited from the late Shah and failed to cure. For example, *Eshteghal-e-Mohojereen Roustai* (1981) concerns the problems facing migrant peasants seeking work in large cities; *Ta'dabir Eghtessa-di-y-Janghi* (1982) deals with the muddles of the Islamic government's war effort;

Rakhshan Bani Etemaad directing
Off the Limits

and *Farahang-e-Massraffi* (1983) critically assesses renewed consumerism in post-revolutionary Iran. Because of their critical tone, these works were not released in Iran.

In 1986 Bani Etemaad left television and joined the mainstream film industry as a freelance director. Her commercial films *Khareje Aze Mahdoudeh/Off the Limits* (1987) and *Zarede Ghaneri/The Yellow Car* (1989) are social comedies set in pre-revolutionary times. Her satirical portrayal of the inefficiencies of the late Shah's bureaucratic administration and its manipulation by the upper classes have a subtle relevance to contemporary conditions and her skillful direction, which deserves special notice for its feminist edge, has now made her popular with the filmgoing public.

Eshteghal-e-Mohojereen Roustai (1981); *Sazemonhayi Moli Yahoud* (1981); *Ta'dabir Eghtessadi-y-Janghi* (1982); *Farahang-e-Massraffi* (1983); *Tamarkoze* (1984); *Rooze Jahoni Koreghar* (1985); *Khareje Aze Mahdoudeh/Off the Limits* (1987); *Zarede Ghaneri/The Yellow Car* (1989)

BR

BARA, THEDA (1890–1955)

Born Theodosia Goodman in Cincinnati, Ohio, Bara, tagged 'the world's greatest vampire,' was the first screen actress to be manufactured as a STAR by the Hollywood studio publicity system. From her name – an anagram of 'arab death' – to the various stories of her mysterious and supernatural origins in the Egyptian desert, to her stunts in black-draped hotel suites heavily scented with oriental incense, the leading edge of this publicity amplified the macabre, evil and unearthly aspects of the Bara persona. Her first starring role in *A Fool There Was* (Frank Powell, 1915) provided the finance which led to the establishment of the Fox studio and launched Bara as the screen VAMP whose sinister powers, sensuous movements and cold-blooded machinations proved the undoing of helpless husbands and faithful wives in a series of followups with such suggestive titles as *Sin* (Herbert Brenon, 1915), *The She-Devil* (J Gordon Edwards, 1919) and *The Siren's Song* (J Gordon Edwards, 1919).

Yet though Bara's dark-ringed eyes, pallor, pantherish sinuosity and snake-like charm have come to represent the essence of the vamp STEREOTYPE, closer scrutiny of her screen roles and press treatment reveals telling contradictions within this early attempt to construct a popular and powerful cinematic construction of FEMININITY. Onscreen, indeed, half of Bara's roles were more innocent than vampirish: in *Kathleen Mavourneen* (1919), for instance, her husband-to-be Charles J Brabin directed her as a fresh-faced Irish colleen. Offscreen, in the pages of fan magazines, Bara was both the child suckled on serpent's milk and the girl-next-door – 'misunderstood vampire.' Nevertheless, it was as vamp that Bara exerted her immense and powerful fascination for both male and female cinema AUDIENCES. While her appeal to a male audience arguably rested upon MASCULINITY's desire for and dread of an active and powerful female SEXUALITY, Bara herself declared that the PLEASURE she offered a female audience was transgressive: 'V. stands for vampire and it stands for vengeance too,' she declared. 'The vampire that I play is the vengeance of my sex upon its exploiters. You see. . . . I have the face of a vampire, perhaps, but the heart of a "feministe".'

Sumiko Higashi, *Virgins Vamps and Flappers: The American Silent Movie Heroine* (Montreal: Eden Press, 1978)   SR

BARDOT, BRIGITTE (1934–)

Born in FRANCE, Bardot rose to world stardom with *Et Dieu créa la femme/And God Created Woman* (1956), directed by her then husband Roger Vadim. While this film has been hailed as a precursor of the NEW WAVE, mostly for its location in St Tropez (which Bardot helped make France's top resort), it launched 'BB,' a former model, as the most potent sexual myth in France's 'unliberated' 1950s and a valuable French export commodity. Bardot's persona was that of the sex kitten, combining 'natural' and unruly sexuality with childish attributes – her body, lithe but with full breasts; her long hair, BLONDE and wild but with a girlish fringe. She went on to star in unremarkable vehicles in the 1960s and early 1970s, though a few films used her intelligently: Henri-Georges Clouzot's *La Vérité/The Truth* (1960), a courtroom drama in which her sexuality itself is on trial, Louis Malle's semibiographical *Vie privée/A Very Private Affair* (1962), and Jean-Luc GODARD's *Le Mépris/Contempt* (1963). The power of the Bardot myth can be gauged by the idolization ('*bardolâtrie*') of which she was the object – her gingham dresses and hairstyle, even her pout, were copied and she modeled for Marianne, the effigy of the French Republic – as well as the extraordinary hostility she aroused; she was viciously abused and physically attacked on several occasions.

Bardot was the archetypal SEX GODDESS, yet she was also rebellious, and showed evident guiltless pleasure in her own body and sexuality. As a result she was box office but she wasn't popular. These contradictions intrigued Simone de Beauvoir, who defended BB as a manifestation of a new, artifice-free type of FEMININITY, 'as much a hunter as she is a prey.' Though Bardot was no positive HEROINE she showed, unlike her contemporary MONROE, stamina and a shrewd business sense. She retired from acting in 1973 and now lives in St Tropez with her numerous dogs, managing her estate and a shop of Bardot memorabilia. She is a devoted campaigner for animal rights.

Simone de Beauvoir, 'Brigitte Bardot and the Lolita syndrome', in *Women and the Cinema*, eds Karyn Kay and Gerald Peary (New York: Dutton, 1977)   GV

BARRY, IRIS (1895–1969)

One of the most dynamic women in the history of FILM CRITICISM and scholarship must be Barry – film critic, historian, and the first film curator of New York's Museum of Modern Art (MOMA). Barry was very nearly the earliest woman film critic in her native BRITAIN: she wrote for the *Spectator* from 1923 to 1930 and was film editor of the *Daily Mail* from 1926 to 1930. In 1926 she published her very popular *Let's Go to the Pictures*. After moving to the United States, Barry wrote her pioneering and still very important book *D. W. Griffith: American Film Master* (New York: Museum of Modern Art, 1940). Even discounting her other achievements, to have popularized the work of the long-neglected GRIFFITH, and explained it in so comprehensive a fashion – with stills, analysis and filmography – is a feat extraordinary enough to secure her a prominent place in the world of film scholarship.

In the USA Barry was also a regular book reviewer for the New York *Herald Tribune*, and her articles appeared in various popular American magazines including *Vogue* and *Town and Country*. With seemingly boundless energy, she gave courses in cinema studies while working at MOMA, wrote program notes for screenings, and produced the first bulletin of its Film Library. Some would say Barry's work as curator was her most significant contribution: she cadged films and books, hustled grant money, and essentially created MOMA's entire film archive. Barry also compiled and edited *The Film Index* – a long volume treating all aspects of film – for the WPA Writers' Project of the Roosevelt era, and during World War II worked to get political refugees out of Europe. She managed to squeeze in translations, biographies and novels too.

Critically speaking, Barry approached cinema in many fresh theoretical ways: nationally, auteuristically, sociologically, and in terms of genre and myth. Despite an occasional tendency to flipness, Iris Barry may well be the most versatile critic of either sex ever to address cinema.

Marsha McCreadie, *Women on Film: The Critical Eye* (New York: Praeger, 1983)
MMc

BAT ADAM, MICHAL (19??–)

Michal Bat Adam, a major ISRAELI woman filmmaker, began her career as an actress, playing the female lead in Moshe Mizrahi's *Ani Ohev Otach Rosa/I Love You, Rosa* (1972). Her first feature, *Moments/Each Other* (US) (1979), an Israeli–French co-production, revolves around a chance meeting on the Tel Aviv–Jerusalem train between two young women, an Israeli writer and a

> **'A last resort for failed filmmakers.'**
> **What questionable line of work is this?**

French photographer on holiday. The film is structured around a flashback to an earlier meeting between the pair, and progressively zooms in on their relationship, so that it becomes a review of past memories, of feelings sensed but

never defined. Bat Adam's oblique refusal to offer the audience decisive confirmation of the protagonists' presumed lesbian interlude recalls Diane Kurys's similar stratagem in her art house hit *Entre nous/At First Sight* (1983). Bat Adam has made three more films – *The Thin Line* (1980), *Ahava Rishona* (1982), and *Hame'ahev* (1986), based on A B Yehoshua's novel – in the same intimist style.

Moments/Each Other (US (1979); *The Thin Line* (1980); *Ahava Rishona/First Love* (1982); *Hame'ahev/The Lover* (1986)

Ella Shohat, *Israeli Cinema: East/West and the Politics of Representation* (Texas: University of Texas Press, 1989)   ES

BATCHELOR, JOY (1914–)

Joy Batchelor formed the ANIMATION partnership Halas and Batchelor with her husband, the Hungarian John Halas. The studio, established in 1940, was the largest animation unit in BRITAIN in the postwar years. It began by making short public information films for the wartime government: for example *Dustbin Parade* (1941) on the importance of saving waste. Later, the studio continued to make information and educational films, but also produced many entertainment shorts, series, and features, the most successful being *Animal Farm* (1954).

Batchelor was active in more than five hundred productions over four decades as writer, producer, or director, alone or in collaboration with Halas. These were all productions of a large studio with at times up to one hundred employees organized into a hierarchical division of labor. It is hard to assess Joy Batchelor's personal authorship in these studio productions, though her talents as a writer and director are undoubted. It is harder still to discern any especially feminist or feminine consciousness in her work. Her reputation unfortunately has tended to be overshadowed by that of her more image-conscious husband, who has been the subject of greater critical and public attention.

Shorts directed with John Halas: *Train Trouble* (1940); *Carnival in the Clothes Cupboard* (1940); *Filling the Gap* (1941); *Dustbin Parade* (1941); *Digging for Victory* (1942); *Jungle Warfare* (1943); *Modern Guide to Health* (1946); *Old Wives' Tales* (1946); *Charley* Series (1946–7); *First Line of Defence* (1947); *This is the Air Force* (1947); *What's Cooking?* (1947); *Dolly Put the Kettle On* (1947); *Oxo Parade* (1948); *Heave Away My Johnny* (1948); *The Shoemaker and the Hatter* (1949); *Fly About the House* (1949); *The Figurehead* (1953); *The Candlemaker* (1956); *The First 99* (1958); *Dam the Delta* (1958); *All Lit Up* (1959); *Piping Hot* (1959); *For Better For Worse* (1959)

Shorts directed alone: *Classic Fairy Tales* Series (1966); *Colombo Plan* (1967); *The Commonwealth* (1967); *Bolly* (1968); *The Five* (1970); *Wet Dot* (1970); *Contact* (1973); *The Ass and the Stick* (1974); *Carry on Milkmaids* (1974)

Features: *Animal Farm* (with John Halas, 1954); *Ruddigore* (1964)

Roger Manvel, *Art and Animation* (London: Halas and Batchelor, 1980) IK

BELGIUM

Since the early 1960s between eight and ten feature films a year have been produced in Belgium, a country divided not only by its cultures but also by its bilingual – French and Flemish – configuration. Such an output is certainly no mean achievement considering the inadequate infrastructure, absence of professional film training schemes, and limited funding. Half of these films are funded either by the Flemish or the Walloon Ministry of Culture. The other half are financed through co-productions with France, the Netherlands, Germany, or Britain. Since Walloon talents tend to migrate to Paris – André Delvaux and Marion HAENSEL are exceptions – it is Flemish rather than francophone cinema

that makes a name for itself in Belgium. In the late 1960s Harry Kuemel achieved fame internationally as well as locally with *Mr Hawarden* (1969) and *Daughters of Darkness* (1970), which have both become lesbian cult movies; the former involving CROSSDRESSING in its plot, the latter LESBIAN VAMPIRES.

In the early 1980s Robbe de Hert gained international recognition with *De witte van Sichen/Whitey* (1980, based on Ernest Claes's book), as did Lili Rademakers, who made *Menuet* (1982) in joint production with the Netherlands. *Menuet* is a film about a young woman living in the country during the fifties, who flouts all sexual morality. Szamy Slingerbaum also received recognition in cinematographic circles for his very individual stylized drama documentary *Bruxelles-Transit* (1982). This is the story of the Jewish mother of a filmmaker, who flees Poland in 1947 with her husband and children to come to Belgium. It shows the problems of adaptation by, and the appalling rootlessness of, all immigrants in the West. Over the past few years, the names of Marc Didden (*Istanbul* [1985]), Dominique Deruddere (*Crazy Love* [1986]) and Patrick Conrad (*Perneke* [1985], *Mascara* [1987]) have become well known not so much because of the special qualities of their films – some of them are undisciplined and others stilted – but because they have managed, by their nonconformity, to draw audiences' attention to Flemish cinema.

No active policy promoting films of artistic value is currently being pursued in Belgium, either on the production level or as far as distribution and exhibition are concerned. In the absence of any subsidies, the three noncommercial distributors (Progrès film, Ciné Libre and De andere Cinema) have to survive by their own efforts: however, out of 450 cinemas, only eight have agreed to program their films. Because of lack of funds – in 1986 its budget was cut by 44 percent – the world-famous collection of the Brussels Royal Film Archives, set up by

Jacques Ledoux, is unable properly to fulfill its public function. However, since the 1920s Henri Storck, who co-directed *Misère au Borinage* (1934) with Joris Ivens, has managed at least to keep the flame of DOCUMENTARY alive. Storck was – and still is – an out-and-out documentary maker. His many films (the majority without commentaries) about Belgian idiosyncrasies, traditions and wrongs bear witness to this, as does his promotion of film documentary, for which he set up the Centre Bruxellois de l'Audiovisuel (CBA): this is a fund which first of all keeps filmmakers such as Robbe de Hart, Chantal AKERMAN, Michel Khleifi and Mary Jimenez in work, and secondly has given several people their first chance in filmmaking. After her first two films, *Piano Bar* (1982) and *La Moitié de l'amour/Love's Half* (1984), Mary Jimenez made *Du Verbe Aimer/About the Verb to Love* in 1983–4 with money from the CBA.

Francis Bolen, *Several Aspects of Belgian Cinema* (Brussels: Ministeries van Cultuur, 1971)   AF

BEMBERG, MARIA LUISA
(1940–)

After raising an upper-class family and divorcing her husband, Bemberg sought out the cinema as an outlet for personal growth and for expressing her developing feminist concerns. She wrote several screenplays for other ARGENTINE directors (for example, *Crónica de una señora/Story of a Lady* (1970) for director Raúl de la Torre) and then used her own capital to help finance her first two productions. Her films and screenplays, which have always dealt with women and the obstacles to independent thought and action they face within traditional patriarchal societies, were not officially sanctioned during the military dictatorship that governed Argentina during the late 1970s and until 1983. From her first feature-length film until today, Bemberg has worked collaboratively with executive producer Lita STANTIC.

Bemberg became famous with her third feature, *Camila* (1984), an Argentine–Spanish co-production (scripted by Bemberg, Juan Bautista Stagnaro and Beda Docampo Feijoo) based on the true story of a nineteenth-century upper-class girl who eloped with a parish priest and was subsequently hunted down and executed with her lover. Camila (Susú Pecoraro) and her lover Ladislao (Imanol Arias) are presented as romantic victims of a mad passion in a traditional melodramatic framework that unfolds in one of the darkest and bloodiest moments of Argentine history. Despite the fact that the film focuses on the romantic tragedy of the star-crossed lovers rather than offering social comment, Bemberg was unable to make the film until after the Argentine redemocratization process ended the long military dictatorship that followed the second fall of Perónism. Bemberg's next film, *Miss Mary* (1986), the story of an English governess imported into 1940s Argentina to educate the children of an upper-class family, was also scripted by the Bemberg–Stagnaro–Feijoo team and produced by Stantic as an international co-production with Julie Christie in the title role. A glossy, expensive production in the international ART CINEMA mold, it was successful in Argentina, but less so than *Camila* had been. It is not as accessible as *Camila*, because of its complex narrative, pictorial superficiality and facile insertions of Perónist politics – which have also made it problematic for the Argentine critical establishment.

Bemberg is now, in 1989, working on her fifth feature project, *Yo, la más pobre de todas/I, the Worst of All*, a biopic about the seventeenth-century Mexican nun and poetess Sor Juana Ines de la Cruz. Sor Juana joined a convent in order to have freedom to explore her broad intellectual and artistic interests, but was forced to renounce her unusual and troublesome gifts and devote herself to caring for the other nuns. To date, Bemberg's greatest achievement is to have become not only the first commercially successful Argentine female film director, but also one of the few Argentine directors whose films are regularly distributed internationally.

El mundo de la mujer/The World of Women (1972); *Juquetes/Toys* (1978); *Momentos/Moments* (1980); *Señora de nadie/Nobody's Wife* (1982); *Camila* (1984); *Miss Mary* (1986)

John King and Nissa Torrents (eds), *The Garden of Forking Paths: Argentine Cinema* (London: British Film Institute, 1987)

ALo

BENACERRAF, MARGOT (1926–)

One of the first LATIN AMERICAN filmmakers to receive professional training at the Institut des Hautes Etudes Cinématographiques in Paris, VENEZUELA – born Benacerraf was widely celebrated for the two documentaries she made in the 1950s, *Reverón* (about the folk artist Armando Reverón) and *Araya* (a feature-length depiction of traditional life on the remote Araya Peninsula). On the strength of this reputation, Gabriel García Márquez asked Benacerraf to direct *Eréndira*, but the project lay idle until taken up a decade later by the Mozambican-born Brazilian director Ruy Guerra. Still revered as one of the pioneers of new Latin American cinema, Benacerraf has never allowed herself to be coaxed out of her premature retirement, not even during the late 1970s when oil revenues encouraged Venezuela's most cinematically prolific period.

Reverón (1952); *Araya* (1958)   JBu

BERGHOLM, EIJA-ELINA (1943–)

Director and scriptwriter Eija-Elina Bergholm is best known in FINLAND as a theater director and director of television drama. Bergholm graduated from the Finnish Theater Institute in 1965 and also studied History of Art and Drama at Helsinki University from 1963 to 1965. Her first job was with Finnish Commercial Television, where she was a director of drama. After that she worked as artistic director of the Helsinki Student Theater; during that time she started writing film scripts. *Punahilkka/Little Red Riding Hood* (1969, directed by Timo Bergholm) was a very famous Finnish film of its time, and was compared with films of the French NEW WAVE. Jorn Donner's *Anna* (1970), based on Bergholm's script, created a good deal of controversy about nudity in film.

The first film directed by Bergholm, *Marja Pieni* (1972), was a great success, winning the Finnish State Award and a prize at the Karlovy Vary film festival. In 1978 Bergholm became a director of TV drama for the Finnish Broadcasting Company, and since then has directed several dramas and films for TV. Her best-known works are two poetic dramas made in 1980 and 1983 based on poems by Arja Tiainen, and Frank Wedekind's play *Lulu*, made in two parts in 1982. All these plays contributed strongly to the renewal of Finnish TV drama. In 1982 Bergholm won a three-year state scholarship, which made it possible for her to return to feature films; she scripted

> French feminist theorist Julia Kristeva devised a brand new form of analysis. What is it called?

and directed *Angelan sota* (1984). This is a story about a Finnish woman, working in a German military hospital, in Finland who falls in love with a German officer. Bergholm's latest major work is a TV film, *Punainen Ruukku*, part of which was shot in Israel. This film won the Finnish State Award in 1987.

Marja Pieni/Poor Maria (1972); *On neidolla punapaula/The Maiden Has a Red Ribbon* (1977); *Tunturisusi/The Mountain Wolf* (1978); *Palava Susi/The Burning Wolf* (1980); *Lulu I and II* (1982); *Isolde Pako-*

lainen/Isolde the Refugee (1983); *Angelan sota/Angela's War* (1984); *Punainen Ruukku/The Red Pot* (1987)

See also: NISKANEN, TUIJA-MAIJA   TA

BERGMAN, INGMAR (1918–   )

From *Crisis* (1946) to *Fanny and Alexander* (1982), SWEDISH director Ingmar Bergman's *oeuvre* spans over forty films. Over the years, these films have been studied from a number of perspectives – existential, social, religious, psychoanalytical. Nor has it escaped critics that many of his leading parts are played by women. Thus, Bergman has long had a reputation for harboring a unique understanding of the female psyche, based on films such as *Waiting Women* (1952), *So Close to Life* (1958) and *Scenes From a Marriage* (1973). Furthermore, he has allowed women to become vehicles for existential themes – indeed, symbols for suffering humanity, a dignity traditionally conferred only on men. An early example of this can be found in *Summer Interlude* (1951), as well as in later films such as *Through a Glass Darkly* (1960), *Persona* (1966) and *Cries and Whispers* (1973).

However, in the 1970s feminist writers revised this view. Thus, according to US critic Joan Mellen, there is a gender-related pattern behind Bergman's philosophical issues. His men fail because their pleas – to God, to existence as such – go unanswered; whereas the lives of his women 'lack meaning because they are rooted in biology. . . . They are depicted as if on a lower notch of the evolutionary scale.' She concludes: 'His men move in an ethical realm, his women in a biological one.' However, although Mellen has a point, she generalizes at the cost of ignoring context and difference. For instance, when Bergman shows women groveling in the dirt, is this not just as much because he allows them to represent humankind in its entirety – the ethical *and* the biological? By comparison, his men come across as strangely arid and incomplete, even such obvious heroes as the knight in *The Seventh Seal* (1957). In

other words, why regard the ethical as somehow intrinsically more 'positive'; if this is the realm Bergman's men inhabit, who wants it?

Bergman's films include: *Kris/Crisis* (1946); *Det regnar på vår kärlek/The Man with an Umbrella/It Rains on Our Love* (1946); *Skepp till Indialand/A Ship to India/The Land of Desire* (1947); *Musik i mörker/Night Is My Future* (1948); *Hamnstad/Port of Call* (1948); *Fängelse/Prison/The Devil's Wanton* (1949); *Törst/Thirst/Three Strange Loves* (1949); *Till glädje/To Joy* (1950); *Sånt händer inte här/This Can't Happen Here/High Tension* (1950); *Sommarlek/Summer Interlude/Illicit Interlude* (1951); *Kvinnors väntan/Waiting Women/Secrets of Women* (1952); *Sommaren med Monika/Summer with Monika/Monika* (1953); *Gycklarnas afton/Sawdust and Tinsel/The Naked Night* (1953); *En lektion i kärlek/A Lesson in Love* (1954); *Kvinnodröm/Journey into Autumn/Dreams* (1955); *Sommarnattens leende/Smiles of a Summer Night* (1955); *Det sjunde inseglet/The Seventh Seal* (1957); *Smultronstället/Wild Strawberries* (1957); *Nära livet/So Close to Life/Brink of Life* (1958); *Ansiktet/The Face/The Magician* (1958); *Jungfrukällan/The Virgin Spring* (1960); *Djävulens öga/The Devil's Eye* (1960); *Såsom i en spegel/Through a Glass Darkly* (1960); *Nattvardsgästerna/Winter Light/The Communicants* (1963); *Tystnaden/The Silence* (1963); *För att inte tala om alla dessa kvinnor/Now About These Women/All These Women* (1964); *Persona* (1966); *Vargtimmen/Hour of the Wolf* (1968); *Skammen/Shame/The Shame* (1968); *Riten/The Rite/The Ritual* (1969); *En passion/A Passion/The Passion of Anna* (1969); *Färödokument/The Faro Document* (1969); *Beröringen/The Touch* (1971); *Viskningar och rop/Cries and Whispers* (1973); *Scener ur ett äktenskap/Scenes From a Marriage* (1973); *Trollflöjten/The Magic Flute* (1975); *Ansikte mot ansikte/Face to Face* (1976); *Das Schlangenei/The Serpent's Egg* (1977); *Herbstsonat/Autumn Sonata* (1978); *Färödokument 1979/The Faro Document 1979* (1979); *Aus dem Leben des Marionetten/From the Life of the*

Marionettes (1980); *Fanny och Alexander/ Fanny and Alexander* (1982); *Efter repetitionen/After the Rehearsal* (1984)

Mellen, Joan, *Women and Their Sexuality in the New Film* (New York: Dell, 1975)
MKo

BEYZAYIE, BAHRAME (1938–)

A filmmaker in IRAN, Beyzayie is a pioneer of the new Iranian cinema. He studied literature at Teheran University and has been a playwright, art critic, and historian of Iranian dramatic art: his publications on the history of drama remain the most authoritative in the field.

With no training in filmmaking, Beyzayie joined the Center for the Intellectual Development of Children and Young Adults in the late 1960s and directed films portraying the lives and times of adolescent Iranians, such as *Amou Sibilou* (1969), and *Safar* (1970). He later made films which combined visual aesthetics with social REALISM (the award-winning *Gharibeh va Maah* [1972], *Ragbar* [1973], centering on personal and psychological relationships, and *Khalaagh* [1975], on the loss of identity suffered by Iranians as a result of westernization). He was appointed Dean of the Faculty of Fine Arts at Teheran University in 1975, but was dismissed by the Islamic government in 1979. Whilst still in post he continued making films, but these were never released in Iran, despite being selected for exhibition in film festivals abroad. *Tcherike-Ye-Tara* (1977), a film exploring the place of women in Iranian history, was selected for the 1980 Cannes Film Festival and later shown at the London Film Festival.

Beyzayie is noted for his sensitive approach to Iranian psychology, especially female psychology, and the detailed manner in which he portrays his female characters. They are neither wives nor whores, but whole individuals with independent lives. Because men play no significant role in the lives of these women, the institution of marriage is marginalized. This has endeared him greatly to women film buffs. Between 1979 and 1985 Beyzayie made no films, but then returned to cinema as editor of *Davandeh/The Runner* (1985) and director of *Shoyad Vaghty Dighar* (1987), a Hollywood thriller parody depicting destructive male jealousy toward women.

Beyzayie's films include: *Amou Sibilou/ The Mustachioed Uncle* (1969); *Safar/The Voyage* (1970); *Ragbar* (1973); *Gharibeh va Maah/The Stranger and the Fog* (1972); *Kalaagh/The Crow* (1975); *Tcherike-Ye-Tara/Ballad of Tara* (1977); *Shoyad Vaghty Dighar/Another Time Perhaps* (1987)

Raphael Bassan, Corine McMullin and Sarah Wappers, 'Bahram Beyzai', *Image et Son*, no. 364 (1981)
BR

BIRRI, FERNANDO (1925–)

A filmmaker and active teacher since the 1950s, Birri – born in ARGENTINA – was an early pioneer and supporter of the new LATIN AMERICAN cinema movement, and today remains an influential filmmaker and educator. After studying filmmaking at the Centro Sperimentale di Roma in the 1950s and being much influenced by Italian NEOREALISM, Birri returned to Argentina ready to create a new NATIONAL CINEMA. Stymied by the constraints of the then struggling commercial Argentine industry, however, Birri returned to his native Santa Fe and began an experimental cinema course at the local university, which later became a fully-fledged cinema school. Birri wanted to develop a regional cinema in Santa Fe which would be national (focused on issues of national concern), realist (rather than commercially stylized), and popular (focusing on and appealing to ordinary people). Working collaboratively with male and female students, Birri and the school produced several films and photo-essays, the best known of which are *Tire dié* (1954), a documentary, and *Los inundados* (1961), a neorealist-inspired picaresque feature about a family displaced by seasonal flooding. Both of these films are unique not only because of their attention to a social class rarely seen on the Argentine screen, but also because of their equal treatment of male and female characters.

Forced to leave Argentina in 1963 by the changing political climate, Birri lived in São Paulo, Brazil, for a few months and contributed to the development of a strong regional documentary movement there. After living in Italy for nearly a decade and producing a few films, Birri returned to active teaching in the late 1970s, teaching special courses in Mexico and Venezuela. Since 1986 he has headed the International Film School in Havana, CUBA, where young male and female Third World students on full scholarships follow a rigorous four-year plan of study in filmmaking. In this new position, Birri continues to be the single most important pedagogical force of the New Latin American cinema.

Birri's films include: *Tire dié/Toss Me a Dime* (1954); *La primera fundación de Buenos Aires/The First Foundation of Buenos Aires* (1959); *Buenos dias, Buenos Aires/Good Morning Buenos Aires* (1960); *Los inundados/Flooded Out* (1961); *Rafel Alberti, un retrato del poeta/Rafael Alberti, Portrait of the Poet* (1983); *Mi hijo el Che/ My Son Che* (1985); *Un viejo con alas enormes/An Old Man With Great Wings* (1988)

Julianne Burton, 'The Roots of Documentary Realism: Interview with Fernando Birri', in *Cinema and Social Change in Latin America* (Austin: University of Texas Press, 1986)   ALo

BLACHE, ALICE GUY *see* GUY, ALICE

BLACK CINEMA

In the USA, representations of black people by black filmmakers began early this century with *The Railroad Porter* (1912), made by William Foster and his Photoplay Company, and continue right up to the present. Early US black independent cinema aimed to counter the

Final scene from *Hair Piece*, by Ayoka Chenzira

negative images, even the absence, of black people in mainstream film: *The Birth of a Race* (1918) was conceived by Emmett Scott, who had been secretary to Booker T Washington, as a rebuttal to D W GRIFFITH's *The Birth of a Nation* (1915). Other black filmmakers attempted to fill the void created by the lack of films tailored to black audiences. The earliest independents were Nobel Johnson and his brother George, founders of the Lincoln Motion Picture Company in 1916. Perhaps the best-known black independent filmmaker was Oscar Micheaux, who wrote, produced, directed, and exhibited more than thirty films between 1919 and 1948. Micheaux's film *Body and Soul* (1924) included the first film role for stage actor and singer Paul Robeson.

Black women independent filmmakers in the USA began making films around the early 1970s. One of the earliest, if not the very first, work of this kind was *I am Somebody* (Madeline Anderson, 1970), a DOCUMENTARY about hospital workers on strike in Charleston, South Carolina. Other independent films created by African-American women include *Your Children Come Back to You* (1979) and *A Different Image* (1982), both by Alile Sharon Larkin; *The Cruz Brothers and Mrs Malloy* (1980) and *Losing Ground* (1982) by Kathleen Collins; *Hair Piece: A Film For Nappy-Headed People* (1981) and *Secret Sounds Screaming: The Sexual Abuse of Children* (1986) by Ayoka CHENZIRA; and *Illusions* (1982) by Julie DASH.

In BRITAIN, black INDEPENDENT CINEMA began around the late 1950s, with *Ten Bob in Winter* (Lloyd Reckord, 1959), followed by Lionel Ngakane's *Jemima and Johnnie* (1964), and *Death Be Your Santa Claus* (1969) by Frankie Dymon, Jr. Today, British black independent filmmakers are creating films which raise important questions about the cultural politics of race and nation, gender, identity, and representation. These are products of mixed black workshops whose objective is to explore new ways of representing the varied experiences of black people within the African diaspora. Significant films include *Handsworth Songs* (John Akomfrah, 1986) and *The Passion of Remembrance* (1986), directed by SANKOFA's Maureen Blackwood and Isaac Julien. *Dreaming Rivers* (Martina Attille, 1988) is an expressive film that challenges prevailing images of BLACK WOMEN in cinema. A number of black and Asian women work in Britain as producers, production managers, and teachers of film and video, as well as directors. These include: Karen Alexander, co-director of the video *Ms Taken Identity* (Albany Video, 1986), Avril Johnson of the Black Audio Film Collective, Seema Gill of Retake Film Collective, and Pratibha Parmar, maker of *Emergence* (1986) and *Sari Red* (1988).

Continental Europe also has a sprinkling of black women filmmakers, and there are more on the horizon as film and video become increasingly recognized by black people as powerful media to which they should have access. Many of these women produce work for television, whilst raising the elusive funding for their own productions. They include Elsie Haas (Haiti/France); Gloria Lowe (Guyana/Netherlands); Veronique Mucret (France) and Harmel Sbraire (France). CARIBBEAN films by and for black people are a relatively recent phenomenon, though the work of two women filmmakers from this area – Sarah MALDOROR and Euzhan PALCY – have achieved international recognition. In AFRICA, Safi FAYE remains the only well-known woman filmmaker.

Mbye B Cham and Claire Andrade-Watkins (eds), *Blackframes: Critical Perspectives on Black Independent Cinema* (Cambridge, MA: MIT Press, 1988)

See also: ABORIGINAL FILM AND VIDEO; ANTI-APARTHEID FILM AND VIDEO; BLACK WOMEN AND FILM THEORY; MAORI FILM; NATIVE AMERICAN FILM; NATIVE CANADIAN FILM   JBo/JG

Pratibha Parmar's *Emergence*

BLACK WOMEN

Within the broader field of RACE AND CINEMA, representations of black women in mainstream film have often been negative: this is a venerable tradition dating back to the earliest years of cinema, beginning with films like *The Wooing and Wedding of a Coon* (1905) and *The Masher* (1907), both made in the USA. In *The Masher*, a white man who makes sexual overtures to every white woman he meets reacts with horror and contempt when he learns that a veiled woman who accepts his advances is black. Since then, STEREOTYPES of black women have included: Aunt Jemimas, whores and seducers, AMAZONS and matriarchs, tragic mulattoes, exotics, and long-suffering spouses.

Although the first two versions of *Show Boat* (Harry Pollard, Universal, 1929; James Whale, Universal, 1936) presented the black woman as a large, overbearing figure, the role of the black woman as 'mammy' is inextricably connected in most filmgoers' minds with Hattie McDaniel's performance in *Gone With the Wind* (Victor Fleming, MGM, 1939). Even though McDaniel was the first black person to win an Academy Award (in 1939 as Best Supporting Actress), the representation of the mammy has continuously come under fire.

The black woman as irresistible seducer has been played out in many films. Nina Mae McKinney played this part in *Hallelujah* (King Vidor, MGM, 1929), while Dorothy DANDRIDGE was virtually confined to such roles, the most notable being in *Porgy and Bess* (Otto Preminger, Columbia, 1959) and *Carmen Jones* (Otto Preminger, Twentieth Century-Fox, 1954). The black woman's perceived ability to endure almost anything was presented in Cicely Tyson's portrayal of Rebecca in *Sounder* (Martin Ritt, 1972), while films of the 'blaxploitation' period (from 1971 to 1975) showed black women simply as sexual repositories for libidinous black male protagonists. Several contemporary representations of black women have been rather scary, high-flung exotics: Tina Turner in *Mad Max: Beyond Thunderdome* (George Miller and George Ogilvie, 1985), and Grace Jones in *A View to Kill* (John Glen, 1985) and *Vamp* (Richard Wenk, 1986).

The mid-1980s film which had the most roles for black women is also one of the most widely debated films about black life. *The Color Purple* (Steven Spielberg, 1985), based upon the Pulitzer Prize-winning novel by Alice Walker, contained a variety of representations of black women, from the reticent protagonist to the strong-willed and aggressive supporting characters. Although the film raised the ire of many black viewers, there was strong support from others. This reaction is similar to that received by an earlier film based on the work of a black woman writer: *A Raisin in the Sun* (Daniel Petrie, 1961), from the play by Lorraine Hansberry, has been criticized for its overbearing matriarch in the character of the mother. Other viewers, however, consider the black women in this film to be well-rounded characterizations.

While independent BLACK CINEMA – especially in the USA – has for many years been trying to counter some of the more negative stereotypes of black people in mainstream cinema, it was not until the 1970s that black filmmakers worldwide began to devote attention specifically to the black female experience.

Edward Mapp, 'Black Women in Films: A Mixed Bag of Tricks', in *Black Films and Film-makers: A Comprehensive Anthology from Stereotype to Superhero*, ed. Lindsay Patterson (New York: Dodd, Mead & Company, 1975)   *JBo*

BLACK WOMEN AND FILM THEORY

Although FILM THEORY gestures in the direction of heterogeneity, much of it has been produced by white, middle-class males. Closing the circle, the audience spoken of, and spoken to, is also usually white and male. FEMINIST FILM THEORY has redressed the situation to some extent, but has not dealt adequately with the social and cultural experiences of all women. Since the 1970s there have been active and productive efforts by black women to develop a method of understanding the creative output of black women and its relevance for a black female AUDIENCE. In literary studies, the work of black female scholars has brought about a different understanding of black women's culture and of the many dimensions of black women's lives. We now know that there is a black woman's literary tradition that began in the nineteenth century. Currently, the black women's writing community – a group composed of creative artists, critics and scholars as well as audience members – is continuing the process of revising black women's social and cultural history. The goal of all these efforts is to challenge and oppose the forces that negatively affect black women's lives and to create and perpetuate images that are

worthwhile for black women. All of this has come about because black women have responded to the need to create a means of representing and critiquing themselves.

This work by black women in literature has established a foundation for analyzing the work of black women in other cultural spheres, including film and television. Black independent filmmakers Martina Attille and Maureen Blackwood of SANKOFA write that what is needed is a theory of the representation of BLACK WOMEN that considers the totality of their lives. The tools of ethnography will help accomplish this. By talking with black women, informally and also through formal interviews, it is possible for a black feminist critic to bring to light their preoccupations and concerns, shared because of their status as black and female in class/caste societies. Additionally, black filmmakers need to talk with other black women at screenings, forums, and discussion sessions. This will help the development of constructive images of black women. Rather than constantly attempting to challenge negative images, black women creative artists, critics, and scholars, as well as cultural consumers, can work together to create relevant new images.

Martina Attille and Maureen Blackwood, 'Black Women and Representation', in *Films for Women*, ed. Charlotte Brunsdon (London: British Film Institute, 1986)

See also: BLACK CINEMA   *JBo*

BLONDES

A term applied to certain types of female roles and stars and generally used figuratively rather than literally. The color of a woman's hair is supposedly associated with a whole range of other attributes: blondeness invariably suggests something about her SEXUALITY and ethnicity, and frequently her mental attributes as well. While the sexual and mental attributes ascribed to blondes have been variable, ethnicity remains constant: the white woman is regarded as the ultimate prize for the white man, and blondeness is the ultimate sign of whiteness, being racially unambiguous. Hence blondes often embody western cultural associations of whiteness and purity, as against blackness and evil – giving rise to the virginal, innocent, and vulnerable blonde threatened by the evil 'black' man/beast, as in films like *Birth of a Nation* (D W Griffith, 1915) or *King Kong* (Schoedsack and Cooper, RKO, 1933); or as distinct from the more tempestuous and sexual brunette or redhead. However STEREOTYPES of blondes are not static, and a range of blonde types can be identified, even within Hollywood cinema: ice-cold blonde beneath whose chilly exterior lurks a smoldering fire (Grace Kelly); the blonde bombshell, whose sexuality is explosive and available to men, though often at a price (Brigitte BARDOT, Jean HARLOW, Mae WEST, Diana DORS), and most famously the 'dumb blonde' epitomized by Marilyn MONROE. Dumb blondes are defined by their combination of overt, 'natural' sexuality (of which they may or may not be aware) with a profound ignorance and innocence manifest in an inability to understand even the most elementary facts of everyday life. It is this lack of understanding of what is 'obvious' to ordinary people that is the basis of dumb blonde humor. However, dumb blonde humor can also contain elements of 'native wit,' which stems from naivety and functions to show up the irrationality and/or the hypocrisy of the social order. To this extent the dumb blonde stereotype has a subversive side which is sometimes overlooked: exposing the dumb blonde stereotype as a stereotype was the theme of Judy Holliday's Oscar-winning performance in George CUKOR's *Born Yesterday* (Columbia, 1950).

Richard Dyer, *The Dumb Blonde Stereotype* (London: British Film Institute, 1979)

See also: DAY, DORIS; DIETRICH, MARLENE; SEX GODDESSES; STANWYCK, BARBARA   TP

BORDEN, LIZZIE (195?–   )

Coming from a privileged Ivy League background, US filmmaker Borden studied painting and art history before becoming involved in cinema, first as an editor and then as an independent filmmaker with her own production company, 'Alternate Current.'

Borden's first feature, *Born in Flames* (1983), set in a post-revolutionary New York City, is a radical futuristic feminist fable about sexual politics, race, class, and the role of the media. The script was evolved in collaboration with the main characters, and the style is formally inventive in its use of complex montage EDITING, pseudo-documentary scenes, and fast-paced MUSIC. The film explicitly addresses the spectator as a feminist, while offering a range of positions for identification. Although *Born in Flames* has become something of a classic of FEMINIST INDEPENDENT FILM, many feminists have taken issue with its central utopian statement that women can work together across class and race lines.

Borden's next film, *Working Girls* (1986), has a more conventional narrative structure and deals in a nonmoralistic way with prostitution as 'a viable economic alternative' for middle-class women, given the general exploitation of women in the labor market. The sex scenes – shot from the women's point of view – are nonvoyeuristic and unerotically demystifying. Since the film is quite sympathetic toward the male clients, dramatic conflict is posed in terms of work relations between the prostitutes and the madam. Many women who had supported the radical feminist implications of *Born in Flames* considered it contradictory that Borden could make this apparently uncritical film on prostitution. However, it is precisely Borden's undogmatic feminism which has allowed her to tackle important – and controversial – issues for women.

Honey in Borden's *Born in Flames*

Regrouping (1976); *Born in Flames* (1983); *Working Girls* (1986)

Teresa de Lauretis, 'Rethinking Women's Cinema: Aesthetics and Feminist Theory', in *Technologies of Gender: Essays on Theory, Film, and Fiction* (Bloomington and Indianapolis: Indiana University Press, 1987)   US

BOX, MURIEL (1905–   )

Muriel Box is the most prolific of British women film directors, and one of the very few to have sustained a career as a filmmaker in BRITAIN. She started out as a typist, then continuity girl, at British Instructional Films (whose most successful films were Mary FIELD's 'Secrets of Nature' series) in the late 1920s. Her career progress was never easy or straightforward: it was many years before she was given the opportunity first to write scripts, and then to direct.

Box (then Muriel Baker) worked in continuity at Elstree Studios, with Michael Powell on 'quota quickies,' and at Gaumont before meeting Sydney Box – whom she later married – in 1932. Together they formed a prolific and successful play-writing partnership. During World War II Sydney established his own production company, Verity Films, which by 1942 had become the biggest producer of DOCUMENTARY films in Britain. Muriel began to direct shorts and documentaries for the company, largely as a result of the shortage of male directors in wartime. After the war ended, Muriel and Sydney moved to GAINSBOROUGH STUDIOS, he as head of production and she as head of the script department. The Box partnership became one of the best known in the industry: they collaborated on the writing and production of numerous films, including *The Seventh Veil* (1945) and *The Brothers* (1948), an extraordinary and somber Scottish MELODRAMA. Muriel's career as a director of features took off in the early 1950s with a topical film centering on the Festival of Britain, *The Happy Family* (1952). The films she directed from then on are notable mainly for their variety, rather than for any specific commitment or point of view, in a way that is typical of the British postwar film industry. Among these were several examples of the WOMAN'S PICTURE (including *Street Corner* (1953), about the women's police force, *The Truth About Women* (1958) and *The Passionate Stranger* (1957)), which at the time were received by critics as merely formula pictures of no great merit; viewed again today, however, they are worthy of attention as quasi-feminist films made within the mainstream of the commercial industry. Other films of Box's can be similarly reclaimed: *Simon and Laura* (1956), for instance, because of the acute way it analyzes the early days of TV sitcom; or *This Other Eden* (1959) – at the time this seemed a weak attempt to exploit a possible Irish market for cinema, but it has recently been analyzed as a surprisingly progressive playing out of Anglo-Irish tensions.

Box's career as a filmmaker ended after she directed the unsuccessful sex comedy *Rattle of a Simple Man* in 1964, and after the partnership with her husband had split up. She began a new career as a novelist, and in 1966 she and the novelist Vera Brittain formed a feminist publishing house, Femina Books.

The Happy Family [GB]/*Mr Lord Says No!* [USA] (1952); *A Prince for Cynthia* (1953); *Street Corner* [GB]/*Both Sides of the Law* [USA] (1953); *The Beachcomber* (1955); *To Dorothy, a Son* [GB]/*Cash on Delivery* [USA] (1956); *Simon and Laura* (1956); *Eyewitness* (1956); *The Passionate Stranger* [GB]/*A Novel Affair* [USA] (1957); *The Truth About Women* (1958); *This Other Eden* (1959); *Subway in the Sky* (1959); *Too Young to Love* (1960); *The Piper's Tune* (1960); *Rattle of a Simple Man* (1964)

Muriel Box, *Odd Woman Out* (London: Leslie Frewin, 1974)   CM

BRAZIL

In 1898, a few months after the Lumières showed their cinematograph in Brazil, Alfonso Segreto, an Italo-Brazilian, began to make documentaries of local scenes and events; but from the outset the unequal distribution of both wealth and technology limited exhibition to the towns. Between 1900 and 1912 over a hundred films were made: documentaries, historical and literary adaptations and fictional reconstruction of famous crimes were the most popular of genres; but massive imports of US and European films put an end to this Golden Age, and hopes for a NATIONAL CINEMA raised by the arrival of sound proved short-lived. In despair, many directors resorted to parodies of foreign – mostly US – genres, while Mario Peixote made Brazil's most famous film, *Límite/Limit* (1930), under the influence of France's avant garde. The one outstanding filmmaker of the 1920s and 1930s was the prolific Humberto Mauro (1897–1983). One of the creators of the national film industry and the only filmmaker who would be respected by Cinema Novo directors, Mauro continued making films until 1975.

It is difficult to assess the contribution of women to the industry in the early years, since they do not appear in the credits; though a number helped their husbands as actresses and by doing various jobs on the set. However, women's presence as producers and directors was surprisingly strong in the 1920s and the 1930s: Gita de Barrios acted in her husband's films in the 1920s and wrote his scripts; in 1930 Cleo de Verberena became Brazil's first woman director; in 1933 actress Carmen Santos founded a studio, Brazil Vita Filme, and in 1948 acted, scripted, produced, and directed *Inconfidência Mineira/Conspiracy in Minas Gerais*. Santos directed other films – which were not, however, released – and in 1979 created a women's film cooperative specializing in animation.

The 1930s were disastrous for the Brazilian film industry, and despite state protectionism it survived only thanks to newsreels and documentaries. In the late 1940s, with the success of a popular genre – the 'chanchada' – the industry picked up and produced its first international film star: Carmen Miranda. The 'chanchadas' were crude farces, despised by the elite, with more music than plot. They often parodied Hollywood genres and satirized the pretensions of the indigenous ruling classes. Unsophisticated urban audiences, who for the first time heard their own language spoken, identified with them. However, the arrival of television in the 1950s signaled the demise of a genre that had by then degenerated into 'pornochanchadas'.

As a response partly to the 'chanchadas', and partly to a desire on the part of the bourgeoisie for 'quality' cinema, the Vera Cruz studios were created in 1949. Prestigious foreign names were called in and investment was enormous. But the studio neglected to develop a national distribution and exhibition network, and without the economic infrastructure to back its Hollywood-type methods went bankrupt in 1954, having achieved a single worldwide success with Lima Barreto's *O cangaçeiro/The Bandit* (1953), shown in over eighty countries. Between 1940 and 1970, women in the film industry worked predominantly as actresses: the exceptions being Maria Basaglia, Carla Civelli, Lygia Pape and, most notably, Gilda de ABREU.

The late 1950s saw the birth of a new type of critical DOCUMENTARY, whose object was the plight of the dispossessed rather than the revolutionary potential of the organized proletariat. Cinéma vérité techniques were used extensively, but by the end of the 1960s documentary makers began to question this approach, proposing as their task interpretation rather than reflection. From the documentary schools of the 1950s emerged CINEMA NOVO, the most important movement of Brazilian cinema and the only LATIN AMERICAN film movement to have had an influence worldwide. But there was no place for women in Cinema Novo; and gender issues were not part of the revolution the filmmakers envisaged. Tereza Trautman shot two features, but Suzana Serena, Rosa Lacreta and Lygia Pape made only documentaries. Alongside Cinema Novo 'pornochanchadas' flourished, with the censors turning a blind eye. In this atmosphere a new movement was born: Udigrudi (Underground), which rejected 'well-made cinema' and audience approval and adopted the aesthetics of garbage as an answer to the political stance of Cinema Novo.

After 1972 a new force entered Brazilian filmmaking: EMBRAFILME, a state-funded enterprise for production and distribution which managed to make Brazilian films popular in their own country. In this new, more favorable atmosphere, Cinema Novo directors continued to make films throughout the 1970s and 1980s, seeking technical excellence and diversifying languages and themes. Carlos Diegues's *Bye Bye Brasil* (1980) was successful both at home and abroad, and the veteran Dos Santos

> Janie's Janie *(Geri Ashur, 1971)* and Joyce at 34 *(Joyce Chopra, 1972)* are examples of which film genre?

found a popular voice that was rewarded at the box office. Arnaldo Jabor and Leon Hirszman produced their best work, which refuses to cover up social contradictions whilst never forgetting that the grotesque and a gaudy sense of humor are integral parts of the nation's culture. In the 1970s women filmmakers who had previously managed only to shoot one feature film or a small number of documentaries began to enter the industry in larger numbers, with television easing their way into a man's world. The intimist approach favored by many 1970s documentaries privileged women's voices. Inés Castillo, Olga Futemma and Regina Jeha are outstanding. Tereza

Trautman, Ana CAROLINA, Suzana AMARAL and Tisuka YAMASAKI began in documentary and went on to features but have not yet been able to create a feminist cinema. Love and the eternal triangle are recurrent themes, and the stable heterosexual couple is seen as eminently desirable. Most of the women characters in their films lack independence and appear to consider work as a transitory stage from which they will be redeemed by a male partner. Feelings are all-powerful, and though female sexuality is beginning to be addressed, there is little awareness of differences between women.

In a country with one of the world's largest external debts, the future of Brazilian cinema is not hopeful. From a peak of 102 films in 1980 production has been sliding, despite the state's continued support (in 1988 Embrafilme's budget was about a hundred million dollars, a unique figure in Latin America) and quotas for compulsory showings of national films. Video, and Brazil's hugely successful television SOAP OPERAS, have also contributed to the decline in cinema attendances.

Randal Johnson and Robert Stam (eds), *Brazilian Cinema* (Rutherford, NJ: Fairleigh Dickinson University Press, 1982)

NT

BREIEN, ANJA (1940–)

Born in NORWAY and trained at the French film school IDHEC, Anja Breien started making short films in the late 1960s. Her first feature film, *Voldtekt* (1971), investigates the issue of rape from the viewpoint of the suspect, focusing on the way the judicial system affects him. *Hustruer* (1975), a feminist riposte to John Cassavetes's *Husbands* (1970), made Breien – and Norwegian cinema in general – internationally known. Three housewives break loose from their families and spend several days exploring and discussing their experiences of womanhood. Both *Hustruer* and its successor

Hustruer ti år etter (1985), with a formally identical structure, are characterized by an irony and sense of humor which emphasize the women's ambivalence about questions of self and sexuality, as they cope with their roles as wives and mothers. Breien wrote the script in close collaboration with the actors, and the spontaneity of the dialogue works in effective contrast with the relatively straightforward images in the film.

Breien has worked in various GENRES. On the one hand, films like *Den allvarsamma leken* (1977) and *Arven* (1979) follow the tradition of Ibsenian drama; on the other, some of her films are BERGMAN-like chamber plays. Breien has also directed a thriller dealing with incest, *Papirfuglen* (1984), and *Forfolgelsen* (1981), a drama about a seventeenth-century woman, who frightens people because of her capacity for strong and passionate love, and is consequently persecuted as a witch.

Short films: *Jostedalsrypa* (1967); *17. maj – en film om ritualer* (1969); *Ansikter* (1969); *Mine soskend Goddad* (1972); *Muren rundt fengslet* (1973); *Arne Bendik Sjur* (1973); *Herbergisterne* (1973); *Gamle* (1975). Feature films: *Voldtekt/Rape* (1971); *Hustruer/Wives* (1975); *Den allvarsamma leken/Games of Love and Loneliness* (1977); *Arven/Next of Kin* (1979); *Forfolgelsen/ The Witch Hunt* (1981); *Papirfuglen/Paper Bird* (1984); *Hustruer ti år etter/Wives – Ten Years After* (1985)

Solrun Hoaas, 'Anja Breien: Film Director', *Cinema Papers*, no. 39 (1982)   *AKo*

:::
The films I Spit on Your Grave (1980) and Lipstick (1981) represent which popular film genre?
:::

BRITAIN

Since its earliest days, British cinema has been expected to survive without significant government support on a small market. One major problem for British

cinema has always been Hollywood. Unlike other countries in Europe, which had a cultural imperative to create films which would ensure the national audience would be supplied with films in their own language and engaging with the country's social and cultural concerns, Britain has been supplied with English-speaking features from America. Another problem has been television – between 1951 and 1960 annual cinema admissions dropped from 1365 million to 501 million – which, apart from drawing audiences away, also to some extent satisfied any perceived 'need' for a cultural product which reflected what might be quintessentially 'British.' The effect of television has recently been further compounded by home video, since Britain has one of the highest rates of video-cassette recorder ownership in the world.

Another major factor militating against British cinema also lies close to home. There is an all-pervasive philistine intellectual climate which has failed to support film (with its mass-culture image) as against 'high art' like theater and opera. As a direct result of this, whilst in the past the British have been keen cinemagoers, FILM CRITICS have been disdainful: one wonders why critics like C A LEJEUNE chose film at all to comment on, since she obviously felt it lacked 'taste' – nor was she alone in her attitude. This relates to one of the dominant strands in British cinema – the notion of its 'quality,' against Hollywood's 'vulgarity.' Many films draw on Britain's literary heritage and in the postwar period numerous film adaptations have been made of established 'classics' – plays or novels by such writers as George Bernard Shaw, Shakespeare, Noël Coward, Graham Greene, E M Forster, and Charles Dickens. Most of these films are overwhelmed by respect for their sources. There seems to have been a crisis of confidence amongst filmmakers about writing and developing original scenarios in favor of the cachet of making films based on successful novels or plays. This was evident even during the heady days of the BRITISH NEW WAVE, when plays and novels about working-class people by writers like John Osborne, Stan Barstow, David Storey and Shelagh Delaney were filmed. This trend continues today, with major British productions of *A Room with a View* (1986), *Little Dorrit* (1987), and *A Passage To India* (1984), amongst others. The 'New Wave' films of the 1960s touch on another major strand in British cinema, a social REALISM derived from the meshing of DOCUMENTARY concerns from the 1930s with the literary conventions of narrative drama.

There have been many dismissals of British cinema, and remarks such as French director François Truffaut's that there is 'a certain incompatibility between the terms "cinema" and "Britain"' are often quoted. The crisis in confidence has frequently encouraged British directors to leave Britain and seek the sunnier economic and creative climes of Hollywood (Alan Parker, Tony Richardson, Alfred HITCHCOCK, John Schlesinger, Ridley Scott, Stephen Frears), but others have remained; and there are other strands, vital and variegated, to be teased out of the mainstream contribution: GAINSBOROUGH STUDIOS, POWELL AND PRESSBURGER, and Hammer HORROR, for example – all of which draw on deeper, darker veins of FANTASY, horror, macabre, and gothic – aspects of British culture not regarded as in the best of taste. At other times, there has been a blossoming of independent filmmaking in Britain – as in the 1950s with Karel Reisz and Lindsay Anderson and the 'Free Cinema' movement, or in the 1960s and early 1970s when cultural and political changes in Britain led to a renewed concern with questions of representation and reporting, and with the institutional control of the media. Around this time, collectives such as the Angry Arts Group, Cinema Action, Berwick Street Film Collective, and the LONDON WOMEN'S FILM GROUP were started. Funding has always been a major problem for this sort of INDEPENDENT CINEMA, but for some at least the advent of CHANNEL FOUR TELEVISION in 1982 solved financial difficulties. The much-vaunted 'New British Cinema' owes its genesis and continuing existence to TELEVISION, ironically, since Channel Four has funded or co-funded a number of innovative and alternative films shown on television as well as in cinemas. 'Film on Four' has contributed money to films such as Irish filmmaker Neil Jordan's *The Company of Wolves* (1984) (based on Angela Carter's feminist reworking of 'Little Red Riding Hood'), Richard Eyre's dissection of Thatcher's Britain at the time of the Falklands War, *The Ploughman's Lunch* (1983), Stephen Frears's *My Beautiful Laundrette* (1985), and many other notable successes.

What then of women in British cinema? Women have not had a high profile in the British film industry – with some notable exceptions: in documentary filmmaking Mary FIELD and Jill CRAIGIE; and during the fifties in feature filmmaking, Wendy TOYE, Betty Box and Muriel BOX. In Britain today, women feature directors can be counted on the fingers of one hand (Sally POTTER, Beeban Kidron, Lezli-An Barrett). However, in television there are more women directors, and since a common way into feature filmmaking is via the small screen, it is to be hoped that women will make this leap too. Certainly the kinds of films that Channel Four has helped fund have gone some way to providing actresses at least with roles which portray a wide range of social and cultural backgrounds. However, in these times it is hard to end on a note of optimism: censorship, repression, political control bite ever deeper, many hardwon freedoms are under threat or are being eroded, and it seems clear that enlightened and oppositional cultural interventions are ever more likely to fall victim to the hungry maw of dominant media forms.

Charles Barr (ed.), *All Our Yesterdays: 90*

Years of British Cinema (London: British Film Institute, 1986)

See also: BARRY, IRIS; BATCHELOR, JOY; BRITISH BOARD OF FILM CENSORS (CLASSIFICATION); BRITISH DOCUMENTARY MOVEMENT; BRITISH FILM INSTITUTE; BRYHER; 'CARRY ON' FILMS; CINEMA OF WOMEN; CIRCLES; DAWSON, JAN; 'DOCTOR' FILMS; DORS, DIANA; EALING STUDIOS; JOHNSTON, CLAIRE; LEIGH, VIVIEN; LAUNDER AND GILLIAT; LEEDS ANIMATION WORKSHOP; MULVEY, LAURA; NEUBAUER, VERA; NICOLSON, ANNABEL; POWELL, DILYS; REINIGER, LOTTE; REVILLE, ALMA; RHODES, LIS; SANKOFA; DE VERE, ALISON; WOMEN'S FILM, TELEVISION AND VIDEO NETWORK   SP

> *'It is said that analyzing pleasure, or beauty, destroys it. That is the intention of this article.' What article? And by which British feminist filmmaker and theorist was this killjoy statement written?*

BRITISH BOARD OF FILM CENSORS (CLASSIFICATION)

The British Board of Film Classification (BBFC) began life in 1912 as the British Board of Film Censors. Faced with mounting CENSORSHIP by local authorities responsible for licensing cinemas, the film industry decided to appoint its own censorship body to 'induce confidence in the minds of the licensing authorities and of those who have in their charge the moral welfare of the community generally.' In this they were largely successful, in that the Board's standards came increasingly to be trusted, and films they had certificated were rarely cut or banned. Similarly, a BBFC-certificated film has never been publicly prosecuted, and private prosecutions of such films have come to grief.

As far as film is concerned, the BBFC, in the words of the venerable judge Lord Denning, 'is not a legal entity. It has no existence known to the law. It is but a name given to the activities of a few persons.' When it comes to VIDEO, on the other hand, the Board does have statutory powers. In 1984, after a considerable flurry in the press and Parliament over 'video nasties,' the government decided that all videocassettes in commercial distribution must be certificated, designating the BBFC as the appropriate body. It is now illegal in BRITAIN to rent or sell a prerecorded feature film which has not been certificated by the BBFC, and illegal to rent or sell a certificated cassette to a person beneath the age specified on the certificate. The BBFC tends to apply stricter standards to videos than to films, since the 1984 Act expressly instructs the Board to have 'special regard to the likelihood of video works . . . being viewed in the home'; 'home' implicitly being taken to include children. However, even in the area of film the Board is strict by western European and North American standards, especially when it is considered that in this instance it is a nonstatutory body. For example, in 1987 it demanded cuts in 16.3 percent of the films to which it granted a PG (parental guidance recommended) certificate, and in 20.6 percent of those given an 18 (no admission to under-eighteens) certificate. The Board also refused to pass any of the various versions of *The Texas Chainsaw Massacre II* submitted to it. In recent years the BBFC has become increasingly concerned about the level of violence in films and videos, especially violence directed toward women. According to its 1987 Annual Report,

> the Board has since the middle seventies had a consistent and firm policy towards violence against women, particularly where the violence is in a sexual context or is sexually motivated. Increasing

evidence has become available in recent years to support the stand the Board has taken. . . . We know of no country other than Britain in which such a considered and unambiguous stand has been taken on this kind of material. It is an aspect of Board policy increasingly vindicated by experimental evidence and by the views of social commentators.

Guy Phelps, *Film Censorship* (London: Victor Gollancz, 1975)   SP

BRITISH DOCUMENTARY MOVEMENT

'It is worth recalling that the British documentary group began not so much in affection for film per se as in affection for national education. If I am to be counted as the founder and leader of the movement, its origins lay in sociological rather than aesthetic ideas.' So wrote Scottish-born mentor and guru of this highly influential school of DOCUMEN-TARY filmmaking, John Grierson. Grierson, who is credited with inventing the term 'documentary,' was a social democrat, and passionately devoted to the ideal of democracy. In film, he saw the most powerful cultural medium for political change: film was capable of informing and engaging the citizen in such a way that he or she could participate more fully in society. In BRITAIN in the late 1920s, Grierson and Stephen Tallents set up the state-sponsored Empire Marketing Board (EMB) Film Unit, which in turn became the General Post Office (GPO) Film Unit and, during World War II, the Crown Film Unit. Under the patronage of these various government-funded bodies, a group of mostly male, middle-class, Oxbridge-educated filmmakers produced numerous documentaries profiling public institutions and exploring social problems of various kinds. Amongst the best-known films associated with the movement are: *Night Mail* (1936), *Industrial Britain* (1931), *Shipyard* (1935), *Coalface* (1935). In *Housing Problems*

(1935), sponsored by the gas industry, working men and women spoke directly to the camera about their lives and living conditions for the first time in the history of cinema. Grierson believed in the 'high bravery of upstanding labor,' an attitude reflecting the interest in and idealization of the working class, common among middle-class intellectuals in the thirties.

Although downplayed in histories of the movement, the handful of women directors associated with it made significant contributions to the development of documentary cinema. Ruby Grierson, for example (a sister to John), played a key role in the production of the pioneering *Housing Problems*: although credited only as an assistant, she was in fact responsible for directing the to-camera interviews which set this film apart from previous documentaries. She later co-directed (with Ralph Bond) *Today We Live* (1937), an affecting – and quite radical – film about people's struggles against the demoralization of unemployment, which has been described as one of the documentary movement's most convincing examples of genuine social concern. Sadly, Ruby Grierson's promising film career was cut short by her early death in 1940. Another of John Grierson's sisters, Marion, joined the EMB film unit in 1930 and was responsible for training many of the 'documentary boys' in editing. In 1935 she became a director of Associated Realist Film Producers, one of several independent production companies formed as a spinoff from the government film units. Marion Grierson's directorial credits include *So This is London* (1933), *London on Parade* (1938), and *Around the Village Green* (1937), which she co-directed with Evelyn Spice. Spice was the documentary movement's most prolific woman director, with at least fifteen films to her credit during the 1930s, the best known of which include *Weather Forecast* (1934) and *Sydney Eastbound* (1938).

The radical impact of the British Documentary Movement waned after the war, and certainly during the seventies it was viewed less than favorably by many critics, who condemned its gradualist attitudes and paternalism. However, in light of more recent political developments the radicalism of these documentaries should not be underrated, for their influence has been far-reaching. Not least, they have informed some aspects of INDEPENDENT CINEMA and FEMINIST INDEPENDENT FILM: through their remarkable sense of social responsibility, their respect for working women and men, and their celebration of the dignity of work of all kinds.

Don Macpherson (ed.), *British Cinema: Traditions of Independence* (London: British Film Institute, 1980)

See also: REINIGER, LOTTE   SP/AKu

> Lotte Reiniger designed her own multiplane camera in the 1920s. For what purpose?

BRITISH FILM INSTITUTE

An official body founded 1933 and now largely funded by the government's Office of Arts and Libraries, the British Film Institute (BFI) sees itself as responsible for 'fostering and encouraging the development, study, preservation and appreciation of the art of film and television.' At a formal level, the institute has never made any commitment to FEMINIST INDEPENDENT FILM and video. But despite a troubled relationship with some autonomous feminist groups, pressure from within and outside the organization has forced the BFI to play an important role in funding and developing feminist work throughout BRITAIN.

During the seventies and early eighties, for instance, the BFI Production Board helped fund a number of noteworthy British feminist films, including *The Song of The Shirt* (Susan Clayton, 1979) and *Doll's Eye* (Jan Worth, 1982).

The BFI fully funded Sally POTTER's *The Gold Diggers* (1983), the first feature-length British film made by an all-woman crew and cast. Since then, however, BFI films have almost all been directed by men, and the increasingly limited funds available for large-scale production have tended to be directed toward a rather literary type of ART CINEMA. In terms of more 'hands-off' funding, however, the BFI has helped support FEMINIST DISTRIBUTION and a chain of regional cinemas, some of which have been central to FEMINIST EXHIBITION policies, and hosting special – and sometimes groundbreaking – women and cinema events. These cinemas have helped blur the boundaries between 'education' and 'pleasurable' cinemagoing, a process in which the BFI's Education Department has played an important role.

Recent changes, many linked to the harsher, more 'rational' atmosphere now dominating British arts funding, suggest that the BFI has a contradictory attitude to feminist work. On the one hand, possibilities for production seem limited; on the other, much feminist exhibition and educational work has found a permanent and thriving place in BFI-supported cinemas and media centers. As the nineties – and further 'rationalizations' – dawn, the question now is how women can encourage the BFI to expand on the partly feminist-inspired rethink of cinema which it nurtured in the 1970s and 1980s.

Patience Coster (ed.), *BFI Yearbook 1988-9* (London: British Film Institute, 1988)   JRo

BRITISH NEW WAVE

Film production in BRITAIN in the late 1950s is characterized by a polarization of GENRES. The uncertainties of the industry in the face of the rapid expansion of broadcast television also resulted in a repetition of accepted formulae, with a consequent stagnation of forms – particularly of the typical EALING STUDIOS and GAINSBOROUGH STUDIOS products so successful and innovative in the 1940s; and the production of series such as the 'DOCTOR' FILMS, 'CARRY ON' FILMS and the LAUNDER/GILLIAT 'St Trinian's' cycle. By the late 1950s there was a marked absence of films dealing with the 'realities' of contemporary British life; and a number of films, innovative in both form and subject, attempted to remedy this lack. Many of the filmmakers concerned, such as Lindsay Anderson, Tony Richardson and Karel Reisz, had been associated with the critical JOURNAL *Sequence* in the early 1950s and had also been engaged with the quasi-avant-garde experimentations with film form known as 'Free Cinema.' The group of films indicated by the term 'New Wave' represented the first forays of this group into 'mainstream' cinema. They were received with great excitement by public and critics alike, and seemed at the time to signal a longed-for resurgence of indigenous British cinema. The ecstatic language of much contemporary criticism recalls that which heralded Ealing's most fruitful phase in the late 1940s, or the more recent success of Goldcrest productions in the 1980s.

In common with other British films of the 1960s, New Wave cinema focuses on the young and their attempts to take a place in adult society. The emphasis is on the individual pitted against the group – in contrast to Ealing's formulation of the interdependent community. Typically, narratives are set in northern cities and concern a working-class milieu and/or hero. In the focus on class mobility, the meritocratic ideals of the 1950s give way to a rather more sceptical recognition of money and power – in its various forms – as the route to the good life. At the same time, there is a rather nostalgic critique of contemporary values expressed in such oppositions as the city versus the country, or television versus the brass band. An emblematic composition recurring in many of the films has the hero in contemplative mood as he sits in the countryside (nature) overlooking the city (culture).

The ambiguity of these films' celebration of contemporary society is most marked in their representations of SEXUALITY, perceived in contemporary critiques as 'permissive.' The representations are permissive in that they routinely depict more overt sexual activity than was previously the norm on the British cinema screen – incidentally rendering superfluous the sexual innuendo which was the stock-in-trade of such popular comedies as the 'Carry On' films – but their representations of women are deeply reactionary. Like many British and American films of the mid 1940s, however, which took problematic aspects of the social positioning of women as their central subject, these films' concentration on the goals, motives, and experience of a charismatic male working-class figure do allow scope for alternative readings. The fate of female characters may warrant our censure, but at the same time the details of the hero's narrative path offer considerable insights into the vicissitudes of contemporary gender politics.

While 1940s films offered powerful, often transgressive HEROINES who, though punished in the story for their transgressions, still presented compelling models to their audiences, the 1960s films offer women as victims: of their mothers, as in *A Taste of Honey* (Tony Richardson, 1961); of their lovers, as in *Poor Cow* (Ken Loach, 1967); or of the social order in general, as in *Room at the Top* (Jack Clayton, 1959); *Saturday Night and Sunday Morning* (Karel Reisz, 1960); and *A Kind of Loving* (Schlesinger, 1962), of which critic Penelope Gilliatt wrote: 'Its real theme is not social discontent but the misogyny that has been simmering under the surface of half the interesting plays and films in England since 1956.'

John Hill, *Sex, Class and Realism* (London: British Film Institute, 1986)   JT

BROOKS, LOUISE (1906–85)

Born in Kansas, USA, Brooks went to New York in 1922 to pursue a career in ballet. As a result of appearances in the Ziegfeld Follies she received an acting contract from PARAMOUNT in 1925, which allowed her to remain in New York until 1927, when she had to move to Hollywood. Although two of her best American productions were filmed there (*A Girl in Every Port* [Howard Hawks, 1928] and *Beggars of Life* [William A Wellmann, 1928]), she despised Hollywood for its superficiality, gossip, and the intrusions of the studios into her private life. At the end of her film career she published critiques of the 'dream-factory' which are acutely informed by her experiences behind the scenes. Thus she was finally able to attain some measure of public self-fulfillment through writing, at a distance from the male-dominated culture-industry of Hollywood.

Her determination not to conform resulted in dismissal from Paramount in 1929, but at the same time led to engagements in GERMANY, where she did her most memorable work. Under the direction of G W Pabst she made *Die Buechse der Pandora/Pandora's Box* (1929) and *Tagebuch einer Verlorenen/Diary of a Lost Girl* (1929). Both films show Brooks in the role of a guiltless, passive seductress with masochistic qualities, a favorite theme of late WEIMAR CINEMA. Back in the USA, Brooks's film appearances were limited to small secondary roles because she refused to be cast in sexually exploitative parts. Though she had the

> **What species of bird is Hata Mari?**

opportunity to appear in the movies again after her revival in 1953 (brought about by a retrospective in France) she refused once more; this time, though, for health reasons.

Louise Brooks, *Lulu in Hollywood* (New York: Alfred A Knopf, 1974)   *VR*

BRUECKNER, JUTTA (1941–)

WEST GERMAN filmmaker Jutta Brueckner is a member of the movement known as NEW GERMAN CINEMA. After studying political science, philosophy, and history, she came to filmmaking with no formal training via the route of writing screenplays. Having developed a passion for writing early in life, Brueckner has written the screenplays for most of her films, as well as scripts for Volker Schloendorff and Ula STOECKL. She was drawn to film because she found it created a public space for women's experience and offered a means of expression that her previously preferred area of literature did not. For her, film visualized, rather than simply imagined, women's physical presence, permitting an intensity of identification that literature could not achieve. In all her film work she has tried to find new forms with which to narrate women's experiences and allow women to recognize their own situation.

Her first feature film, *Ein ganz und gar verwahrlostes Maedchen* (1977), explores the development of a young woman, using semi-documentary techniques. In her next film, *Hungerjahre* (1979), Brueckner focuses on a girl who becomes so alienated from her own body that she finally attempts suicide. The adolescent trauma is built up through repetition of moments and situations drawn from Brueckner's own experiences. In contrast, *Laufen Lernen* (1980) deals with a forty-year-old housewife's bid for emancipation, while a more recent film, *Ein Blick – und die Liebe bricht aus* (1987), is a series of performance pieces exploring female desire, lust, self-humiliation, and aggression.

Brueckner has described her films as autobiographical, and conceives of them as specifically for women as a social group. Most of them deal with questions of female identity and women's relationship to society. With her films she aims to bewilder, disturb, and irritate, but especially to show that large part of female reality which has been traditionally suppressed.

Tue Recht und scheue Niemand/Do Right and Fear Nobody (1975); *Ein ganz und gar verwahrlostes Maedchen/A Thoroughly Neglected Girl* (1977); *Hungerjahre/Years of Hunger* (1979); *Laufen Lernen/Learning to Run* (1980); *Luftwurzeln* (episode in *Erbtoechter/The Daughters' Inheritance*) (1982); *Kolossale Liebe/Colossal Love* (1984); *Ein Blick – und die Liebe bricht aus/One Glance, and Love Breaks Out* (1986)

Patricia Harbord, 'Interview with Jutta Brueckner', *Screen Education*, no. 40 (1981–2)   JK

BRYHER (1896–1983)

Bryher (Winifred Ellerman) was the first European woman film critic to see film in national and sociological terms. She was a co-editor of *Close Up*, the earliest JOURNAL to treat the motion picture as an art form: *Close Up* was published from Switzerland between 1927 and 1933 and counted among its contributors leading intellectuals of the period, including Bryher's friend HD. Bryher's reviews and articles for *Close Up* treated educational films, Soviet films, and protests about censorship. 'A Certificate of Approval,' for example, complains about the British Customs' seizure of a film about Icelandic seals that she was carrying. In another piece she writes on Eisenstein's *The General Line* (1929), calling it possibly 'the finest educational film ever made.'

Bryher's book *Film Problems of Soviet Russia* (1929) is a firsthand account of her visit to the Soviet Union to see the state of Soviet film. Predating even C A LEJEUNE, who had a much wider readership, Bryher writes on individual directors such as Eisenstein, Pudovkin, and Kuleshov, dubbing the latter's *Expiation* (1926) a masterpiece. A chapter is devoted to the Soviet studio system, the state school of cinematography in Moscow, educational films, and what she

calls the 'sociological' film. Befitting her times, Bryher takes an unabashedly leftist line in this book.

Bryher's other writings on film appeared in *Sight and Sound*, in *Cinema Survey* (London: Blue Moon Press, 1937), and in her autobiography, *The Heart to Artemis*.

Bryher, *The Heart to Artemis: A Writer's Memoirs* (New York: Harcourt, Brace and World, 1962)   MMc

BURROUGHS, JACKIE (1938–)

Jackie Burroughs has been a principal figure in film and theater in CANADA for over twenty-five years. Always willing to take risks, infinitely generous with younger artists or new talent, she has worked as an actor at every level of theater – from late-night avant-garde performance clubs to dance/theater; from touring off-Broadway productions to classical theater at Stratford; and in roles that range from Portia to Alfred Jarry. She began working in film when the Canadian feature industry was in its infancy (some say its golden age) in the late 1960s, combining her trained technical skills with improvisation for a low-budget fictional documentary, or alternatively working at the high end of the profession in Hollywood-style features. Her roles in films have varied from working-class delinquents to birdlike elderly spinsters; from whiskey-voiced tarts to turn-of-the-century feminists. She has continued to pursue a career of extraordinarily varied expression, working in a variety of performance media. In 1987 she worked with a filmmaking collective to produce, write, direct, and star in a daring feature based on *Give Sorrow Words*, the letters of Maryse Holder. *A Winter Tan* (1987) tells the story of a woman of a certain age who takes a holiday from feminism in Mexico and loses herself in a bulimic orgy of alcohol, drugs, and desire for young men. Flamboyant, mannered, intelligent, her highly charged performances have been rewarded with every honor that Canadian film and theater can bestow.

A Winter Tan (co-d, 1987)   KA

BUTE, MARY ELLEN (1906–83)

US AVANT-GARDE filmmaker and animator, best known for her poetic, abstract, short musical films, Bute was born in Houston, Texas, and studied painting at the Pennsylvania Academy and the Sorbonne. Settling in New York, she became interested in musical composition and ways of devising pictorial forms which would have the ordered sequence of MUSIC. The constraints of the picture frame soon became too confining, and Bute began to seek ways of introducing the element of time. In the early 1930s she collaborated with musician and electronics pioneer Leon Theremin on experiments with optical devices for projecting color and images synchronized to music. Interested in applying mathematical formulae to the ordering of sequences, Bute worked with mathematician and painter Joseph Schillinger and filmmaker Lewis Jacobs on the uncompleted film *Synchronization* (1932), for which she produced abstract drawings.

Bute made a number of ANIMATION films in the 1930s using drawings, or moving objects photographed using various speeds and lights, all based on sequences of music – for example the black-and-white film *Rhythm in Light* (1934), which uses Grieg's 'Anitra's Dance.' Color was introduced later in films such as *Spook Sport* (1939), animated by experimental filmmaker Norman McLaren.

In the 1950s Bute experimented with choreographing images with an electronically controlled beam of light, using a specially designed oscilloscope, in *Abstronic* (1952–4), combining two films based on music by Aaron Copland and Don Gillis. From the late 1950s she turned to directing live-action films, directing the feature *Passages from Finnegans Wake* (1965), adapted from Mary Manning's play of the same title. Bute was attracted by the poetry of James Joyce's language, recalling the phrase 'Joyce split the word and from it flowed the pure music of "Finnegans Wake".' She made a short film *From the Cradle Endlessly Rocking*, about Walt Whitman, and was working on a film adaptation of a play by Thornton Wilder, *The Skin of our Teeth*, at the time of her death at the age of seventy-seven.

Films include: *Rhythm in Light* (1934); *Synchrony No. 2* (1936); *Evening Star* (1937); *Parabola* (1938); *Escape, Spook Sport* (1939); *Escape* (1940); *Tarantella* (1941); *Polka Graph* (1952); *Mood Contrasts* (1953); *Abstronics* (1954); *The Boy Who Saw Through* (1956); *Passages from Finnegans Wake* (1965)

Robert Russett and Cecile Starr, *Experimental Animation* (New York: da Capo, 1988)   IK

CAMERA MOVEMENT

Shifting of framing in films usually occurs because of camera movement, and some types of camera movement are used so often that they have their own names. A pan occurs when the camera turns left or right on its axis parallel to its base. Tilts are up-and-down pans. When the camera moves along on a tripod, tracking or dolly shots are created, while cranes are movements in which the camera is raised and moved some distance from its regular height. While a zoom has the effect of changing the framing of a shot, it is not technically an aspect of camera movement since the camera itself does not move – a zoom is in fact created through shifting the focal length of the lens.

In CLASSICAL HOLLYWOOD CINEMA the functions of camera movement include following actions and characters, revealing information important to the narrative, or – in combination with EDITING techniques such as the shot/reverse shot – suggesting the subjectivity of a character. Alternative film practices have occasionally confronted the apparent 'omniscience' suggested by the camera's accessibility to privileged sites of vision. For instance, the mobility of the camera in relation to onscreen and offscreen space has been explored by the French filmmaker Marguerite DURAS.

JaS

CAMERA OBSCURA

Formed by four editorial members of the JOURNAL, *WOMEN AND FILM, Camera Obscura* first appeared in the USA in 1976. The initial motivation for forming a new collective to develop work on feminism and film came from a dissatisfaction with a concept of film as reflection (or distortion) of reality and attempts to produce films with feminist content whilst at the same time accepting dominant, 'patriarchal' cinematic forms. The objectives of the journal were to develop a theoretical critique of CLASSICAL HOLLYWOOD CINEMA and the function of images of women within this system. They drew on theories of IDEOLOGY and on SEMIOTIC forms of analysis, as well as looking at how the spectator is positioned according to a PSYCHOANALYTIC model. In an early account of their work, the editors set out their intention to develop a specifically feminist reworking of these newly developed theories. As well as providing an account of NARRATIVE cinema as 'illusionist,' this theoretical work would form part of a project of developing a feminist COUNTERCINEMA to deconstruct the codes and conventions of film, undermining the notion of reality it presented. This was to be part of a challenge to the patriarchal systems through which notions of SEXUALITY are produced and represented.

Camera Obscura's perspective suggests that it is only through work on the way cinema interacts with the spectator that patriarchal meanings can be challenged and reconstructed. While taking inspiration from the work of AVANT-GARDE filmmaking on the material processes of cinema, the journal's editors called for an extension of experimental work to address the construction of woman in patriarchal discourse from a socialist and a feminist perspective. This dual project is supported by documentation of women's film activities in both writing and filmmaking.

Since its beginnings, *Camera Obscura* has regularly published theoretical writings that pursue its interest in how films work as TEXTs and what is referred to as the 'figuration of the feminine,' as well as critical analyses of feminist films that develop a political experimental cinema: this has included the work of Marguerite DURAS, Yvonne RAINER, and Chantal AKERMAN amongst many others. It has explored new theoretical perspectives such as POSTMODERN-ISM, considered the shifting nature of sexuality as it interconnects with class, RACE, and ethnicity, and has recently acquired a more eclectic range of interests to include such topics as SCIENCE FIC-TION and institutional approaches to the female consumer in TELEVISION.

Camera Obscura Collective, 'Chronology,' *Camera Obscura* no. 3–4 (1979) GS

CANADA

The feature film industry in Canada is in a more or less perpetually dismal state. The commercial industry, as in most other countries of the world, is dominated by US production. Distribution and exhibition are also controlled largely by American corporations. On Canadian cinema screens, 93 percent of the films are American. Of the remaining 7 percent from other countries, 2 to 3 percent are Canadian. The disincentives for Canadian feature filmmaking are thus enormous. For women, the situation is even worse. For fifty years, not one woman directed a feature film. For the

> The Hyena's Breakfast (1983), directed by Austrian-born Elfi Mikesch, explores a painful preoccupation. What is it?

next ten years, less than one film per year was completed by a woman. There are larger numbers of women actively engaged in the feature film industry in QUEBEC, though their numbers are currently dwindling, too, in the second term

of a federal conservative government which has engaged only retrogressively with Canadian culture and has opened the doors to America even more widely with the Free Trade Agreement ratified on 1 January 1989.

Nevertheless, the history of Canadian women filmmakers began very early in the history of the cinema itself, with *Back to God's Country* (1919), a silent feature which is in every frame a vehicle for its star and creator, Nell SHIPMAN. It was fifty years before a Canadian woman directed another feature film, but in the meantime women were making their way in documentaries, animation, and experimental films. Donna Conway King was one of the few women working in film in Canada in the 1920s, but by the 1940s women such as Evelyn Spice, Jane Marsh, Judith Crawley, and Gudrun Bjerring-Parker were directing documentaries about Canada's regional life and women's contributions to the war effort.

The NATIONAL FILM BOARD OF CANADA (NFB) played a crucial part in the development of Canada's filmmaking history, and the history of women within it. Although the facts of this history appear to parallel those of other countries – in that women, as usual, made short documentary and children's films which tended to have lower budgets, smaller crews, and little opportunity for financial return – those facts tell only part of the Canadian story. Unlike FRANCE, the SOVIET UNION, the United States, GERMANY, and ITALY – countries which played a significant part in the creation of a mainstream industry dominated by feature films – Canada made no feature films to speak of until the 1960s. Thus the perceived discrimination against women has less meaning here, in that all filmmakers were confined to the short-film ghetto. Moreover, the unique situation of the NFB as the principal source of pre-television films in the farflung regions of the country gave those films and filmmakers an opportunity for influence which exceeded comparative opportunities elsewhere. Thus for Canadians who grew up in the first decades after World War II, films by women, such as *Peoples of the Potlatch* (Laura Boulton, 1944), *Terre de Nos Aieux* (Jane Marsh, 1943), and *Glooscap Country* (Margaret Perry, 1961), have become part of the Canadian collective cultural unconscious. And in 1975 the NFB created a new opportunity for women filmmakers with the founding of STUDIO D, a section dedicated to making films by and about Canadian women.

In TELEVISION and in independent DOCUMENTARY as well, women filmmakers have become central to the Canadian experience in Canada. As in the feature film industry, television networks are dominated by US programming, but Canadian networks have been successful nationally in current affairs and documentary reporting. Although women have largely been confined to daytime and children's programing, in the flagship areas of current affairs there have been a few, such as Beryl FOX and Phyllis Switzer, who have carved out permanent niches in Canadian television history. In the independent sector, Janis COLE and Holly Dale have had successful theatrical runs for feature documentaries, Kay Armatage and Brenda Longfellow have combined feminism and the arts in their experimental documentaries, and Brigitte Berman won an Academy Award for her privately financed feature documentary *Artie Shaw: Time Is All You've Got* (1987).

Memories of childhood in Canada are populated with animated images produced by Canadian women. In the fifties, the country's cultural heritage was recounted in ANIMATIONS of native legends such as *How the Loon Got Its Necklace* (Judith Crawley, 1954), *Kumak the Sleepy Hunter* (Alma Duncan, 1955), and *Legend of the Raven* (Judith Crawley, 1957). Evelyn Lambart created classics such as *L'histoire de Noël* (1973) and *Mr Frog Went A-Courting* (1974) after working for many years as assistant to Norman McLaren. And in the seventies, a bright new star began to shine in the delightful and always innovative films of Caroline LEAF (*Le Mariage du hibou*, 1975; *The Street*, 1976; *Metamorphosis of Mr Samsa*, 1977). It is in the AVANT GARDE that Canadian women have contributed most successfully to cinema as an art form. This is partly the result of significant individual artists such as Joyce WIELAND and Patricia GRUBEN, but their situation has been supported by the funding priorities of federal and provincial granting bodies such as the Canada Council, which has taken as its mandate in film production the support of innovative and experimental work.

Since Sylvia Spring's *Madeleine Is . . .* (1969), Mireille Dansereau's *La vie revée* (1972), and Joyce Wieland's *The Far Shore* (1975), Canadian women have entered the feature film industry in slowly increasing numbers. And in the 1980s, young filmmakers like Sandy Wilson (*My American Cousin* [1985]), Anne Wheeler (*Loyalties* [1986]), and Patricia Rozema (*I've Heard the Mermaids Singing* (1987]) are making news with their aesthetically accomplished, feminist, and economically viable productions. Although the gains have been intermittent and women filmmakers still account for only approximately 3 percent of budgets and productions, nevertheless women are making their presence felt. And feminism has been instrumental in this process: Studio D was a direct result of women's demands. The Canadian women's movement has provided not only the will for women to enter the profession and the support systems (demands for public financing, feminist producers, and women technicians, as well as audiences) which helped them to do so, but subjects and sensibilities as well.

Kass Banning, 'From Didactics to Desire: Building Women's Film Culture', in *Work in Progress: Building Feminist Culture*, ed. Rhea Tregebov (Toronto: The Women's Press, 1987)

See also: BURROUGHS, JACKIE; MONTREAL INTERNATIONAL

CANTRILL, CORINNE (1928–   ) and ARTHUR (1938–   )

The Cantrills are AUSTRALIA's most prolific AVANT-GARDE filmmakers and polemicists. Their partnership began in 1963 with a series of films on child arts and crafts which were televised by the national broadcaster, ABC-TV, during a brief period when shortage of product made Australian television accessible to independent filmmakers. Returning to Australia in 1969 after a four-year stint in London, the Cantrills took up a fellowship at Australian National University and were influential in the National Library's acquisition of avant-garde films. Their multi-screen projection and film-performance work, and their lecture and screening tours of Australia, were vital in disseminating avant-garde film history at a time when a rhetoric of cultural nationalism was agitating for a feature film industry. In 1971 they began editing *Cantrills Filmnotes*, to date publishing nearly sixty issues. Since 1972 the Cantrills have been guests at major international experimental film festivals and screening venues, including a six-month Artists-in-Berlin award in 1985. Their films vary in length from the two-minute *Zap* (1971) to the 148-minute *In This Life's Body* (1984). All their work displays a rigorous investigation into the filmic process, including many three-color separation experiments, multi-screen works, and films concerned with the processes of perception. The preoccupation with landscape, which has marked attempts to produce a distinctive national identity in both documentary and feature film, has taken on a different inflection in the Cantrills' landscape work, from *Home Movie – A Day in the Bush* (1969) to *Bouddi* (1970), *Earth Message* (1970), and the *Touching the Earth* series (1977). Their most recent work,

including *In This Life's Body*, *The Berlin Apartment* (1987 two-screen film) and *Projected Light* (1988 two-screen with slides), demonstrates a deepening preoccupation with personal experience and personal history while maintaining the purism of their experiments with the material of film. *In This Life's Body* attracted particular interest from women because of its use of Corinne's family photographs to compose an impossible autobiography from photographic traces of the self.

The eighty or so films made by the Cantrills include: *Eikon* (1969); *4000 Frames, An Eye-Opener Film* (1970); *Harry Hooton* (1970); *Skin of Your Eye* (1973); *At Eltham* (1974); *Reflections on Three Images by Baldwin Spencer, 1901* (1974); *Three Colour Separation Studies – Landscapes* (1976); *At Uluru* (1977); *Grain of the Voice Series: Rock Wallaby and Blackbird, Two Women, Seven Sisters* (1980); *The Second Journey (To Uluru)* (1981); *Floterian–Hand Paintings From A Film History* (1981); *Waterfall* (1984); *In This Life's Body* (1984); *Note on Berlin, the Divided City* (1986); *Walking Track* (1987); *The Berlin Apartment* (1987)

Barry Kapke, 'Cinema of the Senses: Selected Films of Arthur and Corinne Cantrill', *Cinematograph*, vol. 3 (1988)

FC

CAREER WOMAN

A cultural STEREOTYPE available to describe women who deviate from the normative wife-and-motherhood goal of adult women. Film narratives involving career women are often organized around what is seen as the irresolvable conflict between career and FEMININITY. There are a number of variants of the stereotype: the highly intelligent, ambitious, and single-minded career woman who sacrifices love in the mistaken pursuit of career, only to realize the error of her ways at the end of the film (*All I Desire* [Douglas Sirk, Universal, 1953], *Woman of the Year* [George Stevens, MGM, 1941]); or the equally intelligent and talented career woman whose femininity (warmth and compassion) undermines her career (*Pat and Mike* [George Cukor, MGM, 1942], *Mildred Pierce* [Michael Curtiz, Warner Bros., 1945]) The first spate of Hollywood's career-woman movies came in the 1930s, and STARS like Joan CRAWFORD, Bette DAVIS, Katharine HEPBURN, Rosalind Russell, Barbara STANWYCK are associated with such roles. These films are often fascinating examples not just of misogyny in operation, but also of how a star's PERFORMANCE can work against the grain of a script. Hepburn's performances in particular seem actually to reveal the patriarchal control at work in films such as *Christopher Strong* (Dorothy Arzner, RKO, 1933) and *A Woman Rebels* (Mark Sandrich, RKO, 1936). In the wake of feminism, the career woman has recently been treated more sympathetically, though the basic theme of irresolvable conflict remains (*Rollover* [Alan J Pakula, 1981]). There has also been a parallel (backlash?) development in the form of the 'man as housewife' film, beginning with the alarmingly popular *Kramer vs Kramer* (Robert Benton, 1979).

Molly Haskell, *From Reverence to Rape* (New York: Penguin, 1973)   TP

CARIBBEAN

Film activity in the Caribbean is characterized by consumption rather than production. As with many other regions of the world, the dominance of US cinema and TV is readily apparent, and American productions have been the staple for audiences in the region since these media were introduced there. Film DISTRIBUTION and cinema screens are in the hands of commercial entrepreneurs, who are happy to fill them with US 'B' movies and generous helpings of INDIAN popular films and karate and KUNG FU films.

Film production in the region was monopolized by Hollywood in the 1950s and 1960s, in films in which seas, sands, and lush tropical locations with their colorful, musical, exotic peoples were the backdrop for ROMANCES, gangster movies, and desert island adventures. Many Caribbean countries have nevertheless attempted to start their own film industries: among them Jamaica, Trinidad, Barbados, Martinique, Guadeloupe, and Guyana. In some of these areas, 16mm and 35mm production units were established mainly as commercial ventures; but in Guyana, a state-run film center with full post-production facilities was built in the early 1970s. Today most of these facilities are obsolete and have been little used. The main constraint has been the capital-intensive nature of cinema, which requires considerable support from governments, international cultural bodies, and private investors in order to survive in the face of foreign imports. Thus there is no Caribbean film industry as such; though individual filmmakers work in film and video formats for both cinema and TV. Countries of the Hispanic Caribbean (CUBA, VENEZUELA, Puerto Rico), however, have different histories in relation to cinema and much more developed film industries.

The region as a whole has a rich cultural heritage of literature, theater, music, dance, and the performing arts generally. Given this and the area's geographical qualities, it is not surprising that classics like *The Harder They Come* (Perry Henzell, 1972), *Smile Orange* (Trevor D Rhone, 1974), *Rue cases nègres/Black Shack Alley* (Euzhan Palcy, 1983), and *Wan Pipel/One People* (Pim de la Parra, 1976) would eventually be made. Although most of these films were financed from outside the region, they were made by Caribbean filmmakers or Caribbean writers. Today, video production for television is the main media activity in the region; and outside a few training workshops (in Martinique, for instance), or in the production of advertisements, film is little used. TV has been the vehicle for development of a film culture, though most TV films are still picked up from US satellites. Where local programs are produced, however, these have proved very popular, particularly in Trinidad, Jamaica, and in French 'départements outre-mer' Martinique and Guadeloupe.

Many filmmakers from the Caribbean have turned to Europe and the USA for training in film, and for the resources to pursue their craft. Since the 1970s there has been an increase in activity on the part of Caribbean filmmakers and writers – including those born of Caribbean parents outside the Caribbean – who have been returning to the region to make films drawing on the literature, history, folklore, and sociopolitical realities of the region, as well as from the experiences of Caribbean people in Europe and America. However, these films are too few in number and appear too rarely on Caribbean screens to have any sustained impact on the colonized tastes of the region's audiences.

Women's contribution to all this is difficult to quantify; but it is plain that their participation is small compared to men's, and probably even smaller than it is in the West. However, in the field of feature production two women directors have achieved international recognition: from Martinique, Euzhan PALCY, and from Guadeloupe, Sarah MALDOROR. Euzhan Palcy won recognition with the highly successful *Rue cases nègres*, her first feature film, based on her own adaptation of the Josef Zobel novel of the same name. The film has a strong central character in 'Ma Tine,' through whom the strength and determination black women have brought to the history of black struggle – though recognized only relatively recently – are celebrated. Sarah Maldoror is a radical filmmaker through whose many films black culture and struggle are also documented. Maldoror directed the internationally acclaimed feature film *Sambizanga* (1972), set in Angola and featuring a woman's participation in the struggle for her country's liberation. Both Maldoror and Palcy now live part of the time in Paris.

The work of other Caribbean women filmmakers has been concerned with the social, political, and economic situation of women, their skills, and their contribution to Caribbean culture. Sistren, the Jamaican Woman's Theater Co-op, produced a film called *Sweet Sugar Rage* (Honor Ford-Smith, 1985), which came out of their theater workshops with mostly rural working-class women all over Jamaica. Sistren have an international reputation for their popular innovative style of theater, which they plan to make more widely available through film. Gloria Lowe, a Guyanese director living in the Netherlands, works on 16mm and video, producing a number of documentaries including *With Our Own Hands* (1987), an account of migrant women in the Netherlands, and *Finding Our Own Face* (1987), which documents work of three Surinamese women artists. Elsie Haas, a Haitian filmmaker living in France, works in film and TV and has directed a number of fiction and documentary films, including *Zatrap* (1979), a documentary which follows a day in the life of a domestic in Martinique, through whom we learn about the workings of Martiniquan society. Claudine Boothe's first film, a short entitled *No Virginity, No Nationality* (1981), examines the operation of Britain's racist immigration legislation, in particular as it works against Asian women. Boothe, a journalist from Jamaica, lives and works in Britain and is now working on a series for TV examining the effects of a single European market on black women. Another Jamaican filmmaker, Denis Elmina Davis, who trained and has worked primarily as a camerawoman, made *Omega Rising: Women of Rastafari* (1988) as her directorial debut; this film looks at women in the Rastafarian movement in both Jamaica and Britain.

Most Caribbean filmmakers get their training outside the region, and it is very difficult for anyone at all – let alone women – to obtain experience and work in TV or film in the Caribbean itself. This explains why so many Caribbean

A major feminist film journal is published in West Germany. It is also Europe's only feminist film journal. What is its name?

women filmmakers born in the region live and work in Europe. A number of women film- and videomakers born in Britain of Caribbean parents have featured strong roles for women in their work, which often addresses various aspects of the Caribbean migration experience. They include: Karen Alexander (Guyana), co-director of the video *MsTaken Identity* (1986); Maureen Blackwood (Jamaica), a member of the black independent filmmakers' group, SANKOFA, which made *The Passion of Remembrance* (1986); Martina Attille (St Lucia), maker of *Dreaming Rivers* (1988); and Wendy Williamson (Jamaica), who made *Castles of Sand* (1986).

Maureen Blackwood and June Givanni, 'Black Film-making in Europe', *Screen*, vol. 29, no. 4 (1988)   JG

CAROLINA, ANA (1943–)

BRAZILIAN filmmaker Ana Carolina Teixeira Soares initially trained as a physiotherapist at São Paolo's university. She directed some eleven documentaries, mostly on political subjects, in the 1960s and 1970s. In her DOCUMENTARY work, she deconstructs traditional ideas of the film medium as untampered 'reality,' using it as a vehicle for interpreting 'reality.' She has also made animation films. In 1977 she shot her first feature, *Mar de rosas*, a wittily surrealist farce in which traditional feminine roles are subverted.

Indústria (1969); *Getulio Vargas* (1974); *Mar de rosas/A Sea of Roses* (1977); *Nelson Pereira dos Santos* (1979); *Das tripas coração/With the Heart in the Hands* (1982); *Sohno de valsa/A Waltz-like Dream* (1987)

Simon Hartog, 'Ana Carolina Teixeira Soares: A Conversation', *Framework*, no. 28 (1985)   NT

'CARRY ON' FILMS

The 'Carry On' films [were made in BRI]TAIN between 1958 an[d ... were] never critically acclai[med ... pro]ducts of EALING STU[DIOS ...] popular with British a[udiences for] years. The twenty-eight films made over the two decades were all produced by Peter Rogers and directed by Gerald Thomas, and each engaged practically the same group of performers: Kenneth Williams, Kenneth Connor, Joan Sims, Charles Hawtrey, Sidney James, Hattie Jacques, Jim Dale, Bernard Bresslaw, and Barbara Windsor. The first, *Carry On Sergeant* (1958), was not made to be part of a series: it dealt in outrageously comic fashion with the training of National Service conscripts, and the film's farcical music-hall qualities, which so captured the public's attention were reproduced *ad nauseam* in all 'Carry On' films thereafter. These films are the cinema's equivalent of the rude seaside postcard, replete with images of various kinds of female STEREOTYPES: winsome and pneumatic BLONDE virgins, grim-visaged nagging wives, coy, hoydenish spinsters, mothers-in-law as frosty harridans. The language of the films is loud with puns and innuendos of rampant rudeness, and the plots often revolve around such niceties as the frustrations of honeymoon couples, and people get 'locked in the lavatory' with alarming regularity. If at all possible every character has at some point in the story to be caught, metaphorically or otherwise, with their trousers or knickers (nearly) down. The films are usually set in an institution – an army barracks, school or hospital, say – where people's physical needs, sexual and excretory, are not catered for and the inmates are intent on rigorously repressing all pleasures of the flesh: it is for 'new arrivals' to subvert the status quo in the name, in the words of critic Marion Jordan, of 'a lower-class masculine resistance to "refinement"; an insistence on sexuality, physicality, fun, on the need for drink in a kill-joy world; for shiftiness in an impossibly demand-

...trial society . . .'. For a time, ...arry On' series stayed in uniform ...ry On: Nurse, Teacher, Constable, ...ruising), but in the sixties began to ...mine a richer vein with parodies of other GENRES (Carry On: Spying, Screaming, Cleo, Cowboy, Up the Khyber). In their crudely mocking way, these spoofs displayed variants of the gender dramas inherent in the fictional worlds of the films they parodied, denying any place to women; portraying them, indeed, as gaolers, sexual objects, or unnatural predators.

Marion Jordan, 'Carry On . . . Follow That Stereotype', in *British Cinema History*, ed. James Curran and Vincent Porter (London: Weidenfeld & Nicolson, 1983)   SP

CAVANI, LILIANA (1933–   )

A film director based in ITALY, Cavani is well established in the national film industry, having made ten feature films and seven documentaries for RAI, Italian television. She graduated from the Centro Sperimentale di Cinematografia, Rome's film school, and began her career making documentary films on historical subjects for RAI, by whom her first feature was produced in 1966. Since then, Cavani has primarily made fiction films, commercially distributed. Her films often offer rereadings of historical or mythological figures (*Francesco d'Assisi* (1966); *Galileo* (1968); *I cannibali* (1969); *Milarepa* (1973–4)) and exhibit an attraction for cultural tropes, in particular for German culture (*Al di la' del bene e del male* (1977), about Nietzsche and Lou Andreas Salomé; *Il portiere di notte* (1974), a reconsideration of Nazism in terms of sexual politics; and *Interno berlinese* (1986), a Japanese novel set by Cavani in Germany). The myth of Antigone was interestingly treated in *I cannibali*, and reinterpreted in light of the contemporary political revolt in Italy against authority and state repression.

Although not insensitive to feminist issues, Cavani would not identify with feminism. Her films present a difficult case of analysis for feminist critics. None of her films is really about women and, in any case, men enjoy a privileged position in the cinematic and narrative space. Although she has been critical of the status quo and has questioned knowledge and its relation to power, men are the main subject and object of inquiry (Francesco, Galileo, Milarepa, Nietzsche); though she has treated intriguing female figures like Antigone and psychoanalyst Lou Andreas Salomé. However, Cavani's films strive to exceed sexual difference, present nonconventional models of sexuality, and question the symbolic order. Feminist theorists have therefore suggested interesting ways in which they might be *adaptable* to a feminist reading.

Storia del terzo Reich (1962–3); *L'eta' di Stalin* (1963); *La casa in Italia* (1964); *Philippe Pétain: processo a Vichy* (1965); *La donna nella Resistenza* (1965); *Gesu' mio fratello* (1965); *Il giorno della pace* (1965); *Francesco d'Assisi* (1966); *Galileo* (1968); *I cannibali/The Cannibals* (1969); *L'Ospite/ The Guest* (1971); *Milarepa* (1973–4); *Il portiere di notte/The Night Porter* (1974); *Al di la' del bene e del male/Beyond Good and Evil* (1977); *La pelle/The Skin* (1981); *Oltre la porta/Beyond the Door* (1983); *Interno berlinese/Affair in Berlin* (1986)

Kaja Silverman, 'The Female Authorial Voice', in *The Acoustic Mirror* (Bloomington and Indianapolis: Indiana University Press, 1988)   GB

CECCHI D'AMICO, SUSO (1914–   )

The substantial career of Cecchi D'Amico, a screenwriter working in ITALY, has informed Italian auteur cinema from NEOREALISM to NEW ITALIAN CINEMA. Born into a literary family, Cecchi d'Amico was trained in classics, literature, and foreign languages. In the 1930s and 1940s she worked as a translator of plays and as a journalist, and began writing film scripts after the war. She took part in the formation and development of neorealism: she co-wrote the neorealist classics *Ladri di biciclette/Bicycle Thieves* (Vittorio de Sica, 1948) and *Miracolo a Milano/Miracle in Milan* (Vittorio de Sica, 1951). From 1946 to 1952 she worked with Luigi Zampa, a director of comedies who was also involved in the neorealist experiment. During neorealism she worked very closely with writers Cesare Zavattini and Ennio Flajano, with whom she shared a refined cultural edge and a realist attention to everyday life with an ironic touch.

Cecchi D'Amico has collaborated with major Italian directors. She worked with Michelangelo ANTONIONI on *I vinti/The Vanquished* (1952), *La signora senza camelie/Camille Without Camellias* (1953), and *Le amiche/The Girl Friends* (1955), an intriguing film entirely dominated by women characters and their relationships, adapted from a novel by Cesare Pavese. With Francesco Maselli she made *Gli indifferenti/Time of Indifference* (1964), and with Francesco Rosi *La sfida/The Challenge* (1958), *I magliari* (1959), and *Salvatore Giuliano* (1962). Her long collaboration with Alessandro Blasetti began in 1949 and lasted until 1966, with *Tempi nostri/Anatomy of Love* (1953) and *Peccato che sia una canaglia/Too Bad She is Bad* (1955), for example. She has worked with Franco Zeffirelli, and also written for television. Throughout her whole career she has collaborated extensively with directors interested in comedy – most of all with Luigi Comencini, Mario Camerini and Mario Monicelli.

Her association with Luchino Visconti is most prominent, and most dear to her. Visconti and Cecchi D'Amico established a steady director–screenwriter team. Cecchi D'Amico has co-written almost all Visconti's films after neorealism: *Bellissima* in 1951; *Siamo donne/We the Women* in 1953 (both with actress Anna Magnani); *Senso* in 1954; *Le notti bianche/White Nights* in 1957; *Rocco e i suoi fratelli/Rocco and His Brothers* in 1960; *Il lavoro/The Job* in 1962; *Il Gattopardo/The Leopard* in 1963; *Vaghe stelle dell'Orsa/Sandra* in 1965; *Lo straniero/The Stranger* in 1967; *Ludwig* in 1974 (she promoted the recent restoration of the film after its mutilation at the hands of its distributor); *Gruppo di famiglia in un interno/Conversation Piece* in 1974, and *L'innocente/The Innocent* in 1976. Issues such as models of sexual identity, MOTHERHOOD, women's fantasies and desires, and women's conditions in history are all approached in these films.

Asked about her writing of close to one hundred films, Suso Cecchi D'Amico says: 'I have enjoyed myself very much.'

Marie Christine Questerbere, *Les scénaristes italiens* (Lausanne: Hatier, 1988)   GB

CENSORSHIP

Although in its everyday usage censorship is usually seen purely in repressive terms, implying prevention from publication – usually through cutting or banning – it can in fact be productive. Cinema has attracted more censorship than any preexisting medium, though with the decline in cinema attendances in many parts of the world, this dubious honor is rapidly passing to TELEVISION and VIDEO. In its productivity, however, film censorship has created film GENRES, certain types of film NARRATIVE, film STARS – even the ways in which we understand cinema and its place in society.

Film censorship has taken a variety of forms at different times and places. Censorship can take place before a film is made, at various stages during its production, and/or after its release. Most censorship is actually precensorship, so that cuts and bans in films already made are rare in comparison with less visible forms of censorship – which range from filmmakers' own choices of 'acceptable' topics and treatments through to vetting productions at the idea, script, or preview stages. Film censorship can be institutionalized and legally sanctioned in varying degrees. Commercial film industries tend to object to censorship on grounds of restraint to trade (while noncommercial cinemas might object on grounds of 'artistic freedom'), but many have had to accept it in the face of outside pressures: in which case there is usually a preference for self-regulation. The Hollywood PRODUCTION CODE, or Hays Code, administered by the Motion Picture Producers and Distributors Association, is a classic case of industry self-regulation. However, film censorship may also, or instead, take place in the public sphere, through agencies of central or local government, or through nonstatutory but authoritative bodies such as the BRITISH BOARD OF FILM CENSORS (BBFC).

Objects of censorship also vary: while, for example, the Production Code focused on sex and crime, the BBFC, certainly in the 1930s, exercised a covert political censorship under the guise of avoiding 'controversy.' Before the thirties, film censorship in BRITAIN had been involved in debates about the nature of cinema as a new public sphere. The BBFC had resisted various attempts to embourgeoisify the medium, or to use it for anything except diversion for the working classes: hence its objections to any treatment of 'serious' topics, and indeed to notions of film as an 'art form.'

On the other hand, the Hollywood Production Code – a thoughtful moral document written by a Jesuit – was grounded in the view that cinema could enhance 'spiritual or moral progress.' Its preoccupation with various types and effects of sin make it as much a formula for acceptable modes of film narration as a list of prohibitions. Its insistence on 'compensating moral values' (showing sinful acts is permissible provided the perpetrators receive their just deserts in terms of this moral code) may be associated with the forms of narrative resolution characteristic of CLASSICAL HOLLYWOOD CINEMA, and indeed with the oft-remarked disjunctive or implausible endings of many Hollywood films. The Code's support for the sanctity of matrimony relates to film narratives which set up a threat to a marriage as the 'problem' setting the story in motion, and the resolution of the narrative through the restoration of such a relationship: *Mildred Pierce* (Michael Curtiz, Warner Bros., 1945), and *Christopher Strong* (Dorothy Arzner, RKO, 1933) are just two of countless Hollywood films with such storylines. This in turn has implications for the representation of women in films, with the FEMME FATALE in a sense being a product of censorship – her narrative function precisely to trouble 'the sanctity of marriage and the home.'

While it is generally accepted that – in the West at least – film censorship today is not as strict as it once was, the issue is far from dead. In some parts of the world, especially where cinema continues to be an important medium of communication, censorship – and its productive effects – continue. Political censorship in CHILE, for example, has produced a flourishing Chilean cinema in exile, as well as an active form of video 'samizdat' at home. In INDIA, taboos on sexual representation have given rise to stylized and allusive references to sexual activity in the 'song picturizations' of popular cinema. In the West, film PORNOGRAPHY – whose attraction must be in large part the lure of the forbidden – actually depends upon censorship, is produced by it.

In recent years feminists have become involved in debates on censorship, usually in relation to the treatment of women in violent hardcore pornography, which is more widely circulated in print media than on film. Mainstream cinema – which tries to avoid the 'porn' label – did, however, attract the censure of feminists with the release in the late 1970s and early 1980s of a cycle of 'slasher' films, involving bloody killings of women indulging in 'transgressive' sexual behavior. Feminists, though, have on the whole tended to be more interested in direct action against such films than in supporting existing – or even new

70

– censorship institutions, which are set up to combat 'obscenity' rather than to protect the interests of women.

Annette Kuhn, *Cinema, Censorship and Sexuality, 1909–1925* (London and New York: Routledge, 1988)   *AKu*

CENTRAL AMERICA

The history of film production in the Central American countries – Guatemala, El Salvador, Honduras, Nicaragua, Costa Rica, and Panama – is scant and sporadic. Aggressive control of local EXHIBITION markets by both Hollywood and Mexican producers, chronically limited economic resources, often exploitive political regimes, together with enormous ethnic and cultural variations from one part of the region to another, are all factors which have blocked the development of a local film culture. The political turmoil that has rent much of the region during the 1970s and 1980s is simply the continuing manifestation of unresolved conflicts and contradictions that have been festering since the

> ···
> : *'A comedy of yuppy conformity': this film* :
> : *by West German filmmaker Doris* :
> : *Doerrie focuses on the living habits of* :
> : *what species?* :
> ···

turn of the century. Unlike the conflict with COLOMBIA which 'created' the nation of Panama at the dawn of the century, Augusto César Sandino's resistance to US marine occupation in the 1920s, the peasant massacres in El Salvador in the early 1930s, or the US-engineered overthrow of the liberal Arbenz government in Guatemala in 1954, the current strife has generated a rich audiovisual record, since all sides have enlisted the visual media as a favored weapon of combat. Central American film culture is thus built upon the constants of warfare, repression, and the countervailing drive to establish a sense of national/regional identity and collective purpose.

In this context, Itsmo Films in Costa Rica and Panama's GECU (the Experimental University Film Group, long under the direction of Pedro Rivera) are anomalous in their longevity. INCINE, the Nicaraguan National Film Institute founded in 1979 on the model of CUBA's ICAIC, has been limited by grandiose ambitions, scarce resources, and abundant internal conflict. Other Nicaraguan media groups, both government-sponsored and independent (Videonic, Sistema Sandinista de Televisión, Taller Popular de Video, MIDINRA [the national agrarian reform ministry], AMLAE [the national women's group], and so on), made an early choice to work primarily in VIDEO because of its greater economy and versatility. Radio Venceremos, a guerrilla communications collective in El Salvador which has assembled an impressive body of work under extremely difficult circumstances over the past decade, freely mixes 16mm and video footage, black-and-white and color to create their fascinatingly hybrid stylistic mix. Honduras and Guatemala have only isolated pockets of image-making activity. There, even more than elsewhere in Central America, images tend to be recorded primarily for export and by outsiders.

Given the tenuousness of all these endeavors, the frequent preference or necessity of anonymity, and the shifting composition of many of the above groups, it is difficult to be specific about women's role in contemporary Central American visual culture. Of the six countries, Nicaragua's media-making efforts have received the most exposure. Women's participation has been crucial there. The median age of film and videomakers like Miriam Loasiaga, Amina Luna, Rossana Lacayo, María José Alvarez, and Lylliam Mejía, for example, is barely twenty-five. They have developed quickly, without benefit of background preparation; they have many years of creativity ahead of them, if circumstances permit. Many women from abroad deserve recognition for

71

lending crucial support to the development of Nicaraguan film and video, among them Jackie Reiter (Britain), Berta Navarro, and Margarita Suzán (Mexico), DeeDee Halleck, Martha Wallner, and Julia Lesage (USA). In 1987, as part of the commemoration of the tenth anniversary of the Nicaraguan women's organization, AMLAE published a flyer – 'Nicaragua: Women on Video' – describing twenty-four works related to women's topics (produced by an assortment of nationals and visitors, including several of the women listed above) along with directions for contacting eleven local distributors. Clearly, in Nicaragua at least, women-centered visual culture has become a priority – and a reality.   *JBu*

CHANNEL FOUR TELEVISION

When Channel Four began broadcasting in November 1982 it did so with a brief to innovate, experiment, and produce programs for audiences not catered for by BRITAIN's other commercial TELEVISION channel. A decentered organizational structure was invented, buying programs from a group of newly created – and, at their best, dynamic – independent companies. Here, many previously disenfranchised viewers hoped, was a channel with not merely an inclination but a duty to be 'different' from the rest of television: a channel which would embrace the multicultural society Britain had become, encourage formal experiment, and create a new kind of television less constrained than hitherto by notions of 'balance.'

The position of women in all of this was less clear. Women working inside Channel Four were divided on whether a commissioning editor with direct responsibility for women's programs should be appointed. In the end none was. And although a number of DOCUMENTARY series run by women were commissioned including the weekly current affairs programs *20/20 Vision* and *Broadside*, and the magazine shows *Watch the Woman* and *Woman in View*,

none survived. The fact that they were arguably 'allowed to fail' perhaps indicates television's ambivalent attitude to programs aimed at women audiences. In the less expensive areas of single documentaries and experimental/innovative television, however, feminism did find a more permanent, if perhaps more marginalized, role. Important documentaries such as the award-winning *Maids and Madams* (Mira Hammermesh, 1985) and *Veronica 4 Rose* (Melanie Chait, 1984) were made, and the department responsible for independent film and video became a major source of funding for innovative feminist work such as Lynne Tillman's and Sheila McLaughlin's *Committed* (1984), whilst also supporting Britain's regional film and video workshops. However, women have largely failed to make any impression on the channel's prestigious drama and feature film departments.

Since the early heady days of innovation and selfconscious difference a far more pragmatic, cost and ratings-conscious channel has emerged. Innovative work still takes place – as with the gay and lesbian series *Out On Tuesday* – but some of the earlier intentions have fallen by the wayside, leaving women in Britain a little – but not very much – better served by television than they were before 1982.

Helen Baehr and Gillian Dyer (eds), *Boxed In: Women and Television* (London: Pandora Press, 1987)   *JRo*

CHAUVEL, ELSA (1898–1983) and CHARLES (1897–1959)

When Elsie Wilcox (stage name Elsie Sylvaney) starred in Charles Chauvel's second feature, *Greenhide*, in 1926, she not only reversed an AUSTRALIAN film tradition (exemplified in Chauvel's first feature, *Moth of Moonbi* [1926], in which a country girl learns her lesson in the city) by playing a high-society girl who meets her match in the country, she also embarked on a new career assisting

Charles Chauvel in the production, writing, and direction of the seven features he was to make during the next thirty years. Charles Chauvel's epic vision of Australian life, landscape, and history resulted in ambitious and often physically demanding location shoots in inaccessible terrain, notably in his most successful film, *Sons of Matthew* (1949); and in *Jedda* (1955) – Australia's first color film, which starred aboriginal actors in the leading roles. After the cessation of features production from 1940 onward the Chauvels became the most prominent of those few who managed to produce narrative films in the three decades from World War II to the revival of the Australian film industry in the early 1970s. One of Australia's leading editors from the silent era, Mona Donaldson, reedited Chauvel's *Heritage* (1935) and edited *Uncivilised* (1936) before leaving the film industry after almost twenty years. The Chauvels contributed substantially to the representation of Australia in terms of myths of landscape and pioneers, laying the foundations for the quest for a NATIONAL CINEMA which in the 1970s would attempt to define its difference from Hollywood by reinvoking landscape, light, and the 1890s bush legends of Australian mateship and survival in the hostile antipodes.

The Moth of Moonbi (1926); *Greenhide* (1926); *The Wake of the Bounty* (1933); *Heritage* (1935); *Uncivilised* (1936); *40,000 Horsemen* (1941); *Rats of Tobruk* (1944); *Sons of Matthew* (1949); *Jedda* (1955)

William Routt, 'On the Expression of Colonialism in Early Australian Films – Charles Chauvel and Naive Cinema', in *An Australian Film Reader*, ed. Albert Moran and Tom O'Regan (Sydney: Currency Press, 1985)   FC

CHENZIRA, AYOKA (195?–)

Chenzira is a US independent filmmaker and video artist based in New York City. Her background in dance, theater, music, and still photography prepared

Ayoka Chenzira

her for her current work in the media of film and video. Films such as *Syvilla* (1975) and *Zajota and the Boogie Spirit* (1989) take dance and the African-American experience as their subjects. Chenzira is also an accomplished animator: her short film *Hairpiece: A Film For Nappy-Headed People* (1984) is an animated satire on black women's struggles with racist standards of beauty. Particularly effective in its use of humor and specific address to BLACK WOMEN, *Hairpiece* is an important work in BLACK CINEMA. Chenzira's video work confronts the racist and sexist abuse of power, integrating the perspectives of people of color in exploring feminist issues such as sexual abuse. Chenzira is also a media activist and teacher who presents her work widely and lectures on many topics related to African-Americans and the media.

Syvilla: They Dance to Her Drum (1975); *Hairpiece: A Film For Nappy-Headed*

73

People (1984); *Secret Sounds Screaming: The Sexual Abuse of Children* (1985); *5 Out of 5* (1987); *The Lure and The Lore* (1988); *Zajota and the Boogie Spirit* (1989)   PW

CHILD, ABIGAIL (1948–)

Trained in documentary, US filmmaker Child shifted careers and began making AVANT-GARDE films in San Francisco with *Some Exterior Presence* (1977). She developed a fast-cut and pixillated style with a series of short films in the 1970s which found full form in *Ornamentals* (1979). Child's work, in its concern for the elements of film form (the frame, shot, the phrase of SOUND), has been associated with the Language poets. Since 1981 she has produced a seven-part film, *Is This What You Were Born For?* (1981–9), in which she reworks numerous film GENRES to unpack their latent content and social context. The home movie, DANCE film, FILM NOIR, PORNOGRAPHY, and DOCUMENTARY have all been subjected to analysis through her rigorous and often humorous editing of sound and image. With *Covert Action* (1984) Child placed herself within the feminist debate by directly addressing the image of women in film; and with *Mayhem* (1987) by specifically addressing lesbianism. Child moved to New York in 1980 and has become a central figure in the avant-garde film movement there, teaching and organizing public screenings. She publishes her theoretical writings and poetry frequently in JOURNALS of film and poetics on both east and west coasts of the USA, and distributes her films through Filmmakers Cooperative (New York) and Canyon Cinema Cooperative (San Francisco).

Except the People (1970); *Game* (1972); *Tar People* (1975); *Some Exterior Presence* (1977); *Peripeteia I* (1977); *Daylight Test Section* (1978); *Peripeteia II* (1978); *Pacific Far East Line* (1979); *Ornamentals* (1979); *Is This What You Were Born For?* (1981–9, including *Prefaces, Mutiny, Covert Action, Perils, Mayhem, Both 1 & 2,* and *Mercy*)

Marjorie Keller, 'Is This What You Were Born For?', in *X-Dream*, ed. Saul Levine (Boston: Saul Levine, 1987)   MKe

CHILE

Film production in this LATIN AMERICAN country has been traditionally conditioned by meager possibilities of return from a relatively small market. According to Chilean film historians only seventy-eight features were produced between 1910 and 1931, and since 1931 no more than 120. Among the few silent films that have been preserved is *El húsar de la muerte* (Pedro Sienna, 1925), restored at the University of Chile in 1982. The creation in 1942 of Chile Films – a government-owned company attached to the Corporation of Production Development – included the building of a lavish studio in Santiago. This organization was designed to improve production facilities so that Chilean films could compete with foreign productions – including Spanish-language films – on the domestic market. Film historians claim that features made by Chile Films were poor imitations of the GENRES popularized by the Mexican and Argentinian film industries during the forties; and despite massive investments, these productions failed to recoup costs and the company had to settle for documentary and newsreel production. In 1987, under pressure from independents, the Chilean government enacted fiscal measures to allow producers to sustain a regular yet modest activity. With Patricio Kaulen as executive director, Chile Films renewed its partnership with the independents. German Becker (*Volver* [1969]); Aldo Francia (*Valparaiso, mi amor* [1967]); Patricio Kaulen (*Largo viaje* [1967]); Miguel Littín (*El Chacal de Nahueltoro* [1969]); Raúl Ruiz (*Tres tristes tigres* [1968]); Helvio Soto (*Caliche sangriento* [1967]), and others, made films that addressed current social and political concerns.

DOCUMENTARY has been the most consistent type of production in Chile. Independent directors like Nieves YAN-

COVIC and Jorge di Lauro paved the way for politically innovative documentary. But most of this activity was concentrated at universities, where units like the Experimental Group of the University of Chile – created by Sergio Bravo in 1962, and later directed by Pedro Chaskel – trained young directors and bolstered a socially committed cinema. During the Popular Unity government a revived Chile Films, under the directorship of Miguel Littin, took radical steps to support the production, distribution, and exhibition of Chilean Films, providing facilities for many filmmakers, including women like Marilú MALLET, Valeria SARMIENTO and Angelina Vázquez.

All existing film legislation was revoked by the military government that overthrew Salvador Allende in 1973, and all forms of official support ceased. Archives, university-based film schools and film societies were dismantled, while most filmmakers were forced to leave the country. Affected by stringent censorship laws, cinema was driven out of the public sphere. Since 1978, VIDEO has been a vital medium of audiovisual production for filmmakers – many of them women, community-based groups, and alternative cultural organizations. Video technology has been mobilized against the ideological tenets of the Pinochet regime and developed into a dynamic site of struggle, encouraging new forms of social exchange and giving new vitality to the cultural vanguard by becoming a unique alternative for creative expression. At the same time, the growth of video has prompted the organization of extensive distribution and exhibition networks. In its various forms, Chilean video practice has developed into a major field of political intervention. In its most experimental form, video has been used by visual artists like Eugenio Dittborn, Juan Forch, Catalina Parra, Marcela Serrano, and collectives like CADA, constituted in 1979. A feminist perspective has been developed by Diamela Eltit (*Zona de dolor IV* [1984]) and Lotty Rosenfeld (*Proposición para (entre) cruzar espacious limites* [1983]), Patricia Camiragua (*Popsicles* [1981]) and Tatiana GAVIOLA. In its most political form, video has become an alternative informational tool through collectives, like *Teleanálisis* and *Cine-Ojo*, recording events censored by the official media. Video played a major part in the 1988 referendum campaign that allied popular groups with democratic parties, and in general this oppositional practice communicates the urgency of combating the rightwing ideology of the regime.

Work in film, however, has regained some momentum through dedicated directors maintaining autonomous productions: *Julio Comienza en Julio* (Silvio Caiozzi, 1979), *Los hijos de la guerra fria* (Gonzalo Justiniano, 1986), *La estacion del retorno* (Leo Kocking, 1987) and *Imagen Latente* (Pable Perelman, 1987). These films and videos dramatically confront the national state of crisis. Other Chilean filmmakers – like Patricio Guzmán (Cuba and Spain), Miguel Littin (Mexico and Spain), Orlando Lubbert (Germany), Claudio Sapiain (Sweden), Marilú Mallet (Quebec), and Raúl Ruiz (France) – have pursued their activity in exile. The three parts of *The Battle of Chile* (Grupo Tercer Año and Patricio Guzmán, 1975–9), for example, were completed under the auspices of ICAIC in CUBA, while international solidarity networks funded documentaries condemning state repression, such as *Gracias a la vida* (Angelina Vázquez, 1979), which was made in Finland. While these films deal with the political implications of the institutional break in Chile, others have dealt with a wider range of topics. Raúl Ruiz, for instance, has clearly moved away from a nationally specific problematic. His prolific career in France represents the complex relationship exiles must negotiate with regard to their original and their adopted cultures. Ruiz's innovative aesthetic has endeared him to the critical vanguards in France and Britain. Overall, the Chilean cinema in exile has produced an impressive array of features and documentaries; and although production is spread throughout many countries in Europe and the Americas, these films represent a steadfast – albeit fragmented – continuity for a NATIONAL CINEMA.

Zuzana Pick, 'Chilean Cinema in Exile. The Notion of Exile: a Field of Investigation and a Conceptual Framework', *Framework* no. 34 (1987)   ZP

CHINA

Mainland China's is a cinema in which history and women play prominent parts, and its narrative and visual forms are indebted to traditional operas, *xiaoshuo* ('small talk' or novels), and western influences. The first Chinese-made movie was a piece of 'filmed theater,' *Ding Jun Shan/Ding Jun Mountain* (Liu Zhonglun, 1905), with a Peking Opera actor playing scenes before the camera. An explicit criticism of feudal marriages appeared in the first story feature, *Nan Fu Nan Qi/The Suffering Couple* (Zheng Zhengqiu and Zhang Shichuan, 1913). Early Chinese silents were film adaptations of the 'civilized play,' a form of spoken drama with social themes. A notable adaptation, *Hei Ji Yuanhun/Dead by Dark Injustice* (Zhang Shichuan, 1916), attacked imperialists' opium operations in China and inaugurated the edifying tone Chinese audiences came to expect of serious films. Female impersonation was not uncommon in the silent era: the first woman actress, Yan Shanshan, a student from Canton Northern Expedition Woman's Bombing Team, played a supportive role in *Zhuangzi Shi Qi/Zhuangzi Tests His Wife* (1913), while the main female role was played by her husband, the film's director and screenwriter, Li Minwei. In an OPERA film, *Tiennu Sanhua/Fairy Showering Flowers* (1920) – in which optical effects were first attempted – the director and 'heroine' was Meilanfang, a Peking Opera actor famous for his female impersonations. Women's victimization by urban crime was a favorite subject in features influenced by Hollywood thrillers: in this vein, *Yanruisheng/ The Murder Case* (Chen Shouzhi, 1921)

Peng Xiaolin's *Story of Three Women*

and *Hongfen Kulou/The Pink Skeleton* (Guan Haifeng, 1922) created local sensations.

About 650 silent narrative features were produced between 1921 and 1931 by 170 film companies operating mostly in Shanghai, some of them only very briefly. The most prolific company, Ming Xing, dramatized, through MELODRAMA, various forms of women's oppression, including widows' problems of remarriage – *Yu Li Hun/Jade Pear Death* (Zhang Shichuan, 1923); prostitution – *Shanghai Yi Furen/A Woman in Shanghai* (Zhang Shichuan, 1925), and barriers to woman's education – *Erba Jiaren/Beautiful Sixteen* (Zheng Zhengqiu, 1927). Other studies produced explicit sexist and escapist screen fantasies such as *Pan Si Dong/The Spider's Cave* (Dan Duyu, 1927) and *Dongfang Yetan/The Oriental Nights* (Dan Duyu, 1931). The first movie serial, which ran from 1928 to 1931, *Huoshao Hongliansi/The Burning of Red Lotus Temple* (Zhang Shichuan), had eighteen parts and featured women warriors. China's first sound film, *Genu Hong Mudan/Singsong Girl Peony* (Zhang Shichuan, 1931) attributed a woman's toleration of her husband's violence to her Confucian values.

Newsreels produced by the film companies Ming Xing, Tien Yi and Luan Hua documented the Japanese invasion and the Civil War between the 1930s and the late 1940s. Political censorship of films began with the Kuomintang's Film and Theater Censorship Committee in 1930, while members of the League of Leftist Writers undermined the Republican government by making films in the tradition of SOCIALIST REALISM. Many important classics of this period had anti-Japanese and economic hardship themes, including *Chuncan/Spring Silkworms* (Cheng Bugao, 1933), *Xiao Wanyi/Toys* (Sun Yu, 1933), *Da Lu/The Highway* (Sun Yu, 1934), *Shen Nu/The Goddess* (Wu Yonggang, 1934), *Yu Guang Qu/The Fishermen's Song* (Cai Chusheng, 1934), *Shizi Jietou/The Crossroads* (Shen Xilin, 1937), and *Malu Tienshi/Street Angel* (Yuan Muzhi, 1937). The actress Ruan Lingyu, 'China's Greta Garbo,' rose to stardom from key roles in *Toys* and *The Goddess*. Her suicide in 1935 after playing in *Xin Nuxing/New Women* (Cai Chusheng, 1934) was emblematic of women stars being glamorized, and then crushed by media scrutiny.

The Japanese takeover of Shanghai in 1937 led to the relocation of production centers in Chongqing, Yan'an and HONG KONG. Around seventeen companies confined to the concessions in Shanghai ('orphan island') made about 250 softcore PORNOGRAPHY films between 1937 and 1941. Government studios in Chongqing – China Film Studio and China Central Film Studio – produced about twenty-nine features between 1937 and 1945, including *Babai Zhuangshi/Fight to the Last* (Ying Yunwei, 1938) and *Huan Wo Guxiang/Give Me Back My Country* (Shi Dongshan, 1945). Anti-Japanese sentiments also inspired Chinese ANIMATION, which was pioneered by the Wan brothers in 1937. The heyday of classical Chinese cinema was in the postwar/Civil War period. Disillusion with inflation, joblessness, housing shortages, and a disrupted social and moral order in the aftermath of war gave rise to an indigenous NEOREALISM: these films were sympathetic with humble suffering folk and skeptical about the westernized urban bourgeoisie. Among the best of them were *Yijiang Chunshui Xiang Dongliu/Spring River Flows East* (1947), co-directed by Cai Chusheng and Zheng Junli *Baqianli Lu Yun He Yue/Eight Thousand Miles of Clouds and the Moon* (Shi Dongshan, 1947), and *Xiao Cheng Ji Chun/Spring in a Small City* (Fei Mu, 1948).

After the People's Republic was established in 1949, production, distribution, and exhibition of films targeted for workers, peasants, and soldiers were nationalized and supervised by the Film Bureau under the Ministry of Culture. Chen Boer, ex-actress and an activist in anti-Japanese and leftist women's movements, became first Minister and was later party secretary of Northeast Studio and supervisor of newsreel and feature productions. Films made between 1949 and 1965 played an edifying role in the socialist construction and conversion of China. Changes in national political and economic policies affected filmmaking in terms of style (revolutionary realism), as well as through public criticism (Hundred Flowers, Anti-Rightist movements), censorship, production quotas, and an implicit Han nationalism.

In accord with Party's policy of equality, women were trained as documentary cinematographers, screenwriters, editors, rural projection team members, and progressive actresses; and representation of women on the screen emphasized their emancipation from feudal oppression. By 1958, ten studios were operating in China: Beijing, August First, Changchun, Xian, Tian Shan, Inner Mongolia, Emei, Guangxi, Xiaoxiang, and Pearl River. Nevertheless, only two women were directing features: Dong Kena directed *Kunlun Shanshang Yike Cao/A Blade of Grass in Kunlun Mountain* (1962); Wang Ping, an assimilated Hui minority, made eight pro-revolution films before 1965, including *Liubao De Gushi/Story of Liubao* (1957), *Huaishu Zhuang/Locust Tree Village* (1962), and *Nihongdeng Sha De Shaobing/Sentinels Under the Neon Lights* (1964). Normal filmmaking came to a halt during the Cultural Revolution from 1966 to 1969.

A second, spontaneous Hundred Flowers movement in Chinese cinema, appearing after 1979, was marked by an inquisitive spirit, transgressing political taboos and theatrical influences to redefine film REALISM and reinforce humanist values. New generations of younger filmmakers are inspired by DOCUMENTARY aesthetics and ethnographic sensibilities. Female superheroes have given way to ordinary women crushed by misunderstanding: *Bei Aiqing Yiwang de Jiaoluo/Corner Forsaken by Love* (Zhang Qi and Li Yalin, 1982) and *Ren Dao Zhongnian/At Middle Age* (Wang Qimin and Sun Yu, 1983).

Films by male directors have sought to restore symbolic potency to ordinary men: *Lao Jing/Old Well* (Wu Tianming, 1987), *Furong Zhen/Hibiscus Town* (Xie Jin, 1987), *Hong Gaoliang/Red Sorghum* (Zhang Yimou, 1988) link national spirit with male virility. An open-door policy, along with 'Four Modernizations' politics, has also brought market pressures to the industry: few recent productions were state-financed, and studios have had to balance their budgets with a percentage of box office gross (split with the China Film Distribution Corporation). Entertainment genres, including KUNG FU, COMEDIES and thrillers, have became studio survival staples.

About fourteen women directors have been active in documentary and commercial feature productions in the 1980s. Although most of them would not identify themselves as feminists of any kind, recurring themes of women's independence and sexuality in conflict with social morality are often found in their films, which also emphasize rapport between women: *Hongyi Shaonu/Girl In Red* (Lu Xiaoya, 1984), *Qing Chun Ji/Sacrificed Youth* (Zhang Nuanxin, 1986) are nostalgic about mother–daughter relationships: the professionally independent heroines of *Nuer Lou/Army Nurse* (Hu Mei, 1986), *Nuren De Gushi/Story of Three Women* (Peng Xiaolian, 1988), and *Ren Guai Qing/Woman Demon Human* (Huang Shuqian, 1988) found little understanding from men, or from the world around them.

Jay Leyda, *Dianying, Electric Shadows: An Account of Films and the Film Audience in China* (Cambridge, MA: MIT Press, 1972)

See also: FIFTH GENERATION; REVOLUTIONARY MODEL FILMS; TAIWAN; XIE JIN   EY

CHOPRA, JOYCE, (1938–)

Known in the early years of feminism as the director (and star) of *Joyce at 34*

Smooth Talk, by Joyce Chopra

(1972), a DOCUMENTARY about the dilemma that her own onscreen pregnancy created for her career as filmmaker (with Claudia WEILL behind the camera), US director Joyce Chopra made more documentaries and then came to full public attention with her fiction feature *Smooth Talk* in 1986. Made from Joyce Carol Oates's story 'Where Are You Going, Where Have You Been,' with screenplay by Chopra's husband Tom Coles, the film deals with female adolescence and sexual initiation. It also allows its teen heroine's mother a voice, in contrast not only to CLASSICAL HOLLYWOOD CINEMA, but even to various feminist explorations of mothers and daughters, such as *Daughter Rite* (Michelle Citron, 1978), where the mother's side is often left out by a young woman director. *Smooth Talk* uses and transforms the speech, interactions, sex-and-virginity subject matter – and the all-American mall and fast-food diner settings – that figure in American youth-market films, but removing them entirely from American youth-film banality. Chopra underplays the metaphysical reverberations of Oates's story in favor of the realistic nuances of a young girl's rite of passage. *The Lemon Sisters* (1989), Chopra's second feature film, produced by Diane Keaton and starring Keaton and Carol Kane, centers on three women who grew up in the old Atlantic City.

Joyce at 34 (1972); *Girls at 12* (1975); *Martha Clark Light and Dark: A Dancer's Journal* (1980); *Smooth Talk* (1986); *The Lemon Sisters* (1989)

B Ruby Rich, 'Good Girls, Bad Girls,' *Village Voice*, 15 April 1986   BKQ

CHYTILOVA, VERA (1929–)

The first films by Věra Chytilová coincided with the emergence in the sixties of the Czechoslovak 'New Wave,' of which she became one of the most innovative and radical exponents. Apart from this she is also the first, and still the only, overtly feminist filmmaker in CZECHOSLOVAKIA. Věra Chytilová originally studied philosophy and architecture, and did various jobs – draftswoman, model, script girl – before obtaining a place at the Prague Film School (FAMU), where she studied directing.

Her graduation film, *Strop* (1961), and her debut film at the Barrandov studios, *Pytel blech* (1962), encountered the displeasure of the authorities, and it took a year of negotiation for these two medium-length films to be released. They were shown together in 1962 under the title *U stropu je pytel blech/There's a Bag of Fleas on the Ceiling*. In the style of cinéma vérité, and influenced by American underground cinema, these films offer a personal contemplation of the lot of women and a moralizing, sarcastic tract against hypocrisy. Here, as in most of her later films, Chytilová uses nonactors to achieve the effect of authenticity. Her film *O něčem jiném* (1963) is one of the best produced during the 'New Wave.' In it, she remained true to the cinéma vérité method but introduced a new philosophical note to Czech film by showing the parallelism of success and failure, the relativity of two totally dissimilar 'women's destinies.' As with *Strop* and most of her later films, the subject is looked at from a feminist standpoint and the ending is inconclusive. The director, throughout her work, encourages the viewer to become actively involved in the creation of meaning; and in her search for 'the truth,' form fulfills an important role. Chytilová once declared: 'Beauty is the means and not the end – but if we were to forget that, we might say: if formalism, then beautiful.' This could be said of most of Chytilová's films. On *Sedmikrásky* (1966) and *Ovoce stromů rajských jíme* (1969), Chytilová worked in close cooperation with another leading Czech filmmaker and designer, Ester Krumbachová. These two films, which are also formally innovative, were not appreciated by those in authority. Between 1969 and 1975 Chytilová was unable to work, and despite being invited to numerous WOMEN'S FILM FESTIVALS, was not allowed to attend. In 1975 she finally wrote a letter to President Husák refuting the accusations against her, explaining her work and attributing her problems to male chauvinism within the industry. Since 1976, Chytilová has completed ten short and feature-length films. Her latest film, *Kopytem sem, kopytem tam*, which premiered in 1989, is the first film in EASTERN EUROPE about AIDS.

Strop/Ceiling (short, 1961); *Pytel blech/ A Bagful of Fleas* (short, 1962); *O něčem jiném/About Something Else* (1963); *Automat 'Svět'/Snack-Bar 'World'* (short, 1965); *Sedmikrásky/Daisies* (1966); *Ovoce stromů rajských jíme/We Eat the Fruit of the Trees of Paradise* (1969); *Hra o jablko/The Apple Game* (1976); *Čas je neúprosný/ Inexorable Time* (short, 1978); *Panelstory/ Prefab Story* (1979); *Kalamita/Calamity* (1980); *Faunovo příliš pozdní odpoledne/ The Very Late Afternoon of a Faun* (1983); *Praha, neklidné srdce Europy/Prague, the Restless Heart of Europe* (short, 1985); *Vlčí bouda/Wolf's Hole* (1986); *Šašek a královna/The Jester and the Queen* (1987); *Kopytem sem, kopytem tam/A Tainted Horseplay* (1988)

Věra Chytilová, 'I Want to Work': Letter to President Husák,' *Index on Censorship*, vol. 5, no. 2 (1976)   ZB

CINEMA NOVO

This BRAZILIAN film movement can be divided into three phases. The first, 1960 to 1964, influenced by developmentalist and populist nationalism, is optimistic about the future. Mainly REALIST (Glauber ROCHA being the exception), and concentrating on the rural dispossessed, the films of this period sought to raise people's consciousness to the process of social transformation and contribute to the fight against colonialism, rejecting both Hollywood and commercial Brazilian cinema. The directors, very young and largely schooled in film clubs, looked to Italian NEOREALISM for its

aesthetics, and to France's NEW WAVE for its production methods. Handheld cameras, location shooting, natural sound, and cooperative financing, from being economic necessities, became an aesthetic – 'the aesthetic of hunger.' *Cinco Vezes Favela/Favela Five Times* (1961), with five sketches by different directors; Dos Santos's *Vidas secas/Barren Lives* (1963); Ruy Guerra's *Os fuzis/The Guns* (1964); Carlos Diegues's *Ganga Zumba* (1963), together with two films by Rocha, represent this first phase, which ended with the military coup of April 1964.

The second period, 1964–8, saw repression, exile, and censorship. Filmmakers tried to examine the failure of both populism and the Brazilian left. Mainly urban and anti-illusionist, they became aware of the failure of their work to attract the mass audience without which there could be no true political action. They founded a cooperative for distribution, while Leon Hirszman's *Garota de Ipanema/The Girl from Ipanema* (1967) demystified the myth of the 'golden' girl and became Cinema Novo's first box office success.

> *A Danish star of silent cinema has been claimed as 'the most fascinating personality of the primitive era.' Who is she?*

The third period, 1968–73, coincided with a hardening of repression and opened the way for ellipsis, analogy, and allegory, coded languages of revolt, less vulnerable to censorship. This 'tropicalist' phase gave Cinema Novo its biggest popular success, Joaquim Pedro de Andrade's *Macunaíma* (1969). At the end of the period, many filmmakers were forced into exile or had to go into coproduction as funding became difficult and the Brazilian film industry entered a deep crisis.

Randal Johnson, *Cinema Novo* × 5:

Masters of Contemporary Brazilian Film
(Austin: University of Texas Press,
1984) *NT*

CINEMA OF WOMEN

One of two FEMINIST DISTRIBUTION
organizations in BRITAIN (alongside
CIRCLES), Cinema of Women – or
COW, as it is affectionately known – was
started in 1972 by a group of women
involved in the group Cinesisters, itself a
descendant of the LONDON WOMEN's
FILM GROUP. Ten years later the range
of films distributed is large, from FEM-
INIST INDEPENDENT FILMS such as
Thriller (Sally Potter, 1979) – one of the
first films COW distributed, and still
widely shown – to issue-based campaigning videos and a small but respected
list of international feminist feature
films.

During the mid 1980s Cinema of
Women began distributing feature films
in earnest, attempting to create audiences
for feminist work beyond the relatively
contained, though crucially important,
circuit of venues offered by the women's
groups, educational institutions, and
grant-aided cinemas. Mainstream film
critics responded negatively to films such
as Marleen GORRIS's *A Question of
Silence* (1981), Lizzie BORDEN's *Born In
Flames* (1983) and Lynne Tillman's and
Sheila McLaughlin's *Committed* (1984);
either attacking them with relentless
venom ('the unacceptable face of feminism') or ignoring them completely.
Despite the aggression directed at distribution practices and individual films
which did not, apparently, accept their
'appropriate' cultural place, these features reached wide audiences without
being marketed in a way that compromised their feminist qualities.

The political imperative and physical
opportunities for challenging the mainstream with this kind of 'aggressive'
feminist distribution altered in the late
eighties as British commercial distribution became more interested in, and
receptive to, feminist feature films.

Simultaneously, the central role of nontheatrical work was reestablished by the
new, cheaper technology which transformed VIDEO into an important means
of political and educational organization.
Today, much of Cinema of Women's
most vital work involves the distribution
of nonfiction campaigning films and
videos, sometimes innovative in form,
on subjects such as health hazards at
work, incest, rape, and sexuality.

Jane Root, 'Distributing *A Question of
Silence*: A Cautionary Tale,' in *Films for
Women*, ed. Charlotte Brunsdon (Lon-
don: British Film Institute, 1986) *JRo*

CINEMIEN

With over 350 titles currently in distribution (on 16mm and 35mm or on video),
Cinemien's work in FEMINIST DIS-
TRIBUTION in the NETHERLANDS is
unparalleled: nowhere else in the world is
there such a huge collection of films
made by women permanently available
for exhibition. Cinemien was set up in
Amsterdam in 1974 with a starting subsidy from the United Nations Women's
Year. It has subsequently developed into
a professional organization offering five-
and-a-half jobs. For a decade, the Film
Department at the Dutch Ministry of
Culture refused to subsidize Cinemien,
arguing that films by women did not
give new life to cinema. In 1984, after a
vote in Parliament – and with the help of
press and public campaigns – Cinemien
gained equal treatment with the two
other independent film distributors, and
is now the only one of the three still
surviving.

Cinemien's list includes feature films,
documentaries, experimental films, cartoons, and videos of a great many
nationalities: the collection of films made
by Third World women – from
MOROCCO, EGYPT, ALGERIA, INDIA,
BRAZIL, MEXICO, and elsewhere – is
particularly impressive. Films from
CHINA, the SOVIET UNION, HUN-
GARY, and POLAND are also available.

Cinemien keeps close track of new feminist filmmakers, and about half of the hundred features available are first films. About 10 percent of the collection is distributed nowhere else in the world – often not even in the films' own countries of origin: *Fatma '75* (Selma Baccar, Tunisia, 1975); *Wanda* (Barbara Loden, USA, 1970); *Il valore della donna e il suo silenzio/Woman's Greatest Value is her Silence* (Gertrud Pinkus, Switzerland, 1980); and *Macumba* (Elfi Mikesch, West Germany, 1982). Cinemien was the first distributor for innumerable female filmmakers, and is internationally famous for giving financial and moral support to contemporary women's film work. 'Het Historisch Projekt' (The Historical Project), however, is also very important: this includes films by Lois WEBER, Germaine DULAC, Maya DEREN, and Dorothy ARZNER; and films starring Louise BROOKS and Asta NIELSEN. Cinemien's most successful films over the past few years have been *Via degli specchi/Street of Mirrors* (Giovanna Gagliardo, Italy, 1982); *Rue cases nègres/Black Shack Alley* (Euzhan Palcy, Martinique/France, 1983); *Committed* (Sheila McLaughlin and Lynne Tillman, USA, 1984); *Verfuehrung: die grausame Frau/Seduction, the Cruel Woman* (Elfi Mikesch and Monika Treut, West Germany, 1985); *A hora dele estrela/The Hour of the Star* (Suzana Amaral, Brazil, 1985); *Anne Trister* (Léa Pool, Quebec, 1985) and *Desert Hearts* (Donna Deitch, USA, 1985). Apart from distributing films and videos, Cinemien is an international information center. It regularly collaborates in FILM FESTIVALS, both in the Netherlands and abroad. It also issues publications, and one of its staff members has started her own film production company. In 1988 Cinemien began commercial distribution, and the International Women's Film Archive is currently being set up. *AF*

CINE-MUJER

This COLOMBIA feminist film and video collective was founded in the late 1970s by Sara Bright and Eulalia Carrioza. They were later joined by Fanny Tobón de Romero, Dora Cecilia Ramírez, Clara Riascos, and Patricia Restrepo. One of only a handful of such groups in LATIN AMERICA (Mexico's Cine-Mujer and Brazil's Lilith Video Collective are the other notable examples), the Colombian group is the longest-lived and most successful, since these women have managed for more than a decade to earn their living from production work through a balanced combination of independently generated and commissioned projects.

Cine-mujer's productions are: *A primera vista/At First Glance* (1979), narrative short about the image of women in advertising; *Paraíso artificial/Artificial Paradise* (1980), narrative short about the marital crisis of a woman in her middle years; *Llegaron las feministas/The Feminists Have Arrived* (1981), sixty-minute video report of the first meeting of Latin American and Caribbean feminists in Bogotá, June 1981; ¿Y su mamá que hace?/And What Does Your Mommy Do? (1982), satirical short; *Carmen Carrascal* (1982),

Cine-mujer's *Carmen Carrascal*

medium-length documentary on the daily life of a peasant artisan; *Prolemática de la mujer/Women's Problematic* (1983), television series; *Ni con el pétalo de una rosa/Not Even with a Rose Petal* (1983), television series on violence against women; *¿En que estamos?/Where Are We At?* (1984), report of the second meeting of Latin American and Caribbean feminists in Lima, Peru, in 1983; *Buscando caminos/Searching for Pathways* (1984), video on the Organization of Women From the Popular Sectors of Bogotá; *Momentos de un domingo/Sunday Moments* (1985), period medium-length feature on the differences between male and female upbringing; *Realidades políticas para la mujer campesina/Political Realities for the Peasant Woman* (1985); *Diez años después/Ten Years Later* (1985), documentary about women's struggles in Peru, Jamaica, Guatemala, Nicaragua, and Colombia made for the closing session of the Decade of Women conference in Nairobi; *La mirada de Myriam/Miriam's Stare* (1985), medium-length documentary/fiction hybrid.

Sarah Montgomery, 'From One Country to the Next: Interview with Dora Ramírez', *Screen*, vol. 26, no. 3–4 (1985)

JBu

CIRCLES

One of two FEMINIST DISTRIBUTION organizations in BRITAIN, Circles has had an impact far out of proportion to its small size and chronic financial insecurity. Circles started in 1979, partly as a response to an Arts Council of Great Britain exhibition on experimental film. Feeling that their work on women's involvement in this field was being marginalized, the women on the exhibition committee withdrew their painstakingly researched work and issued an explanatory statement. In many ways, this research was the cornerstone of Circles, which went on to distribute the films by Alice GUY, Germaine DULAC, Maya DEREN, and Lois WEBER which

were to have been discussed in the exhibition.

The 're-presentation' of these historical films stands alongside the distribution of contemporary work by women, on both film and VIDEO. Much, but by no means all, of this might be classified as AVANT-GARDE or experimental, and is linked by a desire to challenge and disturb existing representations of women. These films cannot always be easily 'enjoyed' by audiences unfamiliar with COUNTERCINEMA: indeed, some might be seen as perplexing and 'difficult.' For Circles, such reactions are part of the process of shifting perceptions, a stance which contrasts with that of the other British feminist distributor, CINEMA OF WOMEN, which tends to favor accessible films and videos related to immediate feminist campaigning needs.

This is not to say that Circles is uninterested in questions of audience or political goals; rather that it has chosen to contextualize 'difficult' work with program notes and speakers, and by bringing together films in packages around particular subjects. For instance, the popular 'Black Women and Invisibility' package sets Ayoka CHENZIRA's humorous animated ten-minute film *Hairpiece: A Film For Nappy-Headed People* (1981) alongside Julie DASH's *Four Women* (1978), a stylized, experimental DANCE film, and *Illusions*, (1982), a FILM NOIR-influenced drama set in Hollywood. These particular films are linked under the slogan: 'Some of us are brave, some of us are strong . . . but how many of us do you see?' – a question which echoes Circles' beginnings in historical research, but can also stand for their continuing work of reclaiming the presence of women in film and video.

Jenny Holland and Jane Harris (eds), *Circles Women's Film and Video Distribution Catalogue* (London: Circles, 1987)

See also: NICHOLSON, ANNABEL; RHODES, LIS

JRo

CISSE, SOULEYMANE (1940–)

One of AFRICA's most interesting filmmakers, as a child Cissé played truant to go to the movies; as a student, organized film screenings; and later worked as a photographer and projectionist before becoming a filmmaker. He spent eight years studying filmmaking in Moscow, where he was taught by major Soviet directors and learned from them the importance of developing 'the most practical way of making cinema.' Cissé's first feature film on return to his native Mali, *Den Muso* (1975), revolves around a young mute girl who, ignored by her parents, meets a young drifter and becomes pregnant. Her father throws her out and the young man discards her for another girl. Distraught and unable to communicate her anger, the girl sets fire to her lover's house and returns to her father's, where she commits suicide.

Dounamba Dany Coulibaly

dans

" **den muso** *"*
(la fille)

un film de Souleymane Cissé

Souleymane Cissé's *Den Muso*

Cissé's concern has always been to communicate mainly with his Malian and African audiences, and until now all his films have shown recognizable urban locations in which ordinary Africans may see characters they recognize in entertaining stories full of the minutiae of daily life, plot surprises, and questions to which only they – the spectators – can provide answers. In *Baara* (1978), Cissé again takes a character at the bottom of the social hierarchy – a young man newly arrived from the country who, without a proper job, becomes an illegal porter, an itinerant fetcher-and-carrier. His daily experiences take the audience through the social realities of a capital like Mali's Bamako. In *Finye* (1982) the theme is corruption and education: the traditional leaders have ceded power to the new political bureaucracies, and their former guiding knowledge is all but lost. Students pass exams according to who their parents are, not their ability: neglected and demoralized, some inevitably fall into drug abuse;. but a politicized revolt does eventually take place.

Cissé is continuously developing a personal cinematic style, and in *Yeelen* (1987) has begun to work more on the image – on surfaces, textures, and tones – and on creating atmosphere through space and sound: finding the right music was integral in making this film. In an unspecified, almost metaphysical time, a young man sets out to acquire from his elders the power and knowledge which will enable him to master the surrounding forces. While deeply rooted in African culture, this film has universal significance and won the Prix du Jury at the 1987 Cannes Film Festival.

L'aspirant/The Candidate (1968); *Sources d'inspiration/Sources of Inspiration* (1968); *Cinq jours d'une vie/Five Days in a Life* (1968); *Den Muso/The Girl* (1975); *Baara/Porter* (1978); *Finye/The Wind* (1982); *Yeelen/The Light* (1987)

Angela Martin, *African Films: The Context of Production* (London: British Film Institute, 1982)   AM

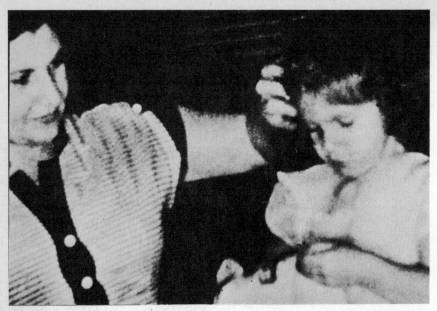

Michelle Citron's *Daughter Rite*

CITRON, MICHELLE (1948–)

In US filmmaker Citron's *Daughter Rite* (1978), the emerging feminist documentary tradition found perhaps its most important expression of feminist content in experimental form and made an important contribution to FEMINIST INDEPENDENT FILM. Two sisters are presented in mock cinéma vérité style discussing their often painful feelings about themselves, each other, and their mother. This 'documentary' space is intercut with home-movie footage accompanied by a woman's voice-over reading journal entries. Citron's film provided a strong emotional identification for – as one critic put it – 'every woman who has a mother.' Although schooled in and drawn to the formal experimentation of the male AVANT GARDE, Citron was concerned that the many women being radicalized by feminism were excluded from such films. Her concern about the accessibility of her films, united with a perception that feminist issues could not be dealt with through a purely formal

cinematic language, led her to experiment with the more familiar conventions of DOCUMENTARY and, indeed, of MELODRAMA. The female AUDIENCE she envisioned could be drawn in through recognition of these GENRES, but also forced to ponder both the absence of women's stories from the mass media and the construction of documentary truth.

Citron's next project, *What You Take For Granted* (1983), looks at women in a range of nontraditional jobs. Again a technique of mock-documentary, here combined with the development of a storyline between two of the 'interviewees,' seems ideally suited to a topic of broad interest to feminists and general audiences. As in *Daughter Rite*, the stories told by the actresses are composites of interviews conducted with many women. Currently working on a script for a feature film entitled *Acting Out*, Michelle Citron is Head of Production in the Radio, TV and Film Department at Northwestern University, Illinois.

Self-Defense (1973); *April 3, 1973* (1973); *Integration* (1974); *Parthenogenesis* (1975); *Daughter Rite* (1978); *What You Take For Granted* (1983); *Mother Right* (1983)

Michelle Citron, 'Women's Film Production: Going Mainstream', in *Female Spectators: Looking at Film and Television*, ed. E Deidre Pribram (London and New York: Verso, 1988)   PW

CLARKE, SHIRLEY (1925–)

A founding figure of the independent film and video movements in the USA, Shirley Clarke began making films in 1953 in New York. Clarke has distinguished herself over a long and productive career by her rendering of controlled improvisation in the cinema. The independent (as opposed to the commercial mainstream *and* the AVANT-GARDE) direction of her work has made her DANCE and DOCUMENTARY films and her videotapes unique in the field. Clarke was one of the founders of the Film-makers' Distribution Center, which later became the Film-makers' Cooperative, the prototype for independent distribution cooperatives worldwide. Her humanist political commitment thus manifests itself both in her own artistic practice and in her dedication to the field of INDEPENDENT CINEMA. Her earliest works are dance films, culminating in *Bridges Go Round* (1958), which transforms the movement between a human viewpoint and an abstract structure into a dance. Clarke's most famous works are cinéma vérité-style documentaries of the New York underground: *The Connection* (1961), *The Cool World* (1963), and *Portrait of Jason* (1967). Clarke was also a pioneer in the field of independent VIDEO, using early video technology for experimental documentaries. Throughout her work there is a commitment to the human figure as the most engaging subject for moving-image representation, and a consistent linking of jazz and black culture with an improvisational mode of artistic creation.

Dance in the Sun (1953); *In Paris Parks* (1954); *Bullfight* (1955); *Moment in Love* (1956); *Bruxelles 'Loops'* (1957); *Bridges Go Round* (1958); *Skyscraper* (1959); *A Scary Time* (1960); *The Connection* (1961); *The Cool World* (1963); *Robert Frost: A Lover's Quarrel With The World* (1964); *Man in the Polar Regions* (1966); *Portrait of Jason* (1967); *Videotapes: Series no. 1* (1972); *Videotapes: Series no. 2* (1973); *Angels of Light* (1972); *Wendy Clarke's Whitney Show* (1976); *24 Frames Per Second* (1977); *Four Journeys Into Mystic Time* (1979); *A Visual Diary* (1980); *Savage/Love* (1981); *Tongues* (1982); *Johanna Went 'Performance'* (1982); *Johanna Went 'The Box'* (1983); *Ornette Coleman – A Jazz Video Game* (1984); *Ornette – Made in America* (1985)

Jonas Mekas, '*The Connection* and the Uncertainty of Man', *Village Voice*, 10 April 1962   MKe

CLASSICAL HOLLYWOOD CINEMA

This term refers to a way of telling a story in film in which style is subordinated to the needs of the NARRATIVE. Although this practice has been adopted worldwide as DOMINANT CINEMA, the term is generally used to refer to films made within the HOLLYWOOD STUDIO SYSTEM, especially from around 1930 until about 1960, a periodization derived from both film style and conditions of film production. By the mid 1910s the norms which guided narrative cinema in the USA and the production conditions which supported it and were to maintain its international dominance were largely in place. By 1930, SOUND was introduced and rapidly adapted to the needs of narrative cinema. From the 1950s independent production rose as the studio system slowly eroded, the influence of European ART CINEMA was felt on Hollywood, and the studios themselves diversified into television production. Classical Hollywood cinema also extends to noncinematic areas (FANDOM, merchandising tie-ins, ADVERTISING,

CONSUMERISM in general) which circulated elements of classical Hollywood cinema in other fields of popular culture. STARS, GENRES, FASHIONS, beauty, and expectations about the 'well-made' film were significant in the widely recognizable ICONOGRAPHY of Hollywood films.

The IDEOLOGIES which inform classical Hollywood cinema – in all its manifestations – have been a central concern of FEMINIST FILM THEORY, criticism, and history. Style, narrative structure, industrial production, and popular discourses are all involved in constructing and distributing knowledge about social life (gender, class, race, nationhood, family, and so on) through films. Feminist perspectives on classical Hollywood cinema have sought to understand the relationship between women (as real, historical beings), women on the screen (representations constrained by the norms of classical Hollywood cinema), and women as AUDIENCE.

STRUCTURALIST analysis reveals that the Hollywood film is characterized by a narrative structure with five primary elements. The beginning: the film begins with its fictional world in a state of equilibrium or stasis. The rupture: something happens to rupture that equilibrium, to disturb the stasis. This poses an enigma which the narrative must and will answer. The cause–effect chain: each scene leads to the next in a logical fashion, driving the narrative forward. The characters: characters have personality traits which are relevant to the narrative; their goals and desires enter into conflict with those of other characters and contribute to the cause–effect chain. The resolution: the film ends when all of its questions are answered. The resolution is a return to a state of equilibrium, a situation which echoes the one which began the film. The 'happy ending' is satisfying because the questions which were posed have been answered, and equilibrium has returned.

The four elements of film style are subordinated to the needs of the narrative. The camera centers on the human body (the characters). Continuity EDITING maintains the illusion of a seamless narrative space. MISE-EN-SCENE is designed to be relevant to the story, providing information about character traits and contributing to verisimilitude. SOUND is centered on the human being (characters' voices) and those sound effects which contribute to the effect of REALISM; MUSIC underscores the film's meanings.

> *Sylvia Lawson is a notable contributor to the reestablishment of which national cinema?*

The ideological power of this type of narrative cinema is a result of its representational qualities. Classical Hollywood cinema attempts clearly to 're-present' human activities within a recognizable world, yet one whose ambiguities are diminished by the films' narration and style. Narrative equilibrium assumes that social life is comfortably ordered with everyone in her proper place. The rupture is a disturbance to this order. As the cause–effect chain moves forward, the ideologies which underpin dramatic conflict are called into question. The resolution is a confirmation of the social equilibrium which began the film. Characters are recognizable as people of gender, class, race, and nationhood, social identities which inform the conflict the film works through. Film style centers on characters and the dilemmas with which they cope. Style assists the audience to chart and understand the ideologies at stake in the characters' problems, and in the narrative. The 'well-made' Hollywood film personalizes social conflict through characters with gendered identities. Ideologies are taken up by a cause–effect chain which moves toward a 'satisfying' resolution, and they are made visible and recognizable through film style.

For example, the meanings offered by

Mildred Pierce (Warner Bros., 1945) are dependent upon a social context of post-World War II working mothers, real women who lived within the socioeconomic conditions and ideologies which the film recognizes as significant to women's self-identities. The film begins with the murder of playboy Monty Beragon (the rupture – a disturbance to systems of law, justice, personal safety). The narrative answers the question of who killed Monty by telling the story of Mildred's life in flashback. The cause –effect chain which resulted in Monty's murder is linked with Mildred's struggle as a businesswoman and her concomitant failure as a mother (conflicting ideologies of post-World War II womanhood: a recognition of woman's capabilities beyond the family and the urge to re-socialize her back into the family). The film resolves its enigma by identifying Mildred's daughter Veda as the killer and by 'blaming' Mildred for spoiling her (Mildred's traits as a character include a desire for her children to have more than she had). The 'happy ending' solves the crime and captures the criminal (law and justice are secure). It also resolves Mildred's story by returning her to her former husband (pulling together the remnants of the original Pierce family prior to the divorce), and implicating Mildred's character traits in the crime (hard work provides the money for upward mobility, but at the cost of 'proper' attention to children).

Film style charts Mildred's progress from ordinary housewife (housedress, apron, making pies in the kitchen of the small Pierce home) to successful postwar businesswoman (furs, padded shoulders, elaborate home, a restaurant chain). Her flashbacks are marked by dissolves and shadows on her face as the police officer probes Mildred, linking her story with the murder in the cause–effect chain. Extracinematic discourses work through contradictory ideologies of womanhood. In promotional material on the film, Joan CRAWFORD (who plays Mildred) is discussed as a star (the comeback of a great actress; lavish Hollywood lifestyle) and as a wife-mother whose devotion to her children and her relatively ordinary husband at the time (Phillip Terry, a minor actor) bear no resemblance to the character she plays. Yet publicity also links Joan with Mildred through their shared commitment to hard work and its resulting upward mobility. Joan, the actress, was able successfully to negotiate these demands, while Mildred was not. Reviews of the film implicitly recognize these ideologies: many blame Mildred for being a bad mother (identify her as the primary causal agent of the film, in other words), whose neglect of her family for business results in Veda's 'sociopathic' personality. While the narrative structure, style, and popular discourses of classical Hollywood cinema attempt to provide a unified ideology, the question remains of how real women perceived its address to their self-identities.

David Bordwell, Janet Staiger and Kristin Thompson, *Classical Hollywood Cinema: Film Style and Mode of Production to 1960* (New York: Columbia University Press, 1985)

See also: ACTING; CLOSEUP; COLOR; LIGHTING; MAKE-UP; PRODUCTION CODE; SILENT CINEMA   *MBH*

CLOSEUP

Shots in which an isolated portion of a character's body (usually the head or hands) or an object fills the frame, closeups control what a spectator can see and consequently function to convey information. As a standard procedure, closeups developed from the early 1910s as a technique that facilitated the visibility of characters' facial expressions – an asset for ACTING styles in SILENT CINEMA. So important were closeups in CLASSICAL HOLLYWOOD CINEMA that cinematographers innovated special lighting equipment and matte boxes to simulate glamor portraits. Closeups of actresses, often associated with particular

LIGHTING effects, were important in the creation of STAR images.   *JaS*

COCINA DE IMAGENES

The first Latin American WOMEN'S FILM FESTIVAL, Cocina de Imagenes, held in October 1987, marked the beginning of a historical moment for LATIN AMERICAN and CARIBBEAN women cineastes. The term Cocina de Imagenes is impossible to translate because of the multiple connotations associated with the word *cocina*. The intention of the gastronomical title was to provide a visual sampling of *'guisos'*/menus which would represent diversity. Held in MEXICO, the festival was organized by a group of Mexican women filmmakers, artists, and volunteers. Zafra, an independent film distribution company, and the Cineteca, a state-operated theater complex, provided space for the numerous screenings. The festival brought together professional filmmakers and video artists, as well as those at the start of their careers. Twelve or more Latin American countries took part, as well as Canada and the United States, as seventy-five women gathered for ten days of screenings and mutual exchange.

Mexican filmmakers Matilde LANDETA, Marcela FERNANDEZ VIOLANTE, Maria NOVARO, Rosa Marta Fernández, Bussi Cortes, Mari Carmen de Lara, Berta Navarro, Maryse SYSTACH, and Liliane Lieberman, among others, participated in symposia which addressed issues related to the specificity of the latina cineaste. One feminist commented on the erroneous assumption which inscribes all latina filmmakers into the role of feminists. Filmmaking, she warned, is contingent upon the filmmaker's ideological position; whether it be from a 'woman's' point of view or from that of a feminist, these two positions are different, and their difference is reflected in the form and content of their final product. Other issues aired included patriarchy within the industry, competition between women, lack of financial assistance, censorship, and difficulties in distribution. Some women contended that economic survival was problematic whenever necessity forced artistic integrity and freedom to be temporarily compromised. Latina filmmakers are seeking alternative financial resources by reaching out to foreign countries for assistance.

> *Notable Russian-born filmmaker and theorist Maya Deren is known as 'The Mother' of what unconventional child?*

The festival ended with overwhelming agreement to create a second film and video festival, to be held in Mexico City. In addition, a quarterly newsletter, *Cine/Video/Mujer*, is now available, providing information related to film and video festivals, publications and exhibitions. Even though the questions posed were not resolved, the festival ignited an important and very significant beginning for latina filmmakers and video artists.

CH-N

COLE, JANIS (1954–) and DALE, HOLLY (1953–)

Cole and Dale are among CANADA's best-known women filmmakers. As independent DOCUMENTARY filmmakers who began to work together as students, they share functions as producer, director, and editor. They have made their reputations by taking on colorful, marginal, underworld subjects in a humanist way. *Cream Soda* (1975), a student film, and *Minimum Charge No Cover* (1976) are about the underworld of petty criminals in the sleazy sex-trade district of Toronto. *The Thin Blue Line* (1977) is a personal and psychological investigation of the criminally insane inmates of a maximum-security prison, and was the first of their films to be widely seen. *P4W Prison for Women* (1981) and *Hookers on Davie* (1984), both feature-length, celebrate the humanity and survival instincts

90

of women prisoners and Vancouver prostitutes respectively, and were among the rare Canadian documentaries to do well in theatrical release. *Calling the Shots* (1988) is about women filmmakers trying to break into the feature film industry. Occasionally criticized for political and cinematic naivety, their films are characterized by direct cinema techniques with an emphasis on colorful and engaging characters who open up remarkably easily for the filmmakers.

Cream Soda (1975); *Minimum Charge No Cover* (1976); *Nowhere To Run* (1977); *Thin Blue Line* (1977); *P4W Prison For Women* (1981); *Hookers on Davie* (1984); *Calling the Shots* (1988)   KA

COLETTE (1873–1954)

Colette (born in FRANCE as Sidonie-Gabrielle Colette) remains one of the most popular novelists of the twentieth century; she came to fame with her four *Claudine* novels (1900–3), originally published under her first husband's name, Willy. Several of her works – *La Vagabonde*, *Chéri*, *Gigi* – are internationally famous, and many have been adapted to film, particularly by women directors: MUSIDORA in the 1910s, Simone Bussi in the 1930s, and Jacqueline AUDRY in the 1940s and 1950s (*Gigi* was adapted a second time by Vincente Minnelli, at MGM, in 1958). Colette also wrote FILM CRITICISM from 1914 to 1939. She contributed scripts and dialogues, notably for Marc Allégret's *Lac aux dames* (1934) and Max OPHULS's *Divine* (1935), based on her own experience on the music-hall stage. She is the subject of a documentary, *Colette* (Yannick Bellon, 1950).

Colette's work always focuses on women, either in the figure of the sexually awakening *gamine*, of which Gigi is the archetype, or of the sensual mature woman, as in *Julie de Carneilhan* (Jacques Manuel, 1949) and *Chéri* (Pierre Billon, 1950). Though often marked by rose-tinted nostalgia, her books, and the films based on them, provide a fascinating portrait of women struggling against the constraining sexual roles available to them in France in the early part of this century.

Alain and Odette Virmaux (eds), *Colette at the Movies* (New York: Ungar, 1980)
GV

COLOMBIA

During the 1970s the Colombian government, like those of BRAZIL and VENEZUELA, took concrete measures to encourage the development of national film production in response to pressures from an active group of independent filmmakers, several of whom took their inspiration from the example of Gabriela SAMPER, and a growing number of European-trained directors. Legislation from 1971 decreed the obligatory exhibition of Colombian-made shorts at first-run theaters and established a rebate system to encourage producers and distributors as well as filmmakers. FOCINE, the national film development agency founded in 1978, made commendable strides in both production (feature as well as documentary) and distribution before collapsing a decade later, the victim of internecine struggles within the government bureaucracy and a no-win economic situation.

The Colombian cultural scene in general, and the film sector in particular, are characterized by a remarkably high level of female leadership. LATIN AMERICA's foremost female art critic, Marta Traba, who established her career in Colombia rather than in her native ARGENTINA partly because the climate was so encouraging to women, was one of the first to draw attention to this fact. The Museum of Modern Art, the Cinemateca Distrital of Bogotá, the regional directorate of Culture and Tourism, are all posts which have been consistently occupied by women of inordinate energy and vision, among them Isadora de

Colombian filmmakers Marta Rodríguez and Jorge Silva

Norden, Gloria Triana, and María Elvira Talero.

The Colombian DOCUMENTARY tradition first received serious attention from abroad in the early 1970s with *Chircales/Brickmakers* (1970) by sociologist Marta RODRIGUEZ and her late husband Jorge Silva. In the 1980s the films and videos of the CINE-MUJER collective have circulated widely in Colombia and abroad. Between 1980 and 1986 Gloria Triana, an anthropologist by training, directed more than forty made-for-television films, using a wealth of different styles and approaches to document and celebrate Colombia's richly idiosyncratic regional folklore. This remarkable body of work remains virtually unknown outside Colombia. The production of serious feature films has been limited during recent years to fewer than five annually. So far no female feature director has come to the fore, but a 1984 Colombia-Cuba co-production directed by Gloria Triana's brother, Jorge Ali Triana, based on a 1966 screenplay by Gabriel García Marquez, deserves special mention as the most eloquent exploration to date of Latin American *machismo* as an almost pathological vicious circle.

Hernando Martínez Pardo, *Historia del cine colombiano* (Bogotá: Editora Guadalupe, 1978) *JBu*

COLOR

Color can reproduce the 'natural' look of the world and thus be an important element in realist filmmaking. Yet color can also draw attention to itself, troubling the illusion of reality and distracting from the action central to the narrative. In CLASSICAL HOLLYWOOD CINEMA, however, conventions were developed to subordinate color to the primacy of NARRATIVE. Color, it was assumed, should contribute to unobtrusive REALISM and not be emphasized unless it carries a specific narrative meaning. Otherwise, color could disturb the proper functioning of more important elements such as character. The color of COSTUMES, for example, should do no more than separate actors from backgrounds and from each other, and reinforce character traits. These apparently 'realist' conventions, though, may also ituate women ideologically. In films such as *Written on the Wind* (Douglas Sirk, Universal, 1956), *Marnie* (Alfred Hitchcock, Universal, 1964) and even the black-and-white *Jezebel* (William Wyler, Warner Bros., 1938), the color red is a signifier of the troubled and troubling sexual identity of the central women characters.

Despite its repression for the sake of realism, color enhances the ability of film to provide pleasure in spectacle. In some genres, such as MUSICALS and FANTASY, color departs from 'unobtrusive' realism, attracting attention to itself and contributing to an aesthetics of spectacle. Transcending all genres is the female lead, the site of both the narrative and the spectacle functions of color. Her appearance has primacy in the color planning of a film. The colors which will most compliment her dominate a film's color system (the background color of sets as well as the costuming and casting of other actors). As she fulfills her narrative role as a gendered protagonist, she is lovely to look at, her colored image soliciting pleasure in looking (SCOPOPHILIA). Color helps to define her as a woman through costuming and MAKE-UP at the same time as it enhances her ideological role in producing visual pleasure through the LOOK.

Steve Neale, *Cinema and Technology: Image, Sound, Color* (Bloomington and Indianapolis: Indiana University Press, 1985)

See also: FILM STOCK   MBH

COLUMBIA

Columbia started as a DISTRIBUTION company in the USA in 1920, adding production in 1924. Unlike other major film companies, Columbia did not purchase theaters in the 1920s. During the Depression years, Columbia managed to remain stable by producing second-bill pictures and shorts. In 1934, the success of *It Happened One Night* (Frank Capra) and *One Night of Love* (Victor Schertzinger) permitted the studio to move into some 'A'-feature filmmaking. Through the next three decades Columbia remained a minor studio, but in 1973 new owners succeeded with blockbuster movies and by diversification. In 1982 Coca-Cola bought Columbia, but spun it off in 1987 (while retaining 49 percent of the outstanding stock). Columbia Pictures Entertainment now includes the old Columbia, Tri-Star Pictures, Columbia Television, a first-run syndication branch, and 635 film theaters.

In the heyday of the HOLLYWOOD STUDIO SYSTEM during the 1930s and 1940s, Columbia contracted with STARS and directors by an arrangement of a specific number of films, encouraging independent productions such as those of director Frank Capra. Columbia was one of the first companies in the early 1930s to employ a unit-production system in which several associate producers supervised six to eight films per year. Stars were usually borrowed for onetime deals, although Rita HAYWORTH spent some time under contract at Columbia.

Ed Buscombe, 'Notes on Columbia Pictures Corporation, 1926–1941', *Screen*, vol. 16, no. 3 (1975)   JaS

COMEDY

The PLEASURE of comedy has been seen as its disruption of conventions, overturning commonsense categories of behavior and reversing expectations. Comedy film therefore represents a GENRE which refuses to be contained by the demands of REALISM. Despite its association with 'play', critics have argued that comedy helps maintain the subordination of some social groups through ridicule and reductive 'typing.' Others have noted comedy's capacity to articulate opposition to norms through the freedom of carnivalesque forms. It might well be that exaggeration and FANTASY also allow for the expression of social and psychic tensions.

Feminist analysis has focused on the use of sexual STEREOTYPES which place women as objects of comedy. Physically typed, women are categorized according to norms of sexual desirability, embodying either the promise of seduction or the threat of marriage. Stereotyped as 'dumb' BLONDE, nubile sex bomb or ageing harridan, these caricature figures can be seen as projections of male fears or desires. Freudian analysis suggests that the pleasure of comedy derives from the liberation of a disturbing idea normally repressed, which is channeled through comedy into something that can be laughed at, thus rendering it harmless. It is also suggested that the overpowering of the disturbing thought demands a victim and implies a sadistic relation to this victim. From this perspective, comedy in film may reveal ambivalence toward women and the insecurities of male sexual identity. In this view, the work of comedy is to defuse threats to the sexual order represented by women.

In Hollywood cinema, comediennes have played on stereotypical features to show up and transgress the boundaries of acceptable FEMININITY, often exploiting the grotesque, as with Bette Midler, for example. Mae WEST's double-entendres satirize sexual propriety and reverse the norm of the passive undemanding woman whose body is only for the enjoyment of men. Others – like Marilyn MONROE and Jean HARLOW – have exaggerated the features of the dumb blonde to parody its assertions of what women are like. In some cases characteristics such as 'crazy' logic are used to propose alternative systems of behavior

or meaning that men cannot understand or master: Judy Holliday, for example, in *Born Yesterday* (George Cukor, Columbia, 1950).

When women take the stage in comedy, they often also seize control of male-centered arenas. The screwball comedy, for example, features a wisecracking, besuited CAREER WOMAN outdoing her male counterparts in the whole of work, taking all the best lines and giving men a hard time trying to win her over. Women's control over language and NARRATIVE in comedy film, and their frenetic movement during slapstick performances, provide a challenge to male control by resisting the decorum appropriate to passive femininity. However, these films are often disappointing in their resolution of disordered femininity, putting female characters in their place in relation to men, usually through marriage. The power of language, movement, and narrative direction is seized from them, diminishing their threat to the established order.

> 'Tackles Oedipal narrative, male psychoanalytic theory, the New Man, attitudes to ageing, US policy towards Central America and the New York housing crisis.' This 1985 film is not called Breathless but The Man Who Envied Women. It is made by a foremost US independent filmmaker. Who is she?

As in MELODRAMA, though, the importance of these moments of identification with active HEROINES may resist narrative closure. Some female stereotypes – the nagging and demanding wife, or perhaps especially the cynical hardboiled spinster – cannot be reharnessed for masculine desire and remain powerful and potentially threatening, even if consigned to the narrative sidelines. Our pleasure in the skill of a star's execution can also endure beyond the subduing of the character, and can be said to represent the power of PERFORMANCE over the power of narrative.

Patricia Mellencamp, 'Situation Comedy, Feminism and Freud: Discourses of Gracie and Lucy', in *Studies in Entertainment: Critical Approaches to Mass Culture*, ed. Tania Modleski (Bloomington and Indianapolis: Indiana University Press, 1986)

See also: SEIDELMAN, SUSAN   GS

CONSUMERISM

Popular films are well integrated into a wider consumer culture, usually through three types of merchandising: lifestyle showcase, formal product tie-in, and star endorsement. Lifestyle showcase is usually a subtle display within a film itself, in which MISE-EN-SCENE supports the realist representation of characters and narrative space through 'desirable' furnishings, clothing, and so on. Less covert is the tie-in which was honed as a merchandising strategy in the HOLLYWOOD STUDIO SYSTEM of the 1930s and 1940s. Based on direct contractual relationships between film studios and retail manufacturers, the latter provided consumer products (watches, appliances, cars) for films, so reducing the studio's overhead costs. The brand-name product was then advertised with the film. A typical means of exploiting the tie-in was a display in a department store window: a cardboard cutout of the star with the product (silk stockings, hat, coiffure – all available in the store) and the title of the film (in which one can see the product in use in the star-character's life) now playing at the local theater. A variation of the film tie-in continues today in media circulation of FASHION looks, hairstyles, soft drinks and beer, and in 'ancillary rights' contracts for music and toys. Star endorsements benefited the career of the STAR, whose public presence enhanced her potential for longevity on the screen. But, as shown by the cosmetic industry's long and profitable relationship with the film industry, star recommendations mask not only the role of specialized film MAKE-UP and cinematography in producing 'natural' beauty, but also the business arrangements behind the endorsements. The most lucrative site of merchandising remains female self-image. By incorporating consumer products in cinematic REALISM, and by coordinating the advertising of stars and films with products, woman's experience with film is dispersed across her everyday existence and into the nation's economic life.

Charles Eckert, 'The Carole Lombard in Macy's Window', *Quarterly Review of Film Studies*, vol. 3, no. 1 (1978)

See also: ADVERTISING; EXHIBITION; FANDOM   MBH

COOLIDGE, MARTHA (1946–)

Originally trained as an actress with Lee Strasberg and Stella Adler, Coolidge studied animation at Rhode Island School of Design before going on to Columbia Graduate Film School in New York. After a spell working for television in Canada in 1968, she returned to the USA in 1970/71 to study at New York University's film school. During the early seventies she was active in the cause of INDEPENDENT CINEMA, writing articles on the difficulties of obtaining funding and distribution, and becoming a founder member of the Association of Independent Video and Film-makers. She made a series of independent documentaries with a personal slant (which she has described as 'portraits'), among them *Not a Pretty Picture* (1975), a semi-autobiographical docudrama about rape which quickly became part of the feminist film canon.

The next phase of her career was fraught with difficulties. In 1978 Francis Coppola's Zoetrope Studio, impressed by Coolidge's previous work, approached her to direct *Photoplay*, a rock 'n' roll love story. She worked on the production for two years until it was abandoned when Zoetrope began to collapse. She returned to TV work and Canada, where she was invited to direct *The City Girl* when the original director dropped out. Basically exploitation material focusing on a woman photographer's search for sexual fulfillment, it was revamped by Coolidge into an exploration of the difficulties of female independence, reminiscent of Claudia WEILL's *Girlfriends* (1978) in its cinéma vérité-style REALISM and ironic humor. Yet again the production was beset by financial problems, until Peter Bogdanovich agreed to finance completion. Even then, the film was unable to find a US distributor until 1984.

Meanwhile Coolidge's next film, *Valley Girl* (1983), a low-budget teen pic, was a huge commercial success and provided her breakthrough into the industry. She was subsequently commissioned by Paramount to make *Joy of Sex* (1984), a standard teen COMEDY into which she was able to inject a degree of feminist comment on subjects such as contraception, menstruation, and pregnancy. Nevertheless, she was at pains to distance herself from the end result, describing herself as a hired hand prepared to make compromises to get into Hollywood. Her first big-budget feature – *Real Genius* (1985), a teen SCIENCE FICTION comedy – followed, to a decidedly mixed critical reception.

Coolidge is nowadays wary of being labeled a feminist, describing her films as 'feminist influenced,' an ambiguous phrase which accurately describes the movies from *The City Girl* onward. Her ambivalence seems to derive from her own difficult experience as a woman director trying to make it in the industry, and from a belief that the major studios are hostile to politics of any kind. Her twenty-year career, spanning radical film and TV documentaries and exploitation subjects, is an object lesson in the compromises facing women seeking big-budget status in mainstream Hollywood.

David: Off and On (1972); *More Than a School* (1973); *An Old-fashioned Woman* (1974); *Not a Pretty Picture* (1975); *Bimbo* (1978); *Photoplay* (1978–80, unfinished); *Employment Discriminations: The Troubleshooters* (1979); *Strawberries and Gold* (1980); *Valley Girl* (1983); *The City Girl* (1984); *Joy of Sex* (1984); *Real Genius* (1985)

Pam Cook, 'Not a Political Picture – Martha Coolidge'; Jane Root, 'Review of *Joy of Sex*'; Pam Cook, 'Review of *City Girl*'; Sylvia Paskin, 'Review of *Real Genius*,' *Monthly Film Bulletin*, vol. 53, no. 635 (1986)   PC

CORDEIRO, MARGARIDA, (1938–) and REIS, ANTONIO (1927–)

This remarkable couple started making films together in PORTUGAL in 1976. Margarida Cordeiro trained as a doctor and Antonio Reis was originally a painter and a poet. The inner vision of Cordeiro's and Reis's films informs the outside world from which they are never cut off: always exploring, they stretch film language to the limits. Disillusioned with modernity, they find the seeds for an authentic national culture in the remotest region of Portugal. Women are at the center of all their work: women on their own (men have been forced to go abroad for work), who live in a mythical and ritual world, close to the essentials. History, technology, and the town are alien male constructs. Plots and words are reduced to a minimum and the beauty of the natural surroundings, filmed with powerful love in a deliberately slow rhythm, suits their chosen setting perfectly.

Trás-os-Montes (1976); *Ana* (1982); *Rosa de areira/A Sand Rose* (1989)   NT

COSTA, JOSE FONSECA E (1933–)

José Fonseca e Costa was born in Angola. Film clubs were his school and he was, briefly, an assistant to ANTONIONI. One of the leaders of PORTUGAL's 'Young Cinema' and the most popular with the public, Costa rejected the slow and nostalgic tempo favored by Portuguese filmmakers, preferring a dry humor that proved very popular. Sex, the army, the family, and marriage are favorite targets. His women characters are not passive victims but witty exploiters of the system, who expose the strong links between patriarchy and fascism. His third film, *Kilas* (1981), was Portugal's biggest ever local success.

O recado/The Message (1971); *Os demónios de Alcácer-Kibir/The Devils of Alcácer-Kibir* (1977–80); *Kilas, o mau da fita/Kilas, the Film's Baddie* (1981); *Música, Moçambique!* (1982); *Sem sombra de pecado/No Trace of Sin* (1982); *A balada da Praia dos Caes/The Ballad of Dog's Beach* (1986); *A mulher do próximo/Thy Neighbour's Wife* (1988)   NT

COSTUMES

In the early 1900s, film performers usually wore their own clothes. By the mid 1910s, however, the longer feature film required a more specialized division of labor in all aspects of film production, including costumes. In the USA, to ensure cost-effective production, the continuity script was broken into a wardrobe plot so that the costumes for each scene would be ready when the scene was shot. In the heyday of the HOLLYWOOD STUDIO SYSTEM, a studio's wardrobe department had five sub-branches, staffed by perhaps a hundred women: dressmaking, stock materials, finished wardrobe, millinery, and fancy dress. As early as the mid 1910s couture designers were frequently hired to dress leading ladies, who often had a designer of their own choice; and until the World War II fabric shortage it was not uncommon for leading men to have individually designed suits. Extras typically wore their

A Hollywood costume conference

own clothing, except for period films when they were costumed by outside firms. Most costume design, however, is the work of the studio costume department. Whether imported or studio-based, a costume designer works with the art director to create costumes appropriate to the film's period and to the traits of the characters.

In supporting characterization, costumes underscore ideologies of FEMININITY and encourage an easily read ICONOGRAPHY: CAREER WOMAN (suits, shoulder pads), VAMP (slinky lowcut gowns), 'shop girl' (ordinary daywear), socialite (glamorous gowns), loose woman (cheap tight dresses), wife-mother (modest dresses), and so on. As a woman's character progresses through the narrative, costumes change to follow her transformation. Costumes circulate and confirm meanings about woman's gendered and class status, and associate woman's appearance with visual PLEASURE. While costumes help to naturalize woman in many social roles, in some film GENRES – MUSICALS in particular – they can also 'stop' the narrative as the costume and the woman combine in a display which objectifies her as spectacle.

Elizabeth Leese, *Costume Design in the Movies* (New York: Ungar, 1977)

See also: ART DIRECTION; FASHION; HEAD, EDITH   *MBH*

COUNTERCINEMA

In the West this term has been used to refer to methods of formal innovation in film drawing primarily upon the MODERNIST tradition, and taking apart or deconstructing the methods of CLASSICAL HOLLYWOOD CINEMA. At the level of content the term has also been used to designate a politically oppositional cinema (usually in opposition to the values of capitalism and to racist, sexist, and homophobic ideologies).

The theory of countercinema emerged in the context of early-1970s debates in Europe and North America concerning the supposed political implications of different formal methods. According to the 'political modernism' of this period, a politically radical cinema could be developed only on the basis of a rejection of the illusionist methods of traditional REALIST cinema. The new method, notably in the work of Jean-Luc GODARD, was thought to exemplify the necessary break with the illusionism of realist representations by calling attention to the constructed nature of film language, and to the process of meaning production itself. Countercinema requires a departure from the pattern of climax and resolution or 'closure' established by classical NARRATIVE, distances the audience from the action by minimizing identification with characters, and rejects the presentation of a unified, coherent narrative in favor of radical narrative digressions and often disturbingly juxtaposed heterogeneous elements. This formally based theory of countercinema establishes the principle of modernist self-referentiality as the new antirealist norm, adopts some of Bertolt Brecht's preferred methods of distanciation and episodic structure, and proposes a fundamental critique of the view of cinema as the most realistic art form.

Some feminist critics and filmmakers have taken up the methods of countercinema as a way of challenging the taken-for-granted sexism of much classic realist storytelling. Claire JOHNSTON, in her article 'Women's Cinema as Counter-Cinema', explores some of the arguments for this kind of formal innovation both inside and outside Hollywood. A number of women filmmakers have deliberately deconstructed traditional methods in both fiction and documentary in the belief that cinema cannot simply and transparently reflect women's experience, but is always necessarily, and through film language, constructing versions of that experience. Among the criticisms of countercinema, however, has been the observation that women viewers have often been puzzled, confused, and disappointed by films adopting antirealist formal methods.

Claire Johnston, 'Women's Cinema as Counter-Cinema', in *Movies and Methods*, ed. Bill Nichols (Berkeley: University of California Press, 1976)

See also: AVANT-GARDE FILM; INDEPENDENT CINEMA; SOCIALIST CINEMA   SHa

CRAIGIE, JILL (1914–   )

In common with several other women in BRITAIN, Jill Craigie was given the opportunity to direct films during World War II. She began her career as a journalist at the age of eighteen: first on a teenage magazine, then as a writer in the London branch of Hearst newspapers. After the outbreak of war Craigie worked for the British Council as a scriptwriter, producing many scripts for documentaries on British culture. She was 'noticed' as a new talent and signed up by Two Cities Films to direct and write DOCUMENTARIES. She made two films for the company: *Out of Chaos* (1944), about the wartime boom in painting, and *The Way We Live* (1947), an extremely well received documentary-drama about postwar reconstruction in Plymouth.

Craigie attracted a good deal of media attention at the time because of the fact that she was a woman, and over her struggles to get her serious, 'nonentertainment' films shown in mainstream cinemas. In 1948 she formed her own production company, Outlook (with the producer William MacQuitty), for her first and only venture into feature filmmaking. *Blue Scar* (1949) – the story of a working-class family in a Welsh mining village before and after the nationalization of the coal industry – was initially refused exhibition by all the major circuits, and was shown to general audiences only after an intense press campaign. Craigie made only one more film, *To Be a Woman* (1951), a documentary arguing forcefully that equal pay for women should be granted as a right. The film was funded by members of women's organizations: interestingly (but perhaps not surprisingly), it excited much less press interest than any of her other films. After Craigie's marriage to the Member of Parliament Michael Foot (later to become leader of the Labour Party) she abandoned filmmaking, though she continued to write scripts for the BBC and feminist articles for the London *Evening Standard*.

Jill Craigie's hallmark as a filmmaker was her ability to bring out the best in 'ordinary people,' her political commitment and her perseverance in achieving her ambition to do what was still considered to be a man's job. Although today she dismisses her films as 'amateur,' they have much to offer contemporary audiences.

Out of Chaos (1944); *The Way We Live* (1947); *Blue Scar* (1949); *To Be A Woman* (1951)   CM

CRAWFORD, JOAN (1904–77)

From her carefree flappers to her crazed women, Joan Crawford was a Hollywood STAR who worked hard at being a star. Every element of her personality seemed to go into her image: an overweening desire to be loved; masochistic conscientiousness; an obsession with perfection vilified by her adopted daughter in the book *Mommie Dearest*.

After a miserable, abused Texan childhood, Crawford was whisked by MGM executive Harry Rapf from a Broadway chorus line to Hollywood in 1925. There she was launched as a FASHION starlet (clothes would always remain an important and influential part of her persona) and her name changed in a competition from Lucille Fay Le Sueuer. In 1928, her rigorous self-training for stardom paid off. As the hedonistic, saucy, but morally upstanding heroine of the silent *Our Dancing Daughters* (Harry Beaumont, MGM) and its followups, Crawford became the jazz baby of the era. In the thirties, however, determined to be a

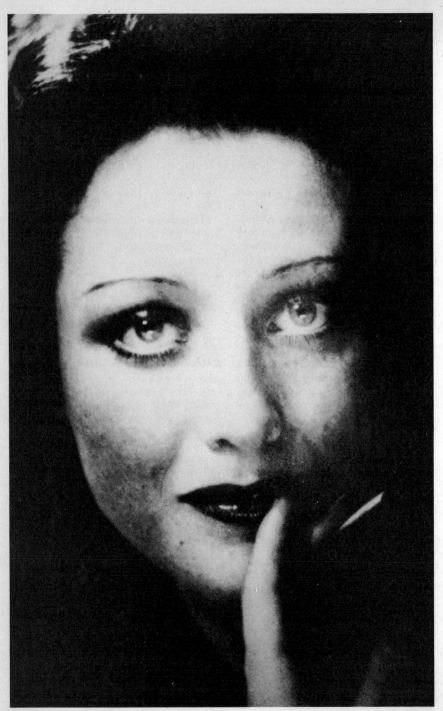

The young Joan Crawford

'real' actress, she starred in MELO-DRAMAS like *Paid* (Sam Wood, MGM, 1930), *Possessed* (Clarence Brown, MGM, 1931), *Letty Lynton* (Clarence Brown, MGM, 1932), *Grand Hotel* (Edmund Goulding, MGM, 1932), and *Mannequin* (Frank Borzage, MGM, 1938), in which she came to typify the honest, aspirational working girl who makes her way up the social ladder but ultimately turns her back on it for true love. While these films admonished the upper classes, they also gave Crawford immense opportunity to model their clothes and lifestyles as long as her heroines embraced them. The one notable exception is her role as a husband-snatching arch bitch in George Cukor's *The Women* (MGM, 1939), made one year after she was declared 'box office poison' by a leading exhibitor.

When her contract at MGM ended in mutual disagreement, Crawford went to WARNER BROS., where she spent much of the next decade playing maturer versions of her previous incarnation: lonely, independent women in search of love, attracted to and betrayed by sexless sugar daddies before finding love with 'real' men. The films include *Humoresque* (Jean Negulesco, Warner Bros., 1946), *Possessed* (Curtis Bernhardt, Warner Bros., 1947), *Flamingo Road* (Michael Curtiz, Warner Bros., 1949) and *Mildred Pierce* (Michael Curtiz, Warner Bros., 1945) – which had the extra dimension of self-sacrificing MOTHERHOOD and an ungrateful daughter. The Crawford look – heavy eyebrows, grim red mouth, padded shoulders, hard sculpted cheekbones – together with these roles, endowed her with what were considered aggressively 'masculine' qualities. In Nicholas Ray's *Johnny Guitar* (Republic, 1954), made once she had gone freelance, that dichotomy between male and female is reflected in her tough-talking, gun-slinging Vienna, equally at home in black male attire or white dress.

The pop-psychology-conscious fifties fine-tuned Crawford's image in films like *Harriet Craig* (Vincent Sherman, Columbia, 1950), *Sudden Fear* (David Miller, RKO, 1950), and *Female on the Beach* (Joseph Pevney, Universal, 1955), in which she played older women falling passionately in love with deceiving or murderous young men. As both achiever and victim, a truster and a neurotic, Crawford's characters play out conflicting desires and drives as pure theater – hence her large gay following. The exaggerations, however, took on a life of their own during the 1960s when, in a series of camp horror thrillers, the only laudable one of which was *Whatever Happened to Baby Jane?* (Robert Aldrich, 1962), the Crawford image became a frenzied caricature of itself.

Richard Dyer, *Stars* (London: British Film Institute, 1979)   ALi

CRETEIL

FRANCE's international WOMEN'S FILM FESTIVAL began in Sceaux in 1979, moving to Créteil (another suburb of Paris) in 1985. The Festival International de Créteil et du Val de Marne – Films de Femmes, to give it its full name – is now permanently housed in Créteil's Maison des Arts, and part-financed by local funds. This annual ten-day event takes place in March and has become the world's largest women's film festival: in 1988 it drew a mixed audience of thirty thousand spectators and showed more than a hundred films (including sixty features) whose common denominator was a woman director. Besides competitions (with cash prizes) for new feature films, documentaries, and shorts, each year features thematic sections and a director's retrospective.

Créteil's trajectory reflects the evolution of women's cinema in the West since the 1970s: from an explicitly feminist ethos, the event has moved toward a more market-oriented strategy. But despite the toning down of its feminism, Créteil has met with only limited success in its aim of improving women's standing in the film industry against professional and media resistance, still very strong in France. Créteil's privileging of ART CINEMA over AVANT-GARDE and VIDEO work has been criticized as conservative, yet within the French context it is logical, corresponding to the dominant industrial and critical framework within which most women directors in western Europe make and exhibit films.

Ginette Vincendeau, 'Women's Cinema, Film Theory and Feminism in France', *Screen*, vol. 28, no. 4 (1987)   GV

CROSSDRESSING

Crossdressing refers to the practice of dressing in clothes conventionally associated with the opposite sex. In film, this generally produces confusions about gender roles, social status, and sexual identity. Crossdressing is associated with film GENRES such as COMEDY and the MUSICAL, where stories often revolve around mistaken identity and misrecognition. Different kinds and degrees of crossdressing can be understood in distinct ways: for example, *Some Like It Hot* (Billy Wilder, United Artists, 1959) and

Ossi Oswalda crossdresses in *I Don't Want To Be a Man* (1918)

Victor/Victoria (Blake Edwards, 1982) employ full sexual disguise to fool other characters about the gender identity of protagonists, whereas *Calamity Jane* (David Butler, Warner Bros., 1953) concerns the TOMBOY appearance of the Doris DAY character and the problem of how she is to be taught the lessons of 'correct' femininity. Generally speaking, there is a marked difference between representations of male and of female characters who crossdress. Female characters, such as Katharine HEPBURN in *Sylvia Scarlett* (George Cukor, RKO, 1935), continue to look sexually attractive and desirable, whilst male characters, such as Dustin Hoffman's *Tootsie* (Sydney Pollack, 1982) tend to appear ridiculous and laughable. This visual distinction can be interpreted as signifying the superiority of masculine status over feminine: feminists argue that this results from the unequal values placed upon MASCULINITY and FEMININITY in a patriarchal culture. Such inequality can also be explained in terms of the place of women as a sexual spectacle in cinema – so much so that even in masculine attire she remains eroticized for the LOOK. Indeed, Marlene DIETRICH's performances in male evening dress in films like *Morocco* (Josef von Sternberg, Paramount, 1930) have been seen as part of her fetishized image.

Crossdressing in cinema is of interest to feminists because it seems to offer the potential of breaking down rigid gender dichotomies and undermining the fixed notions of masculinity and femininity. By producing ambiguities and confusions around gender identity, crossdressing narratives raise the possibility of more fluid forms of sexual and gender identification, both between characters in films and also for the cinema AUDIENCE itself. Furthermore, by making visible the 'constructedness' of gender, through transformations in COSTUME, MAKE-UP, use of space, gestures, LIGHTING, and so on, crossdressing offers a perfect support to the feminist claim that gender is not a biological

Julie Andrews in *Victor/Victoria*

category, but a socially constructed identity. Finally, crossdressing narratives typically investigate 'how the other half lives,' and so may expose male privilege, power, or authority. Female characters often crossdress to gain access to a male world which excludes women (as in *Yentl* [Barbra Streisand, 1983]), and male characters who crossdress often undergo a raising of consciousness about gender inequality as a result of their experience as the 'opposite sex' (as in *Tootsie*). Thus crossdressing films raise the question of what gender difference means, dealing, in greater or lesser degree, with the issue of inequality. However, it can equally be argued that although crossdressing might open up these transgressive possibilities, any radical potential is usually closed off by the films' conventions. The audience's knowledge of the sexual disguise, together with the almost invariably restored 'true' gender identities and the heterosexual couple at the end of the film, in combination with the visual conventions of the male gaze, serve to undermine the subversiveness of these films.

Indeed, cinematic conventions may even reaffirm the 'naturalness' and ultimate fixity of SEXUALITY and gender identity. To what extent, then, do crossdressing films reinforce the status quo, and to what extent do they challenge it?

Crossdressing films have also been of interest to FILM CRITICS interested in lesbian and gay subcultures, where crossdressing has a historical significance as part of a more general challenge to fixed gender identities. Readings of crossdressing films from a gay perspective emphasize the moments of sexual transgression in the text over against the films' endings, and analyze the unusual forms of desire and identification offered the audience by sexually disguised characters. Crossdressing films can also be read within the context of play and 'camp,' producing particular meanings for lesbian and gay audiences.

Annette Kuhn, 'Sexual Disguise and Cinema', in *The Power of the Image* (London: Routledge & Kegan Paul, 1985)

See also: LESBIANISM AND CINEMA

JcS

CUBA

To Cuban historians, the year 1898 signals the inception of three parallel and interrelated historical phenomena: the spread of the film medium, the beginning of the American drive to conquer territory beyond its shores, and Cuba's trajectory as an independent nation-state. That year marked Cuba's transition from Spanish colony to neo-colony of the United States; and in the incorporation of Cuba into the US sphere – as in subsequent North American interventions in the Caribbean, Central and South America – film culture would become a vital weapon. Under the shadow cast by the strong film industries of both the USA and MEXICO, Cuba was the site of only intermittent and faltering attempts to develop a NATIONAL CINEMA. This changed in 1959 with the first cultural decree of the Castro government which

Humberto Solás's *Lucía*

set up ICAIC, the Cuban Institute of Cinematic Art and Industry. Within a decade, the bold and innovative accomplishments of filmmakers like Santiago Alvarez, Tomás Gutiérrez Alea, and Humberto SOLAS, and the 'imperfect cinema' theorized by Julio García Espinosa, had begun drawing international attention, an interest that waned with the return to more conventional modes of filmmaking in the 1980s.

With a handful of exceptions, the Cuban DOCUMENTARY tradition has tended to ignore or to ghettoize women's concerns, encouraged by an official ideology which is reluctant to acknowledge the separate problems of any single sector of the population. Octavio Cortázar's *Con las mujeres cubanas/With the Cuban Women* (1974), however, is an early tribute to women's achievement within the new work roles encouraged by the revolutionary regime; and Rolando Díaz's *Controversia* (1982) playfully depicts the debate around sex roles in a Cuban peasant community as a kind of

duel in song, intercutting ironic images of fighting cocks and dapper horsemen to satirize the revered iconography of machismo. Possibly because of reluctance to be 'confined' to the female sphere, many of Cuba's female documentarists have been reluctant to propose woman-centered topics. In *Cuando una mujer no duerme/When a Woman Doesn't Sleep* (1985), Rebeca Chávez offers a filmed biography of Panchita Rivero, a black doctor well into her nineties when the film was shot. Marisol Trujillo's stylish and evocative *Mujer ante el espejo/Woman in Front of the Mirror* (1983), also biographical, uses the reflections of a ballerina to address the female dilemma of motherhood versus career. Though the husband's lack of involvement is gently satirized, the film makes no real effort to conceptualize early childcare as anything other than a woman's problem. Mayra Vilasís's *Una pareja de oro/A Golden Couple* (1986) extols a mixed-race marriage between two of Cuba's leading athletes in the most idealized terms, unquestioningly reinforcing traditional mythologies of romantic love. Miriam Talavera's *Uno, dos, eso es/One, Two, That's It* (1986), on the other hand, offers an unusual look at boxing which emphasizes the collective (and cross-gender) effort behind this only apparently individualized (and male) endeavor, pointing the way to how a more feminized sensibility might shed new light on familiar themes and social practices.

A number of the most interesting Cuban features since the late 1960s have centered on issues of sex/gender equality – or what the Cubans have preferred to refer to as 'the problematics of the couple.' These include Humberto Solas's *Lucía* (1969), Sara GOMEZ's *One Way or Another* (1975–7), Pastor VEGA's *Portrait of Teresa* (1979) and *Habanera* (1984), Tomás Gutiérrez Alea's *Up to a Point* (1984), to name only the best known. It is notable that only one of these features was directed by a woman, and tragic that Sara Gómez did not live to make another feature ✦but it is inexplicable that since her death in 1974 no other woman has been offered the opportunity to direct a feature film. (The single exception is documentarist Marisol Trujillo, who was invited to prepare her first feature in 1987: a children's film.) ICAIC has a wealth of eager candidates, all of whom are currently directing documentaries. These include the three documentarists already mentioned, as well as Teresa Ordoqui and Belkis Vega. Ironically, Cuba's best-known living woman filmmaker, award-winning documentarist Estela Bravo, has developed her *oeuvre* not within ICAIC but as part of Cuban national television, where women's participation has been much more visible. Feminism, though a growing movement throughout Latin America in the 1980s, has not been widely encouraged or practiced in Cuba. Although Cuba's Family Code, promulgated in the mid 1970s, is one of the most progressive pieces of social legislation anywhere in terms of its equal division of rights and responsibilities between male and female partners, the Cuban government has discouraged feminism because of its ostensibly divisive effect on a country which still perceives itself as under siege. A four-day symposium on Women in the Audio Visual World at the Eighth International Festival of the New Latin American Cinema in Havana in 1987 was therefore a signal event. Drawing the avid participation of dozens of Cuban women within the media sector into a discussion which incorporated participants from around the world, the event prompted new awareness and cemented new alliances. It was followed in 1988 by the thirty-three-film series 'Homenje a Las Pioneras del Cine en América Latina,' the first major retrospective of LATIN AMERICA's women filmmakers to be held anywhere.

Michael Chanan, *The Cuban Image: Cinema and Cultural Politics in Cuba* (Bloomington and Indianapolis: University of Indiana Press, 1985)   JBu

CUKOR, GEORGE (1899–1983)

Cukor was a Hollywood filmmaker (of Hungarian origin) who started his career as a Broadway director. His stage beginnings bear on his screen work in two major ways: play adaptatons (*Dinner at Eight* [MGM, 1933], *The Philadelphia Story* [MGM, 1940], *The Women* [MGM, 1939], *My Fair Lady* [1964]), and an interest in the world of actors (*Sylvia Scarlett* [RKO, 1936], *A Star is Born* [Transcona Enterprises, 1954], *The Actress* [MGM, 1953], *Heller in Pink Tights* [Paramount, 1950]). With this theatrical heritage, Cukor is also *par excellence* a classic Hollywood director who, in his own words, 'learned how to function within what they call the system,' brilliantly showcasing stars (mostly female: GARBO, CRAWFORD, HEPBURN, earning him the reputation of a 'women's director') and orchestrating top technical expertise.

In the course of his long and prolific career, Cukor worked mainly in sophisticated COMEDIES (*Holiday* [Columbia, 1938], *The Philadelphia Story*, *The Women*), melodramas (*A Woman's Face* [MGM, 1941], *Gaslight* [MGM, 1944]), and MUSICALS (*Les Girls* [MGM, 1957], *Let's Make Love* [Twentieth Century-Fox, 1960], *My Fair Lady*), focusing on women characters; many of his films draw on women screenwriters. If they do not necessarily, as Molly HASKELL claims, show 'complete identification . . . with the woman's point of view' (see the misogynistic, though very funny, *The Women*), they are sympathetic representations of women's social/sexual predicament: the courtesan in *Camille* (MGM, 1937), the bourgeois housewife in *Gaslight*, the successful actress in *A Star is Born*. And *Sylvia Scarlett* has attracted feminist interest for its investigation of sexual ambiguity. In the main, though, Cukor's films uphold the heterosexual couple as the desirable norm, but insist on equality between men and women – notoriously in the witty Katharine Hepburn–Spencer Tracy comedies (*Adam's Rib* [MGM,

1949], *Pat and Mike* [MGM, 1952]), and the films starring the great comedienne Judy Holliday (*Born Yesterday* [Columbia, 1950], *It Should Happen to You* [Columbia, 1954], *The Marrying Kind* [Columbia, 1952]).

Molly Haskell, *From Reverence to Rape: The Treatment of Women in the Movies* (New York: Penguin, 1973)   GV

CULTURAL STUDIES

Cultural studies emerged in BRITAIN in the late 1960s, in the same period as FILM THEORY, and is associated particularly with the Centre for Contemporary Cultural Studies at Birmingham University, directed first by Richard Hoggart and then by Stuart Hall. A hybrid, semi-institutionalized academic discipline, cultural studies is partly a product of the more politicized forms of intellectual inquiry demanded by the social movements of the 1960s and 1970s, and partly the academic consequence of interdisciplinary concerns of some sociologists, historians 'from below,' scholars of popular literatures, and those committed to the study of working-class cultures and popular forms of entertainment. Like film theory in Britain in the late 1960s and 1970s, cultural studies has had strong links with adult education, and, arguably, both disciplines inherit the moral imperatives associated with English studies in the 1930s. The contemporary mass media have always been included within its broad definition of culture, and cultural studies has been influential in debates about literature, as well as developing methods for the study of other media.

Cultural studies work has had a range of emphases, using different methodologies at different times. The most clearly identifiable strands include: documenting the lifestyles/cultures and histories of subordinate groups (the working class, youth, gender, and ethnic subcultures); analysis of cultural texts produced or consumed by these groups (for example,

women's magazines, reggae music, romantic fiction); critiques of existing academic disciplines, particularly within arts and social sciences; analysis of the current state and social policies (educational reform, legislation around sexuality); elaboration of appropriate methods for the study of the mass media; a continuing general engagement with critical theories of culture. Although the books which can retrospectively be seen as founding texts of cultural studies – Richard Hoggart's *The Uses Of Literacy* (1957), Raymond Williams's *The Long Revolution* (1961), and Stuart Hall and Paddy Whannel's *The Popular Arts* (1964) – all deal with cinema, they are less concerned with what is specific to cinema than with cinema as a part of contemporary culture. Thus although it is a discipline committed to the study of all forms of contemporary culture, cultural studies has had, as yet, comparatively little to say about cinema as such. Major exceptions here would be work on EALING STUDIOS, on STARS, and on the James Bond films. Although cinema would seem, in theory, to fall within the cultural studies field, historically it has tended not to; for a number of institutional, intellectual and economic reasons. On the other hand, cultural studies approaches have become widespread, affecting disciplines like art history and literary studies, as well as film and media studies: in this sense cultural studies has transformed the field in which cinema is studied.

Cultural studies approaches have been more directly influential on the study of TELEVISION, however, a medium – in a period of declining cinema attendance – perhaps more amenable to the cultural studies interest in popularity, everyday life and the AUDIENCE. It is probably in relation to the latter that cultural studies has had the greatest impact: it has always had a considerable investment in the idea of an active, meaning-creating popular audience – often, indeed, a rather wayward, meaning-wresting one. Ethnographic work done with certain social groups on, say, their television watching

Which Hollywood star, in George Cukor's Born Yesterday (1950), proved that dumb blondes ain't so dumb?

or comic reading would obviously have implications for feminist thinking on women's reception of films: the cultural studies stress on the social reality and activity of audience members can be contrasted with more formal notions of the spectator found in film theory. Finally, stress on the historical dimensions of meaning creation would be a key characteristic of cultural studies.

Stuart Hall, Dorothy Hobson, Andrew Lowe and Paul Willis (eds), *Culture, Media, Language* (London: Hutchinson, 1980) *CB*

CZECHOSLOVAKIA

Czech cinema has a continuous tradition, dating from before the turn of this century, while Slovak cinema started only after World War II. At an early stage Czech cinema demonstrated its ability to adapt to new technical and artistic realities, continuing to flourish after the introduction of sound and proving its flexibility after World War II, when it was able to adjust itself to numerous sociopolitical changes. Probably the best-known director in the history of Czech cinema is Gustav Machatý, who made the famous (and much-censored) poetic film *Extase/Ecstasy* (1932).

After 1945, Czech cinema continued virtually without interruption: indeed, a number of films started and abandoned under German occupation were later completed and released. The Czechoslovak film industry was nationalized in 1945. This meant that, being liberated from the pressures of the market, directors faced no financial worries. At the same time, however, as both producer and distributor, the state gained full artistic and ideological control over the industry. Even today a film does not need to be overtly censored, since it can be stopped at any stage of production or distribution. Nevertheless, apart from heavy-handed didactic 'fairytales,' a number of directors have produced quality work.

After Khrushchev's denunciation of Stalin in 1956 a brief period of thaw took place in Czechoslovak cinema, with films like *Touha/Desire* (Vojtěch Jasný, 1958) – a return to Czech lyricism of the thirties – and also ideologically courageous works such as *Velká samota/Great Seclusion* (Ladislav Helge, 1959). During this period all the EASTERN EUROPEAN cinemas were trying various ways of solving ideological and historical problems, and looking for new styles for expressing reality: these they often found in metaphors. In Czechoslovak cinema, symbols stemmed directly from daily life. The years between 1961 and 1968 saw a spell of relative freedom for Czechoslovak filmmakers which produced the Czechoslovak 'film miracle' or 'New Wave'; an early example of which was *Slnko v sieti/Sunshine in a Net* (Štefan Uher, 1962). This film was closely followed by *Černý Petr/Peter and Paula* (Miloš Forman, 1963); *Křik/The Cry* (Jaromíl Jireš, 1963); *O něčem jiném/About Something Else* (Věra Chytilová, 1963) – all of them concerned with contemporary themes presented in a critical and nonglamorized way. With liberalization it became possible to comment on the horrors and absurdities of the previous decade, as in *O slavnosti a hostech/The Party and the Guests* (Jan Němec, 1966); while directors like Miloš Forman, Evald Schorm or Ivan Passer dealt more directly with the compromises and crises of daily life. The film considered to be the manifesto of the 'New Wave' is *Perlicky na dně/Pearls in the Abyss* (1965). With the exception of Miloš Forman, all the major representatives of the movement took part in this film's production: Jiří Menzel, Věra CHYTILOVA, Jan Němec, Evald Schorm, Jaromil Jireš, Juraj Herz, and Ivan Passer. After the Prague Spring of 1968, Gustav Husák's succession to power signaled the start of a a 'normalization' which for cinema meant an abrupt end of the 'New Wave' and stricter controls. Since that time only a handful of films of any originality have been made.

In features production, women – with the exception of Věra Chytilová – are conspicuous by their absence. Women usually figure lower down the credit list as production assistants, clapper-girls, make-up artists, or at best as script editors or writers. A slightly better situation obtains in the field of short, documentary, or newsreel films. A more important 'female' domain has, however, been puppet, animated, and cartoon films; though even here women mainly work as rank-and-file animators for men directors. Hermína Týrlová was the founder of puppet film production at Zlin (Gottwaldow) studios. She made several series of fairytales, and in her later films drew more on reality, creating a new world of animated objects, often combining puppet animation, live child actors, and special effects. Her pioneering films were well received at festivals all over the world, and Týrlová encouraged many new talents.

Josef Skvorecky, *All the Bright Young Men and Women* (Toronto: Peter Martin Associates Ltd, Take One Film Book Series, 1, 1971)

See also: HOLLAND, AGNIESZKA   ZB

DALE, HOLLY *see* COLE, JANIS and DALE, HOLLY

DANCE

The parallel concerns of movement, illusion, and rhythm link dance and cinema; but dance in film has been used with varied aesthetic and political intention, and with significant cultural implications.

Although women's contribution to dance as an art form has been immense, until recently women in dance have been accepted and recognized only as performers. The power structures of the dance world are similar to those of the film industry, which has prompted some women filmmakers working outside the mainstream in experimental and AVANT-GARDE spheres to work with dance as a means of subjective expression, exploration of SEXUALITY or nonverbal communication. The marginalization of women in both dance and film opens space for women to challenge ideologies of FEMININITY, creating a new cinematic language with movement as an integral part of this language. Examples can be found in the work of Maya DEREN, Yvonne RAINER, Shirley CLARKE, Doris Chase, and Elizabeth Ross. FEMINIST INDEPENDENT FILM has also drawn on dance in its explorations of femininity and patriarchy, in films by Sally POTTER and Julie DASH.

In commercial cinema, dance becomes a vehicle for dominant approaches to NARRATIVE and IDEOLOGY. The emphasis is on the male dancer as athlete; MASCULINITY becomes a spectacle of ritualized process. While gay men have sought refuge in the marginal world of dance, commercial cinema reinstates a dynamic and powerful image of the male dancer, relegating the female to passive accessory (*The Turning Point* [Herbert Ross, 1977]). In recent ballet films, Mikhail Baryshnikov has served Hollywood's purpose to these ends (*White Nights* [Taylor Hackford, 1985], *Dancers* [Herbert Ross, 1987]). His notorious heterosexuality and breathtaking technique legitimize male dancing. He

Four Women, **directed by Julie Dash and performed by Linda Young**

Maya Deren's *Ritual in Transfigured Time*

becomes a star in the sense that he really only plays himself.

Dance often stands as a metaphor for the sexual act; film sensualizes dance by making explicit parallels with sex. While the body as instrument makes dance an obvious metaphor for sexuality, commercial film uses this to reinforce ideol-

ogies of gender, and indeed of race: the erotic and the exotic are brought together when LATINA and BLACK actresses like Carmen Miranda and Dorothy DANDRIDGE feature in dancing roles. Dorothy ARZNER's *Dance, Girl, Dance* (RKO, 1940) is perhaps Hollywood's only exception to this generalization. Working both within and against CLASSICAL HOLLYWOOD CINEMA, this film critiques its endorsement of male voyeurism by juxtaposing a cabaret dancer with a classical dancer and having the latter round on her audience to deliver a denunciation of their (and our, the audience's) voyeurism.

Judith Lynne Hanna, *Dance, Sex and Gender* (Chicago: University of Chicago Press, 1988)

See also: LAMARQUE, LIBERTAD; MUSICAL; PERFORMANCE; TOYE, WENDY   *KL-J*

DANDRIDGE, DOROTHY (1922–65)

Although an accomplished actress and the first BLACK WOMAN to be nominated for an Academy Award for Best Actress, Dorothy Dandridge had a difficult professional and personal life. She was a glamorous and talented singer and actress and yet, because suitable parts for black people were scarce, she had long intervals between acting roles. Dandridge also suffered the fate of other beautiful, fairskinned black 'leading ladies,' in that she was usually cast according to her looks and skin color. Black actresses before her who encountered similar difficulties were Nina Mae McKinney, Fredi Washington, and Lena Horne. Dandridge is best remembered for her portrayal of the sultry vixen in *Carmen Jones* (Otto Preminger, Twentieth Century-Fox, 1954) and as Bess in the Preminger musical *Porgy and Bess* (Columbia, 1959).

Dandridge is credited with a number of firsts. She was the first black actress to appear on the cover of *Life* magazine and the first to be in a screen interracial romantic relationship. The film was *Island in the Sun* (Robert Rossen, Twentieth Century-Fox, 1957). For a time after her role in *Carmen Jones*, she was as talked about and publicized as the 1950s white stars Elizabeth Taylor and Marilyn MONROE. Although Dandridge is best known for her casting as sexy, evil temptress, one of her first dramatic roles was as the committed young teacher who cares about her young students in the film *Bright Road* (Gerald Mayer, MGM, 1953).

Michelle Parkerson, 'The Tragedy of Dorothy Dandridge', *Black Film Review*, vol. 4, no. 2 (1988) *JBo*

DASH, JULIE (1952–)

US independent filmmaker Dash was born in New York City, and is currently based in Atlanta, Georgia. She studied film as an undergraduate and at the American Film Institute before attending film school at the University of California, Los Angeles, in the 1970s. Part of a group of young black filmmakers dubbed by critic Clyde Taylor the 'LA Rebellion' in US BLACK CINEMA, Dash and her films have forged a crucial link between this movement and a women's film culture largely defined by white women.

Each of Dash's films has been centrally concerned with black women's image and self-definition. *Four Women* (1977) is an experimental dance film presenting four archetypal images of black women set to a ballad sung by Nina Simone; and *Diary of an African Nun* (1976) is an adaptation of a short story by Alice Walker. But it is Dash's innovative and powerful thirty-four-minute film *Illusions* (1983) which has attracted the greatest critical attention. The film's narrative centers on two black women employed in very different ways in the Hollywood film industry of the forties:

Illusions, by Julie Dash

Mignon Dupree (Lonette McKee) uses the wartime 'freedom' for women in the job market to ascend to a position of power as an executive in the studio system. To do so, however, she must 'pass' as white. When she befriends a young black woman, Ester Jeeter (Roseann Katon), whose singing voice is synched to a blonde starlet's performance, Dupree's consciousness of the irony of her position in the myth machine becomes crystallized. The film's critique goes to the heart of Hollywood's portrayal of BLACK WOMEN, effectively seizing on the codes of CLASSICAL HOLLYWOOD CINEMA to dramatize enforced invisibility in the two women's stories.

After almost six years of fundraising Dash is currently in production with a 35mm feature film, *Daughters of the Dust*. Telling the story of the women of a Gullah family (descendants of freed slaves living on the sea islands off the coast of South Carolina and Georgia) at the turn of the century, this film is important both as a more mainstream effort by an independent black woman producer and also as a piece of black American history erased by popular culture.

Working Models of Success (1974); *Diary of an African Nun* (1976); *Four Women* (1977); *Illusions* (1983); *We Are Mothers Too Early* . . . (1987)

Clyde Taylor, 'The LA Rebellion: New Spirit in American Film', *Black Film Review*, vol. 2, no. 3 (1986)   PW

DAVIS, BETTE (1908–89)

This great American dramatic actress is one of the STARS of the HOLLYWOOD STUDIO SYSTEM who continued working in the cinema through to the 1980s. She was a repertory player at WARNER BROS. during the 1930s, winning an Oscar in 1938 for her part in *Jezebel* (William Wyler). Two years earlier she had rebelled against the contractual strictures and implicitly sexist treatment of the studio – 'inferior roles, slavelike working conditions' – and traveled to London at the invitation of a British film producer. Warners took out and won a breach-of-contract suit and suspended Bette Davis for a year, but on her return gave her a good role in *Marked Woman* (Lloyd Bacon, 1937). During World War II, when working women comprised the majority of cinema audiences in the USA, Bette Davis's parts improved in such films as *Dark Victory* (Edmund Goulding, Warner Bros., 1939), *The Little Foxes* (William Wyler, Goldwyn, 1941), and *Now Voyager* (Irving Rapper, Warner Bros., 1942). Her performances in these films present feminist audiences of today with questions and paradoxes concerning, for example, the star, FEMININITY, and CLASSICAL HOLLYWOOD CINEMA. Typecast as the 'superfemale' (a term coined by feminist critic Molly HASKELL) or the 'bitch,' Bette Davis played intelligent, independent, sharp women who resisted – even opposed – accepted codes of feminine behavior and the conventions of marriage and family. If the narratives invariably and implacably punish these women, Bette Davis's PERFORMANCE arguably resists such strategies. Following the war, Bette Davis's career declined, though there were notable high points, including *All About Eve* (Joseph L Mankiewicz, Twentieth Century-Fox, 1950); but as a professional character actress she reemerged in the early 1960s to play a series of four female monsters, beginning with Jane Hudson in *Whatever Happened to Baby Jane?* (Robert Aldrich, 1962), with Joan CRAWFORD, through *Hush . . . Hush Sweet Charlotte* (Robert Aldrich, 1964), *The Nanny* (Seth Holt, 1965), and concluding with *The Anniversary* (Roy Ward Baker, 1967), in which her creation of the monster matriarch is fitting, if macabre, testimony to Hollywood's long resistance to representing women as human beings.

Bette Davis with Whitney Stine, *Mother Goddam* (London: W H Allen, 1975)   PB

DAWSON, JAN (1939–80)

Jan Dawson, FILM CRITIC, editor, and translator, taught film studies in Berkeley, California, before returning to her native BRITAIN to join the editorial department of the BRITISH FILM INSTITUTE (BFI) in 1967. She became editor of the BFI's *Monthly Film Bulletin* in 1971, contributing much to the rigor and reliability of its documentation. She left in 1973 to become a freelance writer and contributor to international JOURNALS such as *Take One* (Canada), *Cinema Papers* (Australia), *Film Korrespondenz* (West Germany), as well as *The Listener*, *Film Comment*, and *Sight and Sound* in Britain. She also wrote booklets on Alexander Kluge and Wim Wenders and popularized their work outside WEST GERMANY. Fluent in French and German, she prepared the English-language screenplay for François Truffaut's *The Story of Adèle H.* (1976), and translated Faber's English version of *Conversations with Eugène Ionesco*. She was a confirmed enthusiast for European cinema, and for NEW GERMAN CINEMA in particular: she was preparing a history of it at the time of her death. Her other major contribution to film was as organizer and consultant for FILM FESTIVALS in London, Perth, Edinburgh, Chicago and most notably Berlin, where she was responsible between 1976 and 1980 for a range of publications which set a world standard for festival documentation. Her work in all these different areas is marked by its eclecticism, scrupulous intellectual rigor, and trenchant insight. In 1980, a commemorative annual award was set up in her name, to fund initiatives in film criticism and scholarship.

Marsha McCreadie, *Women on Film: The Critical Eye* (New York: Praeger, 1983)

SP

DAY, DORIS (1924–)

An extremely popular Hollywood STAR, well known for her roles in musicals and sex comedies in the 1950s and 1960s, Day (born Doris von Kappelhoff in Cincinnati, Ohio) was already well known on the radio as a singer before making her first film, *Romance on the High Seas* (Michael Curtiz, Warner Bros., 1948). Between 1948 and 1968 Day made thirty-nine films. Her image was a mixture of the sunny, freckle-faced girl-next-door/TOMBOY and the perpetual 'professional' virgin, an image which became increasingly at odds with the beliefs and attitudes of the 'liberated' sixties. But condescending dismissals of Day as the perpetual virgin were disquietingly inaccurate. In her autobiography she challenges her star image, pointing to the tough dramatic roles she had played (as in *Love Me or Leave Me* [Charles Vidor, MGM, 1955]), and revealing a life which had been far from rosy. In Britain the disquiet surfaced in 1980, when two feminists persuaded the National Film Theatre to mount a retrospective season of Day's films, arguing that many of them prefigured concerns which later became central to the women's movement.

> *French psychoanalytic theorist Catherine Clément links two myth-making machines. One is cinema. What is the other?*

In fact, Day played the girl-next-door in only two of her nearly forty films: *On Moonlight Bay* (Roy del Ruth, Warner Bros., 1951) and *By the Light of the Silvery Moon* (David Butler, Warner Bros., 1953). Her major – and her most famous – tomboy role was in the MUSICAL *Calamity Jane* (David Butler, Warner Bros., 1953). This is a more typical Day film, in so far as it concerns the problem of gender definition – of what is the 'proper' way for a woman to behave (and contrasts with other CROSSDRESSING movies like *Some Like It Hot* [Billy Wilder, United Artists, 1959] and *Victor/Victoria* [Blake Edwards, 1982] which employ full sexual disguise to fool other characters about the gender of the protagonists). Day's crossdressing character spends most of the film caught between the desire to retain her independence and the bizarre attractions of FEMININITY. She succumbs to femininity only in the last few minutes, on discovering she is in love with her erstwhile sparring partner Wild Bill Hickock (Howard Keel). This pattern of a woman torn between an independence and self-determination which the male hero is both attracted to and threatened by is as typical of Day's films as it is of, say, FILM NOIR. The difference is that Day's genre is COMEDY, and her characters rarely use SEXUALITY as a weapon, but are generally trying to assert their right to be considered as something other than sex objects. In *Pajama Game* (Stanley Donen, Warner Bros., 1957), the heroine makes it plain that the union is more important to her than her lover (a member of the management); and in *Pillow Talk* (Michael Gordon, Universal, 1959) she resists the hero's definitions of her as a prude and exposes him as a deceitful womanizer. However, despite the resistance and resilience of Day's characters, they generally capitulated in the end and went – literally or figuratively – to the altar. The value feminists may attach to Day's films depends partly on whether we decide to give final weight to an hour-and-a-half of struggle or to ten minutes of capitulation; and partly on whether we feel Day's PERFORMANCE undermines the strength of the characters she plays.

A E Hotchner, *Doris Day: Her Own Story* (London: W H Allen, 1976)

See also: BLONDES; CAREER WOMAN

TP

DEITCH, DONNA (1945–)

After experience as still photographer for feature films, camerawoman, editor, and director of numerous documentaries, shorts and commercials, US director Donna Deitch made her first feature, *Desert Hearts* (1985), as an independent film, for which she had to spend some years in grueling fundraising. A ROMANCE between two women based on Jane Rule's novel *Desert of the Heart*, the film uses a fifties pop-art setting of bold Western landscapes and music, and Reno gambling tables, as a metaphor for risk-taking. Deitch applies highly commercial filmmaking techniques to a lesbian love story, a subject she felt had not been handled in a frank and real way in American films. It was doubtless her sympathy and skill with women characters and relationships between women, as well as her storytelling skills, that led Oprah Winfrey, of TV talkshow fame, to entrust to Deitch the direction of *The Women of Brewster Place* (1989). This ambitious four-hour TV production based on Gloria Naylor's award-winning novel concerns the intertwined lives of seven black women, ranging from a church woman to a welfare mother to a sophisticated lesbian couple.

Woman to Woman (1975); *The Great Wall of Los Angeles* (1978); *Desert Hearts* (1985); *The Women of Brewster Place* (1989)

Kathi Maio, *Feminist in the Dark: Reviewing the Movies* (Freedom, California: The Crossing Press, 1988)   BKQ

De MILLE, CECIL B (1881–1959)

SILENT CINEMA director Cecil B De Mille was born into a distinguished American theatrical family headed by his strong-willed mother after his father's early death. In 1913 he abandoned a modest stage career to become one of the founders of the Jesse L Lasky Feature Play Company. As Lasky's director-general, De Mille played a pivotal role in establishing the studio's reputation for artistic feature films. Critics praised his first release, *The Squaw Man* (1914), which was partially financed by his mother, and became accustomed to the superior photography, composition, and dramatic lighting effects (labeled 'Rembrandt or Lasky lighting') that characterized his early features. With the release of *The Cheat* in 1915, De Mille achieved international acclaim. During a transition when Lasky merged with Adolph

Zukor's Famous Players (later PARA-MOUNT) in 1916, De Mille directed Metropolitan Opera diva Geraldine Farrar in well-publicized films that brought cultural legitimacy to filmmaking.

De Mille became a trendsetter in the postwar era by making a series of popular sex comedies and melodramas with provocative titles like *Old Wives for New* (1918), *Male and Female* (1919), and *Why Change Your Wife?* (1920). Such spectacles provided a showcase for the 'new woman' intent on conspicuous consumption, typified by Gloria Swanson, and served as etiquette manuals for an expanding middle class. De Mille also directed the famed biblical epics *The Ten Commandments* (1923) and *The King of Kings* (1927) in the silent period. During the early twenties he became less innovative and settled upon formulaic spectacles that became his trademark and endured at the box office for decades. For the most part, his sound films are historical epics or frontier sagas that celebrate American expansionist values.

Donald Hayne (ed.), *The Autobiography of Cecil B. De Mille* (Englewood Cliffs, NJ: Prentice-Hall, 1959; reprinted by Garland, 1985)　　　　　SHi

DEMME, JONATHAN (1944–)

Born in New York and raised in Miami, Demme worked as a publicist at Embassy Pictures and United Artists, and wrote reviews for the New York trade paper *Film Daily*, before moving to London in 1968. There, and subsequently in Los Angeles, he worked on low-budget EXPLOITATION FILMS for Roger Corman, following in the footsteps of directors like Francis Coppola, Martin SCORSESE and Peter Bogdanovitch, who would become key figures in NEW HOLLYWOOD CINEMA.

Demme's quirky style and eye for eccentricity emerged early. For Corman's New World Productions he cowrote and co-produced the biker film *Angels Hard As They Come* (1971) and worked on *The Hot Box* (1972). *Caged Heat* (1973) was Demme's directorial debut and he went on to direct, among others, *Citizen's Band* (1977), *The Last Embrace* (1979), *Melvin and Howard* (1980), *Swing Shift* (1984). His concert film of the band Talking Heads, *Stop Making Sense* (1984), was critically acclaimed, but it was *Something Wild* (1986), starring Melanie Griffith as a modern FEMME FATALE, which brought Demme to the attention of mainstream Hollywood. The film's ironic mishmash of GENRES, its knowing references to the New York AVANT GARDE, and its contradictory approach to the Melanie Griffith character have guaranteed it a place as a cult film. This was followed by *Swimming to Cambodia* (1987) and *Married to the Mob* (1989), which returned to some of the themes of *Something Wild*: physical transformations, explosive violence, predatory women, and a sexually unawakened central male character. Although more populist in approach, the film also contains many 'in-jokes' aimed at a New York ART CINEMA audience, and offers the same unproblematic view of race (black and white citydwellers cohabiting in harmony) for which *Something Wild* has been criticized.

Cameron Bailey, 'Nigger/Lover: The Thin Sheen of Race in *Something Wild*', *Screen*, vol. 29, no. 4 (1988)　　　　LF

DENMARK

Without government support few feature films would be produced in Denmark today. However, Denmark was Europe's most prosperous film center before World War I and the coming of sound. Among the leading directors of that period were Urban Gad, Benjamin Christensen, and Carl Dreyer, filmmakers specializing in melodramatic style, moral or literary subjects, and mystery thrillers. The world-famous star Asta NIELSEN provided a model for the image of the VAMP in Hollywood films.

Since World War II a number of documentaries have been produced;

whilst among features realistic dramas and small-scale comedies dominate. Henning Carlsen, Sven and Lene Grønlykke, and Annelise Hovmand, for example, have worked in the European ART CINEMA tradition. The abolition of film censorship in 1969 launched a profitable output of sex films for domestic and

> The British cinema has produced the cinematic equivalent of the rude seaside postcard. What is this?

international markets; at the same time, though, women took a more significant role as filmmakers. Astrid HENNING-JENSEN, Brita Wielopolska, Ingrid Oustrup Jensen, Lizzie Corfixen, Elisabeth Rygard, and Helle RYSLINGE, among others, have investigated questions of motherhood and problems of female immigrants. In the 1980s, Denmark became known for its films for and about children. *AKo*

DE PALMA, BRIAN (1944–)

A director associated with NEW HOLLYWOOD CINEMA, De Palma is one of a group of 1960s film school graduates (which also includes his friends Martin SCORSESE, Francis Coppola, George Lucas, and Steven Spielberg) who made the leap from low-budget anonymity to the major studios. He began his first feature while still a student, and in 1972 was signed to Warner Bros. to make *Get To Know Your Rabbit*, starring Tommy Smothers; but the project was not a happy one for De Palma and he left before the film was completed. In 1973 he made a murder-thriller, *Sisters*, starring Margot Kidder, which contained elements of the dark humor that characterizes much of his early work. But it was not until the release of *Carrie* (1976), an adaptation of a Stephen King novel starring Sissy Spacek, that De Palma's niche as the ultimate director of mainstream psychological thrillers was established. He went

on to direct more films in the same GENRE, attracting adverse critical attention from feminists for his insistence on the spectator as voyeur and on the female central character as victim, stalked by the camera. Both *Dressed To Kill* (1980) and *Body Double* (1984) had original scripts by De Palma, and both were lambasted by feminists because of what was perceived as excessive violence and near-PORNOGRAPHY. *The Untouchables* (1987) saw a move away from De Palma's earlier themes to a less controversial gangster picture, because, in De Palma's view,

> It's very difficult to have a woman as a person that's in jeopardy now, because you get all the antagonism from the feminist press. And so it becomes a real problem – even though I think, in that genre, women in jeopardy are something that work better than men in jeopardy. It's a convention of the form. But it's something that's sort of going out of fashion . . . .

Giovanna Asselle and Behroze Gandhy, 'Dressed to Kill: A Discussion', *Screen*, vol. 23, nos. 3/4 (1982) *LF*

DEREN, MAYA (1917–61)

Maya Deren is often referred to as the Mother of the US AVANT GARDE because of her indefatigable work on behalf of experimental film in the 1940s and 1950s. Acutely aware of the importance of networking, she wrote, lectured, and toured with her films, organizing screenings, workshops, and symposia (including the 1953 Poetry and Film Symposium in New York, in which she participated with Parker Tyler, Arthur Miller, and Dylan Thomas), and setting up the Creative Film Foundation in 1954. She was equally energetic in publicizing herself, delighting in behaving and dressing unconventionally and helping to create a myth of exoticism which often takes precedence over the many impressive intellectual and artistic achievements

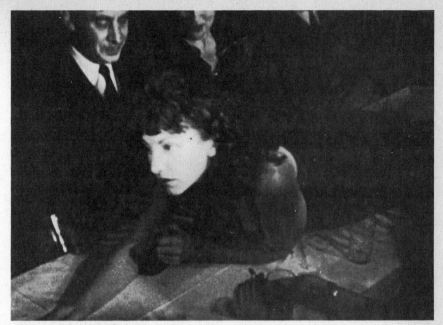

Maya Deren in *At Land*

with which she packed her brief forty-four years. A Russian Jewish émigrée whose family fled to New York in 1922, Deren was a poet, journalist, and left-wing political activist during the thirties. In 1942, while working as assistant to black choreographer/anthropologist Katherine Dunham, she published a key article, 'Religious Possession in Dancing,' which inaugurated a lifelong interest in Haitian myth and ritual. The same year she met her second husband, Czech émigré Alexander (Sasha) Hammid, who introduced her to filmmaking.

In spite of a substantial body of written and other work produced over a twenty-year span, it is for her six completed short films made between 1943 and 1958 that Deren is remembered today. Apart, perhaps, from the pamphlet *An Anagram of Ideas on Art, Form and Film* (1946), her theories are rarely seriously considered. Yet the films are an integral part of the theory, and vice versa (one can hardly imagine Eisenstein's films being discussed without reference to his theories

of montage). In her films, Deren worked through complex ideas about form, consciousness, sexuality, and individual identity, from the dreamlike paranoid narratives of *Meshes of the Afternoon* (1943) and *At Land* (1944), to the abstract 'creative geography' of *A Study in Choreography for Camera* (1945) and the 'cubism in time' of *Meditation on Violence* (1948), each of which crystallizes Deren's ideas about the nature of film art and, more importantly, what cinema might become if freed from traditional notions of space and time. The lyrical beauty of the films (and, indeed, of Deren herself, who appeared in three of them) has tended to obscure their origin in rigorous intellectual thought. Similarly, the unfinished Haitian film footage (compiled after her death as *Divine Horsemen*) and her Haitian Notebooks have fallen into obscurity, perhaps because Deren's involvement with voodoo, in spite of her efforts to be taken seriously (her magisterial anthropological book, *Divine Horsemen: the Living Gods of Haiti*, was published in 1953), has been treated as the bohemian antics of a Greenwich Village eccentric. Fortunately, the efforts of feminists during the seventies to reconstruct and reevaluate the wide range of material left behind by Deren, now bearing fruit in the fascinating *Legend of Maya Deren* project, will enable the record to be put straight.

Meshes of the Afternoon (co-d. Alexander Hammid, 1943); *At Land* (1944); *A Study in Choreography for Camera* (1945); *Ritual in Transfigured Time* (1946); *Meditation on Violence* (1948); *The Very Eye of Night* (1958). Uncompleted: *Witch's Cradle* (1943); *Medusa* (1949); *Divine Horsemen* (1947–51); *Ensemble for Somnambulists* (1951); *Haiku Film Project* (1959–60)

Vèvè A Clark, 'Signatures', in *The Legend of Maya Deren Vol. 1 Part One*, ed. Vèvè A Clark, Millicent Hodson, Catrina Neiman (New York: Anthology Film Archives, 1984); Catrina Neiman, 'Chambers', in *The Legend of Maya Deren Vol. 1 Part Two*, ed. Vèvè A Clark, Millicent Hodson, Catrina Neiman (New York: Anthology Film Archives, 1988)

PC

DERRY FILM AND VIDEO COLLECTIVE

Derry Film and Video Collective (DFVC), established in 1984, was the first INDEPENDENT CINEMA workshop in the northwest of IRELAND. The collective is funded by CHANNEL FOUR TELEVISION. Working in the belief that local people ought to be trained to represent themselves (as a counter to the perceived inadequacies and inaccuracies of mainstream television coverage), the collective began to organize access to equipment and training for local people. Among their projects are *Derry Video News* (1984); *Strip Searching – Security or Subjugation* (1984), which examines how the policy of strip-searching affects women in Armagh prison; and *Planning* (1985), which deals with the history of military involvement in urban planning in nationalist areas in the north.

All of DFVC's work reflects a particular commitment to issues which impinge on women's realities. Their most recent project was *Mother Ireland* (1988), a documentary examining the way in which Ireland as a nation has been represented historically as a woman: this originated in Celtic mythology and has been developed through folklore, literature, and song. A major motif is Ireland as a helpless and subdued woman, awaiting rescue either by a French prince or sometimes by Bonnie Prince Charlie of Scotland: through this allegory political sentiments have been expressed during times of repression in Irish history. The documentary explores the roots of these images, and also examines the image of the Virgin mother propagated by the Catholic Church as a role-model for Irish women. The significance of *Mother Ireland* lies in its attempt to challenge received images of woman, and also to deal with the implications of such a challenge for Irish women today. Due to censorship legislation, however, *Mother Ireland* will not be broadcast either in Ireland or in Britain. DFVC, who own the production, have nevertheless taken steps to distribute it themselves.

Future projects for the collective include *Hush-a-Bye Baby*, which they hope to make on 16mm film. This emerged out of a workshop for young people on sexuality, and marks the collective's move into drama production. The collective is also actively involved in media education through seminars, forums, and training, and sees this as a means of increasing informal distribution of independent film and video work beyond more established channels such as CINEMA OF WOMEN and The Other Cinema.

Lorainne Kennedy, 'Mother Ireland', *Making Sense*, no. 6 (1989)   SM

DE VERE, ALISON (1927–   )

An ANIMATION filmmaker who has worked her way through the studio system to become a renowned designer and independent animator in BRITAIN, de Vere was born in Pakistan and trained as an artist at the Royal Academy Schools. She began her career in animation at the bottom, working her way up through the traditional women's grades such as cel painting and color mixing for studios such as Halas and Batchelor, where she worked from 1951 to 1956. After five years she had reached the position of designer, and went on to work freelance on television commercials, credits, and special effects sequences until in 1968 she was engaged as background supervisor for *Yellow Submarine* (George Dunning, 1968). Although flawed by a poor script, *Yellow Submarine* contains many outstanding and innovative sequences. It is for its design, however, that the film is most widely admired: on this de Vere collaborated with German designer Heinz Edelman.

For ten years from 1970 de Vere worked on commercials for Wyatt Cattaneo Productions. Using their facilities she was also able to make the two personal films which first won her international recognition. *Café Bar* (1975) won a special jury prize at Annecy, and in 1979 *Mr Pascal* won a Gold Award at the same festival. These films are enriched by de Vere's interest in art, poetry, and philosophy; they contain strongly biographical elements, drawing characters from real life and images from her dreams, memories, and fantasies. *Café Bar* is based on a favorite animators' haunt in Soho's Frith Street, and the main character is a self-portrait. The music for *Mr Pascal* was composed and performed by two street musicians – a contingent as well as an artistic decision, since the films received no external funding and were made over a number of years in her spare time.

In the 1980s de Vere continued her independent filmmaking with funding from CHANNEL FOUR TELEVISION. In 1984 she made a half-hour adaptation of George Eliot's *Silas Marner*. She returned to more personal and autobiographical subject matter in *The Black Dog* (1987),

whose heroine, the same character as in *Café Bar*, undertakes a labyrinthine journey through mythological landscapes toward self-understanding. De Vere is now working on an adaptation of *Psyche and Eros*.

Two Faces (1963); *False Friends* (1968); *Café Bar* (1975); *Mr Pascal* (1979); *Silas Marner* (1984); *The Black Dog* (1987)   IK

DIETRICH, MARLENE (1901–   )

Born in GERMANY into a bourgeois Prussian family, Marie Magdalene Dietrich turned to theater after breaking off her early training in music. She joined Max Reinhardt's acting school, and was subsequently cast in the Reinhardt company and in revues and, from 1923 onward, in film roles. Although the notion that she was 'discovered' by Josef von STERNBERG belongs in the realm of myth, Dietrich did make her film breakthrough as Lola-Lola in Sternberg's *Der blaue Engel/The Blue Angel* (1930). The female image crystallized in this film – the fetishistic PHALLIC WOMAN – characterized the subsequent six-year Dietrich–Sternberg collaboration at PARAMOUNT in the USA. From *Morocco* (1930) to *The Devil Is a Woman* (1935) Dietrich played VAMPS whose erotic appeal rested in no small measure upon a spectacle of transsexuality and CROSS-DRESSING. Gaylyn Studlar's notion that 'the subversive quality of von Sternberg's films seems crucially dependent on the masochistic aesthetic embedded in them' applies equally well to the parts played in them by Dietrich.

Between 1935 and 1961 Dietrich, an enduring STAR, appeared in films by various directors, often repeating the successes of the Sternberg era. During World War II (by which time she was a US citizen), she made numerous appearances before American troops at the front, surely exceeding any expectations imposed upon her by the state. This was a foretaste of her second career – as a singer/variety artiste – which she began to pursue toward the end of her film

Marlene Dietrich

career. Marlene Dietrich now lives in Paris.

The fifty-three films in which Marlene Dietrich appeared include: *Tragoedie der Liebe* (Joe May, 1923); *Madame wuenscht keine Kinder/Madame Wants No Children* (Alexander Korda, 1926); *Prinzessin Olala/Art of Love* (Robert Land, 1929); *Der blaue Engel/The Blue Angel* (Josef von Sternberg, 1930); *Morocco* (Sternberg, Paramount, 1930; *Dishonored* (Sternberg, Paramount, 1931); *Shanghai Express* (Sternberg, Paramount, 1932); *Blonde Venus* (Sternberg, Paramount, 1932); *Song of Songs* (Rouben Mamoulian, Paramount, 1933); *The Devil is a Woman* (Sternberg, Paramount, 1935); *Desire* (Frank Borzage, Paramount, 1936); *Angel* (Ernst Lubitsch, Paramount, 1937); *Destry Rides Again* (George Marshall, Universal, 1939); *The Flame of New Orleans* (René Clair, Universal, 1941); *Kismet* (William Dieterle, MGM, 1944); *A Foreign Affair* (Billy Wilder, Paramount, 1948); *Stage Fright* (Alfred Hitchcock, Warner Bros., 1950); *Rancho Notorious* (Fritz Lang, Fidelity Pictures, 1952); *Witness for the Prosecution* (Billy Wilder, Theme Pictures/Edward Small, 1958); *Touch of Evil* (Orson Welles, Universal, 1958); *Judgement at Nuremberg* (Stanley Kramer, 1961); *Schoener Gigolo – armer Gigolo/Just a Gigolo* (David Hemmings, 1978)

Gaylyn Studlar, *In the Realm of Pleasure. Von Sternberg, Dietrich, and the Masochistic Aesthetic* (Urbana and Chicago: University of Illinois Press, 1988)   *VR*

DISTRIBUTION

Films are an unusual commodity, in that they are usually hired out to EXHIBITION rather than sold. The relationship between film production and film distribution differs greatly from country to country, and also historically, distribution arrangements being in varying degrees separated from, or linked to, production. However, in all but the most marginalized of AVANT-GARDE and INDEPENDENT CINEMAS, finance for making a film today depends upon the negotiation of a distribution deal as part of a package: increasingly, such negotiations involve TELEVISION.

In the heyday of the HOLLYWOOD STUDIO SYSTEM, production and distribution (along with exhibition) were all in the hands of the same companies, the 'vertically integrated' major studios. Distribution was dominated by a system of runs and clearances in which the studios ensured that their films would reap the greatest profits. First run was most profitable, with the major studios' films playing for top ticket prices in deluxe downtown movie theaters, 77 per cent of which were owned by the 'Big Five' (MGM, TWENTIETH CENTURY-FOX, PARAMOUNT, WARNER BROS., RKO). Subsequent runs occurred after the film had 'cleared' the first-run theaters. The film was then distributed to theaters designated as second run, third run, and so on, to outlying neighborhoods, small towns, and rural areas, with progressively lower ticket prices. First-run theaters accounted for a disproportionately high percentage of box office receipts. The 1948 anti-trust decision, *US v Paramount et al.*, required the Big Five to divest their theater chains. While exhibitors could now bid for first-run distribution rights to films, the traditional system of runs remains the dominant distribution practice today. The majors were also allowed to retain their distribution networks, and this was a key factor in providing access to the screen and to audiences.

Other distribution methods were the roadshow and the 'four-wall.' Films with spectacular production values were defined as 'special events' through roadshow distribution in prestige theaters for unusually high ticket prices. In recent years, newly restored prints of films have revived the roadshow: *Napoleon* (Abel Gance, 1927) recently played in movie palaces with live orchestras. Independent producers sometimes had to 'four-wall' their films by renting individual theaters, because no distributor would pick up the film. Distribution remains highly influenced by profit maximization: it can easily marginalize 'small' films, independent films, foreign-language films, and films whose subject matter or style questions accepted values, allowing them only to slip in and out of town, if they play at all. Feminist films and films by or about women can fall into several of these marginal categories. Through its production company, Goldwyn, Donna DEITCH's lesbian ROMANCE *Desert Hearts* (1985) received only limited distribution in the USA, and then mainly in urban areas, due to preconceptions about what will 'play' (make money) in small towns and rural communities.

Jason E Squire (ed.), *The Movie Business Book* (New Jersey: Prentice-Hall, 1983)

See also: FEMINIST DISTRIBUTION

MBH

DJEBAR, ASSIA (1936–)

Assia Djebar, born in Algiers, began her career as a novelist and essayist (writing in French) after the independence of ALGERIA. Capitalizing on her recognition as one of the few Algerian women writers, she secured financial support from the state television, RTA, to produce two films. While this gave her freedom during production, it hindered international distribution. As a result this innovative director has, despite her major contribution to ARAB CINEMA, achieved little recognition. Her masterpiece is her debut, *Noubat Nissa Djebel Chenoua* (1978), a daring blend of feature and documentary hitherto unseen in Arab cinema, supported by a poetic use of commentary. At the center of the film are the women, who 'kneaded and washed' the War of Independence. The only man in the film is handicapped, and moves around in a wheelchair. Significantly, perhaps, most of the women on the screen are either elderly or little girls. The silence of Algeria when colonized is paralleled with the silence of women in

Algerian society. *Al Zerda* (1980) is made entirely of archive footage shot by the French during colonial times in North Africa. Djebar organizes her material in chapters crossing over colonial boundaries of Algeria to feature Morocco and Egypt, for example, and asking questions of the images she shows. The result is subversion of the original footage by editing. 'Memory is a woman . . . veiled,' says Djebar in the commentary of this anti-colonialist film.

Noubat Nissa Djebel Chenoua/The Nouba of the Women of Mount Chenoua (1978, also known as *The Nouba of the Women*); *Al Zerda/The Zerda* (1980)   HS

'DOCTOR' FILMS

The enormous popular success of the first of this COMEDY cycle, *Doctor in the House* (Ralph Thomas, 1954) established actor Dirk Bogarde as a major box office attraction in BRITAIN – a position he enjoyed throughout the 1950s. In all, seven 'Doctor' films were made between 1954 and 1970, featuring more or less the same central characters and actors, though Bogarde himself appeared in only four of them. Although production values are relatively elaborate in these films, characterizations are minimal. The eponymous doctor, Simon Sparrow (Dirk Bogarde), moves through a universe of sketches and STEREOTYPES – the generic source of which appears to be the music-hall or variety show – linked only by a tenuous narrative thread, and by the actor's presence. Humor is constructed in two ways: on the difference between 'us' (asserting a shared understanding between the audience and the central character) and 'the other' (referring to alien groups such as foreigners or women) and on the audience's recognition of stereotypical situations more or less associated with the medical profession and its contexts.

The 'Doctor' films – particularly the later ones – have much in common with the contemporary and also very popular

'CARRY ON' series, but are altogether more polite. Through the access offered to the central figure the audience is invited not only to enjoy jokes made at the expense of most other inhabitants of the story but also to enter, occasionally, the selfless and fascinating world of those bound by the Hippocratic Oath. *Doctor in the House*, for example, has a scene where the newly qualified doctor on night call battles through snow to reach, just in time, a patient's delivery of her seventh child: the patient being appropriately grateful for the presence of this expert observer at the birth. *Doctor at Large* (1957), in one of its subtler moments, has a vignette of Dr Sparrow comforting a frightened woman scheduled for surgery. In scenes such as these the films come close to articulating exemplary 'human' values, but the women – the protagonists in such scenes being invariably female – are always passive and supplicant.

The representation of women in general in the 'Doctor' films is reactionary in the extreme; they are either subservient or predatory, a problem or a joke. This reading is reinforced by the episodic structure of the films, which encourages the audience to perceive all other characters through the eyes of the central (male) character. Though in each film Bogarde is 'partnered' by a female lead, such characters function solely as a channel of access for the audience to Bogarde, being rarely, if ever, of interest in themselves: it is always Bogarde's attributes on which the audience is invited to dwell. In so far as these female characters do invite empathy on the part of a female audience, it is in order to participate in the pleasures of Bogarde's charming naivety apropos the politics of gender, or in the delights of his apparent passivity or vulnerability. The performances offer a male fantasy about masculine desirability to women.

The 'Doctor' films were all produced by Betty Box for Rank and directed by Ralph Thomas: *Doctor in the House* (1954); *Doctor at Sea* (1955); *Doctor at Large* (1957); *Doctor in Love* (1960); *Doctor in Distress* (1963); *Doctor in Clover* (1966); *Doctor in Trouble* (1970).

Robert Murphy, *Realism and Tinsel: Cinema and Society in Britain, 1939–1968* (London and New York: Routledge, 1989)   JT

DOCUMENTARY

One of the most commonly held assumptions about the documentary as a film GENRE is that, unlike fiction film, it reveals the truth. It is difficult to find a definition to encompass the varied techniques and approaches in cinema, television, and video to which the word documentary has been applied. Pioneer of the BRITISH DOCUMENTARY MOVEMENT John Grierson once said it was 'all films made from natural material . . . where the camera shot on the spot.' But perhaps another of Grierson's definitions of the genre is nearer the mark: 'the creative treatment of actuality' – with the emphasis on creative. For Grierson, along with many later documentary practitioners and theorists, realized that there can never be in any sense an unmediated 'reflection of reality' through film, nor indeed any revelation of an absolute truth. For whatever is recorded on film is always a construction informed by social and political forces, economic constraints, aesthetic considerations, and whatever technology is at hand. The spectator of the documentary makes an active interpretation of this construction according to her own consciousness. There can never be a single meaning to a film – films' meanings change with time and circumstance, and are read at different times in different ways by their audiences. So despite assumptions to the contrary, documentaries can never be objective.

123

During the early 1970s, the first films made in association with the new women's movement in the West were documentaries. There have been many debates within feminism about the implications and politics of documentary filmmaking. Because film offers a moving image with sound, it is often seen as the best medium for truth-telling, and it was this aspect of film which was so attractive to feminist filmmakers of the time. The documentary could make visible with accuracy, immediacy, and accessibility hitherto hidden aspects of women's personal experience, and these could then be viewed as part of women's wider social and cultural oppression, and used as a means of raising consciousness. Films like *Growing Up Female* (Julia Reichert and Jim Klein, 1969), *Janie's Janie* (Geri Ashur, 1971), *Joyce at 34* (Joyce Chopra, 1972), *Woman to Woman* (Donna Deitch, 1975), often autobiographical, were made by American women filmmakers who were very active in this field. 'Biography, simplicity, trust between woman filmmaker and woman subject, a linear narrative structure, little selfconsciousness about the flexibility of the cinematic medium – these are what characterize the feminist documentaries of the 1970s,' according to feminist film theorist Julia Lesage. But from other quarters came criticism: these filmmakers were deemed privileged in terms of class and ethnicity; the documentary idea of revealing or telling a truth was seen as deceptive because what had in fact been arranged, set up, edited, was presented as if it 'just was,' with nothing more than a neutral, recording camera intervening between audience and actuality. In 1973, Claire JOHNSTON put forward the argument that for feminist cinema to be effective it must be a COUNTERCINEMA. But for all the valid criticisms made of feminist documentary, it nevertheless performs a vital function of informing, educating, activating, and stimulating audiences, particularly in the context of feminist campaigns and resistance movements outside the West. While not necessarily espousing western versions of feminism, documentary film and VIDEO have been important tools of struggle and education – and also areas in which women directors have made significant contributions – in such places as PALESTINE, CUBA, and throughout LATIN AMERICA.

Julia Lesage, 'Political Aesthetics of the Feminist Documentary Film', in *Films for Women*, ed. Charlotte Brunsdon (London: British Film Institute, 1986)

See also: AHRNE, MARIANNE; AMARAL, SUZANA; ANTI-APARTHEID FILM AND VIDEO; CAROLINA, ANA; CLARKE, SHIRLEY; COLE, JANIS, AND DALE, HOLLY; CRAIGIE, JILL; EMBER, JUDIT; ETHNOGRAPHIC FILM; FIELD, MARY; FOX, BERYL; HENNING-JENSEN, ASTRID; KOPPLE, BARBARA; MILLETT, KATE; NAIR, MIRA; NEW DAY FILMS; PERINCIOLA, CRISTINA; SAMPER, GABRIELA; SHUB, ESFIR; SINGER, GAIL; SOLNTSEVA, IULIIA; STUDIO D; SVILOVA, ELISAVETA; VARDA, AGNES; WEILL, CLAUDIA; YAMASAKI, TIZUKA; YANCOVIC, NIEVES   SP

DOERRIE, DORIS (1955–)

Born in WEST GERMANY, Doerrie attended film school in Munich after studying theater acting and film in the United States. A relative newcomer to West German cinema, she shot to international fame with the phenomenal success of her third feature film, *Maenner* (1985). A comedy of middle-class mores and manners, the film is about two seemingly opposite men – one a successful commercial art director, the other a halfhearted dropout.

Originally Doerrie wanted to be an actress, but while in New York she decided she preferred to be behind the camera. Although not particularly well known outside Germany until recently, she has in fact pursued a highly successful and prolific filmmaking career. Her graduation film at Munich, *Der erste Wal-*

zer (1978), was screened at the Hof, Luebeck, and Berlin film festivals, and broadcast on Bavarian television. Since 1978 she has worked for various German television stations making both documentaries and feature films, including the children's film *Paula aus Portugal* (1979) and a film about a teenage girl, *Dazwischen* (1981). Such were the audience ratings for the latter that a West German television station decided to back her first cinema feature, *Mitten ins Herz* (1983). Submitted as the West German entry to the 1984 Venice Film Festival, *Mitten ins Herz* is about a young woman hired by a dentist to live in his house. Her next feature film, *Im Innern des Wals* (1984), is also about a young woman and her relationship to an older man, this time her father.

Whereas in her first two cinema films Doerrie explores the effects of men on women, in *Maenner* she has moved on to examine men themselves. Dismissed by some critics as a comedy of yuppie conformity, *Maenner* has nevertheless collected an array of awards. While critics are obviously divided over the film, Doerrie's success has continued with her latest film, *Paradies* (1986), a story of love and passion starring Katherina Thalbach, who was awarded West Germany's top prize for her performance.

Der erste Walzer/The First Waltz (1978); *Haettest was Gscheits gelernt/If Ya'd Only Learned Something Practical* (1978); *Paula aus Portugal/Paula from Portugal* (1979); *Von Romantik keine Spur: Martina (19) wird Schaeferin/No Trace of Romance: Martina (19) Becomes a Shepherdess* (1980/81); *Dazwischen/In Between* (1981); *Unter lauter Schafen/Among Noisy Sheep* (1981); *Mitten ins Herz/Right in the Heart* (1983); *Im Innern des Wals/In the Belly of the Whale* (1984); *Maenner/Men* (1985); *Paradies/Paradise* (1986)

Marcia Pally, 'Open Doerrie', *Film Comment*, vol. 22, no. 5 (1986)   JK

DOMINANT CINEMA

This term is used in FILM THEORY to refer to the institutions involved in producing films and marketing them internationally to a mass audience, and to the distinctive stylistic characteristics of the films themselves. While Hollywood – or, more precisely, the HOLLYWOOD STUDIO SYSTEM and CLASSICAL HOLLYWOOD CINEMA in combination – is usually considered the limit case of dominant cinema, its characteristic institutions and styles are not confined to this cinema which has dominated the world's screens since the 1910s. In fact, one of the defining features of dominant cinema is its pervasiveness as a model for film industries and filmmakers the world over. This dual pattern of cultural domination has an IDEOLOGICAL component in the expectations audiences bring to their viewing of films. The many varieties of cinema which do not fit these expectations – certain NATIONAL CINEMAs, AVANT-GARDE FILM, COUNTERCINEMA, FEMINIST INDEPENDENT FILM, for example – tend inevitably to be pushed to the cultural margins by dominant cinema, with the result that, with the occasional exception, such cinemas must constantly struggle against the dominant model, be sucked in by it, be raided for new and superficially applied ideas, or be regarded by audiences as 'other,' difficult, inaccessible. One of the objectives of the INDEPENDENT CINEMA movement has been to counter the 'difficult' tag by promoting different ways of viewing – ways which could transform our understanding of mainstream, as well as of 'marginal,' films.

Annette Kuhn, *Women's Pictures: Feminism and Cinema* (London: Routledge & Kegan Paul, 1982)   AKu

DOOLITTLE, HILDA see HD

DORS, DIANA (1931–84)

Dors (born Diana Fluck) stands out among British actresses of the 1950s for her refreshing independence *vis-à-vis* the media and the marketing contexts through which her performances and persona were circulated. Hailed as BRITAIN's answer to those other BLONDE sex symbols Marilyn MONROE and Brigitte BARDOT, she exhibited none of the tragic vulnerability of the former; nor allowed herself to be restricted to the typecast 'sex-kitten' roles of the latter during the high points of their respective careers in the fifties. Although she appeared in sixty-three films between 1946 and 1984, the fifties were undoubtedly Dors's most productive years, and it was unfortunate for her that the straitlaced prurience of the period emphasized the difficulties of her flamboyant private life at the expense of any serious discussion of her performances. One of the most memorable of these was as Ruth Ellis, the last woman in Britain to be hanged for murder, in *Yield to the Night* (J Lee-Thompson, 1956). She spends the major part of the film in the condemned cell, unmade up and wearing a voluminous white nightdress. The rapport between her character and that of her warder, played by Yvonne Mitchell, is a notable portrayal of a relationship between two women, rare in films of this time.

During the 1960s and 1970s Dors's film roles were less frequent, her more successful work being on stage and, latterly, on television, where she briefly hosted a chat show. Interviewed in 1984, she appeared satisfied with her career to date ('I think today I'm regarded as a pretty good all-rounder') and to be looking forward to developing her acting skills free of the constraints of her fifties SEX GODDESS image. She was playing the part of Violet in Joseph Losey's film *Steaming* (1985) when she died of cancer at the early age of fifty-two.

Dors stands out, with hindsight, as an independent woman able to use the structures available in the excessively patriarchal cultural climate of the fifties and sixties to further her career while also, paradoxically, falling victim to the same climate in the successive traumas of her private life.

Diana Dors, *For Adults Only* (London: Star, 1978)   JT

DULAC, GERMAINE (1882–1942)

The first feminist filmmaker and a key figure in the 'first AVANT GARDE' of the 1920s, Dulac was born in FRANCE as Germaine Saisset-Schneider. She started her career as a photographer and wrote for two feminist journals, *La Fronde* and *La Française*. Enthusiasm for the cinema and the greater openings for women created by World War I made her, well in her thirties, start her own production company, Delia Film. Her first films were conventional melodramas, but a chance meeting with theoretician Louis Delluc in 1917 started both of them formulating the tenets of the 'first French avant garde,' also known as French Impressionism. Dulac was at the center – indeed, has been called 'the heart' – of this group of intellectuals and filmmakers (also including Jean and Marie EPSTEIN, Marcel L'Herbier and Abel Gance) devoted to promoting the 'seventh art,' through filmmaking, film education (they created the first *ciné-clubs*), and FILM CRITICISM.

Dulac's films from *Ames de fous* (1917) onward increasingly privileged the representation of atmosphere, impressions, and inner feelings over narrative, and showed her interest in pure movement. Her first critical success was *La Fête espagnole* (1919), scripted by Delluc, but her major work is *La Souriante Madame Beudet/The Smiling Madame Beudet* (1923), a conventional narrative which she transforms into a sympathetic portrayal of the frustrations and desires, and eventual revolt, of a bourgeoise woman against her oppressive husband – using superimpositions, dissolves, and slow motion to make the spectator share the HEROINE's point of view. Dulac alternated avant-garde productions with fairly conventional films like *Gossette* (1923),

Dulac's *The Smiling Madame Beudet*

but still aspired to a more abstract style, what she called 'the integral film . . . a visual symphony made of rhythmic images.' A supreme expression of this is *La Coquille et le clergyman/The Seashell and the Clergyman* (1927), scripted by the Surrealist Antonin Artaud, which opened in Paris before a riotous audience who vilified Dulac for 'feminizing' Artaud. Beyond this controversy, the film remains a rare attempt at rendering the processes of the Unconscious on the screen. She went on to make abstract or documentary film essays on poems, musical pieces, and the famous *Germination d'un haricot* (1928) – the stop-motion record of the germination of a seed – and lectured on film. She was head of Gaumont newsreels until her death.

Aesthetically, Dulac's films have been the object of some controversy. Importantly though, as feminist critic Sandy Flitterman-Lewis points out, what characterizes her work is a deep commitment to feminist issues, and above all a 'search for a new cinematic language capable of expressing female desire.'

Germaine Dulac's films include: *Les Sœurs ennemies* (1916); *Vénus victrix* (1916); *Ames de fous* (1917); *La Cigarette* (1919); *La Fête espagnole* (1919); *La Belle dame sans merci* (1920); *La Mort du soleil* (1921); *Gossette* (1923); *La Souriante Madame Beudet/The Smiling Madame Beudet* (1923); *Ame d'artiste* (1925); *La Coquille et le clergyman/The Seashell and the Clergyman* (1927); *Germination d'un haricot* (1928); *La Princesse Mandane* (1929); *Thèmes et variations* (1929)

Sandy Flitterman-Lewis, *To Desire Differently: Feminism and the French Cinema* (Urbana: University of Illinois Press, 1990)   GV

DUMB BLONDES *see* BLONDES

DURAS, MARGUERITE (1914–)

A novelist, playwright, and filmmaker (born Marguerite Donnadieu in French Indo-China), Duras is a major postwar literary figure in FRANCE, and recently won the Goncourt Prize for *L'Amant/*

The Lover. Duras wrote screenplays – notably for Alain Resnais's *Hiroshima mon amour* (1959) – and co-directed an adaptation of her play *La Musica* (1966) before fully taking on filmmaking in 1969 with *Détruire, dit-elle*. Since then she has conducted writing and filmmaking as interlocking activities, her novels, plays, and films subtly echoing and cross-referencing each other. For instance, her films *La Femme du Gange* (1974) and *India Song* (1975) and the novels *The Vice-Consul, The Ravishing of Lol V. Stein*, and *L'Amour* all rework the same key events and characters.

As a writer and filmmaker Duras is a MODERNIST, deliberately seeking, like Jean-Luc GODARD or Chantal AKERMAN, to deconstruct – or at least to question – the conventions of classical NARRATIVE, and to challenge the spectator into a more active participation in the narrative process. She works on SOUND and image with equal intensity, her lyrical soundtracks – sometimes with her own mesmerizing voice, as in *Le Camion* (1977) – in some cases assuming a separate identity: *Son nom de Venise dans Calcutta désert* (1976) matches an entirely new set of images to the soundtrack of *India Song*. Duras's approach is minimalist and allusive, and she has been criticized for the ahistorical nature of her characters, mostly drawn from the leisured upper classes. However, a social protest, though oblique, is discernible: for example the colonial legacy in *India Song*, and concentration camps in *Aurélia Steiner* (1979).

Duras's vision is bleak, particularly of women's condition, which she describes as 'suicidal.' Though by no means a con-ventional feminist, she concentrates in her films on female desire and on women's experience, in particular in their relation to time and language. For Duras, silence is a form of female resistance. However negative such a worldview, one could agree with French feminist critic Françoise Audé that 'if Marguerite Duras's characters are too intent on being engulfed in "submissiveness" for feminists to adopt them wholeheartedly . . . they painfully endorse the destitution which is at the heart of the feminist protest.'

> *Doris von Kappelhoff made her cinema debut in an unlikely vehicle,* Romance on the High Seas *(1948). Who is this swashbuckler?*

La Musica (1966, co-d. Paul Seban); *Détruire, dit-elle/Destroy, She Said* (1969); *Jaune le soleil* (1971); *Nathalie Granger* (1973); *La Femme du Gange* (1974); *India Song* (1975); *Son nom de Venise dans Calcutta désert* (1976); *Des journées entières dans les arbres/Days in the Trees* (1977); *Baxter, Vera Baxter* (1977); *Le Camion/The Lorry* (1977), *Le Navire Night* (1979); *Aurélia Steiner* (1979)

E Ann Kaplan, 'Silence as Female Resistance in Marguerite Duras's *Nathalie Granger* (1972)', in *Women and Film: Both Sides of the Camera* (London and New York: Methuen, 1983)   GV

DUTCH CINEMA *see* NETHERLANDS

EALING STUDIOS

Looking back at the 1940s and 1950s, it seems that Ealing productions occupy a disproportionate status in the history of BRITAIN's film industry. Perhaps this is because of the sheer number of films produced – nearly a hundred over twenty years. The Ealing COMEDIES, though perhaps the most celebrated of these films, were by no means the only GENRE represented: Ealing studios made MELODRAMAS, police dramas, and even ventured into FANTASY. Contemporary critical acclaim is also undoubtedly a factor: Ealing productions were explicitly associated with culture and quality. Consequently, the reassertion of middle-class hegemony in postwar British cultural life, so disrupted by the popular culture and state socialism of the war period, is elided with an international assertion of British 'quality' in the face of the perceived threat of American culture.

The studios were purpose-built in 1931 in the west London suburb of Ealing by the production company Associated Talking Pictures (ATP). In 1938 Michael Balcon, head of production for ATP, took the name 'Ealing' for the production company itself. As film historian Charles Barr says, 'films were now not only made at Ealing but *by* Ealing.' The forties and early fifties were remarkably stable, thanks partly to a deal which Balcon made in 1944 with the giant Rank Organization which lasted till 1955, when the studios at Ealing were sold. From 1955 until its final demise in 1958, the Ealing production company continued to operate from MGM's studios at Borehamwood. It was at Ealing, however, as Balcon recorded on a plaque at the site, that 'during a quarter of a century were made many films projecting Britain and the British character.' Balcon built up a 'stable' of directors, technicians, and actors, most of whom, it seems, subscribed to his own aspirations to 'put film to work in the national interest in wartime,' as he put it in a 1939 memorandum. Given the middle-class composition of the management and production teams, it is not surprising to find that the most convincing representations in the films are of middle-class characters.

Typically these films deal with communities in which collective and democratic values are tested, proved, and celebrated. Ealing's dominant personnel, however, were not only middle-class but also male. Conventional assumptions about the appropriate social roles of women are – not surprisingly – recycled and confirmed through Ealing's fictions. Rose Sandigate (Googie Withers) in *It Always Rains on Sunday* (Robert Hamer, 1947) is shown to be a transgressive HEROINE during the course of the narrative, but her consequent suffering is emphasized and she is pulled back into the patriarchal order at the story's end. Christine Garland (Phyllis Calvert) in *Mandy* (Alexander Mackendrick, 1952) also flouts her husband's authority, doing so for the sake of her child and at some cost to herself: again narrative resolution entails a reuniting of the family unit. Christine's task has been to persuade her husband to look to the future, to move with the times. The emblematic closing shot of the reunited parents watching their deaf-mute daughter playing with her contemporaries on the bomb site of the Chelsea Embankment summarizes the adult female's role as that

129

of maintaining the social fabric. As such it is typical of Ealing's rather selfconsciously positive contribution to the cohesion of British society – a society, it would seem from the resolutions of Ealing films, in which divisions of race, class, and gender were entirely absent.

Charles Barr, *Ealing Studios* (London: Cameron & Tayleur in association with David & Charles, 1977)   *JT*

EAST GERMANY

Even within EASTERN EUROPE, East German cinema remains relatively unknown outside the German Democratic Republic (GDR) – for a variety of reasons, some GDR-based, some a result of the international climate. Before the GDR gained diplomatic recognition in 1973, western film distributors could not, or would not, buy GDR films. The only GDR film studio, DEFA, has tended also to foster GDR-specific themes in an effort to educate as well as to entertain the East German public, and this has limited GDR films' appeal to wider audiences. In addition DEFA have not encouraged technical and formal innovations, which have often been prerequisites for the entry of East European films into the West's commercial circuits. A third reason was that films had to be dubbed or subtitled in Hungary or West Berlin, costing scarce hard currency: this has meant that very few – and often not the best – GDR films have been available for export. Finally, and perhaps most substantively, the GDR has had few directors of exceptional talent.

It is especially striking that in a country which justifiably vaunts its record on economic, social, and legal support for women's equality, the vast majority of camera operators and sound technicians, as well as directors, are men. The only branch of the industry dominated by women is cutting/editing. The few women film directors there are have emerged only in the last ten years, and there is virtually no published material available about their work. However, in feature films, two women deserve mention: Evelyn Schmitt, for her films *Ein Seitensprung/Escapade* (1979) and *Das Fahrrad/The Bicycle* (1982); and Iris GUSNER. The GDR's television studios produce a number of features, and both Vera Loebner, whose adaptations of GDR novels enjoy great popularity, and Christa Muehl, who has filmed Brecht short stories, are doing interesting work.

The branch of the GDR film industry best known abroad is DOCUMENTARIES. Annelie Thorndike and Gitta Nickel were pioneers in the field, and the male partnership of Heynowski and Scheumann is now internationally known. More recently, Petra Tschoertner's exploration of partner relationships *Hinter den Fenstern/Behind the Windows* (1988?) won prizes in Mannheim. The real box office hit of 1988 in the GDR was Helke Misselwitz's *Winter Ade/Farewell to Winter* (1987), a feature-length documentary based on interviews with women and providing a feminist perspective on East German society.

A theme which dominated many early GDR films – often in overly simplistic, didactic terms as a result of the cultural edicts of SOCIALIST REALISM – is the recent Nazi past and World War II. A common plot line portrays the journey of young boys, seduced from their school desks by tales of heroism and glory in selfless death for the Fatherland, to ultimate disillusion and despair at the reality of Nazi war crimes, and ending with the rosy glow of potential involvement in a humane, socialist future. More recent films have dealt with the fascist past in a more subtle manner. An interesting example of this is the film *Stiehlke, Heinz, Fuenfzehn/Heinz Stiehlke, Fifteen Years Old* (Michael Kann, 1986–7). This follows the 'adventures' of a fifteen-year-old who suddenly discovers he is a social outcast when it transpires that his father, who has fallen at the front as a highly decorated Wehrmacht officer, was in fact Jewish. The Fatherland Heinz had completely identified with now rejects him, and after his mother dies in a bomb raid he becomes an outlaw. The film is not so much about the youth's struggle to survive the final year of World War II as about the psychic confusion triggered in a teenager's search for identity in a world where he no longer fits.

More recent GDR films focus on personal and social problems in contemporary East German society. The depiction of women in early films about the recent past confined them to stock roles not very different from those allotted them by the Nazis, namely, mother or SS concentration camp guard, heartless initiator into the secrets of sex, or innocent young girl symbolizing humane values which could transcend the oppressive Nazi reality: the virgin/whore dichotomy was close to the surface. By contrast, some

> Asked why her films about poets and painters are about famous men, this contemporary Caribbean filmmaker replied: 'Because governments are in the hands of men and I can get money to make films about famous men.' Who is she?

recent films on GDR society portray the real contradictions women face in their everyday personal and social relationships. After the overt politicization of earlier films dealing with the Nazi legacy, it is undoubtedly the films which deal with GDR social reality, and focus on women's struggles to establish their autonomy in the face of ongoing contradictions (despite wide-ranging legislation and social provision in their favor) which currently enjoy the greatest box office success within East Germany.

Heiko R Blum and others, *Film in der DDR* (Munich: Hanser, 1977)

See also: GERMANY; WEST GERMANY   BE

EASTERN EUROPE

It is impossible to speak of 'East European' cinema as a single body of work, just as it is impossible to make general statements about East European literature or politics, or the economies of the East European countries. Far from presenting a monolithic structure, the situation is very diverse, with both practical conditions (training, film studios) and output (amount, quality) differing widely from country to country. However, from the point of view of women in the film industry, some generalizations can safely be made. Women directors, scriptwriters, and producers are very much in the minority. The few 'big name' women directors such as Márta MESZAROS in Hungary or Larissa SHEPITKO in the Soviet Union are individual exceptions, not representative of any trend toward greater parity in the film industry. It remains difficult, despite universal (though very differently realized) policies in favor of equality of opportunity for women in all the East European socialist countries, for women to be taken seriously and to succeed in this industry. A scene in Mészáros's *Napló Szerelmeimnek/Diary for My Loves* in which the central figure is ridiculed for wanting to become a director – acting is surely a much more suitable profession for women – remains as true today as it was for the early 1950s depicted in the film. Difficulties like unsocial hours and travel for directors, or the heavy equipment handling for camera operators, go hand in hand with traditional prejudice to perpetuate the status quo.

The best-known film-producing countries in Eastern Europe outside the SOVIET UNION are undoubtedly CZECHOSLOVAKIA, HUNGARY, and POLAND. In all three, a film industry was well established before World War II. Albania, Bulgaria, Romania, and Yugoslavia have smaller and on the whole less well-established film industries. Among the few women filmmakers working in these countries are Binka

Zhelyazkova of Bulgaria (*When We Were Young* [1960], *Golyamoto Noshtno Kupane/The Big Bath Night* [1980]) and Elisabeta Bostan of Romania, who specializes in children's films. Throughout Eastern Europe, the fortunes of film production since 1945 have fluctuated in line with political developments in the various countries. There was general pressure in the 1950s and early 1960s to produce films which would impart an optimistic and committed view of contemporary reality – building socialism. This cultural policy, developed from the theory of SOCIALIST REALISM, constrained both styles (it was anti-experiment and anti-abstraction) and themes (it favored depictions of concrete social reality in the factory or on the land) of early East European films.

For a variety of reasons – their own countries' cultural policies undoubtedly among them – some directors (such as Miloš Forman of Czechoslovakia or Roman Polanski and Jerzy Skolimowski of Poland) accepted the lure of Hollywood and the West. On the other hand, even prior to glasnost, Hungary, and more recently Romania, have attracted western production companies as venues for autonomous productions or for co-productions. This is because despite bureaucratic difficulties these countries offer low-cost, high-quality facilities and actors.

The 1970s and 1980s, particularly since glasnost, have seen more differentiated developments; so that, for example, Hungarian cinema today – like its Soviet counterpart – is in a ferment of change, producing features and documentaries which rediscover and confront the hidden history of the postwar, and particularly the Stalinist, years. In Czechoslovakia and EAST GERMANY, on the other hand, there is still reluctance to lift the veil on such painful topics. However, socialist control and censorship of scripts in Eastern Europe has never prevented production of some of the greatest films of the postwar period by internationally acclaimed directors.

David W Paul (ed.), *Politics, Art and Committment in the Eastern European Cinema* (New York: St Martin's Press, 1983) BE

EDITING

The selection and arrangement of shots in a film is called editing (or sometimes montage). The main function of editing is to connect segments of material into narrative, spatial, rhythmic, patterned, or rhetorical orders. Film theorists Lev Kuleshov and Sergei Eisenstein argued that editing has the capacity to create filmic meaning: Kuleshov's famous tests of actors intercut with various objects or events, and his 'creative geography' experiments, are used to support such observations. These editing possibilities were also explored by AVANT-GARDE filmmaker Maya DEREN. In the 1920s, Eisenstein theorized the different forms of what he called montage, while the French avant-gardist Germaine DULAC argued that editing should promote optical harmonies and a film ought to be a 'visual symphony made of rhythmic images.'

Certain editing patterns are used very widely. Crosscutting is alternating between two different places; and framing and joining shots so that the camera remains on one side of an imaginary line drawn through characters is the 180-degree rule in the continuity editing system which characterizes CLASSICAL HOLLYWOOD CINEMA. Continuity editing refers to matching actions and ensuring spectators can locate characters easily within a space: eyeline matches and point-of-view shots (when the camera takes the actual position of the character who is looking) are patterns which suggest what characters are looking at; and alternating between shots of two characters in a dialogue is shot/reverse shot editing.

Theorists who claim that editing patterns promote the appearance of continuity or identification with characters argue that editing reassures spectators and promotes their PLEASURE in following film's organization of time and space. Following from this, feminist theories of the LOOK argue that these editing patterns contribute significantly to cinema's objectification of women.

JaS

EGYPT

The oldest and most prolific of ARAB CINEMAS (boasting around two thousand films), Egyptian cinema was born in the 1920s. In the most industrialized and powerful Arab country of the time, it benefited from the solid infrastructure of a real film industry backed by a nascent bourgeoisie, and produced mostly MELODRAMAs void of social content and artistic merit, pale imitations of Hollywood movies. Later on, singers and belly-dancers became an essential ingredient which enabled Egyptian cinema to dominate Arab big (and now small) screens. When social problems surfaced in films, the predicament of women was occasionally dealt with. After 1952, with the arrival of Nasser, the prevailing socially aware and anti-imperialist climate stimulated filmmakers to make more 'patriotic' films such as God is With Us (Ahmad Badrakhan, 1956), about the Suez affair; and Gamila Al Gazaeria/Djamila the Algerian (Youssef Chahine, 1958), about the famous Algerian woman jailed and tortured by the French during Algeria's war of independence. The weight of censorship and market forces had various effects on more gifted or socially aware filmmakers. Fatine Abdelwahab stuck to conventional commercial COMEDIES to convey (occasionally) his social message – which includes support for women's liberation. Salah Abu Seif chose to make 'one film for myself and three for the producers.' Hussein Kamal, after a few honorable films, went back to routine. Youssef Chahine became more personal in style and bold in content, often reaching authorial scope. Radical author Toufic Saleh succumbed to the pressure of repeated banning of his films and years out of work: his Long Days (1981), prais-

ing the fascist Iraqi President Saddam Hussein, was contrary to what he stood for. Attempts at radical cinema such as those by Gamaat Al Cinema al Guedida/ The Group of the New Cinema were shortlived: this group produced a one-off, if interesting, critique of Egyptian society in Oughnia Ala Al Mamar/Song of The Track (Ali Abdelkhalek, 1972). Sporadically, films such as Al Baree/The Innocent (Atef Al Tayyeb, 1986), about the torture of leftwing prisoners, are released – but with a disclaimer denying any link with reality.

Women have played an important part as producers since the earliest days of Egyptian cinema. Aziza Amir produced and starred in Leila (1927), one of the earliest Egyptian films. Assia Dagher, Lebanese-born, prospered as an actress and producer in Cairo, launching her little niece Mary Queeny. Later Queeny, now a STAR, married Ahmed Galal, her aunt's favorite director and scriptwriter, and with him built the 'Galal Studios.' After his death in 1947 she ran the studio alone and started her own film company, 'Mary Queeny Films,' producing and acting. Since the 1930s, actresses have directed films in Egypt. Both Aziz Amir (Ghafferi An Khataouki/Pay for Your Mistake) and Fatma Rouchdi (Al Zawag/The Marriage) produced, played in, and directed their films. Bahiga Hafez directed Leila, bint el Sahra/Leila, Daughter of the Desert (1936) and Leila al Badawiyya/Leila the Bedouin (1943). Amina Mohamed directed a single film, Tita Wong (1936). Apparently, the most powerful of these pioneering women (many of whose films are lost) did not change conventional forms and contents, nor challenge social taboos detrimental to women. But if it did not matter for the film industry whether a he or a she reproduced patriarchal stereotypes, the films did prove, as Mary Queeny put it, that 'Women are as capable as men of doing everything.'

Later Egyptian films show the double moral standard suffered by women. Infringement of social taboos, loss of virginity, and subsequent dishonor lead inevitably to death: *El Bostagui/The Postman* (Hussein Kamal, 1964) is one of the best-made films about this issue. The problems faced by women in a changing society also found expression: *El Abocato Madiha/Madiha the Lawyer* (Youssef Wahba, 1950) rejects modern ideas about women's work; whereas *El Oustaza Fatma/Solicitor Fatma* (Fatine Abdelwahab, 1952) supports women's work and equality with men. *Ana Hourra/I Am Free* (Salah Abu Seif, 1959) poses the problem of women's liberation and its limits in a male-dominated society. Later on, social contradictions – including those of gender – began to be dealt with more openly on the screen, encouraged by Nasser, who appointed a woman minister. *Zawgati, Mudir Am/My Wife is Director-General* (Fatine Abdelwahab, 1966), a commercial film based on an impeccably feminist script by two men (Abdel Hamid Gawda Sahar and Saad Wahba), portrays the difficulty of a top civil servant who becomes her husband's boss in a ministry. She is more efficient, rational, and principled, as well as kinder to her staff, than her male predecessors. Even a devout backward Muslim (a bold attack on religion) is in tears when she resigns after her husband turns her private life into hell before the compulsory happy ending.

After 1967, the political radicalization of directors led to a more true-to-life representation of women. Youssef Chahine abandoned previous STEREO-TYPES to portray women as more revolutionary and politically conscious than men in his best film, *Al Ousfour/The Sparrow* (1975). In *Iskindiria . . . Leh?/Alexandria Why?* (1978) a communist militant daughter of an anti-Zionist Jew has to face the world with an illegitimate child whose father is in prison. In a more commercial vein, *Ouridou Hall/I Want a Solution* (Said Marzouk, 1975) – a film said to have been instrumental in changing the law – demands the right of women to divorce in an Islamic society where this is solely the man's decision. But social reforms in Egypt did not always affect the portrayal of women in films. Shadi Abdelsalam depicts them in a rather traditional way in his haunting *Al Moumia/Nights of Counting the Years* (1969), in which the woman is either a mother representing blind tradition or a prostitute. Post-1967 defeat brought about a revival of documentaries, a genre hitherto connected with government propaganda. Attiat El Abnoudi made her debut with the award-winning short *Hesan El Tin/Horse of Mud* (1971), describing the wretched working conditions of women in a brick factory. The film was banned as being inspired by 'imported ideology.' Her style varies between the ethnological *Sandwich* (1975) and the poetic *Bihar El Atache/Thirsty Sea* (1984). *Permissible Dreams* (1983) contrasts the rationality and progressiveness of a peasant woman eager to educate her daughter with the backwardness of her husband and father-in-law, who spend the miserable family budget on useless western gadgets. Other women, such as Asma Al Bakri, Leila Abu Seif, and Lebanese-born Nabiha Loufti, have also expressed themselves in documentaries. In fiction, most women directors work in Egyptian television, whose head was until recently a woman. However, Nadia Hamza, Nadia Salem, and Ines Daghidi work in mainstream commercial cinema, their films often reflecting women's problems. For example, *Afwan Ayouha Al Kanoun/Sorry, It's the Law* (Ines Daghidi, 1985) exposes the penal code's double standard in regard to adultery through a woman lawyer defending her girlfriend, a university teacher accused of attempted murder. It has been argued, however, that the conventional style of these films defeats their purpose.

M Khan, *An Introduction to the Egyptian Cinema* (London: Informatics, 1969) HS

EIRE *see* IRELAND

EISNER, LOTTE (1896–1983)

Lotte Eisner grew up in Berlin in a Jewish merchant family. She studied archeology and art history, both of which greatly influenced her approach to cinema: elements of style became an important criterion for her, and she described the research she had to do for her books as 'archeological excavations.' In 1927 she became the first well-known woman FILM CRITIC in GERMANY (for the *Film-Kurier*). In the course of this work she met, among others, the directors Fritz Lang, G W Pabst, Bertolt Brecht, and Sergei Eisenstein.

:**************************************:
: *'First run' sounds sporting, but what does* :
: *this term mean for cinema?* :
:**************************************:

In 1933 she had to emigrate to Paris, where she worked as a correspondent for several journals. She subsequently spent some time in a concentration camp. In 1934 she met Henri Langlois, who would later found the Cinémathèque Française, and in 1945 became his closest colleague and chief curator of the Cinémathèque. Together, Eisner and Langlois collected and saved thousands of films. Lotte Eisner arranged programs for retrospectives, festivals, exhibitions, and collections, and published many essays in the JOURNAL *Revue du cinéma* (later *Cahiers du cinéma*). She worked at the Cinémathèque until 1975.

Eisner's first book, *The Haunted Screen*, which is about German Expressionist cinema, was published in 1952: a time when, as she says, 'there was hardly any interest in cinematic art of the past in Germany. . . . Everything seemed cut off from the past, the terrible years had swept away yesterday's culture.' Eisner did not want to see cinema in isolation from German history but, in analyzing its style and content, wanted to include the social history and mentality of the nation from which it was born. It also seemed important to her 'to apply the methods of stylistics and development of style evolved by art historians . . . in order to outline the cinematic history of a nation in broad terms.' In 1964 her study

of F W Murnau was published, followed some years later by her book on Fritz Lang.

Lotte Eisner, *The Haunted Screen: Expressionism in German Film and the Influence of Max Reinhardt* (Berkeley: University of California Press, 1969) *AB*

ELEK, JUDIT (1937–)

Elek entered the Academy of Theater and Film Art as the only woman in her class in 1955. She graduated with István Szabo and others of HUNGARY's 'first generation' directors in 1961, and it was for this group that the Béla Balázs Studio for young directors was founded. Elek is referred to as one of the first exponents of so-called 'cinéma direct' style. The very high regard accorded her work in French-speaking countries is exemplified by the retrospectives of her films at the WOMEN'S FILM FESTIVALS in CRETEIL in 1980 and in MONTREAL in 1986. In 1987 she was awarded the prestigious Chevalier de l'Ordre des Arts et des Lettres by the French government.

Her first film was the short feature *Találkozás/Encounter* (1963), portraying the first meeting of two 'lonely hearts' brought together by an advertisement in the newspaper personal ads section. In 1964 her novel *Awakening* was published. Elek is perhaps best known for her two documentary dramas about the fate of two girls struggling to free themselves from the constraints imposed by traditional attitudes in the Hungarian village where Elek lived for four years while making *Istenmezején 1972–73/A Hungarian Village* (1974) and *Egyszerü történet/A Commonplace Story* (1975). Currently she is working on a feature based on a real historical incident: the trial in the last century of Jews accused of the ritual killing of a young girl.

Találkozás/Encounter (1963); *Kastélyók lakoi/The Inhabitants of Manor Houses* (1966); *Meddig él az ember/How Long does Man Matter?* (1968); *Sziget a szárazföldön/ The Lady from Constantinople* (1969);

Találkozunk 1972-ben/We'll Meet in 1972 (1971); *Istenmezején 1972–73/A Hungarian Village* (1974); *Egyszerü történet/A Commonplace Story* (1975); *Majd holnap/Maybe Tomorrow* (1979); *Martinovics* (1981); *Mária-Nap/Maria's Day* (1983)   BE/ER

EMBER, JUDIT (1935–   )

Ember taught Hungarian and history for five years before training as a film director from 1964 to 1968. For a few years she worked in the studio for popular scientific films, and several of her films have been produced for the Béla Balázs experimental studios in HUNGARY. Ember is considered to be the pioneer of feature-length 'talking heads' DOCUMENTARIES which dig up sometimes uncomfortable historical truths. Her choice of subjects unpopular with the authorities has meant that her scripts often fail to get passed, and her career has been dogged by struggles to get films on important issues accepted. Her film *Pocspetri*, about a village show trial in 1948, was released only in 1988, although it was made in 1982. *Mistletoes* (1978) was a drama documentary about three generations of women in a gypsy family, played by themselves.

20 év múltán/After Twenty Years (1964); *Látogatóban/Visiting* (1965); *Színpad/The Stage* (1967–8); *Tisztavatás/Inauguration of Officers* (1969); *Vitaklub/Discussion Club* (1970); *A Határozat/The Resolution* (1970); *Az emlékezet tartóssága/The Durability of Memory* (1974); *Az olcsóját és a jóját/The Cheap One and the Good One* (1974); *Kavaró/Mixer* (1975); *Tantörténet/Instructive Story* (1976); *Én nem is láttam ilyet, de nem is csináltam/I've Never Seen or Done Anything Like it* (1976); *Fagyöngyök/Mistletoes* (1978); *Pocspetri* (1982)

BE/ER

EMBRAFILME

Founded at the end of the 1960s in BRAZIL, Embrafilme is a state-financed enterprise which contributes to film production and distribution, drawing its funds from a tax on cinema tickets. In 1974, President Geisel appointed as its director filmmaker Roberto Farias, who turned it into a powerful cultural stimulus, financing the work of young filmmakers and ensuring proper distribution for local products. Soon Embrafilme became, after US companies, the largest film distributor in the Americas; their policy of backing national filmmakers paid off and they achieved many box office successes. While not all filmmakers approve of state financing of the industry, even the most rebellious have accepted Embrafilme's distribution. It would seem beyond doubt that without state financing, Brazilian films would not have managed to reach large sectors of the local population.   NT

EPSTEIN, MARIE (1899–   )

A scriptwriter and filmmaker living and working in FRANCE who, when not totally ignored by film histories, is overshadowed by her two collaborators: her brother Jean Epstein, and Jean Benoît-Lévy. Born Marie-Antonine Epstein to Polish parents, she began in the AVANT-GARDE milieu as assistant director and actress in her brother's *Cœur fidèle* (1923); she then contributed several scripts which he directed and which are generally recognized to be among his best. Her major work, however, was with Benoît-Lévy – first as scriptwriter, then as scriptwriter and co-director, starting with *Le Cœur de Paris* (1931). Their second co-directed film, *La Maternelle* (1933), adapted from a populist novel by Léon Frapié, is recognized as one of the best early French sound films. She went on working with Benoît-Lévy throughout the 1930s.

Marie Epstein's work, both as scriptwriter and as director, shows concern for education and social issues, in its observation of popular milieus, children, and youth – in particular *Peau de pêche* (1929), the celebrated *La Maternelle*, and *Altitude 3200* (1938), a film that shares the

Popular Front ethos of a new, healthier, lifestyle – as well as an interest in women (*Hélène* [1936]). After the war she made a documentary on atomic energy and later worked at the Cinémathèque Française, painstakingly restoring silent films, among them some of her brother's, and Abel Gance's *Napoléon*.

Assistant director on *Cœur fidèle* (1923, dir. Jean Epstein). Scripts for Jean Epstein: *L'Affiche* (1924); *Le Double amour* (1925); *Six et demi onze* (1927); *Vive la vie* (1937). Scripts for Jean Benoît-Lévy: *Ames d'enfants* (1928); *Peau de pêche*, *Maternité* (1929). Films scripted by Marie Epstein and co-directed with Jean-Benoît-Lévy: *Le Cœur de Paris* (1931); *La Maternelle* (1933); *Itto* (1934); *Hélène* (1936); *La Mort du cygne* (1937); *Altitude 3200* (1938); *Le Feu de paille* (1939). As director: *La Grande espérance* (1953).

Sandy Flitterman-Lewis, *To Desire Differently: Feminism and the French Cinema* (Urbana: University of Illinois Press, 1990)   GV

EROTICISM

The term eroticism frequently arises in discussions of PORNOGRAPHY. Whereas the latter term tends to be used pejoratively, eroticism is seen as more elevated. The distinction often made is that pornography induces purely genital arousal leading to masturbation, whereas erotica may evoke a whole range of sexual, emotional, and physical responses. The erotic does not have to involve scenes which are sexually explicit. The Surrealists, for instance, saw the erotic as central to mystical experience and as instrumental in the struggle for the reconciliation of opposites such as Eros/Thanatos and Eros/Psyche.

Some feminists distinguish carefully between 'male pornography' and 'woman's erotica,' arguing that male pornography is by definition mechanical, sexist, dehumanizing, impersonal, and obsessed with phallic themes – performance, power, aggression. If feminists were to design their own sexually arousing films, they say, these would not be pornographic but erotic. However, there is as yet no accepted definition of woman's erotica. Drawing on classical definitions, some feminists argue that the erotic is the cord which binds together the physical, emotional, spiritual, and intellectual. Others say that women, like men, may derive erotic pleasure from viewing depictions of impersonal sex. A third group claims that a woman's erotica involve only feelings and desires which are tender, beautiful and soft, and take place within a significant relationship; a view based on a belief that desires which are aggressive, forceful, violent are patriarchal and would not exist at all in a separatist female utopia. Some even argue that women enjoy pornography/erotica only because their desires have been warped by patriarchal conditioning. Others would argue against all these views in favor of an erotica which embraces all bodily sensations, including pain. It would appear that what one woman experiences as erotic another might experience as pornographic. In the cinema, a woman's erotica should at the very least address the female spectator and depict scenarios which are not fixated on the genital and the heterosexual but speak to a whole range of bodily pleasures and sexual preferences.

> 'O glorious, mighty hall – thy magic and thy charm unite us all to worship at beauty's throne.' A 1920s invocation – and to what?

Currently, the only clearly female pornography/erotica available are examples of LESBIAN INDEPENDENT CINEMA such as *She Must Be Seeing Things* (Sheila McLaughlin, 1987), or the films of Barbara HAMMER. These may prove to be quite different from a 'feminist erotica' – in turn, not necessarily the same as 'woman's erotica' – which suggests a set of feminist guidelines to which the material would presumably have to conform. Given the conflicting feminist views on the subject, drawing up such guidelines would probably prove impossible.

'Women and Erotica' issue, *Spare Rib*, no. 191 (1988)   BC

ETHNOGRAPHIC FILM

Ethnographic film may be DOCUMENTARY's most precocious and irritating subgenre: it won't stop asking impossible questions, and it won't go away. If, as ethnographer David McDougall wrote in 1970, an ethnographic film 'seeks to reveal one society to another,' then to succeed it must also reveal itself as a document made up of specific historical, social, political, and cultural assumptions. Critics agree that the category ethnographic film encompasses far more than the kinds of films popularly thought of as 'ethnographic' – museum archival footage, anthropologists' educational films, travelogues, and so on. Ethnography lies in the eyes of the beholder; an ethnographic reading interrogates both the ritual being represented and the ritual of its representation.

Films have been made for ethnographic use as long as films have been made. In 1895, while the Lumière brothers shot their scenes of French life, an anatomical specialist named Félix-Louis Regnault was filming a Wolof woman making pottery at the Paris Exposition. Thomas Edison sent crews to Indian pueblos, Pacific islands and the Holy Land to bring back vignettes for American and European audiences. In the 1920s, filmmaker Robert Flaherty turned this method into *Nanook of the North* (1920) and *Maona* (1926): semi-fictional, semi-documentary accounts of his experiences of – and prolonged intimacy with – Alaskan Eskimos and Samoans. Anthropologists, eager to upgrade their standards of evidence and prove that theirs, too, could be a science, soon turned to film and photography as field tools. Margaret MEAD and Gregory

Bateson's films about family life in Bali are among the first and best examples of this kind of ethnographic film, still being made and still being screened in the world's natural history and science museums. In 1932, Luis Bunuel brought irony to the genre with *Las Hurdes*, a blithe travelogue about a bitterly poor mountain village. In the 1950s, French ethnographer Jean Rouch began experimenting with participatory modes of storytelling, inviting the Africans he was filming to help make up fiction and psychodrama, and in one film, *Jaguar* (1953–5), to provide a voice-over commentary on their own characters.

Ethnographic film, in short, has evolved from a naive discourse of exoticism to a sophisticated genre that questions received social assumptions, about a filmmaker's own society as well as its approach to other societies. As subjects, women have played a prominent role in ethnographic films, the ideal 'native informant' in part because, as 'unconscious' bearers of cultural information, they can be shown passing it on to children (see, again, Margaret Mead and her films on women, childbearing and childrearing in Bali). As filmmakers, women are using ethnographic filmmaking to question patriarchal and colonialist assumptions rife in their own societies and in the societies they examine, often passing on filmmaking skills to members of those societies. Some practitioners include TRINH T Minh-ha, Melissa Llewellyn-Davies (*Diary of a Maasai Village* [1984], *The Women's Olamal* [1984]), Christine Noschese (*Metropolitan Avenue* [1985]), Carolyn Strachan (*Two Laws* [1981], in collaboration with Alessandro Cavadini), and Yolande Zauberman (*Classified People* [1987]).

Paul Hockings (ed.), *Principles of Visual Anthropology* (The Hague: Mouton, 1975)

See also: ABORIGINAL FILM AND VIDEO; MAORI FILM; NATIVE AMERICAN FILM; NATIVE CANADIAN FILM; RODRIGUEZ, MARTA; SAMPER, GABRIELA   JSh

EXHIBITION

The relationship between audiences and films is shaped by conditions of film exhibition: the physical space of the screening environment, the public and private discussions which surround the cinematic experience, and the films available for viewing. The commodity status of popular cinema requires exhibition to a mass AUDIENCE. As consumers of spectacle and entertainment, audiences are made physically and ideologically comfortable in darkened film theaters. In the USA in the years of the HOLLYWOOD STUDIO SYSTEM, exhibitors were strongly encouraged by the studios and the trade press to participate actively in publicizing films with 'ballyhoo,' stunts, and contests designed to affirm the exchange value of films as spectacle and entertainment. For the opening of the Depression feature *Gold Diggers of 1933* (Busby Berkeley, Warner Bros., 1933), for example, $200 in gold coins was buried in a vacant lot in Denver, Colorado. Studio and newspaper cameras snapped as thousands scrabbled in the dirt for the money. More widespread, and continuing to some extent today, are quieter forms of ballyhoo: prizes, games, and publicizing of the spectacle made possible by 'state-of-the-art' technologies of SPECIAL EFFECTS and SOUND systems.

The history of film exhibition shows how changes in a community's population and economy affect the location and design of theaters: from kinetoscope parlors, nickelodeons, downtown 'atmospheric' movie palaces, suburban cinemas, drive-in theaters, art houses, the multi-screen cineplex, to the contemporary well-appointed theater which challenges home video. Alternative types of exhibition call into question the experience offered by mainstream cinema. Rather than the newest release, regional and local film series offer programs organized around social, political, and/or film historical issues. Program notes, lectures, or discussions can raise questions about the ideologies and meanings of films and allow audiences to participate more actively in the exhibition context. This extension of film culture beyond mainstream commodity exhibition is an important venue for feminist and other types of INDEPENDENT CINEMA.

Ben M. Hall, *The Golden Age of the Movie Palace: The Best Remaining Seats* (New York: Clarkson N Potter, 1961)

See also: ADVERTISING; CONSUMERISM; FEMINIST EXHIBITION   MBH

EXPERIMENTAL FILM *see* AVANT-GARDE FILM

EXPLOITATION FILM

As a GENRE, exploitation film capitalizes on the box office success of other more lavish, upmarket productions. They are made on very low budgets, with tight production schedules, low-paid, inexperienced, nonunion personnel, minimal production values, 'sensational' selling campaigns, and widespread saturation bookings aimed at specific markets (predominantly the youth/drive-in audience generally uninterested in critical reviews), all in the interests of making a fast buck. Consequently, they are usually deemed unworthy of serious critical attention because of their blatant commercialism. Being so tightly tied to market forces means that the elements which lend big-budget films their coherence (STARS, psychological REALISM, NARRATIVE development, expensive production values) are often absent from exploitation films. Instead, they offer schematic, minimal narratives, comic-book STEREOTYPES, 'bad' ACTING, and brief film 'cycles' (New World's short-lived student-nurse cycle in the early seventies, for example) which disappear as soon as their audience appeal is exhausted. And in order to attract their audiences, exploitation films contain a high degree of sensationalized sex and/or violence, apparently playing on the more retrograde fantasies of young male viewers.

Given these limitations, the exploitation film may not appear to be congenial material for women filmmakers. Nevertheless, women directors, including a declared feminist like Stephanie ROTHMAN, an ex-UCLA film school graduate, have worked successfully in exploitation. Indeed, during the 1970s Rothman's films were widely shown and discussed on the art-house circuits and at feminist events by audiences quite different from those originally intended. Though clearly aware of the sensitive nature of exploitation material for feminism, Rothman has pointed out that within the necessary economic restraints, the low-budget exploitation director, particularly at New World under producer Roger Corman, had considerable freedom. The 'exploitation' is, to a certain extent, mutual: there is a challenge in the necessity of shooting fast and cheaply, in displaying ingenuity and injecting ideas which do not entirely go along with hardcore exploitation principles. In fact, during the seventies New World gained something of a reputation for feminism: films such as Jack Hill's *The Big Doll House* (1971) or Joe Viola's *The Hot Box* (1972), in response to public demand for more female roles, celebrated a popular version of 'Women's Lib' by putting strong, assertive women characters in action roles usually reserved for men. But Rothman's films go further than this, questioning and undermining the male fantasies underlying violence.

Stephanie Rothman has not traveled the route to mainstream production taken by many of her male counterparts (Joe Dante, Jonathan DEMME, Martin SCORSESE, among others); nevertheless there are now, as there were in the early seventies, a number of women directors working in low-budget exploitation, though the new generation seems more aware of the dangers of ghettoization. Amy Jones's *Love Letters* (1983), produced by Corman, contained some ex-ploitation elements, but was much nearer the ART CINEMA end of the market than her earlier *Slumber Party Massacre* (1982); while Penelope SPHEERIS has disclaimed the exploitation provenance of *Suburbia* (*The Wild Side*) (1984) and *The Boys Next Door* (1985). At a time when the major studios have been steadily moving toward penetration of the exploitation market (Amy Heckerling's youth pic *Fast Times* [1982] was produced by Universal, and her gangster parody *Johnny Dangerously* [1984] by Twentieth Century-Fox), it will be interesting to see where this route leads them.

Pam Cook, 'Exploitation Films and Feminism', *Screen*, vol. 17, no. 2 (1976)
PC

EXPORT, VALIE (1940–)

Born Waltraut Lehner in Austria, Valie Export has gained an international reputation as an AVANT-GARDE film- and videomaker, photographer and performance artist. She also writes on contemporary art history and feminist theory, and has organized and contributed to many international art exhibitions and film festivals.

An important theme in all Export's work is the externalization of internal psychic states and the liberation of the female body from socialization. Since 1967 she has done a series of short feminist and experimental films, including . . . *Remote . . . Remote* (1973), which painfully depicts female self-mutilation. With her 'film happenings' she also explores the notion of an 'expanded cinema' (sometimes in collaboration with Peter Weibel). Films such as *Cutting* (1967–8), *Der Kuss* (1968) and *Tapp und Tast Kino* (1968) often integrate nonvisual sensual/sensory experiences (especially tactile ones) in an attempt to redefine the audience–performer relationship and to extend purely cinematic conventions. A similar concept is expressed in her video installations: for example, *Split Reality* (1969) and *I (Beat [It])* (1978).

Valie Export's *Invisible Adversaries*

Unsichtbare Gegner/Invisible Adversaries (1976), her highly acclaimed prizewinning first feature film, is about female identity and representation, culture and environment. The ambiguous SCIENCE FICTION plot about the Earth being colonized by 'Hyksos' in the guise of aggressive men gives Export an opportunity to incorporate her experimental strategies imaginatively and very effectively. Despite being theoretically and visually challenging, the film succeeds in being entertaining and humorous.

Export's subsequent films continue to explore aesthetic and formal issues in a variety of formats, including experimental, DOCUMENTARY, and narrative film. Many critics support this use of experimental strategies to subvert familiar narrative forms without becoming inaccessible. Many would agree that Valie Export's films represent one of the most exciting contemporary feminist challenges to both mainstream and

avant-garde cinema, and that her transition from experimental shorts to feature films has not compromised her political and aesthetic position.

Menstruationsfilm (1967); *Ars Lucis* (1967–8); *Abstract Film No. 11* (1967/68); *Cutting* (1967–8); *Ohne Titel 1*★ (1968); *Ohne Titel XR*★ (1968); *Der Kuss*★ (1968); *Ein Familienfilm von Waltraut Lehner* (1968); *Instant film*★ (1968); *Valie Export*★ (1968); *Ein Sprachfest*★ (1968); *Gesichtsgrimassen* (1968); *Proselyt* (1968); *Ansprache Aussprache* (1968); *Splitscreen – Solipsismus* (1968); *Tapp und Tast Kino* (1968); *333* (1968); *Ping Pong* (1968); *Sie Suesse Nummer: Ein Konsumerlebnis* (1968); *Sehtext: Fingergedicht* (1968); *Auf + Zu + Ab + An* (1968); *Eine Reise ist eine Reise Wert*★ (1969); *Das Magische Auge*★ (1969); *Split Reality* (1969); *Tonfilm* (1969); *Touching* (1970); *Hauchtext: Liebesgedicht* (1970); *Facing a Family* (1971); *Interrupted Line* (1971/72); *Schnitte* (1972); *Hyperbolie*

(1973); *Asemie* (1973); *Adjungkierte Dislokationen* (1973); *Mann & Frau & Animal* (1973); . . . *Remote . . . Remote* (1973); *Body Politics* (1974); *Raumsehen und Raumhoeren* (1974); *Homo Meter* (1976); *Unsichtbare Gegner/Invisible Adversaries* (1976); *Delta: Ein Stueck* (1977); *I (Beat It)* 1978; *Restringierter Code* (1979); *Menschenfrauen* (1979); *Das Bewaffnete Auge* (1982); *Syntagma* (1983); *Die Praxis der Liebe/The Practice of Love* (1984); *Tischbemerkungen – November 1985* (1985); *Die Zweiheit der Natur* (1986); *Ein Perfectes Paar oder die Unzucht Wechselt Ihre Haut* (section in *Sieben Frauen und Sieben Suenden* 1985); *Yukon Quest*★ (1986); *Mental Images oder der Zugang zur Welt*† (1987); *Maschinenkoerper – Koerpermaschinen – Koerperraum* (1988); *Dokumente zum Internationalen Aktionismus* (1988); *Unica* (1988)

Valie Export, 'The Real and its Double: The Body', *Discourse*, vol. 11, no. 1 (1988) US

★ with Peter Weibel
† in collaboration with others

FANDOM

In the 1910s, film performers' identities were made known to the public, the star system developed, fan magazines appeared, and fans, the vast majority of whom were undoubtedly women, became an important part of the film industry, particularly in the USA during the years of the HOLLYWOOD STUDIO SYSTEM. Interest in behind-the-scenes Hollywood and the offscreen lives of STARS enhanced the film industry's opportunities to promote itself. News and feature stories about Hollywood in magazines and newspapers and on radio helped sustain the audience for film by offering what film theorist John Ellis has called 'the invitation to cinema.' By seeing the film, the desire whetted by publicity will be satisfied. As part of CLASSICAL HOLLYWOOD CINEMA, fan magazines intensified the desire for Hollywood films by detailing Hollywood life. Calling upon readers to share ideologies of family life, work, and heterosexual romance, fan magazines carefully positioned Hollywood within a popular frame of reference. Fan magazines stressed the dual identity of stars (as both ordinary and special) through stories in which stars shared their privileged fashion and beauty knowledge, and by articles on the commonplace of home life and the raising of children. The hard work and personal cost of stardom was affirmed ('The Price They Pay for Fame', 'So You'd Like To Be a Star?'). If a star's career was threatened by a moral backlash, fan magazines could temper the damage by asking for empathy ('Why the Perfect Wife's Marriage Failed' justified Myrna Loy's divorce), or by separating the star from her film role ('Norma Takes a Dare' explained that Shearer's performance as 'the sex-tortured' Nina in *Strange Interlude* [Robert Z Leonard, MGM, 1932] did not derive from her own life experience).

John Ellis, *Visible Fictions* (London and New York: Routledge & Kegan Paul, 1984)

See also: GOSSIP COLUMNS   MBH

FANTASY

The word 'fantasy' has various meanings in relation to cinema. Its most commonly understood meaning relates to fantasy as a GENRE consisting of films which draw on the cinema's ability to use special effects to create an 'unrealistic' or fanciful world. Hollywood cinema has developed the use of fantasy, particularly in the HORROR and SCIENCE FICTION genres; while European directors such as Jean Cocteau made an art of the fantasy film with such productions as *Orphée* (1950) and *La belle et la bête* (1946). Elements of fantasy have also been incorporated in 'realistic' films: for instance in dream sequences in FILM NOIR and bizarre sequences in some COMEDIES. In recent years, the use of the term has been extended and developed in new ways, particularly in relation to the view that fantasy is a distinct NARRATIVE form. One of the most influential works in this area to influence film theorists has been Tzvetan Todorov's *The Fantastic: A Structural Approach to a Literary Genre*.

Extending Todorov's approach, some theorists argue that fantasy should also be seen as an expression of unconscious drives. This view emphasizes the importance of recurring themes and motifs such as the doppelgaenger, mirror images, and bodily transformations.

FEMINIST FILM THEORY is interested in this view of fantasy, arguing that the film text represents 'male' fantasies about the world, particularly in terms of representations of woman. This approach stresses the fact that film is not a direct record of the real world but rather a representation of the (male) director's view of the real world: a mediated or constructed practice. It is argued that since IDEOLOGY speaks through the individual, creative practices such as film serve also to speak the prevailing ideology. Hence the predominance of the (male) 'Oedipal narrative' and the presence of stereotyped images of woman that speak only to male fantasies and desires. By studying the way in which male fantasies are represented within the film system, feminist theorists hope to arrive at a better understanding of the construction of MASCULINITY and FEMININITY and the place of women within society.

A related approach, which draws on Freud's theory of the primal fantasies, has important implications for feminist debates about spectatorship within PSYCHOANALYTIC FILM THEORY. In this view, looking at a film is similar to the experience of fantasizing. Hence the viewer is 'free' to identify with characters on the screen – regardless of their gender. This approach challenges feminist theories of spectatorship which posit the LOOK as central and argue that viewers tend to identify only with their screen surrogate.

'The Fantastic' issue, *Wide Angle*, vol. 10, no. 3 (1988)   *BC*

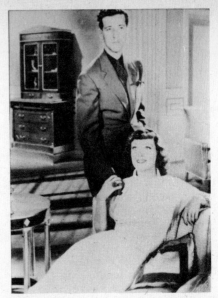

Costume designer Adrian, with Joan Crawford

FASHION

As early as 1910, fashion shows were incorporated into newsreel programs in movie theaters around the world. Soon there were numerous shorts on fashion. Feature films with integrated fashion show sequences were common in US cinemas from the 1920s through the 1940s. These sequences allowed 'shop girl' characters to have access to glamor,

and were given a meager narrative motivation by setting films in locations where fashion shows were plausible: department stores, design houses, or society entertainment. Women's COSTUMES were often quickly copied and made available to the public in department stores. Macy's of New York claimed to have sold 500,000 copies of Adrian's dress design for Joan CRAWFORD in *Letty Lynton* (Clarence Brown, MGM, 1932). The relationship between women STARS and fashion was so strong in Hollywood that when a star was not costumed for fashion, the decision had to be accounted for. When Ginger Rogers played a woman in poverty in *Primrose Path* (Gregory LaCava, RKO, 1939), publicity explained that 'realism' required that her 'costumes' be purchased at a dime store. Even when a star plays a woman of ill-repute, the exigencies of fashion override the ideologies of the role. Bette DAVIS's 'bar girl' role in *Marked Woman* (Warner Bros., 1937) was accompanied by publicity which stressed the gowns for the film as well as the star's fashion sense and beauty regimen. Whether everyday wear or glamorous gowns, costumes have been a primary source of tie-ins between the film and the fashion industries, and a major means of publicizing films. Film costumes sometimes reverberate in fashion. For example, Edith HEAD's exotic sarong for Dorothy Lamour in *The Jungle Princess* (William Thiele, Paramount, 1936) was widely adapted as playwear. More often, costumes adopt the look of contemporary fashion. Even when the designer is uncredited, film costumes enter into public discourse on fashion through media coverage of stars and their film roles.

Mauren Turim, 'Designing Women: The Emergence of the New Sweetheart Line', *Wide Angle*, vol. 6, no. 2 (1984)

See also: ADVERTISING; CONSUMERISM   *MBH*

FASSBINDER, RAINER WERNER (1946–82)

One of the best-known WEST GERMAN film directors, Rainer Werner Fassbinder was the 'Wunderkind' of the NEW GERMAN CINEMA movement. A prolific filmmaker, he made over twenty fulllength feature films and numerous television productions in just over ten years. Moreover, he wrote the scripts for most of these, acted in a good number of them, and even took over the camera in his later years.

While Fassbinder's early films have an autobiographical flavor, his later work starts to address issues of wider social relevance such as homosexuality, immigrant workers, the bankruptcy of the left, and feminist issues. Toward the end of his career he also made what he described as German Hollywood films, epitomized by *Die Ehe der Maria Braun* (1978) and *Lili Marlene* (1981). He has worked with a number of film GENRES, and much has been written about his reworking of the gangster movie and his

use of MELODRAMA. Certain themes, however, recur throughout Fassbinder's work: isolation, alienation, issues around love and relationships, with the lonely outsider frequently featuring as the hero(ine) of his films.

Although much of his work focuses on male relationships, a considerable number of his films feature female protagonists and raise issues of relevance to areas of feminist debate. *Angst Essen Seele Auf* (1973) revolves around an elderly widow who marries a younger man, an immigrant worker. Of particular importance, according to feminist filmmaker Helke SANDER, is the way in which the film demonstrates that 'a woman's sexual, emotional and intellectual life does not end at 50,' and thus challenges traditional representations of older women. *Die bitteren Traenen der Petra von Kant* (1972) addresses the frequently neglected subject of lesbian relationships, and *Fontane Effi Briest* (1974) shows the oppressive workings of patriarchal society.

Fassbinder's films include: *Katzelmacher* (1969); *Warum laeuft Herr R. Amok?/Why Does Mr R. Run Amuck?* (1970); *Der Haendler der vier Jahreszeiten/The Merchant of Four Seasons* (1971); *Die bitteren Traenen der Petra von Kant/The Bitter Tears of Petra von Kant* (1972); *Acht Stunden sind kein Tag/Eight Hours Don't Make a Day* (1972); *Angst Essen Seele Auf/Ali: Fear Eats the Soul* (1973); *Fontane Effi Briest/Effi Briest* (1974); *Faustrecht der Freiheit/Fox and His Friends* (1974); *Mutter Kuesters' Fahrt zum Himmel/Mother Kuesters Goes to Heaven* (1975); *Ich will doch nur, dass ihr mich liebt/I Just Want You to Love Me* (1976); *Frauen in New York/Women in New York* (1977); *Die Ehe der Maria Braun/The Marriage of Maria Braun* (1978); *Lili Marlene* (1981); *Lola* (1981); *Die Sehnsucht Veronika Voss/Veronika Voss* (1982)

Anna K Kuhn, 'Rainer Werner Fassbinder: The Alienated Vision', in *New German Filmmakers*, ed. Klaus Phillips (New York: Ungar, 1984)   *JK*

FAYE, SAFI (1943–)

Having worked for six years as a teacher, Safi Faye took a higher degree in ethnology: her thesis was research in the Serer region of Senegal, AFRICA. She acted in Jean Rouch's *Petit à petit/Little by Little* (1970) and her own short film, *La passante* (1972); and in 1975 made a fictionalized documentary about her own village, Fadial. *Kaddu Beykat* is about the bad effects on the village of an unequal world market economy which imposes single-crop cultivation. The implications are pointed up particularly in the fictional elements of the film: one of the young men of the village leaves to look for work in the city. In 1979 Faye made *Fad Jal* – again in Fadial and again mixing fiction and documentary – about the relationship between popular memory, the oral tradition, and daily village life: this film won the Catholic prize at Carthage in 1980. Faye has also made a documentary for German television, *Man sa yay* (1980), has worked for the UN in New York, and in 1981 made *Les âmes du soleil*, about the terrible conditions in which many women and children are now forced to live in Africa. She is currently working on another feature film, *La toile d'arraignée*.

La passante/The Passer-by (1972); *Kaddu Beykat/News From My Village* (1975); *Fad Jal* (1979); *Goob na nu/The Harvest is Over* (1979); *Man sa yay/I, Your Mother* (1980); *Woman* (1980); *Les âmes du soleil/Souls of the Sun* (1981); *La toile d'arraignée/The Spider's Web* (in production)

Angela Martin, 'Interview with Safi Faye', *Framework*, no. 11 (1979)   AM

FEMALE SPECTATORS *see* AUDIENCE AND SPECTATOR

FEMINALE

WEST GERMANY's main WOMEN'S FILM FESTIVAL, the Feminale has grown from a small national affair into an international forum. Held annually in Cologne, it began in 1984 and expanded in 1986 to include work from Austria and Switzerland. In 1988, to coincide with European Film and Television Year, the festival expanded still further and programmed material from FRANCE, ITALY, BRITAIN, IRELAND, the NETHERLANDS, and SPAIN. Over the years the Feminale has built up a reputation for presenting the latest films and videos by women working in West Germany, and has functioned as something of a showcase for this work. By programming the work of film- and videomakers such as Ruth Becht, Monika Funke Stern, Bettina Gruber, Cathy Joritz, and Maria Vedder, it has also managed to demonstrate the wide range of women's film and video work in West Germany's experimental sector. At the same time the festival has also addressed women's film history, often presenting work by earlier women filmmakers such as Alice GUY, and retrospectives of contemporary ones like Ula STOECKL. Since 1988 it has included a competition, awarding a prize for the best short film and best short video.

> During 1933, in Denver, Colorado, $200 in gold coins was buried. Thousands dug in the dirt to find them. This ballyhoo served to publicize the opening of which Hollywood film?

Alongside the presentation of women's film and video work the Feminale also stresses its role as a forum for information, exchange, and debate. To this end it programs a series of workshops and debates throughout the festival, all of which aim to help the promotion, production, and distribution of women's work throughout Europe. Recent discussions have included debates on such issues as EROTICISM and violence in films made by women, PORNOGRAPHY, women's film and FEMINIST INDEPENDENT FILM, and the idea of a women's television channel has been floated. In its recent expansion, the Feminale aims to become a major international festival: an aim the organizers hope will promote the interest of all women involved in the film and video sectors throughout Europe.

Moira Sweeney, 'Feminale – Fourth Koeln Women's Film Festival', *Independent Media*, no. 83 (1988)　　　JK

FEMININITY

The opposition masculine/feminine underlies a wide range of cultural oppositions in which 'masculine' qualities (agency, activity, courage) are valued over 'feminine' ones (passivity, receptiveness, sensitivity). This metaphorical functioning of gender works in quite contradictory ways in cinema. Cinema audiences are feminized, in one of the governing metaphors of twentieth-century cultural criticism, as passive recipients of the products of the culture industry as against the active consumers of high and avant-garde art. In this view, all consumers of mass culture are feminized. However, since television in the home became widespread, the cinema audience has been 're-virilized' – arguably at the point where the cinema has also been upgraded to an art form.

This division is also apparent in cinema and television GENREs: the femininity – in targeted audience, narrative concerns, and sphere of representation – of certain genres is synonomous with their low critical status. Derogatory terms such as 'weepie' and SOAP OPERA are used for feminine genres, often implying uncritical involvement and overidentification by audiences. However, these despised genres have been reassessed by FEMINIST FILM THEORY in a number of ways: films have been read as offering preferred patterns of femininity – almost like morality tales for the twentieth century; as revealing contradictions in social understandings of gender; as expressing the impossibility of feminine spectatorship; as being the occasion for marketing fantasies in the shape of both CONSUMERISM and film STARS; as giving momentary voice to female desires; as revealing the masculine bias of aesthetic values.

Within cinema there has been extensive use of camera/gun/penis metaphors, so that to look or gaze becomes masculine, to be looked at, feminine. Feminists working within PSYCHOANALYTIC FILM THEORY, and theorists of the metapsychology of cinema, have elaborated extensively on Laura MULVEY's 1975 formulation of a heterosexual division of labor within CLASSICAL HOLLYWOOD CINEMA in which, it is argued, the spectatorial position is masculine. This raises the question of what the position of a feminine spectator could be, and whether it is possible to represent femininity and the female body without resorting to notions of subordination. The solutions proposed depend on how the relationship between the female body and femininity is understood. Most feminists would agree that 'femininity' refers to the cultural, social, and psychic aspects of the biological category 'female'. Femininity is thus a historically and culturally variable category, specific in terms of class, ethnicity, nationality, and so on; which is nevertheless understood in most cultures as a natural one. There is considerable debate on the extent to which traditional feminine attributes (generally in white western culture, it should be noted, though rarely specified as such) are either essentially feminine or historically and socially defined as such. This theoretical argument is of relevance to all aspects of filmmaking. While, for instance, historical understandings of femininity can justify the practice of using an all-woman crew, notions of essential femininity generally underlie the use of cyclical formal structures, or lunar and menstrual imagery. Similarly, it can be argued that women are essentially more peaceful and less competitive than men, and are therefore better at working collectively; or that only women are in a position to understand certain readings of films. Conceptually, the problem is not so much to do with femininity as with the category 'woman.' At one extreme, the argument is that women do indeed have natural attributes which are misrepresented and repressed within patriarchal culture; at the other, that the very idea of what it is to be a woman is always being *made* in any culture – always set up as one side of an axis of sexual difference – against MASCULINITY. It is therefore the construction of sexual difference (and hence also of heterosexuality), rather than the categories femininity or masculinity, which should be analyzed. The parallel question of how difference-as-gender can be understood in relation to difference-as-ethnicity has rarely been addressed, and white scholars tend to ignore the 'whiteness' of their approach.

This perhaps explains why FEMINIST FILM THEORY is so often drawn to extreme cases in discussing femininity – women in male genres, or taking masculine roles; CROSSDRESSING; women marked in relation to vision (girls who wear glasses, women photographers, blind women) – as well as to questions like the nude female body, active feminine desire, and female stars. In relation to the latter, and more generally to notions of femininity as PERFORMANCE, the concept of the MASQUERADE has been explored: here the artificial quality of femininity is accentuated and the display of femininity seen almost as a form of resistance or irony, one way of inhabiting an unavoidable position.

Rosemary Betterton (ed.), *Looking On: Images of Femininity* (London: Pandora Press, 1987)

See also: AUDIENCE AND SPECTATOR; BLACK WOMEN AND FILM THEORY; SEXUALITY   CB

FEMINIST DISTRIBUTION

Closely related to the FEMINIST EXHIBITION movement, feminist distribution emerges from a sense that making films is not enough, and that it is crucial to control the means by which films reach their intended audiences. Commercial DISTRIBUTION organizations were simply not interested in feminist films; and in the 1970s and early 1980s a series of groups dedicated to distribution were started, such as CIRCLES and CINEMA OF WOMEN in Britain, CINEMIEN in the Netherlands, and NEW DAY FILMS in the USA.

While the policies, composition, and funding of individual groups vary, all at their most basic are motivated by a desire to circulate films which would otherwise be ignored by commercial distributors. The range of films, however, can be wide – including formally innovative work, popular feature films, and revivals of older films like Leontine SAGAN's *Maedchen in Uniform* (1931) and Germaine DULAC's *La Souriante Madame Beudet/ The Smiling Madame Beudet* (1923). The most obviously political aspect of feminist film distribution, however, is the circulation of short, issue-based, campaigning films on subjects like abortion, industrial health hazards, and rape. These are often hired for screening in non-cinema settings such as classrooms, political meetings, and women's self-help groups.

At the same time, however, feminist distribution has never limited itself simply to improving the physical availability of films: distributors have always seen this aspect of their work as going hand in hand with a desire to influence the ways films are understood. Framed negatively, this entails a steadfast refusal to distribute films in ways that undermine or distort their central intention. The case of the renting by its commercial distributor of Bonnie Sher Klein's anti-pornography film *Not A Love Story* (1981) to PORNOGRAPHY cinemas helped underline the need for a feminist film distribution system. Feminist distributors see the film itself as just one part of a whole chain of meaning. Film ADVERTISING, for instance, is part of the experience of a film; so, too, is the AUDI-

ENCE. Together, feminist distributors and exhibitors have worked to create viewing situations, such as women-only screenings, which encourage debate. These discussions help define 'feminist film,' whilst locating the films themselves in their own, specifically feminist, history. This means both tracing connections between feminist 'issues' and questions of representation and also, more generally, reclaiming the role played by women in shaping film history.

Charlotte Brunsdon (ed.), *Films for Women* (London: British Film Institute, 1986)

See also: GROUPE INTERVENTION VIDEO; REEL WOMEN; VIDEO FEMMES; WOMEN MAKE MOVIES

JRo

FEMINIST EXHIBITION

Feminist ideas on film exhibition are closely allied with FEMINIST DISTRIBUTION policies. But while the distribution movement is concerned with the availability of films, alternative exhibition is directly involved in actual screenings. In particular, it is interested in creating a new type of relationship between AUDIENCEs and films. Commercial film EXHIBITION treats films as units or commodities. As long as film ADVERTISING emphasizes GENREs and STARS, other sorts of links between films – of history, of politics, of director, of circumstances of production – remain hidden.

Hand in hand with the growth of INDEPENDENT CINEMA, independent exhibition, notably in Britain and the USA, has tried to turn existing models of the relationship between film and audience on its head. With varying degrees of success and longevity, a range of organizations – community cinemas, independent commercial cinemas, film workshops and various educational organizations – attempt to create a situation where films are seen in the context of other films, supported by documentation, and in a context of discussion. In-stead of passive, isolated consumers, the alternative exhibition movement hopes to create audiences who play an active part in the cinematic event. Feminist ideas have been crucial in this area. Complex, 'difficult' works of feminist COUNTERCINEMA need a particular kind of viewing situation. But these imperatives are also linked to a straightforward political desire to show films on feminist subjects in women's groups, trade unions, community centers, and a range of other nontheatrical venues. Sometimes screenings are women-only, or – more recently – black women-only. Drawing from the experience of consciousness-raising and other types of feminist groups, these events allow films to be transformed by viewing circumstances far removed from conventional cinemagoing: seeing *Supergirl* (Jeannot Szwarc, 1984) with a raucous all-women audience is a very different experience from seeing it at a local commercial cinema.

Feminist exhibition is also involved in the reevaluation of early feminist films, such as Leontine SAGAN's *Maedchen in Uniform/Maidens in Uniform* (1931), and also CLASSICAL HOLLYWOOD CINEMA. For instance, the meaning of Douglas SIRK's *Imitation of Life* (Universal, 1959) shifts when it is shown in a season dedicated to reassessing the role of BLACK WOMEN in American commercial cinema; while a screening of *Fatal Attraction* (Adrian Lyne, 1987) becomes a very different experience when prefaced by an introduction and followed by a discussion examining the assumptions it makes about female sexuality. *JRo*

FEMINIST FILM THEORY

'The image of women in the cinema has been an image created by men. The emergent women's cinema has begun the transformation of that image. These notes explore ideas and strategies developed in women's films.' These words are emblazoned on the cover of a pamphlet published in 1973, *Notes on Women's*

Cinema, edited by Claire JOHNSTON. It is significant that words appear where an illustration is usually offered as enticement to the reader. We might reasonably expect a spectacular film frame, a familiar frozen image of some female star. What we get is a declaration. The very presentation of this pamphlet embodies the spirit of its writing: it is concerned to develop a critique and a transformation, to give women words, an analytic and emancipatory language. It is also an act of appropriation (not 'women in the cinema' but 'women's cinema') and it implies – by gesturing toward transformation and strategies – a political project incorporating a new perspective.

Who did film critic Molly Haskell call 'the high priestess of the holy communion of American Romance'?

It was in the early 1970s, in the wake of feminism as a broader cultural movement, that the relationship between women and film was first focused as political. The first WOMEN'S FILM FESTIVALS were organized, and the emergence in 1972 of *Women and Film*, the earliest feminist film JOURNAL, paved the way for feminist criticism. Differing perspectives soon began to emerge, and some voices began to call for a systematic and theoretical approach, stressing the need to develop a body of knowledge (more scientific than impressionistic) that could account for the way cinema in general (not just individual films) reproduces sexist IDEOLOGY. Thus, as the quotation suggests, feminist film theory did not spring into print fully formed but began from 'notes', from explorations, and in dialogue with FILM CRITICISM and historical approaches. Although it has now developed into a somewhat formidable body of work (formidable in terms of quantity, but also because of its increasingly specialized language) feminist film theory is by no means complete or coherent, but rather derives its impetus from debate, and from drawing on adjacent theoretical areas such as SEMIOTICS, PSYCHOANALYTIC FILM THEORY and FILM THEORY in general. In turn, it has had an amazing impact on film studies – so much so that now it is impossible to work in this broader area without taking cognizance of feminist film theory.

Early debates centered on questions of STEREOTYPES versus 'real women,' setting the tone for feminist film theory's almost exclusive preoccupation with Hollywood cinema. One tendency (represented, amongst others, by Molly HASKELL, author of *From Reverence to Rape*) argues that CLASSICAL HOLLYWOOD CINEMA, where it presents negative views of women, poor role models, and absent women (or – the other side of the coin – glamorous unattainable ideals) does not truthfully or adequately reflect the reality of women's lives. A more theoretical tendency (as exemplified by a group of British cinefeminists including Claire Johnston and Laura MULVEY) refuses to buy into the argument about whether or not films reflect true reality, suggesting instead that cinema does not simply reflect the world, but rather mediates, represents ideas *about* the real. REALISM, the dominant mode of Hollywood cinema, is seen as ideological in that it functions as a vehicle to resolve contradictions that cannot in fact be resolved in the social. Moreover, it is argued that in order to understand film as a signifying system (a notion derived from semiotics) it is necessary to situate the female image in terms of film language, and to understand how woman functions in the overall system as a sign (a sign of exchange between men, for instance, within the NARRATIVE). Within this framework is elaborated the notion of 'progressive realism', which posits that sometimes woman is not entirely contained by the Hollywood structure. For instance, in the films of Dorothy ARZNER the discourse of the woman is said to be foregrounded in relation to the prevailing patriarchal discourse. Similarly, various Hollywood GENREs – FILM NOIR, MELODRAMA, the WOMAN'S PICTURE – have been reexamined by feminists for signs of disruption, for points where feminine desire and the female voice break through. Not all feminists, however, agree with the notion of progressive realism and the methods associated with its analysis. The US journal *CAMERA OBSCURA*, for instance, has taken issue with the emphasis on transgressive moments in Hollywood films, arguing that this approach can be misleading when trying to understand how textual effects are produced, and how AUDIENCES respond. *Camera Obscura* emphasizes notions of TEXT and reading, arguing for a more rigorous close reading of Hollywood films in order to understand more precisely how the audience is placed through endlessly varied textual patternings. The generation of PLEASURE and meaning (and their effects) can thus be specified more clearly, even though their production and reception may operate on an unconscious level.

The notion of the Unconscious, which has been important in the development of feminist film theory, indicates its debt to psychoanalysis. Perhaps the most crucial precept has been the Freudian notion that MASCULINITY and FEMININITY are not biological categories (like 'men' and 'women') but are, rather, culturally constructed (not symmetrically but in terms of a power differential) through processes of repression. Thus ideology can be seen as working on an unconscious level – not simply to reflect, but actively to construct ideas of sexual difference and SEXUALITY, and in the process to repress the feminine voice and feminine desire. How does cinema, as a specific cultural site with its own language, work on the unconscious level? Feminist film theorist Laura Mulvey has examined the psychoanalytic concept of pleasure in looking, relating the LOOK to the kinds of pleasures generated in Hollywood cinema. She proposes that all these films are directed at a hypothetical male viewer (for the gratification of male anxieties and desires), so that the female viewer has no choice but to occupy a position of ultimately masochistic pleasure. Polemically, she argues that a feminist COUNTERCINEMA would need to attack traditional cinematic mechanisms and pleasures, and deploy a new filmic language.

Feminist film theory has developed in conjunction with FEMINIST INDEPENDENT FILM, each stimulating the other, though the connection may sometimes be indirect. Examples of early and influential experimental theory-related films are Sally POTTER's *Thriller* (1979) and *Sigmund Freud's Dora* (McCall, Pajaczkowska, Tyndall, Weinstock, 1979). There are now many feminist filmmakers, around some of whom there is a developing body of feminist theoretical writing: Yvonne RAINER, Chantal AKERMAN, Marguerite DURAS, Valie EXPORT, and women filmmakers of the NEW GERMAN CINEMA.

Annette Kuhn, *Women's Pictures: Feminism and Cinema* (London: Routledge & Kegan Paul, 1982)

See also: BLACK WOMEN AND FILM THEORY; ROSEN, MARJORIE   LS

FEMINIST INDEPENDENT FILM

Feminist independent film is a vast category encompassing many different types of 'independence' – and strategies for gaining it. In general, however, feminist independent film defines itself against two categories of filmmaking practice: both mainstream or DOMINANT CINEMA, and (though with somewhat less vigor) male-dominated INDEPENDENT CINEMA. That said, feminist independent cinema does have much in common with independent cinema: notably the objective of making films which proclaim themselves to be aesthetically and politically innovative, and making them outside the funding and distribution systems which organize mainstream

Sally Potter's *Thriller*

film and television. Although women were not powerful in early independent film movements such as the 1930s BRITISH DOCUMENTARY MOVEMENT, or Free Cinema in the fifties, many have worked within the AVANT-GARDE sphere of independence. Others have allied themselves with the socialist DOCUMENTARY movement, making films about working people hitherto unrepresented on film.

In the early seventies, some elements of the socialist documentary approach became allied with the sudden burst of energy accompanying the 'second wave' of the women's movement. A series of films, such as those made in Britain by the LONDON WOMEN'S FILM GROUP and in the USA by the Newsreel Collective and the Women's Labor History Project, documented feminist campaigns, and the social conditions being challenged by feminists. These films contain the beginnings of an aesthetic strategy for 'independence': an approach which encompassed independence from mainstream STEREOTYPES of women, independence from controlling, explaining male voices, and independence from being 'spoken for' even by 'sympathetic' male left filmmakers. The new women's films stress a sense of 'women speaking,' of autobiography, of 'representing ourselves,' an approach which continues to be influential in feminist filmmaking in North America, as well as in certain cinemas of resistance elsewhere in the world. At the same time, these groups were involved in building organizational superstructures, such as women-only production groups and FEMINIST DISTRIBUTION and FEMINIST EXHIBITION practices: necessary conditions for a film culture aiming for any real 'independence.'

As the seventies progressed, the status of feminist work changed within the independent sector as a whole, especially in

Britain. New theoretical work by writers like Pam Cook, Claire JOHNSTON, and Laura MULVEY placed questions of SEXUALITY and gender at the heart of debates about how to make films which were aesthetically and politically innovative in form and content. To filmmakers such as the Berwick Street Collective (*Nightcleaners* [1975]) and the Film and History Project (*Song of The Shirt* [1979]), anti-narrative strategies and new attitudes to the act of looking at films were crucial in any attempt to overturn existing relationships between the sexes. Feminist independent film, then, is distinguished by a link between form and content. It was simply not enough to create films which challenge the forms of mainstream cinema: this work also sought to challenge dominant cinema's conventions of 'appropriate' content for films. Unlike avant-garde independent practices, the subject matter of this 'deconstructive' feminist independent cinema was usually directly political, dealing with women's experiences – such as the exploitive cleaning jobs in *Nighcleaners* – excluded or repressed by mainstream cinema.

There are perhaps two distinct approaches to independent, theoretically inspired, feminist filmmaking. 'Deconstruction' concerns itself with analyzing and then breaking down the codes of mainstream cinema. Films like Sara GOMEZ's *De cierta manera/One Way or Another* (1975–7) aim to create a different relationship between the spectator and dominant cinema. The second approach, a feminist COUNTERCINEMA embodying 'feminine writing,' moves beyond challenging dominant cinema to begin investigating the possibility of a specifically feminine cinematic language. Films like *Thriller* (Sally Potter, 1979), *Daughter Rite* (Michelle Citron, 1978), and *Jeanne Dielman, 23 Quai du Commerce, 1080 Bruxelles* (Chantal Akerman, 1975) perhaps share a desire to create a new kind of cinema speaking a 'feminine voice.' While these films borrow a certain set of concerns from agitational feminist documentaries of the early seventies, as well as many techniques from countercinema, they are to be distinguished from both by their interest in fiction rather than nonfiction and in subjectivity rather than 'truth.'

During the eighties, agitational documentaries and both types of feminist countercinema have continued to be produced. It is possible, though, that toward the end of the decade the power of the idea of 'independence' began to wane – in Britain especially, where the changing political climate under an increasingly entrenched Thatcherism, the creation of CHANNEL FOUR TELEVISION, and changes in distribution and exhibition patterns have all helped blur the categories of 'mainstream' as against 'alternative' or 'independent.' Feminist political positions and aesthetic strategies which had once been easy to define as 'against the mainstream' have become partially incorporated within it. Recent ART CINEMA, for instance, has learned much from the school of 'feminine writing,' while TELEVISION has learned some (but by no means enough) of the techniques of feminist documentary.

Annette Kuhn, *Women's Pictures: Feminism and Cinema* (London: Routledge & Kegan Paul, 1982)

See also: AKERMAN, CHANTAL; BLACK CINEMA; BORDEN, LIZZIE; CINE-MUJER; CHENZIRA, AYOKA; CITRON, MICHELLE; DASH, JULIE; DEITCH, DONNA; GORDON, BETTE; GROUPE INTERVENTION VIDEO; LEEDS ANIMATION WORKSHOP; LESBIAN INDEPENDENT CINEMA; MURPHY, PAT; RAINER, YVONNE; SOCIALIST CINEMA; SROUR, HEINY; SYDNEY WOMEN'S FILM GROUP; VIDEO FEMMES   JRo

FEMME FATALE

Wicked, scheming, creative, sexually potent and deadly to the male, the femme fatale is one of the few powerful female figures in CLASSICAL HOLLYWOOD CINEMA. Originally a character constructed in French romantic literature, the femme fatale in film is particularly associated with FILM NOIR and the thrillers of the 1940s and 1950s. Like her predecessor, the VAMP of the 1920s, the femme fatale is primarily defined by her desirable, but dangerous, SEXUALITY – which brings about the downfall of the male protagonist. Typically, the femme fatale combines glamor and sensuality with driving ambition or self-interest. She lures men into a web of intrigue and robs them of their willpower and rationality, exploiting her irresistibility to make them collude with her schemes. Barbara STANWYCK's Phyllis Dietrichson in *Double Indemnity* (Billy Wilder, Paramount, 1944) is a classic example: the embodiment of the evil woman, seductress, deceiver, and murderer, the icy Stanwyck unflinchingly plots and bears witness to her husband's death. She then doublecrosses her accomplice, the hapless insurance salesman trapped by sexual obsession, but is ultimately murdered by her prey when he discovers her duplicity. Other actresses associated with femme fatale roles are Rita HAYWORTH – defined primarily not by evil but by mystery in *Gilda* (Charles Vidor, Columbia, 1946) and *The Lady from Shanghai* (Orson Welles, Colombia, 1948); and Joan Bennett, the alluring temptress in *Woman in the Window* (Fritz Lang, International, 1944) and *Scarlet Street* (Fritz Lang, Universal, 1945).

Since the power of the femme fatale comes at the expense of men, nothing less than her destruction can control the threat she poses to the patriarchal order. The story often constructs the sexually powerful woman as a threat to the male/moral order, so justifying her loss of power as necessary to the reestablishment of that order. Whether she is murdered (as in *Double Indemnity*), rendered symbolically powerless (as in *Sunset Boulevard* [Billy Wilder, Paramount, 1950]), or unconvincingly married off (as in *Gilda*), the femme fatale's punishment is necessary for narrative closure.

The danger of the sexually independent woman is expressed visually through LIGHTING, camera angles, composition, and other aspects of MISE-EN-SCENE: women visually dominate men in the film frame, suggesting the threat represented by their powerful sexuality. The long-haired, long-legged, cigarette-smoking 'spider women' of film noir live in a sinister, immoral world of shadows and darkness, seeming irresistibly to pull the camera and the LOOK with them when they move. Their duplicitous nature is visually emphasized by mirrors (*Gilda*, *Double Indemnity*, *The Lady from Shanghai*), suggesting split identities and false reflections, or by portraits – the classic idealization of the woman as image – which offer a place for male fantasy and projected fears and desire (*The Woman in the Window*, *Rebecca* [Alfred Hitchcock, Selznick, 1940] and *Laura* [Otto Preminger, Twentieth Century-Fox, 1944]).

Feminists are interested in the femme fatale because she represents an independent and powerful FEMININITY. In the context of the 1940s – a time of shifting definitions of gender in the West – the femme fatale has been read as indicative of the fears the 'new woman' evoked, and as a legitimation of masculine desire to maintain control over women's increasingly independent sexuality. Is the femme fatale a STEREOTYPE which justifies patriarchal control over the strong sexual woman, or does she offer female spectators pleasure in seeing women who are deadly, but sexy, exciting and strong?

E Ann Kaplan (ed.), *Women in Film Noir* (London: British Film Institute, 1980)

See also: AUDIENCE AND SPECTATOR; PHALLIC WOMAN   JcS

FERNANDEZ VIOLANTE, MARCELA (1941–)

Marcela Fernández Violante is one of MEXICO's most gifted, underrated, and persistent filmmakers to have endured the unsettled political climate of a male-dominated film industry. A graduate of the University Center for Cinematographic Studies, Mexico City (CUEC),

Fernández Violante began her career in 1971 with a documentary on artist Frida Kahlo which in 1972 won an Ariel – the equivalent to the Academy Award – for best documentary. In 1974–5 she wrote and directed her first feature film, *De todos modos Juan te llámas/Whatever You Do You Lose*, starring Jorge Russek, Juan Ferrera, and Rocio Brambila, and based on the Cristero insurrection of 1926–9. The film explored the corruption of an ideological political system as seen through the eyes of the general's adolescent daughter. In 1976–7 Fernández Violante, in collaboration with Pedro Miret, wrote the screenplay of her second film, *Cananea*, starring Steve Wilensky and Carlos Bracho, and based on a historical event of 1906 in the mining town of Canaea. The film conveyed a

powerful message against anglo, post-colonial, imperialism. *Misterio/Mystery* (1979–80), starring Juan Ferrera, Helena Rojo and Victor Junco, was based on a novel by Vicente Leñero, and is one of her most complex and critically acclaimed films, with a score of 'Arieles' to its name. In the narrative the 'real' and the 'unreal' overlap and envelop the male protagonist during the filming of a tele-novela/soap opera. The film strongly critiqued Televisa, a privately owned Mexican television monopoly.

In 1980 Fernández Violante directed *En el pais de los pies ligeros o el Niño Raramuri/In The Land of Light Feet*, which describes the life of an indigenous community of Tarahumaras, and how a criollo/white boy is able to bond in friendship with a Raramuri child. Her most recent

Marcela Fernández Violante

and controversially received film, *Nocturno amor que te vas/Departed Love in the Evening* (1987), portrays the strength and vulnerability of a working-class woman who sets out alone to confront the established order, driven to uncover the disappearance of her male companion. Fernández Violante is currently acting director and film professor at the Center for Cinematographic Studies, Universidad Nacional Autonoma, Mexico City.

Frida Kahlo (1971); *De todos modos Juan te llámas/Whatever You Do, You Lose* (1974–5); *Cananea* (1976–7); *Misterio/Mystery* (1979–80); *En el pais de los pies ligeros o el Niño Raramuri/In the Land of Light Feet* (1980); *Nocturno amor que te vas/Departed Love in the Evening* (1987)

Jorge Ayala Blanco, 'Marcela Fernández Violante', in *Cinema and Social Change in Latin America*, ed. Julianne Burton (Austin: University of Texas Press, 1986)
CH-N

FESTIVAL DES FILLES DES VUES DE QUEBEC *see* QUEBEC WOMEN'S FILM AND VIDEO FESTIVAL

FESTIVAL INTERNATIONAL DE CRETEIL ET DU VAL DE MARNE – FILMS DE FEMMES *see* CRETEIL

FIELD, MARY (1896–1968)

A pioneering producer and director of DOCUMENTARY films, Field was a leading figure in this area of BRITAIN's film industry, and an international authority on films for children. Educated at Bedford College for Women, she taught history for a while before being invited in 1926 by Bruce Woolfe (who was associated with the BRITISH DOCUMENTARY MOVEMENT) to join British Instructional Films as education manager. A year later, she moved to the production side and eventually became a

director. She was involved mostly with making nature documentaries for children's education. John Grierson, founder of the British documentary movement, described the *Secrets of Nature* series which she made in the late twenties as 'a long and brilliant line of nature films . . . more continuous in their work, less dramatic at all costs than either the Americans or Germans, more patient, analytic, and in the best sense observant. Here, if anywhere, beauty has come to inhabit the edifice of truth.' In 1934 Field joined GB Instructional Films (GBI), where she made the *Secrets of Life* films. In 1944 she inaugurated the Children's Entertainment Division of GBI, and until 1950 acted as executive producer on all the films made for J Arthur Rank's Children's Cinema clubs. During the Second World War, along with many other documentary filmmakers, she cooperated in making official films for the Ministry of Information. Amongst her many achievements were the introduction and development of moving diagrams in educational films. In 1951 Field became executive officer of another new venture, the Children's Film Foundation, and traveled the world lecturing and attending conferences on this subject. By 1957 she was chairwoman of the International Centre for Films for Children in Brussels, and in 1959 became program consultant for two television companies. She retired in 1963.

Secrets of Nature series (1922–33); *Strictly Business* (1931); *The King's English* (1934); *Secrets of Life* series (1933–43)

Mary Field, *Good Company: The Story of the Children's Entertainment Film Movement in Great Britain, 1943–1950* (London: Longmans, 1952)
SP

FIFTH GENERATION

The 'fifth generation' is a name given to a a group of young graduates of the State Film School (the Beijing Film Academy) who started making *tansuopian* (innovative films) in the People's Republic of

CHINA during a period of artistic freedom in the early 1980s. The directors best known outside China include Chen Kaige, Tian Zhuangzhuang, Huang Jianxin, Wu Ziniu, and cinematographer/actor/director Zhang Yimou. Coming from educated urban families, they experienced the Cultural Revolution in their teens and worked as peasants, factory workers, and soldiers before being trained in film. They started filmmaking in less established regional studios in Guangxi, Inner Mongolia, Xiaoxiang, and also in Xian – where the studio head, filmmaker Wu Tianming, protected their work from bureaucratic and political pressures. Their films are diverse in theme and style, sharing a radical rejection of the Chinese melodramatic tradition, a critical and sometimes skeptical vision of Chinese culture, politics, and society, and an ethnographic sensibility to the lives of Chinese peasants. The work of the male members of the group – Chen's *Huang Tudi/Yellow Earth* (1984), Tian's *Le Chang Zhasa/On the Hunting Ground* (1986), and Huang's *Hei Pao Shi Jian/The Black Cannon Incident* (1985), for example – offer deliberately opaque metaphors of contemporary China.

The two women graduates of this group, Peng Xiaolian and Hu Mei, have worked in the more established Shanghai and August First Studios. Both have been able to circumvent the studios' commercial or military constraints, and their films are more psychological and personal than those of their male colleagues. Hu Mei's *Nuer Lou/Army Nurse* (1986) and Peng's *Nuren De Gushi/Stories of Three Women* (1988) present subtly feminist assertions of women's wishes and desires in their differing interpretations of human relationships in a modernizing China.

Tony Rayns, 'The Sun and the Rain', *Monthly Film Bulletin*, vol. 55, no. 650 (1988)   EY

FILM CENSORSHIP *see* CENSORSHIP

FILM CRITICISM

A term disputed by writers and readers alike, film criticism has been called an art, a craft, a branch of literature, a subbranch of a general discipline of Criticism, a last resort for failed filmmakers, and a high or low form of journalism. Where some critics see their task as aesthetic evaluation, others see it as cultural or political analysis. Some claim only to express their personal tastes, defending the interest of their opinions on such grounds as love and knowledge of cinema, familiarity with the arts in general, or their skills as writers of prose. Many of the most widely read FILM CRITICS in newspapers and magazines primarily provide a 'consumers' guide' – an information service which also generates publicity material ('quotes') for distributors. This is the function of most critics working in radio and television as well, though some are more like historians, framing reruns or specialized programs with a discourse on cinema's past and its value in the present.

Faced with such diversity, it is useful to ask what film criticism *does* rather than trying to define what it *is*. This makes it possible to differentiate practices which may really have little in common. For example, Renata Adler – herself a critic – distinguishes between 'serious intermittent critics' writing from interest or desire, and 'staff critics' paid to write regularly regardless of whether they have anything to say, and so to develop routine marks of personal style. In this case it may eventually be the persona of the reviewer that readers 'consume,' rather than information or opinions about film.

To this we can add that where criticism is flexible in scope, and retrospective in its approach to films (assuming that the reader has seen them), reviewing is obliged to refer prospectively to a narrow range of events in the here and now (a screening 'tonight,' a season 'this month') as though the reader has not seen them. Critics can therefore discuss the endings of narrative films and analyze structure. Reviewers are not supposed to 'give it away,' and tend to create a kind of narrative suspense about film plots, as opposed to analysis. But it is too easy to dismiss reviewing as inferior to criticism rather than different from it. Because reviewing is so institutionalized in the media, and so much part of the commercial process of cinema, it is a powerful source of orthodox ideas of what counts *as* cinema (what is 'good,' 'worthwhile,' 'entertaining,' and what relations these values have to one another). So it is an

> Who is the very first recorded woman film director?

important place for challenging and changing these ideas. The repetition, regularity, and routine phrasing that Adler notes as flaws in the 'staff critic' can also be seen – along with the space, layout, and house-style rules of publications – as formal constraints defining the genre of reviewing. It is with these that feminist reviewers must work to change public perceptions of film.

Meaghan Morris, 'Indigestion: A Rhetoric of Reviewing', in *The Pirate's Fiancée: feminism, reading, postmodernism* (London: Verso, 1988)

See also: GOSSIP COLUMNS   MMo

FILM CRITICS

It is strikingly easy to come up with the names of vast numbers of women who have written about cinema. For, by contrast with other areas of the film industry, in which women have started to flourish only in the last two decades or so, women film critics, reviewers, and historians have been at it for a very long time. It is a continuing tradition, moreover: women critics and historians have been prominent throughout all phases and areas of film art – a fact which led one male critic, writing in the *Observer* in 1964, to wonder sourly if 'the

matriarchy . . . may not have the unfortunate side-effect of planting, deep in the collective unconsciousness, the notion that in order to review films it is necessary to be womanly.'

In Europe in particular, women critics and historians were on the scene early: in the 1920s and 1930s in BRITAIN there were BRYHER, C A LEJEUNE, and Iris BARRY. In Germany in the 1930s film historian and critic Lotte EISNER started publishing her influential books and reviews: her later works on Max Reinhardt, F W Murnau, and Fritz Lang were particular landmarks. In the USA, women film reviewers were ubiquitous. Evelyn Gerstein wrote for major Boston daily newspapers in the 1920s and 1930s, and in the same period Velma Pilcher reviewed for *The Christian Science Monitor*, Helen Lawrenson for *Vanity Fair*, Cecilia Ager for *Vogue*.

One of the reasons for women's prominence, in the periodical field at least, was that film reviewing was originally considered a second-rate activity. Cinema was thought to be many levels below theater, and indeed confusions about film's importance among the arts led many early journalist-critics to write about film pseudonymously. In fact, film reviews would often appear on the 'woman's page' of a daily newspaper, being thought not sufficiently important to take up time and space in the more commercially clout-rich drama section. But women film critics had the last laugh, as – particularly in the 1960s and early 1970s – FILM CRITICISM achieved a kind of superstar status – and writers like Pauline KAEL and Penelope Gilliatt (the latter initially in England and then in the USA) became icons of the merging of popular and high art. Intellectuals such as Claude-Edmonde Magny in France, and Susan SONTAG in the USA, produced critical articles and books which provided theoretical ammunition for regarding film as 'serious' art.

Marsha McCreadie, *Women on Film: The Critical Eye* (New York: Praeger, 1983)

See also: ALTENLOH, EMILIE;
COLETTE; DAWSON, JAN; HD;
LAWSON, SYLVIA; POWELL,
DILYS   *MMc*

FILM DISTRIBUTION *see*
DISTRIBUTION; FEMINIST
DISTRIBUTION

FILM EXHIBITION *see* EXHIBITION;
FEMINIST EXHIBITION

FILM FESTIVALS

The continuing paradox of the relation of
women and women filmmakers to international film festivals is that although
women far outnumber men in the work
of the festivals (running many departments of the large festivals, from guest
liaison to sales offices to corporate spon-
sorship, with press offices of all major
festivals administered by women), they
are rarely in the position of selecting the
films, and films by women filmmakers
number less than 10 percent amongst the
selections. Although the tide may seem
to have been turning in the past few
years, with women Festival Directors in
Toronto, London, and Washington,
always a powerful woman critic on the
New York selection committee, and
male/female teams selecting for two of
Berlin's major sections, still the majority
of Class A festival selections are made –
often single-handedly – by men (Cannes,
Montreal, Los Angeles, Chicago, Melbourne, Sydney, Edinburgh). Nevertheless, there are three major international
festivals where women audiences can
count on a substantial selection of films
by women. Berlin is always a useful excursion for the screenings of new films
by filmmakers from WEST GERMANY,
which tend to include higher numbers of
women than other national cinemas.
Cannes, as the biggest festival in the
world, always yields relatively large
numbers of films by women, and the
market screenings are particularly useful
for viewing commercial films by women

which would not otherwise see wide release or festival exposure. Since Kay
Armatage started selecting for Toronto
in 1982, that festival has become known
by women filmmakers, feminist critics,
women programmers/curators, and audiences as the largest selection of new
films by women outside of the two major
WOMEN'S FILM FESTIVALS.

KA

FILM NOIR

As a GENRE, film noir refers to a Hollywood film movement of the 1940s and
early 1950s. These films are characterized
by darkness – both literal and metaphorical. They present a nighttime world of
dark shadows (evoked by high-contrast
expressionistic LIGHTING), dangerous
city streets, pervasive criminality, and
explosive SEXUALITY. There is also a
bleak evocation of characters groping in
the dark, driven by suspicion, by obsessive preoccupation with the past
(often articulated in fragmented narratives, elaborate flashbacks, framing devices, dream/nightmare sequences) and
with that which is mysterious, unknown, and often, as it turns out (in
unresolved plots), unknowable. The
films are frequently shaped by a structure
in which the hero/detective starts out
investigating a crime, but ends up investigating a woman – it is her mystique that
comes under scrutiny, as in *Laura* (Otto
Preminger, Twentieth Century-Fox,
1944) and *Out of the Past* (Jacques Tourneur, RKO, 1947).

The film noir heroine is recognizably a
FEMME FATALE specializing in murder,
seduction, and revenge – Barbara STAN-
WYCK in Billy Wilder's *Double Indemnity*
(Paramount, 1944) and Joan Bennett in
Fritz Lang's *The Woman in the Window*
(RKO, 1944). Yet in this genre nothing is
what it seems – the heroine is more often
than not presented as quintessentially
ambiguous. Maybe she's innocent (of a
crime *and* of sexuality); maybe she isn't –
in which case she is both desirable *and*

dangerous. Either way, these women are in control of their own sexuality – a threatening proposition. In *Kiss Me Deadly* (Robert Aldrich, United Artists, 1955) the metaphor of female sexuality as explosive is literalized: a search for the 'great whatsit' reveals the object to be an atomic bomb which blows up the world.

Some feminist criticisms of film noir argue that the genre is particularly oppressive in its representation of women, since HEROINES who are shown to be in control of their own sexuality are seen as a threat – ultimately they have to be controlled, put in their place, or killed off by the male order. Other approaches, however, are more positive, arguing that in so far as the genre eschews domestic harmony and facile resolutions it creates a space for exploring (often critically) the contradictions of patriarchal culture. Films such as *Gilda* (Charles Vidor, Columbia, 1946) can be seen as self-reflexive – narrative resolution (the heterosexual couple ultimately united) is seen to be bought at a cost. The apparently 'natural' state of sexual equilibrium is secured on the basis of certain brutal repressions, in particular the repression of female desire and of homosexuality. Rita HAYWORTH's

> 'To put on femininity with a vengeance suggests the power of taking it off.'
> What concept in feminist film theory is being referred to here?

PERFORMANCE as Gilda is seen, at moments, to parody the femme fatale figure, to show 'her' up as a STEREO-TYPE, a projection of male fantasy. Moreover, MASCULINITY, in these films, is often presented as very precarious. Typically, the film noir hero is obsessive and neurotic, sometimes decidedly psychotic. Most importantly, though, he doesn't know what is going on. It is in the female figure that energy and passion are focused.

More recent versions of Hollywood

film noir include *Klute* (Alan J Pakula, 1971), *Chinatown* (Roman Polanski, 1974), *Body Heat* (Lawrence Kasdan, 1981), and *Blood Simple* (Joel Coen, 1984).

E Ann Kaplan (ed.), *Women in Film Noir* (London: British Film Institute, 1978)

LS

FILM STOCK

On a clear, flexible celluloid base, a light-sensitive emulsion contributes significant variables to the characteristics of the film image. Properties of film stocks include contrast, graininess, sensitivities to various aspects of the light spectrum, and sharpness. Because of chemical and physical features, generally the less time needed to expose the image (a fast speed), the grainier, softer, and more contrasty the image.

The earliest black-and-white films were orthochromatic, a film stock which has good sensitivity to the violet and blue range of the light spectrum, less to green and yellow, and none to red. As a result, in early films reds appear black in the photographic image while light blues tend to go to white. Panchromatic (pan) film, which became available as early as 1913 but achieved widespread use only after the late 1920s, is able to pick up as tones of gray reds as well as violets, blues, greens, and yellows. Until the conversion to pan film stock, cinematographers who worked toward a full range of grays compensated for ortho's characteristics by manipulating the MISE-EN-SCENE. Women and men actors were advised against using rouge on the cheeks or red lipstick, but MAKE-UP manuals suggested dotting edges of the eyes with reds to enlarge them, much like eyeliners. Filters can also alter light characteristics: a major advantage of panchromatic film stock was that with proper filters clouds could become visible in light blue skies, and day-for-night shooting was cheaper than shooting after dark with massive amounts of lighting equipment. COLOR film stocks are numerous: famous types are Technicolor, Agfacolor, and Eastman Color. The technology to produce color tones has been biassed in favor of white skin tones.

Brian Winston, 'A Whole Technology of Dyeing: A Note on Ideology and the Apparatus of the Chromatic Moving Image', *Daedalus*, vol. 114, no. 4 (1985)

JaS

FILM THEORY

While several seminal works in film theory were produced during the 1920s and 1930s by academics and scholarly film critics such as Lotte EISNER, Emilie ALTENLOH, and Béla Balázs, systematic analytical sudy of cinema did not get fully under way in the West until after World War II. It took a while longer for film studies in general, and film theory in particular, to find their way onto the curricula of some academic institutions in Europe, Australia, and North America. However, developments in film theory have emerged as often, or more often, from film JOURNALS as from the academy. André Bazin, sometime editor of the French journal *Cahiers du cinéma*, is widely regarded as a founding father of film theory. His writings have inspired many studies of REALISM in cinema, and were a formative influence on theorist Christian Metz, whose work from the late 1960s on laid the foundations of PSYCHOANALYTIC FILM THEORY.

Film theory has tended to borrow its conceptual frameworks and methods from other disciplines – literary studies or sociology, for example – adapting them to a new object, cinema, and developing and challenging them in the process. Where 1960s film theory stemmed from English studies, readings of films and studies of AUTHORSHIP in cinema were often influenced by the Leavisite 'practical criticism' which dominated many university English departments at the time. A controversial move toward STRUCTURALIST modes of film analysis took place in Britain during the 1960s, inspired by the work of the French anthropologist Claude Lévi-Strauss and to some extent by literary theory of the Russian Formalist school. Structuralist approaches were productive in studies of individual film GENREs – the Hollywood WESTERN in particular – in studies of IDEOLOGY in cinema, and latterly in analyses of film NARRATIVE.

With the publication in 1969 of Peter Wollen's *Signs and Meaning in the Cinema* (London: British Film Institute/Secker & Warburg), an approach to cinema based in SEMIOTICS – dealing with cinematic codes, or the processes through which meanings are produced in films – was popularized. While structuralist-inspired film theory quite quickly fell out of favor, semiotics remains a key influence in film theory today. For example, a notion of film as TEXT, or signifying system, is taken for granted in most theoretical work on cinema. The idea of signification also underlies those elements of psychoanalytic film theory influenced by the work on language and subjectivity of psychoanalyst Jacques Lacan. Alongside structuralist-semiotic-psychoanalytic strands of film theory, more social-science-based approaches have informed work on the sociology of cinema, including studies of genre as a sociocultural phenomenon and readings of films as expressive of wider social trends. In recent years, studies of cinema influenced by cognitive psychology, by critical theory of the Frankfurt School, and by CULTURAL STUDIES, have offered a challenge to semiotic/psychoanalytic approaches. FEMINIST FILM THEORY has drawn on most of these tendencies, while arguably remaining dominated by psychoanalytic approaches. But feminist film theory, even of the dominant tendency, has been instrumental in taking on and challenging 'cinepsychoanalysis,' and in bringing about important developments in the wider field of film theory.

Pam Cook (ed.), *The Cinema Book* (London: British Film Institute, 1985)

See also: POSTMODERNISM;
POSTSTRUCTURALISM   *AKu*

FINLAND

The first two decades of this century were a period of experimentation in Finnish cinema, with more ambitious film production beginning only in the early 1920s. Finland's first female film director was Glory Leppänen, though she made only one film (in 1936), and is better remembered as a drama director. She was hired after the sudden death of Erkki Karu, one of the pioneers of Finnish cinema. Although Leppänen had had no experience as a film director, she had spent a year in Vienna studying in Max Reinhardt's theater school. Her film *Onnenpotku/Lucky Stroke* was not a success; but it does provide a vivid picture of a Finland recovering from the Depression. The leading lady of the film was Ester Toivonen, who became a star in Finland after winning a European beauty contest.

One of the most interesting Finnish film directors is Teuvo Tulio. From the thirties to the fifties he made several personal and strongly emotional MELODRAMAS. His films were despised by both the industry and the critics, but were extremely popular, especially with female audiences. In Tulio's melodramas the fate of the woman was to collapse under the pressure of hypocritical Finnish class society. Almost all his films tell the story of an innocent, poor, and naive girl who, because of her beauty and kindness, becomes famous and rich. But in the end her fate is blindness, jail, punishment, misery, and death. Tulio's favorite actress was Regina Linnanheimo, and they continued to make melodramas together from 1930 until the end of the 1950s. One of their best-known films is *Rikollinen nainen/The Criminal Woman* (1952), for which Linnanheimo wrote the script.

Actress Mirjam Kuosmanen is one of the forgotten women in the history of Finnish cinema. She was one of the most popular film stars of the forties and fifties, but it is little known that she was also an 'auteur' of her films: she wrote the scripts and co-directed them. Among the films co-directed by Kuosmanen – without screen credit – was *Valkoinen Peura/The White Reindeer* (1952). Perhaps internationally the most famous Finnish film of all time, *The White Reindeer*, was nominated in Cannes and noticed even in Hollywood. It tells a story of a woman who is a witch without knowing it: she turns into a white reindeer and bewitches men.

It has been characteristic of the Finnish situation that women directors or actresses have occasionally had the opportunity to make a single film. Actress Ansa Ikonen made one film (*Nainen on valttia/The Women are Trumps*) in 1944, while actress/director Ritva Arvelo made her film *Kultainen vasikka/The Golden Calf* in 1961. In this situation many Finnish women have gone abroad in the hope of pursuing a career: director Ingemo Engström went to Germany, and animator Marjut Rimpinen to England. Directors living in Finland have also made films abroad: for example Eija-Elina BERGHOLM and Tuija-Maija NISKANEN have both worked in Sweden.

Peter Cowie, *The Finnish Cinema* (South Brunswick, NJ: A S Barnes, London: Tantivy Press, 1976)   *TA*

FONOROFF, NINA (1956–)

The union of 'personal film' aesthetics with postmodern sensibility is successfully achieved in the films of Nina Fonoroff. One of the youngest of the AVANT-GARDE filmmakers in the USA, Fonoroff came to the cinema with a less romanticized and more socially conscious sensibility than her predecessors, and proceeded to critique film GENREs, particularly FILM NOIR, the Hollywood 'spectacular' and the avant-garde film itself. Fonoroff uses rephotography of appropriated images and sound loops to stop frame, repeat scenes, and distort the material in an attempt to reveal the latent content of common film forms. *Big Story* (1984) re-creates a thriller in abstract form, giving all the clues of suspense, but without any object. *Some Phases of an Empire* (1984) reworks the 1951 version of *Quo Vadis* (Mervyn Le Roy, MGM) by combining it with phrases from the book *Rebecca of Sunnybrook Farm* to comment humorously upon the sexual and political implications of this fantasy of the fall of Rome. *Department of the Interior* (1986) juxtaposes positive and negative imagery of suburban landscape with sound fragments of Menotti's opera *Amal and the Night Visitors* to meditate poetically on mother –daughter relationships as they are revealed through home movies. Fonoroff's work exemplifies an important strain of recent practice by independent filmmakers in the USA.

Empathy (1980); *Misery Index* (1982); *Big Story* (1984); *Some Phases of an Empire* (1984); *Department of the Interior* (1986); *The Substance of Things Hoped For* (1989)

Nina Fonoroff with Lisa Cartwright, 'Narrative is Narrative, So What is New?', *Heresies*, no. 16 (1983)   MKe

FOX, BERYL (1931–   )

For years one of CANADA's most innovative and politically committed DOCUMENTARY filmmakers, Beryl Fox made seminal contributions to the development of television current affairs in the 1960s. She joined the Canadian Broadcasting Corporation as a script assistant and researcher, and co-directed her first film in 1962. Particularly in historically significant investigative series such as *Document* and *This Hour Has Seven Days*, she was a major figure both onscreen and behind the camera. She seemed to be able to strike to the heart of the current political climate, and was the first Canadian to examine American racial tensions, feminism, and the Vietnam War. Although she left

CBC in 1966, she continued to make documentaries for television throughout the seventies, until she began to produce feature fiction films for theatrical markets. Her work is consistently marked by clearly populist sympathies, commitment to social change, and strong liberal feminism.

Television: *Balance of Terror* (with D Leiterman, 1962); *Servant of All* (with D Leiterman, 1962); *One More River* (with D Leiterman, 1963); *Three on a Match* (with D Leiterman, 1963); *The Single Woman and the Double Standard* (1963);

> *Filmmakers Maya Deren, Yvonne Rainer, and Sally Potter have all tried to create a new cinematic language – with what?*

Summer in Mississippi (1963); *The Chief* (with D Leiterman, 1964); *The Mills of the Gods: Viet Nam* (1965); *The Honourable René Levesque* (1966); *Youth: In Search of Morality* (1966); *Saigon: Portrait of a City* (1967); *Last Reflections on a War* (1968); *A View From the 21st Century* (1968); *Memorial to Martin Luther King* (1969); *Be a Man – Sell Out!* (1969); *North with the Spring* (1970); *Here Come the Seventies* series (1970–2); *Travel and Leisure* (1971); *Jerusalem* (1973); *Habitat 2000* (1973); *Man Into Superman* (1974); *Wild Refuge* series (1974); *Take My Hand* (1975); *How to Fight with Your Wife* (1975); *The Visible Woman* (1975); *Return to Kansas City* (1978). Films produced: *Images of the Wild* (1978); *Fields of Endless Days* (1978); *Dr Elizabeth* (1978); *Rose's House* (1979); *Hot Wheels* (1979); *Surfacing* (1979); *By Design* (1981)   KA

FRANCE

Historically, more women have taken an active part in French cinema than in any other national film industry. Yet French cinema is one of the most misogynistic, both in its representation of gender and in its popular GENREs; it has also rarely produced major female stars on the Hollywood model. This paradox is understandable in the context of a patriarchal and Catholic culture which also valorizes individual artists and auteurs, thus providing a space – however marginal – for women.

French cinema ruled world screens until World War I, through a combination of creative talent and entrepreneurial spirit (Pathé and Gaumont). Most of the work of pioneers, including the world's first woman director Alice GUY, Ferdinand Zecca and Georges Méliès, is lost, making a true appreciation of these early years difficult. Nevertheless, two lasting aspects of French cinema emerged: male comedy (Max Linder, Rigadin) and a strong realistic impulse, whether in melodrama, religious scenes, or 'social problem' films. While another popular form, the adventure/crime serial, thrived, the founding in 1908 of the *Film d'Art* company opened the door to highbrow literary adaptations and the tradition of the art film.

The expansion of the American film industry and the upheaval of World War I combined to undermine French world hegemony. While a reduced production of popular films continued up to the late 1920s (serials, bourgeois melodramas, and realist films dominated), AVANT-GARDE movements flourished. In the 'first avant garde,' or French Impressionism, Germaine DULAC, Louis Delluc, Marcel L'Herbier, Abel Gance, Jean and Marie EPSTEIN were searching for a film language capable of rendering subjectivity outside classical NARRATIVE, and attempted to define a NATIONAL CINEMA – in Delluc's words: 'Let French cinema be real cinema, let French cinema be really French!' Dulac, an avowed feminist, put these experiments to the service of a specifically feminine viewpoint. The 'second avant garde' was marked by the work of Surrealist artists such as Man Ray, Luis Buñuel, Salvador Dali, and René Clair. Its most famous film, Buñuel's *L'Age d'or* (1930), shows the ambiguous treatment of women

typical of Surrealism: both idolized and objectified as the bearers of 'subversive' *amour fou.*

Apart from Alice Guy, MUSIDORA, and Germaine Dulac, a few women directed silent films (Renée Carl, Marie-Louise Iribe, Rose Lacau-Pansini in features; Suzanne Devoyod, Elyane Tayar, Lucie Derain in documentaries); only Marie Epstein, Solange Bussi (*La Vagabonde* [1931]) and Marguerite Viel (*La Banque Némo* [1934]), made features in the 1930s, while a few worked in documentaries (Lucie Derain, Lucette Gaudard, Claudine Lenoir). The coming of SOUND deeply affected the structures of the industry and the types of films made. Stage plays from the popular boulevard and vaudeville theater became a major source for films. Historians have often deplored these films as vulgar and 'uncinematic,' yet they defined a specifically French cinema – using colloquial language and styles of performance, and indigenous forms of humor. In this popular tradition, which includes the films of Marcel Pagnol, Sacha Guitry, and a host of lesser-known directors, men occupied center stage and women were often little more than (in playwright Marcel Achard's words) 'the stake of the game.' The subgenre of 'Russian' melodrama – Marcel Carné's *Jenny* (1936), Albert Valentin's *L'Entraîneuse* (1938), or Abel Gance's *Paradis perdu* (1939) – provides interesting exceptions. Alongside the ground-breaking work of Jean RENOIR, one aspect of French film in the 1930s has been widely acclaimed: poetic realism, a pessimistic, FILM NOIR, type of populist drama blending surface realism (contemporary urban settings, working-class characters) with poetic stylization, epitomized by the films of Marcel Carné (*Quai des brumes/ Port of Shadows* [1938], *Le Jour se lève* [1939]), and those of Pierre Chenal, Jacques Feyder, Julien Duvivier, and Jean Grémillon. Though this tradition has produced 'mythical' women characters (Nelly/Michèle Morgan in *Quai des brumes*), the poetic realist drama was always that of the male hero, archetypally embodied by Jean Gabin – 'Oedipus in a cloth cap,' as André Bazin put it.

During the German occupation of France, production at first declined and many prominent filmmakers left the country. Those who stayed tended to shy away from contemporary subjects – hence a proliferation of 'escapist' films and costume dramas culminating in Carné's *Les Enfants du paradis* (1945), though a few works, such as Henri-Georges Clouzot's *Le Corbeau* (1943), viciously satirized the contemporary French provincial bourgeoisie. On the other hand, the years 1940 to 1944 represented a golden age for French films at the box office, without competition from (banned) Anglo-American films. One noticeable development was an increase in women's MELODRAMAS – for instance Abel Gance's *La Vénus aveugle* (1940), Marcel Pagnol's *La Fille du puisatier* (1940), Jean Stelli's *Le Voile bleu* (1942), and Jean Grémillon's *Le Ciel est à vous* (1944). Though it is tempting to see these as simple 'reflections' of the Vichy ideology (exalting motherhood, patriotism, and sacrifice), other factors, such as changing gender roles and the address to a female AUDIENCE, are relevant.

In the postwar period French women were at last given the vote, and Simone de Beauvoir published her crucial feminist essay *The Second Sex* in 1949. Shorts, documentaries, and montage films attracted many women directors: Marie-Anne Colson-Malleville, Denise Dual, Hélène Dassonville, Nicole Védrès (*Paris 1900* [1947]), Yannick Bellon (*Goémons* [1948]). Meanwhile, popular cinema plowed the familiar furrows of *noir* poetic realism (Yves Allégret's *Dédée d'Anvers* [1948]), comedies, and literary adaptations in the French 'tradition of quality,' of which Claude Autant-Lara's *Occupe-toi d'Amélie* (1949), Jacques Becker's *Casque d'Or* (1952), and René Clément's *Gervaise* (1956), are typical. It is in this mainstream that women like Andrée Feix, Caro Canaille, and Jacqueline AUDRY worked (though the latter did inflect the genre). Reworking the American thriller, the *policier* genre emerged then, to become one of the two most popular in France up to the present day (the other being COMEDY). Even in its best early examples – Jacques Becker's *Touchez pas au grisbi* (1954), Jean-Pierre Melville's *Bob le flambeur* (1956) – the French *policier* did nothing to challenge the misogyny of its American counterpart.

Outside genre cinema, a number of directors – Robert Bresson, Jacques Tati, Alain Resnais, Agnès VARDA – worked in ways which, with their small budgets and crews, and emphasis on personal expression and unconventional film language, affirmed the practice of auteur cinema – cinema founded in AUTHORSHIP – at a time when its theoretical basis was being formulated by François Truffaut and his colleagues at *Cahiers du cinéma*. These critics virulently challenged French mainstream cinema and soon turned filmmakers themselves, spearheading the NEW WAVE. But however innovatory in style, New Wave films on the whole failed to take on contemporary issues in 1960s France, or to address women, as either characters, filmmakers, or spectators. It took both the events of May 1968 and the rise of the women's movement for this to happen.

May 1968 may not have brought the 'revolution in and through the cinema' called for by *Cahiers du cinéma*; it nevertheless heralded a shift, in both *auteur* and popular films, toward a more socially conscious cinema (typical are the films of René Allio, Claude Sautet, Maurice Pialat, Louis Malle, Bertrand Tavernier), though with, at the other end of the spectrum, the rise of 'X-rated' PORNOGRAPHY. Many professionally trained women – Nelly Kaplan, Yannick Bellon, Nadine Trintignant, Nina Companeez – entered filmmaking at that point and released their first features. At the same time, a new generation of (often untrained) women directors made militant DOCUMENTARIES on issues such as abortion – the famous *Histoires d'A* (Marielle Issartel and Charles Belmont, 1973) – work, motherhood, mental health, and so on. Actresses such as Anna Karina and Jeanne Moreau turned to direction. The MUSIDORA association was founded in 1973, holding the first women's film festival in Paris in 1974. In 1982 the Centre Simone de Beauvoir was founded by Carole Roussopoulos, Delphine Seyrig, and Ioana Weider, with a brief to promote women's work, particularly in VIDEO; the CRETEIL annual women's film festival, also still in existence, started in 1979. Feminist feature films reached regular cinema circuits: Coline Serreau's *Mais Qu'est-ce qu'elles veulent/What Do They Want?* (1977), Varda's *L'Une chante, l'autre pas/One Sings the Other Doesn't* (1977), Yannick Bellon's *L'Amour violé/Rape of Love* (1978), and the daily *Le Matin* talked, in 1979, of 'the irresistible rise of women directors.' Male directors reacted to feminism in various ways: lucid exposé of male fears (Jean Eustache's *La Maman et la putain/The Mother and the Whore* [1973]), hysteria (Bertrand Blier's *Calmos* [1976]), or cooptation – 'strong' HEROINES began to appear in mainstream films, played by Simone Signoret, Annie Girardot, or new stars like Isabelle Huppert and Miou-Miou.

The 1980s have seen important changes. While an unprecedented number of women directors are now working in the film industry (though still less than 10 percent of French filmmakers), their work has become increasingly diverse, belying the notion of a homogeneous 'women's cinema.' Also, in line with the general ideological retrenchment, low status of feminism, and neglect of FEMINIST FILM THEORY in 1980s France, it is often divorced from feminism. Some women directors have moved toward big-budget ART CINEMA (Diane Kurys's *Coup de foudre/At First Sight* [1984], *Un Homme amoureux/A Man in Love* [1987]), or popular genres (Bellon's *La Triche* [1984], Coline Serreau's box office triumph *Trois hommes et un*

couffin/Three Men and a Cradle* [1986]). Some, like Anne-Marie Miéville or Marguerite DURAS, pursue a modernist line: while others (Juliet Berto, Caroline Roboh) have adopted POSTMODERN aesthetics, like their male counterparts Jean-Jacques Beineix, Leos Carax, or Luc Besson. In these films, a fashionable gender bending, as well as delight in images, surfaces, and lifestyles, have tended to replace the stylistic innovation of the 1950s and 1960s and the ideological challenges of the 1970s.

On the whole, though, the mainstay of women's cinema in France remains the auteur film: it is in this tradition that established directors like Varda, or relative newcomers like Jeanne Labrune, Geneviève Lefèvre, Marie-Claude Treilhou, Charlotte Silvera, Suzanne Schiffman, and Aline Isserman work. Though increasingly threatened by falling attendances, blockbusters (American or French), and deregulated television, it may still be this type of filmmaking which offers a vital section of French directors, male or female, the best chance of survival on the national and international scenes.

Susan Hayward and Ginette Vincendeau (eds), *French Film: Texts and Contexts* (London and New York: Routledge, 1989)

See also: BARDOT, BRIGITTE; COLETTE; HUILLET, DANIELE; OPHULS, MAX   *GV*

FRAUEN UND FILM

Founded in 1974 in WEST GERMANY by filmmaker Helke Sander, *Frauen und Film* (Women and Film) was the first, and remains the only, European feminist film JOURNAL. It has provided a forum for both exploring contemporary women's filmmaking and rescuing the history of women's contribution to cinema throughout the twentieth century. Thus the work of Alice GUY, Esfir SHUB, and Maya DEREN has been discussed alongside that of Chantal AKERMAN,

Marguerite DURAS, Yvonne RAINER, Helke SANDER, Ula STOECKL, Elfi MIKESCH, and many other contemporary women filmmakers.

The journal has focused mainly on the notion of a feminist COUNTER-CINEMA, exploring questions of feminist aesthetics and attempting to define a feminist film culture. In its early years one of the key roles *Frauen und Film* performed was to function as a newsletter. It provided a forum for feminist film politics within the women's movement and carried information about new films by women filmmakers, reports from FILM FESTIVALS, interviews with filmmakers, and the like. Another major concern was to document the extent of women's contribution to cinema, looking not only at women directors but also at editors, producers, viewers, actresses, camerawomen, and film critics. The journal has also attempted to counter patriarchal structures and institutions through its format: it is run by an editorial collective; its title was a deliberate inversion of the name of a fifties woman's magazine, *Film und Frau* (Film and Woman); and at the level of language, the editors initially rejected the use of capitals to signify their rejection of what can be viewed as the dominant male discourse.

Although *Frauen und Film* still appears today, its format underwent a change during the late seventies and early eighties. When Helke Sander withdrew from the editorial board, the journal started to become more the domain of critics and theorists, with less involvement from actual filmmakers. This moved it away from its practical, newsletter orientation and coincided with a loosening of its ties with the women's movement. There has since been a greater emphasis on theory and history, with the journal becoming particularly interested in English and North American FILM THEORY. Although this shift to a more academic orientation is regretted in some circles, *Frauen und Film* nevertheless provides an invaluable documentation of the work and working conditions of West German women filmmakers, who have been so neglected in most critical considerations of West German cinema, and represents an enormous contribution to feminist film culture more generally.

Miriam Hansen, 'Messages in a Bottle?', *Screen*, vol. 28, no. 4 (1987)   JK

FRIEDRICH, SU (1954–)

Having begun making independent films in 1978, Friedrich has made eight films to date. Her contribution to AVANT-GARDE FILM in the USA has been in the integration of varieties of personally informed imagery with texts written in the first-person voice, often directly scratched into the film emulsion. The powerful graphic presence of text *as image* reinforces the content of these highly 'personal films.' *Gently Down the Stream* (1981) incorporates entries from a dream journal into an eclectic series of closeup and handheld images. The language charges otherwise incidental shots with sexual and violent overtones; and the evocation of unconscious levels in the experiences of everyday life is the film's ultimate strength. *The Ties That Bind* (1984) is an experimental documentary about the filmmaker's mother's life in Germany during World War II. The tension inherent in the mother–daughter relationship, as well as the inability of a

Su Friedrich's *Gently Down the Stream*

postwar American filmmaker to comprehend the political life of her mother as a young German woman under Hitler, are explored in the interrelated texts and images. *Damned If You Don't* (1987) is an experimental narrative about a young nun who, in exploring life outside her convent walls, ends up in an erotically powerful lesbian encounter. Friedrich's distinctive style runs through all of the films she makes, crossing experimental, documentary, and narrative boundaries.

Hot Water (1978); *Cool Hands Warm Heart* (1979); *Scar Tissue* (1979); *I Suggest Mine* (1980); *Gently Down the Stream* (1981); *But No One* (1982); *The Ties That Bind* (1984); *Damned If You Don't* (1987)

Scott MacDonald, 'Su Friedrich: Reappropriations', *Film Quarterly*, vol. 41, no. 2 (1987–8)   *MKe*

GAINSBOROUGH STUDIOS

Founded by Michael Balcon in 1924 as a small two-stage studio in Islington, North London, Gainsborough survived the financial upheavals suffered during the twenties and thirties by the film industry in BRITAIN by producing popular low-budget films cheaply and quickly. Under Edward Black's management, a small stable of stars and production personnel was built up, making critically well-received movies directed by the young Carol Reed and Alfred HITCHCOCK (*Young and Innocent* [1937]; *The Lady Vanishes* [1939]). But after the box office success of the costume melodrama *The Man in Grey* (Leslie Arliss, 1943), the studio took a decisive turn. Edward Black left the company, control passed to Maurice Ostrer with his policy of providing 'escapist' fare for an audience sick of war films, and Gainsborough entered its most successful phase with the shortlived series of medium-budget WOMAN'S PICTURES, featuring stars like Margaret Lockwood, Phyllis Calvert, James Mason, Jean Kent and Patricia Roc.

Though the Gainsborough MELODRAMAs were a hit with the public, they met wholesale critical opprobrium. They were attacked not only for their triviality, but for their overt reliance on GENRE conventions. Yet, as recent feminist interest has discovered, this was precisely the films' strength, enabling them successfully to challenge Hollywood's domination of the British market. Women who had experienced the sexual and economic independence offered by the war years responded with delight to a TOMBOY Margaret Lockwood as would-be highwayman Lady

Skelton in *The Wicked Lady* (Leslie Arliss, 1945), or Phyllis Calvert as respectable Italian matron turned gypsy in *Madonna of the Seven Moons* (Arthur Crabtree, 1944). Somehow, the narrative resolutions in which they got their comeuppance could not erase the exhilaration of seeing them act out forbidden desires onscreen. Even those contemporary dramas like *Love Story* (Leslie Arliss, 1944), *They Were Sisters* (Arthur Crabtree, 1944), or *The Root of All Evil* (Brock Williams, 1947), with their atmosphere of female self-sacrifice, gave considerable space to British womanhood as emancipated, active, and capable of fighting for what she wanted – an image crucial to British postwar democratic ideals.

In 1946 Ostrer was succeeded by Sydney Box, who ushered in a new phase of Gainsborough productions. Together with his co-producer/screenwriter wife Muriel BOX, who went on to become a director, Sydney made a number of controversial films, many of which ran into trouble with the BRITISH BOARD OF FILM CENSORS, and all of which were criticized for their preoccupation with squalor and sadism (among them *The Brothers* [David MacDonald, 1947] and *Good-time Girl* [David MacDonald, 1947]). At the end of the forties, Gainsborough, along with the rest of the British film industry, fell on hard times. The Islington studio was closed and the company moved to Pinewood Studios under the Rank umbrella, where unadventurous policies finally put paid to the exotic, transgressive impulse that characterized its heyday. Gainsborough, like Hammer subsequently, successfully capitalized on the dark undercurrents in British society and culture, bringing to the fore themes of sexuality and national identity normally buried beneath a suffocating blanket of taste and respectability.

Robert Murphy and Sue Aspinall (eds), *BFI Dossier No. 18: Gainsborough Melodrama* (London: British Film Institute, 1983) PC

GARBO, GRETA (1905–90)

Starting her career as a plump teenage model in silent film commercials in her native country, SWEDEN, Garbo was a far cry from 'the Divine,' as she was later to be called – or, as Molly HASKELL has put it, 'the high priestess of the holy communion of American Romance.' Born Gustafsson, Greta became Garbo while still in Sweden. The name is usually attributed to her discoverer, director Mauritz Stiller, but was in fact suggested to her by Mimi Pollak, one of her friends in theater school and later one of the very few women in pre-1960s Sweden to direct a film. Arriving in the States in 1924, Garbo became a household name after only two mediocre silent melodramas. Her best-known American films include *Anna Christie* (Clarence Brown, MGM, 1930), *Queen Christina* (Rouben Mamoulian, MGM, 1933), *Anna Karenina* (Clarence Brown, MGM, 1935), *Camille* (George Cukor, MGM, 1937), and *Ninotchka* (Ernst Lubitsch, MGM, 1939).

Garbo's image of European otherness, of enigmatic sphinx, survived the coming of sound: this is attributed partly to her deep, somewhat husky, voice. Her voice, together with her unusual height, broad shoulders, and large hands and feet, are said to have appealed to both male and female audiences (for instance, in her CROSSDRESSING role in *Queen Christina*). This has also made her interesting to latter-day FEMINIST FILM THEORISTS such as Molly Haskell, for whom Garbo, along with Marlene DIETRICH, is 'that other great androgyne . . ., the anima of no single auteur or even society, but . . . a natural force, a principle of beauty that, once set in mo-

tion, becomes autonomous.' This is certainly an interesting point, worth more scrutiny: to what extent can a STAR like Garbo be said to be her own director, an actress perhaps too much aware of her own power to allow herself to be subordinated to a strong director?

Molly Haskell, *From Reverence to Rape* (New York: Penguin, 1979) MKo

GAVIOLA, TATIANA (1956–)

Actively involved in directing and producing video in CHILE, Gaviola graduated from the School of Communication Arts at the Catholic University of Chile in 1979. Although trained as a filmmaker, she has opted for VIDEO as a means of overcoming the financial and political constraints that have limited film production in Chile since the military coup of 1973. Her work, which has been produced by the major video producers, Filmocentro, Ictus, and Promav UC, alternates between documentary and experimental. Gaviola's videos deal with historical issues, but most center upon the lives of women and their struggle for political change. Her work has been shown extensively in Europe and North America, where she has taken part in workshops organized by feminist collectives. With Lotty Rosenfeld, Diamela Eltit, Patricia Camiragua, and others, Gaviola occupies an important place in the contemporary context of Chilean audiovisual production, and their work expresses a repositioning of cultural practice within the extremely repressive conditions that have affected the social and political fabric of the country.

Tiempo para un líder (co-d. Jaime Eyzaguirre, 1982); *Tantas vidas, una historia* (1983); *No le tengo miedo a nada* (1984); *Machalí, fragmentos de una historia* (1984); *Sarah Bernhardt* (1984); *La secreta obcenidad de cada día* (1985); *La ciudad, positivo y negativo* (1985); *José Balmes y Gracia Barrios* (1985); *Muerte en Santa Maria de Iquique* (1986); *Yo me comprometo* (1986); *Acuarela* (1986); *La gallinita ciega* (1987);

Garbo in *Queen Christina*

3000 mujeres + cuatro (1987); *Angeles*
(1988)   ZP

GAZE, THE *see* LOOK, THE

GENRE

The notion of genre has a long history
within literary studies, where it has been
used to make distinctions between types
or kinds of literature. The original Aris-
totelian distinction between lyric, epic,
and dramatic modes has informed much
subsequent discussion, though STRUC-
TURALIST criticism has altered the
emphasis to a notion of genre as a set of
codes and conventions, which alter historically but still provide the arena for an
implied contract between reader and
writer, presenting us with a notion of a
shared, but often unvoiced or unconscious, set of expectations.

The term was originally applied to
cinema as a production category in the
film industry. The industrial production
of films on a large profit-making scale
called for maximizing resources through
specialization in different kinds of film
production. In Hollywood, particular
studios became associated with particular
film genres – as did STARS, directors,
and producers: MGM is associated with
expensive-looking musicals, the director
George CUKOR with the WOMAN'S
PICTURE, and so on. The notion of 'contract' remains, however: studios could
produce and market films within categories which made sense financially, but
were also meaningful in terms of AUDI-
ENCE expectations. This points to one of
the key features of the production of
entertainment as a commodity – 'the
same but different': the constant demand
to produce more of what can be recognized, whilst also offering enough innovation to merit further expenditure by
the cinemagoer.

Within FILM THEORY, particularly in
the 1960s and early 1970s, genre was seen
as a critical category which would allow
recognition of the industrial, social, and
textual aspects of cinema. Genre studies
promised a sustained critical approach to
popular Hollywood cinema, making
possible comparisons of ICONOGRA-
PHY, NARRATIVE structure, and
directorial style within groups of films
which could also be identified as having
shared thematic concerns, or as representing responses to the same cultural
stimulus (World War II, Prohibition, the
changing position of women, and so on).
This promise, however, was to some
extent undone, or displaced, by the shift
within academic film theory to SEMI-
OTICS and PSYCHOANALYTIC FILM
THEORY.

As a critical category, genre has considerable flexibility and can be very useful, despite its central paradox: how can
we define a genre without relying on
deductions made from films which we
have first to assume to be within the
genre? Indeed, it is the very impurity of
the category, its dependence on the
expectations and judgement of both
filmmakers and audience, which makes
genre so interesting. For example, many
women filmmakers have worked over
the terrain of MELODRAMA (the family,
domestic life, sexual desire), while using
formal strategies quite different from
those of Hollywood. Looking at films
like *Film About a Woman Who . . .*
(Yvonne Rainer, 1974), *The Passion of
Remembrance* (Maureen Blackwood,
Sankofa, 1986), or *News From Home*
(Chantal Akerman, 1976) with a knowledge of the history of melodrama as a
genre allows both a critical reflection on
this history, and also a clearer sense of
what is at stake in any attempt to make
innovative representation of FEMININ-
ITY and the family.

Much FEMINIST INDEPENDENT
FILM has worked consciously with existing genre conventions, playing with or
challenging the viewer's expectations.
Sally POTTER's short film *Thriller* (1979)
examines the convention of the early and
tragic death of romantic HEROINES by
having Mimi – the consumptive heroine
of Puccini's opera *La Bohème* – investigate her own death. Work of this kind,

which exposes as conventional what may appear natural, is possible only with a historical notion of genre. The historical dimension of genre allows histories of images, stories, and pleasures to be looked at as separate from – though related to – 'the outside world'; and this is crucial to an understanding of how particular social groups have been represented in films. Genre provides a mediating concept with which what was previously taken for granted (the heroine gets her man) can be made strange (the heroine gets her woman).

The concept of genre allows us to make links between what appear to be dissimilar films. For example, ART CINEMA has been approached as the work of individual directors working in national contexts, and defined in opposition to the formulaic and international qualities of Hollywood genres, so that the former is validated by terms such as 'authenticity,' 'expressiveness,' and 'realism.' However, art cinema can itself be approached as a genre, but one with the defining feature of 'appearing not to be generic,' and with subsidiary features such as complexity of form, unresolved narratives, self-evident AUTHORSHIP, and frequently selfconscious reference to Hollywood genres. Much women's and feminist feature production falls into this genre which, like feminism itself, has a strong leaning toward the autobiographical. FEMINIST FILM THEORY, however, often ignores these generic qualities, approaching films, with all the innocence that greeted art cinema of the 1950s and 1960s, as simple expressions of a feminine sensibility.

Finally, it should perhaps be noted that in French, 'genre' means gender as well as genre. Feminist critics have pioneered work on gendered genres and subgenres such as melodrama and the woman's picture, contributing to the current critical reevaluation of these previously despised genres. Investigation of the gender affiliations of particular genres has unsettled both established critical hierarchies (for example, the common ideas that the melodramatic is somehow inferior to the realistic) and assumptions about the concerns of particular genres. For example, feminist work has pointed to the ways in which HORROR films, marketed at male audiences, are repeatedly concerned with anxieties about sexual difference and the female body.

Christine Gledhill, 'Genre', in *The Cinema Book*, ed. Pam Cook (London: British Film Institute, 1985)

See also: COMEDY; DOCUMENTARY; ETHNOGRAPHIC FILM; EXPLOITATION FILM; FANTASY; FILM NOIR; KUNG FU; MALE MELODRAMA; MUSICAL; PORNOGRAPHY; REVOLUTIONARY MODEL FILM; ROMANCE; SCIENCE FICTION; SOAP OPERA; SWORDPLAY; VAMPIRE FILM; WESTERN; WOMEN IN PERIL; WOMEN'S REVENGE   *CB*

GERMAN DEMOCRATIC REPUBLIC *see* EAST GERMANY

GERMANY

From its beginnings German cinema has stood in the midst of cultural debate, caught between entertainment, education, and art; between emancipation and conservatism. As long as cinema was confined to the fairgrounds – its character similar to the variety show – there was no significant indigenous film production. Although the Skladanowski brothers organized public film screenings at the same time as the Lumière brothers and Thomas Edison; and although Oskar Messter was involved with film as well as with recording and projection equipment, the German market was dominated by American, Italian, and French productions until 1914. The discrepancy between the large number of German screenings of foreign films and the small number of German productions shows that the public – the lower classes, including many women – enjoyed the entertainment.

The rise of a German film industry

began only when going to the movie theater became established as a socially accepted amusement. By 1910 traveling theater had given way to permanent movie palaces, a distribution system was in place, and multiple-reelers, along with film drama, had won favor. The bulk of film production was divided between two companies – Messter-Film and Paul Davidson's Projektion-AG Union – which attempted to bring cinema onto the level of the bourgeois arts. From this emerged the German film d'art, which took its cue from the theater: stage directors and actors were hired, and literary writers encouraged to write screenplays. In addition to this, attempts were made to import movie talent (such as Asta NIELSEN and Stellan Rye) rather than products. Along with structurally rigid films d'art, this practice also generated exceptional films, films which took joy in the reproduction of surface vividness, whose mechanics of production were still visible and thus opened up sensory vistas beyond the everyday experience of much of the public. Since avoiding CENSORSHIP was still relatively easy (each town had its own board of censors), and the movies were not yet a site of culture or education, they were able to work with entertaining topics largely excluded from bourgeois art. Social conventions such as gender difference, the exclusion of the sexual, and class differences – later to be heavily thematized as conflicts – could be ignored in the movies. The bulk of production – detective films, dramas, and serials – did not claim to educate, but provided a screen for the projection of fantasies. These liberating tendencies of cinema provoked resistance from the upper classes; the Kinoreformer (cinema reformers) in particular denounced the reception of this 'trash.' A few of the critics – Emilie ALTENLOH among them – did, however, adopt a more positive attitude toward the penetration of cinema into the bourgeois scene and the democratization of images.

World War I made possible the rise of national film production, since the demand for films remained high while imports ceased. The number of production companies grew; the government stepped in. Deulig (Deutsche Lichtspiel-Gesellschaft) was founded in 1916; through Erich Ludendorff's initiative, the most important film companies – Messter, Projektion-AG Union, and the Danish Nordisk – were united as Ufa (Universum Film AG) in 1917. This concentration of capital heralded the heyday of German film, known as WEIMAR CINEMA. Commercial productions reflected the economic consolidation of the film industry at the aesthetic level: the historical costume drama showed clear signs of escapism; German Expressionism, which became the most artistically significant form, mirrored an introspective mood and sensibility. Expressionism influenced later Weimar films, in which contradictions between repression and freedom, the crisis of the male subject, and the urge for female self-definition tend to be resolved in MELODRAMA.

Despite their connection with Expressionism, the films of Fritz Lang which were based on screenplays by Thea von HARBOU no longer worked with painted backdrops, but rather with monumental, ornamentally built structures, which dwarfed the human body. Another aesthetically interesting project of the Weimar period was the Querschnittsfilm (cross-section film), which broke free of narrative and tried to provide objective insights into everyday life. On the other hand, a subjective point of view was taken up by the usually independently produced Proletarische Film (proletarian films). These films, while at times addressing themselves to women's issues, set class struggle above such questions. Owing to the temporary suspension of censorship at the beginning of the Weimar Republic, the Aufklaerungsfilm (sex education film), which dealt with topics such as prostitution and venereal disease, was able to establish itself. At the same time the AVANT GARDE, which usually showed rigidly formal, abstract, or rhythmic tendencies, and Lotte

REINIGER's poetic, fantastic, shadow-play ANIMATION films, were able to win a space for themselves. Sound films, which appeared at the end of the Weimar period, were heavily indebted to the American example provided by the MUSICAL; independent innovations with SOUND could first be heard in films of the early 1930s. The anchoring of gender difference in the voice began with these films, as stressed by film theorist Kaja Silverman in *The Acoustic Mirror* (Bloomington and Indianapolis: Indiana University Press, 1988).

Despite the aesthetic diversity of its products, the German film industry soon found itself in financial difficulties: it was primarily American competition which forced Ufa to borrow extensively from MGM and PARAMOUNT in 1926. Even these loans were not enough to save Ufa; only the radical rightwing publisher Hugenberg, in cooperation with IG Farben and the Deutsche Bank, was able to bring this about. The web of capital, political interest, and film was not perfected, however, until Adolf Hitler rose to power in 1933: the National Socialists saw film as an effective means of influencing the masses, and in 1933 founded the Reichsfilmkammer (Reich Film Organization) which, by blacklisting nonmembers, was able to exclude political and aesthetic nonconformists, and most of all Jews, from the film industry. A wave of emigration by German film talent followed this blacklist. The Reichslichtspielgesetz (Reich Cinema Law) of 1934 subjected all films – even those produced before 1933 – to a rigid censorship, which was no longer bound to definable criteria. In 1936 film criticism was outlawed, to be replaced by film reports; by 1938 the state was the major shareholder in all the sizeable film enterprises (Ufa, Tobis, and Bavaria); and finally, in 1942, all film enterprises were merged into the state-owned Ufi (Ufa Film GmbH). Under these conditions, scarcely any film could be produced outside a propaganda-serving agenda. It was not only the *Staatsfilm* (state film, directly commissioned by the state) which was steeped in political doctrine, but also – indeed, especially – films meant as entertainment, historical costume dramas, and *Kulturfilme* (cultural films).

The aesthetic framework of the National Socialist film used the stylistic forms developed in the Weimar period. In order to produce an imaginary male identity, NAZI CINEMA radically excluded the otherness of the female sex, other nationalities, other religions, and liberating viewpoints and topics. Robbed of all artistic and enlightening qualities, cinema degenerated into a propaganda machine of power.

Anton Kaes and others, *Deutsche Filmgeschichte* (Stuttgart: J B Metzlerische Verlagsbuchhandlung, forthcoming)

See also: DIETRICH, MARLENE; EAST GERMANY; EISNER, LOTTE; WEST GERMANY   *VR*

GERMANY, EAST *see* EAST GERMANY

Maeve and Anne Devlin have in common a fine feminist filmmaker. Who is she?

GERMANY, WEST *see* WEST GERMANY

GILLIAT, SIDNEY *see* LAUNDER, FRANK AND GILLIAT, SIDNEY

GISH, LILLIAN (1896–)

A child actress who had spent most of her life in theatrical touring companies, Lillian Gish was in her teens when US director D W GRIFFITH engaged her to appear in Biograph films. Griffith cast Gish in numerous one-reelers and in such historic epics as *The Birth of a Nation* (1915) and *Intolerance* (1916). Gish also starred in successful Griffith MELODRA-MAs during and after World War I, notably *Hearts of the World* (1918), *True Heart Susie* (1919), *Broken Blossoms* (1919), *Way Down East* (1920) and *Orphans of the Storm* (1922). Proving her competence behind the camera as well, she directed her sister Dorothy in a comedy, *Remodelling Her Husband*, distributed by PARAMOUNT (1919). By the time her career with Griffith ended, Gish had acquired enough expertise to exert considerable control over features she made for Inspiration Pictures – *The White Sister* (Henry King, 1923) and *Romola* (Henry King, 1924) – and at MGM, notably *La Bohème* (King Vidor, 1926), *The Scarlet Letter* (Victor Seastrom, 1926), and *The Wind* (Victor Seastrom, 1927).

Unquestionably one of the great actresses of SILENT CINEMA, Gish displayed even more subtlety and range in her last features, but remained a symbol of Victorian womanhood. A child-woman with flowing blonde hair, wide eyes, and a rosebud mouth, she represented a feminine ideal that became outmoded during the Jazz Age. As an ethereal vision, however, she inspired adulation in writers who paid tribute to her ineffable charm and characterized her beauty in terms of a Botticelli painting. Actually Gish proved quite durable, both as a virginal heroine buffeted about in a cruel world and as an actress. After the silent era she pursued a stage career, resumed screen acting in character roles, and recently starred with Bette DAVIS in *The Whales of August* (Lindsay Anderson, 1987).

Lillian Gish, *The Movies, Mr Griffith and Me* (New York: Prentice-Hall, 1969)

SHi

GODARD, JEAN-LUC (1930–)

Originally a film critic, Godard became a central figure of the NEW WAVE in FRANCE with his first feature, *A bout de souffle/Breathless* (1959), and is arguably the most influential director in French postwar cinema. Godard's early films in-augurated his lifelong reflection on the film medium (as in *Le Mépris/Contempt* [1963]) and the existential despair of male characters (*Pierrot le fou* [1965]); but importantly others conducted a quasi-sociological exploration of France during the 1960s consumer boom, positing prostitution as literally the condition of women (*Vivre sa vie* [1962], *Deux ou trois choses que je sais d'elle/Two or Three Things I Know About Her* [1967]) and metaphorically the alienated human condition (including that of the artist) under capitalism. Anticipating May 1968, *La Chinoise* (1967) began Godard's 'political' period, which produced increasingly experimental COUNTERCINEMA under the Dziga Vertov group (*Pravda* [1969], *Vent d'Est* [1970]). 1974 marked the beginning of Godard's collaboration with Anne-Marie Miéville and their work on video (*Numéro deux* [1975]). In 1979 Godard, with Miéville, returned to actual filmmaking and, in a more pessimistic mode, to early concerns like prostitution, notably in *Sauve qui peut (la vie)/Slow Motion* (1980), which also offers an illuminating, if negative, account of the problems involved in male–female collaboration.

Godard is a problematic figure for feminists. Though often blatantly misogynistic, he has, in the words of Colin MacCabe and Laura MULVEY, 'more than any other single filmmaker . . . shown up the exploitation of woman as an image in consumer society'; good examples are *Une Femme mariée* (1964), or *Numéro deux*. But, as these writers also point out, Godard's use of images of women is simultaneously critical and complicit. Furthermore, even in his most politically aware works Godard tends to equate women with SEXUALITY and guilt, thus ultimately reproducing classic patriarchal myths.

Godard's films include: *A bout de souffle/ Breathless* (1959); *Le petit soldat* (1960); *Une Femme est une femme/A Woman Is a Woman* (1961); *Vivre sa vie/It's My Life* [UK]/*My Life To Live* [USA] (1962): *Les*

Carabiniers (1963); Le Mépris/Contempt (1963); Bande à part/Band of Outsiders, Une Femme mariée/A Married Woman (1964); Alphaville, Pierrot le fou (1965); Masculin-féminin/Masculine-Feminine (1966); Deux ou trois choses que je sais d'elle/Two or Three Things I Know About Her, Made in USA, La Chinoise, Weekend (1967); Le Gai savoir (1968); One Plus One (Sympathy for the Devil), British Sounds, Pravda (1969); Vent d'Est, Luttes en Italie/Struggle in Italy, Vladimir et Rosa (1970); Tout va bien, Letter to Jane (1972). With Anne-Marie Miéville: Ici et ailleurs (1974), Numéro deux (1975), Comment ça va, Six fois deux (1976); France/tour/détour/deux/enfants (1978); Sauve qui peut (la vie)/Slow Motion (1980); Passion (1981); Prénom Carmen (1982); Je vous salue Marie/Hail Mary! (1983); Détective (1984); Soigne ta droite (1987).

Laura Mulvey and Colin MacCabe, 'Images of Woman, Images of Sexuality', in Godard: Images, Sounds, Politics, ed. Colin MacCabe (London: British Film Institute/Macmillan, 1980)   GV

GOGOBERIDZE, LANA (1928–)

Gogoberidze, one of the foremost contemporary SOVIET directors, originally intended to pursue an academic career as a literary scholar. She wrote her doctoral thesis on the American poet Walt Whitman at the University of Tbilisi (in the Soviet republic of Georgia) before moving to Moscow to study film direction at the state institute of cinematography (VGIK). After graduating from VGIK, Gogoberidze made her first feature film, Pod odnim nebom (1961), three stories about Georgian women from different periods of Georgian history. Since then, Gogoberidze has directed steadily, with eight feature films and three documentaries to her credit. These films mainly deal with the lives of women and are notable for their exceptional frankness and lack of sentimentality.

Gogoberidze's first work to come to the attention of western audiences was Neskolko interviu po lichnym voprosam/Several Interviews on Personal Questions (1979), an intensely moving portrayal of a woman struggling to cope with her career as a reporter and a disintegrating marriage. Interviews was shown at many international film festivals and won several prizes. Her 1984 movie Den dlinnee nochi was the official Soviet entry at the Cannes Film Festival, and Krugovorot (1986) won the director's prize at the Tokyo Film Festival. Gogoberidze chairs the film direction department at the Rustaveli Theatre Institute in Tbilisi; in 1987 she was elected president of the International Association of Women Filmmakers.

Gelati (1957); Tbilisi 1500 let/Tbilisi, 1500 Years Old (1959); Pod odnim nebom/Under One Sky (1961); Ia vizhu solntse/I Can See the Sun (1965); Rubezhi/Borderlines (1970); Kogda zatsvel mindal/When Almond Trees Were in Blossom (1973); Perepolokh/Confusion (1976); Neskolko interviu po lichnym voprosam/Several Interviews on Personal Questions (1979); Poslednoe pismo detiam/The Last Letter to Children (1980); Den dlinnee nochi/Day Longer than Night (1984); Krugovorot/Turnover (1986)   DJY

GOMEZ, SARA (1943–74)

Raised in a middle-class black family in Havana, CUBA, Sara Gómez studied literature, piano and, later, Afro-Cuban ethnography. She worked as a journalist prior to joining ICAIC, the newly formed Cuban Film Institute, in 1961; here she subsequently served as assistant director to Cuban filmmakers Jorge Fraga and Tomás Gutiérrez Alea, as well as to the visiting French director Agnès VARDA. One of two black filmmakers at ICAIC at the time, and for several years the Institute's only woman director, Gómez made a series of documentary shorts on assigned topics before earning the freedom to direct her first feature. Her screenplay for The Miraflores Housing Project, a love story based loosely on her own relationship with soundman

One Way Or Another, **by Sara Gómez**

Germinal Hernández, was notable for its unconventional mixture of fiction and documentary, professional and social actors, its will to challenge established conventions of the genre, and its frank interrogation of the limits and contradictions of the Cuban revolutionary process. While the film was in postproduction, Gómez died of an acute asthma attack. The film, retitled *De cierta manera/One Way or Another*, was completed by Tomás Gutiérrez Alea, and though screened at Pesaro in 1975, it was not released in Cuba until 1977 due, according to Cuban sources, to 'problems with the negative.'

One Way or Another (a more faithful English translation would be 'In a Way' or 'To a Degree' or 'More or Less') has been acclaimed in the West as a paradigmatic example of Third World cinefeminism. As is characteristic of feminist efforts in the LATIN AMERICAN context, the film frames its interrogation of gender difference in the context of paral-

lel interrogations regarding race and class bias. In Cuba its impact has been marked and prolonged. Its close look at marginalized black urban culture catalyzed parallel artistic explorations in theater and fiction. Tomás Gutiérrez Alea's feature *Hasta cierto punto* (*Up to a Point*, 1984), makes homage to the Gómez film not only in its title but in its modes of production and representation, which imitate the mixture of 'real and fictional' people and events which characterized *One Way or Another*. Work of other women filmmakers from north and south America – Lizzie BORDEN's *Born in Flames* (1983) and Tizuka YAMASAKI's *Patriamada/Beloved Motherland* (1985), to cite only two examples – also suggest debts to this now-classic feature.

Iré a Santiago/I Shall Go to Santiago (1964); *Excursion a Vueltabajo/Outing to Vueltabajo* (1965); *Y tenemos sabor/And We've Got 'Sabor'* (1967); *En la otra isla/ On the Other Island* (1968); *Isla del tesoro/*

Treasure Island (1969); *Poder local, poder popular/Local Power, People's Power* (1970); *Un documental a propósito del transito/A Documentary About Mass Transit* (1971); *Atención pre-natal año uno/Prenatal Care in the First Year* (1972); *Sobre horas extras y trabajo voluntario/About Overtime and Voluntary Labor* (1973); *De cierta manera/One Way or Another* (1975–7)

E Ann Kaplan, 'The Woman Director in the Third World: Sara Gómez's *One Way or Another*', in *Women and Film: Both Sides of the Camera* (New York and London: Methuen, 1983)   JBu

GORDON, BETTE (1950–)

New York-based filmmaker Gordon's best-known works are FEMINIST INDEPENDENT FILMS which wed an interest in feminist theory to rigorous explorations of narrative forms and their economies. *Variety* (1983), for example, both parodies and turns the tables on the male quest for the 'truth' of female SEXUALITY. It is the story of a woman obsessed by the PORNOGRAPHY industry: a Times Square porn theater ticket-taker, she spends much of the film tailing a Mafia don. *Variety* creates but frustrates a seemingly straightforward NARRATIVE – we see what our heroine is seeing, but we don't know what it tells her. We're not sure how the man she's following responds – which leaves the audience both titillated and unfulfilled. The film's strength lies in the tension of its non-ending: the absurdity of the sacrifices required for narrative closure become all too clear. All the film can allow is a symbolic stand-off between female and male characters.

Gordon's earliest films, made in collaboration with her then husband, James Benning, while she was a graduate student at the University of Wisconsin at Madison and later a professor at the University of Wisconsin at Milwaukee, were strictly AVANT-GARDE. In 1979 she moved to New York and in 1980 made *Empty Suitcases*, which combines the fractured style she had evolved in Wisconsin with a kind of autobiographical psychodrama reminiscent of Yvonne RAINER. The film also nodded to Super-8mm punk filmmaking, a tradition she would mine further in the script for *Variety*, written by Kathy Acker (who comes from downtown New York). Gordon has said that *Variety*'s protagonist's fascination with images of male power expresses her own sense that women making films from a woman's point of view are doing 'something illegal.' She has also defended herself against critics who call her heroine's fascination with pornography a naive reversal of male exploitation of women's images by saying: 'I believe that women can enter into a male discourse and trouble it.' In her contribution to the omnibus women's film *Seven Women, Seven Sins* (1986), a segment called *Greed*, Gordon makes money, not pornography, the object of the quest, describing how a bathroom attendant's oppressive job and class jealousy lead to murder. Gordon is currently working on episodes for a television series on monsters, which she describes as a mix of FILM NOIR and HORROR.

Michigan Avenue (1973); *I–94* (1974); *United States of America* (1975); *Central Times and Noyes* (1976); *An Algorithm* (1977); *Empty Suitcases* (1980); *Variety* (1983); *Greed* (1986)

Jane Root, 'Women X: Interview with Bette Gordon,' *Monthly Film Bulletin*, vol. 51, no. 604 (1984)   JSh

GORRIS, MARLEEN (1948–)

Gorris began making films with little experience of cinema, after studying drama at home and abroad. Not only in her native NETHERLANDS but also internationally, her two features have proved that it is possible to make films which are commercially appealing and also, in both content and cinematic form, uncompromising in their feminism. Gorris's first film, *De Stilte Rond Christine*

Broken Mirrors, by Marleen Gorris

them up, and allows them to die of hunger and neglect. *Broken Mirrors* is about the sexual threats all women know about. Nevertheless, no matter how demoralizing its story may sound, the film – far from inspiring anguish – manages to conjure up a spirit of strength and resistance.

At present Gorris has two feature films in preparation, one of them, *Antonia's Life*, being about several generations of women living in Limburg, her native region.

De Stilte Rond Christine M/A Question of Silence (1981); *Gebrokene Spiegels/Broken Mirrors* (1984)

Mary C Gentile, 'Feminist or Tendentious? Marleen Gorris' *A Question of Silence*', in *Film Feminisms: Theory and Practice* (Westport, CT: Greenwood Press, 1985)   AF

M/A Question of Silence (1981), is a crime film turned upside-down. A man, chosen at random, is murdered by three women who do not know each other. The women do not deny the deed, but the question remains: why did they do it? The women refuse to divulge their motive. As the film proceeds, Gorris analyzes lack of understanding of the act as being a logical consequence of a specific point of view, that of male society. When the judge asks the women whether they could equally well have murdered a woman, they burst into irrepressible laughter, together with a number of other women (in the audience as well as in the film itself). In both narrative and cinematic terms, *A Question of Silence* is a highly subversive film.

Broken Mirrors (1984), Gorris's next film, is even more radical than her first. It has two storylines: one shows the life of seven prostitutes in a brothel in an ironical and realistic way; in the other a nondescript man – practically invisible in the film itself – knocks down women, locks

GOSSIP COLUMNS

The Hollywood gossip column contributes to an essential aspect of the STAR system: the blurring of personal life with professional life. Like its antecedents in small-town and urban newspapers, the gossip column shares the social doings of the 'local community' through accounts of public activities (charity benefits, parties, houseguests, who was with whom). By defining people and events as worthy of coverage or as influential (the A-list and B-list for parties), the gossip column advances a Hollywoodian form of class relations. By taking sides in affairs of the heart and political activism (through expressions of understanding, support, reproach, censure) the gossip columnist can contribute to, or help avert, a career-threatening scandal. In its coverage of personal life, the gossip column has taken up subjects considered ideologically dangerous for the film industry: divorce, pregnancy, motherhood. And, by suppressing knowledge of homosexuality, the gossip columnist has helped homosexuals to remain in the closet and on the screen.

Gossip columnists were most prominent during the 1930s and 1940s, when the film industry relied heavily on the star system. By the late 1920s, Louella PARSONS was well established in Hollywood. In the late 1930s, Hedda Hopper was welcomed by the studios as her principal rival. Since being noticed (or ignored) could affect a star's 'bankability' and a studio's profits, gossip columnists regularly received lavish gifts and inside information. While this informal arrangement could be mutually profitable, gossip columns were by no means simple conduits for press agentry. Each columnist had a network of sources which reached beyond those approved by her subjects. These included the people who performed service functions for the film industry: delivery people, servants, florists, caretakers, and even medical personnel.

Christopher Finch and Linda Rosenkrantz, *Gone Hollywood* (Garden City, NY: Doubleday, 1979)   MBH

GREAT BRITAIN *see* BRITAIN

GRIFFITH, D W (1874–1948)

Born into a Victorian patriarchal Confederate family, but sensitized early to Southern values of romance and chivalry, Griffith's early ambition was to be a playwright in a nineteenth-century melodramatic vein. Instead he became a film director, valued by critics and historians of SILENT CINEMA for developing techniques of cinematic NARRATIVE structure and REALISM such as crosscutting and the closeup.

Griffith's HEROINES and the STAR actresses he schooled – most notably Lillian GISH – are central to this paradox. Griffith's pictorial compositions venerate his actresses, who combine Victorian innocence with American robustness; details of local incident and ordinary human behavior revitalize the long-suffering heroines of MELODRAMA, infusing sentimental scenarios with human warmth and intensity of feeling; and crosscutting between parallel or opposing characters, images, and events offers authorial comment on the trials and tribulations undergone by these women.

MASCULINITY is a major problem of the narratives of Griffith's films, which chastise the excesses of patriarchy – the sexual double standard, religious bigotry, adherence to the letter of the law – rather than empathize with its victims. These failings are exemplified in male figures preserved from Victorian melodrama in such films as *Broken Blossoms* (1919), *Way Down East* (1920), and *Orphans of the Storm* (1922). By way of contrast with these patriarchs and seducers, Griffith offers a 'new man' who rejects patriarchal excesses and is sufficiently feminized to become soulmate and ally to the heroine. The perverse – often incestuous – overtones of such scenarios have not escaped latter-day feminist critics, even though we may be grateful for the respect and humanity with which Griffith approached his female characters.

Notable among the hundreds of films made by Griffith are: *A Drunkard's Reformation* (1909); *Enoch Arden* (1911); *The Mender of Nets* (1912); *Judith of Bethulia* (1914); *The Birth of A Nation* (1915); *Intolerance* (1916); *Hearts of the World* (1918); *A Romance of Happy Valley* (1919); *True Heart Susie* (1919); *Broken Blossoms* (1919); *Way Down East* (1920); *Orphans of the Storm* (1922); *Isn't Life Wonderful* (1924)

Julia Lesage, 'Artful Racism, Artful Rape: Griffith's *Broken Blossoms*', in *Home Is Where the Heart Is: Studies in Melodrama and the Woman's Film*, ed. Christine Gledhill (London: British Film Institute, 1987)   CG

GROUPE INTERVENTION VIDEO

A QUEBEC VIDEO production and FEMINIST DISTRIBUTION collective,

GIV was formed in Montreal in 1975. At first a mixed men's and women's group, GIV converted itself to an exclusively women's collective in 1979. In its development, GIV became part of the social and aesthetic upheaval which was transforming Quebec society in the 1970s. The tendency to accept the existence of a link between the form and the content of social intervention, and the popularity of VIDEO as the tool of choice for social struggle, were characteristic of thinking in the arts in Quebec at the time; and GIV chose video to witness the vitality of the women's movement. In this period, the group produced *Chaperons rouges/Red Riding Hood* (Hélène Bourgault and Helen Doyle, co-produced with VIDEO FEMMES, 1979), about the consequences of rape; *Femmes de rêves . . .* (Louise Gendron, 1979), about publicity's stereotypes; and *La Perle rare* (Diane Poitras, 1980), about pink-collar workers. At the beginning of the 1980s, the collective suffered from financial difficulties. Unable to move from half-inch to the now dominant three-quarter-inch

....
: *Who and what is Winifred Ellerman?* :
....

video format, the group was forced to abandon production for a five-year period. It continued nevertheless to distribute the work of several women video artists who, determined to continue producing, formed their own production companies organized in association with GIV. Videos produced in these circumstances include Diane Poitras's *Pense à ton désir/Make a Wish* (1984), a fiction about women at the age of menopause; *Comptines* (1986), a video clip using images from an Irish women's protest against the death of a prisoner; and Nancy Marcotte's *Reportage Brésil: 1* (1986), about a women's police station in São Paolo; as well as *Pour qui tourne la roue* (1983) and *On voulait pas des miracles . . .* (1985), both by the collective 'Actions féministes par l'image'; and both about working conditions of women in industry. In the mid 1980s several of these video artists inspired a renaissance of production at GIV, creating, amongst others, *Une maison de naissances* (Irène Demcauk, 1987), *Le Plaisir* (Lynda Peers, 1987), and *Une fille de ma gang* (Marilyn Burgess, 1989). Playing a role similar to Video Femmes in Quebec City, GIV created both a vast repertoire of feminist engaged videos and a solid network of distribution to work in conjunction with the feminist movement in Quebec.   BF

GRUBEN, PATRICIA (1947–)

Patricia Gruben studied film at the University of Texas before moving to CANADA in the early 1970s. For almost a decade she worked as assistant, props person, and set decorator at various levels of the film industry, from children's programming to television commercials and feature films. In 1979 she made her first film, a complex and meticulously crafted short which received immediate attention as the work of a major new figure in Canada's AVANT GARDE. Densely worked and multilayered, *The Central Character* uses optically treated multiple images, maps, blueprints and other texts, minimal and repeated images combined with a fragmentary, hallucinatory, and looped voice/sound composition on the audio track to produce a delicately nuanced investigation of disintegrating feminine subjectivity. With *Sifted Evidence* (1982), a forty-minute avant-garde narrative, Gruben achieved international recognition. Combining parody, drama, fictional autobiography, travelog, and educational documentary, the narrative tells of a woman's romantic ambivalence and futile quest for the Mexican source of ancient goddess figures. The film combines richly textured images, using front-screen projection and staged studio incident as well as location shooting, maps, slides, and other textual insertions, and the largely asynchronous audio track makes evocative use of different forms of address, voice, language, music, and silence. *Low Visibility* (1985), Gruben's first feature-length film, carries on her investigation of language and subjectivity and forms of cinematic illusion, the media of visual representation, and the formations of personal vision in a narrative of a man who has lost both memory and powers of speech. Able to speak only in curses and expletives, he is cared for by nurses who communicate only in jokes and by psychiatrists whose language is purely clinical; and he is under investigation for a suspected murder by a television news team, a clairvoyant, police investigators, and a battery of video surveillance cameras. Since 1984 Gruben has taught film production at Simon Frazer University in British Columbia, and has also founded Praxis, a professional training workshop for feature writers and directors. She is currently in production with a new avant-garde personal feature and has several dramatic scripts optioned and in development for future productions. One of the most accomplished filmmakers in Canada, and clearly the most intelligent and complex, her work is consistently marked by a rare combination of scientific theory (ranging from archeology to medicine, botany to psychoanalysis, architecture to linguistics), autobiography, formal structural complexity, and a remarkably sensual and poetic use of the cinematic apparatus.

The Central Character (1979); *Sifted Evidence* (1982); *Low Visibility* (1985)

Kaja Silverman, *The Acoustic Mirror: The Female Voice in Psychoanalysis and Cinema* (Bloomington and Indianapolis: Indiana University Press, 1987)   KA

GUIDO, BEATRIZ (1924–88)

ARGENTINE short story writer and novelist, Guido had a longstanding professional collaboration with director and producer Leopoldo TORRE-NILSSON, who was also her husband. She authored all of Torre-Nilsson's screenplays, from *La casa del angel/The House of the Angel*

(1957) to *Piedra libre/Free Stone* (1976), assisted him in his productions, wrote screenplays for other directors, and published many novels which brought her international recognition as one of the 'angry' writers of the 1955 generation. Born into a progressive upper-class family which believed in equal education for girls, Guido studied philosophy in Italy and in France (with Gabriel Marcel, the existentialist). Her fiction – novels, stories, and screenplays – always deals with closed, claustrophobic worlds with atmospheres of decadence and sexual repression. Serving as a metaphor for the effects of social norms on individuals, this sexual repression/decadence makes love impossible, sex always violent, and incest likely, especially for female characters with limited contacts with non-family males. Although she would have rejected the label 'feminist writer,' Guido appropriated a fictional space – the erotic – and a defiant, aggressive position toward it not traditionally available to women of her generation and class in Argentina.   ALo

GUSNER, IRIS (1941–)

The first EAST GERMAN woman feature film director to become widely known, Gusner was born in Trautenau in the Soviet Union, and studied film in Moscow from 1961 to 1967. She then worked for GDR television before moving to the DEFA film studios, where she has been a director since 1972.

Gusner's first feature to attract attention for its feminist perspective was *Alle meine Maedchen/All My Girls* (1979), set in a factory and telling the stories of five young women workers and their forewoman. Women workers at the real NARVA factory where the fictional plot is set commented that the film was entertaining, but that the women seemed superficial, their lives too simple. Their own lives were much more complicated, full of conflict and contradiction. Gusner accepted this criticism, but moved sideways from this near-documentary feature on the lives of working women to the domain of the love story, where she has remained ever since. *Waere die Erde nicht rund . . .* (1980–1) remained semi-autobiographical rather than offering commentary on the difficulties inherent in crosscultural relationships, or a feminist view of marriage as doomed by unreconstructed male chauvinism. The central theme of Gusner's more recent films is often a love story, but without emphasis on the difficulties of running a nonsexist relationship based on equality and mutual respect.

Some commentators regard Gusner's recent films as lightweight, and her contribution as a feminist filmmaker over-rated. Her reputation derives in part from the fact that East Germany suffers a dearth of women directors, and Gusner is often cited or sent as token woman filmmaker to represent the GDR at international film festivals. A real difficulty for Gusner herself is that as of 1986 DEFA had not subtitled or dubbed any of her films, so that they are virtually unknown outside the GDR.

Die Taube auf dem Dach/The Dove on the Roof (1972–3); *Was halten Sie von Leuten, die malen?/What Do You Think of People Who Paint?* (1974); *Das blaue Licht/The Blue Light* (1975–6); *Man nennt mich jetzt Mimi . . ./They Call me Mimi Now . . .* (1976); *Einer muss die Leiche sein/Someone Has to be the Corpse* (1977); *Alle meine Maedchen/All My Girls* (1979); *Waere die Erde nicht rund . . ./If the Earth Wasn't Round* (1980–1); *Kaskade rueckwaerts/Backwards Somersault* (1985–6); *Ich liebe dich April, April/April, April, I Love You* (1987–8)

Wilhelm Roth, 'Iris Gusner: Romantik und Satire, Kitsch und Komik', *Film (W. Germany)*, no. 1 (1985)   BE

GUY, ALICE (1873?–1968)

Alice Guy, born in FRANCE, was the world's first woman director and possibly the first director ever of a fiction film. She worked as Léon Gaumont's

A House Divided, by Alice Guy

secretary in Paris in 1895 when the first Lumière cameras were exhibited. Fascinated by the new technology and recognizing its narrative potential, she sought Gaumont's permission to direct a few little sketches which she herself scripted. The first one (and, according to some sources, the first scripted fiction film ever), *La Fée aux choux/The Cabbage Fairy* (1896), was a joky fairytale about children born in cabbages. Gaumont soon delegated his growing film production department to her, and there followed a period of intense activity until 1906, during which she shot about two hundred one-reelers, acting as scriptwriter, director, producer, and head of wardrobe. The heady and anarchic beginnings of the film industry gave women like Alice Guy far greater scope and power than any other period of film history, allowing Guy also to experiment with photographic effects, SOUND, and hand-painting. Her extremely successful films spanned the spectrum of popular French GENREs, from slapstick and melodrama to ambitious historical reconstructions and biblical epics. Ferdinand Zecca, Victorin Jasset and Louis Feuillade – all three to become France's star SILENT CINEMA directors – were at one point employed as her assistants.

In 1907 she married the Englishman Herbert Blaché and the couple emigrated to the USA, where Blaché was to supervise Gaumont's distribution subsidiary in New York. After the birth of her first child in 1909, Guy founded the Solax film company in Flushing, NY (later in Fort Lee, NJ), directing its first production, *A Child's Sacrifice*, in 1910; subsequently Solax released more than three hundred films, many of which Guy directed herself. As a director, she worked in popular American genres – WESTERNs, thrillers, MELODRAMAs – and experimented with various aspects of REALISM.

In 1913–14, Solax became Blaché Features Inc., specializing in four-reel dramas (fourteen by Guy) and later the Guy-Blachés founded various shortlived companies, including Famous Players and Plays, devoted to adapting stage hits, before being driven out of business in 1917 by the restructuring of the American film industry. Guy stopped filmmaking after *Tarnished Reputations* (1920). She had directed at least seventy American two-reelers and features, and had achieved some notoriety in the USA as the 'charming Frenchwoman' director. Guy and Blaché were divorced in 1922 and she returned to France with her two children, unsuccessfully trying to revive her film career, and struggling (with equally little success) to correct film histories which regularly attributed her French films to male directors such as Jasset and Emile Cohl.

Alice Guy was belatedly celebrated by the Cinémathèque Française and awarded the French Legion of Honour in 1953, but it was only in the 1970s that her pioneering role in the film industry was widely recognized. Few of her films have survived, but among these *A House Divided* (1913) shows her technical skill and a humorously critical view of marital relationships. Though the feminist content of Guy's films as a whole can only be surmised, there is evidence of her interest in women's issues. Her exemplary career certainly gave credence to her famous statement that 'there is nothing connected with the staging of a motion picture that a woman cannot do as easily as a man' (1913).

Alice Guy has been credited with the direction of more than four hundred one-reelers in France between 1896 and 1907, and with more than three hundred one-reelers in the USA between 1910 and late 1913. Her feature films are: *Shadows of the Moulin Rouge* (1913); *Beneath the Czar* (1914); *The Monster and the Girl* (1914); *The Million Dollar Robbery* (1914); *The Woman of Mystery* (1914); *The Yellow Traffic* (1914); *The Lure* (1914); *The Tigress* (1914); *The Heart of a Painted Woman* (1915); *Greater Love Hath No Man* (1915); *The Vampire* (1915); *My Madonna* (1915); *What Will People Say?* (1916); *The Ocean Waif* (1916); *The Adventurer* (1917); *The Empress* (1917); *A Man and the Woman* (1917); *House of Cards* (1917); *When You and I Were Young* (1917); *Behind the Mask* (1917); *The Great Adventure* (1918); *Tarnished Reputations* (1920)

Anthony Slide (ed.), *The Memoirs of Alice Guy-Blaché* (Metuchen, NJ: Scarecrow Press, 1986)   GV

GYARMATHY, LIVIA (1932–)

Originally a chemical engineer in a factory in Budapest, HUNGARY, Gyarmathy subsequently chose, jointly with her husband and collaborator Géza Böszörményi, to make filmmaking their profession. She graduated from the Academy of Theater and Film Art in 1964, followed four years later by her husband. Their partnership involves each writing screenplays for the other's films. Gyarmathy is best known as a highly accomplished documentary director, but she has also made features, ironical comedies conveying hard-hitting social comment, usually on the dilemmas facing working women. Her films are beautifully made, while displaying seriousness of purpose and political commitment.

The most recent documentary made by Gyarmathy and her husband, *Recsk 1950–53* (1988), is the story of a secret forced labor camp of which Böszörményi was himself an inmate. Gyarmathy spent two-and-a-half years tracking down ex-guards and secret police who were the perpetrators of atrocities at this Hungarian Gulag. Her interviewing technique adds greatly to the drama of the film.

58 másodperc/58 Seconds (short, 1964); *Üzenet/Message* (1967); *Ismeri a szandimandit?/Do You Know 'Sunday-Monday'?* (1969); *Tisztelt Cím!/Dear Address!* (short, 1972); *Álljon meg a menet!/Wait a Sec!* (1973); *Magányosok klubja/The Lonely Persons' Club* (short, 1976); *Kilencedik emelet/Ninth Floor* (short, 1977); *Minden szerdán/Every Wednesday* (1979); *Koportos* (1979); *Együttélés/Co-existence* (1982); *Egy kicsit én . . . egy kicsit te . . ./Now it's My Turn, Now it's Yours* (1985); *Vakvilágban/Blind Endeavour* (1986); *Faludy György Költo/The Poet George Faludy* (1987); *Recsk 1950–53/The Story of a Secret Forced Labour Camp* (1988) BE/ER

HAENSEL, MARION (1952–)

Marion Haensel attended the French Circus School (the Fratellini Circus) and also trained as a mime artiste in France. She later studied drama in Brussels and attended classes at the Lee Strasberg Actors' Studio in New York. For many years she worked as an actress, and since 1977 has produced and directed films in BELGIUM. Although her three feature films are based on novels, they surpass literature. *Le lit* (1982), based on Dominique Rolin's novel of the same name, is a film about life in opposition to death: a woman is looking after her husband, who is on his deathbed. If *Le lit* is about love, Haensel's two other films are poignant indictments of its absence. In *Dust* (1984), based on J M Coetzee's novel, a grown-up daughter (Jane Birkin) yearns for the love of her father (Trevor Howard), and finally kills him in order to keep him to herself. In *Les noces barbares* (1986), based on Yann Queffelec's novel, a young man does the same to his mother (Marianne Baisler), who cannot possibly love him because he is the result of a rape.

Through wonderfully stylized pellucid images, Haensel creates the sharpest possible contrast with the violence with which these characters treat each other – violence that invariably stems from social evils: in *Dust*, it emerges from relationships between men and women and between blacks and whites in South Africa; in *Les noces barbares* from rape and its disastrous impact on a young

Marion Haensel's *Les noces barbares*

woman's life. However, both MISE-EN-SCENE and script avoid any kind of moralizing. The meaning of these films emerges as a matter of course through their style: one recognizes bitterly that such things should never ever be allowed to happen.

Equilibre (1977); *Sannu Bature, Gongola, Hydraulip II, Bakh* (1979); *Le lit/The Bed* (1982); *Dust* (1984); *Les noces barbares/The Cruel Embrace* (1987)   AF

HAMMER, BARBARA (1939–   )

US independent feminist filmmaker Hammer has made fifty short films and videos in more than fifteen years as an artist. Her career as a formally experimental, lesbian–identified filmmaker has spanned many debates and trends within American feminism and the INDEPENDENT CINEMA community. Merging influences as seemingly incompatible as AVANT-GARDE filmmaking and the goddess movement, Hammer's films convey a personal vision which has been a significant touchstone in attempts to construct a LESBIAN INDEPENDENT CINEMA, and more generally to define a lesbian aesthetic in art.

Hammer's films of the 1970s – such as *Dyketactics* (1974), *Double Strength* (1978), *Sappho* (1978), and *Women I Love* (1979) – are rhythmic, erotic evocations of lesbian love and lifestyles. Her dreamlike montages draw on imagery from nature, ancient art, myth, and women's bodies, and often focus on Hammer's own relationships with other women. The films have occasionally drawn criticism for what is seen as a romantic celebration of an essential female spirit based on biological difference. In later work Hammer has explored the eroticism of texture and the play of light, using optical printing and animation techniques. Recently, she has brought her radical feminist politics and aesthetic concerns to her work in VIDEO.

The subject of major retrospectives in Berlin and Paris, and recipient of

Barbara Hammer

numerous awards and solo screenings worldwide, Hammer has been a unique, outspoken, and highly visible proponent of independent women's filmmaking. She has also taught film production at several universities and art institutes.

Films include: *'X'* (1973); *Dyketactics* (1974); *Superdyke Meets Madame X* (1977); *Double Strength, Multiple Orgasm, Menses, Sisters!, Women's Rites, Haircut* (1978); *The Great Goddess* (1978?); *Eggs, Sappho, Women I Love* (1979); *Our Trip* (1980); *Arequipa, Sync Touch, Pictures for Barbara, Pools* (1981); *Audience, Stone Circle* (1983); *Bent Time, Doll House, Tourist* (1984); *Optic Nerve* (1985); *No No Nooky TV, Place Mattes* (1987); *Endangered* (1988). Videotapes include: *Snow Job: The Media Hysteria of Aids* (1986); *Bedtime Stories I, II & III, History of the World According to a Lesbian, Two Bad Daughters* (1988); *TV Tart, Hot Flash* (1989)

Claudia Gorbman, 'Bodies Displaced, Places Discovered', *Jump Cut*, no. 32 (1987)   PW

HARBOU, THEA VON (1888–1954)

Thea von Harbou began her career as a screenplay writer when already a successful author in GERMANY. She published bombastic and racist novels, novellas, and essays that glorified the German nation and laid down the appropriate role of women: to support and provide for her warrior man. 'August 1914,' writes Harbou in *Die deutsche Frau im Weltkrieg* (Leipzig: Hesse und Becker, 1916), 'saw the birth of the new German woman.' After writing her first screenplay in 1919 she met Fritz Lang, with whom she worked closely and successfully until his emigration in 1933; despite the collaboration, the melodramatic tendency of Harbou's work remained largely unchanged over this period. Slight traces of critical perspective can be found, though, in *Dr Mabuse, der Spieler* (Fritz Lang, 1922) and *Das Testament des Dr Mabuse* (Fritz Lang, 1933). Her activism on behalf of the legalization of abortion is reflected in *Das erste Recht des Kindes* (Fritz Wendhausen, 1932). The ensuing differences between Harbou and the National Socialist authorities were quickly resolved in light of her nationalistic and chauvinistic stance and her instinct for popular taste, and she was engaged to work on a number of 'state films' in the era of NAZI CINEMA.

After the war, Harbou was able to reestablish herself in the film culture of the Federal Republic of Germany. Having been banned from filmmaking under the Allied government from 1945 to 1949, she wrote successful scripts (including *Dr Holl* [Rudolf Hansen, 1951]), and was the subject of a retrospective at the International Film Festival in Berlin in 1954.

Reinhold Keiner, *Thea von Harbou und der Deutsche Film bis 1933* (Hildesheim: Georg Olms, 1984)   *VR*

HARLOW, JEAN (1911–37)

Jean Harlow's career as a Hollywood STAR spanned five years, from 1932 until her death in 1937 at the age of twenty-six. She was taken up by MGM and made thirty-two feature-length films during those years. A talented comedienne, she was seldom able to fulfill that talent. The case of Jean Harlow uncovers not only the ways in which the HOLLYWOOD STUDIO SYSTEM created, managed, and manipulated female star images on and off the screen, but also the ways in which books, magazines, and many biopics since have reinforced that misogynist mythology. British writer Leslie Halliwell, for example, defines Harlow in his *Filmgoer's Companion* as 'a wisecracking "platinum blonde" with a private life to suit her public image.' In fact the studio manufactured that merged private/public image, much as the Hollywood machine was to manufacture that of Marilyn MONROE, to whom Harlow is often seen as precursor. In such films as *Red Dust* (Victor Fleming, MGM, 1932) and *China Seas* (Tay Garnett, MGM, 1935), both with her 'regular' leading man Clark Gable, she played the swaggering, wisecracking, sexy and 'common' woman who goes through many humiliations but triumphs in the end by revealing that she is a trouper. Jean

Jean Harlow

Harlow, labeled the original platinum BLONDE, achieved a breakthrough in playing a *Red Headed Woman* (Jack Conway, MGM, 1932) with a fine script by Anita LOOS, from which comes Harlow's memorable line 'Gentlemen prefer blondes. Sez who?'. Other notable Harlow performances are in *Dinner at Eight* (George Cukor, MGM, 1933) and *Libeled Lady* (Jack Conway, MGM, 1936).   PB

HASKELL, MOLLY (1939–)

In the early 1970s in the USA, Molly Haskell was one of three women critics to found a career on being a feminist film critic (the other two were journalist Marjorie ROSEN and academic Joan Mellen). Haskell, whose husband is *Village Voice* chief film reviewer Andrew Sarris, started freelance FILM CRITICISM for the *Village Voice*, *Film Comment*, and *Film Heritage* in the early seventies, and later went on to become a regular film reviewer for *Voice*, *New York* magazine, and *Vogue* in the late seventies and early eighties; though at present she is not reviewing regularly for any periodical. Haskell's most outstanding and lasting contribution, and the one that has brought her the greatest acclaim, is her 1974 book *From Reverence to Rape*. Pioneering in its view that women's roles in films have deteriorated over the years, this book has been credited not only with the attention given to women's widespread degradation in cinema, but also with the spate of films by and about women which appeared in the mid seventies.

One influential mark of Haskell's work is her strong identification, as both woman and critic, with the stars she viewed as a teenager and an adult: it is in this way that Haskell underscores the influence of film on women's lives. This is exemplified by her comment that François Truffaut's *Jules and Jim* 'couldn't have been anybody but me and my two dearest male friends at college in Ann Arbor [Michigan].'

Haskell is unusual in providing strong conceptual groundings for her criticisms, blending contemporary feminist thinking with some strongly-held Freudian notions, laying the groundwork for FEMINIST FILM THEORY.

Molly Haskell, *From Reverence to Rape: The Treatment of Women in the Movies* (New York: Holt, Rinehart & Winston, 1974)   MMc

HAWKS, HOWARD (1896–1977)

Hollywood director Howard Hawks made movies in almost every GENRE and for nearly every major studio. Prolific and professional, he eschewed formal experimentation, but his technical craftsmanship, ear for dialogue, eye for scene construction, and ability to exact superb performances from actors made many of the films he turned out yearly – screwball COMEDIES, private-eye and gangster thrillers, MELODRAMAs, and WESTERNs – the ranking classics in their categories.

Hawks earned a degree in mechanical engineering, won a junior championship in tennis, and raced cars and airplanes professionally before getting his first break at the Famous Players-Lasky company (now Paramount), directing several scenes of a Mary PICKFORD vehicle, *The Little Princess* (1917). He then worked as a scenarist, editor and producer, eventually directing the unsuccessful *The Road to Glory* (1926). In 1930 Hawks began producing his own movies, becoming one of the very few directors during the era of the HOLLYWOOD STUDIO SYSTEM to work steadily without a studio contract. In forty-four years he directed, produced, and co-wrote – often with writers such as Ernest Hemingway, William Faulkner, and Ben Hecht – forty-five films, and co-produced and/or co-wrote countless others.

Admired by French film buffs since the 1930s, Hawks was 'rediscovered' by American proponents of film AUTHORSHIP in the late 1950s; and in the 1970s historians began viewing his work as exemplary of classical Hollywood style and ideology. In her 1975 article 'Visual Pleasure and Narrative Cinema,' FEMINIST FILM THEORIST Laura MULVEY uses Hawks's films to illustrate the argument that images of women in Hollywood films solicit the male LOOK. Compared with other Hollywood women, however, Hawks's female characters tend toward the extraordinary. Although 'the Hawksian woman' capitulates to men in the end, she is none the less independent, smart, and often career-minded (Rosalind Russell in *His Girl Friday* [1940], for example), with 'masculine' traits enough to thrive in Hawks's rugged world of aviators, detectives, and cowboys (Lauren BACALL in *To Have and Have Not* [1944]), or to subdue a comic hero (Ann Sheridan in *I Was a Male War Bride* [1949]).

The best known among Hawks's films are: *Scarface* (United Artists, 1930); *Twentieth Century* (Columbia, 1934); *Come and Get It* (Goldwyn, 1936); *Bringing Up Baby* (RKO, 1938); *Only Angels Have Wings* (Columbia, 1939); *His Girl Friday* (Columbia, 1940); *To Have and Have Not* (Warner Bros., 1944); *The Big Sleep* (Warner Bros., 1946); *Red River* (United Artists, 1948); *I Was a Male War Bride* (Twentieth Century-Fox, 1949); *The Big Sky* (RKO, 1952); *Monkey Business* (Twentieth Century-Fox, 1952); *Gentlemen Prefer Blondes* (Twentieth Century-Fox, 1953); *Rio Bravo* (Warner Bros., 1959); *Rio Lobo* (1970)

Molly Haskell, 'Man's Favorite Sport? – Revisited', in *Focus on Howard Hawks*, ed. Joseph McBride (Englewood Cliffs, NJ: Prentice-Hall, 1972)   JSh

HAYS CODE *see* PRODUCTION CODE

HAYWORTH, RITA (1918–87)

Hollywood's forties SEX GODDESS and one of COLUMBIA's biggest STARS was born Margarita Carmen Cansino, of half-Spanish extraction, in New York. Trained to dance by her teacher father, she began her screen career in bit dancing parts for Fox. When Fox merged with Twentieth Century in 1936 Hayworth was dropped, only to pick up a seven-year contract with Columbia the following year. There, under the watchful eye of Columbia boss Harry Cohn, her black hair was dyed red as she underwent rigorous star grooming. Her first big break came as the flirtatious wife of an air pilot in Howard HAWKS's *Only Angels Have Wings* (Columbia, 1939). From then on, she was launched as a glamorous pinup: a sultry temptress in *Blood and Sand* (Rouben Mamoulian, Twentieth Century-Fox, 1941) and then in a series of lighthearted dance-oriented films such as *You'll Never Get Rich* (Sidney Lanfield, Columbia, 1941) and *You Were Never Lovelier* (William A Seiter, Columbia, 1942) with Fred Astaire, and *Cover Girl* (Charles Vidor, Columbia, 1944) with Gene Kelly. However, it was with Vidor's *Gilda* (Columbia, 1946) that the Hayworth image reached its apotheosis. As the wild, flirtatious dancer, Hayworth's sensual use of her hair and hip-swaying dance-cum-striptease in 'Put the Blame on Mame' endowed her with an extraordinary liberated sexual energy, at odds with the static quality of the usual female pinup. Matched against Glenn Ford in a perversely sadomasochistic relationship, Hayworth's Gilda emerged as a FEMME FATALE without the wicked ways of most of her ilk. But in Orson Welles's *The Lady from Shanghai* (Columbia, 1948), made as the couple were on the point of divorce, she appeared as the other side of that coin: her hair shorn and dyed blonde under Welles's orders, Hayworth's Elsa was an incarnation of greed and evil. The film was less than successful.

Dogged viciously by the press, Hayworth stayed out of movies for the next couple of years while she was married to Prince Aly Khan. Her return to Hollywood in 1951 was marked by Columbia's attempt to recapture the

Rita Hayworth as *Gilda*

spirit of *Gilda* in the senseless *Affair in Trinidad* (Vincent Sherman, Columbia, 1952). Although it brought hefty box office returns, the day of the sex goddess was starting to wane. Cohn could not, or would not, find the right vehicles for her, and after *Pal Joey* (George Sidney, Columbia, 1957) Hayworth appeared intermittently as losers in mediocre films. Hampered by a vengeful studio boss who felt he owned her, Hayworth, like Marilyn MONROE later, was trapped by the sex deity created in her name. As she said in 1973: 'I was certainly a well trained dancer. I'm a good actress. I have depth. I have feeling. But they don't care. All they want is the image.'

Richard Dyer, 'Resistance through Charisma: Rita Hayworth and *Gilda*', in *Women in Film Noir*, ed. E Ann Kaplan (London: British Film Institute, 1980)
ALi

HD (1886–1961)

Hilda Doolittle, an American poet and novelist who signed herself HD, is best known for her experimental poems on classical themes, and for co-founding the 'Imagist' movement with her sometime lover, Ezra Pound. But HD also wrote FILM CRITICISM, acted in films, and probably co-edited one of the first English-language films to reflect Eisensteinian editing techniques.

Between 1927 and 1929, HD contributed reviews to *Close Up*, which was published by her friends Kenneth Macpherson and BRYHER. *Close Up*, the first JOURNAL devoted to film as art, the first to explore links between psychoanalysis and cinema, and the first to translate S M Eisenstein's writings into English, enjoyed an international readership: other contributors included Gertrude Stein, Dorothy Richardson, Marianne Moore, and psychoanalysts such as Hans Sachs. HD's reviews filtered contemporary films through her extremely personal voice, her theories of classical aesthetics, and her passion for concrete imagery as a storytelling device.

HD also acted in two short films, *Wing Beat* and *Foothills*, produced by Bryher and Macpherson's film production company, POOL, between 1927 and 1930. In 1930 the three collaborated on and acted in a longer film, *Borderline*, a MELODRAMA about an interracial love triangle in a Swiss village; the film co-starred Paul Robeson and his wife Eslanda. According to a publicity pamphlet HD is believed to have written, the poet played 'Astrid the white cerebral,' who 'is and is not outcast, is and is not a social alien, is and is not a normal human being, she is borderline.' Although Macpherson directed and took most production credits, HD and Bryher probably edited the film, which combined intellectual montage with an insistent Freudian interiorization of everyday events. *Borderline*'s enthusiasts included G W Pabst and Lotte Lenya, both of whom singled out HD for praise. The public, however, found the film impenetrable: it was rarely screened in Europe and in the United States was impounded by the Customs Service, possibly because it was thought to advocate miscegenation.

HD's writings on film include reviews in *Close Up* between 1927 and 1929, and a pamphlet: Borderline: *A POOL film with Paul Robeson* (London: Mercury Press, 1930)

Anne Friedberg, 'Approaching *Borderline*', in *HD: Woman and Poet*, ed. Michael King (Orono, ME: National Poetry Foundation, 1986)
JSh

HEAD, EDITH (1907–81)

Edith Head is the most recognized COSTUME designer in the history of film, and the first woman to head a studio design department. After teaching Spanish in public school, Head began to study art. In 1923 she was hired by PARAMOUNT as a sketch artist. She was Head Designer at Paramount from 1938 to 1967, after which she became Head Designer at UNIVERSAL until her retirement in the late 1970s. She also worked on films for MGM, WARNER BROS., COLUMBIA, and TWENTIETH CENTURY-FOX. Head and her team were nominated for thirty-four Academy Awards, receiving eight. Head also extensively advised women in lectures, in magazines and on radio and television. She co-authored two books, *The Dress Doctor* (1959, on her career) and *How to Dress for Success* (1967). In the latter, Head's guidance derives from the role of costume design in films: 'When Hollywood stars dress for specific roles, the clothes they wear are of tremendous importance in projecting the feeling and the personality of each character . . . what you wear at all times must be chosen for appropriateness as well as for flattery.'

Exotica: *Cleopatra* (Cecil B De Mille, Paramount, 1934), Claudette Colbert; *The Jungle Princess* (William Thiele, Paramount, 1936), Dorothy Lamour's sarong; *Samson and Delilah* (Cecil B De Mille, Paramount, 1950), Hedy Lamarr, Victor Mature

Period dress: *Union Pacific* (Cecil B De Mille, Paramount, 1939), Barbara Stanwyck; *The Heiress* (William Wyler, Paramount, 1949), Olivia de Havilland; *The Man Who Shot Liberty Valance* (John Ford, 1962), Vera Miles, James Stewart, John Wayne; *The Sting* (George Roy Hill, 1973), Robert Redford, Paul Newman

Contemporary: *All About Eve* (Joseph L Mankiewicz, Twentieth Century-Fox, 1950), Bette Davis, Anne Baxter, Marilyn Monroe; *A Place in the Sun* (George Stevens, Paramount, 1951), Elizabeth Taylor, Shelley Winters; *Roman Holiday* (William Wyler, Paramount, 1953), Audrey Hepburn; *Sabrina* (Billy Wilder, Paramount, 1954), Audrey Hepburn's 'Sabrina neckline'; *Rear Window* (Alfred Hitchcock, Paramount, 1954), Grace Kelly; *The Facts of Life* (Melvin Frank, 1960), Lucille Ball

Edith Head and Jane Kesner Ardmore, *Dress Doctor* (Boston: Little, Brown, 1959)   MBH

Sketch by Edith Head for *Samson and Delilah*

HEIN, BIRGIT (1942–)

Birgit and her husband Wilhelm Hein are leading radical avant-garde filmmakers in WEST GERMANY. They have been collaborating since the late 1960s, making experimental films and staging multi-media events and performances. Frustrated by being typecast in the role of filmmaker's wife, Birgit Hein has also established herself independently as an art historian and critic of AVANT-

Kali, by Wilhelm Hein and Birgit Hein

GARDE FILM. In their early films, the notoriously aggressive *Rohfilm* and *Reproductions 3* (both 1968), the Heins engaged with the language of cinema in an attempt to manipulate the perceptual effects of their work. However, by the mid 1970s their audiences had become unresponsive and felt alienated by the couple's radical formal aestheticism. As a consequence, the Heins shifted strategy and focused – with transgressive explicitness – on their private problems.

Birgit Hein rejects notions of a specific female aesthetic. She argues that even a film like *Love Stinks* (1982), despite its focus on female sexuality, remains very much a joint project with Wilhelm Hein. Their autobiographical films attempt to demonstrate that it is possible for women to work with men in depicting female sexuality without becoming voyeuristic.

S&W, Und Sie (1967); *Gruen, Rohfilm, Reproductions 3* (1968); *625, Work in Progress Part A* (1969); *Portraets I, Madison, Wis, Replay, Foto-Film, Filmraum: Reproduktionsimmanente Aesthetik* (1970); *Dop-pelprojektion I, Videotape I* (1971); *Doppelprojektion II–IV, Kurt Schwitters I, II, III, Dokumentation, Fussball* (1972); *Ausdatiertes Material, God Bless America, Stills, London* (1973); *Strukturelle Studien* (1974); *Portraets II* (1975); *Materialfilme I, Materialfilme II* (1976); *Portraets III* (1970–7); *Verdammt in alle Ewigkeit* (1978–9); *Superman und Superwoman* (1980/81); *Love Stinks – Bilder des taeglichen Wahnsinns, American Graffiti* (1982); *Verbotene Bilder* (1985); contributing *Fusswaschung* to the *Jesusfilm* (1986)

Mo Beyerle, Noll Brinckmann, Karola Gramann and Katharina Sykora, 'Ein Interview mit Birgit Hein', *Frauen und Film*, no. 37 (1984)   US

HENNING-JENSEN, ASTRID (1914–)

Having begun her career in the 1930s as an actress, Henning-Jensen started making films at the outbreak of World War II, which coincided with the beginning of the DOCUMENTARY movement in DENMARK. She and her husband Bjarne co-directed and co-scripted several films, the best known of which is *Ditte Mennes-kebarn* (1946). Astrid made her first solo film in 1945, and has subsequently made a number of documentaries and feature films both in Denmark and abroad: in the 1950s she worked in Norway and also for Unesco in Geneva.

Women, children and marriage have been central themes in Henning-Jensen's films, including those made in collaboration with her husband. Children feature centrally in her early films *De pokkers unger* (1947) and *Palle Allene i Verden* (1949), as well as in her recent *Barndommens gade* (1986), which portrays an important phase in a young girl's life, as leaving school and confirmation coincide with the onset of puberty. Stylistically, Henning-Jensen's work is in the tradition of social REALISM: she charts the everyday life and experiences of people in small towns and working-class districts. For children in her films, harsh reality is often contrasted with fantasies and dreamworlds.

Vinterboern (1978) investigates women's feelings about pregnancy and childbirth, focusing on their hopes and fears in the intimate atmosphere of the maternity clinic. Although her themes are of feminist interest, Henning-Jensen has not hitherto been regarded as a maker of 'kvindefilm' (feminist films); though her work is now being rediscovered by filmmakers and writers working in the context of the women's movement.

Films on which Henning-Jensen was assistant director, co-director or director: *Cykledrengene i torvegraven* (short, co-d., 1940); *SOS Kindtand* (short, co-d., 1943); *Når man kun er ung* (ass. d., 1943); *De danske sydhavsoer* (short, co-d., 1944); *Flyktningar finnar en hamn* (short, co-d., 1944); *Dansk politi i Sverige* (short, co-d., 1945); *Skibet er ladet med* (short, co-d., 1945); *Ditte Menneskebarn/Ditte, Child of Man* (ass. d., 1946); *Stemning i April* (co-d., 1947); *De pokkers unger* (co-d., 1947);

Denmark Grows Up (short, co-d., 1947); *Kristinus Bergman* (co-d., 1948); *Palle Allene i Verden* (1949); *Vesterhavsdrenge* (co-d., 1950); *Kranes konditori* (1951); *Ukjent man* (1951); *Better Than Cure* (short, co-d., 1953); *Solstik* (co-d., 1953); *Tivoligarden spiller* (short, co-d., 1954); *Ballettens boern* (short, 1954); *Kaerlighed på kredit* (1955); *Hest på sommerferie/Horse on Holiday* (short, 1959); *Et brev til en son* (1961); *Forraederiet* (1962); *Kvinden og soldaten* (1962); *Een blandt mange* (1962); *Den jagede* (1963); *Der er noget i luften* (1964); *Et minde om to mandage* (1964); *Vend dig ikke om* (1964); *De blå undulater* (1965); *Min bedstefar er en stok* (1967); *Nille* (1968); *Mig og Dig/Mej och dej* (1969); *Vinterboern/Winterborn* (1978); *Ojeblikket* (1980); *Hodja fra Pjort* (1985); *Barndommens gade/Street of My Childhood* (1986)

AKo

HEPBURN, KATHARINE (1907–)

Idolized now as a combination of patrician beauty, cultured intelligence, and independence, Hepburn's Hollywood STAR persona, onscreen and offscreen, did not always win her success. Born in New England into a well-off, freethinking family and educated at Bryn Mawr, Hepburn began her acting career in summer stock. Her willful behavior had her fired and rehired regularly, but when she scored a hit on Broadway with *The Warrior Husband* in 1932, RKO signed her for a phenomenal $1500 a week to make *A Bill of Divorcement* with George CUKOR. Of the thirteen subsequent films she starred in for RKO, only *Morning Glory* (Lowell Sherman, 1933) and *Little Women* (George Cukor, 1933) were successes. *Stage Door* (Gregory La Cava, 1937) and more specifically *Bringing Up Baby* (Howard Hawks, 1938) would later become cult favorites; Dorothy ARZNER's *Christopher Strong* (1933), *Sylvia Scarlett* (George Cukor, 1936) and *A Woman Rebels* (Mark Sandrich, 1936) have recently been reassessed by feminist critics for their portrayals of the rebellious woman, their challenge to the male viewpoint and the notion of FEMININ-

Hepburn with Cary Grant in *Bringing Up Baby*

ITY in Hollywood, and the subversive SEXUALITY of the androgynous TOMBOY heroine, Sylvia Scarlett. However, by 1938 Hepburn's other failures, plus her refusal to talk to the press and her unorthodox behavior – wearing men's clothes and indulging in numerous pranks – led her to be labeled 'box office poison' by a major exhibitor. Undeterred, she bounced back to popularity with her portrayal of determined society belle Tracy Lord in *The Philadelphia Story* (George Cukor, MGM, 1940), a role she had created on stage. *Woman of the Year* (George Stevens, MGM, 1942), which marked the start of her long partnership with Spencer Tracy, also established her finally as the spirit of the educated free woman engaged in battle with the opposite sex. Some feminists have argued that her characters are punished for their independence by opting for oppression in the form of romantic love. Others contend that her rebellious screen persona leaves a more forceful impression than any narrative resolution. It is clear, however, that the Hepburn/Tracy partnership placed her in a firmly heterosexual framework, as distinct from the sexual ambiguities of some of her earlier films.

Hepburn's lengthy movie (and stage) career, which has continued with the likes of *Adam's Rib* (George Cukor, MGM, 1949), *The African Queen* (John Huston, United Artists, 1951), *Summertime* (David Lean, United Artists, 1955), *Suddenly Last Summer* (Joseph L Mankiewicz, Columbia, 1959), *Guess Who's Coming to Dinner* (Stanley Kramer, 1967) right up to *On Golden Pond* (Mark Rydell, 1981) and *The Ultimate Solution of Grace Quigley* (Anthony Harvey, 1984), won her three Oscars and has made her an icon of survival: a mature version of her young, headstrong, gifted heroines – disarmed, perhaps, no longer by a man, but by her age.

Andrew Britton, *Katharine Hepburn – The Thirties and After* (Newcastle: Tyneside Cinema Publications, 1985)   *ALi*

HEROINES

The film heroine can change according to context. In CLASSICAL HOLLYWOOD CINEMA, heroines tended to be either romantic figures or the more active and calculating women typified by the FEMME FATALE of FILM NOIR. In the fifties, examples of the heroine taking on more overtly masculine characteristics appeared in the guise of the TOMBOY, the classic example being Doris DAY's role in *Calamity Jane* (David Butler, Warner Bros., 1953). During the seventies it became possible to think of the Hollywood heroine in terms of a female protagonist moving the narrative forward as she examines and deals (though not always successfully) with problems in her own life – as, for instance, in *Alice Doesn't Live Here Anymore* (Martin Scorsese, 1974). During the eighties the rise of a more aggressive heroine is witnessed in such films as *Aliens* (James Cameron, 1986). Hollywood heroines are often STEREOTYPES, defined more by appearance than by action, and frequently unable to resolve the problems that face them without the help of a male protagonist: in this sense, the heroine's ambitions and actions are defined in terms of male heroic values.

Outside Hollywood, however, other types of heroine may emerge. In the cinemas of the SOVIET UNION and other socialist countries, for instance, the positive working-class hero of SOCIALIST REALISM is occasionally a woman; and FEMINIST INDEPENDENT FILM has created some heroines who seize narrative viewpoint and narrative agency, whilst avoiding the individualistic qualities of the Hollywood hero(ine): feminist films such as *Carry Greenham Home* (Beeban Kidron and Amanda Richardson, 1983) convey the heroism of the collectivity of women. For a character to achieve the status of heroine, audience members must reach some identification with that character. How they do so, however, depends upon their own position in relation to what they are seeing on the screen. For feminists, this simple statement presents interesting, and often encouraging, possibilities. For example, Vienna (Joan CRAWFORD), strange heroine of *Johnny Guitar* (Nicholas Ray, Republic, 1954) will have different meanings as heroine for male heterosexuals and for lesbian audiences. Nor need the female STAR of a film necessarily be its heroine: the heroine of *Imitation of Life* (Douglas Sirk, Universal, 1959) is arguably not its star, Lana Turner; that honor is reserved for Annie (Juanita Moore), with her extraordinarily overdetermined funeral parade.   *JRy/PB*

HEYNS, KATINKA (1947–   )

Katinka Heyns made her early reputation as an actress, first coming to prominence in *Katrina* (Jans Rautenbach, 1969) and later starring in a number of television series. With her husband, noted Afrikaans novelist and critic Chris Barnard, she established her own film company, Sonneblom Films, most of whose work has been for television – notably *Major Sommer*, *De Dood van Elmien Alder, 1945*, and *Tekwan*. *Fiela se Kind* (1988) is Heyns's first venture in feature film production and an important milestone in SOUTH AFRICA's film industry, in that it refocuses the gender and race STEREOTYPES of previous commercial films.

Set in the barren landscape of the nineteenth-century Cape, the story follows the life of a young 'white' orphan who is found and raised by the Koemoeties, successful farmers who are 'colored.' When this is discovered he is returned to an impoverished, depraved, and dehumanized family who live in the Knysna forests. The message is clear: the British colonial authorities of the 1880s could not tolerate a 'white' child being brought up in a 'colored' family. A notable feature of the film is its reversal of race roles: for example, where the central female character of many South African films is traditionally the 'white' Afrikaans *boerevrou* (farm wife), here the

> Woodpeckers Don't Get Headaches *is one of the notable films, directed in 1975, by this filmmaker. Who is she?*

boerevrou is 'colored.' She is dominant and highly visible, hardworking, God-fearing, nurturing, and benevolent. Her stylized physical image embodies the ICONOGRAPHY of the positively valued Afrikaner STEREOTYPE: plump body, and the traditional emblems of good housekeeping – aprons and headscarves.

Fiela se Kind/Fiela's Child (1988)

WJA/RET

HIDARI, SACHIKO (1930–)

Hidari is known as an actress for her various roles in films such as *Jochukko/ The Maid's Kid* (1955) by Tomotaka Tasaka, to Shohei Imamura's *Nippon Konchuki/The Insect Woman* (1963). Within an eight-year period Hidari's talent allowed her to play roles ranging from an innocent country girl who heads for Tokyo to a woman in postwar Japan grubbing through the earth like an insect for survival.

JAPAN's New Wave Cinema (1959–69) initiated a new image of woman and Hidari has said of this period: 'only now are we beginning to have a society which is almost ready to accept women as complete human beings.' Hidari was awarded the Berlin Film Festival Best Actress Award for her role as a wife who begins to question traditional expectations in Susumu Hani's (her former husband's) *Kanojo to Kare/She and He* (1963).

Hidari considers this to have been her most difficult role because she was instructed to act 'naturally.' Hidari's most challenging task to date was her first feature film as director, *Toi Ippon no Michi/The Far Road* (1977), commissioned by the Japan National Railway Union. For this film, Hidari not only did rigorous preliminary research, including interviewing railway workers and their wives, but also directed, produced, and starred as Satoko, the wife of Ichizo, who retires from the railway system stripped by 'progress' of his pride. Hidari neither romanticizes nor aggrandizes the Japanese working-class woman, who cares for her children and home, cajoles her husband, denies him his sexual needs because of her fatigue, supplements the household income by doing piecework at home, and is willing and able to challenge the injustices of progress. The film presents a realistic interpretation of women rarely seen in Japanese cinema, by a woman who is still willing to direct if given the chance.

Toi Ippon no Michi/The Far Road (1977)

Joan Mellen, *Voices from the Japanese Cinema* (New York: Liveright, 1975)

JYY

HITCHCOCK, ALFRED (1899–1980)

One of the most complex and controversial of film directors, Hitchcock was born and educated in London at St Ignatius College, a Jesuit school. He began his career in film at the Famous Players-Lasky studios in 1920, when he met Alma REVILLE, who was to work with him on many of his films. He began by designing subtitles for silent films, later graduating to producing and finally to directing. He made more than fifty feature films in his career – the first being *The Pleasure Garden* in 1925. His British work spans a number of GENREs, from ROMANCE to MUSICAL to COMEDY, but also includes a number of crime films such as *Blackmail* (1929), *Murder!* (1930), *The Man Who Knew Too Much* (1934),

The *Thirty-nine Steps* (1935), and *The Lady Vanishes* (1938). All these films explore questions such as the transference of guilt and the ambiguity of moral values, themes to which he would return with greater and more varied emphasis in his later output. In spite of his imaginative and inventive handling of narrative structure, the narrow-minded critical consensus was that Hitchcock was a clever-clever technician with nothing to say and a rather dubious and 'inartistic' interest in manipulating audiences' emotional reactions. It is not surprising that, like many other directors, he left Britain to work in the far more congenial cinematic climate of Hollywood. From 1940 onward he worked for various of the major Hollywood studios, directing such thriller classics as *Rebecca* (Selznick, 1940), *Notorious* (RKO, 1946), *Stage Fright* (Warner Bros., 1950), *Rear Window* (Paramount, 1954), *Vertigo* (Paramount, 1958), *North by North-West* (MGM, 1959), *Psycho* (Shamley, 1960), *The Birds* (Universal, 1963), and *Marnie* (Universal, 1964).

It was Hitchcock's 'Hollywood period' that earned him the title of 'Master of Suspense,' but once again for his British and American critics he largely remained a minor English artist, a major English entertainer. Indeed, the first radical reassessment of Hitchcock came (in the 1950s) in the columns of the French JOURNAL *Cahiers du cinéma*: perhaps the French, sharing his staunchly Catholic background, were more sensitized to some of his moral preoccupations. Since the 1950s, the limited and limiting appraisal given Hitchcock by some of his contemporary critics has been subsumed by a vast weight of theoretical attention to his films from many different perspectives, including feminist ones. But, as film theorist Tania Modleski points out, it is 'the issue of sexual violence which must be central to any feminist analysis of the films of Alfred Hitchcock. In film studies, Hitchcock is often viewed as the archetypal misogynist who invites his audience to

indulge their most sadistic fantasies against the female.' In Laura MULVEY's essay, seminal in PSYCHOANALYTIC FILM THEORY, 'Visual Pleasure and Narrative Cinema (1975),' she focuses on his films in order to reveal how women in CLASSICAL HOLLYWOOD CINEMA are made into passive objects of male voyeuristic and sadistic impulses, and how by implication women in the audience can only have a masochistic relation to the cinema. Modleski, in her rereading of several of Hitchcock's films, including the early British thrillers, says that Hitchcock 'reveals a fascinated and fascinating tension, an oscillation between attraction to the feminine – his identification with women . . . and a corresponding need to erect, sometimes brutally, a barrier to the femininity which is perceived as all-absorbing.'

Tania Modleski, *The Women Who Knew Too Much* (London and New York: Methuen, 1988)   SP

HOFMAN-UDDGREN, ANNA (1868–1947)

Actress and owner of a music-hall theater in fin-de-siècle Stockholm, Anna Hofman-Uddgren was also SWEDEN's first woman film director (and, after Alice GUY, the second in the world). Indeed, she was one of her country's film pioneers, showing films in her theater as early as 1898 as part of a music-hall program. As for her own filmmaking, she began as a pioneer in a field related to cinema – commercials: her first film was called *Stockholmsfrestelser* (*The Temptations of Stockholm* [1911]). She was also the first person to persuade August Strindberg – that most staunchly patriarchal, not to say misogynist, of men – to agree to her filming his plays *Miss Julie* and *The Father*. According to Swedish film historian Bengt Idestam-Almquist, in these films – now lost – she showed an 'instinctive' understanding for the new medium. Thus, in *Miss Julie*, Hofman-Uddgren included the suicide scene

Anna Hofman-Uddgren

(which is never shown on stage); and in *The Father* made a visually dramatic point with a traveling sequence involving a stagecoach, from an event conveyed only verbally in the play. However, these were the last films Hofman-Uddgren directed, due largely to her financier/producer's death in 1912.

Blott en dröm (1911); *Stockholmsfrestelser* (1911); *Stockholmsdamernas älskling* (1911); *Systrarna* (1912); *Fröken Julie* (1912); *The Father* (1912)

Bengt Idestam-Almquist, *Svensk film före Gösta Berling* (Stockholm: Norstedts, 1974)   MKo

HOLLAND *see* NETHERLANDS

HOLLAND, AGNIESZKA (1948–)

Agnieszka Holland is a leading filmmaker in POLAND, who began her film career as assistant director to Krzysztof Zanussi on *Illuminacja/Illumination* (1973). During the following few years, Holland

was involved mainly in theater direction and television work. Her first films, made for television, bear a strong imprint of CZECHOSLOVAKIA's 'New Wave' cinema, the heyday of which Holland enjoyed at first hand whilst studying in Prague. She graduated in 1971 from the Prague Film School, and soon developed a distinctive personal style. *Aktorzy prowincjonalni* (1978) is set in a small town, with the backstage tensions of a theater company serving as a witty metaphor for the political situation; it received the FIPRESCI prize in Cannes in 1980. By that time Agnieszka Holland was already considered a prominent representative of the Polish New Wave, labeled by reviewers a 'cinema of moral unrest' – this, in Holland's view, being 'just a roundabout way of saying that it was a critical, political cinema.' In *Gorączka* (1980), Holland went back to the 1905 revolution, the period which saw the sudden birth of a workers' and national revival movement in Poland. She finished editing the film *Kobieta samotna*, a very sensitive but harrowing portrayal of the daily drudgery of a single mother living in the provinces, just before the imposition of martial law in Poland in December 1981.

Since late 1981 Holland has been based in Paris, where she has made two documentaries for French television. Her 1984 feature film *Bittere Ernte*, set during World War II, examines the relationship between a gentile farmer and the Jewish woman he is hiding. In 1986 this film was nominated for an Academy Award for Best Foreign Language Film.

Agnieszka Holland is a close associate of Andrzej Wajda: she co-scripted his film *Bez znieczulenia/Rough Treatment* (1978) and worked with him on, among other films, *Danton* (1982).

Wieczór u Abdona/Evening at Abdon's (1974); *Niedzielne dzieci/Sunday Children* (1976); *Coś za coś/Something for Something* (1977); *Zdjęcia próbne/Screen Test* (co-d., 1977); *Aktorzy prowincjonalni/Provincial Actors* (1978); *Gorączka/Fever* (1980); *Kobieta samotna/A Woman Alone* (1982);

Agnieszka Holland with her daughter, Kasia

Bittere Ernte/Angry Harvest (1984); *To Kill a Priest* (1988)

Andrew Short, 'Lost Generation', *Index on Censorship*, vol. 11, no. 5 (1982)   ZB

HOLLYWOOD

In the 1910s, the US film industry shifted base from the East Coast to the California desert, in search of good weather for year-round shooting, cheap labor, plentiful real estate – Hollywood at this time was a rural outpost of Los Angeles – and, some say, relatively laissez-faire attitudes toward business legalities. By the early 1910s, films had increased in length from the one- or two-reel shorts of the early days to the multiple-reel precursors of the fiction feature; and by the mid to late 1910s the formal and stylistic features of what would come to be called CLASSICAL HOLLYWOOD CINEMA were more or less in place. And while, as a consequence of the disruption to European cinemas wrought by World War I, US films were beginning to dominate world markets, the American film industry was taking its first steps to developing the structures for organizing the production and merchandizing of films which, by the late 1920s, would become fully developed in the 'mature oligopoly' of the HOLLYWOOD STUDIO SYSTEM.

The Hollywood films exported all over the world influenced film styles and modes of production in many NATIONAL CINEMAS, some of which – particularly in LATIN AMERICA and throughout the western world – have consciously struggled against Hollywood's economic, cultural, and ideological domination. Such efforts have often required state subsidy in order simply to survive. Other areas, however – INDIA and EGYPT, for example – have for various reasons been able to sustain thriving indigenous commercial cinemas over long periods of time. Nevertheless, and despite the transformations undergone in Hollywood's film (and increasingly now television) industry in the past three decades, classical Hollywood cinema remains an almost universal touchstone, for cinemagoers and filmmakers alike – to be embraced or resisted, but never to be ignored. In ideological terms, Hollywood's continuing influence is inseparable from its dubious and often irresistible PLEASUREs: its ideals of MASCULINITY and FEMININITY, of normative SEXUALITY, of desirable lifestyles – all embedded in a worldview which holds not only that conflicts have to do solely with individuals, but that all conflicts can be resolved.

Tino Balio (ed.), *The American Film Industry* (Madison: University of Wisconsin Press, 1976)

See also: ARZNER, DOROTHY; COOLIDGE, MARTHA; CUKOR, GEORGE; DE MILLE, CECIL B;

GRIFFITH, D W; HAWKS, HOWARD; HITCHCOCK, ALFRED; LUPINO, IDA; MAY, ELAINE; NEW HOLLYWOOD CINEMA; OPHULS, MAX; ROTHMAN, STEPHANIE; SEIDELMAN, SUSAN; SILVER, JOAN MICKLIN; SIRK, DOUGLAS; SPHEERIS, PENELOPE; STERNBERG, JOSEF VON; WEILL, CLAUDIA; WEBER, LOIS   AKu

HOLLYWOOD STUDIO SYSTEM

The studio system originated with the major US film companies which called their production facilities 'studios'; and the term is often applied to a specific period of filmmaking, that of Hollywood from the early 1920s until about 1960. The studio system has also become a prototypical method of organization for mass-production film industries in other nations: the term can now refer to any mode of film production typified by division and specializations of labor, hierarchies of authority, routine sequences of work activities, detailed paper planning and record-keeping, and the perception of individuals as workers to be fitted into a job line.

:::
: *Who was Russia's first female film*
: *director?*
:::

Within US fiction film production between about 1895 and 1909, film work was organized in several ways. One method involved a single worker who determined subject matter (pre-production), framing and shooting (production), and editing (post-production). Alternatively, two or three individuals might be jointly involved in all these tasks. By about 1903, however, a theatrical model appeared in which a producer-director organized work functions, including supervising set design, LIGHTING, and ACTING. This division and hierarchization of labor developed in part because of increased demand for product, with fiction films being easy to produce efficiently and regularly. As far

as is known, at this point no women held positions as single, collaborative or producer-director filmmakers. Nor were women employed as professional cinematographers. However, once the theatrical model was employed, women were hired in areas associated with 'feminine' talents – as story writers, costumers, and actresses. At this time, producer-directors edited shots into narrative sequences, but women were hired for the routine work of assembling rough cuts, as well as for routine manufacture of exhibition prints from the master negative.

Between 1909 and 1914, production output increased and regularized as the US film industry solidified into a distribution oligarchy. Departments developed, accountants were employed, stories became scripts, and physical plants resembling large factories were built. The STAR system became an important method of differentiating between the products of different companies. In the early to mid 1910s, several women moved into major positions of authority, or even started their own production firms. Among the most notable of these were Alice GUY (president of Solax), directors Marguerite Bertsch, Jeannie Macpherson, Lois WEBER, and independent producer-stars Gene Gauntier, Ethel Grandin, Marion Leonard, and Norma Talmadge.

However, as film companies merged and vertically integrated, two changes diminished top management opportunities for women. First of all, although independent companies continued to be a viable option in the market, their ability to secure returns on product was hampered by the major companies – which combined production with DISTRIBUTION and, after 1920, EXHIBITION. Most stars found that contracts with the majors were more profitable than self-employment. The division of labor was also transforming itself into the system which would come to dominate the US film industry. A central producer became studio head, organizing numerous films simultaneously and having authority over pre- and post-production as well as over the hiring of directors to be in charge of the production phase. Using a fully detailed continuity script which had every shot, as well as camera angles and special effects, specified, the central producer could ensure product quality and production efficiency. In the early 1930s the central producer system underwent a minor change, with several associate producers taking over management of six to eight films per year. Until the appearance in the late 1970s of several women – including Sherry Lansing and Jane Wagner – as producers and studio heads, the central producers and their immediate subordinates were always men.

While the studio system as such no longer exists in Hollywood, the current division of labor remains true to its origins. During the 1950s, the US film industry cut back its contract labor and shifted toward financing specialized products. Whereas the studio system had implied guaranteed employment, the new 'package-unit' system works on profit-loss accounting for individual film projects. However, the division of labor remains much the same, with unions still having jurisdiction over work tasks. A hierarchy of managers tops middle- and lower-line workers. Mobility for women has increased somewhat, and a few women directors have broken into Hollywood, usually with one-off projects: Gillian ARMSTRONG, Martha COOLIDGE and Claudia WEILL, for instance. But in relation to the workforce as a whole, women are still very much in the minority in top jobs. They remain predominantly employed in story and SCREENWRITING areas, COSTUMES and MAKE-UP, acting, and EDITING. Their route to positions of greater authority has often been through work as agents to positions as producers.

David Bordwell, Janet Staiger and Kristin Thompson, *The Classical Hollywood Cinema: Film Style and Mode of Production*

to 1960 (London: Routledge & Kegan Paul, 1985)

See also: ADVERTISING; ART DIRECTION; COLUMBIA; CONSUMERISM; MGM; PARAMOUNT; PRODUCTION CODE; RKO; TWENTIETH CENTURY-FOX; UNIVERSAL; WARNER BROS.   JaS

HONDO, MED (1936–   )

A filmmaker from Mauritania – formally one of the ARAB countries – whose sensibility belongs rather to AFRICA, Abid Mohamed Medoun Hondo began his career as an actor in Paris, where he started his own performance group, Shango, in 1966. He wrote the script for his first feature film in 1965, but production of *Soleil Ô* was completed only in 1969, with minimal means, snatched time, and the contribution of friends and actors. The film was selected for the Cannes Festival's Critics' Week in 1970 for its exciting cinematic treatment of the experiences of immigrant workers in France, but banned in several African countries at the request of French ambassadors. In his subsequent documentaries Hondo shows equal awareness of the need to combat imperialist cinema on its own formal ground, as well as in terms of content. *Nous aurons toute la mort pour dormir* (1977), about the Polisario Front's struggle for independence in the Western Sahara, also shows the development of a truly egalitarian social organization. For *West Indies, ou les nègres marrons de la liberté* (1979) – a grand musical tracing the story of slavery from Africa to the West Indies and the subsequent migration to Europe – Hondo avoided naturalistic settings and filmed the entire action on a wooden ship constructed in a disused Citroën factory in Paris. The spectacular *Sarraounia* (1986), on the other hand, was filmed on location: it tells the story of the powerful woman chief of the Azmas who led resistance against colonization and of the French forces ranged against her. The film, a co-production between Hondo's company, Les Films Soleil Ô, and the

Burkina Faso government, has received widespread critical acclaim.

Ballade aux sources/Roots Ballad (1969); *Partout ou peut-être nulle part/Everywhere or Perhaps Nowhere* (1969); *Mes voisins/My Neighbours, Soleil Ô* (1969); *Les bicots-nègres, vos voisins/Your Neighbours the Niggers* (1973); *Nous aurons toute la mort pour dormir/We'll Have the Whole of Eternity for Sleeping* (1977); *Polisario, un peuple en armes/Polisario, a People in Arms* (1978); *West Indies, ou les nègres marrons de la liberté/West Indies Story* (1979); *Sarraounia* (1986)

Françoise Pfaff, Med Hondo and Mark Reid, 'The Films of Med Hondo', *Jump Cut*, no. 31 (1980)   AM

HONG KONG

Until the 1940s, the history of cinema in Hong Kong was coterminous with that of CHINA. Immigrants from the mainland fleeing Japanese invasion, civil war and socialist takeover formed the base of Hong Kong's rapid postwar development, fostered by the laissez-faire policy of British colonial capitalism. A mixed cultural heritage influenced the forms and content of Hong Kong cinema: narrative techniques adopted from vernacular forms of contemporary Chinese literature, from Cantonese operas, and from Hollywood melodramas; generic formulae and visual modes already popular in Shanghai; dialects and subcultures of the immigrants and the Cantonese. MELODRAMA, with its emphasis on family ethics, was both a popular GENRE in the 1950s and 1960s and also a mode with which all other genres (including the martial arts 'KUNG FU' and 'wuxia' (SWORDPLAY) films of the 1960s and early 1970s, and the romantic comedies and urban crime films of the 1980s have close connections. Recurrent themes of degeneration of patriarchal authority, sacrifices made by women on behalf of their families, subjugation of personal goals for the sake of survival, as well as fantastic displacements of political and

social anxieties, have been the thematic preoccupations of an immigrant cultural complex. However, heavy dependence on convoluted plots, dialogue, STEREOTYPES and, in the 1980s, fast-paced editing and flashy spectacle rather than subtle MISE-EN-SCENE, set most of these quickly assembled films apart from 'serious' art as well as from the Hollywood melodramas more familiar to audiences outside Hong Kong. This partly accounts for the fact that overseas reception of these films has been limited mainly to Chinese audiences.

> *It was launched in the USA in 1976, and devoted itself to critiquing classical cinema and how images of women function within it. What is it?*

Hong Kong nevertheless has one of the world's most prolific film industries: second only to INDIA's, it is characterized by low-budget productions (post-dubbed into Mandarin and Cantonese for export), by medium-sized companies, short exhibition schedules in small theater chains, and an enthusiastic and young moviegoing public composed mainly of urban workers and students. Shaw Brothers and Golden Harvest, two major studios, became a southeast Asian phenomenon in the 1960s and 1970s, making huge profits from 'kung fu' films that entered the international market. In the mid 1970s, television started to influence filmmaking through generic crossovers: this led to a rise in the popularity of urban crime films and comedies, and rigorous local competition from new companies, such as Cinema City and Film Workshop. An introduction of new styles also took place, as television directors and film school graduates Allen Fong, Ann Hui, Patrick Tam, and Hark Tsui, among others, made their film directing debuts between 1979 and 1982. Inevitably succumbing to the pressures of an escapist entertainment industry, the work of these young directors nevertheless offers insights into the undercurrents of alienation and insecurity beneath Hong Kong's growing prosperity; and their films show a selfconscious handling of generic conventions. *Fuzi Qing/Father and Son* (Allen Fong, 1981), *Feng Jie/The Secret* (Ann Hui, 1979), *Ming Jian/The Sword* (Patrick Tam, 1980), and *Do Ma Dan/Peking Opera Blues* (Hark Tsui, 1986) capture the consciousness of living in a borrowed place on borrowed time.

Hong Kong films are organized predominantly according to male desires, male friendship, and masculine point of view. Most of them are overtly sexist, except for the unusual reversal in the swordswoman's tradition in martial art films. A very reactionary voyeurism has been cultivated, and is still considered by production companies crucial for box office success. Other than as actresses, women in the film industry work as assistant producers, assistant directors, continuity persons, in costumes and in catering, and are usually hired on a per-film basis. There are only a handful of women directors, most of them film school graduates who have gained experience through working on television drama series. Thematically and stylistically, their films vary, sharing perhaps an awareness of the psychological undercurrents beneath reality and of subtleties in cultural politics related to women's roles. Shu Shuen's *Dong Furen/The Arch* (1970) remains an exemplary commentary on the repression of women within the family. The prolific Ann Hui, more preoccupied with social themes, boasts *Feng Jie/The Secret* and the Vietnam trilogies (including the better-known *Tou Bin Nuhai/The Boat People* [1982]) among her more notable credits.

Hong Kong Urban Council, *Hong Kong International Film Festival: Special Topic Monographs* (Hong Kong: The Urban Council, 1978–86)   EY

HORROR

Horror has enjoyed the unusual status of being both one of the most popular yet most denigrated of film GENREs. Its history begins with the SILENT CINEMA and includes such classics as *The Phantom of the Opera* (Rupert Julian, 1925) and *Nosferatu* (F W Murnau, 1922). Although the thirties, which spawned some of the cinema's great monsters (Frankenstein, Dracula, King Kong), are usually recognized as the golden age of horror, every decade saw new developments. Producer Val Lewton dominated the forties with classics such as *I Walked With A Zombie* (RKO, 1943) and *Cat People* (RKO, 1942). In the fifties, US producer/director Roger Corman drew on the works of Edgar Allan Poe, while the Hammer Studios in BRITAIN began to remake the classics. The sixties gave birth to the psychological horror film, such as Alfred HITCHCOCK's *Psycho* (Shamley, 1960) and Michael POWELL's *Peeping Tom* (1960). The past two decades have been dominated by the splatter movie and a spate of WOMEN IN PERIL exploitation films.

French critics began to take the genre seriously when, in the fifties and sixties, they discussed the horror film as part of the 'fantastique.' In other countries, however, horror was discussed primarily in terms of its harmful effects on society. By the seventies, some writers had argued for the horror film as an art form and also discussed important influences: the gothic novel, Surrealism, and German Expressionism. Film critic Robin Wood is interested in the relationship between horror and society. He argues that in the American horror film 'normality' has always been represented by the heterosexual, monogamous couple and the institutions of the family, police, church, and military. The monster, frequently a sympathetic figure, represents our unconscious desires to destroy the norms which oppress us. Wood argues for the potential progressiveness of horror, citing such examples as *The Texas Chainsaw Massacre* (Tobe Hooper, 1974) and *The Omen* (Richard Donner, 1976).

In the late seventies and early eighties, feminist groups protested against misogynistic representation of women in slasher films such as Brian DE PALMA's *Dressed To Kill* (1980), linking it with the way women were represented in violent PORNOGRAPHY. They argued that women were portrayed as victims, their bleeding, battered bodies depicted in graphic detail, indicating that pleasure in viewing is linked directly to the representation of violence against women.

In his monograph *Genre* (London: British Film Institute, 1980), film theorist Steve Neale argues that the monster, invariably associated with the castration scenario, signifies the terrifying aspects of female SEXUALITY. Drawing on Julia Kristeva's theory of the abject, another approach proposes that woman is constructed in horror as the 'monstrous-feminine' in a passive and an active way. In some films, woman signifies the monstrous-feminine through the image of her bleeding, disfigured body. In others, she is represented as the monstrous-feminine in an active capacity: for instance, as witch (*The Exorcist* [William Friedkin, 1973]); lesbian vampire (*The Hunger* [Tony Scott, 1983]); and primeval mother (*Aliens* [James Cameron, 1986]). These representations signify a more terrifying aspect of woman, and connect her image to those of the Sphinx, Medusa, and Hecate. It is possible, however, that the female spectator may derive PLEASURE and power from watching such potent figures.

Barbara Creed, *The Monstrous-Feminine: Women in the Horror Film* (London and New York: Routledge, forthcoming)

See also: SCIENCE FICTION; VAMPIRE FILM; WOMEN'S REVENGE   BC

HUILLET, DANIELE (1936–)

The name of Danièle Huillet, French-born filmmaker who has worked in WEST GERMANY for most of her career, is closely linked with that of her companion, the filmmaker Jean-Marie Straub. But although she shares scripting and directing credit on all their work, Huillet's contribution to the collaboration is usually played down or ignored. On the other hand, their working collaboration is so close that it would not necessarily be meaningful to separate it along gender lines (Huillet has, however, indicated that she tends to be in charge of sound and editing, while Straub does most of the camerawork). Huillet sees the issue of women as falling within a left/revolutionary framework, rather than being a separate political issue.

Huillet and Straub's work is MODERNIST, oppositional, intellectually demanding, and considered difficult; and in spite of their efforts it is rarely seen outside the international film festival circuit. Their films have their roots in European (mostly German) high culture: literature – Brecht, Boell, Kafka – or music – Bach, Schoenberg – and are particularly concerned with an exploration of history. They are politically committed – sometimes explicitly so, as in *Fortini/Cani* (1976), which reworks material about the Israeli–Palestinian conflict; but this is more often evident in their approach to the material. It is a cinema which is, in critic Maureen Turim's words, 'theoretical, elliptical, innovative, and challenging.'

In collaboration with Jean-Marie Straub: *Machorka-Muff* (short, 1962); *Nicht Versoehnt, oder es Hilft nur Gewalt, wo Gewalt herrscht/Not Reconciled* (1965); *Chronik der Anna Magdalena Bach/The Chronicle of Anna Magdalena Bach* (1968); *Der Braeutigam, die Komoediantin und der Zuhalter/ The Bridegroom, the Comedienne and the Pimp* (short, 1968); *Les Yeux ne veulent pas en tout temps se fermer, ou peut-être qu'un jour Rome se permettra de choisir à son tour/ Othon* (1969); *Geschichtsunterricht/History Lessons* (1972); *Einleitung zu Arnold Schoenbergs Begleitmusik zu einer Lichtspielszene/Introduction to Arnold Schoenberg's Accompaniment to a Cinematographic Scene* (short, 1972); *Moses und Aaron/ Moses and Aaron* (1975); *Fortini/Cani* (1976); *Toute Révolution est un coup de dés/Every Revolution is a Throw of Dice* (short, 1977); *Dalla Nube alla Resistenza/*

The Chronicle of Anna Magdalena Bach

From the Cloud to the Resistance (1979); *Trop tôt trop tard/Too Early Too Late* (1981); *En rachachant* (short, 1982); *Amerika Klassenverhaeltnisse/Class Relations* (1983)

Maureen Turim, 'Oblique Angles on Film as Ideological Intervention: Jean-Marie Straub and Danièle Huillet', in *New German Filmmakers*, ed. Klaus Phillips (New York: Ungar, 1984) GV

HUNGARY

From a feminist standpoint, Hungary must be regarded as one of the most exciting countries as far as cinema is concerned, not only in EASTERN EUROPE, but worldwide. Institutional, financial, and gender constraints mean that very few women directors elsewhere have succeeded in producing an entire body of films, as Hungarian Márta MESZAROS has done. And, while Mészáros claims she is not a feminist, she does assert that the subordination of women is the 'prob-

lem of the century.' In substance, her films – focusing on working women, women struggling to assert their autonomy, women's sexuality, and strong friendships between women – can be regarded as having made a very substantial contribution to feminist cinema. Indeed, it is as a result of her perspective on women that Mészáros's films have until recently failed to gain the recognition they deserve in Hungary itself.

Aside from Mészáros's contribution, Hungary is perhaps the only country apart from WEST GERMANY with a large number of successful women directors, both in documentary and in feature films. Judit ELEK's drama documentaries on the constraints imposed on women in rural Hungary, and Judit EMBER's *Mistletoes* (1978), about three generations of gypsy women, are noteworthy not only for their subject matter but also for the approach taken by their directors. The films rely on a relationship of trust with the people they portray: Elek lived in the village she portrays for four years, and so knows her characters intimately; in Ember's film the gypsy women play themselves. This kind of drama documentary in which real-life protagonists play themselves is a technique developed particularly by Hungarian women directors, including Livia GYARMATHY and Györgyi Szalai. Ildiko Enyedi's first feature, *My Twentieth Century* (1989), won the Caméra d'Or at the 1989 Cannes Film Festival, suggesting that this director has a bright future. Unlike Enyedi, who rejects feminism as too narrow a conceptual framework, Maria Sos, with her first feature, *The Unhappy Hat* (1980), made an overtly feminist film about the lives of four middle-aged women who have emancipated themselves from their weak men. Hungary is also well known for ANIMATION films, and Katalin MACSKASSY's films are innovative in their mix of animation and live action.

As might be expected from a country where the specifically Hungarian versions of glasnost and perestroika are producing much open debate and major political change, the film industry too is in a state of excitement and flux. Hungarian cinema is perhaps the best known of Eastern Europe in the international arena, a distinction exemplified in the recognition won by Márta Mészáros with *Adoption* (Golden Bear at the Berlinale, 1975) and *Diary for My Children* (Grand Prix of the Jury at Cannes, 1984; Grand Prix, Budapest, 1984; several other international prizes): and István Szabo with his films *Mephisto* (Academy Award, Oscars for best film and best actor – Klaus Maria Brandauer – as well as British Film Critics' Award for best foreign film in 1982) and *Colonel Redl* (West German Golden Film Band; and Jury Prize at Cannes, 1985). This international acclaim reflects not only the talent and creativity of Hungarian directors, but also the excellent studio facilities they enjoy. It is furthered by the annual Hungarian Film Festival held in early February, immediately preceding the Berlin Film Festival. The February 1989 festival provided stunning illustration of how far the democratization process has accelerated since it began in 1988, with a previously unheard-of degree of free speech and freedom of expression. Filmmakers are at the forefront of this process. Of the thirteen features and eleven documentaries shown at the 1989 festival, the great majority were concerned with 'hidden history,' the history of the postwar and Stalinist years which does not appear in school textbooks, but which it has now become possible to tell. Hungarian historians acknowledge that filmmakers are uncovering the painful past more boldly than they themselves, or any other branch of scholarship or the arts, have yet done. Hungarian television in particular has been slow to adapt to the new climate.

Hungarian cinema has a long and active history. Perhaps its best-known name remains Alexander Korda, who wrote the first regular film column in Hungary in 1912 and launched the first film periodical, *Pesti Mozi*, before turning to directing. By 1918 he had made nineteen films. One of Korda's innovations still used today was the 'dramaturg,' or story editor. During the shortlived Hungarian Republic of Councils from April to August 1919, the film industry was nationalized and Korda appointed commissioner for film production. This made the Hungarian film industry the first nationalized industry anywhere – preceding the SOVIET UNION by a few months – and marks a significant period in its history. On the collapse of the Republic, Korda and several more of Hungary's best directors fled arrest or persecution by the rightwing regent Admiral Horthy. As a consequence, the 1920s were paradoxically a low point for the Hungarian film industry, by contrast with the 'golden age' of film elsewhere. The film industry was again nationalized in 1948, initially producing films geared to raising socialist consciousness.

Today the Hungarian film industry is based on a state-funded studio system producing around twenty-two films per year. Directors receive a low basic salary which is considerably augmented when they are in production. Production, and the government's annual subsidy to each studio, are administered by Mafilm, which employs around 2500 people. Mafilm also provides facilities, both for local productions and for the increasing number of co-productions being made in Hungary. While Mafilm administers the production side, Hungarofilm organizes film distribution and sales, import and export, as well as Hungarian film weeks abroad. Hungarofilm is headed by István Szabo, who came to Hungarofilm from the Film Board at the Ministry of Culture. Hungary also has a Film Institute run by István Nemeskürty, for twenty-six years the highly respected head of the Budapest Studios. The Film Institute publishes a monthly film magazine, *Filmkultura*, and runs its own cinema in Budapest, the Filmmuseum. Nemeskürty is also known as the author of a history of Hungarian cinema.

The four main studios are Objektiv, Dialog, Hunnia and Budapest. A fifth studio, Pannonia, makes mostly animation films. There is also a partially state-funded independent film studio, Mozgokep Innovacios Tarsulas (Inno-vation Studio), set up by a group of independent filmmakers out of what used to be the fifth largest studio. Its directors make alternative and politically hard-hitting films not destined for mass audiences, and shown since February 1989 in their own independent Budapest cinema. Finally, the Béla Balázs Studio (BBS) – named after the renowned Hungarian film theorist and teacher – is the young directors' studio, giving film school graduates the opportunity to make their mark. BBS is also subsidized by the Ministry of Culture's film department, and its status allows its directors to make experimental cinema and video films, since they are under no obligation to exhibit their product publicly. Recently a 'video magazine,' *The Black Box*, has been produced under BBS's auspices, showing in its first three issues footage of pro-environment demonstrations in Budapest and at the Danube Dam site, material which TV will not show. In Hungary, cassettes of *The Black Box* can be borrowed from libraries, or purchased.

Graham Petrie, *History Must Answer to Man: The Contemporary Hungarian Cinema* (Budapest: Corvina Kiadó, 1978)
BE/ER

ICELAND

Films were first shown in Iceland in 1903, and the first permanent cinema was established there in 1906. In 1912 the number of cinemas increased to two and remained thus until 1930, when a third was added. Today there are altogether thirteen cinemas in the capital, Reykjavik, whose population is one hundred thousand. Icelanders did not make films before World War I, but filmmakers from Sweden, France, Denmark, and Switzerland went to Iceland during that period to shoot films. In 1917 Swedish director Victor Sjöström/Seastrom premiered *Berg-Ejvind ock hans hustru/The Outlaw*, based on a play by Icelandic author Johann Sigurjonsson, but World War I prevented the making of this famous film on location in Iceland. Only one all-Icelandic fiction film was made during the silent era: *Avintyri Jons og Gvendar/The Adventures of Jon and Gvendur*, a short directed by Loftur Gudmundsson in 1923. Feature films were not made in Iceland until 1948, when Gudmundsson made the first Icelandic sound film, *Milli fjalls og fjöru/Between Mountain and Shore*. Iceland's first full-length documentary was Loftur Gudmundsson's *Island i lifandi myndum/Iceland in Moving Pictures*, made in 1925. In subsequent years Gudmundsson made a large number of documentaries about manual and industrial labor in Iceland on both sea and land.

During the interwar years foreign filmmakers visited Iceland frequently, but it was not until the beginning of World War II that Icelandic filmmakers began to emerge. Oskar Gislason was the most influential filmmaker of this and the postwar period: he made several documentary films and features during the 1940s and 1950s. The high point came in 1951, when Gislason and Gudmundsson premiered Icelandic films, both shot on 16mm.

Icelandic Television was founded in 1966, bringing about – among other things – the establishment of Felag Kvikmyndagerdarmanna, the Icelandic Filmmakers' Association. In the years 1972 to 1978 the Icelandic Cultural Council offered only small grants for making films, all of which were devoted to documentary production. However, the Reykjavik Film Festival meant a new beginning for Icelandic film culture: first held in 1978, this is now an annual event. The Icelandic Film Fund and Film Archive were established in 1979.

> 'Pure, blond, virginal, naive, pleasant and capable.' This unlikely vision of femininity gave rise to a genre in which national cinema?

August Gudmundsson's *Land og Synir/Land and Sons* (1979) marked a new beginning for the continuous production of Icelandic feature films. Almost a third of Iceland's population of 250 000 saw the film. *Utlaginn/Outlaw: The Saga of Gisli* (1981), directed by August Gudmundsson, was the first attempt to adapt one of the Icelandic sagas for the screen. *A hjara veraldar/Rainbow's End* (1983), by Kristin JOHANNESDOTTIR, was the first Icelandic film made by a woman director. *Rainbow's End* can also be considered a feminist film, with demanding symbolism and visual insight as well as a very personal voice. Other female directors in Iceland are Kristin Palsdottir (*Skilabod til*

Söndru/Message to Sandra [1984]); Thorhildur Thorleifsdottir (*Stella i orlofi/ The Icelandic Shock Station* [1986]); and Gudny Halldorsdottir (*Kristnihald undir jokli* [1988]).

Icelandic Film Fund, *Icelandic Films* (Reykjavik: Icelandic Film Fund, 1980/83, 1984/86, 1979/88)   TA

ICONOGRAPHY

A method of analyzing visual motifs and style in films, iconography derives from art history but can be applied to a range of media. In film, iconography is associated with examinations of the visual aspects of GENRE and MISE-EN-SCENE. Iconography, in identifying and classifying dominant motifs and resulting subject matters or themes, can work on various levels of analysis, from the overall visual construction of a film to specific symbols within it. The strength of iconography as a method of analysis is that it can bring to light certain styles or techniques associated with particular genres: for instance, the essentially painterly conventions light contrast in FILM NOIR, or the particular image compositions found in the WESTERN. Iconography not only identifies visual facts or motifs, but also interprets these in terms of socially significant themes and meanings: for example, the visual presentation of women in the thematic context of film noir relates to certain understandings of female SEXUALITY.

Iconographical analysis of films involves three stages. In the first, visual facts making up the dominant motifs are identified. In the second, the theme or subject matter arising from recognition of the motifs is examined. The final stage of analysis identifies the socially significant meanings which inform the film's subject matter or theme. Underlying these stages are changes in levels of meaning. During the first stage meaning is based on individual reaction to – and simple recognition of – dominant motifs. By the second stage meaning has become inclusive of social, religious, sexual factors, and so on. A woman dressed in black, say, may become symbolic of a certain kind of sexuality, in the context of the overall theme or subject of the film. The third level of meaning combines the social significance of the theme with some understanding of its cultural and historical context. Iconography suggests that the meaning of a particular motif or theme is cultural, in that it can only be understood by, and relevant to, a specific AUDIENCE.

Erwin Panofsky, *Meaning in the Visual Arts* (London: Peregrine, 1983)   JRy

IDEMITSU, MAKO (1940–   )

Currently, Mako Idemitsu is JAPAN's only female VIDEO artist concerned with the psychological make-up of the Japanese woman from a female perspective. Her primary concern is to encourage an awareness of the Japanese woman's situation – which is dictated by traditional expectations – and through this awareness to bring about much-needed change. Idemitsu's objective must be seen against a backdrop of social values in which girls are traditionally expected to work until their twenty-fifth birthday and 'retire' from the workforce between the ages of twenty-six and twenty-nine, to devote their lives to childrearing and household responsibilities. It is not uncommon for mothers to find vicarious satisfaction through their children, sons especially, since husbands are expected to play the role of the 'salaryman,' which involves long working hours and after-hours peer socialization, or one to two-year postings abroad. 'The situation is not healthy,' Idemitsu states.

Idemitsu's concern becomes apparent in works like *Hideo-chan, Mama-Yo* (1983) and *Yoji, Do-shita-no?* (1987). In both *Hideo* and *Yoji*, the mothers are obsessed with their sons. Idemitsu's technique of including a television monitor in the narrative underlines the bonding of Hideo's mother with her son, and in *Yoji*, the inset monitor reveals the psychological reasoning behind the mother's manipulative behavior. Idemitsu's work not only exemplifies her understanding of social problems, but also shows her technical skill – in the simultaneous intermixing of two video images which has become her signature.

As early as 1973, Idemitsu was exploring the psychological make-up of her genre. Early works (*Shadows, Parts I and II* and *Animus, Parts I and II*) explore, through Jungian concepts, the suppressed and repressed aspects of personalities. Idemitsu credits her years in America between 1962 and 1973 (when she was married to painter Sam Francis, had two sons, and first experimented with Super-8mm and 16mm film) with her desire to promote a Japanese feminist awakening by revealing Japanese woman as she is.

Idemitsu's work includes: *Hideo-chan, Mama-Yo/Hideo Dear, It's Me, Mama* (1983); *Great Mother Series* (*Harumi*, 1983; *Yumiko*, 1983; *Sachiko*, 1984); *Yasushi no Keikon/The Marriage of Yasushi* (1986); *Yoji, Do-shita-no?/Yoji, What's Wrong With You?* (1987); *Kiyoko no Kurushimeru/ Kiyoko's Situation* (1988)

Micki McGee, 'Domestic Disharmony: Mako Idemitsu's Psychodramas', *The Independent*, vol. 9, no. 3 (1986)   JYY

IDEOLOGY

At its simplest, 'ideology' refers to how a particular belief system explains society. But Karl Marx pointed out that the class which rules by virtue of its ownership of the means of production (of a society's wealth) has power thereby to disseminate a society's 'ruling ideas.' The ideology of the ruling class explains society in terms of its natural fitness to rule, and thus misrepresents the place of other classes or groups in that society's power relations. From this stems the conception of ideology as 'false consciousness.' Marxist social theory opposes ideology by analyzing the unequal power relations that underlie social appearances.

The political problem here is that the 'false consciousness' whereby the oppressed accept their inequality is rarely dispelled by simple demonstration of 'true' social models. Feminists, in particular, find this true of patriarchy, where unequal sexual relations are embedded in

Ideologies of romantic love pervade dominant cinema

213

ideologies of romantic love, family, maternity. The French marxist philosopher Louis Althusser extended ideology to include not only fully formulated ideas but also commonsense wisdoms, images, everyday practices. Ideology operates not just in the head, but in the assumptions that shape the way we do things. Ideology in this sense is systematized in the institutional practices of the home, school, church, and media, and in the representational practices of journalism, fiction, film, television, advertising, etc. Drawing on the ideas of French psychoanalyst Jacques Lacan, Althusser suggests the profoundly 'unconscious' way dominant ideology infiltrates not only everyday life, but our identities as 'subjects' at the center of our world.

This definition of ideology enables feminists to analyze how patriarchal ideologies continue to perpetuate unequal relations between the sexes in countries or institutions which claim to support sexual equality. Representations create ideologically gendered subjects, who find unequal economic, legal, sexual, and emotional divisions between men and women natural. The theory of 'dominant' ideology has been criticized for its apparently inescapable determinism. However, its mixture of ideas, images and commonsense wisdoms, arising out of diverse institutional practices often having contradictory aims, means that 'dominant' ideology is also fragmented and incoherent, and that competing or oppositional ideologies cannot be prevented from making themselves heard.

The notion of ideology as internally contradictory has inspired a good deal of FILM THEORY, where the method of ideological analysis aims to expose ideological contradictions at work in film TEXTS, notably those of DOMINANT CINEMA. Some FEMINIST FILM THEORY, and feminist tendencies within PSYCHOANALYTIC FILM THEORY, concern themselves particularly with ideologies concerning SEXUALITY, FEMININITY, and MASCULINITY as these are played out in cinema; and with seeking to exploit ideological contradictions in these areas to create alternative or resistant practices both of reading, and – through FEMINIST INDEPENDENT FILM – of making, cinema.

Annette Kuhn, *Women's Pictures: Feminism and Cinema* (London: Routledge & Kegan Paul, 1982) CG

INCONTRI INTERNAZIONALI DI CINEMA E DONNE

An ongoing WOMEN'S FILM FESTIVAL in ITALY, Incontri takes place annually in Florence and is directed by Maresa D'Arcangelo and Paola Paoli. A showcase for films made by women from all over the world, it has been running for more than a decade. The festival's aim is to inquire into geographical areas and the history of women. Each year either one NATIONAL CINEMA or theme is explored. Topics include 'the mirror gaze,' 'island cinema,' 'imaginary origins,' and 'the house and the world.' A catalogue accompanying the festival's program includes filmographic information, interviews, filmmakers' statements, critical texts by feminist writers, and photographs.

Another well-established feminist showcase for international films in Italy is a section of the Incontri Internazionali del Cinema di Sorrento (Naples). The feminist section has been directed since its beginnings in 1976 by Lina Mangiacapre, leader of the feminist filmmaking collective 'Le Nemesiache.' Contemporary women's films are also presented in the general programs of Italian FILM FESTIVALS dedicated to INDEPENDENT CINEMA. Most prominently among these, the annual Cinema Giovani in Turin and the biennial Filmmaker in Milan both dedicate space to women's films.

Laboratorio Immagine Donna (eds), *XI Incontro Internazionale di Cinema e Donne* (Florence: Press 80, forthcoming) GB

INDEPENDENT CINEMA

This is a term used to describe the forms of cinema that exist outside of a popular or commercial mainstream film industry. Independent films are usually characterized by a rejection of the aesthetic or ideological norms of the dominant industry, and independent cinema is generally thought of as a marginalized, alternative, or oppositional cinema within capitalist societies, fighting for a voice in relation to more economically and socially powerful forms of communication. It has developed in conjunction with movements for social emancipation – including the struggle for women's liberation, recognizing the need for an independent voice for women – since the late 1960s.

The high cost of manufacturing moving pictures, and desire on the part of governments and business interests to control the circulation of ideas in this powerful medium, have resulted, in most countries, in various forms of restriction on access to the means of audiovisual expression. Independent film and VIDEO have developed in response to such pressures of exclusion or CENSORSHIP. In capitalist societies independent film movements often make the demand that public money be used to facilitate freedom and diversity of expression in a realm of communication otherwise dominated by the imperatives of the market. In poorer and smaller nations, and in many Third World countries, a whole emerging indigenous NATIONAL CINEMA may be described as independent, in the sense that it is born out of the struggle against limitations imposed by colonial history, or by an excessive domination of the home market by foreign, imported films.

Historical examples of independent cinema in the West include attempts made by the various Workers' Film and Photo Leagues in the 1930s (in the USA, Britain, and many European countries) to provide a space for the expression of independent working-class views, in opposition to what was seen as the escapism and anti-collectivism of the Hollywood cinema of the time.

Independent cinema also embraces aesthetic and formal AVANT-GARDE movements, such as the American 'underground' and other Surrealist, MODERNIST, poetic, and structural-materialist currents in Europe and North America. These movements include important work by women filmmakers such as Germaine DULAC, Maya DEREN, Carolee SCHNEEMANN, Yvonne RAINER, Joyce WIELAND, Chantal AKERMAN, Laura MULVEY, Lis RHODES, and Sally POTTER. Internationally, independent cinema has also included a strong element of campaigning on women's issues and for the recovery of suppressed women's histories. Examples would include the work of NEW DAY FILMS in the USA, of the LONDON WOMEN'S FILM GROUP in Britain, of the DERRY FILM AND VIDEO COLLECTIVE in Ireland, and of the Colombian collective CINE-MUJER.

Sylvia Harvey, 'The Other Cinema in Britain: Unfinished Business in Oppositional and Independent Film, 1929–1984', in *All Our Yesterdays: Ninety Years of British Cinema*, ed. Charles Barr (London: British Film Institute, 1986)

See also: ABORIGINAL FILM AND VIDEO; BLACK CINEMA; COUNTERCINEMA; FEMINIST INDEPENDENT FILM; LESBIAN INDEPENDENT CINEMA; MAORI FILM; NATIVE AMERICAN FILM; NATIVE CANADIAN FILM; SOCIALIST CINEMA   SHa

INDIA

The world's most prolific film industry comprises a dominant Bombay-based Hindi cinema, more than a dozen regional language film production centers, and a small but strong and diverse tradition of alternative or 'parallel' cinema. Indian cinema history is little shorter than western cinema's: the Lumières reached Bombay with their cinematograph in July 1896 and the first completely Indian feature, introducing a uniquely Indian GENRE – the mythological – was released in 1913. With a vast domestic market to sustain the industry, Indian cinema could develop without conforming to expectations of international audiences and, although Hollywood has always been influential, a distinctive form of mainstream cinema has evolved which owes much to traditional entertainment forms, notably village dramatizations of mythological epics and the colorful spectacle and melodrama of urban Parsee theater. Featuring song, DANCE, and stars in almost every film, the mainstream Hindi cinema, though less than 20 percent of national production, has influenced most regional production, and it alone has pan-Indian distribution. It has also been widely distributed throughout the Third World and even the Soviet Union.

> Helena Nogueira's 1988 film **Quest for Truth** is a landmark in the history of women in cinema. Why is this so?

Although Hindi mainstream films play on nationalist and traditionalist sentiment, the industry has had scant support from national government. It is an anarchic free market – refused institutional finance, heavily taxed, harshly censored, and offered no effective protection against rampant video piracy. The studio system that evolved in the 1930s broke down in the 1940s when wartime profiteers with 'black' money to launder lured stars away from the studios with huge fees. A pernicious star system developed, and the industry is still awash with 'black' money. It is also extraordinarily fragmented, comprising hundreds of small producers, distributors, and exhibitors. National government has funded documentaries (via the Films Division, established in 1947) and some alternative filmmaking since 1960 when,

embarrassed by the international acclaim of Satyajit Ray's *Pather Panchali* at Cannes, it founded the Film Finance Corporation (later the National Film Development Corporation). However, NFDC's impact has been minimal, as no exhibition outlets for alternative cinema were developed within India, and its successes are primarily through international festivals. Only regional cinemas have viable state support, largely because state governments see the political advantage of films exploiting regional chauvinism. There is also a tradition of direct political involvement: local film stars have become Chief Ministers of Tamil Nadu and Andhra Pradesh.

CENSORSHIP has been a major issue. While filmmakers have overcome bans on explicit sexual activity by developing extravagantly suggestive song picturizations (which eroticize the female body equally 'well'), political censorship has been a more serious battleground. Even representations of corrupt police or politicians were mostly taboo until 1983, when pressures from regional and alternative cinemas successfully challenged this. Strict political censorship is, however, a legacy of British rule. Most major film producers of the 1930s and 1940s supported the Congress Party, and a tradition of socially critical filmmaking developed. Even some of the popular mythological, costume and stunt genres subtly subverted British censorship strictures – for example, audiences recognized stunt films starring Fearless Nadia (a blonde whip-cracking wonder woman who regularly saved oppressed peoples from wicked tyrants) as anti-British allegories.

More significantly, in tune with the contemporary interest in defining a 'modern' Indian identity, some major 1930s studios – including Poona's Prabhat (notably V. Shantaram), Calcutta's New Theaters, and Bombay Talkies – produced MELODRAMAs dealing overtly with social injustice, including women's oppression, and criticized traditions of child marriage, dowry iniquities, taboos on widow remarriage, and on love outside arranged marriage. Similar themes continued – alongside more conservative ROMANCEs – through the 1950s classics of Raj Kapoor, Guru Dutt, Bimal Roy, Mehboob Khan, and others, who worked with female STARS of considerable stature – NARGIS, Madhubala, Meena Kumari, Vijayanti-mala, Waheeda Rehman – who were given powerful central roles. However, profound ambivalence has surrounded this chivalrous championing of women's issues, which has ranged from quiet integrity to ingenuous outrage, from patronizing idealization of women to cynical exploitation of fashionable 'mod-ern' themes, including the titillating vi-sion of the sexually independent woman. In the 1970s and 1980s, popular cinema's purported concern with women's issues has become particularly opportunistic with, for example, the fetishized aveng-ing angels of the 1980s WOMEN'S RE-VENGE movies. The industry assumes that urban working-class men are the prime audience for these and the recent cycle of gore and violence movies, and that this audience must be catered for since female audiences (who are charac-terized as enjoying family melodramas, romances, and – until the 1970s, when they virtually died out – mythologicals and devotional films) are dwindling. This is probably a self-fulfilling expecta-tion. Meanwhile, women have always had very little power within the film industry, and virtually no opportunities to make films themselves. Only a hand-ful of women have directed feature films – all in the 1980s – most notably Sai Paranjpee and Arunaraje Desai in the Hindi mainstream, Aparna Sen in Ben-gal, and Prema Karanth in Karnataka. Even female stars are paid considerably less than their male counterparts, and a film's value to distributors is calculated primarily on the male star's box office appeal.

While the polarization of 'art' versus 'commercial' cinema masks considerable heterogeneity within each category, the work of Satyajit Ray and Ritwik Ghatak in the 1950s was a significant interven-tion and catalyst for a 'new' cinema. Concerned with the meaning of the tra-ditional in contemporary India, but re-fusing what they saw as the excesses and naive populism of their commercial con-temporaries, Ray and Ghatak explored new forms. Ray drew on Italian NEO-REALISM, Jean RENOIR, and CLASSI-CAL HOLLYWOOD CINEMA to tackle a wide range of subjects, often rooted in Bengali literature and folklore, and he received immediate wide acclaim in the West. The more iconoclastic Ghatak eschewed conventions of both the Indian mainstream and of bourgeois western humanism and devoted himself to de-veloping an 'epic cinema' (akin to Brecht's vision) which drew on Indian material traditions and mythic arche-types. Combining excruciating melo-drama with remarkable subtleties, Ghatak's work includes, amongst other themes, exploration of women's oppres-sion within wider political contexts – and of the female archetypes located in Hindu goddesses – that underpin this. Ghatak, long marginalized in India and the West, has influenced the work of Kumar Sha-hani and Mani Kaul, and is currently hailed by a new generation of film stu-dents. However, these films have had minimal exhibition opportunities within India, and it was Mrinal Sen and Shyam Benegal who began to bridge the gap between 'art' and the mainstream with a 'middle cinema' that has gradually found a lucrative middle-class audience niche. The 'middle cinema' regularly takes women's exploitation as a theme, but again, almost all its filmmakers are men. Perhaps its greatest contribution for women was in launching two powerful actresses for the 1970s and 1980s, Smita PATIL and Shabana AZMI. Both have worked successfully across the board of commercial and alternative cinemas, and although both have been controversial, they have established strong popular public identities as intelligent young women concerned with feminist issues.

The issues are on the agenda. The hope for the future is that more spaces open up for women to make films themselves.

Rosie Thomas, 'Mythologies of Modern India', in *World Cinema since 1945*, ed. William Luhr (New York: Ungar, 1987)

See also: NAIR, MIRA   *RT*

IRAN

The label 'cinema of parody' has been attached to the work of directors making films in post-revolutionary Iran with finance from various governmental bodies. Among these directors are Mohsen Makhmalbaffe, maker of *Dastfouroush/The Peddler* (1986), Nasser Taghvayie, maker of *Nakhouda Khourshid/Captain Khourshid* (1986), and Dariush Farahang, maker of *Telesm/The Spell* (1987). Although diverse, films by these and other directors are all based on western literature and all copy western film GENREs.

Cinematography was introduced to Iran in 1900 by King Mozafarrull Din Shah, of the Ghaajar dynasty. The first filmmakers were allowed only to make documentaries, mainly of royal events and celebrations. Later on, all films were subjected to royal censorship. This left filmmakers with little alternative but to copy western approaches to cinema. Then as now, the curbing of 'artistic freedom' was seen as essential in preserving the autocratic rule of governments.

However, a new Iranian cinema was born during the late 1960s and early 1970s under the auspices of the Empress Faraah, who took two steps to ensure the development of a film industry. First she launched the Teheran International Film Festival, which gave Iranians their only opportunity to familiarize themselves with the world's INDEPENDENT CINEMA. Second, she established the Center for the Intellectual Development of Children and Young Adults, with a cinema affairs division which financed independent filmmaking. These two institutions were reinforced by the state-owned tele-

vision's move into training new talent. It set up the Academy for Cinema and Television, which provided training in all aspects of filmmaking, and also set up production studios around the country and financed experimental work by young film school graduates. The Center for Intellectual Development of Children and Young Adults became the common factor linking the directors who created the new Iranian cinema. Among the best known of this group are Abbasse Kia Rostamy, Bahrame BEYZAYIE, Feraidoun Rahnama, Sohrabe Shahid Sallesse, and Dariush Mehrejouyie, and their work is characterized by an authentic representation of Iranian experience. New Iranian cinema deals with such themes as socioeconomic deterioration caused by rapid westernization, the clash of traditional and modern cultures, and the consequences of economic domination by western powers: in consequence it was bitterly critical of the late Shah's administration.

But new Iranian cinema fostered very little female talent. In the late 1960s and early 1970s, the removal of cultural taboos regarding the place of women made possible the admission of female students to universities and film schools, and women also found employment in the cinema industry. A small number were able to move through the ranks, via apprenticeships as assistant directors, editors and writers, to become directors. Although these women were careful not to define themselves as feminists, their work did concern itself with the problems of modern Iranian women: the alienation and despair suffered by those torn between traditional and western values, as in *The Sealed Soil* (Marva Nabili, 1977); male hypocrites reaping the benefits of both new and old cultures in *Bita* (Goly Tarragy, 1971). Certain other themes also crop up: the exploration of a mother–daughter relationship in *Maryam va Monny* (Kobra Sai'idy, 1978); an erotic friendship between women in *Ghaire aze Khoudo Hitch Kasse Naboud* (Tahmineh Mir Mirany, 1975). However, these films were never released in Iran, for they coincided with the uprisings of 1977 to 1979, and were banned – along with the women who made them. It was now made illegal even for women to go to movies alone, to appear in films unveiled, or to work alongside men on film crews. The 1981 Censorship Act made the depiction of romantic relationships, of music and dance, and any physical contact between male and female actors, illegal. Holding hands, embraces between husband and wife, parents and children, were banned. Today, because of the difficulties, male filmmakers often choose not to work with women at all.

Since 1986, however, as a result of international pressure, the Islamic Republic has relaxed its reactionary measures. Female filmmakers have since produced mainstream MELODRAMAs such as *Parendeh Kouchake Khoushbakhty/ Little Bird of Happiness* (Pouran Derakhshandeh, 1988) and social comedies such as *Khareje aze Mahdoudeh/Off the Limits* (Rakhshan Bani Etemaad, 1987), both of which have been box office successes. But their directors received government funding only by complying with the compulsory veil and avoiding lesbian and feminist themes: the difference between these films and those made by men is purely the sex of the director. Therefore, apart from a brief interlude in the late 1960s and early 1970s, Iranian women have never yet been able to make films depicting their own experience.

Bahman Maghsoudlou, *Iranian Cinema* (New York: New York University Press, 1987)

See also: BANI ETEMAAD, RAKHSHAN; TAI'IDI, FARZANEH   BR

IRAQ
Oil-rich Iraq has produced an embryonic NATIONAL CINEMA with *Said Effendi/ Mr Said* (Kameran Hassani, 1957), whose NEOREALIST style is said to owe a great deal to the contribution of scriptwriter and actor Youssef El Ani, a well-known theater man. It describes, in true-to-life fashion, an Iraqi teacher. Under the present Iraqi government, however, chilling stories are heard: fine films slightly critical of the government burned, filmmakers terrorized into making state propaganda films, Ministry of Culture and Information bureaucrats stopping shooting and changing scripts, directors fearing death squads, and so on. No real national cinema has emerged here, despite the building of new studios and labs and the expenditure of huge sums of money on state-inspired products. A number of Iraqi talents have emigrated to neighboring countries: Kais El Zoubaidi worked in SYRIA, then with the Resistance in PALESTINE; Qasim Hawal also works with the Palestinian Resistance. Well-known talents have been imported from EGYPT to shoot government films: the anti-Iranian *Al Qadissiya* (1981), with the biggest budget of the ARAB world, is said to be the director Salah Abu Seif's worst film; the same is true of *Al Ayyam Al Tawila/The Long Days* (1980), by Egyptian director Toufic Saleh.   HS

IRELAND
It is a feature of all discussions about Irish film that the national term is itself problematic. Films have been made in Ireland since 1896, but while the subject matter might have been Irish, control over the material was largely in the hands of foreign companies. This problem – the use of Ireland as a facilities base or a scenic setting for foreign production companies – has disabled attempts by indigenous filmmakers to construct images within the social and political contours of Irish experience; and the fraught history of filmmaking in Ireland has repercussions for the development of feminist perspectives in production, as well as in exhibition and distribution. Moreover, the absence of any substantial state training facilities means that young women interested in a career in film have no clear route to training in Ireland.

A serious lack of production funding has also inhibited the development of an indigenous film industry. Until the mid 1970s, the Arts Council in Ireland did not have film within its brief; though with the establishment of the Arts Council Film Script award in 1977, modest amounts of money became available and generated a sense of optimism. During this period, several indigenous projects were produced which marked a breakthrough in the reevaluation and reinterpretation of Irish identity and society. Against a backdrop of continuing economic recession and crisis in Northern Ireland came a cultural and artistic resurgence of which filmmaking formed a key part. With the growth of the women's and gay movements, there was a gradual opening up of hitherto 'taboo' issues such as contraception, abortion, divorce, adoption, and illegitimacy. Organizing around equal pay and the right to information on contraception, and violence against women, the women's movement began to voice its growing concern with the mechanisms of patriarchal oppression and to involve itself in social and political life, while the dominance of male discourse came under heavy challenge. While the films made during this period were all by men, their concerns – history, the role of the family, sexuality, the oppressive influence of the Catholic Church – raised issues relevant to women's oppression, however obliquely. Moreover, the work of Joe Comerford, Cathal Black, Bob Quinn, and Kieran Hickey (whose films *Exposure* [1978] and *Criminal Conversation* [1980] directly confront women's experience) moved through conventional narrative structures and formal innovations, reflecting a critical engagement with the film TEXT, as well as with contemporary social realities and versions of history.

These developments continued through to the 1980s, with work now extending across drama and drama-documentary; and the eventual establishment of the Irish Film Board in 1981 seemed to offer further hope for indigenous film. Alongside this institutional support for film culture emerged the revamped Irish Film Institute, which initiated plans to establish an Irish Film Archive (still a large gap in Irish heritage) within a larger Irish Film Center, and also started up courses in film studies. Women were involved in these initiatives at every level, and the success of Pat MURPHY's films sharpened the focus on women's activity on both sides of the camera. The growth of film and video courses and critical and theoretical studies in adult and higher education contributed to a growing optimism. However, the 'Pro-Life Amendment' constitutional referendum of 1983 on abortion, and the rise of a 'New Right' (on questions of law and order as well as on 'the preservation of the Catholic ethos and the family unit' in education and media), signaled a polarization of political debate and a loss of the ground gained in the late 1970s. While these losses were strongly felt, there was still growing confidence within the film community. Development money from the Film Board's modest budget acted as an incentive to other potential investors like RTE (Irish Television), CHANNEL FOUR TELEVISION, and private sponsors. But although a number of these projects got off the ground, optimism was shortlived: in June 1987 the Film Board was abolished. A tax incentive scheme replacing the Board's investment is largely inappropriate for low-budget film production, and resources are likely to be concentrated in fewer and larger-scale productions: a situation which bodes ill for INDEPENDENT CINEMA in Ireland. However, recent films such as *Reefer and the Model* (Joe Comerford, 1988), *Budawanny* (Bob Quinn, 1986), *Clash of the Ash* (Fergus Tighe, 1987), *Sometime City* (Joe Lee and Frank Deasy, 1986), *Boom Babies* (Siobhan Twomey, 1987) continue to chart responses to a specifically Irish experience. Male domination of film production roles is being eroded, as more and more women become involved in all stages of production and are visible in organizations such as Film Makers Ireland, FilmBase, and the Irish Film Institute. Women often make up more than 50 percent of intakes to training courses, and throughout the independent sector there is a willingness to share knowledge and skills. Women like Trish McAdam (director of several documentaries on health issues in education, and of one of the funniest shorts this decade – *The Drip* [1986]), Jane Gogan (producer), Martha O'Neill (chairperson of FilmBase and involved in a number of productions), Edel Quinn (director of the award-winning short *Bread and Honey* [1988], which combines live action and animation), Lelia Doolan (producer of *Reefer and the Model*), and Pat Murphy continue with enormous energy, commitment, and competence, and considerable style.

Kevin Rockett, John Hill and Luke Gibbons, *Cinema and Ireland* (London: Croom Helm, 1987)

See also: DERRY FILM AND VIDEO COLLECTIVE; WALSH, AISLING   SM

ISRAEL

The Israeli film industry has not only been dominated by men but has also privileged male-oriented concerns. Until the 1970s, women's issues were addressed only in so far as they seemed relevant to nationalist and ethnic rhetoric. Already during the Yishuv (the pre-1948 Jewish settlement in PALESTINE), 'Pioneer' films such as *Sabra* (Alexander Ford, 1933) suggested the superiority of Jewish over Arab society through the comparative portrayal of the status of women. Images of women working the land and, in the post-1948 nationalist-heroic films, wielding weapons, further strengthened this egalitarian mystique. In fact Israeli women have been largely limited to traditional roles, even in the socialist communes and in the Army.

The pre-1948 Pioneer films and the 'heroic-nationalist' films dedicated to the Israeli–Arab conflict directly correlate female equality with conformity to nationalist ideals. The few films which privilege female protagonists exalt the woman's sacrifice for the nation, as in the portrayal of the Great Mother in *Heym Hayu Asara/They Were Ten* (Baruch Dienar, 1961), and the war widow in *The Hero's Wife* (Peter Frey, 1963). The occasional exalted heroic image of the Sabra woman as both valiant fighter and nurse in such films as *Pillar of Fire* (Larry Frisch, 1959) and *Target Tiran* (Raphael Neussbaum, 1968) have circulated more widely in the United States than in Israel, as part of a commercial appeal aimed at western spectators. This led to the satire of the Sabra woman in *Portnoy's Complaint* (Ernest Lehman, 1972), based on the novel by Philip Roth. Hebrew novels displayed a passive Sabra woman character more in accord with the Israeli popular culture. Other nationalist uses of women are seen in films such as *Hill 24 Doesn't Answer* (Thorold Dickinson, 1955). In this film, the ethnic 'inferiority' of the 'exotic' Sephardi woman is compensated for by her heroic sacrifice for the country, implying the 'acceptance' of Sephardim (Jews from Arab and Muslim countries, who form the majority of the Jewish population yet are denied access to political, economic, and cultural power). In films such as *Rebels Against the Light* (Alexander Ramati, 1964) and *Sinaia* (Ilan Eldad, 1964), similarly, any 'positive' portrayal of a noble 'exotic' Palestinian or Bedouin woman requires devotion to the Israeli cause. In the comic 'Bourekas' genre, which largely thematizes ethnic tensions between Ashkenazi (European) and Sephardi Jews, gender relations are subjected to a more implicit nationalist IDEOLOGY in which youthful mixed couples allegorically unite conflicting communities.

In the 1970s, with the decline of the mythic heroic Sabra, Israel's new movement of personal cinema focused on sensitive, vulnerable male characters, thus indirectly opening up some space for women protagonists. This same period witnessed the emergence of women filmmakers, notably Michal BAT ADAM, Edit Shchory and Mira Rekanati, who, like their male colleagues, tend to highlight the quest for self through intimate relationships. Yet, as with the male filmmakers, the focus on women is rarely an explicitly feminist one.

> *'Woman as bloodsucker' is signified in films of the silent era by which popular stereotype?*

Ella Shohat, *Israeli Cinema: East/West and the Politics of Representation* (Austin: University of Texas Press, 1989)   ES

ITALY

Italian silent cinema was brought to international attention by its role in the rise of the feature-length film. From the 1910s, a star system established the ICONOGRAPHY of the 'diva': among female 'stars' were Francesca Bertini and Lyda Borelli, who played VAMPs. Throughout the 1910s and well into the 1920s, large numbers of 'super-spectacles' were produced. These historical films were costume or literary epics employing many extras and using grandiose MISE-EN-SCENE. The GENRE's elaborate choreography and traveling shots were influential but, contrary to common belief, the 'super-spectacles' are not Italy's sole or main contribution to the art of SILENT CINEMA. Important regional differences marked a film industry decentralized in Turin, Milan, Rome, and Naples. Predating the influential neorealist aesthetic, the Neapolitan school produced films of crude REALISM, shot on location, integrating the city street-life with socially conscious portrayals of the underclass. A pioneer woman filmmaker, Elvira NOTARI, contributed greatly to the creation of this aesthetic, enriching it with a concern for women's conditions and female fantasy

and desire. Notari, whose name and work have been canceled out of history, made sixty features and one hundred documentaries.

Fascist domination between the early 1920s and the 1940s had its effects on cinema. The Futurists, who had made experimental films in the 1910s, were lured by the rise of the fascist 'revolution'; and the fascist ideology of the vigorous male body entered the new athletic-acrobatic and mythological genres, posing interesting questions about female spectatorship. In the sound era, apart from fiction films and newsreels openly propagandizing the regime, a huge number of 'white telephone' films were made: these romantic, operatic MELODRAMAs or sentimental COMEDIES offer a wealth of intriguing material to feminist critics.

The end of World War II and the fall of fascism are the historical conditions of the internationally acclaimed Italian film movement, NEOREALISM. Roughly between 1945 and 1953, directors such as Roberto Rossellini, Vittorio de Sica (with screenwriter Cesare Zavattini), Luchino Visconti and Giuseppe De Santis made socially conscious films, shot on location with natural lighting and often nonprofessional actors, using a documentary attitude toward stories of common people framed in recent history.

Italy has developed a strong auteur cinema, directors usually being involved in scripting their films. A first generation of auteurs includes Federico Fellini and Michelangelo ANTONIONI, as well as Rossellini and Visconti – who worked steadily with a woman screenwriter, Suso CECCHI D'AMICO, after the heyday of neorealism. In the 1960s a new group of directors emerged. In different ways, the cinema of Pier Paolo Pasolini, Paolo and Vittorio Taviani, Bernardo Bertolucci, Marco Bellocchio, Marco Ferreri, Francesco Maselli, Francesco Rosi, and Gillo Pontecorvo during the sixties and into the seventies is part of a revolt against the social and political status quo. This movement has been named

NEW ITALIAN CINEMA. Since fascism and neorealism did not foster female talents (with the exception of Lorenza Mazzetti in the 1950s), it was basically not until the sixties that women auteurs emerged. Among the new generation, two women, Liliana CAVANI and Lina WERTMULLER, have established themselves in commercial production. Feminism has opened a space for female voices; and a strong women's movement, beginning in the seventies, has generated practices of individual and collective authorship of women's films, of militant cinema, and of feminist critical writings and publications. A Roman filmmakers' collective, among them Annabella Miscuglio and Roni Daopoulo, has made a number of DOCUMENTARY films (*Processo per stupro/Trial for Rape* [1978]; *AAA Offresi* [1979]; *I fantasmi del fallo* [1980]) on issues such as rape, prostitution, and PORNOGRAPHY. Miscuglio, active as a filmmaker since 1971, has curated retrospectives of women's films and in 1967 co-founded the Filmstudio 70 in Rome, a showcase for independent and AVANT-GARDE films. Other feminist collectives include the 'Alice Guy Collective'; the Neapolitan group 'Nemesiache,' led by Lina Mangiacapre, who believes in super-8mm as a vehicle for liberating female fantasy; and the recently formed Camera Women in Turin, which is engaged in film work with women political prisoners. Lu Leone promoted the production of a women-only film, *Io sono mia* (Sofia Scandurra, 1977), based on a novel by feminist writer Dacia Maraini, who is herself a filmmaker and scriptwriter (she has recently worked with Margarethe von TROTTA). In 1972 Elda Tattoli made *Planeta Venere*, about a woman oppressed by class and sex.

In the 1970s, with the disappearance of the adventurous producers of the 1960s, Italian television (RAI) has taken over the role of financing auteur cinema. Among women's films, RAI produced *Maternale* (1975), a landmark film on maternal love directed by Giovanna Gagliardo, screenwriter for Miklós Jancsó. *Improvviso*, made by Edith Bruck in 1979, was also produced by RAI. Like Loredana Dordi (*Fratelli* [1985]), a number of women filmmakers, many of them feminists, have found shelter (but also difficulties) within RAI's system. As for TV programs, between 1977 and 1981 feminist editor Tilde Capomazza and a female editorial team made *Si dice donna*, a weekly women's news program broadcast on RAI in prime time.

A recent state law in support of cinema, 'Articolo 28,' provides funding for auteur films, with the objective of fostering new talent. Films by young male and female directors are shown at the annual FILM FESTIVAL Cinema Giovani in Turin, and the biennial Filmmaker in Milan. Female talents of the 1980s include Gabriella Rosaleva, whose independent films are particularly attentive to form and aesthetics (her *Processo a Caterina Ross/The Trial of Caterina Ross* [1982] is a feminist representation of a witchcraft trial); Fiorella Infascelli, maker of experimental videos (her 1980 *Ritratto di donna distesa* is a real-time depiction of a psychoanalytic session) and of the acclaimed feature *La Maschera* (1988), about a male 'masquerade'; and Adriana Monti, director of an independent film school in Milan in 1983–4 and maker of feminist films on women's rapport (*Scuola senza fine* [1983]; *Gentili signore* [1988]). Cinzia Torrini (*Giocare d'azzardo* [1982] and *Hotel Colonial* [1987]); Francesca Archibugi (*Mignon e partita/Mignon Has Come to Stay* [1988]); and Francesca Comencini (*Pianoforte* [1984]) have all successfully entered the 35mm market. Annual showcases specifically for women's films include a WOMEN'S FILM FESTIVAL, INCONTRI INTERNAZIONALI DI CINEMA E DONNE in Florence, and a section of the Incontri Internazionali del Cinema in Sorrento.

Giuliana Bruno and Maria Nadotti (eds), *Off Screen: Women and Film in Italy* (London and New York: Routledge, 1988)

GB

JAKUBOWSKA, WANDA (1907–)

Although Jakubowska has been making films in POLAND for over fifty years, her significance to Polish film history is largely restricted to the period around World War II, and in particular her film *Ostatni Etap* (1946). In 1929 Jakubowska was a founder member of START (Stowarzyszenie Milosnikow Filmu Artystycznego/Society for Devotees of Artistic Film). The society was formed in reaction against an existing cinema shaped by commercial dictates and lack of production facilities. It campaigned for films of artistic and social commitment, and acted as a production base; though its members' films were produced largely outside the group, which ultimately failed in its objectives. It has nevertheless been described as a forerunner of the French NEW WAVE and of the British Free Cinema movement. *The Last Step* has the distinction of being the second feature produced by the state film board, Film Polski, after the war, and the first to receive widespread distribution abroad. Jakubowska spent the war years in Poland; she was interned for part of that period at Auschwitz, which provided the film's subject matter. It details the lives and relationships of women prisoners in the camp. The tone changes radically in the second half, when it becomes an escape thriller with a dash of romance. The film is the first part of a trilogy, the second and third parts appearing at twenty-year intervals: *Koniec Naszegoswiata* in 1964 and *Zaproszenie* in 1987.

Reportaz nr 1/Report Number One (short, 1930); *Budujemy/We're Building* (short, 1934); *Nad Niemnem/On the River Niemen* (1939); *Budujemy nowe Wsie/We're Building New Villages* (short, 1946); *Ostatni Etap/The Last Step* (1946); *Zolnierz Zwyciestwa/Soldier of Victory* (1953); *Opowiesc Atlantycka/Atlantic Story* (1955); *Pozegnanie z Diablem/Farewell to the Devil* (1957); *Krol Macius/King Mat* (1958); *Spotkania w mroku/Meeting at Dusk* (1960); *Koniec Naszegoswiata/The End of Our World* (1964); *Goraca Linia/The Hot Line* (1965); *150 na Godzine/At One Hundred and Fifty Km an Hour* (1971); *Bialy Mazur/Dance In Chains* (1978); *Zaproszenie/Invitation* (1985); *Kolory Kochania/Colours of Love* (1987)

Frank Bren, *World Cinema 1: Poland* (London: Flick Books, 1986)   AG

JANDA, KRYSTYNA (1952–)

Janda is a film and theater actress in POLAND whose first film, *Czlowiek z Marmaru/Man of Marble* (Andrzej Wajda, 1977), is now recognized as the beginning of the 'Cinema of Moral Anxiety,' a movement in Polish cinema that addressed issues of personal responsibility and corruption in society. Janda came to embody an integrity and aggressive commitment that became so strongly identified with her that it carried over into her role in the Hungarian production *Mephisto* (István Szabo, 1981). Her performances in a number of Andrzej Wajda's films are also significant in that his women characters had, until *Man of Marble*, been absent, passive, or negatively represented: for example, the wife and the lover in *Polowanie na Muchy/Hunting Flies* (1972), who from being objects of desire become identified with parasitic flies. Janda is the only actress whom Wajda has repeatedly featured.

His collaborations with Janda, and with Agnieszka HOLLAND as screenwriter, were crucial in effecting greater attention to details of hard political reality in his films, after a series of vast historical epics in the sixties and early seventies. Poland's 'Cinema of Moral Anxiety' came to an end with the banned *Przesluchanie/Interrogation* (Ryszard Bugajski, 1981), in which Janda plays a woman subjected to police brutality in a prison in Stalinist Poland. With the transition to post-martial-law Poland, Janda's STAR persona was adapted to fill available roles in the currently predominant SCIENCE FICTION and sex comedies. Her committed campaigner has been displaced in the late eighties by actress Katarzyna Figura's STEREOTYPES of dumb BLONDES. However, in 1986 some interesting casting re-created the couple of Wajda's two *Man* films, placing Janda alongside Jerzy Radziwillowicz for *W Zawieszeniy/ Suspended* (Waldemar Kryszek).

Frank Bren, *World Cinema 1: Poland* (London: Flick Books, 1986)   AG

JAPAN

In 1896, two years after their European contemporaries, the Japanese were introduced to the moving image via the Edison Kinetoscope; and a year later imports of the Lumière brothers' films made movie viewing a mass experience. As an adjunct to these imports, the Japanese were quick to adapt from their theater tradition (*Kabuki* and *Bunraku*) a film tradition of their own – the *benshi* (silent movie narrator) system, which developed into a virtual star system: the *benshi* eventually became the box office draw. By the 1930s, works of American directors like Lewis Milestone and Curtis Bernhardt introduced the talkies to the Japanese, still with the aid of the *benshi*. The Yoshizawa Company (importers of the Lumière Cinematograph), however, had been attempting to produce sound films since 1902; but the first sound success was Heinosuke Gosho's *Madamu to Nyobo/The Neighbor's Wife and Mine* (1931). Gosho's social observation of the contrasting behaviors of the overworked Japanese husband who becomes infatuated with the 'modern' girl next door, and of his traditional, neglected wife who displays discontent through her bouts of silence, begins to define the woman's role in Japanese cinema. In the 1930s, when Japan's Great Depression widened the gap between rich and poor, Japanese audiences – unlike their American counterparts, who escaped through Hollywood's glitter – demanded *shomen-geki* (films reflecting the everyday plight of the lower classes). During Japan's first 'golden age' of film production, the *shomen-geki* developed images of, for example, the sacrificing mother, the enduring wife, and the jilted mistress. Through these images the basic message – hard times must be endured as part of one's duty – was projected. This trend continued into the postwar era. Westerners became familiar with Japanese directors of the industry's second 'golden age' after World War II: MIZOGUCHI, Kurosawa, Ichikawa, Ozu, and Naruse. For these directors, woman's role and point of view can best be summarized as accepting of fate, self-sacrificing, submissive, subtle, and male-dominated: if the 1930s had set the tone of the *shomen-geki*, the postwar directors perfected it.

If the *shomen-geki* were interpreted in western feminist terms, the conclusion would probably be that these films are generally male-dominated and devoid of any representation of female self-definition. Non-Japanese audiences viewing works by directors of Japan's second 'golden age' are likely to feel that they are viewing the feminine role from a male point of view. Would this also be true for a Japanese woman? In considering this question, definitions of 'feminism' must be seen as culturally specific. Cultural elements are projected through the director's technical style as well as through his interpretation of characters. So, for instance, Ozu's woman is resigned to her fate – *Tokyo Monogatari/*

Tokyo Story (1953), *Soshun/Early Spring* (1956); Kurosawa's woman is a catalyst of the plot's progress – *Ikiru/To Live* (1952), *Kumo no Sujo/Throne of Blood* (1957); Mizoguchi's woman embodies a sense of tragedy – *Saikaku Ichidai Onna/ Life of Oharu* (1952), *Sansho Dayu/Sancho, the Bailiff* (1954); Naruse's woman bears with acceptance fate's many negative plights – *Ukigumo/Floating Clouds* (1955), *Nagareru/Flowing* (1956). These cultural elements (acceptance of fate, self-sacrifice, and so on) projected through women characters were in fact the expected norms for the postwar Japanese woman. To understand this in terms of the supposition that art mirrors society's mores, and to understand the 'typical' Japanese female viewer's value system, it is necessary to understand how Japanese history and culture differ from those of the West.

For example, Japan has never provided fertile ground for the emergence of a notion of self as the westerner perceives it. Without the self to define its own life parameters, there can never be an initiative for individuals to seek out others in order to change the status quo. This and philosophical precepts such as sense of duty, loss of face, honor, and acceptance of fate have hindered any Japanese feminist awakening of a kind that can be equated with the 1960s and 1970s western women's movements. The image of woman in Japanese culture must be understood in relation to these cultural factors.

The work of two women actresses turned directors, Kinuyo TANAKA (*Koibumi/Love Letter* [1953] and *Tsuki ga Agarinu/The Moon Has Risen* [1955]); and Sachiko HIDARI (*Toi Ippon no Michi/ The Far Road* [1977]), is relevant here. Tanaka's work reflects the masculine interpretation of the *shomen-geki*, but Hidari's film provides a realistic portrayal of the domestic Japanese woman, and of women's strength. Nevertheless, it is still a male-dominated film. Hidari's interpretation of 'woman-as-she-is' has its roots in the 1960s in the work of such

directors as Susumu Hani (*Mitasareta Seikatsu/A Full Life* [1962]; *Kanojo to Kare/She and He* [1963]) and Shohei Imamura (*Buta to Gunkan/Pigs and Battleships* [1961]; *Nippon Konchuki/The Insect Woman* [1963]). Hani and Imamura provided new screen images of women. However, Hani's woman is still on the verge of self-affirmation, while Imamura's is, generally speaking, of mythic dimensions. The mythic image of woman can also be found in recent works by independents such as Mitsuo Yanagimachi (*Himatsuri/Fire Festival* [1984]) and Juzo Itami, with her CAREER WOMAN heroine of *Marusa no Onna/A Taxing Woman, I and II* (1986 and 1987).

But new images of women in Japanese cinema are slow to emerge, because of traditional definitions of woman's position in society. In the video works of Mako IDEMITSU, however, there is some evidence of beginnings of the awareness required for the emergence of an independent sense of self. Idemitsu's statement is direct: Japanese woman, see yourself as you are. Recognition is the first step toward awareness, and from this perspective Idemitsu's attempt seems to be the only 'voice' in Japanese cinema that can truly be labeled feminist. In her latest work, *Kiyoko no Kurushimeru/Kiyoko's Situation* (1989), Idemitsu points her finger at the reasons for the latency of a Japanese feminist movement: the protagonist recognizes and acknowledges herself, but society is not ready to allow her self-affirmation.

Joseph L Anderson and Donald Richie, *The Japanese Film* (New Jersey: Princeton University Press, 1982)   JYY

JOHANNESDOTTIR, KRISTIN (1948–)

Kristin Johannesdottir is one of the most individual and stylistically conscious film directors in ICELAND. She studied literature and cinematography at the Université Paul Valéry in Montpellier, southern France, from 1974 to 1977, and also studied television, video and filmmaking at Vincennes, Paris VIII, and film direction in the Conservatoire Libre de Cinéma Français in 1978. During her years in France Johannesdottir made a few short films: *Arthur et Rosa* is an interpretation of the filmmaker's ruminations on what might have happened had Arthur Rimbaud and Rosa Luxemburg met. *Lendemains moroses* deals with the depression of hangovers.

In 1982 Johannesdottir founded the Voluspa Film production company; and in the following year made her first feature film, *A hjara veraldar*. She has also directed plays for Icelandic television: *Lif til Einhvers/A Purpose in Life* (1983), written by Nina Bjork Arnadottir and directed by Johannesdottir, is one of Icelandic TV's most memorable plays. Johannesdottir's latest production, *Svo a jördu sem a himni* (1988), like her first film, is based on her own screenplay.

Arthur et Rosa; *Lendemains moroses*; *A hjara veraldar/Rainbow's End* (1983); *Svo a jördu sem a himni/On Earth As It Is In Heaven* (1988)   TA

JOHNSTON, CLAIRE (1940–87)

A key figure in the development of FEMINIST FILM THEORY in BRITAIN, Johnston co-organized the first Women and Cinema Event at the Edinburgh Film Festival in 1972. This gave rise to *Notes on Women's Cinema*, from which Johnston's essay 'Women's Cinema as Counter-cinema' still remains one of the basic statements of a feminist politics of film. She proposed an analysis of 'woman' as myth in cinema, a history of women directors like Dorothy ARZNER and Ida LUPINO, and a defense of Hollywood rather than European ART CINEMA in terms of the representation of women. During the mid 1970s she worked both on Hollywood (Tashlin, Walsh, Tourneur, Arzner) and on Brecht and INDEPENDENT CINEMA. These interests were linked by her argument that the task of writing history was to provide tools for struggle in the present. She was one of the first to use PSYCHOANALYTIC

FILM THEORY to deal with feminist questions about memory and identity as well as representation. This led her to take up the issue of cultural difference, particularly in relation to cinema and politics in IRELAND. After some years of distress, Johnston committed suicide in 1987.

In her remembrance of Johnston, Lesley Stern writes that 'not only did her writing have an immense impact, so too did her performance.' Johnston thought that the significance of an argument depended on the context in which it was made, and she stressed the importance of different *ways* of working. During the 1970s Johnston co-organized Special Events at the Edinburgh Festival; she was on the executive of the Society for Education in Film and Television, an editorial board member of the JOURNAL *Screen*, and a member of the LONDON WOMEN'S FILM GROUP.

Claire Johnston's publications include: 'Women's Cinema as Counter-cinema,' *Notes on Women's Cinema* (London: SEFT, 1973); (ed.) *Dorothy Arzner: Towards a Feminist Cinema* (London: British Film Institute, 1975); 'The Subject of Feminist Film Theory/Practice,' *Screen*, vol. 21, no. 2 (1980).

Lesley Stern, Laleen Jayamanne and Helen Grace, 'Remembering Claire Johnston', *Framework*, no. 35 (1988)
MMo

JOURNALS

There have been many journals devoted to film, but considering the impact feminism has made on FILM THEORY there are surprisingly few given over to specifically feminist debates on cinema. The general body of film journals consists of those providing FILM CRITICISM, information, and comment (*Sight and Sound*, *Monthly Film Bulletin*, *Films and Filming*, *Film Comment*, *Cineaste*, and so on); those which offer communication for a network around INDEPENDENT CINEMA (*Independent Video*, *The Independent*); and those whose purpose is to provide a forum for debating critical theory. This last category is probably the most important for feminism, since it is here that FEMINIST FILM THEORY and critical practice have been developed. Some journals have developed around a theoretical position which leaves little space for feminist intervention: for example, *Cahiers du cinéma* in France and *Movie* in Britain took AUTHORSHIP theory as their key explanatory framework in the fifties and sixties.

In the seventies, the retheorization of notions of IDEOLOGY and representation provided a way of constructing a political critique of film as representation in terms of its textual strategies and production of meaning. While this took place in a number of journals, the British journal *Screen* was particularly significant in compiling work around SEMIOTICS and STRUCTURALISM, as it was also for its debates on the use of PSYCHOANALYTIC FILM THEORY in understanding representations of SEXUALITY and patterns of desire and identification elicited from spectators. This had obvious implications for feminism, and particularly influential was Laura MULVEY's article 'Visual Pleasure and Narrative Cinema,' published in 1975, which linked a psychoanalytic understanding of 'woman' as object of sexual PLEASURE for a masculine spectator with an argument for a feminist COUNTERCINEMA that would break with these patterns to produce new forms.

This kind of analysis, along with a more general approach to the 'deconstruction,' or taking apart, of the meanings of gender, was taken up across the range of theoretical journals, examples including *Quarterly Review of Film Studies* from the USA, and *The Australian Journal of Screen Theory*. While journals of the AVANT GARDE, such as British *Afterimage* and later *Undercut*, provide some space for theoretical and polemical writing around a specifically feminist avant-garde film practice, the US journal *CAMERA OBSCURA* links these issues to questions raised for feminism by popular cultural forms.

In recent years journals whose work addresses popular cinema have incorporated debates on reading, address, reception, and the AUDIENCE as well as providing writing on policy debates such as CENSORSHIP. Currently, journals reflect the broadened focus of film theory and criticism and, partly under the influence of feminism, have become more eclectic. From Britain, *Cultural Studies*, *Formations* and *New Formations* look at diverse cultural forms and discourses of gender and sexuality within a wider social and cultural framework and since the seventies and early eighties *Framework* has addressed cinema across diverse cultures, as well as incorporating theories of sexual representation. Its recent critical work on both independent cinema and cinemas in different contexts, especially the Third World, bring questions of sexuality into contact with those of ethnicity and class in a historical framework.

Some aspects of feminist film theory and criticism have been taken up in journals of feminist theory or women's studies. The British journal *m/f*, for example, theorized sexual difference from marxist, feminist, and psychoanalytic perspectives. Its work has been important for looking at the multiple discourses which position women in relation to SEXUALITY, film being seen as one among a number of systems of representation proposing defined places for women within the social framework. British *Feminist Review* also publishes occasional articles on the representation of women in film, grouped interestingly with articles on women's history, social policy debates, and so on. Publications associated with the western women's movement, such as *Ms* (in the US) and *Spare Rib* (in Britain), regularly include journalistic writing on film as part of a redefinition of women's identities and spheres.

See also: FILM CRITICS; *FRAUEN UND FILM*; *WOMEN AND FILM*   GS

KAEL, PAULINE (1919–   )

Described as 'the most celebrated critic in the history of American cinema,' Kael began in the 1940s writing scripts for experimental films, running a small art cinema in Berkeley, California, and contributing freelance to magazines. Her book *I Lost It at the Movies* became a bestseller in 1965, and she moved from California to New York. When she was sacked from *McCalls* after panning *The Sound of Music*, then resigned when *New Republic* rejected her praise for *Bonnie and Clyde*, Kael established a reputation for integrity and independence. She joined the *New Yorker* as a weekly columnist in 1968 (alternating every six months with Penelope Gilliatt) and stayed there until 1979, when she went briefly to Hollywood as a producer for Warren Beatty. On returning to the *New Yorker* she became the magazine's sole FILM CRITIC, but contributed less frequently.

Said to have considerable box office impact, Kael's work may have had its greatest influence in forming an image of FILM CRITICISM itself. With her resistance to editorial and film-industry pressure, her decisive value judgements and her strong prose style, she developed a media myth of the critic as a forceful personality. This helped to move film criticism away from the cultivated tradition associated in the United States with James Agee, and made it a more popular genre. But she also fostered a cult of 'unpredictability,' and a code of flamboyance that could turn into a rigid anti-intellectualism. In the early 1960s she attacked both the German philosopher Siegfried Kracauer, and the American popularizer of AUTHORSHIP theory Andrew Sarris, claiming that systematic thought was inimical to cinema and criticism. In 1980 she in turn was personally attacked in the *Village Voice* by Sarris, and by critic Renata Adler in the *New York Review of Books*. Analyzing Kael's style for its sadistic metaphors, 'strident knowingness' and repetitive mannerisms, Adler identified serious problems in Kael's later work. But both attacks were so intemperate that together they say more about the threat that a powerful woman can still pose to intellectual culture than they do about Kael's criticism itself.

Pauline Kael's publications include: *I Lost It At the Movies* (New York: Little, Brown & Co., 1965); *Kiss Kiss Bang Bang* (New York: Little, Brown & Co., 1968); *Going Steady* (New York: Temple Smith, 1970); *The Citizen Kane Book* (London: Secker & Warburg, 1971); and a debate with Jean-Luc Godard on criticism in *Camera Obscura*, no. 8–9–10 (1982)

Marsha MacCreadie. *Women on Film: The Critical Eye* (New York: Praeger, 1983)   MMo

> *Of which paragon in which British film was it written in 1945: 'Without manufactured glamour or conventional good looks, she magnificently portrays the wife and mother meeting passion for the first time, who wants to die because of it.'?*

KOPPLE, BARBARA (1946–   )

Best known for *Harlan County, USA* (1976), an Academy Award-winning documentary about a miners' strike in

Kentucky, Kopple began making films in a clinical psychology class at college in West Virginia. She then worked professionally as an editor, soundwoman and camerawoman, often with the Maysles brothers, who made DOCUMENTARIES in the cinéma vérité tradition. She was camerawoman on a video about Young Republicans for Nixon at a Republican Convention, and soundwoman on a film about Year of the Woman at a Democratic Convention.

In 1972, at the age of twenty-six, Kopple moved to the coalfields of Harlan County to film a union struggle at the Brookside Mine. The miners had voted to join the United Mine Workers, and the Eastover Mining Co., a subsidiary of a large power company, refused to negotiate with them. *Harlan County USA*, finished four years later, tells the story of the strike, its ensuing violence, and the strikers' efforts to force not only management but the union leadership to respond to their demands. The film unfolds entirely from the mining families' point of view, the result of Kopple's intimacy with the families and her commitment to their fight. It focuses particularly on the miners' wives, many of whom woke up to politics during the strike and went on to become the main political force behind it. Critical reactions to the film, both in the mainstream press and among film theorists, praised its militancy and frankness, as well as its use of music to engage the viewer – the song 'Which Side Are You On?', repeated at key moments, addressed the spectator as often as it addressed the strikers. One critic, Julia Lesage, writing in 1978, saw it as proof of how the feminist documentary had evolved from the consciousness-raising group by focusing 'on problems of identity in the private sphere – how one strikeleader's husband views her union organizing unenthusiastically, or how miners' wives reach a new solidarity only by overcoming sexual suspicions or jealousies.' She also justifies the film's unquestioning use of REALISM as part of a strategy to make

it more widely accessible and thus more politically effective. Critic Noel King, however, in a 1981 attack on realist documentary, criticizes the film's use of traditional Hollywood narrative devices to smooth over ideological contradictions and provide a false sense of conclusion and knowledge. In response, feminist film theorist E Ann Kaplan, in her 1983 book *Women and Film*, attacks King's position as 'too monolithic,' arguing that films evoking an 'active response' from spectators do challenge assumptions about cinema, even if they exploit some of these assumptions to do so.

Since *Harlan County* Kopple has co-directed, with Haskell Wexler, *No Nukes* (1979), a concert documentary about Musicians United for Safe Energy. She has also directed and produced *Keeping On* (1983), a fiction film about organizing textile workers in the South, and plans the 1990 release of a documentary about meat-packers in the Midwest.

Harlan County, USA (1976); *No Nukes* (co-d. Haskell Wexler, 1979); *Keeping On* (1983)

Noel King, 'Recent "Political" Documentary', *Screen*, vol. 22, no. 2 (1981). Julia Lesage, 'The Political Aesthetics of the Feminist Documentary Film', in *Films for Women*, ed. Charlotte Brunsdon (London: British Film Institute, 1986)   JSh

KUNG FU

Kung fu is a Chinese martial arts film GENRE, distinguishable from the SWORDPLAY film by virtue of its prominent display of unarmed male bodies in fighting sequences involving choreographed fist fights, kicks, and leaps. The cult of the male body had its origins in the Buddhist Shaolin temple in China's Jiulianshan and in the secret societies of *Yi Ho Tuan* (the Boxers) of Shantung, which became prominent from the mid nineteenth century in the Han people's resistance against the oppression of the

Manchu government and against foreign aggression. The strenuous training of young men through a rigid master–disciple relationship, friendship among men, and the struggle for survival in a hostile world, relate to a masculine sado-masochism and a fetishization of men's willpower and persistence in kung fu films – escapism for men only.

The kung fu serials made in HONG KONG in the 1950s underlined a simplistic morality in the figure of mature master Huang Feihong, who curbed urban crimes and preached a credo of patience. In the early 1970s, the Golden Harvest studio combined the spectacular power of human bodies in fighting movements with the chilling attraction of violent crimes in *Tang Shan Da Xing/The Big Boss* (Lo Wei, 1971), *Jing Wu Men/Fists of Fury* (Lo Wei, 1972), and *Meng Long Guo Jiang/Enter the Dragon* (Lo Wei, 1972), entering an international market captured by Bruce Lee's quintessential martial arts performances. Box office success led to more low-budget productions, and to negative critical reaction. After its popularity outside China had begun to wane, the genre continued to be renewed by experienced martial arts masters from various schools who became film directors, such as Liu Jialiang (*Shaolin Sanshi-liu Fang/The 36th Chamber of Shaolin* [1978]), Samo Hung (*Fei Long Guo Jiang/Enter the Fat Dragon* [1978]) and Jackie Chan (*A Jihua/Project A, part II* [1987]), whose touches of REALISM, tragi-comic integration of male body power with urban themes, and cross-generic references have kept the kung fu genre alive.

In the 1990s, this action genre for repressed males is still commercially viable, and not only among male working-class audiences in southeast Asia: it is also gaining popularity in the People's Republic of CHINA.

Eighth Hong Kong International Film Festival, *A Study of the Hong Kong Martial Arts Film* (Hong Kong: The Urban Council, 1980)

See also: WESTERN   EY

> 'Cabaret' film is a genre central to the 1940s development of which national cinema?

KUWAIT

Cinema in Kuwait – one of the ARAB countries – is virtually a one-man show: Khaled Al Siddiq achieved international breakthrough with *Bas Ya Bahr/The Cruel Sea* (1972), a beautiful film about the life of the poor pearl-divers in his country before the arrival of the oil manna. The film criticizes women's oppression under feudal traditions and the hold of religion. Less radical and more light-hearted, his second film is based on a novel by the great Sudanese writer Al Tayyeb Saleh: *Urs Al Zein/The Wedding of Zein* (1976) is about the unlikely marriage of the local buffoon to his cousin, the most desirable girl in the village. *Shahin* (1985), shot in India, is based on a tale from Boccaccio. Women filmmakers work mainly in Kuwaiti television.   HS

LAMARQUE, LIBERTAD (1908–   )

Renowned for her beauty and already a popular singer in ARGENTINA before 1930, Lamarque became an internationally known diva and the first superstar of the Argentine cinema through her work in the tango-melodramas of the early sound cinema. Although she had already appeared in *Tango!* (1933), a musical revue, her work with director Agustin 'El Negro' Ferreyra catapulted her to fame. Ferreyra's artisanal and improvisational adaptations of tangos – music, lyrics and plot lines – helped develop an indigenous musical MELODRAMA subgenre aimed primarily at female audiences. In his films *Help Me to Live* (1936), *Besos brujos/Bewitched Kisses* (1937), and *La ley que olvidaron/The Law They Forgot* (1937), Lamarque defined her cinematic persona: the humble young girl, who, wanting to become a singer, is besieged by men and an intolerant society, and must undergo much personal pain and suffering and shed many tears before she can achieve success. Always exemplified by the motto *sufrir cantando* (to suffer singing), in these and a number of other tango-melodramas which were quickly made to capitalize on her popularity, Lamarque's characters were idolized by female audiences and helped to circulate this Argentine definition of the feminine ideal throughout Latin America.

Lamarque made over two dozen films in Argentina, but in the 1940s, as the Argentine industry declined, she moved on to Mexico and later to Spain. She was active in filmmaking until the late 1970s.

ALo

LANCTOT, MICHELINE (1947–   )

QUEBEC (Canadian) filmmaker Lanctôt began her career in the ANIMATION studios of the NATIONAL FILM BOARD OF CANADA (NFB). At that time, however, she was more widely known for her success as an actress, working in both French and English. Her role as the free-spirited idealist Bernadette in Gilles Carle's *La vraie nature de Bernadette* (1972) earned her the Canadian Film Award for best actress in 1972. She was nominated again for the award in 1978 for her role as Lucky in *Blood and Guts* (Claude Chabrol, 1977), and won international acclaim for her part in *The Apprenticeship of Duddy Kravitz* (Ted Kotcheff, 1974), in which she co-starred with Richard Dreyfuss. No subsequent role, however, matched the strength and challenge of the character she played in *Bernadette* and, tired of playing female clichés, she left acting and moved to Hollywood. She claims to have hated the values and the cultural void she found there, and returned to Quebec with several scripts written during her three-year sojourn. Again at the NFB, she wrote and directed her first film, a humorous animated short about female stereotyping called *A Token Gesture* (1975). Her later films were all an expression of her fascination with the themes of marginality and social chaos, the first of these being *L'homme à tout faire* (1980), which won a silver medal at the San Sebastian Festival. Her next film, *Sonatine* (1983) – not a film about teenage suicide as it is often described, but rather a study of adolescent despair at growing up in a society that has little to offer – won her a Genie (Canadian Academy Award) for best director in 1985 and a Silver Lion in Venice in 1984. *La poursuite de bonheur* (1987), an indictment of the americanization of Quebec culture, was one of a series on the subject sponsored by the NFB. Lanctôt's passion for the theater has not died; if she left her career as an actress, it was because she was disillusioned. A history of being obliged to play secondary, supportive roles, and

> Mexican director and actress Maria Elena Velasco created a character well known to Mexican audiences. Who is she?

exasperation at being 'looked at,' have inspired Lanctôt's interest in writing about the crisis regarding the lack of real, intelligent, and strong women's roles in film. Her next project is a personal mythology called *A Hero's Life*, in which she is scripting recognizable women. However, Lanctôt decries the term feminist, describing herself as simply a woman making films.

A Token Gesture (1975); *Trailer* (1976); *L'homme à tout faire/The Handyman* (1980); *Sonatine* (1983); *La poursuite de bonheur/The Pursuit of Happiness* (1987)

C Tadros and M Dorland, '"*Sonatine*: film maudit": A Conversation with Micheline Lanctôt', *Cinéma Canada*, no. 110 (1984)   SB

LANDETA, MATILDE (1913–)

A pioneering filmmaker in MEXICO who was determined enough to break into a male-dominated industry that sought to keep her out because her gender represented a threat, Landeta began her film career in 1933 as a 'script girl.' It was not until 1945 that she was given the opportunity to assist some of the best-known Mexican film directors of the time: Emilio 'El Indio' Fernández, Julio Bracho and Roberto Gavaldon, among others. Aware of the limitations imposed on her by the industry, Landeta, in collaboration with actors and film technicians, formed an independent film company, Tecnicos Y Actores Cinematograficos Asociados (TACMA).

In 1948 she directed her first film, *Lola Casanova*, starring Meche Barba, Armando Silvestre, and Isabela Corona, and based on an ethnographic novel by Francisco Rojas Gonzalez. Her second, and most successful and critically acclaimed film, *La negra Angustias/The Black Angustias* (1949), starring Maria Elena Marquez and Ramón Gay, was based on another Gonzalez novel which Landeta adapted to the screen, dramatically changing the character of Angustias. The filmmaker's feminist position is clearly marked in this film, in which she explored tensions of race and class as well as of gender. Her last film, *Trotacalles* (1951), starring Miroslava and Ernesto Corona, addresses the problematic condition of two latinas caught inside the vice of exploitation and male power relations. Between 1956 and 1962 Landeta was barred from the Mexican film industry as a result of a confrontation with the director of the National Cinematographic Bank.

Among her many screenplays, *Tribunal para menores/Juvenile Court* stands out as one of her most important winning achievements: in 1956 it won the Ariel – equivalent to an Academy Award. In the 1980s Landeta was rediscovered by Mexican/Latin American feminists and film critics, and in the past few years has been honored at numerous FILM FESTIVALS. She is an active member of the Academy of Film Arts and Sciences and remains committed to her writing.

Lola Casanova (1948); *La negra Angustias/ The Black Angustias* (1949); *Trotacalles/ Streetwalker* (1951)

Carmen Huaco-Nuzum, 'Matilde Landeta: An Introduction to the Work of a Pioneer Mexican Filmmaker', *Screen*, vol. 28, no. 4 (1987)   CH-N

LATIN AMERICA

The history of women's role in the evolution of Latin American film culture has yet to be written. Incipient attempts over the past few years have too frequently obscured more than they illuminate: thus 'A Brief Overview of Women's Filmmaking in Latin America,' written in 1989 for a major US distributor of women's films, can make the egregious assertion that Carmen Santos, founder of Brasil Vita Filme studios in Rio in 1932 and producer of several of the most important films by Brazil's foremost auteur, Humberto Mauro, was 'known in Hollywood as "Carmen Miranda".' This is the equivalent of claiming that Dorothy ARZNER was 'known in Latin America as Dorothy Lamour'!

The 1980s were marked by the 'sudden' prominence of women in every field of Latin American film culture – directing, producing, screenwriting, professional training, history, and criticism. This shift toward greater gender balance in a field long dominated by men was without precedent only in its scale. In virtually every country where female participation is currently high, the women involved have discovered that they are not the first, and have begun the difficult but exhilarating task of rescuing their foremothers from oblivion.

MEXICO's Marcela FERNANDEZ VIOLANTE, the first female member of the national film directors' union, exemplifies this phenomenon. Through her personal initiatives in research, writing, and television program production during the late 1970s and early 1980s, three forgotten women who played key roles in the development of Mexican cinema – directors Matilde LANDETA and Adela SEQUEYRO and compiler-editor Carmen Toscano – have begun to earn the belated recognition they so richly deserve. Historians Elice Munerato and Maria Helena Darcy de Oliveira have done extensive research on the participation and depiction of women throughout the long and rich history of cinema in BRAZIL. Leaving Carmen Miranda to one side, for the obvious reason that her career played itself out primarily in the USA, Munerato and Oliveira are investigating the contributions of a number of women active between 1914 and 1950 in addition to Carmen Santos: among them Cleo de Verberena, Georgina Marchiani, Gita de Barrios, and especially Gilda de ABREU. ARGENTINA has had a long history of outstanding female screenwriters – from Beatríz GUIDO, screenwriter-collaborator and wife of Argentina's foremost auteur, Leopoldo TORRE-NILSSON, to Aída Bortnik, co-scripter of the Academy Award-winning *La historia oficial/The Official Story* (1986). In contrast, the work of pioneer directors Emilia Saleny and María V de Celestina, who filmed before 1920, has only recently received acknowledgement. The forty-year gap between Celestina and Vlasta Lah, the next Argentine woman director, responsible for two features in the early sixties, reappears in other national filmographies as well. The history of these lacunae also cries out for investigation.

In those Latin American countries where film production has been more discontinuous, figures like VENEZUELA's Margot BENACERRAF, COLOMBIA's Gabriela SAMPER, CHILE's Nieves YANCOVIC, and CUBA's Sara GOMEZ have assumed the almost mythical status of very distant ancestors, though in fact they emerged relatively recently – in the 1950s and 1960s. Even the 1970s generation – documentarists Nora de Izcue in Peru and Marta RODRIGUEZ in Colombia; producer/co-director Beatriz Palacios in Bolivia (who works in collaboration with her husband, director Jorge Sanjinés); Chileans Valeria SARMIENTO (exiled in France) and Marilú MALLET (exiled in Quebec), renowned Argentine feature filmmaker María Luisa BEMBERG – are still seen as 'new pioneers' because they opened the doors through which, in the subsequent decade, large numbers of women cineastes were to pass.

It is impossible in a short space to name all the women on the contemporary Latin American film scene when, for example, a partial list of documentaries made in Brazil between 1970 and 1988 by female directors includes over three hundred films made by scores of different women, while another thirty women have made features in Brazil during the same period. (Among Brazil's most notable feature directors are Tizuka YAMASAKI, Susana AMARAL, Ana CAROLINA, and Tereza Trautman.) VIDEO production in Brazil virtually outstrips that of all other Latin American countries combined. Here, too, women are at the forefront. Lilith Video, based in São Paulo (Jacira Melo, Marcia Meireles and Silvana Afram) produces some of the most exciting feminist media on the continent. No other country rivals this scope or scale of participation, but the Mexican film scene now has several dozen women actively involved, as do much less prolific film-producing countries like Colombia, Venezuela, Nicaragua (see CENTRAL AMERICA), Peru, and Chile.

Although the situation in Cuba is not so favorable for women, that country does deserve recognition for organizing a massive international symposium on Women in the Audio-Visual World in 1986, in conjunction with the 8th Havana Film Festival, and for putting together the first major retrospective of films by Latin American women – thirty-four films from thirteen different countries – the following year. Cuba has also undertaken the most ambitious audiovisual training program in Latin America: the Escuela Internacional de Cine, Television y Video (The International School of Film, Television and Video) opened outside Havana at San Antonio de los Banos in 1987. The School, which draws its students from Asia, Africa, and all the countries of Latin America, makes an effort to ensure that a representative proportion of students are female. Perhaps the most important single event in terms of women's participation in the Latin American visual media, however, was the COCINA DE IMAGENES encounter held in Mexico City in October 1987 under the auspices of Zafra, Mexico's major independent distributor. At the Cocina, more than seventy women from fifteen countries gathered for ten days to screen films and videos, participate in symposia, and create networks for future communication and exchange. The Cocina event was the historical equivalent of the 1967 festival in Viña del Mar from which the history of the New Latin American Cinema is dated: that founding moment when what have previously seemed individual concerns and isolated pursuits come into focus as a *movement*, a concerted endeavor that spans geographical borders and cultural, material, and political differences.

Teresa Toledo (ed.), *Realizadoras Latinoamericanas/Latin American Women Filmmakers, 1917–1987: Cronología/Chronology* (New York: Circulo de Cultura Cubana, 1987) JBu

LATINAS

Representations of Hispanic and Latin American women in films have varied at different times and places, though in Hollywood at least there has been a tendency toward STEREOTYPES which emphasize the exotic and the sexual. The years of the HOLLYWOOD STUDIO SYSTEM saw an extravagant, almost obsessive, interest in Latin America, with a number of studios importing latina STARS. Mexican Dolores del Rio, contracted to RKO and WARNER BROS. during the 1930s, played classy Latin ladies in films like *Flying Down to Rio* (Thornton Freeland, RKO, 1933) and *I Live for Love* (Busby Berkeley, Warner Bros., 1935). Del Rio's characters are highly attractive to men, their flirtations subtle, their objects always 'anglo.'

The exoticism of del Rio's fellow countrywoman Lupe Velez, however, has an altogether more fiery quality. Publicized as 'the hot baby of Hollywood' and 'the Mexican spitfire,' Velez played a series of hot-blooded Latin women in films whose titles say it all: *Tiger Rose* (George Fitzmaurice, Warner

Rosaura Revueltas in *Salt of the Earth*

Bros., 1929); *Hot Pepper* (John G Blystone, Twentieth Century-Fox, 1933); *Strictly Dynamite* (Elliott Nugent, RKO, 1934). During World War II, RKO made a series of films featuring Velez, aimed this time at the Mexican market. The raw sensuality, which would have offended this audience, was now toned down somewhat. The 1940s vehicles of tropical fruit-bedecked Brazilian performer Carmen Miranda were another attempt by Hollywood to cater for Latin American audiences. Nevertheless, the staging of 'The Girl With the Tutti-Frutti Hat,' Miranda's famous song in *The Gang's All Here* (USA)/*The Girls He Left Behind* (GB) (Busby Berkeley, Twentieth Century-Fox, 1943), shares the spectacularly erotic quality of most of Busby Berkeley's production numbers.

For a time after the war ended, Hollywood, in a further attempt to woo the Latin American market, began making efforts to tone down derogatory representations of Latin characters: with this in view, studios were offered a script vetting service. This effort, however, seems to have been devoted largely to male characters: though even in films with positively drawn latino heroes – such as *Viva Zapata* (Elia Kazan, Twentieth Century-Fox, 1952), with Marlon Brando in the title role – there was reluctance to cast Latin actors in leading roles. A lone exception on both counts, however, and a far cry from the exotic/erotic latina image, is *Salt of the Earth* (Herbert Biberman, 1953), a SOCIALIST REALIST film whose working-class latina HEROINE and narrator is played by Mexican actress Rosaura Revueltas: it is significant, however, that this film was made outside Hollywood, by former Hollywood filmmakers exiled by the McCarthyite blacklistings of the period.

Allen L Woll, *The Latin Image in American Film*, rev. edn (Los Angeles: UCLA Latin American Center Publications, 1980)   *AKu*

LAUNDER, FRANK (1907–) and GILLIAT, SIDNEY (1908–)

A close study of Launder and Gilliat's collaboration, which began in 1928 when they were screenwriters, yields some illuminating insights into BRITAIN's cinema history. Their range of subject matter was broad – as Gilliat wrote in 1974, 'versatility was always our curse' – and they were consequently never identified with particular genres, themes, or stars. Yet their output of modest and popular films was prolific, having in common a gentle, subtle handling of COMEDY, always in the service of some more generalized proposition, often a mildly subversive one. In this sense they recall the populist films of, for example, Frank Capra.

In the first film they directed, *Millions Like Us* (1943), they offer, in line with Ministry of Information requirements, a propagandist explanation of the need for female conscription during World War II. But they also present a more controversial debate about the long-term goals of the war. In an emblematic moment, which anticipates a scene ubiquitous in the BRITISH NEW WAVE cinema of the 1960s, the foreman Charlie (Eric Portman) and the upper-class Jenny (Anne Crawford) sit in the hills overlooking the city, discussing their future. Charlie questions the possibility of their marriage because: 'What's going to happen after the war? The world's made up of two kinds of people – your kind and my kind. We're all pulling together now because there's a war on. I'm not marrying you, Jenny, till I see what happens after.'

The comic absurdities of stereotypical Britishness are played up in the celebrated St Trinians cycle, but the critique is always accompanied by affection for the characters portrayed and a profound interest in the so-called 'ordinary.' The family drama *Waterloo Road* (1944) exemplifies this aspect of Launder and Gilliat's work, which was appreciated at the box office despite an often lukewarm critical reception. No British institution was immune from their scrutiny. The democratic process is the butt of the comedy in *Left Right and Centre* (1959). *Only Two Can Play* (1962) explores the perennially popular fictional device of the romantic triangle. The extramarital entanglement of librarian John Lewis (Peter Sellers) with the library committee chairman's wife Liz (Mai ZETTERLING) actually offers – beyond the delightful opportunities for slapstick, which Sellers exploits to the hilt – a study of the realities of such an affair for Lewis's wife Jean (Virginia Maskell) which is unusually perceptive for the period.

Such acute but underplayed social commentary extends to a recognition of the practical details of daily life for contemporary women. Thus although the conventional female goals of romance, marriage, and childrearing are apparently upheld, the fine details of narrative development always entail close attention to the minutiae of domestic routines, and hence a validation of the actuality of women's lives conspicuous by its absence in most films of the fifties and sixties.

Films produced and/or directed by Launder and Gilliat include: *Two Thousand Women* (1944); *I See a Dark Stranger* (1946); *Green for Danger* (1946); *The Happiest Days of Your Life* (1950); *The Belles of St Trinians* (1954); *Blue Murder at St Trinians* (1957); *The Pure Hell of St Trinians* (1960); *The Great St Trinians Train Robbery* (1966); *Endless Night* (1972)

Geoff Brown, *Launder and Gilliat* (London: British Film Institute, 1977) *JT*

LAWSON, SYLVIA (1932–)

A distinguished writer and historian, Lawson was one of a group of critics who campaigned in the late 1960s and early 1970s to reestablish a national cinema in AUSTRALIA. In her columns for *Nation* (1960–72) and *The Australian* (1970–1) she demanded state support for Australian film, and argued for a reevaluation of Australia's 'forgotten' silent cinema –

presenting it as an original form of NEOREALISM and comparing the director Raymond Longford to Vittorio de Sica. While she referred primarily to European cinema rather than to Hollywood, Lawson early on rejected the 'high/low culture' distinction which influenced subsequent Australian policy debates about funding 'quality' *or* 'entertainment,' 'art' *or* 'commercial' cinema. She insisted on critical engagement with the full range of social and cultural life, and on participation in accessible public media.

In her FILM CRITICISM, Lawson practiced a kind of interventionist cultural politics that feminist critics later theorized as an ideal. Since the late 1970s she has written substantial essays on cultural history, media policy, and the concept of NATIONAL CINEMA. Her award-winning book *The Archibald Paradox* was both a biography of an influential nineteenth-century editor, and a theory of the 'cultural journalism' that she sees as crucial to politics today.

Sylvia Lawson's publications include: 'Not for the Likes of Us' (1965), in *An Australian Film Reader*, ed. Albert Moran and Tom O'Regan (Sydney: Currency Press, 1985); 'Towards Decolonization: Some Problems and Issues for Film History in Australia', *Film Reader*, no. 4 (1979); *The Archibald Paradox: A Strange Case of Authorship* (London: Penguin Books, 1983) *MMo*

LEAF, CAROLINE (1946–)

An independent filmmaker working in CANADA best known for her animated short films such as *The Street* (1976), made for the NATIONAL FILM BOARD OF CANADA (NFB), Leaf, like a number of North American women animators, resents the dominance of the Hollywood cartoon. She has said she finds traditional cartoon or 'cel' ANIMATION somehow male, lacking in emotion with its stock of stereotyped characters and gags, and dislikes the way that the production process is elaborately divided up. In her early work she developed a personal, low-budget handmade style produced intensively directly under the camera, and too individual to be recuperated for commercial production.

In several films including her first, *Sand, or Peter and the Wolf* (1969), made whilst a student at Harvard, Leaf used sand on backlit glass. The sand was formed into images, using implements such as a fork, directly under the camera; it would be moved about slightly between frames, creating a subtly metamorphosing, chiaroscuro effect in black and white. This technique was also used in later films such as *The Owl Who Married a Goose* (1974) and *The Metamorphosis of Mr Samsa* (1977). Introducing color, Leaf used liquid paint on glass in *The Street* (1976), made for the NFB under its remit to 'interpret Canada to Canadians and to the rest of the world,' and nominated for an Oscar. It is based on a short story by Mordecai Richler about life in a Montreal Jewish community, and told from the viewpoint of a nine-year-old boy who is awaiting the death of his grandmother so that he can have her bedroom. Leaf subtly conveys the small boy's self-interest, tinged with mawkish fascination at his first close experience of illness and death, struggling with his awareness of his mother's distress and finally surprised by his own grief at the loss of his granny.

In 1979 Leaf worked with Veronica Soul on *Interview*, a film about self-awareness, mixing DOCUMENTARY with animation. She then made several nonanimation films, both documentary and dramatic, for the NFB. In 1985 she returned to literary adaptation with *The Owl and the Pussycat*, a theatrical experiment in film with live actors in animal costumes performing against drawn backgrounds. She has recently returned to animation, and is making a film by scratching minute images directly onto black leader.

Sand, or Peter and the Wolf (1969); *Orfeo* (1972); *The Owl Who Married a Goose* (1974); *The Street* (1976); *The Metamorphosis of Mr Samsa* (1977); *Interview* (co-d. Veronica Soul, 1979); *Kate and Anna McGarrigle* (1981); *An Equal Opportunity* ('People at Work' series, 1982); *The Owl and the Pussycat* (1985)

Barbara Halpern Martineau, 'Women and Cartoon Animation, or Why Women Don't Make Cartoons, or Do They?', in *The American Animated Cartoon: A Critical Anthology*, ed. Gerald Peary and Danny Peary (New York: Dutton, 1980)   IK

LEBANON

Until the Civil War in 1975, Lebanon had an active film industry catering mainly for neighboring ARAB COUNTRIES. However, the destruction of labs and studios and the emigration of film technicians did not prevent the emergence of a new wave of Lebanese filmmakers – fostering, unusually, equal numbers of women and men. As the Civil War approached, *Saat El Tahrir Dakkat/The Hour of Liberation* (Heiny Srour, 1974) about the struggle in Oman, and *Kfar-Kassem* (Borhan Alaouie, 1975) about the Palestinians' struggle, achieved international recognition; while *Beirut, O Beirut* (Maroun Baghdadi, 1975) looked at a Beirut buzzing with social and sectarian tensions. During the Civil War documentaries flourished, often sponsored by political factions: the Lebanese National Movement sponsored Maroun Baghdadi and the Palestinian Resistance sponsored female director Randa Chahal (*Khatwa, Khatwa/Step by Step* [1976]) and Jean Chamoun. Joceline Saab, a prolific documentarist whose films include *Le Liban dans la tourmente/Lebanon in Turmoil* (1975), and *Beyrouth ma ville/Beirut My Town* (1982), adopted a mainly journalistic style: western TV formed her market as she also filmed Iran, Egypt, and the Polisario Liberation Front. She later made a feature film, *Ghazi El Banat/Adolescent Sweet Love* (1985). With the help of Francis Ford Coppola, Maroun Baghdadi made *Houroub Saghira/Little*

Wars (1982) before settling in France, where he made *L'homme voilé* (1986) with French stars. Since the departure of the Palestinian Resistance after the siege of Beirut in 1982, filming has become far more dangerous. Some filmmakers cannot film in Lebanon due to their religious background. Portrayals of women have varied: as shadowy, helpless, brainless victims incapable of political reflection, as in *Kfar-Kassem*; buzzing with questions, as in *Beirut, O Beirut*; tossed about by the whims of sectarian violence in *Little Wars*; swimming in it like fish in water in *Adolescent Sweet Love*; subjects of conscious reflection about history and who writes it in Heiny SROUR's *Leila Wal Zi'ab/Leila and the Wolves* (1984).

See also: PALESTINE; SYRIA   HS

LEEDS ANIMATION WORKSHOP

An all-women collective in BRITAIN making animated films on feminist and other political themes, the Leeds Animation Workshop was formed in 1976 to make a film to campaign for workplace nurseries – *Who Needs Nurseries? We Do!*. Completed in 1978, this film makes its argument from the children's point of view and, like all the Workshop's films, advocates positive action.

The Workshop operates under principles of independent film production similar to those established at the GPO and Crown Film Units of the 1930s BRITISH DOCUMENTARY MOVEMENT. The group works collectively, avoiding the hierarchical division of labor characteristic of the commercial ANIMATION studio system, and no individual credits are given. The films are distributed by the Workshop itself or by FEMINIST DISTRIBUTION organizations, and they circulate widely amongst

campaign and community groups, colleges, women's groups, and local authorities, avoiding the commercial cinema circuit. They are intended to provoke discussion rather than simply to entertain. The Workshop survives mainly on public-sector funding, from varied sources such as the BRITISH FILM INSTITUTE, local authorities, Yorkshire Arts association, and more recently from CHANNEL FOUR TELEVISION. Its activities have recently expanded to include training.

The Workshop considers cel animation to be the most accessible for audiences, often combined with cutout images to provide a useful low-budget technique. In *Give Us a Smile* (1983), cel is effectively combined with found images from magazine advertisements, fine art and PORNOGRAPHY to show the way women are both bombarded from all sides to conform to stereotypes and also harassed on the streets by men. The film was made in the aftermath of the notorious Yorkshire Ripper case, when women in the area were subjected to even more pressures on the street than usual, and campaign groups such as Women Against Violence Against Women were particularly active. The film aroused controversy for its ending, which advocated fighting back in ways which included setting fire to pornography shops.

Other subjects the Workshop have addressed include workplace safety in *Risky Business* (1980); nuclear war in *Pretend You'll Survive* (1981); the politics of food in *Crops and Robbers* (1986); and homelessness in *Home and Dry* (1987).

Who Needs Nurseries? We Do! (1978); *Risky Business* (1980); *Pretend You'll Survive* (1981); *Give Us a Smile* (1983); *Council Matters* (1984); *Crops and Robbers* (1986); *Home and Dry* (1987)   IK

LEIGH, VIVIEN (1913–67)

A stage and film actress, Leigh was born in India, but was sent at the age of seven to convent boarding schools in England

and later elsewhere in Europe. She studied ballet and drama at the Royal Academy of Dramatic Art in London, and made her first film appearance in a 1934 GAINSBOROUGH STUDIOS production entitled *Things Are Looking Up*. Some two years before her death, she said in an interview: 'In Britain, an attractive woman is somehow suspect. If there is talent as well, it is overshadowed. Beauty and brains just can't be entertained: someone has been too extravagant. . . .' Certainly in her early film roles, Leigh specialized in the part of 'spoilt beauty,' encapsulating a willful, self-destructive, capricious FEMININITY: she was Scarlett O'Hara in David O Selznick's now mythic *Gone With the Wind* in 1939, and Cleopatra in the 1944 film version of George Bernard Shaw's *Caesar and Cleopatra*. Her relationship with, and subsequent marriage to, actor Laurence Olivier and the aura surrounding the couple had a style, audacity and glamor which triumphed over the austerity and grimness of wartime and post-war BRITAIN. They appeared together in 1941, in Alexander Korda's *Lady Hamilton*, a film designed to inspire pro-British feeling in the USA, Olivier playing Nelson and Leigh Emma Hamilton. Her portrayal of the tragic moral downfall of a beautiful woman prefigured the roles she was to play in her later film career: the neurotic and wistful Blanche Dubois in *A Streetcar Named Desire* (Elia Kazan, Warner Bros., 1951) and the exploited, ageing American actress in *The Roman Spring of Mrs Stone* (Jose Quintero) in 1961. The tragic fate of women in parts such as these, women whose lives are finally destroyed by their vulnerability and incipient mental instability, has been seen by some observers as a commentary on Vivien Leigh's own racked private life, which was plagued by illnesses of various kinds. But the fate of the female characters in these stories is also a comment on society's punitive attitudes to gifted women – attitudes of which Vivien Leigh herself was clearly only too well aware.

Hugo Vickers, *Vivien Leigh* (London: Hamish Hamilton, 1988)   SP

LEJEUNE, C A (1897–1973)

Brought up and educated in Manchester, Lejeune is notable for being the first woman in BRITAIN to write regularly and seriously about film – though Iris BARRY runs her a close second. In 1922 Lejeune became FILM CRITIC of the *Manchester Guardian*, and moved to the *Observer* in 1928. She also contributed to magazines and JOURNALS as diverse as the *New York Times*, the *Sketch*, *Sight and Sound*, *Good Housekeeping*, and even *Farmer's Weekly*. She wrote several books: *Cinema* (1931), *For Filmgoers Only* (1934), *Chestnuts in her Lap* (1947); and in 1964 published her autobiography, *Thank You For Having Me*. By 1960, when she retired from the *Observer* after thirty-two years, Lejeune had become a national institution, broadcasting regularly on radio. But when one learns that she retired because of the 'sex and savagery' she perceived in contemporary cinema, the tenor of her FILM CRITICISM becomes apparent. She did not believe in cinema as an art form in its own right, and rejected what she termed 'critical jargon' and 'highbrow nonsense.' She was, however, an enthusiastic champion of the 'quality' tradition of British cinema. Her criticism of film was firmly rooted in a strong Christian and moral outlook: she believed in the triumph of good over evil and rejected films which violated this code. She held 'normalcy' to be an ideal and disliked, for example, films offering psychological explanations and motives. Allied to this was her dislike of films which showed complex or confused family relationships, or films she deemed pessimistic, sad, or gloomy. She left her seat as critic at the point when a new generation of critics, with very different attitudes, was about to take over.

Marsha McCreadie, *Women on Film: The Critical Eye* (New York: Praeger, 1983)   SP

LESBIAN INDEPENDENT CINEMA

Lesbian independent cinema is a growing body of film characterized by two common qualities: it is produced independently of the commercial film industry, and it attempts to provide a more compelling and engaging representation of lesbianism than is offered by DOMINANT CINEMA. Lesbian independent cinema spans a number of western countries and utilizes a variety of film strategies and styles, including DOCUMENTARY, fiction, ANIMATION, and AVANT GARDE, and makes efforts to break down barriers between these categories. It emerged in the late 1960s and early 1970s in conjunction with the development of lighter, more accessible 16mm film equipment, and the advent of the women's and gay liberation movements of that period.

Pioneering lesbian filmmakers such as Jan Oxenberg and Barbara HAMMER began in the early 1970s to make short personal films affirming their sexuality and experiences, Oxenberg drawing upon narrative and documentary styles and Hammer upon the American avant-garde tradition. The 1970s and early 1980s saw the creation of an unprecedented range of low-budget lesbian films: short personal narratives about the experience of first 'coming out' or initiating relationships, such as Janet Meyers's *Getting Ready* (1977) and Greta Schiller's *Greta's Girls* (1978); collectively made documentaries on lesbian motherhood or on individual lesbian lives, both remarkable and 'ordinary,' such as Iris Films' *In the Best Interest of the Children* (1977) and Ishtar Films' *World of Light: A Portrait of May Sarton* (1981); avant-garde films that experimented with nonvoyeuristic approaches to lesbian sexuality, such as Chantal AKERMAN's *Je Tu Il Elle* (1974) and Su FRIEDRICH's *Gently Down the Stream* (1981). Lizzie BORDEN's no-

The Ties That Bind, by Su Friedrich

budget sci-fi feature *Born in Flames* (1983) is considered an exemplary work of lesbian independent cinema, in that it combines radical feminist politics, black and lesbian central characters, and a fast-paced adventure story that keeps the film from being considered 'worthy but deadly' – the fate of some of the more politically rhetorical and technically unsophisticated films to come out of the early lesbian independent cinema movement.

As more women work in independent film, the contours of lesbian independent cinema are changing and broadening. American filmmaker Donna DEITCH made *Desert Hearts* (1985) as an independent film – raising the budget herself and maintaining artistic control – but she chose to present a 'nice' lesbian ROMANCE in a style that fits all the narrative conventions of a Hollywood studio production. On the other hand, West German director Monika Treut shot a gritty black-and-white narrative, *Virgin Machine* (1988), about a young German woman's initiation into the lesbian sexual underground of San Francisco. Treut eschewed both a conventional Hollywood look and a simplistic 'positive' image of lesbianism to fascinate and disturb lesbian viewers.

In considering these and other recent lesbian films, key questions of representation and spectatorship arise: What does it mean for a film to address the 'lesbian gaze'? Can lesbian viewers be the object of cinematic address in a film that relies on the conventions of CLASSICAL HOLLYWOOD CINEMA? Is it necessary – or possible – to create entirely new ways of representing sexual difference? What effect does the intended audience have on the ways lesbian independent cinema represents lesbian sexuality?

Andrea Weiss, *Vampires and Violets: Lesbian Representation in the Cinema* (London: Pandora Press, 1990)

See also: AUDIENCE AND SPECTATOR; MIKESCH, ELFI; OTTINGER, ULRIKE   *AW*

LESBIAN VAMPIRE

The female vampire film is a particularly interesting variant of the VAMPIRE FILM; invariably, female vampire films represent lesbian desire as the female, like her male counterpart, also feeds on the blood of virgins. There are two major historical sources from which the female vampire in film is drawn: the Countess Elisabeth Bathory, a sixteenth-century Hungarian noblewoman, and the Countess Carmilla Karnstein, ill-fated heroine of Sheridan Le Fanu's gothic novella *Carmilla* (1871).

Elisabeth Bathory, reputed to have been one of the most beautiful women in Europe, was accused of slaughtering as many as six hundred young girls whose blood she was supposed to have bathed in, believing it would keep her young. Films based on the Countess Bathory include *Daughters of Darkness* (Harry Kuemel, 1970) and *Ritual of Blood* (Jorge Grau, 1973). In a fascinating book, *Dracula was a Woman* (London: Hamlyn, 1984), Raymond McNally argues convincingly that Bram Stoker's Dracula was not based on the historical figure Vlad the Impaler (1431–76) but was inspired by the Countess Bathory.

Le Fanu's *Carmilla* represented the first major treatment of a female vampire in literature. Carmilla seeks out young women who are like herself; with each new conquest/killing, she symbolically lives out her own death. Film adaptations of Le Fanu's tale include *Blood and Roses* (Roger Vadim, 1960); *Terror in the Crypt* (Camillo Matrocinque, 1963), and *The Vampire Lovers* (Roy Ward Baker, 1970).

Not all lesbian vampire films draw on these two historical figures. For instance, the women in *Vampyres* (Joseph Larraz, 1974) were murdered by an enraged man because they were lesbians. They return as lesbian vampires, seeking out men as their victims. Lesbian desire is de-eroticized in some vampire films. *Vampire Lovers*, however, is a definite exception. Carmilla makes love to her victims, bringing them to the heights of erotic pleasure, before she drinks their blood. A recent film, *The Hunger* (Tony Scott, 1983), represents scenarios of lesbian desire in a highly eroticized context.

Unlike many films which deal with lesbianism, the sexual encounters in the lesbian vampire film are not always dealt with in a pejorative way. The punishment of the female vampire is related more to her status as one of the undead than to the fact that she seduces young virgins. In some examples of this GENRE, such as *Vampyres*, the main protagonists are not punished for their deviant sexual behavior. These films raise interesting questions about spectatorship and identification. How do female members of the AUDIENCE relate to such films when erotic encounters are depicted between two women? Do female viewers respond differently from male viewers? How do theories about the LOOK apply to such films? How does recent feminist work on FANTASY and the female spectator relate to this genre? The fact that lesbian sexual desire is represented free of moralistic proselytizing in some versions of the female vampire film, a genre which does not enjoy a 'high art' status, suggests that popular film genres may have much to offer the female spectator.

Andrea Weiss, *Vampires and Violets: Lesbianism in the Cinema* (London: Pandora Press, 1991)

See also: EROTICISM; HORROR; LESBIANISM AND CINEMA   BC

LESBIANISM AND CINEMA

These two terms may seem incongruous, perhaps even contradictory, since in CLASSICAL HOLLYWOOD CINEMA – and, indeed, elsewhere – narratives often revolve around heterosexual ROMANCE. When the occasional lesbian character, image, or relationship is offered, it is usually in the form of a problem to the heterosexual 'equilibrium' which the NARRATIVE seeks to restore. And lesbian characters are

further marginalized by the fact that their SEXUALITY is rarely named; rather, we recognize them as lesbian by a reliance on stereotyped images, visual associations with deviance (through camera angles, LIGHTING, COSTUMES connoting the odd or sinister) or their disruptive narrative function. The character of Miss Fellowes (Grayson Hall) in *Night of the Iguana* (John Huston, 1964) offers a good example of how lesbian codes operate in cinema. First, she fits the third of three classic lesbian STEREOTYPES: the mannish lesbian; the predatory, sophisticated lesbian; and the neurotic, usually closeted lesbian. As a neurotic lesbian, Fellowes serves both as obstacle to the uneasy heterosexual coupling of the film's main characters (played by Richard Burton and Ava Gardner) and as counterpoint to Ava Gardner's 'natural,' unrepressed (hetero)sexuality. Furthermore, the lesbian character's deviance is highlighted in the juxtaposition of her 'artificial' visual image with the film's 'natural' setting. While suggestions of lesbianism in Hollywood cinema have largely remained at this subtextual level, they are nonetheless encoded precisely in such a way as to encourage particular readings of lesbianism – as social deviance, as sexual titillation or threat, as boundary against which 'normal' women's sexuality and social role are to be defined.

> That it is desirable for feminist cinema to be countercinema was the seductive argument of which notable British writer on film?

In mainstream cinema, lesbianism remained unspoken, and was often visually excised as well, during the reign of Hollywood's Motion Picture PRODUCTION CODE between the mid 1930s and late 1960s. Calling homosexuality a 'sexual perversion,' the Code ensured that American film scripts were altered to accommodate this view – for example, the lesbian 'secret' in Lillian Hellman's play *The Children's Hour* became hetero-sexual adultery in its screen adaptation, *These Three* (William Wyler, Goldwyn, 1936). But the Production Code concerned itself primarily with direct references in the script, the elimination of which in no way insured against possible lesbian readings. For example, a lesbian dynamic can be perceived as the unspoken motivation in Nicholas Ray's *Johnny Guitar* (Republic, 1954) and, more apparently, in Alfred HITCHCOCK's *Rebecca* (David Selznick Productions, 1940).

More than CENSORSHIP itself, the dominant mode of cinematic address that speaks to the spectator as heterosexual, white and male has rendered lesbianism virtually invisible and has determined the ways in which lesbianism is permitted to surface. Lesbian viewers have had to read against the preferred meanings generated by films – meanings affirming heterosexuality and the normative female role.

It has often been suggested, though, that gay men and women have had a special relationship to the cinema. Lesbian audiences today often look to certain films of the 1930s for satisfying lesbian representations, as well as to Hollywood CAREER WOMAN pictures of the 1940s. In part this is because the more open expression of sexuality in films made prior to the Production Code provides greater room for potential lesbian readings. Because of the ways in which the Hollywood STAR system worked, a stance or gesture of a certain actress – such as Marlene DIETRICH's or Greta GARBO's CROSSDRESSING and kissing women in *Morocco* (Josef von Sternberg, Paramount, 1930) or *Queen Christina* (Rouben Mamoulian, MGM, 1933) – had, and continue to have, special resonance for most lesbian viewers. In the films of the 1940s, the transgressions of strong female characters (though in the realm of work rather than of sexuality) also hold greater appeal to lesbians than do more explicit lesbian characters – such as Beryl Reid in the title role of *The Killing of Sister George* (Robert Aldrich,

1968) – whose obvious deviance hinders the viewer's ability to be drawn into identification. The lesbians of European ART CINEMA, beginning perhaps with Leontine SAGAN's *Maedchen in Uniform* (1931), have also offered interesting alternatives.

Although a survey of lesbian representations in Hollywood cinema must inevitably point up the suicides, heterosexual resolutions, and other forms of lesbian denial, DOMINANT CINEMA has also offered rare, poignant moments of lesbian sensuality that are beginning to be retrieved by gay and feminist film theorists. In addition, LESBIAN INDEPENDENT CINEMA has widened the range of representations, often challenging Hollywood conventions and addressing lesbian audiences.

Vito Russo, *The Celluloid Closet: Homosexuality in the Movies* (New York: Harper & Row, 1981)

See also: AUDIENCE AND SPECTATOR; AUDRY, JACQUELINE; LESBIAN VAMPIRE; PHALLIC WOMAN   AW

LIGHTING

An aspect of MISE-EN-SCENE, film lighting can have many functions, foremost among which is visibility of selected actions. Dominant lighting styles for fiction filmmaking were in place by about 1915. Three lights, in a near-triangular arrangement above the bodies of actors, typifies most Hollywood-style films: a key light on one side is supplemented by a lower-illumination fill light on the other, and backlighting shines from the rear. This configuration gives a sense of depth and separates characters from their surroundings. In CLASSICAL HOLLYWOOD CINEMA, various permutations on this basic practice exist, often motivated by GENRE conventions, aesthetic preferences, and ideologies of representation. For instance, hardness or softness of lighting, or top or underlighting, can connote traits of character. FILM NOIR is marked, for example, by its prevalent use of low-key lighting (most of the image is in shadow, with only a few areas of key lighting). Hard-to-achieve low-level and dramatic illuminations have been used by some cinematographers as signature styles. Lighting techniques can also promote IDEOLOGIES of female or male attractiveness, while various complicated procedures have been used to enhance facial contours of STARS such as Greta GARBO and Marlene DIETRICH.

Peter Baxter, 'On the History and Ideology of Film Lighting', *Screen*, vol. 16, no. 3 (1975)   JaS

LONDON WOMEN'S FILM GROUP

Formed in 1972, the London Women's Film Group (LWFG) started with the aim of working in the context of the then burgeoning women's movement, pioneering FEMINIST INDEPENDENT FILM in BRITAIN. Many of their films, such as the early *Betteshanger, Kent 1972* (1972), made after the successful 1972 miners' strike, and *Whose Choice?* (1976) on abortion, were tied into the immediacies of particular political campaigns. Others, like *Miss/Mrs* (1972), criticized STEREOTYPES of women in the dominant media, while *Women of the Rhondda* (1972) uncovered the hidden role played by women in the Welsh miners' strikes of the twenties and thirties. All these films were marked by the group's desire to replace traditional DOCUMENTARY 'objectivity' with new direct images of 'real women.' As Christine Gledhill records: '. . . The first concern of the Movement was simply to put women recognizable to us as women, in the picture. The first independent women's film groups grabbed film or video and went to talk to women about their lives and experiences.' There is a sense of excitement and political charge in these 'women-talking' documentaries, 'which are centrally concerned with what it is to be a woman and with bringing visibility to 'a woman's point of view.'

Women of the Rhondda

While some of the LWFG's later work – especially the political burlesque of *The Amazing Equal Pay Show* (1974) and the mixed fiction/documentary form of *Whose Choice?* (1976) – moved away REALISM and questioned the relationship between spectator and documentary, the desire to speak for a collective feminist 'we' remained. However, this does raise problems: in particular, although this new 'we' sought to speak for all women, the common experience claimed (and sought) was frequently that of women who were privileged in terms of class and ethnicity.

Aside from laying the groundwork for future discussions of the relationship between explicit feminist politics and film, the LWFG did much to change and radicalize INDEPENDENT CINEMA. They made films collectively, sharing practical skills, and even in some cases rotating technical roles. Their policy of accompanying films to screenings was influential in the development of FEMINIST DISTRIBUTION and FEMINIST EXHIBITION. Some members were also active in film union activities, helping to challenge hierarchical attitudes and pushing for equal opportunities within the industry. Although the group disbanded in 1977, several of its members are still active in film culture.

Christine Gledhill, '*Whose Choice? –* Teaching Films About Abortion', *Screen Education*, no. 24 (1977)   JRo

LOOK, THE

One tendency within PSYCHOANALYTIC FILM THEORY draws on the ideas of psychoanalysts Sigmund Freud and Jacques Lacan to explain aspects of the relationship between film TEXT and spectator. Looking (within a particular context – the darkened auditorium – and with a particular object – the screen from which the object of the look is 'primordially absent') distinguishes cinema from other media. But if the most obvious instance of the look in cinema is that of the spectator, there are other looks as well. The idea that cinema 'addresses' the spectator, for instance, implies a look *at* the spectator; there are exchanges of looks between characters within the

fictional space of the film itself; and in a sense the spectator's look is also that of the camera. Freud's work on the libido drives has been invoked in considering in particular the spectator's look, and here the concept of SCOPOPHILIA – the drive to pleasurable looking – has been put to use in considering the specific qualities of cinematic PLEASURE as a set of largely unconscious processes. Film theorists argue that looking involves not only voyeurism – in that the screen image, the object of the spectator's gaze, is distanced from her/him in such a way that a return of the look is impossible – but also narcissism – in that the spectator recognizes and identifies with the human figure on the screen. The concept of the look has been taken up and developed in FEMINIST FILM THEORY in the argument first advanced by Laura MULVEY that in CLASSICAL HOLLYWOOD CINEMA the female figure on the screen is set up preeminently as an object 'to-be-looked-at,' in a spectator–text relationship which constructs a psychically masculine

Woman as 'to-be-looked-at': Jane Russell in *The Revolt of Mamie Stover* (1956)

subject position for the spectator, regardless of her or his social gender. If, as this suggests, there can be no spectatorial look from or to the position of the feminine, can real women's pleasure in cinema be gained only at the cost of psychic crossdressing?

Linda Williams, 'When the Woman Looks', in *Re-vision: Essays in Feminist Film Criticism*, ed. Patricia Mellencamp, Mary Ann Doane and Linda Williams (Los Angeles: American Film Institute, 1984)

See also: AUDIENCE AND SPECTATOR AKu

LOOS, ANITA (1888–1981)

Witty, elegant, and prolific, US writer Anita Loos made a public splash with the novel that remains her masterpiece, *Gentlemen Prefer Blondes*, in 1925. A sardonic sendup of sexual politics in the flapper era, it purports to be the diary of a very pragmatic blonde golddigger. Edith Wharton, her tongue perhaps only half in cheek, called it 'the greatest novel since *Manon Lescaut*'; and the book spawned two movies, a Broadway play, and a Broadway musical.

By 1925, however, Loos had already written scores of screenplays, mostly for D W GRIFFITH's studio. She began her career in her teens as a San Francisco stage actress and started SCREENWRITING at the age of twenty-four. She then moved to Hollywood, where she collaborated with and married director John Emerson. Emerson was to add his name to Loos's scripts for years, although it is unlikely that after the first few years he contributed much besides the punctuation.

During several decades in Hollywood, first with Griffith, then at MGM, Loos worked as scenarist, script doctor, title writer, and dialogist. Her scripts were light and full of puns and gags, and her best characters were women like herself: worldly and sharp-tongued. After World War II she wrote a string of Broadway

plays, among them an adaptation of COLETTE's *Gigi*, as well as a sequel to *Gentlemen*, and her memoirs.

Films scripted by Loos include: *The New York Hat* (1912); *The Power of the Camera* (1913); *Highbrow Love* (1913); *A Cure for Suffragettes* (1913); *The Meal Ticket* (1914); *At the Road's End* (1914); *Intolerance* (titles only, 1916); *The Social Secretary* (1916); *The Americano* (1916); *In Again Out Again* (1917); *American Aristocracy* (1916); *Down to Earth* (1917); *Wild and Woolly* (1917); *Reaching for the Moon* (1917); *Blonde of the Follies* (MGM, 1931); *Red-Headed Woman* (MGM, 1932); *Hold Your Man* (MGM, 1933); *San Francisco* (MGM, 1936); *The Women* (MGM, 1939); *Blossoms in the Dust* (MGM, 1941); *When Ladies Meet* (MGM, 1941); *Gentlemen Prefer Blondes* (Twentieth Century-Fox, 1953)

Gary Carey, *Anita Loos* (New York: Alfred A Knopf, 1981) JSh

LUPINO, IDA (1918–)

Ida Lupino is a film actress, director, producer, and writer, and now directs, and occasionally acts in, television. She was born in Brixton, London, daughter of comedian Stanley Lupino and actress Connie Emerald, and studied at the Royal Academy of Dramatic Art. She soon moved to the USA, and in 1940 won a contract with Warner Bros. In 1941 *Picturegoer* reported that 'she gave up a contract at $1,700 a week rather than play in unsuitable stories.' Some have argued that Lupino's acting career suffered because Warners also had Bette DAVIS under contract at the same time. Her first role to be taken seriously was in *The Light That Failed* (William Wellman, Paramount, 1939). She acted in over fifty Hollywood films, including *They Drive By Night* (Raoul Walsh, Warner Bros., 1940); *High Sierra* (Raoul Walsh, Warner Bros., 1941); and *The Hard Way* (Raoul Walsh, Warner Bros., 1943).

Lupino began directing films in 1949, with *Not Wanted*, on which she took no

Ida Lupino

directorial credit. The film is credited to Elmer Clifton, who was taken ill three days into shooting; Lupino, who had co-written the screenplay, took over. She then formed her own company, Emerald Productions, later known as Filmmakers Inc. and then Bridget Productions. In 1972, she said of her work: 'Frankly, I was more interested in getting stories together than directing. Our company did stories back then that were very daring – rape (*Outrage*, 1950), unwed mothers (*Not Wanted*, 1949), bigamy (*The Bigamist*, 1953). You name it and we did it, but it was in good taste.' Lupino's films depict alienation and displacement in small-city, postwar America. They use an almost documentary sense of place, from city streets to a home for unmarried mothers, to create an intense atmosphere in which disillusioned characters are trapped by their surroundings or try to protect themselves from intrusion from the outside world. Issues of class and shifting social structures are strong elements in her work. Lupino was criticized in the 1970s for making 'feminist films from an antifeminist point of view,' portraying women as passive and victimized. However, she was interested in capturing how women are rendered passive and powerless by society's narrow morality, and in showing female rites of passage into womanhood, into nightmare, into loss of control. Lupino saw her films as liberal rather than overtly feminist: 'They were not only about women's problems, they were definitely about men's too.'

Not Wanted (Emerald, 1949); *Never Fear* (Emerald, 1950); *Outrage* (Filmmakers, 1950); *Hard, Fast and Beautiful* (RKO/ Filmmakers, 1951); *The Bigamist* (Filmmakers, 1953); *The Hitchhiker* (Filmmakers, 1953); *The Trouble With Angels* (1966)

Louise Heck-Rabi, *Women Filmmakers: A Critical Reception* (Metuchen, NJ: Scarecrow Press, 1984)   CS

LYELL, LOTTIE (1890–1925)

With Raymond Longford (1878–1959), Lottie Lyell was part of the most hallowed of film partnerships in AUSTRALIAN silent cinema. Although only one-fifth of the films made in the silent era survive (and even these have sketchy credits), a number of historians have pieced together an impressive record of women's on- and offscreen participation in all aspects of film production in this period. Lyell – like many women involved in film production, including Kate Howarde, who was the first Australian woman to produce and direct a film (*Possum Paddock* [1921]) – began her career in theater. She joined forces with Longford in 1909, and they embarked together on their film career in 1911, along with producer Charles Cozens

Spencer and cinematographer Arthur Higgins. Among their first commercial successes were *The Fatal Wedding* and *The Romantic Story of Margaret Catchpole* (both 1911). Until her untimely death in 1925 from tuberculosis, Lyell worked on twenty-eight films with Longford, starring in twenty-one of them and contributing as writer, co-director, art director, and co-producer. She was the only woman to work behind and in front of the camera for over a decade. Most returned to the stage after a few films, or – like Enid Bennett, Sylvia Bremer, Jocelyn Howarth, Annette Kellerman, Shirley Ann Richards, and Lotus Thompson – pursued their careers in Hollywood. Lyell and Longford's best-known film, *The Sentimental Bloke* (1919), is the outstanding Australian film of the silent era, renowned for its naturalistic performances and its use of socially and psychologically credible actors rather than star types. Many of Lyell's roles, notably that of the seduced woman in *The Woman Suffers* (1918), turned female STEREOTYPES around, and her naturalistic style created individualized variations on wellworn types. After Lyell's death Longford continued to battle the trade monopoly, but his output declined rapidly after the 1920s.

Lottie Lyell's films include: *The Fatal Wedding* (1911); *The Romantic Story of Margaret Catchpole* (1911); *The Tide of Death* (1912); *'Neath Austral Skies* (1913); *The Silence of Dean Maitland* (1914); *The Mutiny on the Bounty* (1916); *The Church and the Woman* (1917); *The Woman Suffers* (1918); *The Sentimental Bloke* (1919); *Ginger Mick* (1920); *Rudd's New Selection* (1921); *The Blue Mountains Mystery* (1921); *The Dinkum Bloke* (1923); *Fisher's Ghost* (1924); *The Bushwackers* (1925); *The Pioneers* (1926).

Andree Wright, *Brilliant Careers: Women in Australian Cinema* (Sydney: Pan Books, 1986)   FC

MACLEAN, ALISON (1958–)

The most accomplished of the younger generation of NEW ZEALAND women filmmakers, Alison Maclean was born in Canada in 1958. She came to New Zealand as a teenager and studied at the Elam School of Fine Arts in Auckland, majoring in film and sculpture. Although she has made only three films so far, they illustrate the growth in sophistication in terms of subjects and methods of New Zealand women filmmakers in general.

Maclean's first film, *Rud's Wife* (1985), is a thirty-minute reflection and dissection of the unsatisfactory family life of an elderly mother and widow inhabiting one of many similar houses in a good-mannered, dull, typical New Zealand suburb. Simply shot, with short sequences enlivened by the techniques of the novice filmmaker (flashbacks, photographs, central character speaking to camera), this film expresses a great deal of the hopelessness and alienation of lives stunted by repressive social structures.

Talkback (1987) moves from consciousness-raising to possibility, with an intricately structured tale of a woman technician's sudden elevation to the position of talkback radio host. Over the period of a night, in a film reminiscent in its tolerance and optimism of Chantal AKERMAN's *Toute une nuit* (1982), she comes to terms with the idea that, for now, she rules the airwaves and can say what she wants.

With *Kitchen Sink* (1989), Maclean has plunged right into the issues of fear and desire. A woman tugs on a hair sticking out of a plughole and pulls out a fetus which grows into a man, with whom she then proceeds to fall in love. The concentrated horror of this piece is achieved through tight montage-directing, expressionistic camerawork, and a tense, wordless soundtrack. Although only twelve minutes long, it is probably the most powerful New Zealand film yet. It was accepted for competition at Cannes in 1989.

Rud's Wife (1985); *Talkback* (1987); *Kitchen Sink* (1989)   AH

MACSKASSY, KATALIN (1942–)

Born in Budapest, HUNGARY, daughter of Gyula Macskássy (1912–72), one of the founders of Hungarian animation, Katalin Macskássy graduated from the Academy of Theater and Film Art in 1971 after working as black-and-white artist and editor for Pannonia Film Studio from 1960. She mixes live action with ANIMATION. She has also traveled around Hungary gathering material on folk art in order to present to children their own heritage.

It Could Happen in Budapest, If . . . (1970); *Gombnyomasra/Push Button* (1973); *Nem igaz!/It Cannot be True* (1974); *Nekem az élet teccik nagyon/I Think Life's Great Fun* (1976); *Children's Rights* (1978); *Aunt Lenke* (1980); *Our Feasts* (1982); *Family Picture* (1983); *Another Planet* (1986); *The Cricket and the Ant* (1988); *Vision* (1988)

BE/ER

MAKE-UP

Film make-up is an effect of the technical needs of film, the centrality of the human face to film style, and ideologies of feminine beauty. In the USA, performers typically applied their own make-up until the mid 1920s and the rise of the

HOLLYWOOD STUDIO SYSTEM, when studio make-up departments assured quality and uniformity of make-up across each film, contributing to the life-like appearance of CLASSICAL HOLLY-WOOD CINEMA. Make-up charts, a map of the face which identified the treatment needed for each area (cheekbones, uneven eyebrows, jawline, and so on), maintained a star's look across her films. In the research lab of Max Factor, the major make-up supply firm, make-up formulae were adjusted for technological innovations in FILM STOCK and LIGHTING, thus contributing to the standardization of both make-up and feminine beauty. A flawless screen complexion was achieved by pancake make-up which eliminated pores, and by powders which shimmered. For CLOSEUPS, the actress was lit to avoid shadows and then the make-up artist ensured that any physical 'imperfections' were covered. Women stars often had a favorite make-up artist and cinematographer, a man whom she could trust with her appearance and thus with her career. Except for major dental problems, character make-up, or physical transformations, men were given much less cosmetic attention than women. Shadows, scars, or imperfect noses could only enhance rugged MASCULINITY, while the same on a woman detracts from prescriptive white FEMININITY. Joan CRAWFORD's high cheekbones were attained through make-up which also covered her freckles. The transformation of Margarita Cansino into Rita HAYWORTH was accomplished through electrolysis which eliminated her low hairline, and by dyeing her natural dark brunette hair to auburn. Anglicized, and thus feminized, Hayworth became a Hollywood beauty. Unlike other technical aspects of filmmaking, information about Hollywood make-up was widely circulated in magazine articles which detailed the physical 'flaws' of the stars and advised readers on the step-by-step make-up procedures which would correct these inadequacies.

Frank Westmore and Muriel Davidson, *The Westmores of Hollywood* (New York: Lippincott, 1976)   MBH

MALDOROR, SARAH (19??–   )

Sarah Maldoror – with Euzhan PALCY, one of the two internationally renowned CARIBBEAN women filmmakers – is perhaps best known for her films made in AFRICA. Maldoror, originally from the island of Guadeloupe, has produced many documentaries, but it was her fiction feature film *Sambizanga* (1972) which brought her greatest acclaim, winning the grand prize at the Carthage Film Festival. *Sambizanga* is a portrait of a woman whose husband, a revolutionary, is arrested and imprisoned, and who is awakened to the true meaning of colonial oppression and the need for struggle. However, Maldoror says that if she were to make that film now, she would make it more powerful: 'The woman would have foreseen that independence would be a failure. I didn't realize when I was making the film that independence would be a failure.'

Maldoror does not deny that she is interested in the problems of women, but says she does not really find any common 'female characteristics' in films made by women. She says: 'Every woman director makes films according to her own personality, just like men do.' On the portrayal of women, Maldoror has said she is interested only in women who struggle, and that these are the women she wants in her films: 'These women can be beautiful, but they are not lifeless dolls.' She offers work to women (not only in front of the camera) as much as possible on her productions, arguing that women can work in whatever field they wish to – including film – and that the crucial ingredient is strong motivation. Men are unlikely to help women to do that . . . 'that is why she has to liberate herself.'

Maldoror, who has been documenting African liberation struggles since 1971, trained at the Moscow film school, where she first met Senegalese director Ousmane SEMBENE. Her debut film was a short documentary on the French use of torture in the Algerian war, *Monangambeee* (1969), which received several awards. From there she went to Guinea-Bissau to make the film *Des fusils pour Banta/Guns for Banta* (1970) with an Algerian Army crew. However, she has not forgotten the Caribbean, and her most recent film *Aimé Césaire, le masque des mots* (1987), is a portrait of the Martiniquan poet and writer who founded the literary, artistic and cultural movement known as 'négritude.' Maldoror was also a founder member of the Paris theater group 'Les Griots,' for which she adapted works by Jean-Paul Sartre and Aimé Césaire. Asked why her films about poets and painters all feature great men, Sarah once said: '. . . because governments are in the hands of men and I can get money to make films about famous men.' Should she be able to realize one of her dearest wishes, however, she would give the world a film based on the novel *Mulatresse Solitude (A Mulatta called Solitude)* by the Guadeloupe author Simone Schwarz-Bart.

Monangambeee (1969); *Des fusils pour Banta/Guns for Banta* (1970); *The Future of Saint Denis* (1971); *Sambizanga* (1972); *Un dessert pour Constance/A Dessert for Constance* (1980); *Aimé Césaire, le masque des mots* (1987)

Sylvia Harvey, Sarah Maldoror, Nadja Kasji, Elin Clason, 'Third World Perspectives: Focus on Sarah Maldoror', *Women and Film*, vol. 1, nos. 5–6 (1974)
JG

MALE MELODRAMA

The very notion of a 'male' melodrama seems incongruous. This is because the MELODRAMA, together with its subgenre, the WOMAN'S PICTURE, has generally been seen as belonging to female audiences – GENREs dealing with such 'unmanly' topics as love and abandonment, pleasure and pain, family and

generation. This does not mean that cinema ignores the emotional problems of men. On the contrary, popular films deal almost exclusively with such issues; these films, however, are given more laudatory generic titles such as FILM NOIR, or the WESTERN, gangster, or private eye film. Films by European male directors such as Michelangelo ANTONIONI – which also deal with themes central to the melodrama – are rarely discussed in these terms. Rather, they are defined as adult drama, as psychological drama, or as ART CINEMA.

> *A British film critic became noted for her overall distaste for the cinema. Who was she?*

Laura MULVEY is one of the few theorists to have analyzed the representation of men in melodrama. In her discussion of Douglas SIRK's films, she argues that melodrama 'can be seen as having an ideological *function* in working certain contradictions through to the surface and re-presenting them in an aesthetic form.' She claims that the 'male melodrama' is primarily concerned with problems which arise from the overvaluation of phallic masculinity in patriarchal cultures. This stress placed on 'phallocentric' values and behavior is at odds with the masculine qualities which are actually needed for the effective and harmonious functioning of the family unit. Male melodramas such as *Home from the Hill* (Vincente Minnelli, MGM, 1960) 'represent a positive male figure who rejects rampant virility'; whereas *Written on the Wind* (Douglas Sirk, Universal, 1956) traces the tragedy of a male figure destroyed by his failure to live up to the demands of an aggressive patriarchal order. Mulvey also argues that the male melodrama is structured differently, and that Sirk's male melodramas approach the complexities of tragedy. This is because the melodramatic hero is usually somewhat aware of his fate – an awareness generally denied the female protagonists of the Sirkian melodrama.

Recently, some FEMINIST FILM THEORY has become preoccupied with the representation of MASCULINITY in film, particularly in relation to male hysteria. These discussions have opened up new ways of speaking about melodrama, particularly in relation to films in which the hero is clearly represented as suffering from clinical forms of hysteria. In *Random Harvest* (Mervyn LeRoy, MGM, 1942), for instance, the hero suffers from amnesia; while in the more recent male melodrama *Paris, Texas* (Wim Wenders, 1984), the hero actually refuses to speak. In both these films, the hysterical symptom is directly related to questions of SEXUALITY and sexual difference. Other noteworthy contemporary male melodramas are *The Accidental Tourist* (Lawrence Kasdan, 1988) and the films of Australian director Paul Cox – particularly *Man of Flowers* (1983) and *My First Wife* (1984).

Laura Mulvey, 'Notes on Sirk and Melodrama', in *Home is Where the Heart Is*, ed. Christine Gledhill (London: British Film Institute, 1987)

See also: SCORSESE, MARTIN   BC

MALLET, MARILU (1945–)

This prolific filmmaker and writer was born in CHILE. An architecture graduate, Mallet began her career in film during the Popular Unity period, but left the country in 1973 after the military coup that overthrew the socialist government of Salvador Allende. Mallet settled in Montreal, QUEBEC, where she has directed documentaries and worked for television. Two collections of her short stories have been published in French. Her best-known film, *Journal inachevé* (1982), deals with the subjective experience of exile through a highly innovative blend of documentary and fictional devices. Mallet's documentary films reveal the poetry of everyday gestures by their striking ability to capture subjective and collective experience. Her filming is based on improvisations in which protagonists act out their own situations, blending fictional performance with social testimony. Many of her films center on the experiences of immigrants in Canada, particularly *Les Borges* (1977), made for the NATIONAL FILM BOARD OF CANADA, which draws a moving portrait of several generations of a Portuguese family. Her films on Latin America have dealt with the impact of development and change. *L'evangile à Solentiname* (1979) is a rare document of the Christian community set up by Ernesto Cardenal in Nicaragua which was bombed by the Somoza airforce in 1979 as a reprisal against the Sandinista-led insurrection against his regime.

Amuhuelai-Mi (1971); *A.E.I.* (1972); *Donde voy a encontrar otra Violeta* (unfinished, 1973); *Lentement/Slowly* (1974); *Les Borges* (1977); *L'evangile à Solentiname* (1979); *Musique d'Amérique latine* (1979); *Les femmes de l'Amérique latine* (1980); *Journal inachevé/Unfinished Diary* (1982); *Mémoires d'un enfant des Andes* (1985)

Zuzana Pick, 'Chilean Cinema in Exile (1973–1986). The Notion of Exile: a Field of Investigation and its Conceptual Framework', *Framework*, no. 34 (1987)

ZP

MAORI FILM

The Maori, the indigenous people of NEW ZEALAND, have been a popular subject for the lenses of colonist filmmakers ever since the earliest New Zealand feature, *Hinemoa*, was made in 1914. Projected upon them have been all the attributes of the Other – mystery, sensuality, savagery, nobility – with Maori women in particular functioning in numerous romances as symbols both of dangerous yet tameable sexuality and of the 'new' country which must be conquered by the European (Pakeha) settlers. Rudall Hayward was the most prolific of these early directors, but it is believed that his wife, Ramai, a photographer and actor, was the first Maori woman to direct in New Zealand (*Eel History Is A Mystery* [date uncertain]).

As the decades and the film industry have progressed, the portrayal of Maori has become more subtle, with several Pakeha filmmakers – John O'Shea (*Broken Barrier* [1952]), Paul Maunder (*Sons For The Return Home* [1979]), Geoff Murphy (*Utu* [1983]) – making efforts to expose and analyze the underlying racial problems of the country. However, Maori critics still see these directors as working largely within a discourse of domination. For the Maori themselves, appropriation of image is an important issue, tied up with the appropriation of their land and the survival of their culture. The last decade has seen the growth of regular Maori-language television and the first feature films originated and directed by Maori – beginning with Merata MITA's feature-length partisan documentary on the riots accompanying the 1981 Springbok tour of New Zealand, *Patu!* (1984). Barry Barclay's *Ngati* (1987), a deceptively relaxed film about a young part-Maori doctor returning to seek his roots in a community on the isolated East Coast, a community whose land is being threatened by the Pakeha, has met with recognition from indigenous peoples in many parts of the world, as well as being popular with general audiences in New Zealand and showing during Critics' Week at Cannes. Merata Mita has gone on to make *Mauri* (1988), about the confusion that results when one loses one's 'Mauri' or spiritual centre through the process of adapting to Pakeha culture.

Maori culture is traditionally oral, collective, and marae-based: translated into film, this can mean extensive use of the kinds of ritual speech and performance given on a marae (tribal meeting place), together with a tendency to disperse point of view across a large number of characters. Fragments of whaikorero (speeches), waiata (songs) and karakia (prayers) may join together with anecdotes (rather than extended, goal-directed narratives), to re-create the atmosphere of a 'hui' (a large meeting, which may go on for several days, called to celebrate something or to discuss and resolve an issue). It takes status and a high degree of conviction to call a hui, and there is a similar sense of social responsibility in making a film, which takes up huge resources, both in money and in the time and trust of the community.

The ambivalent position of Maori women, in relation both to feminism and to film, can be seen in the fact that many tribes do not allow women to speak on the marae; and although this prohibition does not extend explicitly to film, it does mean that many women face the double barrier of lack of experience in public self-expression and lack of access to the resources necessary for filmmaking.

Barry Barclay, *The Control of One's Own Image* (Auckland: Longman Paul, forthcoming)   AH

MASCULINITY

Masculinity in cinema has been thrown into relief in a number of ways by FEMINIST FILM THEORY. The recurrent drama of 'How to be a real man?' – how, as a man, to place yourself in relation to fathers, mothers, the law, other men, and sexual women – propels the narratives of numerous films across a range of scenarios with differing ICONOGRAPHIES. An academically (and popularly) respected film GENRE such as the Hollywood WESTERN is centrally concerned with certain myths: not just of the hero, but of the white hero, and the conflicting demands of true heterosexual masculinity (heroism) and the constraints of social life. Over the many years when Westerns were made, changing attitudes to the hero and the atmosphere in which a man does what a man's gotta do can be discerned. The same conflicts can also be seen in many other genres, though with differing stresses and resolutions. British war films of World War II assemble socially and regionally disparate groups of men to weld them together as united fighting forces; while the heroes of FILM NOIR usually discover that their initial cynicism, solitude, and distrust of women are fully justified.

While relations between these changing representations and wider social and cultural change have not been fully explored, some generalizations can be made. For example, in western cinemas, white heterosexual masculinity is always the unmarked norm within which a range of class types of masculinity can be differentiated. Black or 'native' masculinity, despite changing stereotypes, constantly usurps virility, and is generally represented as both more sexual and less human. This history of the representation of the black man as body produces particular difficulties for representing middle-class black men, as with Sidney Poitier's role in *Guess Who's Coming to Dinner* (Stanley Kramer, 1967). The AIDS crisis has produced a rash of more sympathetic (though necessarily unhappy) representations of gay men, with MELODRAMAs such as *Parting Glances* (Bill Sherwood, 1985) and *Buddies* (Arthur Bressan, 1985). Arguably, some recent shifts in representations of masculinity can be directly associated with feminism: for example, the late-1970s phenomenon of nurturing men in films featuring white men as mothers, such as *Kramer vs Kramer* (Benton, 1979) and *Ordinary People* (Redford, 1980); or the unappealing current boys-in-men's-bodies group, which includes films like *Big* (Penny Marshall, 1988) and *Vice Versa* (Brian Gilbert, 1988). Representations of masculinity in male action genres in non-western cinemas (SWORDPLAY and KUNG FU films, for instance) have yet to be properly analyzed.

There is considerable debate about whether masculinity is an attribute of people with male bodies, or whether it is more usefully regarded as an attribute of NARRATIVE and spectatorship in cinema. In the latter view, to be a hero necessarily entails occupying a masculine position in the story – initiating action, making things happen – whether the character be male or female. However, if a woman appears in this type of role there is usually a hysterical affirmation of her femininity, or she is constantly marked as 'exceptional'; or the story seems implausible: for example, *Johnny Guitar* (Nicholas Ray, Republic Pictures, 1954); *Seven Women* (John Ford, 1965); and *Coma* (Michael Crichton, 1977). A parallel point can be made about men as objects of sexual desire, where it is argued that the male body can sustain a desiring LOOK (a conventionally feminine position) only if the body in question is clearly pursuing a narrative aim (riding across a frontier, winning a dance contest, defending a community). Otherwise, masculinity is diminished, particularly if unsupported by the sort of MISE-EN-SCENE we find in Wade Hunnicutt's study in *Home from the Hill* (Vincente Minnelli, MGM, 1960), or by the relentless iconography of guns, pipes, hats, horses, and cars which supports so many screen heroes.

This debate can be extended into a discussion of how CLASSICAL HOLLYWOOD CINEMA produces PLEASURE and reassurance for its viewers. Summarized in the question 'Is the gaze male?', this debate focuses on the metapsychology of cinema, in which it has been argued that the spectator is offered a masculine position from which to view; and, further, that the structure of classical Hollywood cinema functions very precisely to reenact – and dispel – masculine anxieties about (and pleasures in) narcissism, fetishism, and voyeurism. There are fierce arguments within feminism about what happens to the female spectator within this model, and about whether this PSYCHOANALYTIC approach to the workings of cinema is useful in the first place.

Throughout the history of cinema there have been representations of the man with a camera, or the man in some way inscribed as a 'looker,' gaining both power and pleasure in his pursuit of sights – from Dziga Vertov's 1929 Soviet avant-garde film *Man with a Movie Camera*; through HITCHCOCK's work; Michael POWELL's scandalous 1960 *Peeping Tom*; and ANTONIONI's *Blow-up* (1966) to the male work of avant-garde filmmakers such as Stan Brakhage and Steve Dwoskin. These privileged cameramen of cinema, to whom a reflection on the nature of the medium is always also a meditation on men looking at women, would certainly seem to support a designation of the practice of cinema as (heterosexual) masculine. Whether this is necessarily the case is a key concern of contemporary FEMINIST INDEPENDENT FILM.

Kobena Mercer and Isaac Julien, 'Race, Sexual Politics and Black Masculinity: A Dossier', in *Male Order*, ed. Rowena Chapman and Jonathan Rutherford (London: Lawrence & Wishart, 1988)

See also: AUDIENCE AND SPECTATOR; MALE MELODRAMA; PORNOGRAPHY   CB

MASQUERADE

The dictionary defines 'masquerade' as 'acting or living under false pretences; false outward show; pretence.' FEMINIST FILM THEORY takes up these everyday meanings of the term in order to interpret the highly sexualized, excessively 'feminine,' screen images of such female STARS as Marlene DIETRICH, Marilyn MONROE, and Diana DORS, seeing them as ironic and parodic commodifications of the female body. When we watch Dietrich as a cabaret performer, for example, we are watching a woman demonstrating the representation of a woman's body. Masquerading doubles representation: flaunting FEMININITY by exaggeration of its accouterments shows that 'femininity' is actually an artifice constructed in and through representation.

As originally developed in the 1920s by psychoanalyst Joan Riviere in her studies of female psychology, 'womanliness as masquerade' referred to the exaggeration by some women of 'feminine' attributes and behaviors as a defense mechanism. The term was introduced into FILM THEORY in 1975 by Claire JOHNSTON, who used it simply in the sense of CROSSDRESSING; but with the development of PSYCHOANALYTIC FILM THEORY, masquerade has taken on more specific meanings.

Film theorist Mary Ann Doane, for example, applies the concept of masquerade to a metapsychology of film, arguing that for women, masquerading can be a form of resistance to patriarchal positioning, in that it holds the cultural construction of femininity at a distance, creating a gap between the woman and the image. In this view, 'womanliness' is a mask that can be put on or taken off, a PERFORMANCE. By destabilizing the image, masquerading confounds the masculine structure of the LOOK, and generates the possibility of the female image being manipulated, produced, and read by women. In other words, the act of putting on femininity with a vengeance suggests also the power of taking it off.

Mary Ann Doane, 'Film and the Masquerade: Theorising the Female Spectator', *Screen*, vol. 23, no. 3–4 (1982)

See also: LOOK, THE   AKo

MAY, ELAINE (1932–   )

The *éminence grise* of Hollywood women directors, if there is one, Elaine May entered show business at the age of six as an actress, spending her childhood on the road with her father's traveling theater company. Her stage partnership with Mike Nichols, renowned for its unique kind of dark psychological comedy, lasted from 1954 to 1961. May then turned to playwriting, film acting roles, and screenwriting. As a valued and much-sought-after 'script doctor,' May has weathered intervals between the films she has directed. Although her films work very much within Hollywood GENRE forms, they often contain somber haunting undercurrents that resonate beyond the work itself. They also feature some of the most derogatory images of women on screen: the basket-case incompetence of the heroine of *A New Leaf* (1971), played by May herself; the unprepossessing young Jewish bride of *Heartbreak Kid* (1972), played by May's daughter. May's disturbing view of women, and her predilection for working through male characters' point of view, bring to mind Lina WERTMULLER, also shaped before feminism, who also had to make her way as a director early on, virtually alone in a film culture inhospitable to women.

Although in her third feature, *Mikey and Nicky* (1976), May works with the male world of two petty mobsters and within FILM NOIR conventions, what is most fascinating about the film is its complex, bitter exploration of friendship – even, perhaps, a sibling bond – and the way it addresses the lifelong emotional destitution of being an unloved child. Unfortunately, the new growth and ambition evidenced by this film were anything but welcomed by the studio, Paramount. *Ishtar* (1987), made at Columbia with the largest budget ever entrusted to a woman director, brought with it correspondingly huge expectations. May turns in this film to the Hollywood male-buddies-on-the-road genre (like the old Bob Hope–Bing Crosby road comedies) – a genre that takes her back to the show business world she knows so well. With the recent shattering box office fiasco (though artistic victory) of *Mikey and Nicky* just behind her and the stakes so high, the pressures must have been enormous in the direction of safe light entertainment. Even so, *Ishtar*, like May's other films, presents beneath its humor a remarkably dark world, where everyone betrays everyone else.

A New Leaf (1971); *Heartbreak Kid* (1972); *Mikey and Nicky* (1976); *Ishtar* (1987)

Barbara Koenig Quart, *Women Directors: The Emergence of a New Cinema* (New York: Praeger, 1988) BKQ

McDONAGH SISTERS

Only two of the four features produced by the McDonagh sisters Paulette (1901–78), Isobel (1899–1982), and Phyllis (1900–78) between 1926 and 1933 survive in almost complete form. Their films depart completely from the indigenous AUSTRALIAN genres and their heroines (played by Isobel under her stage and screen name Marie Lorraine) tend to be innocent victims of paternal machinations which separate them from their lovers until a twist of fate brings them together after much hardship and suffering. Born and educated in Sydney, the McDonagh sisters developed a love of the cinema which brought them into film production at the end of the silent era. Paulette, writer, director, and avid cinemagoer, was critical of the Australian bush comedies for their lack of sophistication, and studied Hollywood techniques for producing more subtle rhythms. After a stint at P J Ramster's acting school, frequented by high society, Paulette hired Ramster to direct their first film, *Those Who Love* (1926), but took over directing to get the results she wanted. With Phyllis as business manager, art director, and publicist, and

> Mary Field (1896–1968) is known for her work in what specific genre?

Isobel in the leading roles, Paulette directed their two surviving silent features *The Far Paradise* (1928) and *The Cheaters* (1930), followed by their final sound epic, *Two Minutes' Silence* (1933). The films were noted for their low budgets, for Isobel's naturalistic acting, and for their lavish settings – which included the McDonaghs' family home. The McDonaghs' attempt to add sound sequences to *The Cheaters* resulted in a disastrous premiere. However, the silent version of the film has been widely screened since the revival of feature production in the 1970s renewed women's interest in the

McDonagh sisters as screen pioneers. Paulette also directed a series of documentaries on Australian sporting heroes, including the racehorse Phar Lap. Her decision to remain in Australia rather than follow many of her colleagues to Hollywood marked the end of her cinema career. It was to be another forty-six years before a woman would again direct a feature in Australia – Gillian ARMSTRONG's *My Brilliant Career* (1979).

Those Who Love (1926); *The Far Paradise* (1928); *The Cheaters* (1930); *Two Minutes' Silence* (1933)

Andree Wright, *Brilliant Careers: Women in Australian Cinema* (Sydney: Pan Books, 1986)   FC

MEAD, MARGARET (1901–78)

US anthropologist Mead (1901–78), known by social scientists for her works on gender and culture in the South Pacific and by the general public for her outspoken views on women's rights, nuclear proliferation, race relations, and educational reform, was also a pioneer in the field of ETHNOGRAPHIC FILM. Mead, an extraordinarily thorough notetaker, was drawn to film because of what she perceived as its capacity to record data neutrally. In 1936, while gathering material for a study of gesture in Balinese society, Mead and her husband, Gregory Bateson, filmed 22,000 feet of film which later became a series of short traditional documentaries, complete with explanatory voice-overs. In a famous debate with Bateson, Mead argued that the ethnographic camera should not move and should fade into the background 'so as to give people access to the material, as comparable as possible to the access you had.' Bateson took the other view, arguing for an active use of the camera and saying that the presence of a camera inevitably transformed events being filmed.

Mead filmed tens of thousands of feet of film during the course of her life; two-thirds of it remain uncatalogued, though, due to lack of funds, at the US Library of Congress. She also staunchly advocated a wider use of film in anthropology, encouraging young filmmakers, writing film reviews, and disparaging the 'verbalist bias' she said afflicted anthropology and limited anthropologists to their notebooks. In 1977 the American Museum of Natural History, where she was curator emeritus of ethnography, organized the Margaret Mead Film Festival of ethnographic films in her honor. The festival was so successful that it is now held every year.

A Balinese Family, Bathing Babies in Three Cultures, Childhood Rivalry in Bali and New Guinea, First Days in the Life of a New Guinea Baby, Karba's First Years (with Gregory Bateson, 1952); *Trance and Dance in Bali* (with Bateson and Jane Belo, 1952); *Margaret Mead's New Guinea Journal* (produced and directed by Craig Gilbert, 1968)

Margaret Mead, 'Visual Anthropology in a Discipline of Words', in *Principles of Visual Anthropology*, ed. Paul Hockings (The Hague: Mouton, 1975)   JSh

MELODRAMA

Early SILENT CINEMA inherited and developed many of the features of nineteenth-century stage melodrama. Lack of dialogue produced a highly stylized language of bodily gesture, facial expression, and music. With an emphasis on spectacle, sensational plots, and a MISE-EN-SCENE in excess of naturalism, silent melodrama presented a distinctive if restricted repertoire of character types. These types, recurring in plots revolving around a conflict between innocence and villainy, were gendered almost to the point of caricature. D W GRIFFITH's work exemplifies these tendencies, particularly in those films which personalize political and historical themes. This personalization, brought about by soliciting sentimental and emotional responses, tends to mark the GENRE as feminine in comparison to a masculine genre like the WESTERN or thriller. This might seem to be at odds with feminist approaches, particularly combined with the caricature of sexual difference in which woman functions as victim caught between hero and villain. Yet it is precisely here, where caricature and personalization meet, that feminist interest is engaged. It is by viewing the excessive as evidence of 'trouble,' specifically the trouble that FEMININITY poses to patriarchy, that analysis can begin.

As melodrama was incorporated into SOUND cinema the codification became less theatrical, but elements contributing to an intensification of the emotional persist. Although melodrama has been an important feature of many NATIONAL CINEMAS – of CHINA and INDIA, for example – the attention of FEMINIST FILM THEORY has been directed largely at Hollywood family melodramas of the fifties, particularly those directed by Vincente Minnelli, Douglas SIRK, Max OPHULS, and Nicholas Ray. It is argued that these films frequently criticize the very subject matter and social context they seem to be validating – the bourgeois family. Everything repressed at the level of dialogue and plot (inadmissible desires and psychic violence) 'returns,' it is argued, in mise-en-scène and MUSIC. Signs of excess, instead of being interpreted as stylistic indulgence, are thus read symptomatically – as symptoms of the troubled chaos that underlies the shiny surface of bourgeois life and Hollywood cinema. Feminist critiques focus on the way films such as *Letter from an Unknown Woman* (Max Ophuls, Universal, 1948), *Now, Voyager* (Irving Rapper, Warner Bros., 1942), and *Stella Dallas* (King Vidor, Goldwyn, 1937) can be read as exposing the violence involved in an accommodation to the 'correct' codes of femininity, the price to be paid for a failure to take up a recognizable position in the family scenario.

On a more positive note, the pleasures of melodrama have provided a way into more general theorizations of PLEASURE and female spectatorship. Similarly, FEMINIST INDEPENDENT FILM has used melodramatic elements either to comment quite selfconsciously on the genre, or to develop a female point of view or a cinematic language that is feminine: for example, Yvonne RAINER (*Lives of Performers* [1972]), Chantal AKERMAN (*Jeanne Dielmain, 23 Quai du Commerce, 1080 Bruxelles* [1975]), Sally POTTER (*Gold Diggers* [1983]).

Christine Gledhill (ed.), *Home is Where the Heart Is: Studies in Melodrama and the Woman's Film* (London: British Film Institute, 1987)

See also: FASSBINDER, RAINER WERNER; SOAP OPERA; WOMAN'S PICTURE; XIE JIN   LS

MENKEN, MARIE (1910–71)

US painter turned filmmaker Marie Menken made her first film as a tribute to the sculptor Noguchi. *Visual Variations on Noguchi* (1945) is a rhythmic study of the curved forms of Noguchi's sculpture and the first work of AVANT-GARDE FILM based on individual vision and human movement mediated by the camera. Menken and her husband Willard Maas, along with Maya DEREN, formed the core of the US independent cinema movement in New York in the 1940s. Menken's work established what avant-garde critic and filmmaker Jonas Mekas calls the 'third period' of 'film poetry free of obvious symbolism and literary influences' (the first two having been the French Surrealist, as represented by Germaine DULAC, and the American experimental, as represented by Maya Deren). Menken's influence is perhaps most evident in the work of Stan Brakhage, one of the best-known figures of the US avant garde: whole passages of Brakhage's films can be traced to Menken's *Notebook* (1962), *Glimpse of the Garden* (1957), and *Arabesque for Kenneth Anger* (1961). *Notebook* is viewed by women filmmakers in the independent tradition as a primary source extolling the values of the commonplace and the personal as apt subjects for film, and using the rhythm of the human body (rather than the tripod or steadycam) as the central parameter of CAMERA MOVEMENT. Menken's underground classic *Hurry! Hurry!* (1957) hilariously follows the movements of sperm cells under a microscope in their random and futile dance: the gentle wit and irony of this film foreshadows a great many films by women which undermine traditional notions of sexual empowerment.

Visual Variations on Noguchi (1945); *Hurry! Hurry!* (1957); *Glimpse of the Garden* (1957); *Dwightiana* (1959); *Eye Music in Red Major* (1961); *Arabesque for Kenneth Anger* (1961); *Bagatelle for Willard Maas* (1961); *Mood Mondrian* (1961); *Notebook* (1962); *Moonplay* (1962); *Here And There With My Octoscope* (1962); *Go! Go! Go!* (1963); *Drips and Strips* (1965); *Sidewalks* (1966); *Lights* (1966); *Watts with Eggs* (1967); *Excursion* (1968)

Marie Menken and Willard Maas, special issue, *Filmwise*, no. 5–6 (1987)   MKe

MESZAROS, MARTA (1931–   )

Mészáros returned to HUNGARY in 1946 from the Soviet Union, where her family had emigrated in 1936, later returning again to study film. In 1938 her father, the sculptor László Mészáros, was arrested and interned in the Soviet Union, never to reappear. *Diary for My Children* (1982) illustrates the centrality of this early childhood trauma for Mészáros's creative work, followed closely as it was by the death of her mother in a typhoid epidemic. In many of her films, as she says herself, Mészáros explores the possibility of establishing stable and caring relationships based on mutual respect and companionship, but also on the necessity for the individuals involved to have space and autonomy. Although Mészáros rejects some of the connotations of the feminist label, her focus has remained, since her first film *The Girl* (1968), the aspirations, the daily struggles, the despair and hopes of women: 'It is woman's state of being subjected to men, on historical, emotional and social levels, that I am concerned with. . . .

Marta Mészáros's *Diary for My Children*

Women have great difficulty switching over to discovering themselves: they always attempt to gain their emancipation through men.' The female protagonists in Mészáros's films, on the contrary, are forced by a situation requiring decisive action or change to come to an understanding of themselves and the direction of their lives. Strong friendships between women often assist this process of self-discovery.

Mészáros is one of very few women directors, not only in EASTERN EUROPE but worldwide, to have made a consistent body of feature films. Although briefly championed by western feminists during the 1970s, she is not as widely known in the West as her work merits. Her two *Diary* films with actress Zsuzsa Czinkóczi have at last brought her international acclaim and long-deserved acceptance in Hungary. *Diary for My Loves* (1987) describes her struggles to be accepted as a woman film student, with interviewing bodies insisting she must surely want to become an actress, not a film director. The same film deals very courageously with the events in Hungary in 1956, before the process of democratization had lifted the taboo on this subject.

Eltávozott nap/The Girl (1968); *A holdudvar/Binding Sentiments* (1969); *Szép lányok, ne sírjatok/Don't Cry, Pretty Girls* (1970); *Szabad lélegzet/Riddance* (1973); *Örökbefogadás/Adoption* (1975); *Kilenc hónap/Nine Months* (1976); *Ök ketten/The Two of Them (Women)* (1977); *Olyan mint otthon/Just Like at Home* (1978); *Útközben/On the Move* (1979); *Örökség/The Heiresses* (1980); *Anna/Mother and Daughter* (1981); *Napló gyermekeimnek/Diary for My Children* (1982); *Délibábok országa/The Land of Mirages* (1983); *Napló szerelmeimnek/Diary for My Loves* (1987); *Little Red Riding Hood – Year 2000* (1989)

Mary C Gentile, 'Márta Mészáros and *Women*: Learning to Accept Multiplicity', in *Film Feminisms: Theory and Practice* (Westport, CT: Greenwood Press, 1985)   BE/ER

METRO-GOLDWYN-MAYER *see* MGM

MEXICO

Mexican national cinema, with rare exceptions, has been a male-dominated industry. Female filmmakers have had to endure major patriarchal opposition, hostility, and professional jealousy, which has confined them from the earliest days.

Cinema had its beginnings in Mexico in 1896, when Gabriel Vayre introduced silent films to Mexican audiences. This era is represented by documentaries about historical meetings and popular festivities of the time, such as *Porfirio Diaz and William Taft in El Paso Texas, 1908*, filmed by Enrique Rosas. With the growing internal unrest felt throughout Mexico, the revolution of 1910 brought to a close the opulent decadence of the 'Porfiriato,' better known as 'la belle époque.' Salvador Toscano and Enrique Rosas became well known as the leading documentarists of the period. By 1916, the documentary made way for fictional dramas as the early twentieth century saw the beginning of industrialization and continuous internal strife.

During the 1920s, Hollywood began to dominate much of the Mexican film industry. Themes of the revolution were substituted for cosmopolitan urban narratives in an attempt to dispel the erroneous world image which some Mexican nationals felt the country had acquired during the 1910 revolution. One of the outstanding films of the silent era is *La banda del automovil gris* (Enrique Rosas, 1919), a serial of fifteen episodes based on real-life events that took place in Mexico City. In 1919 Mimi Derba, a character actress in Mexican cinema, formed the Azteca Film company in collaboration with Enrique Rosas. She wrote three of the films produced by the company, including the only film she directed, in 1917, *La tigresa*. After Azteca Film went out of business, Derba fell into obscurity until her reappearance in 1931 in Mexico's first talking film, *Santa* (Antonio Moreno), in which she played a secondary role.

The early thirties plunged the Mexican film industry into a crisis caused mainly by the limitation of foreign markets and a poor distribution system. The presidency of Lazaro Cardens (1934–40) was marked by significant social changes which included a closer relationship between government and film industry. The administration supported the construction of Cinematografía Latino Americana Sociedad Anonima (CLASA) film studios. Melodramatic themes of prostitution and incest emerged in Mexican films of this period in which female characters wrestled in moral conflict with the established order. *La mujer del puerto* (Arcady Boytler, 1933) best exemplified this new genre of film. Sergei Eisenstein's influence could be noted in films like *Janitzio* (Carlos Navarro, 1934) and *Redes* (Fred Zinnemann, 1934), social allegories that valorized the indigenous culture in an attempt to recapture its lost heritage. *Alla en el rancho grande* (Fernando de Fuentes, 1935) was the financial success that opened up a foreign market in North America and paved the way for a popular NATIONAL CINEMA and a genre of films known as 'rancheras.' This type of film personified the classic phallocentric representation of the macho male. The female protagonist, on the other hand, was defined solely in relation to his image, as she remained subordinate, unable to articulate her desire. In this period Eva Liminana, a Chilean national known as 'La Duquese Olga,' initiated her film career in 1933 by writing a screenplay for *La sangre manda* (Jose Bohr). In 1942 she wrote, produced and directed her first and last film, *Mi lupe y mi caballo*, which was not released until two years later. Soon after this, Liminana retired from films.

The 1940s initiated a period in Mexican cinema known as 'La epoca de oro' (the golden age), in which the Mexican film industry benefited from North American financial assistance and industrial development. World War II proved beneficial, reducing competition from foreign markets: many of the Hollywood war films produced during this period proved of little interest to a Latin American public. After 1947, rural Mexican popular themes were replaced by urban melodramas. Emilio Fernández 'El Indio' stands out as a creative force who gained international recognition with his films, including *Flor Sylvestre* (1943), *Maria Candelaria* (1943), and *La perla* (1945). The forties also marked the beginning of a 'star system' with, among others, Dolores del Rio, Arturo de Cordova, Cantiflas, Jorge Negrete, Pedro Armendariz, Pedro Infante, and Marian Felix. Hollywood continued to influence Mexican cinema, which on many occasions appeared to mimic North American GENREs. *La devoradora* (Fernando de Fuentes, 1946); *La mujer de todos* (Julio Bracho, 1946); *La diosa arrodillada* (Roberto Gavaldon, 1947); *Dona diabla* (Tito Davison, 1949); and *La mujer que yo ame* (Tito Davison, 1959) conflated elements of FILM NOIR, the WOMAN'S PICTURE, detective and urban MELODRAMAs. They were films in which women in an environment of moral decay were posited as passive, masochistic figures on the edge of mental instability. The genre of 'cabaret' films which grew in popularity during this period included MUSICALS and melodramas that focused on the objectification of women. Narratives of incest, loss of virginity, social alienation, and suicide were prevalent in these films, best exemplified in *Amor de la calle* (Ernesto Cortazar, 1949); *Perdida* (Fernando Rivero, 1949); and *La mujer del puerto* (Emilio Gomez Muriel, 1949). During the forties and early fifties, Matilde LANDETA was the only active female filmmaker in the Mexican film industry.

The National Cinematographic Bank, founded in 1942 during the presidency of Avila Camacho, helped provide a more stable environment for the Mexican film industry, but also monopolized production and distribution of films. The 'golden age' of Mexican cinema came to an end after World War II, when Hollywood reestablished its foothold in LATIN AMERICA. By the end of the forties, Churubusco film studios had been purchased by RKO in collaboration with Mexican financiers. North American consortia, with the backing of Mexican industrialists, controlled 80 percent of theaters in Mexico. The 1950s brought another reorganization of the National Cinematographic Bank, and by the end of the decade the state once again purchased back Churubusco studios. Given the restrictive production climate, independent production companies, such as 'Estudios America,' sprang up with the support of foreign capital to produce low-budget films which could be finished in two or three weeks. 1950, with 124 films made, was the year of highest cinematographic production, surpassing even ARGENTINA. In 1950 Carmen Toscano wrote, produced, and directed a very important feature-length documentary film of the revolution: *Memorias de un mexicano/Memories of a Mexican*, based on footage taken by her father (Salvador Toscano) of the 1910 revolution. In 1977, in collaboration with Matilde Landeta, Toscano began filming *Ronda revolucionaria/Revolutionary Watch*, which was never completed due to her failing health.

In 1953 *Raices* (Benito Alazraki), filmed on location in Yucatan and Chiapas, reopened the autochthonous theme, initiated the low-budget art film, and signaled the beginning of an independent cinema whose films began to gain international recognition. During the late 1940s and early 1950s, the genre of 'cabaret' films reached its peak. In most of these films women were either confined to the private sphere of domesticity and self-abnegating motherhood, or made to frequent the urban underground world of prostitution. During the presidency of Adolfo Ruiz Cortines censorship again surfaced, imposing a contradictory climate of morality. While cabarets were forced to close early and prostitution was openly persecuted, 'erotic' films emerged in the form of *La fuerza del deseo* (Miguel Delgado, 1955) and *Juventud desenfrenada* (Jose Diaz Morales, 1955), in which actresses like Ana Luisa Peluffo appeared nude for the first time to a receptive public.

The sixties mark the beginning of experimental and independent filmmaking in Mexico. At the same time, low-budget serials patterned after Hollywood were mass produced in an effort to give the film industry an inexpensive formula with which to entertain. Fictional dramas continued to be popular, and films of prostitution persisted. Luis Buñuel's presence retained its strong influence over the film industry in such films as *Nazarin* (1958); *Viridiana* (1961); and *El angel exterminador/The Exterminating Angel* (1962). After Matilde Landeta's last film, *Trotacalles* (1951), there is a complete eclipse of women filmmakers until the late sixties with the emerging presence of Marcela FERNANDEZ VIOLANTE. Esther Morales Galvez directed a short film, *Pulqueria 'La Rosita'*, in 1964. In 1963, Carmen Toscano organized the Mexican film archives which were later to be housed in the Cineteca Nacional in Mexico City. In the same year the first national film school, Centro de Estudios Cinematograficos (CUEC), was founded in Mexico City: Marcela Fernández Violante is its first female director.

With Gustavo Diaz Ordaz in office, censorship again surfaced, and 1968 remains a memorable year of violence, with student uprisings against the policies of the Ordaz administration. With the advent of Luis Echeveria's presidency, the film industry relaxed some of the censorship imposed by the previous administration, and films like *Canoa* (Felipe Cazals, 1975) were allowed to be shown. This film critiqued the social isolation of a small community outside Puebla, which in 1968 led to violence between the townspeople and the visiting students. During the seventies, the State once again took control of the Cinematographic Bank and Churubusco film studios, and established three main production companies known as Corporacion Nacional Cinematografica (CONACINE) and Corporacion Nacional Cinematografica de Trabajadores y Estado (CONACITE I & II). In 1978 the state production companies were sold and the National Cinematographic Bank was dissolved. During the early seventies the second film school in Mexico City, Centro de Capacitacion Cinematografica (CCC), was built: here filmmakers like Humberto Hermosillo, Bussi Cortes, and Maryse SYSTACH were trained. One of the darkest periods for the Mexican film industry was the presidency of José Lopez Portillo, when he appointed his sister, Margarita Lopez Portillo, as director of film, radio, and television. Poorly advised, she alienated the film community with her courtship of foreign filmmakers and investors.

> A scarlet woman reflects: 'In Britain, an attractive woman is somehow suspect. . . . Beauty and brains just can't be entertained: someone has been too extravagant.' Who was she?

In this period, however, women's voices began to be heard in some short films: *Acaso irreparable* (Dorotea Guerra, 1976); *El encuentro* (Rosario Hernandez, 1976); *La misma vieja historia* (Maribel Varga, 1977–8); *Naturaleza muerta* (Adriana Contreras, 1979); *Los Buenromero* (Bussi Cortes, 1979). Other short political feminist films and documentaries that appeared during this period are: *La carta de deberes y derechos* (1976); *El tiempo del desprecio* (Margarita Suzan, 1978); *Cosa de mujeres* (Rosa Marta Fernández, 1978); and *Vicios de cocina* (Beatriz Mira, 1978), which examines the routinized tedium and sexual oppression of a housewife. *Rezar* (Maripi Saenz de la Calzada, 1979) investigates themes of control, sexism, and the subordination of women inside a religious institution of learning. Berta Novarro is a politicized social documentarist whose work is best exemplified by *Nicaragua: los que haran la libertad* (1978); *Cronica del olvido* (1979); and *Mexico, historia de su poblacion* (1987). *Rompiendo el silencio* (Rosa Marta Fernández, 1979) addresses the social problem of rape in Mexico City. *La vida toda* (Carolina Fernández, 1978) examines the social conditions of female indigenous domestics employed in the capital.

The 1980s brought a new wave of women filmmakers involved in documentaries, short subject and fictional feminist feature films addressing sexual politics, prostitution, abortion and other sociopolitical issues. *Espontanea belleza* (1980) and *Lugares comunes* (Lilian Liberman, 1983) delve into female/male sexual politics. *Preludio* (1982); *Desde el cristal con que se mira* (1983); *No le pedimos un viaje a la luna* (Maria del Carmen Lara, 1986); *Yaltecas* (Sonia Fritz, 1984); *Historia de vida* (Adriana Contreras, 1981); *Monse* (Gloria Ribe, 1980); and *No es por gusto* (Maria Eugenia Tames and Mari Carmen de Lara, 1981) address the social conditions of prostitutes in Mexico City. The phenomenon of Maria Elena Velasco, better known as 'La India Maria,' remains an anomaly within the film industry. In the seventies she became a television personality by portraying the character known as 'simpleminded Maria' (the indigenous, often illiterate, woman who is relocated from country to city). In the past few years Velasco has directed films in which she stars in the character of 'Maria.' This has led film critics to condemn the portrayal of 'Maria' as pejorative toward women: nevertheless, Velasco's films – such as *Ni de aqui ni de alla* (1987) – have broken box office records.

At present, the Mexican film industry is confronting political and financial crisis, partly due to monetary inflation in the country. Foreign producers have again leased Churubusco film studios, and Hollywood film stars have purchased many of the independent studios.

265

Carl J Mora, *Mexican Cinema: Reflections of a Society, 1896–1980* (Los Angeles: University of California Press, 1982)

See also: COCINA DE IMAGENES; LATINAS; NOVARO, MARIA; SEQUEYRO, ADELA   CH-N

MGM

Promoted as the home of the stars, the Metro-Goldwyn-Mayer studio appeared in the USA in 1924 from a merger of three firms. The parent company, Loew's, began in 1904 and developed into a prominent New York City theater chain. MGM weathered the Depression and, as a publicly owned firm, experienced several serious proxy battles in the 1950s and 1960s. In 1969 Kirk Kerkovian gained control, selling off assets and rearranging the firm several times (including purchasing United Artists).

In the 1930s through the 1950s, in the heyday of the HOLLYWOOD STUDIO SYSTEM, MGM's picture policy was that investments produced profits: the per-picture budget averaged higher than any other Hollywood studio. To organize production, between 1933 and 1948 MGM used several associate producers who tried to maintain production units from film to film. MGM, however, routinely employed multiple writers and editors on one film, and retakes, sometimes by another director, were common after extensive previewing. A major force at MGM during this period was Editorial Supervisor Margaret Booth, who appears to have had significant control over EDITING and protected the Hollywood style of continuity editing. MGM was one of the studios that groomed women to be STARS; its major box office attraction in the early 1930s was Marie Dressler. Other stars who spent significant time at MGM were Greta GARBO, Joan CRAWFORD, Norma Shearer, Greer Garson, and Judy Garland.

John Douglas Eames, *The MGM Story: The Complete History of Over Fifty Roaring Years* (New York: Crown, 1976)   JaS

MIKESCH, ELFI (1940–)

An Austrian-born filmmaker living in WEST GERMANY, Elfi Mikesch is loosely connected with the movement known as NEW GERMAN CINEMA. Having trained as a photographer, she moved to Berlin in the sixties and worked under the pseudonym 'Oh Muvie.' From photography she crossed over into filmmaking and worked extensively as a cameraperson. She has since become closely associated with West German lesbian and gay cinema, frequently working on the films of Rosa von Praunheim. Since the late seventies, Mikesch has also been directing her own films. Her early films tended to fall between the DOCUMENTARY and AVANT-GARDE traditions of filmmaking. *Ich denke oft an Hawaii* (1978), for example, presents fragmentary images of a real-life family, moving between the fantasy world and everyday reality of the sixteen-year-old daughter. *Was soll'n wir denn machen ohne den Tod* (1980), is a lyrical documentary about two women in an old people's home which foregrounds the needs of the elderly; while her next film, *Macumba* (1982), is a poetic, nonlinear film which examines the conventions of storytelling.

More recently, Mikesch has become interested in the theme of sadomasochism. Her first cinematic exploration of this subject came in 1983 with the making of *Das Fruehstueck der Hyaene*, an unsettling portrait of one woman's masochistic fantasies. This has been followed by *Verfuehrung: die grausame Frau* (1985), a collaboration with filmmaker Monika Treut. An exploration of the images of women in the literature of de Sade and Sacher-Masoch, *Verfuehrung* has achieved almost cult status in West Germany, and proved popular in both the United States and Australia. Mikesch has been described by German critics as one of the most formally innovative German women filmmakers. In particular she has gained a reputation for her poetic mode of expression, especially in her documentary films, and her beautiful camerawork. She has also been involved in the design of FRAUEN UND FILM, Europe's only feminist film JOURNAL.

Ich denke oft an Hawaii/I Often Think of Hawaii (1978); *Execution – A Study of Mary* (1979); *Was soll'n wir denn machen ohne den Tod/What Would We Do Without Death* (1980); *Macumba* (1982); *Die blaue Distanz/The Blue Distance* (1983); *Das Fruehstueck der Hyaene/The Hyena's Breakfast* (1983); *Verfuehrung: die grausame Frau/Seduction: The Cruel Woman* (1985)

Julia Knight, *Women and the New German Cinema* (London: Verso, 1990) JK

MILLETT, KATE (1934–)

US feminist author, sculptor, and activist Millett had become known for her manifesto – originally a PhD thesis – *Sexual Politics* when she produced the film *Three Lives* in 1970. An early and straightforward feminist DOCUMENTARY, it features three American women – a young married middle-class woman, an older woman, and a young bisexual woman in the New York theater world – talking to camera about their lives. The film was produced by an all-woman crew and contains all of the elements cited by Julia Lesage in her anatomy of the feminist documentary film: 'biography, simplicity, trust between woman filmmaker and woman subject, a linear narrative structure, little self-consciousness about flexibility of the cinematic medium.' Louisa Irvine, who directed *Three Lives*, has added that Millett's work with cage sculptures also influenced the film: 'We wanted to show three cultural cages.'

Three Lives (1970)

Julia Lesage, 'The Political Aesthetics of the Feminist Documentary Film', in *Films for Women*, ed. Charlotte Brunsdon (London: British Film Institute, 1986) JSh

MIRO, PILAR (1940–   )

After early studies in law and journalism, Pilar Miro graduated in scriptwriting from SPAIN's Official Film School in Madrid. She became a teacher at this institution and in 1960 joined Spanish television (TVE) as a program assistant. In 1963, at the age of twenty-three, she became Spain's first woman television director. Her first feature film, *La peticion* (1976), was followed in 1979 by *El crimen de Cuenca,* which made her internationally known. Her next two films confirmed her as a major director: *Gary Cooper que estas en los cielos* (1980) and *Hablamos esta noche* (1982). Perhaps the most controversial film personality in Spain, Miro has left a decisive and indelible mark on contemporary cinema. From 1983 to 1986, as director of the Film Department of the Ministry of Culture, she undertook the legal reform of national subsidies to film production: this is undoubtedly responsible for the recent boom in Spanish cinema. She left the Ministry of Culture to direct a feature based on Goethe's novel *Werther* (1986). Shortly after this she became director of TVE, but resigned after a political scandal which exposed the misogynistic situation faced, even in freer post-Franco Spain, by women who attain a certain position of power. She is currently working on a new film project.

La peticion/The Engagement Party (1976); *El crimen de Cuenca/The Cuenca Crime* (1979); *Gary Cooper que estas en los cielos/ Gary Cooper Who Art in Heaven* (1980); *Hablamos esta noche/Let's Talk Tonight* (1982)

Ronald Schwartz, 'Pilar Miro', in *Spanish Film Directors (1950–1985): Twenty-one Profiles* (Metuchen, NJ: Scarecrow Press, 1986) RB

MISE-EN-SCENE

Literally meaning 'staged,' the term mise-en-scène is used in theater to refer to the contents of the stage and their arrangement; in FILM THEORY, however, it refers to the contents of the film frame. This includes the arrangement of the profilmic event (elements of the 'real world' which are set up for the camera, or which the camera captures – persons, settings, COSTUMES, props). Mise-en-scène also covers what the spectator actually sees on the screen – the LIGHTING, ICONOGRAPHY, and composition of the film image, for example; and the relationship between onscreen and offscreen space created by the framing of the image, in particular through the 'mobile framing' produced by the use of telephoto (zoom) lenses or CAMERA MOVEMENT. Mise-en-scène produces meaning in films, even if only by providing visual information about the fictional world of a narrative. In some films, however, mise-en-scène can be a site of extraordinarily complex and subtle meanings, as is the case in the films of Hollywood director Douglas SIRK. In CLASSICAL HOLLYWOOD CINEMA more generally, certain notions of FEMININITY may be set up through the costumes, lighting, and framing of female characters: for example, in key-lit and backlit lingering soft-focus CLOSEUPS, Amy Jolly, the Marlene DIETRICH character in Josef von STERNBERG's *Morocco* (Paramount, 1930), is constructed as a spectacle – glamorous, alluring, but ultimately enigmatic in her femininity. Films may also carry other sorts of messages through their mise-en-scène. For women AUDIENCES in particular, the 'staging' of particular styles of interior decor and FASHION may not only assist in merchandizing certain products, but may contribute more generally to an IDEOLOGY of CONSUMERISM.

David Bordwell and Kristin Thompson, *Film Art: An Introduction* (Reading, MA: Addison-Wesley, 1979)

See also: ART DIRECTION; COLOR; SPECIAL EFFECTS   AKu

MITA, MERATA (1942–   )

Merata Mita was producer and director of NEW ZEALAND's most controversial documentary, *Patu!* (1984); but with the completion of *Mauri* (1988) she became the first MAORI woman ever to direct a feature film. Born at Maketu, in the Bay of Plenty, she is of the Ngati Pikiao tribe and, one of nine children, received a traditional Maori upbringing. She trained as a home science teacher, but moved into filmmaking through being asked to do liaison work for Pakeha (European) film crews working on Maori subjects. A large number of her projects have been made as collaborations, often with men, because, she says, it has been easier to get equipment and money that way. Always political in her work, she has made documentaries about union disputes and Maori issues, culminating in *Patu!*, shot during the riots surrounding the Springbok tour of New Zealand in 1981. *Patu!* does not pretend to be an objective DOCUMENTARY: the violence in it is enhanced by a highly wrought soundtrack, and it draws parallels between the situation in South Africa and the state of race relations in New Zealand. The fact that it was funded in part by public money created considerable controversy, and its release was delayed for several years; but it remains a powerful interpretation of a highly important event in New Zealand's recent history.

Merata Mita hesitates to describe herself as a feminist director, because she feels that the energies of Maori women are still directed toward basic cultural survival rather than toward the refinements of western feminist theory. Nevertheless, her feature *Mauri* has a very strong grandmother figure as its central character, and it is her opinion that the best roles for women in New Zealand cinema will be those created by Maori filmmakers, because Maori women still have both physical and spiritual power, whereas Pakeha women have lost a great deal of their spirituality.

Karanga Hokianga (1979); *Bastion Point: Day 507* (co-d., 1980); *The Hammer And The Anvil* (co-d., 1980); *Keskidee – Aroha*

(co-d., 1981); *The Bridge: A Story Of Men In Dispute* (co-d., 1982); *Patu!* (1984); *Mauri* (1988)   AH

MIZOGUCHI, KENJI (1898–1956)

Mizoguchi began his career as an assistant director in 1922, and began directing a year later. By the 1930s he was focusing on the situation of women. Because of this, in JAPAN he has been labeled a feminist – a usage of the term, however, not to be equated with its western sense of proponent of women's rights, equality, or liberation. Mizoguchi's feminist stance is not political; rather, it falls within traditional Japanese notions of worship and indulgence of women. Mizoguchi's ideal woman accepts what fate decrees for her. The ideal is to become selfless, like the character Taki in *Taki no Shirato/The Water Magician* (1933), and to comply with what is expected of her – or negative consequences will follow, as in *Saikaku Ichidai Onna* (1952). Throughout this film, Mizoguchi includes Buddhist sutras in his soundtrack. This technique, together with the use of the long shot – which clearly states that the human condition is part of a larger whole – reinforces Mizoguchi's basic attitude to women.

From a western feminist perspective, Mizoguchi's woman is always victimized. However, the Japanese woman's concept of love encourages dependence, motherly indulgence, forgiveness, and self-sacrifice. The filmmaker's art merely reflects this.

The eighty or more films directed by Mizoguchi include: *Naniwa Ereji/Osaka Elegy* (1936); *Utamaro o Meguru no Onna/Utamaro and His Five Women* (1946); *Waga Koi wa Moenu/My Love Burns* (1949); *Saikaku Ichidai no Onna/ The Life of Oharu* (1952); *Ugetsu Monogatari/Ugetsu* (1953); *Sansho Dayu/Sansho the Bailiff* (1954)

Audie Bock, *Japanese Film Directors*, rev. edn (Tokyo: Kodansha International Ltd, 1980)   JYY

MODERNISM

Modernism is a term applied to various developments in the visual arts and the media during the early to late twentieth century, developments having in common a move from figurative representation to abstraction, and a self-consciousness about form and materials. In film, modernism encompasses the montage innovations of Sergei Eisenstein, the open and broken NARRATIVE of directors such as Jean-Luc GODARD, the rise of ART CINEMA, and the film experiments of artists such as the Dadaists and Surrealists and of individuals such as Andy Warhol. Modernism also embraces AVANT-GARDE FILM as a distinct artistic practice with its own history. Basically, modernism emphasizes idea and process over content: in the visual arts, for instance, attention is drawn to the material qualities of the media used rather than to the image itself or to the content of the end result. Modernist films stress visual presentation of narrative, though often rejecting classical or realist narrative in the first place. The idea of a modernist cinema based around a politics of style gives rise to the concept of COUNTERCINEMA. In reality, however, it is impossible clearly or neatly to define what modernist film or art is, for it comprises many – often conflicting – strands and styles.

Feminist film theorist E Ann Kaplan argues, however, that it is important to acknowledge the influence of modernism on FEMINIST INDEPENDENT FILM. She draws attention to the work of filmmakers such as Germaine DULAC and Maya DEREN, who can be seen as pioneers of modernism in cinema; and to the rise of a more politically direct feminist cinema involving figures such as Chantal AKERMAN, Agnes VARDA, Claudia WEILL, and Margarethe von TROTTA. It is also important to recognize the contribution of feminist fine artists to modernist film: Mary Kelly's involvement in the LONDON WOMEN'S FILM GROUP and in *The Nightcleaners* (Berwick Street Film

Collective, 1975), for example, or the installation works of groups of artists such as Feministo. Modernism's relationship to feminism also keys into important theoretical debates revolving around STRUCTURALISM, POSTSTRUCTURALISM, PSYCHOANALYTIC FILM THEORY, and POSTMODERNISM.

E Ann Kaplan, *Women and Film: Both Sides of the Camera* (London and New York: Methuen, 1983)   JRy

MOLINA, JOSEFINA (1936–)

Born in Cordoba, after early studies in political science Josefina Molina became the first woman to obtain a degree in directing from SPAIN's Official Film School. In 1967 she went to work for Spanish television (TVE) as an assistant director, and a year later made her directorial debut with *Aqui Espana* and *Fiesta*. Having adapted and directed more than fifty TV dramas, Molina is also active as a film critic on radio, and as a theater director. Of her huge body of TV work, particularly outstanding is a 1984 series on the life of *Teresa de Jesús*, which won her acclaim from critics and public alike and quickly became a classic of Spanish television.

Aside from many shorts, Molina's filmography includes: *Vera . . . un cuento cruel/Vera . . . a Cruel Story* (1973); *Cuentos eróticos* (one episode, 'The Lindenblossom Tea', 1979); *Funcion de noche/ Evening Performance* (1981); *Esquilache* (TV drama, 1988); *A Doll's House* (1971); *Eleonora* (1971); *Hedda Gabler* (1975); *Anna Christie* (1976); *Teresa de Jesús* (1984)   RB

MONROE, MARILYN (1926–62)

Actress, STAR, and 1950s icon, Monroe graduated through pinups and television commercials to make her film debut in the late forties with a string of minor parts in low-budget pictures. In 1950 she appeared in two major features as the 'ideal' dumb BLONDE: in *The Asphalt Jungle* (John Huston, Twentieth Century-Fox) she is a gangster's moll; in *All About Eve* (Joseph L Mankiewicz, 1950) she is Miss Caswell, a theater critic's wide-eyed plaything. Her role as the sexy woman with a childlike quality was to be the pervasive Monroe star image across many films, including *Niagara* (Henry Hathaway, Twentieth Century-Fox, 1953); *The Seven-Year Itch* (Billy Wilder, Twentieth Century-Fox 1954) – in which director Wilder provided voyeurs with the famous subway grating scene – and *Some Like It Hot* (Billy Wilder, Twentieth Century-Fox, 1959). In *Some Like It Hot*, Monroe demonstrates her talents as a comic actress, yet remains true to the star image created for her; which raises the question of the tension between the cinema's construction of a star image and the performer's creation of a character, discussed in relation to Monroe's role in *Gentlemen Prefer Blondes* (Howard Hawks, Twentieth Century-Fox, 1953) by Richard Dyer in his book *Stars* (London: British Film Institute, 1979). Marilyn Monroe is one of the very few female stars – perhaps the only female star – to appeal equally to female and male audiences.

Monroe's last major film was *The Misfits* (John Huston, 1961). Her image, and particularly her SEXUALITY, disguised the real acting ability she displayed in films such as this and the earlier *Bus Stop* (Joshua Logan, Twentieth Century-Fox, 1956). Her 'dumb blonde' persona actively worked against appreciation of her as a serious actress, despite her own attempts to improve her craft by studying 'The Method' at Lee Strasberg's Actors' Studio in New York. At the same time her very public private life and her marriages to celebrity figures such as baseball player Joe DiMaggio and playwright Arthur Miller contributed yet further to an emphasis on her qualities as a SEX GODDESS.

The Monroe image has become a major icon – the blonde with molded hairstyle, red lips, and partly open mouth has appeared everywhere, and the vast array of representations of her image – on posters, as photographs, as 'art product,' as book – is central to western culture today. Yet this instantly recognizable image becomes increasingly confusing and distanced in terms of Monroe the woman. The continuing controversy over the circumstances of Monroe's death and her friendship with the Kennedys has further overshadowed her abilities as an actress and brought about conflicting views concerning Monroe's own awareness, and use, of her sexuality.

Gloria Steinem, *Marilyn* (London: Victor Gollancz, 1987)   *JRy/PB*

MONTREAL INTERNATIONAL FESTIVAL OF FILMS AND VIDEOS BY WOMEN

Founded in 1985, this is a WOMEN'S FILM FESTIVAL of consistent quality and increasing significance for feminist film culture in CANADA and QUEBEC. Held annually in June, the festival selection is a result of a year's work by directors Carolynn Rafman-Lisser and Albanie Morin. The festival screenings take place in two small state-of-the-art cinemas, complete with high-definition video projection, in the heart of Montreal's busy and glamorous latin quarter. Although finances have been rocky in the past, and competition from the Montreal World Film Festival and the Montreal Festivale de Nouveau Cinéma make it

> In 1903, Edwin S Porter directed the first of the US cinema's negative representations of black people. It was an adaptation of which novel?

difficult for the women's festival to attract high-profile films and guests, this festival is now established as an annual event which emphasizes the discovery of new films and rising filmmakers. It presents a rigorously feminist but eclectic selection that includes drama, DOCU-MENTARY, and AVANT-GARDE video and films, with an appropriate attention to Canadian films; and attracts feminist writers, curators, exhibitors, and distributors from across North America, as well as a loyal Montreal audience. There are public prizes for est feature and best short film, and a jury prize for documentary films and videos.

KA

MOROCCO

With the distribution and import of films left to market forces, commercial cinema has exerted a strong influence since the early days of cinema in Morocco, one of the ARAB countries. A filmmaker as gifted as Hamid Benani, for example, has not yet managed to direct a second feature film. His *Wechma/Traces* (1970) tells the story of a young orphan in a backward society, in which female characters are either tender mothers or prostitutes. Souheil Benbarka provided another milestone in Moroccan cinema with the beautiful and moving *Mille et une mains/One Thousand and One Hands* (1977), which exposes the ruthless exploitation of carpet workers by the bourgeoisie. Women's predicament is the subject chosen by one of Morocco's most innovative filmmakers, Moumen Smihi. *El Chergui* (1976) is about a woman who drowns during a ritual aimed at preventing her husband from taking a second wife. A similar indictment of a backward society whose traditions paralyze women's aspirations is the focus of Smihi's more experimental feature *44, ou les récits de la nuit/44, or The Tales of the Night* (1982). Other Moroccan filmmakers include Farida Bourquia, Morocco's first woman film and TV director, who in *Al Jamra/The Ember* (1984) describes in NEOREALIST style the persecution of a group of pariahs living in a cave. Ahmed Maanouni, director of the innovative *Alyam, Alyam/O the Days* (1978) and *Transes/Trances* (1981), blends poetic documentary with fiction. Mustapha El Derkaoui chooses a hermetic style to express the alienation of a woman singer manipulated by men in *Les beaux jours de Sheherazade/The Beautiful Days of Sheherazade* (1982).

The theme of dispossession is a favorite of Moroccan cinema: heroes find themselves dispossessed of their beloved (*Le Coiffeur des quartiers pauvres/The Hairdresser of the Poor Neighbourhoods* [Mohmed Reggab, 1982]) or of their land (*Zeft/Tar* [Tayyeb Siddiki, 1984]), or of their belongings (*Le grand voyage/The Great Voyage* [Abdel Rahmane El Tazi, 1982]). Dispossession is also the theme of *Arayiss Min Kasab/Straw Dolls* (Jilali Farhati, 1981), a touching indictment of what a Muslim society does to a woman. Little Aisha is deprived of free choice at the age of twelve, when she is married off to her cousin. Widowed at eighteen, she loses custody of her children on refusing the traditional path of marrying her brother-in-law. Society's cruel double standard is tempered by women's traditional solidarity in misfortune: Aisha's mother-in-law stands by Aisha against her own son. This film owes a lot to Farida Belyazid, its scriptwriter-producer; but Belyazid apparently takes a different path in her first feature film as director: *Bab Ala Al Sama/A Door on the Sky* (1988) seems to preach the virtues of a return to Islam as a solution for women, and for a generation torn apart. The heroine is the center of a spiritual interrogation about national identity and traditional, as against modern, values. Significantly, in 1988 the heroine of a film made by a woman chooses an Islam of tolerance, love, and charity; while in a film made by a man twelve years earlier (*El Chergui*) a woman unveils herself before a stranger, an unthinkable act of defiance: it seems that a number of Moroccan intellectuals – including feminist writers – are bowing before Islamic fundamentalism. Censorship at home notwithstanding, other directors, such as Souheil Benbarka, have taken a more internationalist path: *La guerre du pétrole n'aura pas lieu/The Oil War Won't Happen* (1975), an ambitious film about the oil-producing countries, 'the richest and yet the poorest of this planet,' was banned by five successive ministers of information. His *Noces de sang/Blood Wedding* (1980), adapted from Lorca's novel, and *Amok* (1982), about apartheid, both use international stars. Benbarka had to freeze the building of an ambitious complex of studios and laboratories, Le Dawliz, to become director of CCM, the Moroccan Cinema Center, a state body which is playing an increasing role in helping to foster local talent. Meanwhile Moroccan technicians and studios are catering for an increasing number of commercial European and American films, most of which embody racist attitudes toward Arab-Islamic culture.

See also: AFRICA   HS

MOTHERHOOD

Motherhood became a focus of feminist literary and film studies in the 1980s. While mothers obviously figure in films of all kinds, worldwide, the question of motherhood and cinema has been rather more narrowly addressed in FEMINIST FILM THEORY, which has pointed to the mother's absence from, or marginality in, traditional Hollywood male genres. Attention has also been directed at the Hollywood WOMAN'S PICTURE, since there at least plots dealing with mother–child relationships can be found. A variety of approaches exist within such studies: STRUCTURALIST research analyzes the maternal MELODRAMA by looking at what happens to mother figures in the NARRATIVE as a whole, or to mother–child relations in particular Hollywood films – *Stella Dallas* (King Vidor, Goldwyn, 1937) and *Mildred Pierce* (Michael Curtiz, Warner Bros., 1945) have been much discussed in these terms; IDEOLOGICAL studies examine mother figures in relation to motherhood and the nuclear family as a patriarchal institution; and PSYCHOANALYTIC studies explore how film TEXTS play out processes of separation and individuation, or problems around identification.

As we enter the 1990s, however, such conventional mother-images are being disturbed. In the West at least, 'motherhood' is no longer a secure 'given,' and this has created immense cultural anxiety, evident in a deep ambivalence about this shift, about the loss of a secure, mythic mother – support, nurturer, inspirer. Most startling, perhaps, in this context is the fetal imagery appearing in popular film and literature, coinciding with dramatic advances in male-dominated reproductive technologies.

E Ann Kaplan, *Motherhood and Representation: Feminism, Psychoanalysis and the Maternal American Melodrama, 1830 to 1980* (London and New York: Routledge, 1989)   *EAK*

MULVEY, LAURA (1941–)

A feminist filmmaker and theorist working in BRITAIN, Mulvey has situated her work in the meeting between feminist politics, psychoanalytic theory, and AVANT-GARDE aesthetics influential in the 1970s. Most widely known for her path-breaking essay 'Visual Pleasure and Narrative Cinema' (1975), she has co-directed with Peter Wollen a number of important avant-garde films.

Mulvey began by writing articles for *Seven Days* and *Spare Rib*, including a controversial piece on fetishism in the work of Allen Jones, an artist who made a name from a sculpture show called 'Women as Furniture.' In 1972 she co-organized the Women's Event at the Edinburgh Film Festival with Claire JOHNSTON and Lynda Myles, and co-edited a book, *Douglas Sirk*. In 1974 she made her first film with Wollen, *Penthesilea, Queen of the Amazons*. Starting from a play by Kleist, the film explores the relations between myth and history, asking whether a new order of language (represented in fantasy by the AMAZONS) can come into history through feminist and class struggle, or whether it can exist only in a space and time 'outside.' It was also concerned with the way images of woman have been used to define the idea of such a space as an archaic stage either of history (Matriarchy) or of individual experience (the pre-Oedipal relationship to the mother).

'Visual Pleasure and Narrative Cinema' took up the question of how male fantasies about women and castration structure the LOOK and PLEASURE in cinema, both through the conditions of spectatorship in the film theater and also in the representation of sexual difference on the screen. Although it was taken up in FEMINIST FILM THEORY as a timeless theoretical statement, the essay was written as a strong polemic clearing a space for a different cinema ('It is said that analyzing pleasure, or beauty, destroys it. That is the intention of this article'). In her subsequent films, especially *Riddles of the Sphinx* (1977), which returned to the issue of myth and maternity, Mulvey has explored the possibilities for a 'different' pleasure, using stories always grounded in histories of struggle.

Mulvey's name has been so tightly associated with the critique of 'visual pleasure' (and with what she herself called the 'aesthetic "scorched earth policy"' of the 1970s marxist-feminist avant-garde) that the richness of her work has not always been appreciated. However, it may be more useful now to think of it as an ongoing reflection on myth, memory, and the processes of change – how 'to build from one historical context to another without the endless loss inherent in the "tradition of the new".'

(Co-directed with Peter Wollen): *Penthesilea, Queen of the Amazons* (1974); *Riddles of the Sphinx* (1977); *Amy* (1980); *Frida and Tina* (1982); *Crystal Gazing* (1982); *The Bad Sister* (1983)

Laura Mulvey's publications include: 'Visual Pleasure and Narrative Cinema', *Screen*, vol. 16, no. 3 (1975); *Frida Kahlo and Tina Modotti*, catalogue of exhibition co-organized with Peter Wollen (London: Whitechapel Art Gallery, 1982);

'Changes: Thoughts on Myth, Narrative and Historical Experience', *History Workshop*, no. 23 (1987)   MMo

MURATOVA, KIRA (1934–)

Having had the films she directed banned and her career interrupted in the 1970s, Muratova emerged with glasnost in the mid 1980s as one of the most important revelations of the 'proscribed' SOVIET cinema. A pupil of Sergei Gerasimov at the State Film School VGIK, she co-directed her 1961 diploma short with her husband Aleksandr Muratov. Her first directorial solo, *Short Encounters* (1967), in which she successfully played the leading part of a high-ranking provincial-town official, established her poetic, somewhat Chekhovian, dramatic style. The film – a study of a triangle – got only a limited release. Her subsequent two scenarios were turned down. The next film, *Long Farewells* (1971) – an exploration of the mother–son relationship – was banned as 'too gloomy'; and *Among Grey Stones* (1983) was so drastically reedited that Muratova chose to withdraw her name from it.

Muratova, who always writes her own scripts, puts her female protagonists into situations of suspense and emotional insecurity. They have jobs and careers, but no personal happiness or peace of mind. Their longing for a stable existence is thwarted by the adventurous spirit of men: husbands, lovers, sons. This restless spirit, however, wins out in later films: in *Getting to Know the Wide World* (1979), every character, male or female, leads a nomadic existence, and the misfits of earlier films return as vagabonds in *Among Grey Stones*. This disturbing, strikingly concrete and at the same time ephemeral world is created through free-floating plots, unsettling cinematography and editing, and a weaving together of sound and image.

U krutogo yara/By the Steep Ravine (short, 1961); *Nash chestnyi khleb/Our Honest Bread* (1964); *Korotkie vstrechi/Short Encounters* (1967); *Dolgiie proshchaniia/Long Farewells* (1971, released 1986); *Poznavaia belyi svet/Getting to Know the Wide World* (1979); *Sredi serikh kamney/Among Grey Stones* (directed pseudonymously as Ivan Sidorov, 1983); *Peremena uchasti/Change of Fortune* 1987)

Victor Boiovitch, 'Retrospective d'un âme', *Catalogue of the Festival International de Films de Femmes (Créteil), 1988*   ME

MURPHY, PAT (1951–)

Pat Murphy is a prominent filmmaker in IRELAND whose work reflects a strong engagement with FEMINIST FILM THEORY and FEMINIST INDEPENDENT FILM. She began her career in film whilst still at art school in London, producing a short called *Rituals of Memory* (1977). Her projects on returning to Ireland include *Maeve* (1981) and *Anne Devlin* (1984), both financed largely from Irish sources and setting the agenda for an excavation of Irish identity and history from a feminist perspective. While *Maeve* is set in contemporary Northern Ireland, *Anne Devlin* attempts to retrieve a woman's place in history through focusing on events in early-nineteenth-century Ireland. Issues of class and gender are emphasized. Traditional female roles are represented, but these images are gradually eroded to reveal Anne Devlin as an involved participant in historical events. The motif of women's silence, heralded at the film's opening, is repeated throughout. Refusing language, associated with a male 'voice' and controlling vision, Anne resorts to silent defiance in the face of colonial authority, emphatically asserting her own choice in her history. This film's conventional NARRATIVE structure charts the roots of a history which have resonances in the present, returning to a history to which women have hitherto been denied access.

Murphy's earlier film, *Maeve*, represents a break with dominant narrative form, exploring the need for feminist cinema to challenge conventional structures of storytelling and representation.

Anne Devlin, by Pat Murphy

In this experimental narrative, the heroine voices her alienation from a male republican tradition, and charts her efforts to construct an identity in relation to received notions of Irish history and culture. The broader question of feminism's relation to republicanism (also the subject of *Mother Ireland* [Derry Film and Video Collective, 1988]) is refracted through Maeve's exploration. Murphy's next project, *Fire in a Concrete Box*, from a script written by feminist writer Evelyn Conlon, has received Arts Council development funding.

Rituals of Memory (1977); *Maeve* (1981); *Anne Devlin* (1984)

Claire Johnston, '*Maeve*' and 'Interview with Pat Murphy', *Screen*, vol. 22, no. 4 (1981) SM

MUSIC

There are two kinds of music in film: diegetic and nondiegetic, or extradiegetic. Diegetic music is also called source music, since its source can be seen or accounted for by the diegesis, or the fictional world of the story. Music that does not emerge from this fictional world, such as violins that play during romantic scenes or music that accompanies credits or titles, functions nondiegetically. This is sometimes referred to as background music, a term that is less accurate than it is symptomatic of how music – particularly in mainstream cinema – is often assigned a 'background' function.

Many kinds of music have been used in cinema – ethnic, jazz, electronic, atonal, and rock. But the most influential by far, certainly in the West, has been 'classical' western art music. Even before the advent of SOUND, classical scores were used to lend a legitimacy to film and to ennoble it aesthetically. During the heyday of CLASSICAL HOLLYWOOD CINEMA, scoring was heavily influenced by nineteenth-century romanticism, and followed its basic forms and compositional style. Especially important here was the work of Richard Wagner. Like Wagner, many film practitioners believed that music should play a passive 'feminine' role in the dramatic work and that it should be a vehicle for creating and sustaining emotional effects – and little more. Primers warned budding composers to keep their scores from interfering with the more 'important' task of film narrative, and advised them that the best music was music that the auditor would not notice.

This feminization of film music (an argument that can also be applied to other aspects of the soundtrack) has been extended at the level of metaphor and theory. Theoretically music, like most conceptions of FEMININITY, has been associated with unsteadiness and duplicity, since the effects it produces are so often emotional, irrational, and intensely pleasurable. For this, traditional commentators have disparaged film music (labeling scores 'hysterical' or 'seductive,' especially if they exceed their 'proper' subservient 'place'), while some feminists have found in these same properties a way to consider music as a momentary refuge from traditional forms of patriarchal language. As if to support this connection, music plays an important role in two film genres that have had tremendous appeal to female audiences historically, namely the MUSICAL and the MELODRAMA.

See also: OPERA; ROCK MUSIC   CF

MUSICAL

A film GENRE that combines narrative with MUSIC and DANCE numbers, the musical is known for its heavy stylization, its 'staginess,' and its selfconscious form. Long ignored by film scholars who have considered it an 'escapist,' 'frivolous,' and 'girlish' genre, the musical finally came to be recognized as an object of serious critical inquiry in the 1970s.

Production of the Hollywood musical peaked in the late 1920s, when heavily melodramatic features such as *Applause* (Rouben Mamoulian, Paramount, 1929) and *Hallelujah* (King Vidor, MGM, 1929) were produced. In the 1930s, Depression musicals included Busby Berkeley films at WARNER BROS. and the Astaire/Rogers cycle at RKO. It is MGM, however, Hollywood's largest and most financially secure studio, that is usually regarded as 'home' to classical musicals, producing such lavish examples as *Meet Me in St Louis* (Vincente Minnelli, 1944); *Singin' in the Rain* (Stanley Donen, 1952); and *The Wizard of Oz* (Victor Fleming, 1939). In the 1950s and 1960s, musicals were adapted from established Broadway hits: *Oklahoma* (Fred Zinnemann, Magna/Rodgers and Hammerstein, 1955); *My Fair Lady* (George Cukor, Warner Bros., 1964). Since then production has declined, and the genre's con-

> A film with an unusual heroine was made twice in Hollywood; first at Universal in 1934 and again at Universal in 1959. What is its name, and why is the heroine unusual?

ventions have changed dramatically: the once-classic 'boy meets girl' formula has been replaced by a multi-character cast (*Nashville* [Robert Altman, 1975], *Hair* [Milos Forman, 1979]); and generic boundaries have become increasingly blurred (*The Big Chill* [Lawrence Kasdan, 1983], *Aria* [various directors, 1987]). It remains to be seen how the proliferation of music video will affect the genre, but its influence on films like *Flashdance* (Adrian Lyne, 1983) already suggests that the exaggerated 'escapist' style of earlier musicals might be on the rebound.

Gender shapes Hollywood musicals in several ways. Narrative resolution often centers on the romantic pairing of two seemingly irreconcilable people (*Top Hat* [Mark Sandrich, RKO, 1935] and *Grease* [Randal Kleiser, 1978]). Moreover, their differences are often established in terms of class and aesthetic preference, with female characters representing the 'highbrow' art forms and lifestyles that musicals often attack as stuffy and pretentious

(Ginger Rogers and Olivia Newton-John in the above films). The musical's focus on PERFORMANCE also raises issues for feminists, since women are so crucial to the genre's idea of spectacle. Finally, there is the simple fact that the musical – in its various forms in different NATIONAL CINEMAs has enjoyed great popularity with female audiences (in INDIA and EGYPT, for example). Unlike MELODRAMA (another genre associated both with music and a large female following), however, the musical has neither prompted much debate in FEMINIST FILM THEORY, nor – Chantal AKERMAN's *The Golden Eighties* (1986) notwithstanding – inspired feminist filmmakers.

Rick Altman (ed.), *Genre: The Musical* (London: Routledge & Kegan Paul, 1981)

See also: DANDRIDGE, DOROTHY; LAMARQUE, LIBERTAD; ROCK MUSIC   CF

MUSIDORA (1889–1957)

One of the greatest stars of SILENT CINEMA in FRANCE, Musidora (born Jeanne Roques) owes her reputation to the part of Irma Vep (an anagram of vampire) in Louis Feuillade's popular adventure serial *Les Vampires* (1915–16). There she created France's first cinematic VAMP, a sexy villainess in black leotards – a persona she carried (though without the leotards) into Feuillade's *Judex* (1916), and exploited in contemporary stage acts. Irma Vep caught the imagination of popular audiences and of the Surrealists, who worshipped her 'sub-versive' EROTICISM. Among her close friends were COLETTE, Germaine DULAC, Louis Delluc, and Marcel L'Herbier; she dazzled Paris with her flamboyant lifestyle.

An exceptionally talented and cultured woman, Musidora was more than simply a fashionable actress. She wrote a first novel at fifteen, and was a painter, dancer, novelist, and songwriter, as well as a playwright. Last but not least, she was a filmmaker with her own production company. After adaptations of Colette's *Minne* and *La Vagabonde*, and a third film based on an original script by Colette (*La Flamme cachée* [1918]), she directed four films which showed her taste for real locations and stylistic experimentation; these rarely met with popular success. Musidora was crowned 'queen of the cinema' in 1926, but her film career ended with the coming of sound (save for a short compilation film in 1951). She went on writing and, after 1946, worked at the Cinémathèque Française. Musidora's legend as sexually alluring muse has endured, but the importance of her other persona as talented and courageous filmmaker and artist was recognized when her name was claimed by the association of women who organized the first WOMEN'S FILM FESTIVAL in Paris in 1974.

Musidora's filmography includes: as director/scriptwriter: *Minne* (1916, unfinished); *La Vagabonde* (1917); *La Flamme cachée* (1918); *Vicenta* (1919); *Pour Don Carlos* (1920); *Sol y sombra* (1922); *La Tierra de los toros* (1924); *La Magique Image* (1951)

Francis Lacassin, *L'Avant-scène du cinéma, no. 108*; *Musidora* (1970)   GV

NAIR, MIRA (1957–)

Mira Nair made a remarkable debut with the international success of her first feature, *Salaam Bombay!* (1988), a documentation of street life in Bombay which follows the adventures of a young runaway boy who arrives in the city and survives on his wits among a community of lowlife characters. A tour de force of direction which combines compassion and humor, the film has been a significant box office success in both INDIA and the West – a major breakthrough in distribution terms – and has won many accolades, including the new director's award in Cannes in 1988 and an Oscar nomination in 1989. Working with Sooni Taraporevala on the screenplay, Mira Nair set up the series of improvisational theater workshops with street children in Bombay through which the film was developed, and found and trained her key actors. Profits from the film will be plowed back into a foundation to help educate homeless children in Bombay.

Born in Orissa, East India, and educated in Simla and Delhi University, Mira Nair won a scholarship in 1976 to Harvard, where she studied sociology and cinema and met her cinematographer husband, Mitch Epstein. Her early work was in DOCUMENTARY, including a controversial film on Bombay's cabaret dancers, *India Cabaret* (1985). She lives in New York and is currently working on a film about Indians settled in the USA.

Jama Masjid/Street Journal (1979); *So Far from India* (1982); *India Cabaret* (1985); *Children of Desired Sex* (1987); *Salaam Bombay!* (1988)   RT

NARGIS (1929–81)

Nargis was a key film star in INDIA in the 1940s and 1950s whose screen persona encompassed a range of models of FEMININITY in post-Independence India, and who herself played out some of its most marked contradictions. Her roles ranged from coy coquette to educated independent 'westernized' career woman. She was a powerful screen presence and talented actress who combined extraordinary dignity with a rebellious joie de vivre and, although she was in some ways deeply conservative, her intelligence, outspokenness, and forceful independence made a significant mark. Nargis is particularly remembered for her role in the all-time classic *Mother India* (Mehboob Khan, 1957), playing a resilient peasant woman who struggles against all odds to defend her self-respect, and finally kills her own son to defend the honor of the women of her community.

Born in north India and brought up in Bombay, a fourteen-year-old Nargis – who wanted to study medicine – was pushed unwillingly into films by her ambitious courtesan mother. From the reaction of her schoolfriends Nargis soon experienced the stigma that attached to women working in the film industry. She was an immediate box office success, but with her professional and personal partnership with actor/producer/director Raj Kapoor she shot to superstardom. The couple worked closely on a number of Indian cinema's greatest classics, notably *Awaara/The Vagabond* (Raj Kapoor, 1951) and *Shree 420/Mr 420* (Raj Kapoor, 1955), and their legendary romance was the focus of obsessive public

Nargis in *Mother India*

interest: they were an internationally feted glamorous young couple; but as he was a married man the affair was considered decidedly scandalous. She retired from acting in 1957 following her marriage to actor/producer Sunil Dutt but, in addition to her work as both mother and charity worker, remained involved in film industry activities as a respected senior figure, campaigning through her friendship with Indira Gandhi for better conditions for filmmakers. In 1980 she entered politics as a member of the Rajya Sabha (Upper House of Parliament). *RT*

NARRATIVE

While this term is widely used as a synonym for 'story,' in FILM THEORY it has more specialized meanings. Inspired by STRUCTURALIST studies of literary and folk narratives – studies which presuppose that individual stories are expressions of underlying structures or ground rules common to large groups of narratives – film theorists have looked at narrative structure in film, focusing especially on CLASSICAL HOLLYWOOD CINEMA, but using methods which can be applied also to other types of narrative cinema. Hollywood's version of narrative REALISM is associated, among other things, with a particular kind of ordering of narrative events, or plot structure: the story moves from an initial state of equilibrium in the fictional world; this is disrupted by a problem of some sort – an 'enigma' – that sets the narrative in motion; the ensuing events unfold in a logical sequence; this leads ultimately to the resolution of enigma(s) and narrative closure.

In addition to cause–effect logic and narrative closure, a key feature of realist narrative is the function, or agency in the plot, of characters – fictional individuals whose desires, motives, and personal traits move the story along: for events to appear logical, characters must seem plausible. The logic of narrative events,

279

and the plausibility of characters and their agency in these events, contribute to the verisimilitude, or lifelike quality, of realist narrative. Verisimilitude is powerfully served when this type of narrative structure is given expression through cinema, with its capacity to produce images resembling the 'real world.' In actuality, however, cinema's appearance of reality is an artifice, an effect of the interaction of cinematic codes such as MISE-EN-SCENE, EDITING, LIGHTING. Together, these codes create a coherent and plausible visual setting for the fiction, while always remaining unobtrusively subservient to the demands of the narrative.

FEMINIST FILM THEORY is interested in looking at narrative structure in cinema for what it can reveal about the function or agency of female characters in films, about the place of female characters in the plot, and about female characters' control (or lack of it) of the story through narrative point of view. It is also interested in how more abstract notions of FEMININITY and female SEXUALITY may govern plots and resolutions in films. For example, in *The Big Sleep* (Howard Hawks, Warner Bros., 1946), a classic FILM NOIR, the initial disruption – which gets Philip Marlowe (Humphrey Bogart) into the ambit of the Sternwoods – is the disappearance of Shawn Reagan, aide to the the ailing paterfamilias. But immediately Marlowe enters the Sternwoods' mansion, the story turns to a quite different problem: the enigma of female sexuality, here in the form of Vivian Sternwood (Lauren BACALL) and her sister Carmen (Martha Vickers). The search for the missing Reagan soon gets sidetracked into a quest around the two women – Vivian especially – as told from the detective hero's point of view. Female characters motivate the narrative, therefore, but at the same time become its object. Alternative approaches to female agency, narrative viewpoint and narrative closure have been attempted in FEMINIST INDEPENDENT FILM – in the work, for example, of Sally POTTER and Bette GORDON. Potter's short film *Thriller* (1979), for instance, retells the story of Puccini's opera *La Bohème* from the HEROINE Mimi's point of view. The narrative 'enigma' becomes Mimi's death – how and why? – and is investigated by Mimi herself, who becomes 'the subject, not the object, of this story.'

Pam Cook (ed.), *The Cinema Book* (London: British Film Institute, 1985)

See also: TEXT   AKu

NATIONAL CINEMA

The idea of 'national cinema' in traditional film history tends to be a US-centric construct: it means non-Hollywood (and conversely, each country defines its own cinema against Hollywood). National cinemas also tend to be equated with groups of directors (Italian cinema = Rossellini, Fellini, ANTONIONI. . . ; BERGMAN = Swedish cinema) or movements (WEIMAR CINEMA and NEW GERMAN CINEMA for Germany, the Popular Front and the NEW WAVE in France, the BRITISH DOCUMENTARY MOVEMENT, EALING STUDIOS and the BRITISH NEW WAVE for Britain), leaving huge unexplored gaps between periods and individuals. These auteur- or movement-based definitions, however, are largely restricted to Europe. Other parts of the world remain more nebulous: labels such as 'Indian cinema' or 'Latin American cinema' not only designate, on the whole, just a few individuals or works, they also erase large differences between provinces or countries.

Invariably, too, the English-speaking history of 'national cinemas,' such as it is, defines them overwhelmingly as the province of high art rather than of popular culture. This is partly a function of the stranglehold of American distributors on worldwide exhibition, which lets only a handful of non-anglophone films reach cinema screens in Britain and the USA. It also has to do with a reluctance on the part of film audiences and historians alike to engage with the indigenous popular cultures of continental European and of non-European countries. And the concentration on high art – which tends to be male and white – often elides contributions made by, and/or representations of, women and nonwhite or minority ethnic groups. Nonsexist and nonracist histories of national cinemas which take into account the economic basis of their industries, their indigenous genres, national stars, and popular culture still remain to be written.   GV

NATIONAL FILM BOARD OF CANADA

The National Film Board of CANADA (NFB) was established by an Act of Parliament in 1939 under the direction of John Grierson. Its mandate, 'to interpret Canada to Canadians,' was facilitated not only by the production of films, but also by the establishment of distribution offices in hundreds of communities across the country. The films were given out free to any individual or group who requested them. Needless to say, the Board was stupendously successful in getting its product used, and at least two generations grew up believing that Canadian film *was* the NFB. Although Grierson is sometimes praised for hiring a half dozen women as producers/directors during World War II, he is also on record as saying that film production was an area 'where [women] had ideas above the station to which it had pleased God to call them.' Women in the Board tended to be confined to short documentaries and children's films (for which they were paid far less than the men filmmakers) and the animation of native legends.

Nevertheless, the unique situation of the NFB as the principal source of pretelevision films in the farflung regions of the country gave those films and filmmakers an opportunity for influence which exceeded comparative opportunities elsewhere. Thus for Canadians who grew up in the first decades after World War II, films by women such as *Peoples of the Potlatch* (Laura Boulton, 1944), *Terre de nos aieux* (Jane Marsh, 1943), and *Glooscap Country* (Margaret Perry, 1961) have become part of a collective cultural unconscious. Moreover, the Board was a valuable training ground for women in the profession, and the single source of permanent employment for women filmmakers in the country, employing for over twenty-five years such staffers as Anne-Claire POIRIER and Kathleen SHANNON. To a significant extent, such women filmmakers had the freedom to generate their own projects on subjects of their own choosing, and the luxury of production budgets that were consistently higher than any independent woman filmmaker could ever dream of. In 1975 the NFB created a new opportunity for women filmmakers with the founding of STUDIO D, a section dedicated to making films by and about Canadian women.

D B Jones, *Movies and Memoranda* (Ottawa: Canadian Film Institute/ Deneau Publishers, 1981)

See also: LEAF, CAROLINE; NATIVE CANADIAN FILM; POOL, LEA; SINGER, GAIL   KA

NATIVE AMERICAN FILM

Since the beginning of fiction filmmaking, the approximately 250 existing native American and Inuit tribes in north America have been the subject, or perhaps the object, of countless Hollywood WESTERNs depicting 'Indians' in a negative light, as well as of many ETHNOGRAPHIC FILMS. Not until the 1970s did they get a chance to speak back.

In the wake of native American takeovers at Wounded Knee and Alcatraz, the US and Canadian governments began funding native American training programs in radio and television, as well as independent film projects. Tribal communications societies formed in Canada; film and video series were made throughout the United States, many with native American staff and consultants, and the Native American Public

Broadcasting Consortium (NAPBC) was formed. During the 1970s the first television series presenting a native American critique of STEREOTYPES in the media, *Images of Indians*, was broadcast in the USA. Two festivals – the American Indian Film Festival in San Francisco and the Native American Film and Video Festival in New York – began screening work rarely distributed through mainstream channels and broadcasting networks. As one Seattle video documentarian, Sandra Sunrising Osawa, director of *The Black Hills Are Not For Sale* (1981), observed: 'Our problem is not that we are stereotyped, although this is true. The real problem is that for most non-Indians we are invisible.'

In the 1980s, under the Reagan administration, funding grew scarce and the number of projects decreased. Still, many tribes – notable examples include the Muscogee Creek Nation (Oklahoma) and the Ute Indian tribe (Utah) – have developed their own audiovisual departments with tribal money, or have helped independents within the tribes obtain money, most often for educational projects.

Female native Americans face the same obstacles – severe poverty, racism in the media – as do their male colleagues, with the added obstacle of sexism. Thus there are few independent female native American filmmakers, Osawa being an exception. Generally, women work in radio and television, or participate on productions headed by men. Although the problems of women do not occupy center stage in native American films – tribes' problems with the white government, economic woes, and other concerns have loomed larger – women do figure prominently in many films. They often speak with the voice of tradition, explaining to the viewer a threatened skill, art, or way of life. Girls' initiation rites have also been a popular theme, and an array of films containing discussions of tribal matrilineality implicitly or explicitly challenge the sexism of the dominant white culture.

Of particular interest are films by Osawa; and also *Annie Mae, Brave Hearted Woman* (Lan Brooke Ritz, 1979); *Concerns of American Indian Women*, a 1977 Public Broadcasting Service (PBS) documentary; *The Enchanted Arts: Pablita Velarde* (Irene-Aimee Depke, 1977); *Great Spirit Within The Hole* (Chris Spotted Eagle, 1983); *People of the First Light Series* (1979); *Seasons of a Navajo*, a 1984 NAPBC/PBS film; *A Weave of Time* (1986), directed by Susan Fanshel.

Elizabeth Weatherford and Emilia Seubert (eds), *Native Americans On Film and Video*, volumes I and II (New York: Museum of the American Indian, 1981 and 1983)

See also: NATIVE CANADIAN FILM   JSh

NATIVE CANADIAN FILM

Native filmmakers are few in CANADA. Where they have been active, however, their role has been significant in the rebuilding of communities where identity and values have been lost. Their films and videos stimulate native communities and inform the outside world of their plight. Most native filmmakers received their training at the NATIONAL FILM BOARD OF CANADA (NFB) which, during the 1960s, conducted two two-year training sessions for six to eight potential filmmakers at a time. From these training sessions a number of filmmakers have remained active: Buckley Patewabano, from the Mistassinni community in the James Bay area of Quebec, makes films supported by organizations in the area which document the community's cultural aspects, and was active in helping to install local radio stations; Bob Charlie, who lives in the Yukon territory in northwest Canada, works with a number of communities in his area, often with the support of the Canadian Broadcasting Corporation (CBC); Mike Mitchell, from St Regis, Quebec, was formerly the chief of his community; Willy Dunn, from Montreal, best known for his film *Ballad of*

Which US avant-garde filmmaker brings together Quo Vadis and Rebecca of Sunnybrook Farm in her 1984 film Some Phases of an Empire?

Crowfoot, is a singer and writer as well as a filmmaker; and Gil Cardinal is active in the area around Edmonton, in the province of Alberta. The original training sessions did not create any women filmmakers – Barbara Wilson, in the first group, did not continue. The most significant native woman filmmaker in Canada today, however, is Alanis OBOMSAWIN. Carol Giddes, a young filmmaker from the Yukon who made Doctor, Lawyer, Indian Chief with the NFB's STUDIO D, was trained in the film program at Concordia University.

In Frobisher Bay, in the far north, the CBC has designated specific hours for native programming. These programs are often made by members of the communities. The animation films made in this context are noteworthy, filmmakers again trained by the NFB. Two festivals – one at Pincher Creek, Alberta, which has twice organized events, and a new, small festival in Montreal – have had retrospectives of native filmmaking, as did the Festival of Amiens, France, in 1987.

See also: NATIVE AMERICAN FILM   JL

NAZI CINEMA

Hardly a film was made during the National Socialist period in GERMANY which could be said to be free of some sort of propagandist purpose. The Nazis discovered film was a potent – because unconscious – medium for manipulating the masses. Yet films which explicitly rallied support for National Socialism – such as Hitlerjunge Quex (Hans Steinhoff, 1933) and SA Mann Brand (Franz Seltz, 1933) – were prohibited after 1933: the Party and its institutions, as concrete manifestations of power, were taboo as subjects for films. Power and its struc-

tures became masked, for the effectiveness of indoctrination depended in large part on this concealment. However, not only 'state' films – those directly commissioned by the government – but also, indeed especially, seemingly 'innocent' entertainment films, Leni RIEFENSTAHL's 'culture films,' and historical costume films, all staged the subjugation of the masses to one leader and a moral code devoid of human rights: militarism, racism, colonialism, and the desexualization of women. Women's urge for social independence and mobility, female desire and fantasy, were radically excluded; women were dispossessed of their emancipation to the benefit of patriarchal power structures and a masculine identity which was projected onto the image of the 'Fuehrer.' 'Strong' female figures in National Socialist films suggest a fake autonomy, for in fact identification with imaginary power takes the place of genuine self-determination, and the existence of the female body is negated. Pathos no longer takes the form of unfulfillable female desire but is resolved in the imaginary, in a brutal monumentality of image and MISE-EN-SCENE. The ambivalences which had characterized WEIMAR CINEMA no longer existed. This repression at the level of content was accompanied by a suppression of innovative and emancipatory stylistic conventions. The propagandist purpose of Nazi films demanded a strictly formal organization of cinematic materials: rigid restriction of the field of vision, transparent film language, linear narrative structure, mutual reinforcement of image and sound, and denial of the production process.

The representation of the 'Other' serves exclusively to produce identity, from which sexuality is banished as well. This is demonstrated by nationalistic and antisemitic films which attack both the VAMP (for example, Mazurka [Willi Forst, 1935]) and the erotic male (as in Jud Suess [Veit Harlan, 1940]); both of these are laden with negative connotations. Antisemitic agitation films like Jud

Suess, *Die Rothschilds* (Erich Waschneck, 1940) and *Der ewige Jude: Ein Dokumentarfilm ueber das Weltjudentum/The Eternal Jew* (Fritz Hippler, 1940) occupy a particular position, in that they were produced and screened in the period leading up to the deportations and the Holocaust. Similarly, the film *Ich klage an/I Accuse* (Wolfgang Liebeneier, 1941) was meant to increase the population's acceptance of organized murder, by justifying the killing of the sick and mentally handicapped in the name of euthanasia.

Toward the end of the 1930s, at the threshold of World War II, militarism was foregrounded, not only in war films but also in entertainment films like *Wir tanzen um die Welt/We Dance Around the World* (Karl Anton, 1939), in which uniforms cover the bodies of the dancing girls, exchanging the female body for an imaginary masculine fetish. Rather than feature a series of spectacular musical numbers, National Socialist productions paid special attention to the narrative glue binding the story together: solidarity amongst the troops and the subservience of the individual take the place of Hollywood-style stories about the rise of a star. Toward the end of National Socialism, when the German defeat in World War II had become clear to the population, a series of films was produced encouraging people to hold out; for example, Veit Harlan's *Kohlberg* (1945). Even during the last few days of the war, production was zealously kept up on films which were later completed in the Western or the Eastern occupied zones.

Julian Petley, *Capital and Culture: German Cinema 1933–1945* (London: British Film Institute, 1979)

See also: HARBOU, THEA VON; NEGRI, POLA VR

NEGRI, POLA (1897?–1987)

Born Barbara Apolonia Chalupez, this SILENT CINEMA actress stands – along with Theda BARA – for a type of woman new to the cinema of the 1910s: the VAMP. This STEREOTYPE is characterized by an apparently autonomous female SEXUALITY – which is not to be confused with any real self-determination. The dominating female figures embodied by Negri attain self-realization through erotic-emotional relationships which sidestep established social norms; these women and their objects of desire are in consequence regularly plummeted into misfortune. Negri's background played a significant part in this sexualization of her roles. Born in Poland, she first attended ballet school, then acting school. Having made the transition from Polish to GERMAN cinema in 1917, she was regularly cast in the role of 'exotic, foreign' seductress. This was the role she was expected to retain in her films in the USA, where she was imported, as Hollywood's first European actor, in 1923.

The rise of 'talkies' ended Negri's American career in 1930. She returned to Nazi Germany in 1934 upon an invitation from Propaganda Minister Joseph Goebbels, and was to provide incalculable service to the fascist rulers. Negri offered the Nazis an opportunity – through strategic deployment of an old star – to challenge the autonomous female sexuality which had been depicted in WEIMAR CINEMA. The paradigm of 'exotic vamp' was already associated with sexual repression, but in NAZI CINEMA that paradigm is deployed to defame other nations, set against the stereotype of the thoroughly desexualized German 'Frau.' Negri left Germany in 1939 and returned to the USA, where she appeared in two more films.

Pola Negri's films include: *Die Augen der Mumie Mâ/The Eyes of the Mummy* (Ernst Lubitsch, 1918); *Carmen/Gypsy Blood* (Ernst Lubitsch, 1918); *Madame Dubarry/Passion* (Ernst Lubitsch, 1919); *Sumurun/One Arabian Night* (Ernst Lubitsch, 1920); *Forbidden Paradise* (Ernst Lubitsch, 1924); *Mazurak* (Willy Forst, 1935); *Madame Bovary* (Gerhard Lamprecht, 1937)

Renate Lippert, '"Was wisst ihr denn, was Liebe ist": Pola Negri in *Mazurka*, 1935', *Frauen und Film*, no. 44/45 (1988)

VR

NEOREALISM

Neorealism is a film movement which arose in ITALY during the period following the end of World War II and the fall of fascism, in which socially conscious fictions document recent historical events from the viewpoint of the common people. Films were shot on location with natural lighting and often non-professional actors. Neorealism has remained an important point of reference for subsequent filmmakers, especially outside the West. It has been formative in the NATIONAL CINEMAs of, for instance, CHINA and INDIA, and throughout LATIN AMERICA, influencing BRAZIL's CINEMA NOVO and the work of individual – invariably male – directors such as Fernando BIRRI and Glauber ROCHA.

In Italy, important neorealist directors include Roberto Rossellini, Vittorio de Sica, Cesare Zavattini, Luchino Visconti, and Giuseppe De Santis. Neorealism, however, did not foster female directors, though screenwriter Suso CECCHI D'AMICO wrote neorealist films such as *Ladri di biciclette/Bicycle Thieves* (1948). Actress Anna Magnani's performance in *Roma città aperta/Rome Open City* (Rossellini, 1945) of the life and death of a working-class woman in the Resistance has become an icon of neorealism. The opposition between the good down-to-earth 'popolana' versus the negatively portrayed FEMME FATALE is indicative of the period. Following Rossellini's *L'Amore/Love* (1947–8), Magnani's powerful presence marked films about women by directors such as Visconti (*Bellissima* [1952]; *Siamo donne/We the Women* [1953]) and Pier Paolo Pasolini (*Mamma Roma* [1962]). An intriguing portrait of FEMININITY is to be found in the neorealist hybrid *Riso amaro/Bitter Rice* (De Santis, 1949), about female rice workers. This film represents the transition between the neorealist model of the partisan woman and 1950s popular cinema, which brought back glamor, offering female audiences SEX GODDESSES like Silvana Mangano, Sophia Loren, and Gina Lollobrigida. Rossellini left neorealism behind in the 1950s, but retained a stark neorealist attitude in his deglamorization of the star Ingrid Bergman and in the documentary feel of his films.

Federico Fellini, who began his career as a writer of neorealist films, made very different films as a director. Often challenged by feminists for his questionable portrayals of women and of sex roles, Fellini responded in 1980 with a parody of feminism in *La città delle donne/City of Women*.

Millicent Marcus, *Italian Film in the Light of Neorealism* (Princeton: Princeton University Press, 1986)

See also: DOCUMENTARY; SOCIALIST REALISM   GB

NETHERLANDS

Only since the late 1960s has a national feature film industry developed on a continuous basis in the Netherlands. Before that time, chronic lack of finance and imports – mostly of American films – set the scene. Exceptions were during World War I and in the latter half of the thirties, when German expatriate directors such as Max OPHULS and Douglas SIRK worked in the Netherlands. The very first champions of film as an autonomous art form were the founders of Filmliga (1927), amongst whom Mannus Franken and Joris Ivens are the best known. The group organized showings of films of the international AVANT GARDE of the period, and published a JOURNAL (*Filmliga*, 1927–31) in which Dutch people could read serious FILM CRITICISM for the first time. It is widely accepted that Filmliga was the source of Ivens's subsequent success as a documentary filmmaker; however, it is little known that the group was organized entirely by Helen van Dongen, Ivens's wife at the time. Nor, as a rule, is mention made in film literature of van Dongen's part in the making of Ivens's films between 1929 and 1940: for example, *Regen/Rain* (1929); *Nieuwe Gronden/New Grounds* (1934), *Spaanse Aarde/Spanish Earth* (1937). She was not only the editor, as the credits mention, but also acted as producer, general assistant, sound woman, and sometimes even as camerawoman; Ivens used to leave the overall finishing touches to his films to van Dongen, very often without specific instructions. Helen van Dongen also edited Robert Flaherty's *The Land* (1941) and *Louisiana Story* (1948), and directed and edited three compilation films: *Russians at War* (USA, 1942), *News Review 2* (USA, 1944–5) and *Of Human Rights* (USA, 1949–50).

DOCUMENTARY has traditionally been a much practiced and respected film genre in the Netherlands. Today, along with commissioned films, documentaries form by far the largest branch of Dutch film production; and since the mid 1970s many directors have been involved in this area. REALISM and social commitment speak to the freedom-loving qualities of this small nation. Currently favored documentary topics include the growing self-awareness of the Third World; the Netherlands' former colonies; social and economic problems; and women's subjects. Such films are financed by independent funds, by the government, and by television. Recent successful examples include: *Het Land van Mijn Ouders/My Parents' Country* (Marion Bloen, 1983), which is about the crosscultural identity of an Indonesian girl who grew up in the Netherlands; *Gezocht: Lieve Vader en Moeder/Wanted: Loving Father and Mother* (Sarah Marijnissen and Agna Rudolph, 1987), a film about child sexual abuse within the family which voices the victims' point of view; and *Het Oog Boven de Put/The Eye Above the Well* (Johan van der Keuken, 1988), impressions of daily and religious life in India through the eyes of a sympathetic and sincere western filmmaker.

In the 1960s the establishment of the Dutch Film Academy and the Production Fund, which administers official grants to commercial feature films, made it possible for film production to grow steadily to an average of fifteen films a year. Whereas at the outset most directors tended to imitate the French NEW WAVE, over the past few years scripts based on the American model have done well. Several successful films by the duo Pim de la Parra and Wim Verstappen illustrate this: *Blue Movie* (1971); all the Paul Verhoeven films, for example *Turks Fruit/Turkish Delight* (1973); *Charlotte* (Frans Weisz, 1980); *Het Meisje met het Rode Haar/The Red-headed Girl* (Ben Verbong, 1981); *De Stilte Rond Christine M./A Question of Silence* (Marleen Gorris, 1981); *Flodder/Tatters* (Ruud van Hemert, 1986); *De Lift/The Lift* (Dick Maas, 1988), *De Aanslag/The Attack* (Fons Rademakers, 1986); and *Een Maand Later/A Month Later* (Nouchka van Brakel, 1987).

Fifty years after the founding of Filmliga, discussion flared up again about cinema as a committed art form as against film as commercial entertainment. A great deal happened during the stormy seventies. The Rotterdam Film Festival was founded, and the newly established distributor Film International began promoting films which represented a cinematographic revival but were being ignored by commercial distributors. Film International introduced NEW GERMAN CINEMA to the Netherlands, along with films from POLAND, the SOVIET UNION, CHINA, and JAPAN. At about the same time, but quite independently, two other noncommercial distributors were founded: Fugitive Cinema Holland, which promoted socially committed films; and CINEMIEN, which was to become the world's largest distributor of women's films. A national network of cinemas and theaters showing films imported by these distributors was also successfully established:

in 1986 there were 115 such theaters as opposed to 457 commercial cinemas. By 1988, however, of the three subsidized distributors only Cinemien remained. Fugitive Cinema's and Film International's demise were partly due to a condition imposed by commercial cinema owners – which Filmliga had also contested in its time – that they could do business only with each other, and exceptionally with third parties with special dispensation. Since subsidized distributors are denied the right to release their films in the commercial circuit, they are unable to keep up with the growing recognition and exploitation of directors for whom they have blazed a trail. Moreover, they remain dependent on the government's relatively small film budget.

Nevertheless these developments have given rise to a notion of 'cinematic quality,' which has played a large part in the philosophy which currently sets the tone of Dutch film work. Consequently, a very interesting sector halfway between commercial and avant-garde films shows signs of emerging. This group includes not only male directors like Eric de Kuyper (*Casta Diva* [1983]; *A Strange Love Affair* [1985]) and Gerrard Verhage (*Afzien* [1986]), but also a number of women, for instance Hedy Honigmann with *De Deur van het Huis/The House Door* (1985) and *Hersenschinnen/Illusions* (1988); Digna Sinke with *De Stille Oceaan/The Quiet Ocean* (1985); Annette Apon with *Golven/The Waves* (1982) and *Giovanni* (1983); Lili Rademakers with *Menuet/Minuet* (1982) and *Dagbork van een Oude Dwaas/The Diary of an Old Fool* (1987); and Ine Schankkan with *Vroeger is Dood/Bygones* (1986). Although varied in style as well as theme, all these films are very much concerned with human emotions. Very often the story revolves around a man, which does not in the least mean that female characters are less important. Female directors do not make women's consciousness a central theme, but embody it as a natural feature in both characters and events. All these films are more subtle stylistically and more demanding formally than they could possibly be were they big cinema hits.

During the 1980s, many Dutch films by male directors dealt with the trauma caused by World War II. On the other hand, however, the three women who regularly make successful commercial films are more interested in contemporary topics and are all of a (perhaps rather conventional) feminist persuasion. The third woman, along with Nouchka van BRAKEL and Marleen GORRIS, is Mady Saks. A self-made woman, Saks rose from being a production assistant and director's assistant to directing documentary films – mostly about women in the Third World – and later became a feature film director, She has achieved two successes, both starring Monique van de Ven. Shot in documentary style, *Ademloos/Breathless* (1982) is the story of a woman who manages to get over postnatal depression because she understands that it is her isolation as a woman that caused it in the first place; *Iris* (1985) is a thriller about a young woman vet who starts her own practice in the country and manages to prove herself despite sexist prejudice.

Peter Cowie, *Dutch Cinema: An Illustrated History* (London: Tantivy Press, 1979)   AF

NEUBAUER, VERA (1948–)

Neubauer is a feminist experimental filmmaker who has developed a collage style using an array of techniques, combining animated sequences with documentary and constructed live action. Her work explores personal, feminist, and other political themes, threaded with recurring motifs such as motherhood, childhood, and old age, and often featuring herself or her children as players.

Neubauer was born in Czechoslovakia, and studied art in Prague, Dusseldorf and Stuttgart before settling in Britain in 1968. From 1970 to 1972 she studied at the Royal College of Art, where she made her first, short experimental animations, *Genetics*, *Animation Allega-*

Vera Neubauer's *The Decision*

tion, and *Cannon Fodder*. In these films, Neubauer's quirky and irreverent images flicker and boil erratically, creating a life of their own, true to the material nature of ANIMATION in which movement is produced by projecting sequences of still drawings. They are closer to the mesmerizing flicker of early animated films by pioneers such as the Frenchman Emile Cohl, or recent avant gardists such as Robert Breer, than to the classic naturalist cartoon style perfected by Disney, which erases any sign of individual frames.

Reference to the material of film and animation is a leitmotif of Neubauer's work. *Animation for Live Action* (1978) is partly about the difficulties of creating a film and of being a mother and wife. Neubauer herself is the central actor, simultaneously subject and object, her authorship denied by the introductory male voice-over saying 'this is a film about my wife . . .'. Her animated alter ego gets caught up literally in the cinema apparatus, spinning wildly on the editing machine, and enters into dialogue and struggle with the filmmaker within the live-action film. Contradictions between roles, and between fantasy and reality for

women, are deftly interwoven and held in place by Neubauer's anti-realist collage technique, which defies a simple linear reading. In *The Decision* (1981) the fantasy prompted by a fairytale told on the radio is constantly interrupted by harsh realities such as an extreme closeup of a soiled baby's bottom. The spinning wheel of a zoetrope (one of the optical toys of animation's prehistory) is watched with fascination by a little girl – or is she a fairytale princess? The repeating cycle of images is wryly echoed later by the repetitive cycle of drudgery of household chores and factory assembly line, and of the husband whose drunken violence leads to remorse and reconciliation, which in turn leads to another baby and to more household drudgery.

The World of Children (1984) is the first of a short series of films made by Neubauer for CHANNEL FOUR TELEVISION on the subject of age. It deals with racism, authority, and childhood. Racist myths and taboos are shown as institutionalized by the authority of language. *Midair* (1986) introduced three-dimensional puppet, as well as drawn, animation with live action. A comic opera in which bored housewives learn to be witches at nightschool, the film hypothesizes, via a misspelt graffiti, that war = mentruation envy. A spell is cast, leading to the film's most controversial shot – of woman's 'curse' visited on policemen patrolling the women's peace camp at Greenham Common. Last in the series is *Passing On* (1989), a moving montage of live-action documentary about old age, shot in India and China as well as in Britain.

Genetics, Animation Allegation, and *Cannon Fodder* (1970–2); *Pip and Bessie* (series of six animated shorts, 1973–5); *Fate* (1976); *Animation for Live Action* (1978); *The Decision* (1981); *The World of Children* (1984); *Midair* (1986); *The Mummy's Curse* (1987); *Passing On* (1989)

Claire Barwell, 'Interview with Vera Neubauer', *Undercut*, no. 6 (1982/3)   *IK*

NEW DAY FILMS

This mixed US FEMINIST DISTRIBU-TION cooperative was founded in 1972 by four filmmakers – Lianne Brandon (*Anything You Want To Be* [1971]), Jim Klein and Julia Reichert (*Growing Up Female* [1971]) and Amalie Rothschild (*It Happens To Us* [1972]). They were convinced that there was a strong, viable market for feminist films which commercial distributors had ignored. The coop's pioneering effort in self-distribution for filmmakers was shared with the wider film community in the book *Doing It Yourself*. This 'bible' of self-distribution was updated in the late 1980s. The initial films were soon joined by many classics of feminist DOCU-MENTARY, among them *Joyce At 34* (Claudia Weill and Joyce Chopra, 1972), *Union Maids* (Miles Mogulescu, Julia Reichert and Jim Klein, 1976), *With Babies and Banners* (Lorraine Gray, 1978), *Yudie* (Mirra Bank, 1975), and *The Other Half of the Sky* (Claudia Weill, 1974). By the late seventies, feminists saw that all of society needed to be explored and that change had to happen throughout the whole of society, not just in women's lives. Feminist filmmakers began to produce films on an increasingly wide range of social issues. This was true also of the New Day filmmakers, and in response to their work the collection was broadened to include films on subjects ranging from health and safety on the job (*Song of the Canary* [Josh Hanig and David Davis, 1978]) to sexuality (*Am I Normal* [Debra Franco and David Shepard, 1980]), women in China (*Small Happiness* [Carma Hinton and Richard Gordon, 1984]) and AIDS education (*All of Us and Aids* [Catherine Jordan, 1988]). While the coop has grown to a membership of forty filmmakers, it continues to be run democratically by its whole membership. They choose the films which will be brought into the collection and make all major decisions. The coop is dedicated to the notion that distribution is an extension of production, and that in bringing together the filmmaker and her audience they are creating more responsible productions.   LR

NEW GERMAN CINEMA

This is the name given to the films of a group of directors in WEST GERMANY from the late 1960s onward, only a few of whom have achieved international acclaim: among them Wim Wenders, Werner Herzog, Volker Schloendorff, and Rainer Werner FASSBINDER. Although the films of these and other new German cinema filmmakers are quite diverse, in terms of both content and form, a number of recurrent themes do emerge: there is a concern, for example, with the Nazi past and its legacy, with American culture, and with contemporary West German terrorism. While many of the early films are marked by a mood of despair and rebellion, a preponderance of literary adaptations characterized the mid to late 1970s, and the 1980s witnessed an increasing number of more mainstream international co-productions. The origins of this movement lie in what has become known as the Oberhausen Manifesto, signed by twenty-six would-be feature film directors in 1962. This manifesto expressed dissatisfaction with the current state of West German cinema and demanded the freedom to create a 'new German cinema.' For a combination of reasons the state was responsive to these demands, and during the sixties and seventies introduced a publicly funded film subsidy system. It has been this state funding, together with the setting up of film and television schools, that has enabled the new German cinema to develop.

Whilst most accounts of New German Cinema concentrate on the work of a small number of male directors, the movement has also succeeded in fostering a wealth of female talent. Women filmmakers such as Margarethe von TROTTA, Helma SANDERS-BRAHMS, and Alexandra von Grote are now well-known figures both inside and outside Germany. It has been from television

Alexandra von Grote's
Novembermond

financing in particular that women filmmakers have benefited, helping to produce films by Ula STOECKL, Jutta BRUECKNER, Ulrike OTTINGER, Helke SANDER, and Ingemo Engstroem, among others. Although women's contribution to new German cinema is frequently discussed as if it constituted a single film GENRE, their work in fact spans an enormous variety of forms and styles: from the arthouse REALISM of von Trotta's and Sanders-Brahms's feature films, through the DOCUMENTARY work of Helga Reidemeister and Erika Runge, to the more radical and formally innovative work of Ulrike Ottinger and Elfi MIKESCH. Thematically, however, there are similarities. Several films deal with the Nazi and uneasy postwar periods through autobiography, as in *Hungerjahre/Years of Hunger* (Jutta Brueckner, 1979), *Deutschland, bleiche Mutter/Germany, Pale Mother* (Helma Sanders-Brahms, 1979), and *Peppermint Frieden/Peppermint Freedom* (Marianne Rosebaum, 1984). Others, such as *Novembermond/November Moon* (Alexandra von Grote, 1984), *Madame X – Eine*

absolute Herrscherin/Madame X – an Absolute Ruler (Ulrike Ottinger, 1977), and *Das zweite Erwachen der Christa Klages/The Second Awakening of Christa Klages* (Margarethe von Trotta, 1978), explicitly or implicitly explore erotic friendships between women. Another recurring concern has been to represent women's experiences and explore how women see themselves, as in the work of Ula Stoeckl and Helke Sander.

Julia Knight, *Women and the New German Cinema* (London: Verso, 1990)

See also: PERINCIOLI, CRISTINA   JK

NEW HOLLYWOOD CINEMA

This term applies to the work of a group of directors, mostly male, working in Hollywood since the 1960s, which includes Peter Bogdanovich, Michael Cimino, Francis Coppola, Jonathan DEMME, Brian DE PALMA, Martin SCORSESE, and Robert ALTMAN. Their films have certain common characteristics: a fragmented, often open-ended, NARRATIVE and complex characters replacing the linear narrative and straightforward heroes of CLASSICAL HOLLYWOOD CINEMA; while the use of devices like the zoom and telephoto shots, split screen and slow motion contribute to the destruction of classical MISE-EN-SCENE. Often trained in film schools and with a film history background, these directors share a tendency to make films full of allusion to past Hollywood GENREs, evoking the styles of earlier admired directors like HITCHCOCK, HAWKS, and Ford. The rise of new Hollywood cinema has been attributed to various sociocultural factors, including the loss of audiences to television – resulting in films targeted at smaller social subgroups, and the collapse of the HOLLYWOOD STUDIO SYSTEM and its replacement by the 'package' system of production, which has led to an increase in the perceived importance of the director's AUTHORSHIP. In addition the collapse of confidence in traditional

American values brought about by events like the Vietnam War, race riots, Watergate, and so on, has been seen as contributing to these changes in the Hollywood product.

Feminist critics have noted shifts in representations of women accompanying these changes. Many Hollywood films of the early 1960s show women as victims in increasingly violent narratives, and the powerful female STAR virtually disappeared. Other films of the period show independent female characters contained and confined by home and family, mental institutions, or violence and murder. However, in the 1970s a number of films appeared with female protagonists who were not conventionally glamorous, and whose narratives centered on women's self-discovery and independence (*Alice Doesn't Live Here Anymore* [Martin Scorsese, 1974]; *Starting Over* [Alan J Pakula, 1979]; and *An Unmarried Woman* [Paul Mazursky, 1977]). It is significant that many of the new Hollywood directors passed through the studio of American International Pictures in the 1960s and through New World Productions in the 1970s, under the aegis of Roger Corman, director of many EXPLOITATION FILMS. Corman's films, with their aggressive vengeful HEROINES who shape their own destinies, may be seen as instrumental in changing the ways women are represented in new Hollywood cinema.

Steve Neale, '"New Hollywood Cinema"', *Screen*, vol. 17, no. 2 (1976)   *LF*

NEW ITALIAN CINEMA

New Italian cinema, a cinema of engagement, was born in ITALY in the early-sixties atmosphere of rebellion against the sociopolitical status quo which climaxed in the leftist revolt of 1968. Marco Bellocchio's 1971 film *Nel nome del padre/In The Name of the Father* exemplifies one of the concerns of this movement, a concern relevant to women: the questioning of authority and the revolt against the father. New Italian cinema rebels against the '*padre padrone*,' the father of the nuclear family, religious fathers, political fathers, and in general against all structures of authority as externalized in society and internalized in the superego. Directors Bernardo Bertolucci and Bellocchio acknowledge both the political and the psychological level of the revolt. For other directors – the Taviani Brothers, Gillo Pontecorvo, Francesco Maselli, and Francesco Rosi – the political fathers are the target. From a different standpoint, Ettore Scola has also been sensitive to the father issue, and has treated female '*passione d'amore*.' The couple and traditional roles were questioned in the early black comedies of Marco Ferreri, whose later films show evidence of a male post-feminist discourse. Pier Paolo Pasolini's polyphonic cinema and theoretical writings are intriguing and significant for FEMINIST FILM THEORY: Pasolini questions sexual difference, the body, 'passion and ideology,' and the authorial self. His complex treatment of the Oedipal confrontation with the father includes rapport with the mother. For new Italian cinema, confronting the father also includes the 'fathers' of NEOREALISM and fascism. In so far as a pivotal narrative matrix of this movement is the revolt of son against father (and most new Italian cinema directors are male), the articulation of a specific female viewpoint is limited. Even Liliana CAVANI's inquiries into authority and language center mainly around male figures. Italian feminism and women's cinema have developed 'after the revolution,' as a product and an outcome of the 1968 political revolt. In developing a language of its own, feminist cinema has had to confront and rebel against the heritage of all fathers, all *authorities* – including the authors of new Italian cinema.

R T Witcombe, *The New Italian Cinema* (New York: Oxford University Press, 1982)   *GB*

NEW WAVE

The New Wave is a film movement of the late 1950s and early 1960s which brought major changes in filmmaking practices and styles in many countries, but especially in FRANCE, where the term was coined ('La Nouvelle Vague'), to designate a 'free' approach to film, outside traditional production and stylistic constraints (studios, literary adaptations, large budgets, stars), and to privilege spontaneity and individual artistic expression. A number of factors account for its emergence: lighter and cheaper equipment allowed for on-location shooting, while the advent of television introduced new concepts of REALISM; the demise of the HOLLYWOOD STUDIO SYSTEM created opportunities to promote national film styles; and the postwar fashion for youth helped shake older values and promote a younger generation of filmmakers.

In France, the critical roots of the movement lie in André Bazin's influential writings, in Alexandre Astruc's advocacy of the 'caméra-stylo,' and in François Truffaut's vitriolic (and with hindsight not entirely fair) attack on the 'tradition of quality': films such as those of René Clément, Marcel Carné, Henri Verneuil, Julien Duvivier, Claude Autant-Lara, which seemed forever set in the aesthetics of the late 1930s. Truffaut, with Claude Chabrol, Eric ROHMER, Jacques RIVETTE, and Jean-Luc GODARD, launched this critical onslaught from the influential JOURNAL Cahiers du cinéma. Their aim was to champion their own pantheon of directors (Jean RENOIR, Alfred HITCHCOCK, Howard HAWKS . . .) and to formulate the auteur theory, positing the importance of a director's AUTHORSHIP, of personal vision and of MISE-EN-SCENE, over content and themes – a theory that paved the way for a new concept of filmmaking that was soon to be their own.

The New Wave was never a cohesive movement: between 1958 and 1962 an unprecedented one hundred new directors made a first film in France. There were also isolated precursors: Agnès VARDA's La pointe courte (1954), the films of Robert Bresson, Roger Vadim's Et Dieu créa la femme/And God Created Woman (1956) starring Brigitte BARDOT, and so on. Central to its definition, however, are the Cahiers critics' own films: Godard's À bout de souffle/Breathless (1959), almost a New Wave manifesto with its location shooting, rule-breaking editing, offhand acting, and narrative inspired by American 'B' FILM NOIR, Truffaut's Les 400 coups/The 400 Blows (1959), and Chabrol's Le Beau Serge and Les Cousins (both 1958). Though stylistically innovative and exhilarating, these films (together with those of Pierre Kast, Rohmer, and Rivette) generally lacked any interest in politics and social issues – ignoring the conservatism of the Fifth

She started her career as director by making stars of skunks and raccoons, and went on to become the only woman in Canadian cinema to write, produce, direct and, what's more, star in her own feature films. Who is she?

Republic, or the Algerian war. However, another strand in 1950s French cinema opposed the mainstream and showed greater political awareness: its main representatives were Chris Marker (Dimanche à Pékin [1956], Cuba si! [1962]), Alain Resnais (Nuit et brouillard/Night and Fog [1955], Hiroshima mon amour [1959], Muriel [1963]), and Varda. The ethnographic cinéma vérité of Jean Rouch was equally novel and a major influence on other New Wave directors, particularly Godard.

Whether in its socially conscious strand or in the classic acceptance of the term, however, the 'newness' of the New Wave rarely touched women, and the explosion of new directors bypassed them entirely (Varda and Yannick Bellon predated the movement). Although some films presented 'unconventional' heroines portrayed by emerging stars Bernadette Laffont, Stéphane Audran, Jeanne Moreau, or Anna Karina, New Wave films as a whole, when they were not downright misogynistic (Chabrol's *Les bonnes femmes* [1960]), concentrated on the romantic tribulations of young male heroes – *Breathless*, Truffaut's *Les 400 coups* – and perpetuated, in a more fashionable and sexually explicit way, old patriarchal myths about women (woman as muse, castrating mother or treacherous temptress, or as expression of male angst).

However, while the New Wave reinforced an individualistic and – some would argue – inherently male concept of the director as romantic artist, it also helped institutionalize (with state subsidy) a strong framework for auteur cinema in France, one that proved useful for the generation of women filmmakers which was to emerge in the wake of the May 1968 events and the advent of the women's movement.

Susan Hayward and Ginette Vincendeau (eds), *French Film: Texts and Contexts* (London and New York: Routledge, 1989)

See also: BRITISH NEW WAVE; CINEMA NOVO; NUEVA OLA, LA   GV

NEW ZEALAND

With a population of just over three million it is extremely difficult, financially, for an indigenous film industry to exist in New Zealand. Almost all those who direct feature films have to support themselves by doing other kinds of work, so that there is a large degree of crossover between the film, television, and advertising industries. Deregulation of all sectors of the economy since 1982 has involved the removal of tax shelters for filmmaking, seriously endangering the future of all filmmaking in the country. The only films currently being made are those supported by the government-funded New Zealand Film Commission.

The first films shot in New Zealand –

The Opening of the Auckland Exhibition and *Uhlan Winning the Auckland Cup* – were taken in 1898 by an intinerant showman, A H Whitehouse. The country, with its beautiful scenery and exotic 'natives' (the Maori), soon became a popular location for both overseas filmmakers (including Gaston Méliès in 1912) and local, colonist (Pakeha) directors. The earliest feature, *Hinemoa*, based – as were many early films – on a Maori legend, was made in 1914, directed by George Tarr. The most prolific director of the next thirty years was Rudall Hayward, who made six features, most of them concentrating on Maori–Pakeha themes.

Paradoxically, New Zealand's most famous filmmaker is one who is little known in his own country. Len Lye was an avant-garde artist who left New Zealand for Australia in 1921 because his country was poorly supplied with filmmaking equipment. He eventually joined the Seven and Five Group in London in 1926, pioneering the making of 'direct' film and 'scratch' film, and making a brilliant series of films for the GPO Film Unit, beginning in 1935. His experiments with film as fine art have had few sustained followers in New Zealand, with the exception of Auckland artists and filmmakers Merylyn Tweedie and Bronwyn Sprague.

From 1940 to 1970 only three indigenous feature films were made, all of them by the Wellington company Pacific Films Ltd. *Broken Barrier* (1952) was about a love affair between a Maori woman and a Pakeha man. But the company's next two films, *Runaway* (1964) and *Don't Let It Get You* (1966), in a situation typical of the New Zealand market, did not return their costs; and so plans for further features were shelved. In the meantime the state-run National Film Unit was formed in 1941 out of what had previously been the Government Publicity Studios, and for the next thirty-seven years it produced newsreels called the *Weekly Review* and subsequently a monthly *Pictorial Parade*, as well as documentaries and the occasional drama: these now form one of the few pictorial records of life at that time. The National Film Unit is currently up for sale to private bidders.

Changes in the organization of television in the early 1970s meant there was less work available for independent directors, and with the help of generous tax legislation and the establishment of the New Zealand Film Commission in 1978, a boom began in the New Zealand film industry, with some sixty feature films produced in the next thirteen years, all but five of them directed by men. In many of these films a liberal conscience is visible in relation to issues of political authority and of racial difference, with New Zealand's most popular director, Geoff Murphy (*Goodbye Pork Pie* [1981]; *Utu* [1983]; *The Quiet Earth* [1985]) known in particular as a 'counterculture' personality with a delight in anarchy. But in relation to women the conscience is much less active. It is rare for a woman in a New Zealand film to escape the peripheral roles of 'romantic interest,' symbol of untamed Nature, or sexual convenience. Even in a film such as *The Scarecrow* (1982), which its director Sam Pillsbury says is concerned specifically with 'corrupt male sexuality and aggression,' the voyeuristic nature of the cinematography is such that any 'progressive' message which may be implied is overwhelmed.

Instead, the real energy of many films by male directors resides in the relationship between the leading male characters, 'mateship' (a slow smile, a shared silence, a slap on the back) being one of chief supports of New Zealand society in its 150-year post-colonial history. Roger Donaldson's *Smash Palace* (1982) is probably the best example of the genre: beginning with a portrait of a marriage, it ends with a reconciliation between two 'best mates.' But to be fair, there is a sense in which these films, by concentrating on male paranoia, anxiety, and aggressiveness, are critiquing the concept of 'maleness' in New Zealand as well as entrenching it. Indeed, Vincent Ward, the country's most critically successful director, with his myth-making tales of androgynous adolescence (*Vigil* [1985]; *The Navigator: A Medieval Odyssey* [1988]), goes so far as to ask the most basic questions about the construction of sexed identity.

Women have become visibly active as directors in film and television only in the last ten years, with *The Silent One* (Yvonne Mackay) and *Trial Run* (Melanie Read), both released as features in 1984. Stylistically, the work of New Zealand's female feature directors tends to be mainstream and unexceptional, partly because it is so difficult for them to get financial backing that their films must appeal to as wide an audience as possible. And once the films are finished it is near-impossible for them to get distribution through either of the country's two main exhibitors, to the extent that Gaylene PRESTON and Melanie READ, in conjunction with their producers, have both had to arrange screenings of their own work. Nevertheless, both of them have made 'feminist thrillers' which interrogate the techniques of the conventional WOMEN IN PERIL film, and Melanie Read has gone on to make *Send a Gorilla* (1988), a stylish, fast-paced feminist comedy. Merata MITA's film *Mauri* (1988) is doubly interesting, being only the second feature ever to be written, directed, and largely crewed by Maori.

Many more women are gaining experience as directors in the area of short films, supported by the Queen Elizabeth the Second Arts Council and the Short Film Fund, established as a division of the Film Commission in 1985. Alison MACLEAN's 'bonsai epic' *The Kitchen Sink* (1989) was selected for competition at Cannes, while Shereen Maloney, Pat Robyns, and Kathy Dudding are other notable filmmakers gaining reputations as makers of short dramas and political documentaries.

While FEMINIST FILM THEORY as such has not had a great or visible influence on most New Zealand filmmakers, Helen Martin of the weekly journal *The Listener* has consistently put out intelligent and perceptive reviews for many years, and there was a great deal of useful information to be found in the JOURNAL *Alternative Cinema*, published in Auckland between the mid 1970s and the early 1980s. Roger Horrocks of Auckland University has been a prolific analyst of the cinema as well as a supporter of many young filmmakers of both sexes; and three years ago *Illusions* magazine, a quarterly put out by a collective based at Victoria University, Wellington, began publishing film, television and theater criticism, much of it contributed by feminist critics.

New Zealand films are often not well supported by the audience they are made for (even an extremely accessible film like *Goodbye Pork Pie* achieved its largest audience only when it was shown on national television – 50.3 percent of people over the age of five), and there is considerable tension over the relative necessities of making an internationally acceptable 'product' to attract international funding, as opposed to making films which specifically and imaginatively reflect New Zealand's unique culture. At present, with the future of the film industry in doubt because of a dearth of subsidies, this is a matter of fierce debate; and many of the country's best directors have recently left to work elsewhere.

See also: MAORI FILM   AH

NICARAGUA *see* CENTRAL AMERICA

NICHOLSON, ANNABEL (1946–)
The work of Nicholson, an artist working with film, has been extensively exhibited and performed in BRITAIN and abroad. She studied in London at Hornsey College of Art and later at St Martin's School of Art. She has lectured part-time in various departments of art colleges, and was actively involved in the development of the London Film-Makers' Co-

operative, a key focus for experimental and AVANT-GARDE work, where she was Cinema Organizer. She is also a co-founder of CIRCLES and a signatory to the women's statement in the Arts Council's 1979 'Film as Film' exhibition catalogue, which details the women's withdrawal from the exhibition because of its misrepresentation and neglect of women's role in film history. In 1983 Nicholson worked in an editorial/scriptwriting capacity on the CHANNEL FOUR TELEVISION documentary 'Seeing For Ourselves,' which explored the work of four women filmmakers and showed the role of Circles in providing a historical and contemporary context for women working with film.

The characteristically MODERNIST interest in the material qualities of film which has dominated European, and especially British, avant-garde film marks all of Nicholson's work as a filmmaker. Rejecting illusionist elements of cinema, it stresses film as material and as a set of conventional assumptions. By foregrounding the former, the latter is challenged and subverted. Whilst preoccupations with the structural and plastic nature of film are crucial to Nicholson's work, she has written:

Since 1973, I have been working away from film, towards more circumstantial situations. The aspects of projection which interest me have always been the transient, fragile qualities of light beaming through space. The accidental, the inadvertent light sources which crept into projection situations give me a point of departure. These performances change shape depending on who helps to perform them. This inevitably creates a risk around the work. At the moment I am thinking about the difficulty of retaining a balance between formal work and improvised risk.

Slides (1971); *Flavia* (1973); *Jaded Vision* (1973); *Reel Time* (1973); *Precarious Vision* (1973); *Depth of Filmed* (1973); *To the*

Diary (1975); *Piano Film* (1976); *Fire Film* (1981)

Malcolm Le Grice, *Abstract Film and Beyond* (London: Studio Vista, 1977)

SP

NIELSEN, ASTA (1882–1972)

Hailed as 'the most fascinating personality of the primitive era,' Asta Nielsen made well over seventy films during her twenty-two-year acting career. Born in DENMARK, she worked in the theater for a decade before making her film debut in the 1910 Danish film *Afgrunden/ The Abyss*. Despite the reservations of colleagues, the film was a resounding success, winning Nielsen not only critical acclaim but also the offer of a contract from a film company in GERMANY. By 1914 her name was known all over the world.

Noted for her acting, which was restrained and naturalistic, in direct contrast to the dominant SILENT CINEMA style of exaggerated gesticulation, Nielsen believed in 'living herself into' the characters she was to portray. However, she also involved herself closely in many other areas of the filmmaking process, including the selection of material, locations and props, the development of characters and costumes, casting, and publicity. Although remembered primarily for her tragic and melodramatic roles in films such as *Die Verraeterin/The Traitress* (1911) and *Vanina* (1922), Nielsen worked hard to develop her versatility as an actress. Not only has she been described as 'the most erotic screen actress of her time,' but – based on the evidence of comedies such as *Das Liebes-ABC/The ABC of Love* (1916) and *Das Eskimobaby/The Eskimo Baby* (1916) – American critic Robert C Allen maintains that 'she might well have developed into one of the finest comediennes of her age.'

Nielsen formed her own production company in 1920, but her silent film career came to an end in 1927. She reluctantly made one sound film, *Unmoegliche*

Liebe/Impossible Love, in 1932, and then retired from screen life permanently.

Robert C Allen, 'Asta Nielsen – The Silent Muse', *Sight and Sound*, vol. 42, no. 4 (1973)

JK

NISKANEN, TUIJA-MAIJA (1943–   )

Based in FINLAND, filmmaker Niskanen studied directing at the Finnish Theater Institute, and Drama at Helsinki University. On her graduation in 1968 she became a director in the Finnish Television Broadcasting Company, where she has worked ever since. Over the years she has made several TV dramas and films based on plays and stories by female writers. One of her earliest works is the TV film *Klyftan* (1972), which deals with the 1917–18 civil war in Finland from the viewpoint of a ten-year-old girl. This film, which is in Swedish, won the Finnish State Award in 1972. *Landet som icke är* (1977) is Niskanen's best-known TV feature. It is the life story of Finnish-Swedish poet Edith Södergran (1892–1923). The script was written by another woman director, Eija-Elina BERGHOLM, who also scripted *The Chasm*, and is based on Södergran's poems and diaries.

As a feature film director, Niskanen made her debut in 1980 with *Avskedet*. This film, made with Swedish funding, was filmed in Finland and tells the story of a Finnish-Swedish family. The main character is the daughter, who realizes she is a lesbian and fights to become a theater director. The film paints a vivid picture of her growing pains in the shadow of a patriarchal father and the fascistic atmosphere of the war years in Finland. Niskanen's second feature film is based on Mika Waltari's 1928 novel *The Grand Illusion*.

Niskanen's work often deals with the question of SEXUALITY, especially homosexuality, and has been of great importance in Finland, where these matters are very much taboo.

Nukkekoti/The Doll's House (1968); *Ajolanto/Gotta Run!* (1969); *Malli/The Model* (1971); *Lokki/The Seagull* (1971); *Klyftan/The Chasm* (1972); *Valitsen rohkeuden/I Will Choose Courage* (1977); *Landet som icke är (Maa jota ei ole)/The Land that Does Not Exist* (1977); *Seth Mattsonin tarina/The Story of Seth Mattson* (1979); *Avskedet (Jäähyväiset)/The Farewell* (1980); *Yksinäinen nainen/The Donna* (1982); *Kolme sisarta/The Three Sisters* (1983); *Suuri Illuusio/The Grand Illusion* (1985)   TA

NOFAL, EMIL *see* RAUTENBACH, JANS and NOFAL, EMIL

NOGUEIRA, HELENA (1962–)

Born in Mozambique, Nogueira moved to SOUTH AFRICA following the political upheavals and subsequent independence of her native country under Samora Michel. She graduated from the University of Natal in music, speech, and drama. While at university, she directed two films: *Visages* and *Blood of the Walsungs*. In 1980 she studied film at the Paris Institut des Hautes Etudes Cinématographiques (IDHEC). Employment as a film editor with the South African Broadcasting Corporation followed, and it was there that she produced her feature debut, *Fugard's People* (1982), at the age of twenty. This was the first South African production to be bought by the British Broadcasting Corporation.

In 1986 Nogueira set up temporary residence in Portugal to research and co-write *Farewell to Africa*, a film on the subject of decolonization and independence in Mozambique: she is currently working on this project. *Quest for Truth/Quest for Love* (1988), South Africa's first woman-directed full-length feature for the commercial circuit, is based on an original script developed from Gertrude Stein's *Q.E.D.* It has been screened at the Cannes Film Festival, at the Mifed Festival in Milan, and at the WOMEN'S FILM FESTIVALS at CRETEIL and MONT-

Helena Nogueira (left) on set in *Quest for Love*

REAL. *Quest for Truth* is a woman's film rather than a feminist film. It explores, explicitly and sympathetically, a lesbian triangle: three women are on a yacht sailing to a post-independence state – Mozania – where political freedom has been accompanied by hardship and poverty. The film also exposes the South African Defence Force's destabilizing activities in a neighboring state, and deals with detention without trial, torture, and a security police murder and cover-up operation.

Fugard's People (1982); *Quest for Truth/ Quest for Love* (1988); *Farewell to Africa* (in production)   WJA/RET

NORWAY

Norwegian film production started slowly and with feeble results: by 1920 only twenty films had been produced. Film exhibition in urban areas, however, was established early. In the 1930s, national film production on a somewhat larger scale was started with the founding of Norsk Film A/S. Most of these films were adaptations of well-loved literary works. During the wartime German occupation Norwegian film and cinemas were taken over by the Nazis.

In the postwar era extensive state support has proved vital for the maintenance of a NATIONAL CINEMA – whose main concerns include cultural and economic contradictions between towns and countryside, and the traumatic wartime occupation. In the past decade, Norwegian cinema has attracted international attention – mainly because of its female directors. The films of Anja BREIEN (*Hustruer/Wives* (1975]), Vibeke Løkkeberg (*Loperjenten/The Story of Camilla* [1981]) and Laila Mikkelsen (*Liten Ida/ Growing Up* [1981]) investigate issues of female sexuality, and of growing up and ageing as a woman in Norway. Pioneering work in overtly feminist filmmaking has been done by Nicole Mace in *3* (1971); while Eva Dahr and Eva Isaksen represent the new generation in this field.

In the 1980s independent companies producing low-budget films have also emerged, as well as filmmaking by and for a large cultural minority, the Lapps.

'Cinema of Norway: 70 Years of a Singular System', in *International Film Guide 1988*, ed. Peter Cowie (London: Tantivy Press, 1987)   AKo

NOTARI, ELVIRA (1875–1946)

The earliest and most prolific woman director in ITALY, between 1906 and 1930 Notari made about sixty feature films, one hundred documentaries, and numerous shorts for her own production house, Dora Film. She chose the stories, wrote the screenplays, directed and co-produced all films at Dora. Her name has long been canceled out of history and to date her contribution to the history and development of Italian and world cinema remains unacknowledged.

Although not uneducated, Elvira was of modest social origins. Born Elvira Coda in 1875 near Naples, she married Nicola Notari and founded Dora Film with her husband. This independent production house was a family enterprise. The use of her husband's last name has added to misunderstandings and lack of acknowledgement of her authorship. But it was unquestionably Elvira who wrote and directed all films at Dora: Nicola worked as cameraman. The couple jointly supervised the whole production process from financing to editing. Their son Edoardo played 'Gennariello,' an ever-present character whom screenwriter Elvira kept modifying as he grew up.

This woman's obscured contribution to the development of cinema presents several questions for the history of film. One is the 'uniqueness' of Italian NEO-REALISM. In opposition to the Italian 'super-spectacles,' Elvira Notari's cinema predates the aesthetic of neorealism in style of direction, MISE-EN-SCENE, and subject matter. From the 1910s, her fictions were shot on location, in the streets and dwellings of the city of Naples, often with nonprofessional actors. They documented, with crude REALISM, the conditions of urban living for the underclass. The suppression of female authorship is intertwined with that of historical forms of popular culture. Notari drew the subjects of her MELODRAMAs from the repertoire of Neapolitan popular culture, nineteenth-century popular novels as well as Italian popular romantic fiction directed at female audiences and centered on female characters. Her films offer insights into female viewpoints, desires, and transgressive social behaviors.

Dora Film 'silent' productions specialized in color and 'talking pictures.' Films were hand-painted frame by frame and synchronized 'live' with singing and music. Notari's films were distributed internationally as well as nationally, reaching Italian immigrants abroad. Also, a number of documentary films were produced specifically for, and often commissioned by, such immigrants. These films function as documents of personal and social history, and of cultural identity.

Notari's films encountered difficulties with fascist censorship which opposed her cinema's criticism of the law, its display of poverty and crime, and its use of regional popular culture and dialect. The coming of sound and fascist censorship put an end to her work.

Gli arrivederci and *Gli augurali* (1906–12): this series of short films and documentaries includes *La campagnola*; *I campagnuoli*; *Ballo delle farfalle*; *Musica a ballo*; *Ballerina e buffoncello*; *Colombi e birichino*; *Valzer d'amore*; *Colombi viaggiatori*; *Il cherubino*; *Folletto di fiamma*; *Cuoco Sansone*; *Coscritto*; *Alla Luigi XIV*; *Fotografia a sorspresa*; *Fra le stelle*; *Bebé va a letto*; *La preghiera di bebé*; *Bebé in salotto*; *Bebé vi saluta*; *Scugnizzo napoletano*; *Sui fili telefonici*; *Bebé in giardino*; *Cucú setté*; *La tarantella*; *Buona sera piccante*; *Buone feste*; *Posillipo da Napoli*; *Capri incantevole*; *La San Giorgio*; *Cattura di un pazzo a Bagnoli*. Other

documentaries include: *L'accalappiacani* (1909); *Il processo Cuocolo* (1909); *Fuga del gatto* (1910). Fictions include: *Maria Rosa di Santa Flavia* (1911); *Bufera d'anime* (1911); *Carmela la pazza* (1912); *Ritorna all'onda* (1912); *La figlia del vesuvio* (1912); *I nomadi* (1912); *Guerra italo-turca tra scugnizzi napoletani* (1912); *L'eroismo di un aviatore a Tripoli* (1912); *Povera Tisa, povera madre* (1913); *Tricolore* (1913); *A Marechiaro ce sta 'na fenesta* (1913); *Addio mia bella addio . . . l'armata se ne va . . .* (1915); *Figlio del reggimento* (1915); *Sempre avanti, Savoia* (1915); *Ciccio, il pizzaiuolo del Carmine* (1916); *Gloria ai caduti* (1916); *Carmela la sartina di Montesanto* (1916); *Nano rosso* (1917); *Mandolinata a mare* (1917); *La maschera del vizio* (1917); *Il barcaioulo d'Amalfi* (1918); *Pusilleco Addiruso* or *Rimpianto* (1918); *Gnesella* (1918); *Chiarina la modista* (1919); *Gabriele il lampionaio del porto* (1919); *Medea di Portamedina* (1919); *A Piedigrotta* (1920); *'A Legge* (1920); *'A mala nova* (1920); *Gennariello il figlio del galeotto* (1921); *Gennariello polizziotto* (1921); *Luciella* (1921); *'O munaciello* (1921); *Cielo celeste* (1922); *Cielo 'e Napule* (1922); *E' piccerella* (1922); *Il miracolo della Madonna di Pompei* (1922); *'A Santanotte* (1922); *Scugnizza* (1923); *Pupatella* (1923); *Reginella* (1923); *Core 'e frate* (1923); *'O cuppe' d'a morte* (1923); *Sotto il carcere di San Francisco* or *Sotto San Francisco* or *'N Galera* (1923); *A Marechiaro ce sta 'na fenesta* (remake, 1924); *La fata di Borgo Loreto* (1924, remake of *Nano rosso*); *'Nfama* or *Voglio a tte* (1924); *Piange Pierrot* or *Cosi piange Pierrot* (1924); *8 e 90* (1924); *Mettete l'avvocato* (1924); *Fenesta ca lucive* (1925, remake of *Addio mia bella addio*); *Fantasia 'e surdato* (1927); *L'Italia s'é desta* (1927); *La leggenda di Napoli* (1928); *Napoli terra d'amore* (1928); *La madonnina del pescatore* (1928, remake of *A Marechiaro ce sta 'na fenesta*); *Napoli sirena della canzone* (1929); *Duie Paravise* (1929); *Passa a bandiera* (1930); *Trionfo cristiano* (1930)

Giuliana Bruno, 'Le films di Elvira Notari (1875–1946)', *Lapis*, no. 2 (1988)

GB

NOUVELLE VAGUE *see* NEW WAVE

NOVARO, MARIA (1951–)

A graduate of the University Center for Cinematographic Studies in Mexico City (CUEC), Novaro has accumulated a substantial and impressive body of work. She stands out as one of the young, promising, politicized feminist film-makers in MEXICO whose films inhabit an aesthetically complex world of two realities. Novaro began her professional career in 1981 with super-8mm films, producing *Lavaderos; Sobre las olas;* and *De encaje y azucar.* In the same year, as part of the Mexican film collective Cine Mujer, she directed (in collaboration with Beatriz Mira, Sonia Fritz, and Angeles Necoechea) *Es premera vez.* In 1982 Novaro wrote the screenplay for her first film, *Conmigo las pasaras muy bien,* in which she delves into the notions of fantasy and desire, portraying a tired

> A 1931 German film, directed by Leontine Sagan, was banned by Goebbels. What is its name?

housewife who, with the flick of a magic wand, makes her demanding spouse and child disappear. *7AM* (1982) is a short allegory about the restrictiveness of a woman's working day as seen through the eyes of the female protagonist who, on waking, conjures images of leisure which are contrasted against shots of concrete and urban traffic. *Querida Carmen* (1983) again explores the limits of fantasy and desire, as well as the juxtaposition of the two realities of a young professional woman who daydreams of being Calamity Jane and confronting the untamed Wild West. *Una isla rodeada de agua* (1984) is one of Novaro's best-known films. Shot along Guerrero, the beautiful coast of Costa Grande, the film explores the longing of an orphan female adolescent in search for her displaced

mother. In 1988 Novaro completed *La que quiere azul celeste* as part of a trilogy which addresses issues of class, innocence, ascribed values and the acculturation of a young woman who moves from the country to the capital in search of her lover. Toward the end of 1988 Novaro began filming *Lola,* written in collaboration with her sister. The film is a social commentary focusing on one of the many shanty towns on the outskirts of Mexico City, towns which were most affected by the earthquake of 1985. The film explores urban social issues and the sexual politics of a relationship between a female street peddler and her male companion who is a 'rockanrolero' (rock 'n' roll aficionado).

Lavaderos/Laundry Shed (1981); *Sobre la olas/Over the Waves* (1981); *De encaje y azucar/Of Lace and Sugar* (1981); *Es primera vez/For the First Time* (1981); *Conmigo las pasaras muy bien/With Me You Will Enjoy Yourself* (1982); *7AM* (1982); *Querida Carmen* (1983); *Una isla rodeada de agua/An Island Surrounded by Water* (1984); *Pervertida/Depraved* (1985); *La que quiere azul celeste/In Search of the Pale Blue Horizon* (1988); *Lola* (1988–9)

Jorge Ayala Blanco, *La condicion del cine mexicano, 1973–1985* (Mexico City: Editorial Posada, 1986)   CH-N

NUEVA OLA, LA

Like the similarly named French NEW WAVE, this Argentine film movement was characterized by the simultaneous appearance between 1959 and 1961 of a number of young male filmmakers who, having gained their knowledge of films in cine-clubs and by making shorts in film workshops rather than as apprentices within the established industry, attempted permanently to change the character of national cinematic production in ARGENTINA. Stimulated by the technical fluidity and intellectual ambitions of Leopoldo TORRE-NILSSON's cinema, young cineastes took advantage of a serious creative and financial crisis within the established industry to obtain state-guaranteed loans for independent productions, and adopted the cinema as a medium for personal expression. Simon Feldman, José A Martínez Suárez, Manuel Antín, David José Kohon, Rodolfo Kuhn, and Lautaro Murúa made their feature debuts between 1959 and 1961 with a series of films that were narratively experimental, personal, and cosmopolitan, exploiting the streets of Buenos Aires as locales for *intimiste*, almost autobiographical, expression.

The *nueva ola* coheres as the product of a specific historical moment in Argentina (defined by political optimism, the state's film subsidy programs, and the growth of cinema culture), and is unified as a movement by its class positions and ambivalences. It was primarily an intellectualized cinema designed for a small, elite, Buenos Aires audience that revolted against the conservatism of its cinematic predecessors and exulted in the exploration of sexual/religious freedom and existential morality. Like other film movements of the period, the *nueva ola* included no women directors, and offered questionable representations of women in the actual films, in which women are often objects of fear and desire and a source of much existential angst.

Unlike the French New Wave, the *nueva ola* did not transform the Argentine industry. Not only were the films not great commercial successes nationally, Argentina's position in the international film market also largely precluded their being exported; and the movement was in effect crippled by national economic problems, its own social limitations, and Argentina's political instability.

John King and Nissa Torrents (eds), *The Garden of Forking Paths: Argentine Cinema* (London: British Film Institute, 1987)

ALo

OBOMSAWIN, ALANIS (1932–)

CANADA's best-known native film-maker, Obomsawin began her career in the arts as a singer and storyteller especially interested in giving children a concrete and meaningful sense of her people. Obomsawin's childhood and education were difficult, as they are for so many native people. From Odansk, in the Abenaki reserve northeast of Montreal, she went to Trois Rivieres, a small city in Quebec where she was the only native child. The humiliations wrought by both teachers and other children finally caused her to rebel at the age of twelve. She moved to Montreal in the late 1950s and became part of a circle of writers, photographers, and artists. Gradually she began to emerge as a singer. As a result of her growing fame, she was invited to the NATIONAL FILM BOARD OF CANADA (NFB) to consult on several projects. She then began making her own films and devising multi-media education kits for children. Her work in NATIVE CANADIAN FILM has always focused on her people. *Christmas at Moose Factory* (1971), her first film, tells the story of Moose Factory through the drawings and paintings of its children. *Mother of Many Children* (1977) travels cross-country to introduce us to the lives of girls and women of many different tribes. *Amisk* (1977) documents a concert, the final event of a week of performances in Montreal by native singers and dancers from across Canada in support of the people of James Bay, whose way of life was threatened by the Quebec government's building of a mammoth hydroelectric project in the area. *Incident at Restigouche* (1984) confronts another political issue, the Quebec Provincial Police's invasion of the Mic-

mac reserve with the excuse that the handful of Micmac fishermen had exceeded their salmon quotas: the film deals with the issue of native rights. *Richard Cardinal: Cry from a Diary of a Metis Child* (1986) uses a boy's diary to tell the story of a life of foster homes, institutions, and uncaring that ends with the child's suicide at age fourteen. Obomsawin's latest film, *Poundmaker's Lodge: A Healing Place* (1987), is about a place in the countryside near Edmonton, Alberta, which uses a unique blend of native healing, exercises, and Alcoholics Anonymous meetings to cure native addicts and to offer them a return to their traditions. Although Obomsawin received the Governor-General's Award, Canada's highest award, in 1983, her films have never been accepted for broadcast on CBC television.

Christmas at Moose Factory (1971); *Mother of Many Children* (1977); *Amisk* (1977); *Old Crow* and *Gabriel Goes to the City* (1979, for the series of school telecasts *Sounds from Our People*); *Incident at Restigouche* (1984); *Richard Cardinal: Cry from a Diary of a Metis Child* (1986); *Poundmaker's Lodge: A Healing Place* (1987)

Susan Schouten, 'The Long Walk of Alanis Obomsawin', *Cinema Canada*, no. 147 (1987)   JL

OLIVEIRA, MANOEL (1908–)

Manoel Oliveira, the sole international figure of PORTUGAL's cinema, was born in Oporto and made his first documentary in 1929. *Douro, faina fluvial/Douro, River Work* is an outstanding first work that broke the accepted language of the genre. His early documentaries were optimistic, as was his first feature, *Aniki-Bóbó* (1942), which anticipated the language and themes of Italian NEOREALISM. Unable to get funds, his next film, *O acto da primavera* (1962), was made some eleven years later, but since then he has continued making films with a regularity not possible for any other Portuguese filmmaker. His attempt to fuse DOCUMENTARY and fiction, MELODRAMA and OPERA, and rely on ritual and representation (theater, film as film, fiction), has led to a complex cinematic language applauded abroad but misunderstood at home, where his work is revered but remains largely unseen. A patrician Catholicism, haunted by sexuality and frustration – at all levels – pervades Oliveira's later work.

Oliveira's films include: *Aniki-Bóbó* (1942); *O acto da primavera/A Passion Play* (1962); *O passado e o presente/The Past and the Present* (1971); *Benilde ou a Virgem Mãe/Benilde, the Virgin Mother* (1975); *Amor de perdiçao/Ill-Fated Love* (1976): *Francisca* (1981); *Le soulier de satin/The Satin Shoe* (1985); *O meu caso/My Case* (1986): *Os canibais/The Cannibals* (1988)

Jean-Loup Passek (ed.), *Le cinema portugais* (Paris: Centre Georges Pompidou, 1982)   NT

OPERA

A centuries-old form of stylized music drama, opera has influenced film in two ways – first by providing cinema with an aesthetic model, and second by supplying it with stories for adaptation. In the early days of film, MUSIC from opera was used to instill a sense of 'high art' in the new massified entertainment form. The 'film d'art' movement at the beginning of this century devoted itself to establishing cinema as an art form: Camille Saint-Saëns's score for *The Assassination of the Duke of Guise* (1908) featured prominently in this. Adaptations of well-known operas quickly became common fare, although their association with high art and the upper class have arguably kept them from achieving the widescale popularity enjoyed by Broadway musicals. Most opera movies have been produced as ART CINEMA (Ingmar BERGMAN's *Trollflojten/The Magic Flute* [1975], for example), and sometimes only vaguely resemble their original source (Carlos Saura and Jean-Luc GODARD's 1983 versions of *Carmen*).

The aesthetics of opera have had a tremendous impact on film, especially on scoring techniques. In Hollywood, studio composers relied heavily on the Wagnerian leitmotif, a short musical theme that was used as 'background' SOUND to stand in for characters, places, or ideas. Wagner's aesthetics were influential in other ways as well. Film was often hailed as a 'total art-work,' one that synthesized the individual arts of poetry, music, drama, dance, and so on, just as Wagner had argued for his own operas. Both Wagner and film commentators have insisted that music's role is a primarily emotional, feminine one. Opera continues to influence film production after the heyday of the HOLLYWOOD STUDIO SYSTEM – the 'rock operas' of the early 1970s are indebted to it; Jean-Jacques Beineix's *Diva* (1981) uses it as a narrative theme; it has been influential in non-western cinemas as, for example, in CHINA's REVOLUTIONARY MODEL FILM; and opera's opulent style has been frequently linked to NEW GERMAN CINEMA directors Syberberg and FASSBINDER.

Film opera raises issues for women, since adaptations – even (and perhaps especially) those of the art cinema – uncritically transmit opera's preoccupation with FEMININITY and female sacrifice. Feminists have begun to question this obsession, as Catherine Clément does in her book *Opera, or the Undoing of Women*, and as Sally POTTER does in films like *Thriller* (1979).

Catherine Clément, *Opera, or the Undoing*

of *Women* (Minneapolis: University of Minnesota Press, 1988)

See also: ROCK MUSIC   CF

OPHULS, MAX (1902–57)

Born in Saarbrucken, Ophuls worked as a stage director in Germany in the 1920s, but spent most of his film career in exile: France in the 1930s (where he moved following the Nazis' rise to power), the USA in the 1940s, and France again in the 1950s. Despite such diverse (and sometimes adverse) working conditions, Ophuls's work shows a remarkable stylistic consistency: a taste for costume films and ornate decor (typically, but not exclusively, turn-of-the-century Vienna) and, above all, breathtakingly fluid and intricate CAMERA MOVEMENT.

From a generic point of view, Ophuls's work was also extremely coherent, falling mostly within 'women's genres': bittersweet ROMANCE and MELODRAMA. Accordingly, his critical reputation was relatively low in his lifetime. He was, however, championed as an auteur in the 1960s, and *Madame de . . .* (1953), *La Ronde* (1950) and *Lola Montès* (1955) – the most baroque expression of his MISE-EN-SCENE – are art-house classics. More recently, with the revival of melodrama, feminist critics have singled out *Letter from an Unknown Woman* (1948) for its exploration of feminine desire and romance, *The Reckless Moment* (1949) for its exposition of the constraints put on the figure of the mother by the patriarchal family in middle-class America, and *Caught* (1949) for showing (as film theorist Mary Ann Doane puts it) 'the inscription of femininity as absence.'

Ophuls's films include: *Liebelei* (German and French versions, 1933); *On a volé un homme* (France, 1934); *La signora di tutti* (Italy, 1934); *Divine* (France, 1935); *Komoedie vom Geld* (Netherlands, 1936); *La Tendre ennemie/The Tender Enemy* (France, 1936); *Yoshiwara* (France, 1937);

Joan Fontaine in Ophuls's *Letter from an Unknown Woman*

Werther (France, 1938); *Sans lendemain, De Mayerling à Sarajevo/Mayerling to Sarajevo* (both France, 1940); *The Exile* (USA, Universal/International, 1947); *Letter from an Unknown Woman* (USA, Universal, 1948); *Caught* (USA, MGM, 1949); *The Reckless Moment* (USA, Columbia, 1949); *La Ronde* (France, 1950); *Le Plaisir/House of Pleasure* (France, 1952); *Madame de . . ./The Earrings of Madame de . . .* (France, 1953); *Lola Montès* (France, 1955)

Mary Ann Doane, *The Desire to Desire: The Woman's Film of the 1940s* (Bloomington and Indianapolis: Indiana University Press, 1987)   *GV*

OSTEN, SUZANNE (1944–)

A SWEDISH film and theater director and committed feminist, Suzanne Osten has often participated in debates on current issues and reflected upon them in her plays. While studying Literature and History of Art at the University of Lund, she was active in the student theater, which she left in order to become the director of Fickteatern, one of the first 'free' theater groups in Sweden. From there she moved to the Municipal Theater of Stockholm in 1971, and ten years later was appointed Artistic Leader of Unga Klara (The Children and Youth Theater of the Municipal Theater).

In Unga Klara, Suzanne Osten has directed numerous celebrated experimental plays, many written by herself. She worked with the same group of actors and developed a style with a basis in the grotesque and involving improvisation. In her films, Osten continues this style, constantly pushing at the border between the imaginary and the real, stretching herself toward an expression, a language, of her own. Her first film, *Our Life is Now* (1982), is relatively realistic, however: a homage to her mother, the eminent film critic Gerd Osten, who always dreamed of film directing. Her daughter made that dream come true. *The Mozart Brothers* (1986) is a comedy

Suzanne Osten directing *The Mozart Brothers*

about staging an opera, a film that intricately builds into itself the plot and music of *Don Giovanni*, the Mozart opera that is in the process of being staged. This film brought Suzanne Osten the 1986 Swedish Film Institute award for best director.

Mamma/Our Life is Now (1982); *Bröderna Mozart/The Mozart Brothers* (1986); *Livsfarlig film/Lethal Film* (1988)   *TS*

OTTINGER, ULRIKE (1942–)

A West German filmmaker associated with the more experimental end of the movement known as NEW GERMAN CINEMA, Ottinger began by studying art. Frustrated with her work as an artist in Paris during the sixties, Ottinger moved into filmmaking with no formal training. After experimenting with photo-documentation and happenings, she realized her first film project, *Laokoon und Soehne*, in 1972. With this film she also began her long collaboration with Tabea Blumenschein, who acts in and

Delphine Seyrig in *Dorian Gray im Spiegel der Boulevardpresse*

designs costumes for many of Ottinger's films. Writing, producing, directing, and filming virtually all her projects, Ottinger has experimented with camera, LIGHTING and COLOR to become one of the most formally innovative filmmakers in WEST GERMANY. As one critic has observed: 'Through exaggeration, parody, visual metaphor and unexpected juxtaposition of sound and image, Ottinger constructs a world suffused with fantasy and possible meanings . . .'.

Much of Ottinger's work is centered around the theme of rebellion against alienated forms of living and working, with the aim of making people more conscious of their reality. Her concern with women is also evident in her first feature-length film, *Madame X – Eine absolute Herrscherin* (1977), which explores the lesbian matriarchy of pirate queen Madame X, ruler of the China Sea. Her next film, *Bildnis einer Trinkerin – aller jamais retour* (1979), combines semidocumentary techniques with highly stylized images to examine the rela-

tionship between two women alcoholics. Such work has led feminist critics to haîl Ottinger's films as landmarks in the development of an erotic women's cinema.

More recently Ottinger has been working on a two-part project on China. The first part, *China – Die Kuenste – Der Alltag* (1985), is a documentary recording the filmmaker's direct encounter with China and its culture. The second part, *Johanna d'Arc of Mongolia* (1988), is a feature film focusing on four western women traveling on the Trans-Siberian Railway.

Laokoon und Soehñe/Laocoon and Sons (1972/3); *Die Betoenung der blauen Matrosen/The Bewitchment of Drunken Sailors* (1975); *Madame X – Eine absolute Herrscherin/Madame X – An Absolute Ruler* (1977); *Bildnis einer Trinkerin – aller jamais retour/Portrait of a Female Alcoholic – Ticket of No Return* (1979); *Freak Orlando: Kleines Welttheater in fuenf Episoden/Freak Orlando: Small Theatre of the World in Five Episodes* (1981); *Dorian Gray im Spiegel der Boulevardpresse/Dorian Gray in the Mirror of the Popular Press* (1984); *China – Die Kuenste – Der Alltag/China – The Arts – Everyday Life* (1985); *Johanna d'Arc of Mongolia* (1988)

Erica Carter, 'Interview with Ulrike Ottinger', *Screen Education*, no. 41 (1982)

JK

PALCY, EUZHAN (1957–)

CARIBBEAN filmmaker Euzhan Palcy achieved international recognition with her universally acclaimed film *Rue cases nègres* (1983), a worldwide success which brought her to the notice of Hollywood. She has since become the first black woman to direct a film for a major Hollywood studio, *A Dry White Season* (1989) for MGM, based on André Brink's novel.

From an early age Palcy was a talented writer of poetry, songs, and drama, and her gifts were encouraged by her father. She wrote for local magazines and papers in her native Martinique, and it was in her young impressionable teens that she read two novels which were to be a major influence on her subsequent career in film: Alan Paton's *Cry the Beloved Country*, about apartheid; and *La rue cases nègres*, a Martiniquan classic by Josef Zobel. The latter was to be the inspiration for her first feature film (she wrote the first draft of the screenplay at the age of seventeen), while *A Dry White Season* was based on a novel about apartheid.

Palcy believes women can and should achieve anything they want through their own resolve. She had chosen filmmaking as a career at a very early age, and was seventeen when she wrote, directed, and acted in *La messagère* (1974), a fifty-two-minute play for TV, the first TV drama from any of the French 'départements outre-mer.' She then became a student of literature at the Sorbonne in Paris, at the same time studying cinema at the Rue Lumière School, with the help of a French grant awarded in a script competition for her adaptation of *Rue cases nègres*. French TV, which was to co-produce the film, asked Palcy to prove her skills by making a short film.

She wrote and raised funding for *The Devil's Workshop* (1981–2), which was to become the prototype for *Rue cases nègres*. *A Dry White Season* was guided by the woman Hollywood producer, Paula Weinstein. Palcy says of her work that she has many ideas about things she would like to say – not just as a director, but as a woman director.

La messagère/The Messenger (1974); *L'atelier du diable/The Devil's Workshop* (1981–2); *Rue cases nègres/Black Shack Alley* (1983); *A Dry White Season* (1989)

Susan Linfield, 'Sugar Cane Alley: An Interview with Euzhan Palcy', *Cineaste*, vol. 13, no. 4 (1984)   JG

PALESTINE

Born of the Palestinian Resistance which flourished after the defeat of June 1967, cinema in Palestine – one of the ARAB countries – like most of the Palestinian people, lives in exile. The earliest and major source of documentary production was the Palestine Cinema Unit. Founded in 1968 in Amman in Jordan, the Unit was moved to Beirut in LEBANON in the early 1970s. Other Palestinian organizations soon sponsored filmmakers like Iraqi Qasim Hawal or Lebanese Rafic Hajjar, Jean Chamoun, Randa El Chahhal, and Nabiha Loufti. Some of the best documentaries to emerge have been *Al Miftah/The Key* (by Palestinian Ghaleb Shaas [1976]) and *Falastine, Zakirat Shaab/Palestine, Chronicle of a People* (by Iraqi Kais Al Zoubeidi [1982]), both of which use archive material to analyze the history of the Palestinians. But this is still a men-only history: women's liberation was not high on the agenda, and was considered a diversion from the nationalist struggle.

However, when women do appear in documentaries or newsreels, they are not defeatist and conservative, as they often are in features such as *Kfar Kassem* (Alaouie, 1975) or *The Cheated* (Saleh, 1972). Far from it: Palestinian women appear politically conscious, principled, and determined to fight until the final victory.

May Masri was the first professional Palestinian woman filmmaker. She co-directs her films with Lebanese Jean Chamoun. *Tahta Al Ankad/Under the Rubble* (1982), about the siege of Beirut, does not neglect to show the heroism of Lebanese and Palestinian women resisting Israeli invasion. This was followed by *Zahrat al Koundoul/Women from South Lebanon* (1986), centered on women in the South of Lebanon bravely resisting Israeli occupation. The most daring and talented documentary, however, was made by a Palestinian man: *Al Zakira A Khasiba/Fertile Memory* (1980). Director Michel Khleifi, one of the most inspired

> This pioneering Italian filmmaker made one hundred and sixty films and was an important early influence on the neorealist aesthetic. She was then forgotten. Who is she?

Palestinian filmmakers, made a political and aesthetic landmark with this film, which shows the predicament of Palestinian women suffering not only from the Israeli occupation in the West Bank but also from sexism. Khleifi made an equally gifted and poetic feature, *Urs fil Jalil/Marriage in Galilee*, in 1987: politically controversial and flawed by sexploitation, this film nevertheless portrays women as brave and politically mature.

Heiny Srour, 'L'image de la femme Palestinienne', in *La Palestine et le cinéma*, ed. Guy Hennebelle and Khemais Khayati (Paris: E100, 1977)

See also: ISRAEL; SYRIA   HS

PARAMOUNT

In 1916 several US production companies, including Famous Players and Lasky, merged with the strong DISTRIBUTION company Paramount. In 1919 the company began purchasing theater chains, making it one of the earliest Hollywood studios to achieve full vertical integration. Needing to supply films to its one thousand-plus theaters, Paramount produced forty to fifty films per year. Struggles over control of the publicly owned firm resulted in several changes in top management during the Depression years. In 1936 Barney Balaban became president, a position he held until 1964. By the mid 1960s, Paramount was in serious difficulties and released only nine films in 1965. The company had few interests in the emerging television production market. Gulf & Western later bought control of the company, and restructured it. Several blockbusters in the 1970s, and some smart investments in the leisure industry, have revived Paramount as a significant distributor of films.

During the heyday of the HOLLYWOOD STUDIO SYSTEM from the 1930s to the 1950s, Paramount chose a looser production organization than other Hollywood firms. At times a strong production chief controlled significant portions of the product; at other times associate producers or producer-directors were in charge of several films per year. However, its middle-line management remained fairly consistent throughout the period. In the early 1930s, Mae WEST was a major asset for the studio, but Paramount's profits in later years came through the skills of their director Cecil B DE MILLE and several male stars (Bob Hope and Bing Crosby in particular). Other major women stars at Paramount in these years were Barbara STANWYCK, Paulette Goddard, Hedy Lamarr, and Dorothy Lamour.

Douglas Gomery, The *Hollywood Studio System* (London: Macmillan, 1986)   JaS

PARSONS, LOUELLA (1880–1972)

Louella Parsons began her career as a story editor for Essanay in Chicago in the 1900s. In the late 1910s she wrote movie reviews and columns for newspapers in Chicago and then New York. In the early 1920s Parsons was named motion picture editor of William Randolph Hearst's New York *American*. This promotion has been attributed in part to her friendship with Marion Davies (Hearst's extramarital partner) and her praise for Davies's early films. Parsons developed her GOSSIP COLUMN format in New York, prior to moving to Los Angeles in 1926. There, aided by an impressive network of sources (including her husband, a staff doctor for TWENTIETH CENTURY-FOX), Parsons's daily column and regular feature stories established her as the premier gossip columnist of the film industry. In her search for information, she is credited with breaking the studios' taboo about making public the marital status of stars. Parsons's position with the Hearst newspapers and her continual acclaim for Davies's performances were mocked in the fictional Susan Alexander Kane's opera career in *Citizen Kane* (Orson Welles, RKO, 1940). After the film's release, Parsons joined the Hearst press to punish RKO with unfavorable reviews and, even worse, silence about RKO's stars and films. Parsons wrote two memoirs, *The Gay Illiterate* (1944) and *Tell It to Louella* (1961).

Christopher Finch and Linda Rosenkrantz, *Gone Hollywood* (Garden City, NY: Doubleday, 1979)   MBH

PATIL, SMITA (1955–86)

A key figure in the rise of INDIA's 'parallel cinema' in the seventies and early eighties, actress Smita Patil epitomized the 'new Indian woman,' projecting a strong self-assured sexuality, independence, and intelligent concern with the world about her. Refusing the saccharine glamor of the mainstream film industry, she set a new style for stardom – and femininity – in the eighties, celebrating a sensuality and simplicity associated with Indian traditional lifestyles, while pas-

Smita Patil in *Bhumika*

sionately critical of women's oppression within traditional systems.

Brought up in Poona, the daughter of a social worker mother and a Maharashtrian government minister, Smita began acting in student films and working as a television newscaster while still at college. Her break came when Shyam Benegal offered her a role in *Manthan/The Churning* (1975), but she arrived as a major actress with *Bhumika/The Role* (Shyam Benegal, 1977). Playing the 1940s Marathi film star Hansa Wadkar – who had lived a short and tempestuous life attempting to reconcile the contradictory demands of family and career while fighting the exploitation of women and double standards of the film industry – Smita showed the range of her talent and an uncomfortable foreboding of her own future. Offers followed from Mrinal Sen, Satyajit Ray, and many others, and Smita soon developed a reputation as a formidable actress with an intensity, directness, and raw energy unique in Indian cinema. She also became known for her integrity and commitment, working if necessary for minimal fees for a 'new' cinema that would challenge the Hindi mainstream both formally and politically, in particular in its representation of women.

In the early 1980s Smita gave in to pressure to accept roles in mainstream films, not only because they were lucrative, but also because she recognized that her self-imposed marginality was helping no one – without a 'name' and market potential in mainstream cinema, she could have little effect on public consciousness or on the development of a more popular alternative cinema practice. She rode the contradictions uneasily: her personal life became fodder for a prurient gossip press, and several of her new roles were undignified and exploitative. She continued to champion women's issues, becoming actively involved in setting up a women's refuge in Bombay, and her heart was throughout with the alternative cinema, where her performances won her national prizes

and something of an international reputation, most notably for *Tarang/Vibrations*, (Kumar Shahani, 1984), *Chidambaram* (G Aravindan, 1985), *Umbartha/Subah/The Threshold*, (Jabbar Patel, 1981), *Ardh Satya/Half Truths* (Govind Nihalani, 1983). Her move to commercial cinema was vindicated when films such as *Ardh Satya* and *Umbartha* became box office successes and put an alternative cinema on the map within and outside India. She died of postnatal complications shortly after her first child was born.   RT

PERFORMANCE

Film HEROINES are notorious for putting on an act, playing up, performing for the camera. There is a view of Hollywood that designates it a dream factory, and implicitly, in this view, women are situated on the side of fiction and spectacle. To counteract this, a certain feminist tendency (both in filmmaking and in criticism) has turned to DOCUMENTARY as more authentic (no acting, simply women 'being themselves'). However, other approaches contest the implied conflation of the terms 'fiction,' 'performance,' 'acting,' as against 'real women.' Film ACTING can be seen as simply one element of filmic performance, no more important than camera performance, say, or the landscape as a performative element. Here the film is thought of as a performance TEXT, in which audiences and readings are also involved as performative elements. From this perspective every appearance in a documentary film (as well as fiction) is seen as a performance. The usefulness of this approach lies in the fact that it provides a framework both for analyzing ways in which FEMININITY is produced *as* performance in cinema, and also for making films that employ performance strategies different from those of DOMINANT CINEMA, that attempt new registers of the feminine.

Two famous examples of female

performance are provided by scenes from Dorothy ARZNER's *Dance, Girl, Dance* (RKO, 1940) and Charles Vidor's *Gilda* (Columbia, 1946): in both instances, characters perform on stage to a primarily male audience, and arguably a critique is made of femininity as performance, wherein the female is set up as object of a voyeuristic and sadistic male LOOK. This 'acting out' of femininity, and its implications for the viewer, have been analyzed by film theorist Mary Ann Doane in her essay 'Film and the Masquerade.' Films which interestingly complicate the notion of female performance include Yvonne RAINER's *Lives of Performers* (1972), Ulrike OTTINGER's *Freak Orlando* (1981), and Jean-Luc GODARD's *Two or Three Things I Know About Her* (1966).

Mary Ann Doane, 'Film and the Masquerade: Theorising the Female Spectator', *Screen*, vol. 23, no. 3–4 (1982)

See also: DANCE; MASQUERADE; STARS   LS

PERINCIOLI, CRISTINA (1946–   )

Born in Switzerland, Cristina Perincioli studied at the Berlin Film and Television Academy, where she gained extensive training in documentary filmmaking. Perincioli has direct links with the women's movement in WEST GERMANY, and from the early 1970s has been making films that focus on female protagonists. For instance, *Fuer Frauen – 1. Kapitel* (1971) deals with the struggle of four supermarket saleswomen who strike for equal pay for the same work as their male colleagues; and *Frauen hinter der Kamera* (1972) looks at women involved in the technical side of filmmaking.

Perincioli has concentrated on contemporary social problems – nuclear power and the military, as well as on women's issues – and has criticized her

The Power of Men is the Patience of Women, by Cristina Perincioli

women colleagues for avoiding politically controversial subjects. Her first full-length feature film, *Die Macht der Maenner ist die Geduld der Frauen* (1978), for instance, is about domestic violence. Made with women from West Germany's first women's refuge, which Perincioli helped to found, *Die Macht der Maenner* focuses on one woman's experience of domestic violence, and is intended both to involve the viewer emotionally and to communicate information. It was made collectively, evolving to a certain extent during the production process. As Perincioli explains, '. . . we rehearsed almost every scene in front of the video cameras. Then we watched the scene together and talked about it and made any necessary changes. It is a method that I like to use because we can all learn together.'

Perincioli prefers to work collaboratively with women, and sees such work as an important contribution to women's emancipation. However, funding bodies have proved unsympathetic to such practices, often rejecting or censoring women's projects. Even during the 1970s, Perincioli was replaced with a male director on one of her own television projects, *Anna und Edith/Anna and Edith*. More recently Perincioli has worked in theater, and has been exploring the possibilities offered by the combination of video and computer-generated music and animation.

Striking My Eyes (1966); *Nixonbesuch und Hochschulkampf/Nixon's Visit and the University Struggle* (1968); *Besetzung und Selbstverwaltung eines Studentenwohnheims/Occupation and Self-Administration of a Student Hall of Residence* (1969); *Gegeninformation in Italien/Alternative Information in Italy* (1970); *Fuer Frauen – 1. Kapitel/For Women – Chapter 1* (1971); *Kreuzberg gehoert uns/Kreuzberg Belongs to Us* (1972); *Frauen hinter der Kamera/Women Behind the Camera* (1972); *Die Macht der Maenner ist die Geduld der Frauen/The Power of Men is the Patience of Women* (1978); *Die Frauen von Harrisburg/The Women of Harrisburg* (1981); *Mit den Waffen einer Frau/With the Weapons of a Woman* (1986)

Marc Silberman and Gretchen Elsner-Sommer, 'Women's Movement Art – Interview with Cristina Perincioli', *Jump Cut*, no. 29 (1984)   JK

PHALLIC WOMAN

The image of the phallic woman is most clearly seen in PORNOGRAPHY. In the male bondage film, one of the subgenres of film pornography, the phallic woman or dominatrix dresses in such a way as to suggest she has a penis. This effect is accomplished in at least two ways: she either wears a dildo or she adorns her whole body with phallic trappings (long black boots, whips, chains, and so on) which suggest that her actual body is a penis or phallic substitute. In this type of pornography the male plays the masochist, begging the phallic woman to humiliate and degrade him.

The most obvious representation of the phallic woman in mainstream cinema is the FEMME FATALE of FILM NOIR: her phallicism is suggested by her clothing (black dresses, long pointed fingernails, cigarette holders, and so on) and by the fact that she frequently carries a gun. Dangerous, deceptive, exciting, sensuous – the femme fatale presents a challenge to male power, particularly the power of the father, a sin for which she must ultimately be destroyed. Some of the more memorable phallic women of film noir are Barbara Stanwyck in *Double Indemnity* (Billy Wilder, Paramount 1944); Gloria Swanson in *Sunset Boulevard* (Billy Wilder, Paramount, 1950); and Jane Greer in *Out of the Past* (Jacques Tourneur, RKO, 1947).

FEMINIST FILM THEORY is interested in the phallic woman because her image, by inverting the power dynamics within male–female relationships, points to a crisis within the workings of sexist IDEOLOGY. Freudian psychoanalytic theory holds that the male child initially believes that the mother, whom he desires emotionally and physically, is exactly like himself – that is, that she too has a penis. His later realization that she is without a penis arouses in him fears about his own possible castration. His anxiety is likely to be increased if he mistakes her menstrual blood for the blood which he believes is flowing from her wound. Rather than acknowledge the real nature of the female genitals, he may set up a fetish which comes to stand in for them. Frequently, this fetish is a part of woman's anatomy which is reassuring and does not remind him of the possibility of castration. Often it is that part on which his averted glance first fell immediately after he turned away in shock from the sight of her genital area. Hence, fetish objects are frequently a woman's legs or shoes, or fur (which stands in for pubic hair). Recently, some feminist theorists have turned their attention to the notion of the phallic woman in order to develop a theory of identification and the LOOK which places the male in a subordinate, masochistic position rather than in a sadistic one.

Gaylyn Studlar, 'Masochism and the Perverse Pleasures of the Cinema', *Quarterly Review of Film Studies*, vol. 9, no. 4 (1984)

See also: AMAZONS; VAMP   BC

PICKFORD, MARY (1894–1979)

Born Gladys Marie Smith in Canada, Mary Pickford went on the stage at five years of age, making her film debut in her teens as an extra in D W GRIFFITH's *Her First Biscuits* (1909), and moving almost immediately into lead roles in many more Griffith films. By the early 1910s she was a major box office attraction, becoming one of the earliest STARS of cinema. In addition to acting, Pickford soon became involved in the production and distribution sides of the film industry, with the founding in 1919 of her own brainchild, United Artists. By the 1920s, 'America's sweetheart' had become one of the world's richest women, and the

lifestyle of the Mary Pickford–Douglas Fairbanks couple added greatly to Hollywood's glitter. Pickford retired from the screen in 1933, having made literally hundreds of films, in most of which she portrayed innocent, uncomplicated young women: she had in the end become trapped by the STEREOTYPE.

But it is impossible to portray Mary Pickford as a victim of the system – a role assigned to numerous female Hollywood stars by latter-day critics. On the contrary, she was a highly astute woman who understood her profession and her audience extremely well. Her fans, she knew, were mostly working-class and female: 'I am a woman's woman. My success has been due to the fact that women like the pictures in which I appear.' If, in accord with the mores of the time, Pickford achieved success by bringing to the screen an unsullied FEMININITY, her screen persona never had the vulnerability of, say, Lillian GISH's. Pickford's lively and spirited characters could take care of themselves, with good humor and determination: it is this, perhaps, which earned her the adulation of female cinemagoers all over the world.

Mary Pickford's best-loved films include: *Tess of the Storm Country* (Edwin S Porter, 1914); *Rags* (James Kirkwood, 1915); *Rebecca of Sunnybrook Farm* (Marshall Neilan, 1917); *The Poor Little Rich Girl* (Maurice Tourneur, 1917); *Little Lord Fauntleroy* (Alfred E Green and Jack Pickford, 1922); *Little Annie Rooney* (William Beaudine, 1925)

Sumiko Higashi, *Virgins, Vamps and Flappers: The American Silent Movie Heroine* (Montreal: Eden Press, 1978)
                                        AKu

PLEASURE

While the everyday meanings attached to this word have undergone much elaboration at the hands of FILM THEORY, its mundane associations of simple enjoyment constantly haunt attempts to theorize it. Nevertheless, two sets of ideas in particular have become associated, in studies of cinema, with the concept of pleasure. Drawing on work by the French cultural theorist Roland Barthes, studies of film and NARRATIVE invoke pleasure as a response solicited by REALIST texts, with their logical sequence of narrative events culminating in resolution: Barthes sets this against the 'bliss' [jouissance] of certain other modes of narration. In this context, the pleasures associated with CLASSICAL HOLLYWOOD CINEMA take on a particular kind of significance. Film theorists are also interested in the particular pleasures involved in looking at a moving image on a screen in a darkened auditorium. For example, the unconscious processes at work in film spectatorship are the domain of some PSYCHOANALYTIC FILM THEORY. Feminists adopting the view that the LOOK in classical cinema is masculine have sought to challenge Hollywood's pleasures, through FEMINIST INDEPENDENT FILM as well as FEMINIST FILM THEORY. Others, working in both areas, have sought to inquire into the nature and possibility of specifically feminine forms of pleasure in cinema.

Roland Barthes, *The Pleasure of the Text* (New York: Hill & Wang, 1975)

See also: AUDIENCE AND SPECTATOR

AKu

feature made by a woman and inaugurated a feminist dialogue in Québécois cinema. With this success behind her she established – with Jeanne Morazin and Monique Larocque – a program for women at the NFB called 'En tant que femmes.' During the life of the program (1972 to 1975), Poirier produced six films by women. For the first time, Québécois women were given the chance to reflect seriously on their condition and to record their thoughts on film. It was at this time that Poirier met scriptwriter Marthe Blackburn, and they formed a working relationship that has continued ever since. As Poirier's work developed, she began to form the style of filmmaking that is characteristic of her output. With her film *Les filles du roy* (1974), which explores the history of a number of destitute young women who were paid by the King of France to leave for 'La nouvelle France,' we see the emergence of Poirier's interest in a broken, rhythmic montage. *Mourir à tue-tête* (1979), which followed, provoked a number of controversial discussions. In this film Poirier sought to demystify our

> Mimi investigates her own death. Which feminist film features this tragic heroine and this plotline? From which feminist filmmaker?

POIRIER, ANNE-CLAIRE (1932–)

QUEBEC director, editor and film producer Poirier works in the French section of the NATIONAL FILM BOARD OF CANADA (NFB). Before making her first film at the NFB, a television documentary called *Trente minutes Mr Plummer* (1963), Poirier worked in various capacities in the media and in theater. Gradually, in her role as both director and producer, she developed a resolutely feminist approach within the state structure of filmmaking. Her film *De mère en fille* (1967), about pregnancy and motherhood, was the first Quebec

stereotyping of both the victim and the aggressor of rape. However, she was not entirely successful in avoiding the traps of voyeurism and victimization in her treatment of the subject. Despite this, the film was an international success. Since then she has made two other fiction films, both more linear in their approach: one, *La quarantaine*, about ageing; the other, *Salut Victor!*, on friendship.

Trente minutes Mr Plummer/Thirty Minutes Mr Plummer (1963); *La fin des étés/At the End of Summer* (1964); *De mère en fille/Mother-to-be* (1967); *L'impot de tout . . . de tout* (1969); *Le savoir-faire s'impose*

(1971); *Les filles du roy/They called us 'Les Filles du Roy'* (1974); *Le temps de l'avant/ Before the Time Comes* (1979); *Mourir à tue-tête/A Scream from Silence* (1979); *La quarantaine/Turning Forty* (1982); *Salut Victor!* (1988)

F Prevost and A Reiter, 'The Disturbing Dialectic of Anne-Claire Poirier', *Cinema Canada*, no. 90–91 (1982)   BF

POLAND

The almost total absence of engagement with feminism in the Polish film industry can be understood only within the context of the country's social, political, and cultural history, which in the last two hundred years has been turbulent and violent, with a long period of partition in the nineteenth century, a brief period of interwar independence followed by Nazi occupation, and then the imposition of Soviet Communism in 1945. In conjunction with the fervent espousal of Roman Catholicism, the national identity is complex, but must provide the context for any considerations of a political nature, such as feminism. Women automatically gained the vote when Poland emerged from 123 years of partition after World War I. The conjunction of such factors as the importance of women in estates' management during the partitions, when the men had been conscripted into the three opposing partitioning armies, and the Roman Catholic cult of the Virgin Mary, combined to create a quasi-matriarchal society. However, in the postwar film industry women have not featured greatly, other than in a few exceptional cases. Of note are directors Agnieszka HOLLAND, Wanda JAKUBOWSKA, Barbara SASS, and Ewa Petelska, and producer Barbara Pec-Slesicka.

The close relationship between national and social structures and cinema is compounded by the nature of film production and finance. In 1945, when the Nazi occupation was replaced by Soviet Communism, the Polish film industry – like those elsewhere in EAST-ERN EUROPE – was nationalized under the auspices of the state film board, Film Polski. Since then, it has been directly controlled in all aspects by government agencies. This remains the case even though production is apparently decentralized under the Zespoly Filmowe ('Film Groups') system, established in 1956. Zespoly Filmowe form a federation under which the separate groups operate. Budgets are planned by this federation, and funds distributed around the groups. The box office is the source of funding, with the state as ultimate underwriter. A film's success abroad in the hard currency market makes possible imports of foreign films for national distribution, profits from which then go back into the film fund. Polish feature production stands at approximately thirty per year. Each new Film Group is guaranteed a life of three years, and provides the initial professional training for film school graduates. Ultimate responsibility for the film industry lies with the Ministry of Arts and Culture, and is administered through the Central Office for Polish Cinematography. All films must be submitted to the censor.

Polish cinema, and culture generally, have consistently been concerned with a number of key issues related to national identity. Within cinema, these include assessments of the nation's troubled past, culpability, guilt, personal responsibility, and power and its effects. Narratives have predominantly been concerned with moments in the national history in which such issues could be explicitly foregrounded – World War II, the period of Stalinism, and the situation in postmartial-law Poland. However, these moments are also called upon in films whose treatment of the past is of a more allegorical nature. Even in the populist SCIENCE FICTION adventures of the eighties, in which social comment is less apparent than at any time in Polish postwar film history, the settings are rundown, not hi-tech, a reference to the past more than to the future. Against concerns with psychological probing of a nation which has consistently been a battleground of other nations' aspirations, issues such as gender have been rejected as not urgently in need of examination; indeed, feminism is generally viewed in Poland as 'a luxury we can't afford.' Feminist approaches, then, are absent at every level: in film production in terms of directors and producers; in film education; in developments in the use of film form; and in film narratives themselves.

To a more or less overt extent, the issues already mentioned have been central topics of Polish cinema since 1945. The films of 'The Polish School' (1954–63) are predominantly assessments of the war years in Poland and adaptations of the classics of the national literature. The concern with national past and national identity is most explicit in Andrzej Wajda's films of the period – for example, Lotna (1959), so weighted with symbolic references to national icons as to be almost incomprehensible to a viewer from outside Poland. The change in tone away from the romantic pessimism of the 'Polish School' evident in the films of the 'Cinema of Moral Anxiety' (1977–81) began with the emergence of the 'Second Generation' in the mid 1960s, most notably in directors Jerzy Skolimowski and Roman Polanski. The focus of attention became the daily realities of national life in a world where each person must face responsibility for the status quo. Before these themes found their full and dynamic expression in the late seventies (a period of relative stagnation in the film industry and political life after the crises and shakeups of the late sixties), the films of the 'Third Cinema' (1970–77) displayed an intensification of the themes of alienation and despair that had begun to emerge in the previous decade: Andrzej Zulawski's Treczia Czesc Nocy/The Third Part of the Night (1971) is a key example. The 'Cinema of Moral Anxiety' came about partly as a result of the proposals of a group of documentary filmmakers to translate documentary principles into feature production, and

directors such as Krzysztof Kieslowski successfully made the transition. Kieslowski's film Amator/Camera Buff (1979) is a less obvious, but nevertheless important, example of the films of this period, highlighting the concerns with personal responsibility and perspectives on culpability already mentioned.

The performances of the actress Krystyna JANDA in the films of this period did much to focus the attention of viewers and filmmakers alike on the experience of women. Her characterization of the film student and activist Agnieszka in Wajda's Czlowiek z Marmaru/Man of Marble (1977) and Czlowiek z Zelaza/Man of Iron (1981) developed from an aggressive and engaged commitment in 1977 to something of a madonna-type victim in 1981. Overall, the trend in Polish cinema of the 1980s has been toward second-rate attempts at popular forms, whose aping of western mores, combined with a traditional Polish conservatism, has proved more pervasively sexist than many of the offerings of western cinemas.

Frank Bren, *World Cinema 1: Poland* (London: Flick Books, 1986)   AG

POOL, LEA (1950–)

Québécoise (Canadian) film director of Swiss origin, Pool came to Canada in 1975 to study film and video. After collectively producing a number of student films (including *Laurent Lamerre Portier* [1978], her final school project), Pool made the low-budget short feature *Strass Café* in 1980. An experimental fiction,

> In Marta Mészáros's film Nine Months, actress Lili Monori achieved fame for a heroic act. What was it?

Strass Café employs strongly evocative black-and-white images and a poetic and rhythmical voice-over to speak of the city, of exile, solitude and the search for identity, and of a woman and a man who desire each other but never meet. The film won prizes at several festivals, most importantly the WOMEN'S FILM FESTIVAL at CRETEIL. This festival continued to honor Pool's later films. From 1978 to 1983 Pool taught film and video at the University of Quebec. Between 1980 and 1983 she simultaneously directed a series of programs on cultural minorities for Quebec television. Her second feature, *La femme de l'hôtel* (1984), again uses the city images that have become characteristic of her work. Constructed around three women characters, a filmmaker who befriends a strange, hotel-dwelling woman, and a singer who becomes the filmmaker's incarnation of the strange hotel-dweller, the film charmed audiences and the press with its evocation of the process of creation and the intermeshing of cinema and life. *Anne Trister* (1986) takes again the subject of exile in Pool's partly autobiographical story of a young Jewess, an artist, who leaves her native Switzerland after the death of her father to find her identity in Quebec with a woman friend. Her efforts take concrete form as she attempts to create an environmental painting in her studio, raising again the question of art and reality. Pool's 1988 feature *A corps perdu*, is centered on a male character, but like Pool's women protagonists he is an artist (a photographer), and again a displaced person. The photographer returns to Montreal from a work experience in Nicaragua which has unsettled the ethics of his art. In Montreal he finds that his previously idyllic threesome, a woman and a man lover, has now ended. Attempting to drown his pain, he photographs Montreal and takes another male lover, a deaf-mute. Pool is the only QUEBEC director/writer of popular film sympathetically and openly to treat the theme of homosexual relationships. At present, she is preparing a film for the NATIONAL FILM BOARD OF CANADA series entitled 'The Myth of America.'

Laurent Lamerre Portier (1978); *Strass Café* (1980); *La femme de l'hôtel/A Woman in Transit* (1984); *Anne Trister* (1986); *A corps perdu* (1988)

Edith Madore, '"J'ai besoin d'avoir un regard sur mon regard",' *Ciné bulles*, vol. 8, no. 1 (1988)   JL

PORNOGRAPHY

In cinema, the term 'pornography,' usually defined as distinct from EROTICISM, refers to films designed to arouse sexual desire in viewers – predominantly male. Attempts to make pornography illegal have usually failed; partly because of the difficulty in arriving at a definition. It has been argued that pornography is the inevitable consequence of prudery, and that it represents a deliberate defiance of conventional morality.

Although the term is used as if all pornographic texts were the same, a great diversity exists. Some of the subgenres are: nonviolent erotica; female bondage; male bondage; comedy-porn; genre-porn (based on mainstream film GENRES – for instance, *A Dirty Western* [David Fleetwood, 1975]); lesbian pornography (for male viewers); and a violent rape category in which the victims are women. Male homosexual pornography is made specifically for gay men. Unlike mainstream narrative film, the narrative structure of pornographic texts is slight: pornography is primarily concerned with scenarios of sex presented through closeup shots of genitalia and their interactions.

Pornography in cinema has attracted the attention of the women's movement and feminist critics in recent years. Although all feminists oppose the notorious 'snuff' movies and child pornography, they are not united in their response to pornography depicting adults. On the one hand, many regard pornography as a form of woman-hating and would like to see a total ban on it. They argue that pornography presents only one view of women – as carnal creatures always available to please men. They hold that watching pornography reinforces men's sexist attitudes to women. Extending the argument further, some argue that all 'images' of women (including advertising images) are pornographic, in that they represent only a male view of women, and should also be banned.

A different feminist argument is that pornographic films are primarily about male sexual fantasies. Rather than inciting men to rape, watching pornography may have a cathartic effect. Furthermore, the fact that there is a subgenre of male bondage films (the male as victim is tortured by a powerful, dominating woman) suggests that some pornography is designed to appeal to masochistic desires in men. Given that our society places strong taboos on the expression of male masochism, it is not surprising that such desires are represented primarily in an illicit form of entertainment. They argue that banning pornography would only send the sex industry underground and worsen even further women's working conditions. They tend to support legalization of pornography, in the hope that workers in the sex industry will then have some control over conditions, better pay, and the right to exercise some control over the films in which they appear.

Another issue which has arisen around the pornography debate concerns female PLEASURE. Some feminists argue that female spectators may derive pleasure from watching some forms of pornography. Pornography has been addressed to some extent in FEMINIST INDEPENDENT FILM: in Bette GORDON's *Variety* (USA, 1983), for example; and from a very different standpoint, Bonnie Sher Klein's *Not a Love Story* (Canada, 1980). And if women were to make their own pornography, how would it differ from male pornography?

Carol S Vance (ed.), *Pleasure and Danger: Exploring Female Sexuality* (London: Routledge & Kegan Paul, 1984)

See also: CENSORSHIP; EXPLOITATION FILM; PHALLIC WOMAN   BC

PORTUGAL

Portugal's film industry began in 1896 with a documentary made by Aurelio da Paz dos Rei. The first film theater in Lisbon dates from 1904, and the first film studio, Portugalia Films, from 1909. In 1911, Joao Tavares made Portugal's first box office success: *Os crimes de Diogo Alves/The Crimes of Diogo Alves*. But from the outset, the scarcity of local technicians and financial and commercial problems hindered the development of the industry. Women film directors or technicians were unthinkable in this early period – with one notable exception: Virginia Castro e Almeida, a writer living in Paris, created Fortuna Films in 1922, producing several films which were exported throughout Europe. Almeida's work includes *A sereia de pedra/The Stone Mermaid* (1922) and *Os olhos da alma/The Eyes of the Soul* (1923).

Under Portugal's own branch of fascism, which lasted from the late 1920s until 1968, censorship and propaganda were foremost. Documentaries and features idealized the family; banished class conflict; exalted gentlemen farmers, their bulls and their humble peasants; praised the nation's glorious past and its great writers; and presented an image of Catholic spirituality in opposition to the materialism of European democracies. The image of women promoted by the fascist Catholic hierarchy was that of the good mother, the demure fiancée, the hardworking peasant or fisherwoman, and the FEMME FATALE – often a foreigner. But there was no place for women filmmakers, and even now women are rare in Portugal's film industry.

In the late 1950s the government, worried by the state of the film industry, began sending promising young filmmakers to Europe to study. Inevitably, 'cinema d'auteur' was favored, a trend exaggerated by the unique presence of Manoel de OLIVEIRA, the sole international figure of Portuguese cinema. The main influences on Portugal's

319

Young Cinema (Cinema Novo) were Italian NEOREALISM, Mexican and French poetic realism, and British Free Cinema; but these soon gave way to France's NEW WAVE, with the JOURNAL *Cahiers du cinéma* becoming the main theoretical reference. The young filmmakers wanted to have their say and also to create their own technicians, producers, and distributors, making a clean break with the past. A loose coalition, they shared a desire to make a cinema of resistance to the culture of dictatorship. They found new languages and diverse themes, using allegory and symbolism – as well as self-restraint – to avoid censorship, believing in film as a privileged means of intervening in the larger social process.

After the dictator Salazar's fall from power in 1968, filmmakers had to look for alternative means of finance; and in 1970 a protocol was signed between the Centro Portugues de Cinema and the Gulbenkian Foundation, whereby the Gulbenkian financed documentaries and features on a grant-like basis. Filmmakers, freed from the constraints of the market, forgot their audience, and no amount of effort could persuade the Portuguese public to see their own films. The directors, mostly men, strove for an international style that could be presented in European forums. Only Jose Fonseca e COSTA's *O recado/The Message* (1971), an overtly political film, managed to reach a local audience. An alarming proportion of films from this period were never previewed, and the lack of dialogue between directors and their public exacerbated a divorce that has yet to be resolved. Nevertheless, Portugal's Cinema Novo created a film culture which has done much to nourish later generations of filmmakers.

The euphoria unleashed by the 1974 revolution resulted in a boom in documentaries and cooperative ventures. Filmmakers wanted to record the momentous changes. Censorship was banished; there were no more forbidden subjects, and collective themes were favored. A budding experimental cinema in super-8mm started, and women filmmakers and women's themes began to make themselves felt; but soon, with the institutionalization of the revolution, pre-1974 patterns of production were reestablished.

In the 1980s most filmmakers adopted a POSTMODERNIST language, without ever having used a MODERNIST one. Intertextuality became another form of elitism, and the state, which appears to believe that a NATIONAL CINEMA can come out of subsidies, continued to back films ignored by a public which prefers to see Hollywood films. A hopeful sign, however, is the number of new directors who have joined those who started filming after the 1970s. Women, often coming from television, are making their presence felt in all areas of the industry, and it is their growing numbers which is the salient feature of Portuguese cinema today.

Jean-Loup Passek (ed.) *Le cinéma portugais* (Paris: Centre Georges Pompidou, 1982)

See also: CORDEIRO, MARGARIDA AND REIS, ANTONIO; RUTLER, MONIQUE   NT

POSTMODERNISM

A controversial term, postmodernism has provoked widespread debate in recent years: even such a fundamental question as whether postmodernism signals a break with MODERNISM has not been resolved. Postmodernism has been variously defined as a new historical period, an artistic practice, a theory, a style.

Many definitions concentrate on postmodernism as the aftermath of the modern industrial age brought about by dramatic developments in technology. Cultural critic Jean Baudrillard sees a postmodern world as one dominated by electronic mass media and characterized by simulation: he laments the death of the individual and the loss of distinction between representation and the real. Marxist literary theorist Fredric Jameson has theorized a relationship between postmodernism as a cultural movement, its stylistic manifestations and its economic bases. In cinema, he argues, the dominant stylistic mode is pastiche (evident in the remake), and this signifies a nostalgic desire to return to an earlier, less problematic, time. This refusal to think historically Jameson sees as symptomatic of the 'schizophrenia' (a term favored also by Baudrillard) of consumer society. Critic Jean-François Lyotard defines postmodernism as a crisis in the legitimizing function of NARRATIVE.

> *'Oh dear, I've got to go through another day of kissing John Gilbert.' Which Mimi in MGM's film of La Bohème nearly lost her job for this complaint?*

Cultural theory is the area where postmodernism and feminism have most in common. Here, the feminist critique of patriarchy and the postmodern critique of knowledge intersect: both endorse Lyotard's thesis that there has been a loss of credibility in the *grands récits*, or 'master narratives', of the West – narratives once used to legitimate scientific research and the pursuit of knowledge. Both feminism and postmodernism are critical of any narrative which posits universal truths, such as Progress or Religion; both offer a critique of representation as a system of power which favors the viewpoint of the (white, middle-class) male subject; both are critical of binarism, a conceptual strategy which classifies in terms of oppositions (man/woman; white/black) in order to define the 'other' (woman, black) as inferior; both legitimate the equality of all cultures and voices within artistic practice. The difference, it seems, is that where postmodernism is engaged in a debate with modernist modes of representation,

feminism locates patriarchal IDEOLOGY as the oppressive system.

Feminist cultural theorist Alice Jardine has explored more closely the relationship between postmodernism and feminism in the writings of various French theorists such as Jacques Lacan, Jacques Derrida, and Gilles Deleuze. Their work is marked by what she terms a process of 'gynesis' – that is, a rethinking of the key topics of philosophy (Man, Truth, History) brought about by the collapse of the master narratives. This reconceptualization involves that which has always eluded the master narratives – a 'space' of some kind which is coded as 'feminine.' For instance, Derrida uses terms such as 'hymen' and 'invaginated text.' However, these (male) theorists never relate this process of gynesis to actual women or to feminism, which has always been concerned with these 'spaces.' Jardine argues that postmodern thinking is more indebted to feminism than it will acknowledge.

'Postmodern Screen', *Screen*, vol. 28, no. 2 (1987)

See also: POSTSTRUCTURALISM   BC

POSTSTRUCTURALISM

Poststructuralism refers to an influential contemporary movement which represents both a continuation of STRUCTURALISM and a challenge to it. It represents a methodological shift, a 'working through' of the major insights of structuralism within various fields of inquiry. Poststructuralism covers so many practices that it is difficult, if not impossible, to define. Specifically, poststructuralism challenges the concept of the unified self or subject, the notion of structure as a stable system and the practice of explaining phenomena in terms of origins. The most important single contribution has come from Jacques Derrida and his strategy of deconstruction; other influential theories include Louis Althusser's work on IDEOLOGY, Jacques Lacan's on subjectivity, and

Hélène Cixous's and Luce Irigaray's on FEMININITY.

Poststructuralism provides strategies for understanding language and for reading texts. It holds that a TEXT cannot be 'mastered' or given a definitive interpretation because of the very nature of language. A text must be located in its own historical time, place, and culture, for these factors will always affect its meanings. Poststructuralism sees as misguided efforts to appeal to AUTHORSHIP – to the author as an outside authority able to authenticate the text. Such a desire represents a nostalgia for the presence of a God or Truth. Furthermore, the belief that the individual is somehow 'fully present' to her/himself is a delusion, for we must all speak a language which already has meanings conferred on it by the sociocultural system – language speaks us, we do not speak language.

Building on Ferdinand de Saussure's theory of the 'sign,' on which SEMIOTICS is based, poststructuralism extends some of its insights. In its critique of the fixed nature of the Saussurean sign, it argues that language is a system which exists in competing discourses. For instance, words such as 'woman' are given different meaning in different discourses – medicine, religion, law. 'Woman' can also be constructed differently across film GENREs and within a single film text. The thesis that everything is constructed in and through language also provides a basis for the feminist critique of REALISM in cinema; feminist criticism examines the way cinematic codes are used to construct representations of femininity and MASCULINITY while at the same time making invisible the marks of this construction. The Derridean critique of the 'metaphysics of presence' is of interest to feminism, which views concepts such as Author, God, and Truth as synonymous with logocentrism and male power. Using deconstructive methods, feminists are able to isolate those 'gaps' or blind spots in the filmic text where male domination/power is represented as 'normal.' Also of importance is the critique of binarism – defining phenomena in terms of oppositions (man/woman, white/black) and 'naturalizing' these while giving ascendancy to those which uphold patriarchy (constructing 'woman' and 'black' as other). Lacanian accounts of the decentered subject and of sexual difference produced through language provide an understanding of how patriarchal ideology is constituted differently within women and men: however, there is some debate as to whether this should be seen as descriptive or prescriptive. Film theorist Laura MULVEY's important concept of the LOOK originates in Lacanian theory.

Chris Weedon, *Feminist Practice and Poststructuralist Theory* (Oxford: Basil Blackwell, 1987)

See also: POSTMODERNISM; PSYCHOANALYTIC FILM THEORY   BC

POTTER, SALLY (1949–)

A filmmaker working mainly in BRITAIN, Potter is also a dancer, choreographer, performance artist, and composer, and has been an active member of several feminist performance troupes. Her work in film began in 1968 when she started 8mm productions. *Thriller*, which was released in 1979, has already become something of a classic of FEMINIST INDEPENDENT FILM. Potter calls *The Gold Diggers* (1983), her first feature, 'a musical describing a female quest.'

This idea of a 'female quest' is important more generally to Potter's films, which follow inquiries centered around female sleuths trying to understand and revise woman's roles in film and other art forms. Potter places great weight on the idea of looking and being looked at. Her work also stresses MUSIC and SOUND: *Thriller* quotes freely from the OPERA *La Bohème* and the score of Alfred HITCHCOCK's film *Psycho* as it examines the sacrifices of their two HEROINES. *The*

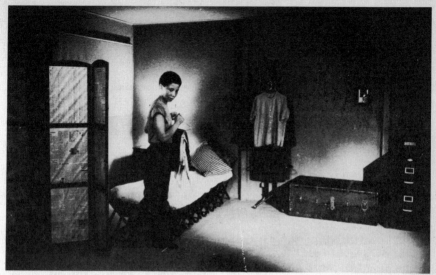

The Gold Diggers, by Sally Potter

Gold Diggers deploys conventions of classical MUSICALs – the dream-sequence, dance numbers, improvisation – while at the same time overturning them, refusing the heterosexual 'boy meets girl' narrative contract and filming in black and white, for example.

Potter's commitment to women in film extends to the selection of her production crew, which for *The Gold Diggers* was all-female (and every member was paid the same daily wage, including Julie Christie, one of the film's leads).

Thriller (1979); *The Gold Diggers* (1983); *The London Story* (1987)

Gillian Swanson and Lucy Moy-Thomas, 'An Interview with Sally Potter', *Undercut*, no. 1 (1981)

See also: DANCE   CF

POWELL, DILYS (1902–)

As a prominent FILM CRITIC for almost fifty years, Dilys Powell's role in British film culture cannot be overestimated. She worked as film critic of *The Sunday Times* from 1939 until 1976, and later for *Punch*; during the 1940s and for many years afterward her FILM CRITICISM (along with that of C A LEJEUNE of the *Observer*) dominated the attention of 'discriminating' filmgoers and many filmmakers, in a way that has no contemporary equivalent. At a time when the critical establishment in BRITAIN was still hidebound by notions of good taste, family values, and REALISM, Powell was expressing her enthusiasm for HITCHCOCK's *Psycho* (Shamley, 1960) and championing popular Hollywood genres, particularly WESTERNs and thrillers. Today many of her judgements (especially about British cinema – the films of POWELL AND PRESSBURGER, for instance) may seem common sense: at the time, however, Dilys Powell's voice was surprisingly strong and progressive. Although she has never described herself as a feminist, nor taken a particular interest in women's cinema, in the 1950s Powell wrote supportively about some of the women stars (such as Diana DORS) who tended to be dismissed or despised by other critics.

Much admired for her integrity, genuine enthusiasm for cinema, and unpretentious approach, Dilys Powell has remained an essentially humanist critic: she strongly dislikes the 'incomprehensible' world of FILM THEORY, particularly SEMIOTICS and STRUCTURALISM. Today Dilys Powell is well known to British audiences as a radio broadcaster. She has produced only one booklet about cinema, *Films Since 1939* (1946), but has written several books about Greece, based on her extensive travels there in the early 1930s and on her work in the Greek section of the wartime Political Warfare Executive. The most popular of these is *An Affair of the Heart* (1957).

Gerald Pratley, 'Dilys Powell', *Films in Review*, vol. 35, no. 4 (1984)   CM

POWELL, MICHAEL (1905–90) and PRESSBURGER, EMERIC (1902–88)

In recent years, much effort has gone into writing about a strand of BRITAIN's cinema that offers an alternative to its dominant strain of REALISM – a vein of FANTASY that explores the sexuality and violence seething under the polite surface. Central to such an exploration must be the work of Powell and Pressburger, whose extraordinary films were at first adversely received by critics, who held that they undermined 'quality' British filmmaking. Alexander Korda (the nearest British equivalent to a movie mogul) was responsible for introducing Michael Powell, born in Canterbury, Kent, to Emeric Pressburger, like Korda a native of Hungary. The partnership was unique in British film history, a challenge to notions of AUTHORSHIP in film, since they collaborated totally on writing, producing, and directing their marvelously visual films. They managed to achieve a remarkable degree of autonomy, starting their own production company The Archers, in 1942, from which emanated a stream of extraordinarily sumptuous films. *A Canterbury Tale* (1944) explores the mystic and arcane in British landscape; and *I Know Where I'm Going* (1945) the pagan, Celtic spirit of the past. They created extravagantly baroque MUSICAL fantasies in *The Red Shoes* (1948) and *The Tales of Hoffmann* (1951).

The elements of sadomasochism and misogyny evident in Powell/Pressburger films are not surprising, given that their maverick imagination owes much to romanticism and the gothic. Punishment is meted out to 'aberrant' women like Vicky in *The Red Shoes*, who, faced with an impossible dilemma – her art or her love – finally chooses death. In *Black Narcissus* (1947) a nun tries to kill her Mother Superior before falling to her own death, driven by hysterically repressed sexual feelings toward the film's hero. Michael Powell's solo directorial project *Peeping Tom* (1960) explicitly links the obsessional hero's murderous gaze at women with the voyeurism of the film camera, which is also his murder weapon.

Powell and Pressburger's films include: *The Life and Death of Colonel Blimp* (1943); *A Canterbury Tale* (1944); *I Know Where I'm Going* (1945); *A Matter of Life and Death* (1946); *Black Narcissus* (1947); *The Red Shoes* (1948); *The Small Back Room* (1949); *Gone to Earth* (1950); *The Tales of Hoffmann* (1951)

Ian Christie (ed.), *Powell, Pressburger and Others* (London: British Film Institute, 1978)   SP

PREOBRAZHENSKAIA, OLGA (1881–1971)

Preobrazhenskaia – actress, director, and scenarist – is probably the single most important woman to have worked in Russian and SOVIET cinema. Trained as an actress at the Moscow Art Theater, she worked in provincial Russian theaters before starring in her first film, the phenomenally popular *Kliuchakh schastia/Keys to Happiness* (1913), based on the equally popular novel of the same name by Anastasiia Verbitskaia. Preobrazhenskaia starred in numerous other big-budget movies in the pre-revolutionary period, and was one of

Preobrazhenskaia's *Peasant Women of Riazan*

Russia's leading film actresses. In 1916 she turned her cinematic talents to directing (*Baryshnia-krestianka*, co-directed with Vladimir Gardin), thereby becoming Russia's first female director.

After the 1917 Revolution, Preobrazhenskaia taught in the first Soviet film school for several years before returning to film direction in 1926 with *Kashtanka* (1926) and *Ania* (1927), two films for children. From 1927 to 1941 she collaborated exclusively with director Ivan Pravov. Their first effort is also their best known, *Baby riazanskie* (1927). The story of a traditional young married woman who is raped by her father-in-law, this is one of the greatest films to come from early Soviet cinema – and also one of the most controversial (its critics charging it, unjustly, with sensationalism). Preobrazhenskaia directed continuously throughout the difficult thirties, the best known of her films of this period being her adaptation of the Civil War novel *Tikhii Don* (1931) and the historical epic *Stepan Razin* (1939).

Baryshnia-krestianka/The Lady Peasant (1916); *Viktoriia* (1917); *Kashtanka* (1926); *Ania* (1927); *Baby riazanskie/Peasant Women of Riazan* (1927); *Svetlii gorod/ Bright City* (1928); *Poslednii attraktsion/ The Last Attraction* (1929); *Tikhii Don/ The Quiet Don* (1931); *Vrazhi tropi/ Enemy Paths* (1935); *Stepan Razin* (1939); *Paren iz taigi/Boy from the Taiga* (1941)

Charles Ford, 'Olga Preobrajenskaia et "le village du péché"', in *Femmes cinéastes, ou le triomphe de la volonté* (Paris: Denoël/Gonthier, 1972)   DJY

PRESSBURGER, EMERIC *see*
POWELL, MICHAEL and
PRESSBURGER, EMERIC

PRESTON, GAYLENE (1947–)
Gaylene Preston is a NEW ZEALAND filmmaker who sees herself as an unashamed propagandist, saying that her movies always contain a fairly definite message, although she would be disappointed if they got so preachy as to be dull rather than inspirational. An art therapist turned filmmaker, Preston is probably the most commercial and successful of the handful of New Zealand

women directors: she makes advertisements and documentaries, as well as features when she can get the funding. Her documentaries tend to be creative, imaginative studies of groups of young people, particularly those who are handicapped in some way; though she has also made music clips, a documentary for British television on Booker Prize winner Keri Hulme, and an experimental video about an obnoxious male art critic who gets thrown out of the window on a long car journey.

Male aggression and female resourcefulness are the subjects of her first feature film, *Mr Wrong* (1985), a clever, humorous yet effective thriller in which the traditionally voyeuristic camerawork of that genre is used to set up expectations of danger which the heroine adroitly escapes. The climax of the film is unfortunately taken out of the heroine's hands, a fact on which many critics have commented unfavorably; but the overall impression is of good entertainment set firmly in the terms of a feminist analysis of male–female relationships. A second feature, *Ruby and Rata*, is currently in production.

The Animals and the Lawn Mower (1972); *Draw Me a Circle* (1973); *Mojak Kojak* (1975); *Creeps on the Crescent* (1976); *Beresford Street Primary School* (1977); *Toheroamania* (1977); *Dat's Show Biz* (1977); *Water the Way You Want It* (1977); *All the Way Up There* (1978); *Learning Fast* (1981); *Holdup* (1981); *How I Threw Art Out the Window* (1981); *Making Utu* (1982); *Taking Over* (1982); *The Only One You Need* (1983); *Angel Of the Junk Heap* (1983); *Mindout* (1984); *Mr Wrong* (1985); *Kai Purakau* (1987)   AH

PRODUCTION CODE

The ideologies of CLASSICAL HOLLYWOOD CINEMA were conditioned to a great extent by the Production Code, sometimes called the Hays Code, a detailed set of self-CENSORSHIP guidelines. The Code was written in 1930,

after many attempts by the Motion Picture Producers and Distributors Association (MPPDA) to develop a self-censorship system. It did not become enforceable until 1934, when the major Hollywood studios signed the 'Resolution for Uniform Interpretation,' which gave authority over interpretation of the Code to a central agency, the Production Code Administration (PCA), also known as the Hays Office or the Breen Office. The 1934 decision came about for many reasons: the Catholic Legion of Decency organized interfaith opposition to Hollywood; early 1930s gangster films such as *The Public Enemy* (William Wellman, Warner Bros., 1931) were criticized for making gangsters sympathetic characters and for suggesting that illegal activities could result in economic welfare; the early 1930s 'kept woman' film cycle raised concerns about women living comfortable lives by exchanging sexual favors for economic security, as in *Red-Headed Woman* (Jack Conway, MGM, 1932); and the United States Congress proposed legislation asking that a government censor be installed in the studios to watch over film production. The film industry chose to self-censor or self-regulate through enforcing the Production Code. Films made before 1934 are known as 'pre-Code' films.

The three general principles of the Code were:

> No picture shall be produced which will lower the moral standards of those who see it. Correct standards of life, subject only to the requirements of drama and entertainment, shall be presented. Law – divine, natural, or human – shall not be ridiculed, nor shall sympathy be created for its violation.

In its 'Particular Applications' section, the Code detailed proscriptions on the representation of SEXUALITY and violence, and required that social institutions such as the family, law, government, and religion not be held up to scrutiny or criticism. Prior to shooting, all scripts were read line by line by the PCA, which required revisions or the elimination of dialogue and scenes. The completed films were also screened by the PCA. If passed, they were given the Seal of Approval, which was required before films could be exhibited.

The Production Code was not without its contradictions. Interpretation of films included attention to 'proper compensating moral values.' Good (moral) characters would be rewarded with happiness (true love, success), while bad (immoral) characters would be punished (death, dishonor, unhappiness). Thus, the ending of a film was privileged: films could represent immoral or illegal activities to a limited extent, keeping in mind that the NARRATIVE structure was so designed that the ending would properly 'compensate' the characters in terms of the Code's moral values. The Hollywood 'happy ending' is inextricably tied to 'appropriate' moral and social values. The authority of the PCA and the Production Code was slowly eroded in the 1950s, for several reasons. Because it was administered by the MPPDA, the Code was dependent upon the cooperation of the major studios, whose power was loosened through independent production and the erosion of the HOLLYWOOD STUDIO SYSTEM. Attempts to draw the waning film audience away from television included films with 'adult themes' (sex, violence). By 1968 the Code had been replaced with a Ratings System, which allows more flexibility in subject matter and treatment. However, the ideologies which informed the Code and Hollywood films for more than twenty years remain well entrenched.

Lea Jacobs, 'Censorship and the Fallen Woman Cycle', in *Home is Where the Heart Is: Studies in Melodrama and the Woman's Film*, ed. Christine Gledhill (London: British Film Institute, 1987)

MBH

PSYCHOANALYTIC FILM THEORY

The idea of films as dreams and the cinema industry as a 'dream factory' – hinting at the exploitation of forces we do not understand – must be almost as old as the medium itself, as is an often unspoken association between cinema and the erotic. A comment, made in 1931 by a moral reformer writing in the *Vigilance Record*, that '. . . instead of affecting the mind and still less so the heart, [film dramas] affect, above all, the sexual instincts. . . . In that lies the mysterious secret of the astonishing success of the cinemas,' is very telling indeed: while perhaps taking issue with the censorious tone, few latter-day film theorists would disagree with the analysis.

It was not, however, until the late 1960s and early 1970s that FILM THEORY began more or less systematically to raid the insights of certain schools of psychoanalysis in the quest to explain how films and cinema work at the unconscious level, and the writings in this area of French theorist Christian Metz became widely disseminated in anglophone film theory. Metz and others drew on concepts such as Sigmund Freud's libido drives and Jacques Lacan's mirror phase to advance a model of cinematic representation as *constructing* its spectators/subjects through the reenactment of unconscious processes involved in the acquisition of language, of sexual difference, and of autonomous selfhood, or subjectivity. Since the early 1970s, psychoanalytic film theory has developed into a considerable, complex, and often uneven body of work, in which three main tendencies may be identified: first, a concern with cinema as a machine producing its subjects within an 'apparatus' which includes not only films and spectators but the entire context of reception, including auditorium, screen, projector, and so on; secondly, a more specific preoccupation with the relationship between film TEXTS and spectators, with particular reference to unconscious processes involved in visual PLEASURE in cinema; and thirdly, an approach to 'reading' films which treats texts as 'material for interpretation,' using the same techniques psychoanalysts would use in deciphering dreams, bodily symptoms, or 'Freudian slips.'

The latter two tendencies have been particularly influential on FEMINIST FILM THEORY – and, indeed, vice versa. Since Laura MULVEY's pioneering 1975 essay 'Visual Pleasure and Narrative Cinema,' in which psychoanalytic categories are drawn on in an implied critique of the gender-blindness of preexisting psychoanalytic film theory, feminism has been the real driving force behind 'cinepsychoanalysis.' In the area of spectator–text relations, Mulvey's ideas about sexual difference and the LOOK in cinema have been a fruitful source of research and debate, provoking challenging questions concerning female spectatorship, and the relationship between on the one hand female/feminine spectators as subjects constructed through unconscious processes, and on the other the female audience as a social group. In the area of textual analysis, psychoanalytic theory has provided tools for prying layers of 'unconscious' meaning from film texts. Feminist psychoanalytic readings of texts of CLASSICAL HOLLYWOOD CINEMA have excavated deeply embedded meanings around FEMININITY and SEXUALITY, meanings often at odds with outward appearances, and highly informative about the deeper cultural levels at which patriarchy operates. Reading DOMINANT CINEMA 'against the grain' can be a form of resistance to Hollywood's lures, but a resistance which does not necessarily involve renouncing certain forms of pleasure– the pleasure of resistance itself, for instance, or that of deciphering a cultural puzzle.

Christian Metz, *Psychoanalysis and Cinema: The Imaginary Signifier* (London: Macmillan, 1982)

See also: AUDIENCE AND SPECTATOR; SCOPOPHILIA   *AKu*

QUEBEC

The first period of the history of women's filmmaking in Quebec is really also a history of the NATIONAL FILM BOARD OF CANADA (NFB). In 1956 the NFB moved from Ottawa to Montreal, a bilingual city, providing enormous impetus to both French- and English-speaking filmmakers. Although the Board is a national institution, the presence of its headquarters in Montreal has had a significant impact on Quebec filmmaking and the cultural identity of the province. At the beginning of the sixties, French Quebec was undergoing significant changes as a result of the 'Quiet Revolution' [*La révolution tranquille*] which overthrew the power of the church and opened up universities and cultural institutions for the first time. The NFB provided a critical outlet for this liberated expression.

During World War II, many talented English-speaking women from Quebec – Jane Marsh, Gudrun Parker, Evelyn Spice, Laura Boulton, and Margaret Pettery – suddenly had 'access' to the newly formed NFB (still in Ottawa at the time). French-speaking women from Quebec were absent from this awakening, remaining almost totally silent in this period. However, the NFB's story of women taking up traditionally male professions during the war follows the typical pattern: as soon as the war ends, women are forced to return to their domestic labors. This impressive body of work by women directors stops almost exactly at the end of the war. It was to be another twenty-five years before women's voices began to reemerge in the history of Quebec cinema. These voices found their expression in 'cinéma direct,' the dominant style of Quebec DOCUMENTARY, to be distinguished from cinéma vérité by its sympathetic engagement with its subjects. The first major step in breaking the now almost exclusively male domination of the NFB was taken in the seventies, in the French sector, with a program called 'En tant que femmes' (1971–5) pioneered by Anne-Claire POIRIER. This program enabled women like Aimée Danis and Hélène Girard to make their first documentary films: a few of them, including Poirier and Mireille Dansereau, later went on to make feature films. Poirier's *Les filles du roy* (1974), which was made in this program, is commonly referred to as Quebec's first resolutely feminist film.

> *Who is the girl with the tutti-frutti hat?*

In the private sector, Mireille Dansereau's *La vie rêvée* (1972) was the first feature film made by a woman in Quebec, and the first feature made by the newly formed film coop ACPAV (Association Coopérative de Productions Audio-Visuelles). However, it was the NFB that continued, and still continues, to be the major funder of women's productions, both experimental and documentary. The most notable productions from the seventies in the public and private sector are Paule Baillargeon's experimental fiction *Anastasie oh ma chérie* (1977); the documentary *Some American Feminists* by Luce Guilbault and Nicole Brossard (1978); the feature documentary by Hélène Girard, *La p'tite violence* (1978); Bonnie Klein's *Patricia's Moving Picture* (1978), and Poirier's *Mourir à tue-tête* (1979).

329

The rebirth of women's filmmaking in the anglophone section of the NFB began a few years later with the funding of a series of films called *Working Mothers* by Kathleen SHANNON. In 1974 Shannon was made head of a new English women's studio, STUDIO D. Through its funding of independent films and its apprenticeship programs, Studio D has been a major force in supporting the work of English women filmmakers in Quebec. At its inception the Studio's mandate was to make films by and for women, either collectively or individually. Although it continues to be underfunded, the Studio has made films of Oscar-winning caliber, such as Terri Nash's *If You Love This Planet* (1982) and Cynthia Scott's *Flamenco at 5.15* (1983). The Studio's year-long training program, organized to coincide with International Youth Year in 1981, took on trainees chosen primarily from film school graduates, among whom were a number of women from ethnic communities. These women are now all actively working in the film industry. Also in 1981 the NFB established the Federal Women's Film Program, a unique women's collective, working in both French and English and making socially and politically committed documentary films. Despite the Employment Equity Agreement signed by the NFB in 1987, however, it is still not easy to combat male prejudices about the role of women in the industry. Outside Montreal, women in Quebec City in the collective VIDEO FEMMES organized to establish the QUEBEC WOMEN'S FILM AND VIDEO FESTIVAL, which survived eleven years. The organizers, Hélène Roy, Nicole Giguère and Hélène Girard, are themselves filmmakers and videomakers.

In 1986 the French branch of the NFB set up its Studio D equivalent, 'Regard des femmes.' Like Studio D, 'Regard des femmes' exclusively engaged women filmmakers from the independent sector. Women making documentary films in Quebec, as elsewhere in CANADA, are still, however, almost entirely dependent on the NFB for most of their funding. Filmmakers in Quebec – such as Sophie Bissonnette (*Une histoire de femmes* [1980]), Sylvie van Brabant, Monique Crouillère, Marie Decary, Hélène Doyle, Jeanine Gagne, Nicole Giguère, Luce Guilbault, Sylvie Groulx (*Le grand remue-ménage* [1978]), Anne Henderson, Tina Horne, Hélène Klodawski, Jacqueline Levitin, Micheline LANCTOT, Marilú MALLET (*Journal inachevé* [1983]), Michelle Perusse, Iolande Rossignol, Lois Siegal and Tanya Tree, and now staff filmmakers Diane Beaudry, Alanis OBOMSAWIN, Beverly Shaffer and Tahani Rached – all began their careers by establishing portfolios with support from one of the many programs at the NFB.

Production in fiction filmmaking remains largely the domain of the private sector. Government funding for filmmaking in Quebec has been available since the foundation of the 'Institut du cinema québécois' in 1978. Since then, SOGIC (Société générale des industries culturelles de Quebec) has offered financial support to filmmakers, recently changing its criteria to allow support for documentary as well as fiction filmmaking. Though not always obviously feminist, a number of feature films have been made by women directors in Quebec: *La cuisine rouge* (1980) by Paule Baillargeon, and films by Mireille Dansereau, Lea POOL, and Brigitte Sauriol. Graduates from the Cinema Department at Montreal's Concordia University set up Mainfilm in 1982, replacing ACPAV as the alternative filmmakers' cooperative. It has produced a significant body of experimental filmmaking, including the work of feminist experimental fiction filmmaker Jeanne Crepeau. Cinema departments at Concordia and other universities have played a critical part in the training of many women filmmakers now working in the industry. A few, such as Nathalie Barton, Mary Armstrong and Louise Carré – who runs a production company for women filmmakers, *La maison des quatre Inc.* – work independently in both documentary and fiction filmmaking. Women have also been very active in the union of Quebec filmmakers, the ARRFQ (Association des réalisateurs et réalisatrices de films du Quebec) and in the independent technicians' union, the STCYQ (Syndicat des techniciennes et techniciens du cinéma et de video de Quebec).

VIDEO has its own history in Quebec. For a while, in the seventies, it was a lively concern at the NFB, and developed as a medium during the Board's *Challenge for Change* program. In 1975 and 1976 the NFB ran a series of workshops for women involved in videomaking. However, it became obvious that the Board's priority was the film format, and the 'Reseau video femmes' (now 'Réseau vidé-elle') became an independent organization. Videographe and PRIM, video production companies, encourage women directors and technicians in the field. The GROUPE INTERVENTION VIDEO, a video distribution company, deals exclusively with work by women. In Quebec City, Video Femmes has had a long and important history in videomaking.

The state-financed Cinémathèque Québécoise has always provided an important forum for the screening of films made by Quebec women, as well as an archival service. The year 1985 marked the birth of the MONTREAL INTERNATIONAL FESTIVAL OF FILMS AND VIDEOS BY WOMEN, which has also been a showcase for many Quebec women filmmakers' work. In 1989, in its fifth year, the festival has achieved a scale and a reputation which make it unique in North America.

Louise Carriere, *Femmes et cinéma québécois* (Montreal: Les Editions Boreal Express, 1983)

See also: NATIVE CANADIAN FILM   *SB*

QUEBEC WOMEN'S FILM AND VIDEO FESTIVAL/FESTIVAL DES FILLES DES VUES DE QUEBEC

A noncompetitive WOMEN'S FILM FESTIVAL organized in 1977 by VIDEO FEMMES in Quebec City, QUEBEC, the festival held its event annually until forced to fold in 1989 for lack of financing. The CRETEIL film festival paid homage to the Quebec festival in 1987, celebrating its status as the oldest annual festival of women's cinema in the world.

BF

RACE AND CINEMA

Racism and colonialism in cinema were present at the medium's inception, suggest film critics Robert Stam and Louise Spence. The unflattering portrayal of people of color coincided with the height of European imperialism, they contend, in 'the long parade of lazy Mexicans, shifty Arabs, savage Africans and exotic Asiatics that have disgraced our movie screens,' and in persistent representations of native Americans as 'beasts and cannibals,' and of latinos as 'greasers and bandidos.'

Negative and demeaning representations of BLACK WOMEN and men, for example, have become standard in mainstream Hollywood productions, beginning with *Uncle Tom's Cabin* (Edwin S Porter, 1903) through D W GRIFFITH's paean to white supremacy in *The Birth of a Nation* (1915), and continuing to the present. Black people have been presented as vicious sex-crazed brutes, docile and faithful slaves and servants, tragically doomed fairskinned women, and clownish buffoonish louts. Five black STEREOTYPES have been identified in early US films: toms, coons, mulattoes, mammies, and bucks. Variations on these basic types have appeared throughout the history of black representation in films, but most images retain the essence of the original five.

NATIVE AMERICANS have been portrayed as cunning and savage 'Red Indians,' their inexplicable and unpredictable bloodlust directed toward white settlers of the American West providing dramatic tension and occasioning lively action sequences in a long line of Hollywood WESTERNs. It is significant that, while in these films native Americans usually appear in groups–with the consequence that characters are neither individualized nor developed – in those rare instances where an Indian is set off from the pack and treated as a character in his own right (as, for example, in *Sign of the Pagan* [Douglas Sirk, Universal, 1954], starring Rock Hudson), he is always played by a white actor; even so, events in the narrative are never constructed from his point of view. Native American women in Westerns are invariably no more than a backcloth to the action. The IDEOLOGICAL contradictions with which such representations are fraught are brought close to the surface in some of John Ford's Westerns. In *The Searchers* (Warner Bros., 1956) the topic of miscegenation is addressed more or less directly in that the hero (John Wayne) is shown quite critically to be pathological in his dread of interracial sex – his native American alter ego is called Scar (played by white actor Henry Brandon). Nevertheless, the resolution of the film is the rescue of the white girl from the 'savages' with whom she has been living for ten years, and the restoration of the proper civilized pioneer family. Ford's later Westerns, notably *Cheyenne Autumn* (Warner Bros., 1964), herald a shift in white attitudes toward native Americans, their history, and their relation to the land. This has coincided with a decline in the Western, suggesting that the 'otherness' of the 'Indians' performed key functions – at the levels of both theme and ICONOGRAPHY – in this GENRE.

By contrast with portrayals of native Americans, the otherness of Latin characters in Hollywood films tends to be sexualized. Unrepressed or wayward SEXUALITY, as a stereotype, is associated with deviousness and untrust-worthiness; and in filmic representations of latins there has often been a sexual division of labor here, with latinos being portrayed as lazy and cunning, and LATINAS as exotic, fiery, sultry, and unpredictable.

For many years, interracial relation-ships were regarded as taboo as themes for films. The Hollywood PRODUC-TION CODE, for example, expressly forbade such storylines ('*Miscegenation* [sex relationship between the white and black races] is forbidden'). In the 1930s the BRITISH BOARD OF FILM CEN-SORS banned Frank Capra's *The Bitter Tea of General Yen* (Columbia, 1932), which dealt with the love of a Chinese warlord for an American girl. While such themes may no longer attract outright CENSORSHIP, the milk-and-water *Guess Who's Coming to Dinner* (Stanley Kramer, 1967) notwithstanding, they do continue to be regarded as too difficult for mainstream cinema to handle.

Robert Stam and Louise Spence, 'Col-onialism, Racism and Representation: An Introduction', in *Movies and Methods*

Volume 2, ed. Bill Nichols (Berkeley: University of California Press, 1985)

See also: ETHNOGRAPHIC FILM   *JBo*

RADIO-KEITH-ORPHEUM *see* RKO

RAINER, YVONNE (1934–)
During the 1950s Rainer trained with Martha Graham and Merce Cunning-ham, co-founding the Judson Dance Workshop in New York with Steve Pax-ton in 1962 and becoming an influential figure in US modern DANCE in the six-ties and early seventies. In 1968 she began to integrate slides and short films into live performances, and her first feature film, *Lives of Performers* (1972), evolved directly from her performance work. Since 1975 she has devoted herself ex-clusively to independent filmmaking, becoming more and more concerned with theoretical and political issues of narrative and representation.

Formally, her films belong with the New York-based minimalist/structural movement of the early seventies, exem-plified by the work of Michael Snow,

Yvonne Rainer's *The Man Who Envied Women*

Joyce WIELAND, George Landow, and Hollis Frampton. But Rainer has been increasingly at odds with the purism of the American AVANT GARDE, with its emphasis on the materiality of film at the expense of psychology, emotion, and politics, and has aligned herself more closely with the work of Jean-Luc GODARD. While sharing an antipathy to NARRATIVE born of a distrust of Hollywood's grip on the audience's hearts and minds, Rainer's interest in human (and specifically power) relationships requires a degree of characterization, and this has prevented her from simply abandoning or rejecting narrative form. At the same time, her political roots in sixties collectivism and seventies feminism have fed an anarchic impulse to deconstruct CLASSICAL HOLLYWOOD CINEMA in order to defuse its authority.

Her feminism also led her to question very early on (*Lives of Performers*; *Film About a Woman Who . . .* [1974]) mainstream cinema's inbuilt voyeurism and dependence on women's bodies as spectacle – well before Laura MULVEY's influential 'Visual Pleasure' article in 1975. Rainer shares with Mulvey (and other avant-garde apologists) a certain puritanism (characteristic also of Godard's COUNTERCINEMA and of some 1970s FEMINIST INDEPENDENT FILM) – seasoned, fortunately, with the saving grace of a playful wit. As well as making liberal use of Brechtian 'alienation' effects, Rainer's work evinces a POSTMODERNIST concern with intertextuality – combining and recombining snippets from many different media and art forms. Since *Kristina Talking Pictures* (1976), her films have become ever more dense and multi-layered, coinciding with a growing commitment to FEMINIST FILM THEORY. Her most recent film, *The Man Who Envied Women* (1985), tackles Oedipal narrative, male psychoanalytic theory, the New Man, attitudes to ageing, US policy toward Central America, and the New York housing crisis, and contains large chunks of quotations from critical theorists such as Michel Foucault, Fredric Jameson, Julia Kristeva, and Meaghan Morris. Perhaps her most theoreticist work, almost requiring a reading list to help the viewer disentangle its complexities, this film nevertheless manifests the characteristic Rainer combination of irony, passion, self-interrogation, and intellect.

Volleyball (short, 1968); *Hand Movie* (short, 1968); *Rhode Island Red* (short, 1968); *Trio Film* (short, 1969); *Line* (short, 1969); *Lives of Performers* (1972); *Film About a Woman Who . . .* (1974); *Kristina Talking Pictures* (1976); *Working Title: Journeys from Berlin/1971* (1980); *The Man Who Envied Women* (1985)

Yvonne Rainer, *Work 1961–73* (New York: New York University Press, 1974) PC

RAUTENBACH, JANS (1936–   ) and NOFAL, EMIL (1926–86)

Trained originally as a psychologist, SOUTH AFRICAN filmmaker Jans Rautenbach joined Emil Nofal in 1964 to form a production company. Rautenbach's first documentary, *The Ever Free* (1967), gained an award at the 1968 Milan Film Festival. His partnership with Emil Nofal saw the production of *Wilde Seison* (1967), *Die Kandidaat* (1968) and *Katrina* (1969). Rautenbach then directed and produced two films from his own production company – *Jannie Totsiens* (1970) and *Pappa Lap* (1971) – before rejoining Nofal for *Ongewenste Vreemdeling* (1974). Nofal's early work was also in the field of documentary, his first fiction film being *Rip van Wyk* (1960). The contentious nature of many of Nofal's early films led him into protracted engagement with the Publications Control Board and with the National Party and Dutch Reformed Church establishments.

Jans Rautenbach's and Emil Nofal's collaborative films come the closest to representing a film movement in South Africa. The heavily allegorical-symbolic style, particularly in the later ones, disguises their inner meanings, both from both from the censors – who nevertheless fiercely attacked them – and also from more conservative South Africans. Rautenbach and Nofal use many of the genre STEREOTYPES found in earlier South African films. However, their radically different treatment of NARRATIVE and ICONOGRAPHIC conventions ensure that these are challenged.

The heroine of *Katrina*, for example, is designated under apartheid as 'colored.' She 'tries for white,' but is rejected. The tragedy of Katrina's situation is that her place in society is doomed, her suicide inevitable: psychologically, she cannot make herself 'white'; physically, she cannot return to the desolation of the 'colored' village. In *Jannie Totsiens* a brilliant young man, in an effort to resist his domineering mother, lapses into catatonic silence. He regains sanity through his relationship with two women, both of whom are incapable of emerging from their own twilight world.

Despite the centrality of women in both these films, women's status in Rautenbach's and Nofal's work is ambiguous. In *Jannie Totsiens*, for example, all three women characters are demented or deluded, with no firm grasp on reality. Liz, the only English-speaking character in the film, is plagued by insecurity and loneliness, and can face the world only through a veil of drug-induced euphoria. Linda (played by Katinka HEYNS), irreversibly scarred by her parents' concept of sin, pathologically remains a child. In these films, women are portrayed as powerful – but untrustworthy.

Wilde Seison/Wild Season (1967); *Die Kandidaat* (1968); *Katrina* (1969); *Jannie Totsiens* (1970); *Ongewenste Vreemdeling* (1974)

Barry Ronge, 'Jans Rautenbach in Retrospect', *New Nation*, vol. 4, no. 2 (1970)   WJA/RET

READ, MELANIE (1955–)

Melanie Read is the only one of NEW ZEALAND's major female directors to identify herself as a 'radical lesbian feminist.' However, the two feature films she has made so far – *Trial Run* (1984) and *Send a Gorilla* (1988) – operate at the 'feminist' end of that continuum, probably in order to obtain the best possible commercial release and distribution.

Read's early life was spent in Malaysia and Australia. She moved to New Zealand as late as 1977, having already started work in Australia as a film editor with television. She has found it easier to make films which display a feminist consciousness in New Zealand, saying that political filmmakers in Australia have tended to be shunted off into the low-budget 'underground,' whereas New Zealand directors such as Gaylene PRESTON and Merata MITA have always been able to demonstrate a high degree of political awareness. Her first feature, *Trial Run*, is a feminist thriller: a woman photographer leaves her family and moves to an isolated cottage for six months, in order to do a photographic essay on some rare birds. She uses the time to improve her running as well; but someone is trying to frighten her. The film looks at fear and anger, female friendship, and the little-represented details of ordinary life at the same time as it attempts to develop a nonsexist visual language. In the attempt it loses a degree of narrative clarity, and the climactic moments are not well timed, so that the impact of the identity of the woman's aggressor (her son) is not as strong as it could be. *Send a Gorilla* is an unusual film in that much of the material in it is the result of a collaboration between a group of female actors. A critique of the commercialization of Valentine's Day, the film has a lot of crazy energy and there are some fine comedic moments, particularly in the performance of Carmel McGlone, a singing telegram-deliverer who has a habit of getting stuck in her gorilla suit. A more serious subtext, which suggests a pervasive misanthropy, occasionally disrupts the comic mood but makes the film more interesting from a feminist perspective. It was selected for the Women's Film Festival at CRETEIL in 1989.

Surfacing (1982); *Hooks and Feelers* (1982); *Trial Run* (1984); *The Minders* (1984); *Send a Gorilla* (1988)

Roger Horrocks, *Interview with Melanie Read* (Auckland: City Art Gallery, 1985)
                                                    AH

REALISM

The term realism was used to describe a movement in nineteenth-century art and literature which arose in opposition to classical idealism. Its aim was to represent people and things as they really are, to mirror the real world. In practice, this meant a focus on the experience of ordinary people – bourgeois housewives, rural workers, and slum dwellers – rather than on that of the great and the powerful; and a preoccupation with contemporary social experience, rather than the mythical past or the projected future. In cinema, the term has been used to cover such a wide variety of historical styles and national movements that it has become almost meaningless as a descriptive term. Some attempt to distinguish between different realisms has been made in the proliferation of subcategories of realism: the realism of CLASSICAL HOLLYWOOD CINEMA, Italian NEOREALISM, social realist fiction, DOCUMENTARY, SOCIALIST REALISM, psychological realism, poetic realism, magical realism. . . .

In FILM THEORY, the major proponent of realism was the French critic André Bazin. He argued that the mechanical nature of photographic reproduction makes film an objective medium ideally suited to recording the real world. Technical advances – the introduction of SOUND, deep-focus cinematography, COLOR, handheld movie cameras, wide-screen projection – enabled film to reproduce reality increasingly accurately, to approximate more and more to our experience of nonfilmic reality. Bazin valued the qualities of transparency, fluidity, and ambiguity in the films of RENOIR, Welles and Wyler, Rossellini and de Sica, Murnau and Flaherty. He found their use of the long take and deep-focus cinematography less didactic and disruptive, and more true to the ambiguities and temporal flow of reality, than the jolting montage of 1920s Soviet cinema and the distorted images of German Expressionist cinema of the same period.

The issue of realism assumed prominence in debates around FEMINIST FILM THEORY and FEMINIST INDEPENDENT FILM in the 1970s. Feminist filmmakers tended to favor social realist documentary as a form to represent the struggles of women. This form was adopted for ideological as well as practical reasons: mainstream commercial cinema, Hollywood in particular, was perceived as restricting the roles of women to limited and oppressive STEREOTYPES bearing no relation to the lives of real women and their struggles against oppression. However, marxist and feminist theorists centered around the JOURNAL *Screen* began to question the realist aesthetic and to advocate its abandonment. They argued that the realist text is complicit with dominant western IDEOLOGIES – bourgeois capitalism, liberal humanism, and patriarchy. Through its failure to unsettle the conventional viewer–screen relationship, it encouraged passivity in the audience. The transparency and fluidity of the realist text, praised by Bazin, masked its ideological operations, its exclusions, its closures. In the process of constructing the real, but masking that construction, it 'naturalized' patriarchal representations of woman and her subordinate position in society. A flight from realism into COUNTERCINEMA and an experimental AVANT GARDE was the solution proffered by this group. Their wholesale dismissal of realism tended to be justified on evidence derived from male-directed classical era Hollywood GENRE films. Recent Hollywood cinema, however, has demonstrated some accommodation with liberal feminism, both onscreen and off; and genre films with strong women protagonists as well as social realist films (documentary and fiction) directed by women continue to be popular with women audiences.

Terry Lovell, *Pictures of Reality* (London: British Film Institute, 1980)

See also: MODERNISM   FF

REEL WOMEN

A Melbourne-based organization active in FEMINIST EXHIBITION and FEMINIST DISTRIBUTION from 1979, Reel Women represents one instance of Melbourne's many efforts to form organizations strong enough to counter Sydney's dominance of AUSTRALIA's feature and independent sectors. Many of the films produced in Melbourne during the 1970s came out of tertiary institutions, and tended to be shorter and more interested in narrative than their Sydney counterparts. Sporadic training workshops were held in Melbourne as well as in Adelaide and Perth, and, starting with the Womenvision Film Festival of 1975, several successful exhibition programs filled the gap left by the closure of the Melbourne Filmmakers' Co-op and cinema. Women from art, theater, and film pooled their resources to produce *Lip: A Feminist Arts Journal*, which made significant contributions to theoretical debates. A number of filmmakers emerged from these alliances, including Monique Schwarz (*Pauses* [1978] and *Eine Familie Braun* [1982]); Carole Sklan (*Farewell to Charms* [1979] and *Fifty-Fifty* [1986]); Sue Ford (*Faces* [1979] and *Egami* [1985]); Claire Jager (*Take the Plunge* [1979] and *No Myth* [1987]); Madelon Wilkins (*Women Seen* [1979] and *Taking a Look* [1985]). Since Reel Women wound up its activities after its peak period from 1980 to 1982, the Victorian Women's Film Unit has given new impetus to women's film activity by employing thirty-six women to make six short films. Several

Melbourne-based women have directed features or telemovies – Nadia Tass (*Malcolm* [1986], *Rikky and Pete* [1988]); Monique Schwarz (*Pieta* [1987]); Rivka Hartman (*Bachelor Girl* [1987]); Ann Turner (*Celia* [1988]), and others, like Solrun Hoaas and Corinne CANTRILL, have produced bodies of work in respectively ETHNOGRAPHIC and AVANT-GARDE filmmaking.

Annette Blonski, Barbara Creed and Freda Freiberg (eds), *Don't Shoot Darling!* (Melbourne: Greenhouse, 1987)   FC

REINIGER, LOTTE (1899–1981)

GERMAN experimental filmmaker Reiniger pioneered a technique of paper cutout ANIMATION, with figures lit from behind to create silhouettes. The technique was partly inspired by Chinese shadow puppets and the expressionist theater lighting of Max Reinhardt, with whom Reiniger studied briefly. She began her film career with the short *The Ornament of the Loving Heart* (1919), and became part of the circle of experimental filmmakers in 1920s Berlin which included Paul Wegener, Walter Ruttman, Berthold Bartosch, Hans Richter, and Carl Koch, whom she married. She collaborated with Koch, and several of the others also worked with her on some of her films. In 1923, at the age of twenty-four, Reiniger began directing one of the very first ever animated feature films (more than ten years before Disney's *Snow White* [1937], often credited as the first ever animated feature). Reiniger completed *The Adventures of Prince Achmed* in 1926. Adapted from the *Arabian Nights*, it is a tale of magic and sorcery in the orientalist fashion adopted by many European artists and designers in the 1920s. Aimed at a general audience including children, it nevertheless contains several abstract sequences, using experimental techniques involving sliced wax, or sand on backlit glass. Reiniger designed and had built a 'multiplane' camera which separated out foreground from background layers, again anticipating later technical innovations by Disney.

In the mid 1930s Reiniger left Germany for BRITAIN, working for the Crown and GPO Film Units, for whom she made *The Tocher* (1938). She settled permanently in Britain after the war and made many short films, often based on legends and fairy stories, for children's television. Reiniger's work and reputation unfortunately suffered from being relegated to the nursery; the later films, which have colored backgrounds and often sentimental narration, lack the experimental edge of her work during the twenties.

Films made in Germany include: *Aschenputtel/Cinderella* (1922); *Die Abenteuer des Prinzen Achmed/The Adventures of Prince Achmed* (1926); *Harlequin* (1931); *Carmen* (1933); *Papagenus* (1935); *Das Kleine Schornsteinfeger* (1935); *Galathea* (1936). Films made in Britain include: *The King's Breakfast* (1937); *The Tocher* (1938); *Caliph Stork* (1955)

Robert Russett and Cecile Starr, *Experimental Animation* (New York: Da Capo, 1988)   IK

REIS, ANTONIO see CORDEIRO, MARGARIDA and REIS, ANTONIO

> She wrote scripts for the French cinema and criticism of its films, but she is known internationally as a writer of fiction. Who is she?

RENOIR, JEAN (1894–1979)

Often hailed as FRANCE's greatest director, Jean Renoir (the son of Impressionist painter Auguste Renoir) indeed produced, in a career spanning almost fifty years, an impressive body of classics: *Boudu sauvé des eaux* (1932), *La Grande Illusion* (1937), *La Règle du jeu* (1939), *Le Fleuve* (1951), and *French Cancan* (1955)

are among the best known. Renoir's most original work was in the 1930s, combining daring technical innovations (deep focus) with socially conscious but candid REALISM (sometimes using non-professional actors – including himself – and location shooting) and a benign and sensual humanism. 'Everyone has their reasons,' as one character in *La Règle du jeu* says, can stand as his overall philosophy. This did not preclude Renoir's commitment to Popular Front ideals: *Le Crime de Monsieur Lange* (1935), the supervision of the Communist Party-sponsored *La Vie est à nous* (1936) and the direction of a union-financed hymn to the French Revolution, *La Marseillaise* (1937).

Renoir's eclecticism makes it impossible to pin down a consistent notion of the 'Renoirian woman.' Parallel to his concern for realism, a love of theatricality runs through his films, sometimes showcasing women as spectacle: Catherine Hessling in *Nana* (1926), Anna Magnani in *Le Carosse d'or* (1953). On the whole, however, Renoir's representation of women is bound to his realist aesthetics and to his grand-bourgeois bohemian culture. Some of his 1930s women characters – notably Valentine in *Le Crime de Monsieur Lange* – are remarkably free of conventional morality and, importantly, have a social and class identity. On the other hand, many Renoir HEROINES are classic embodiments of the myth of woman as nature (in his terms a positive value). This is particularly strong in *Une Partie de campagne* (1936) and *Le Déjeuner sur l'herbe* (1959). Renoir also produced, in *La Chienne* (1931) and *La Bête humaine* (1938), two classic figures of woman as temptress; both films were remade by Fritz Lang in Hollywood, in the FILM NOIR genre: *Scarlet Street* (Universal, 1945) and *Human Desire* (Columbia, 1954).

Renoir's films include: in France – *La Fille de l'eau* (1924); *Nana* (1926); *La Petite marchande d'allumettes* (1928); *La Chienne* (1931); *Boudu sauvé des eaux/Boudu Saved*

From Drowning (1932); *Madame Bovary*, *Toni* (1934); *Le Crime de Monsieur Lange* (1935); *Une Partie de campagne, La Vie est à nous, Les Bas-fonds* (1936); *La Grande Illusion/Grand Illusion, La Marseillaise* (1937); *La Bête humaine/The Human Beast* (1938); *La Règle du jeu/Rules of the Game* (1939): in the USA – *Swamp Water* (Columbia/Warner Bros., 1941); *This Land is Mine* (RKO, 1943); *The Southerner* (1945); *The Diary of a Chambermaid* (Camden Productions, 1946), *The Woman on the beach* (RKO, 1946): in India – *Le Fleuve/The River* (1951): in Italy – *Le Carosse d'or/The Golden Coach* (1953): in France – *French Cancan* (1955); *Eléna et les hommes* (1956); *Le Déjeuner sur l'herbe*; *Le Testament du docteur Cordelier* (1959); *Le Caporal épinglé* (1962); *Le Petit théâtre de Jean Renoir* (1969)

André Bazin, *Jean Renoir* (London: W H Allen, 1976)   GV

REVILLE, ALMA (1899–1982)

Brought up around the corner from Twickenham Film Studios, where her father worked, at the age of fifteen Reville took a job there as a rewind girl in the cutting rooms. Thence she progressed rapidly to editor/continuity girl (in those days in BRITAIN's film industry the jobs were often combined) and worked on several films, most notably the first screen version of *The Prisoner of Zenda* in 1915. She then moved over to the Famous Players-Lasky Studios and in 1922, whilst working on her first assignment for them, met Alfred HITCHCOCK. They both went to work at the UFA Studios in Berlin, assisting British director Graham Cutts on five films. When Hitchcock became a fully fledged director in 1925 with *The Pleasure Garden* for GAINSBOROUGH STUDIOS, Alma was his assistant director. From then on, their personal and professional lives were always linked (they married in 1936) and she worked almost exclusively with him. She was assistant director on *The Lodger* (1926) and worked on the screenplays of:

The Ring (1927), *Juno and the Paycock* (1930), *Murder!* (1930), *The Skin Game* (1931), *Rich and Strange* (1932), *Waltzes From Vienna* (1933), *The Thirty-Nine Steps* (1935), *Young and Innocent* (1937), *Suspicion* (RKO, 1941), *Shadow of A Doubt* (Universal, 1943), and *The Paradine Case* (Selznick, 1947). Reville was also adept at screen adaptations: she adapted *The Secret Agent* (1936), *Sabotage* (1936), *The Lady Vanishes* (1938), *Jamaica Inn* (Mayflower, 1939), and in 1950 *Stage Fright* for Associated British.

At the formal level, Alma Reville's contribution to Hitchcock's career was as screenwriter and adaptor, but in another sense it was incalculable, for she provided him with constructive criticism and advice throughout his entire career. She was for him 'the ultimate authority.' She did, however, write scripts for other directors: *The Constant Nymph* (1928) for Adrian Brunel, *After the Verdict* (1929) for Henry Galen, and *The Fifth Chair/It's in the Bag* (1945) for Richard Wallace.

Joseph McBride, 'Mr and Mrs Hitchcock', *Sight and Sound*, vol. 45, no. 4 (1976)   SP

REVOLUTIONARY MODEL FILMS

This term refers to films made in the People's Republic of CHINA during the later years of the Cultural Revolution (1970–76). There were two types of revolutionary model film: celluloid versions of the eight *geming yangbanxi* (revolutionary model operas) performed during the Cultural Revolution; and films echoing these operas in stories of revolution, in character types, and in formal organization. Revolutionary model opera transformed the ancient art of Peking Opera to accommodate contemporary themes of class struggle. Its beginning was officially announced in Peking in July 1964, with Jiang Qing, ex-actress and wife of Chairman Mao Zedong, heading a radical political faction preventing artists from criticizing Mao's leadership through allegorical uses of traditional OPERA. Thereafter, changes in subject matter, form, and stylization that appeared in the model operas bore the stamp of Jiang's personal censorship. Stories of revolution involving workers, peasants, and soldiers replaced romantic fantasies or tragedies involving ghosts, gods, emperors, generals, scholars, and beauties. A somewhat naturalistic MISE-EN-SCENE coexisted with traditional symbolizations. Characterization followed a strict logic of the 'three highlights': from among the group, highlight the positive characters, the heroes/heroines, and then the most inspiring hero/heroine. Traditional Peking Opera's formalized use of condensed poetic language, singing, and stylized performances (including choreographed fights) was modified to suit new scenarios. Jiang's influence may be credited for the prohibition of romance or marital relationships between characters, and for the creation of superheroic woman types as bold and persistent as men in leading the revolution.

Feature filmmaking in China stopped from 1966 to 1969, during which period many films made between 1949 and 1965 were identified by Jiang's faction as 'poisonous weeds,' and many artists sent to May Seventh Cadres Schools for reform. Filmed performances of revolutionary model operas released from 1970 onward were almost the only films permitted on screen (excluding a few imports from North Korea and Romania). After 1974 production gradually resumed, though films still dealt with themes of class struggle with a militant style reminiscent of the rhetorical and aesthetic organization of the model operas.

Notable revolutionary model films include: *Zhiqu Weihushan/Taking Tiger Mountain by Strategy* (Xie Tieli, 1970); *Hongdeng Ji/The Red Lantern* (Cheng Yin, 1970); *Shajiabang/Shajiabang* (Wu Zhaodi, 1971); *Baimaonu/The White-Haired Girl* (Sang Hu, 1972); *Qija Baihutuan/Raid on White Tiger Regiment* (Su Li and Wang Yen, 1972); *Haigang/On the Docks* (Xie Tieli and Xie Jin, 1972); *Hongse Niangzijun/Red Detachment of Women* (Cheng Yin, 1972); *Long Jiang Sung/Eulogy of the Dragon River* (Xie Tieli, 1972); *Chuangye/The Pioneers* (Yu Yanfu, 1974); *Fanji/Counterattack* (Li Wenhua, 1976)

Godwin C Chu (ed.), *Popular Media in China: Shaping New Cultural Patterns* (Honolulu: University Press of Hawaii, 1978)   EY

RHODES, LIS (1942–)

Artist and filmmaker Lis Rhodes was brought up in the west of England and studied Film and Television at the Royal College of Art in BRITAIN. She sees her art as a social, not an isolated, practice, and has been a part-time lecturer in various colleges, including London University's Slade. She has also worked at the London Filmmakers' Cooperative and is a co-founder of the feminist distribution network CIRCLES. In 1979, Rhodes was on the exhibition committee of the Arts Council 'Film as Film' event –

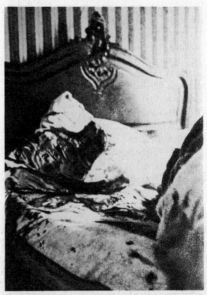

Lis Rhodes's *Light Reading*

an international retrospective of AVANT-GARDE cinema: the women on the panel wanted to include the work of Germaine DULAC, Alice GUY, and Maya DEREN alongside that of contemporary women artists and filmmakers, but in the end felt obliged to withdraw from the event because of its lack of commitment to feminist principles. In 1983 Rhodes produced a booklet (*Her Image Fades as Her Voice Rises*) to accompany a package of four films made by women – Germaine Dulac, Alice Guy, Joanna Davis, and Rhodes herself – which drew together the shared preoccupations in the work of these filmmakers.

Rhodes's own films have the density, concentration, and allusiveness of poetry. Like other British women avant-garde filmmakers, she is concerned with the articulation of language in a culture where 'women's language' is elided.

Dresden Dynamo (1971/2); *Amensuensis* (1973); *Light Music* (1975); *Light Reading* (1978); *Pictures on Pink Paper* (1982); *Hang On A Minute* (with Joanna Davies, 1984/5); *A Cold Draft* (1988)

Susan Stein, 'On *Pictures on Pink Paper* by Lis Rhodes', *Undercut*, no. 14–15 (1985)
SP

RIEFENSTAHL, LENI (1902–)

After a short but highly successful career as a dancer, Leni Riefenstahl became the star actress in the pre-fascist mountain films of Arnold Fanck, who taught her the technical side of the film trade. In her directorial debut film, *Das blaue Licht* (1932), Riefenstahl already shows the mythologizing approach to nature which characterizes fascist films in general, and continues through to the photographic volumes of the 1970s that made her an award-winning photographer.

After Hitler's seizure of power in 1933, many artists left GERMANY because of Nazi antisemitism and the terrorist persecution of political dissidents. Leni Riefenstahl, however, became the most important director of NAZI CINEMA. Her film productions (all four so-called documentaries were commissioned by Adolf Hitler) were not only self-congratulatory of the regime, but also helped perpetuate its ideologies. With the release of *Tiefland* in 1954, Riefenstahl's gradual rehabilitation was begun; and in the 1960s she even enjoyed something of a comeback. Her films were reshown – without comment – in cinemas and on television, and numerous articles were written and interviews made – again with no critical analysis.

Riefenstahl's fourth career as a photographer began with her work, under the name of Helen Jacobs, as a photojournalist for the British *Sunday Times* during the 1972 Olympic Games in Munich. In 1973 and 1976 two photographic books showing the East African tribe of Nuba were published. The glorification of their beautiful, strong and healthy bodies not only adopts the aesthetics of the Olympiad film, but also expresses the Nazi doctrine of racist eugenics. Judgements of Riefenstahl range from 'forerunner of fascism' through 'fellow-traveler' to 'innocent, genial artist.' It was not only the American women's movement, with its commitment to forgotten women artists, which made it possible for Leni Riefenstahl's films to be shown at WOMEN'S FILM FESTIVALS under the 'pure' aspect of 'fascinating' aesthetics: this was encouraged also by a view of art which fails to see politics in aesthetics. Consequently, films initially produced in support of national-socialist ideology have been fetishized and reinstated as masterpieces.

Das blaue Licht/The Blue Light (1932); *Sieg des Glaubens/Victory of Faith* (1933); *Triumph des Willens/Triumph of the Will* (1935); *Tag der Freiheit: Unsere Wehrmacht/Day of Freedom: Our Armed Forces* (1935); *Olympia*. Part 1: *Fest der Voelker/Festival of Nations*, Part 2: *Fest der Schoenheit/Festival of Beauty* (1938); *Tiefland/Lowlands* (1954)

'Come-back for Leni Riefenstahl', special issue of *Film Comment*, vol. 3, no. 1 (1965)

See also: SONTAG, SUSAN   AB

RIVETTE, JACQUES (1928–   )

With his first feature, *Paris nous appartient* (1960), and his work as film critic and theoretician, Rivette was a central figure in the NEW WAVE in FRANCE and, with Jean-Luc GODARD, the most experimental director in this movement. Rivette's films often privilege improvisation and frequently mix DOCUMENTARY and fiction. A dual motif – that of the plot (in the sense of conspiracy) and that of PERFORMANCE – turns them into complex reflections on the NARRATIVE process as well as on creativity, fiction, and imagination (see for instance *L'Amour fou* [1968], and *L'Amour par terre* [1984]).

....
: *Cannibals and the Tropics become 'isms'* :
: *for which national cinema?* :
....

Because of their unconventional narratives and length (some exceed four hours), Rivette's films are unfortunately rarely shown, yet they are both rewarding and pleasurable. They are also of interest to feminists for their focus on women characters. The celebrated *Céline et Julie vont en bateau* (1974) remains the most consummate expression of Rivette's challenge to narrative and patriarchal structures: Céline and Julie control their destiny (as the actresses did with the script), live by their wits, and reject men and marriage; their relationship is both positive and fun (though not explicitly sexual). *Le Pont du Nord* (1981) and *Love on the Ground* are also centered on two women protagonists and, like *Céline and Julie*, involved the actresses in the writing process.

Le Coup du berger (short, 1956); *Paris nous appartient/Paris Belongs to Us* (1960); *La Religieuse/The Nun* (1966); *Jean Renoir, le patron* (1966); *L'Amour fou* (1968); *Out 1: noli me tangere* (1971); *Out 1: spectre* (1972); *Céline et Julie vont en bateau/Céline and Julie Go Boating* (1974); *Duelle/Twilight, Noroît/Nor'west* (1976); *Merry go round* (1978); *Le Pont du Nord* (1981); *L'Amour par terre/Love on the Ground* (1984); *Wuthering Heights* (1985)

Jonathan Rosenbaum (ed.), *Rivette, Texts and Interviews* (London: British Film Institute, 1977)   GV

RKO

A product of US big business, Radio-Keith-Orpheum was organized by RCA as a means to exploit its sound patents. In 1928 it purchased and merged the Film Booking Office and the theater circuits of Keith-Albee and Orpheum. In 1931 RKO purchased Pathé's studios and distribution exchanges. However, debts and the effects of the Depression caused RKO to move into receivership in 1933, and then into bankruptcy. It reorganized in the following years as RCA and the Rockefellers gradually sold its shares to Atlas, from which Howard Hughes bought control in 1948. By 1955, however, Hughes had sold off most of RKO's assets.

During the years of the HOLLYWOOD STUDIO SYSTEM, the production section, RKO Radio Pictures, had several heads who kept changing studio policies. At times high-cost 'A' pictures were emphasized; at others, formula low-budget movies were stressed. At the same time, management systems ranged from strong producers to unit production. RKO also had a tradition of supporting independent production. The Fred Astaire–Ginger Rogers MUSICALS are excellent examples of the style of film RKO was able to produce with its regular staff in the 1930s. Katharine HEPBURN began her film career at RKO, but left in the mid 1930s. In the 1930s and 1940s, RKO produced a number of films emphasizing Latin American themes, including movies starring LATI-

NA actresses Dolores del Rio, Carmen Miranda, and Lupe Velez. During Hughes's tenure, his exploitation of Jane Russell failed – enormous publicity notwithstanding – to turn the studio into a profitable enterprise.

Richard Jewell and Vernon Harbin, *The RKO Story* (New York: Arlington House, 1982) *JaS*

ROCHA, GLAUBER (1938–81)

Glauber Rocha was the leading personality of the BRAZILIAN film movement CINEMA NOVO, and his films and theoretical writings have had a worldwide influence. Film societies were his school, and he began his career as a critic. He was influenced by the cinematic language of Orson Welles, the political violence of Eisenstein, the concern for poverty of Italian NEOREALISM, and the operatic language of John Ford's WESTERNs. For Rocha, who developed what he called an aesthetic of hunger, violence represented the public voice of underdevelopment, the response of the colonized to oppression. A rebel-rouser, he rejected analysis and relied on the possibility of miracles in preference to social transformation. His film language uses popular myth, fable, and rituals; and this fusion of an archaic culture with an AVANT-GARDE language resulted in a unique style that eschewed REALISM and accumulated plots and subplots, images, and sounds. An ambiguous and complex discourse was its outcome, welcomed in the ART CINEMA circuits of the West, but ignored by the very people whose culture he was supposed to reveal.

Rocha's films include: *Barravento* (1962); *Deus e o diabo na terra do sol/Black God, White Devil* (1964); *Terra em transe/Land in Anguish* (1967); *António das mortes* (1969); *Der leone had sept cabeças/The Lion Has Seven Heads* (1970); *Cabezas cortadas/Severed Heads* (1971); *A idade da terra/The Age of the Earth* (1980)

Randal Johnson, *Cinema Novo × 5: Masters of Contemporary Brazilian Film* (Austin: University of Texas Press, 1984) *NT*

ROCK MUSIC

When it emerged in the 1950s, rock 'n' roll made an immediate impact on film, and the film industry was quick to capitalize on its tremendous popularity among movie and record consumers. Rock dramatically changed the function of the musical score, with producers interested less in downplaying its presence (as had been done with film 'background' MUSIC throughout the 1930s and 1940s) than in actually displaying it. Moreover, because rock has always had a massified popular base, it could not instill the same sense of 'high art' into cinema as neoclassical music and OPERA had done, nor could it produce the same kinds of effects. Rock's use has had more in common with the way earlier popular songs had been used in film.

Rock influenced many popular GENREs of the 1950s and early 1960s: the MUSICAL (*Rock Around the Clock* [Fred Sears, Columbia, 1956]), teen beach pictures, even the WESTERN and historical drama (Ricky Nelson sings in Howard HAWKS's *Rio Bravo* [Warner Bros., 1959]), and the US Civil War was the backdrop for Elvis Presley's balled *Love Me Tender* [Robert Webb, Twentieth Century-Fox, 1956]). Parodies of the new rock film, such as Frank Tashlin's 1956 *The Girl Can't Help It* (Twentieth Century-Fox), quickly emerged. In the 1960s, films continued to feature music of successful rock performers (the Beatles' *Yellow Submarine* [George Dunning, 1968]); pop tunes were frequently tied in as theme songs or in diegetic performances like Lulu's 'To Sir With Love' in the film of the same name (James Clavell, 1967). There was the rock opera of the 1970s (The Who's *Tommy* [Ken Russell, 1975] and Tim Rice and Andrew Lloyd Webber's *Jesus Christ Superstar* [Norman Jewison, 1973]), and 'rockumentaries' such as *Gimme Shelter*

(David Maysles, 1970) and Jonathan DEMME's *Stop Making Sense* (1984), as well as baroque takeoffs like Rob Reiner's *This is Spinal Tap* (1984). Abetted by the skyrocketing music video business of the 1980s, rock's commercial vitality appears more secure than ever, and it has a solid place in the film industry, with soundtracks and films relying on one another for revenue.

Critics have argued that the increased commodification of rock has 'softened' its once seditious edge. Yet as sociologists Angela McRobbie and Simon Frith have suggested, the rebellion associated with 'hard' rock has been predominantly masculine in conceit, with rock's ICONOGRAPHY, lyrics, and driving beat geared chiefly to the male libido. By contrast, female rock performers have largely been aligned with 'soft' pop music (a discourse deemed somehow less authentic and more commercial than the presumably 'authentic' one of male singers), and this notion of inauthenticity has been extended to describe pop's listeners as well. The response to female rockers who don't fit the soft, 'pop' stereotype has been interesting. Many are discussed in terms of their androgyny (for example, Annie Lennox) or their 'masculine' aggression (Janis Joplin), categories which require vast amounts of feminine MASQUERADE. One critic labels Madonna – arguably rock's mistress of the masquerade – a 'post-feminist' heroine, something which raises the question of whether these descriptions actually challenge traditional gender boundaries or if they simply jettison the idea of the feminine altogether.

Indeed, rock seems still largely a man's game. Of the few films about female rockers, *Satisfaction* (Joan Freeman, 1988) derives its name from the hit by the Rolling Stones, the 'bad boys' of rock 'n' roll, and its featured 'girl group' exists only in flickering images. *Sid and Nancy* (Alex Cox, 1986), a popular cult film, might well be called 'Sid kills Nancy'; and Mark Rydell's *The Rose* (1979) chronicles a Janis Joplin-style character whose charisma and charm are outdone only by her masochism and insecurity.

Simon Frith and Angela McRobbie, 'Rock and Sexuality', *Screen Education*, no. 29 (1979)

See also: SPHEERIS, PENELOPE   CF

RODRIGUEZ, MARTA (1938–   )

Marta Rodríguez studied sociology in Paris and, upon her return to her native COLOMBIA, became active in that country's first sociology department, founded by her mentor, Camilo Torres, the priest who in 1967 became a legendary martyr to the cause of Latin American guerrilla insurgency. Working as a team with minimal resources, she and her husband, photographer Jorge Silva, made a series of medium-length sociological and ETHNOGRAPHIC FILMS which simultaneously challenged and subverted the 'scientific' approach to DOCUMENTARY by attending to dimensions of subjectivity, myth, and FANTASY. After a long period of economic, political, and personal difficulties, she has recently founded her own production company which includes her son, Luis Rodríguez Silva.

Chircales/Brickmakers (1968–70); *Planas: testimonio de un etnicidio/Planas: Testimony of an Act of Ethnocide* (1970); *Campesinos/ Peasants* (1976); *Nuestra voz de tierra, memoria y futuro/Our Voice Made of Earth, Memory and Future* (1984); *Nacer de nuevo/ To Be Born Anew* (1987); *Las flores/ Flowers* (1988, working title)

'Cine-Sociology and Social Change,' in *Cinema and Social Change in Latin America: Conversations with Filmmakers*, ed. Julianne Burton (Austin: University of Texas Press, 1986)   JBu

ROHMER, ERIC (1920–   )

A director (born Jean-Marie Scherer) and former academic and film critic, Rohmer like other NEW WAVE directors in FRANCE, began making films in the

1950s; but it was not until *Ma nuit chez Maud* (1969) that he became internationally recognized. His films, most of them divided into 'moral tales' (1962–72) and 'comedies and proverbs' (since 1980), are intimate chamber pieces, focusing on the moral, intellectual, and romantic dilemmas of highly articulate characters, which has led to Rohmer's characterization as a 'literary' filmmaker. But while clearly in the tradition of psychological and realist French literature, Rohmer's work is also eminently cinematic – both in its mastery of a classical, economical, style, and in its recourse to cinéma vérité techniques.

Even when apparently focusing on the dilemmas of male protagonists, Rohmer's films give women a prominent place. The title character in *Maud* is the prototypical 'moral tales' heroine: sensually and intellectually far superior to the prim and rather 'boring' hero(es). With the 'comedies and proverbs' Rohmer has increasingly become a 'woman's director,' and his semi-artisanal methods often closely involve his actresses – for instance Marie Rivière, who inspired and stars in *Le Rayon vert* (1986). In these later films, in the words of feminist critic Bérénice Reynaud, Rohmer, 'instead of presenting his heroines as pure objects of desire . . . makes desiring subjects out of them and it is their desire – and not the man's – that constitutes the motion of the fiction.' The fact that this desire is, in most cases, ultimately thwarted (as in the brilliant *Les Nuits de la pleine lune* [1984]) may be experienced by women spectators as unsatisfactory, but Rohmer's films at least provide a space for the representation of female desire, usually repressed in mainstream cinema.

Rohmer's films include: *La Collectionneuse* (1967); *Ma nuit chez Maud/My Night with Maud* (1969); *Le Genou de Claire/Claire's Knee* (1970); *L'Amour l'après-midi/Love in the Afternoon* (1970); *La Femme de l'aviateur/The Aviator's Wife* (1981); *Le Beau mariage* (1982); *Pauline à la plage/Pauline at the Beach* (1983); *Les Nuits de la pleine lune/Full Moon in Paris* (1984); *Le Rayon vert/The Green Ray* (1986); *Quatre aventures de Reinette et Mirabelle/Four Adventures of Reinette and Mirabelle*, *L'Ami de mon amie/My Best Friend's Boyfriend* (1987)

Bérénice Reynaud, 'Representing the Sexual Impasse', and Norman King, 'Eye for Irony', in *French Film: Texts and Contexts*, eds Susan Hayward and Ginette Vincendeau (London and New York: Routledge, 1989)   GV

ROMANCE

A popular film GENRE which, like MELODRAMA and the WOMAN'S PICTURE, appeals largely to a female AUDIENCE, dealing with the so-called 'private sphere' of love, marriage, and relationships associated with FEMININITY in western and other cultures. Romance narratives typically revolve around a potential heterosexual love relationship which must overcome a series of obstacles before being fulfilled. The barriers to fulfillment might be another lover or spouse (*Rebecca* [Alfred Hitchcock, David O Selznick, 1940]); an illness (*Love Story* [Arthur Hiller, 1970]); a journey (*Brief Encounter* [David Lean, 1945]); class, race, or nationality differences (*Guess Who's Coming to Dinner* [Stanley Kramer, 1967]); the attraction not at first being mutual (*Pillow Talk* [Michael Gordon, Universal/Arwin, 1959]); or indeed all of the above (*Camille* [George Cukor, MGM, 1936]). Whatever the problems, they are ultimately overcome and a relationship established, which may result in marriage and promised permanent monogamy, or be followed by tragic loss and painful suffering. Will they or won't they? (or how will they?) live happily ever after is the question that sustains NARRATIVE tension, and desire, passion and loss/fulfillment offer PLEASURES of emotional intensity to the audience. Typically, it is the woman, the heroine,

345

whose pain is on display: romantic HEROINES have been associated with denial (*Now Voyager* [Irving Rapper, Warner Bros., 1942]); repression (*Brief Encounter*); suffering (*Blonde Venus* [Josef von Sternberg, Paramount, 1932]); self-sacrifice (*Jezebel* [William Wilder, Warner Bros., 1938]): illness (*Camille*); and punishment (*The Wicked Lady* [Leslie Arliss, 1945]). In visual terms, the romance film is associated with an ICONOGRAPHY of images associated with 'nature' – empty beaches, countryside, open fires, sunsets. Closeup shots establish intimacy between characters, with soft focus suggesting a fusion or a merging of identities.

Given that romance films are all about gender and SEXUALITY, it is surprising how little feminist critical work has been done on the genre; though a number of feminist critics have looked at romantic novels and their readers. In such work, romance as an IDEOLOGY has sometimes been criticized for offering women a fantasy of everlasting love and commitment and of the family as the place of emotional happiness, safety, and sanctuary, while mythic scenarios of knights in shining armor and princes on white horses reinforce patriarchal notions of male dominance and female passivity. On the other hand, some feminists argue that romantic fiction should not be dismissed as simply reproducing patriarchal ideologies: romance perhaps expresses the difficulties and contradictions of heterosexual womanhood, while the activity of reading romantic novels can even be regarded as a form of resistance to the constant demands made on women in the domestic sphere. Can romances offer their readers any sorts of pleasure other than resistance, though? Are the romantic trajectories of merging, loss of self in another, and intimacy specifically feminine forms of subjectivity? If, as is sometimes suggested, feminine identity is formed in a relationship of similarity to the mother, while MASCULINITY is founded on difference and separation, perhaps the pleasures of romance appeal particularly to the feminine psyche?

While romance as a film genre usually deals with heterosexual relationships, it is also to be found in gay and LESBIAN INDEPENDENT CINEMA, and in mainstream films about lesbians. Since sexuality and relationships are important to lesbian and gay identities, this should not be surprising. But what happens if a lesbian (or a gay) relationship is substituted into a genre primarily concerned with heterosexual relationships? To some extent lesbian romance films follow the genre's conventions: obstacles to a relationship are constructed and overcome – or not, as the case may be. Be the obstacle a heterosexual male rival (*Personal Best* [Robert Towne, 1982]); suicide (*The Children's Hour* [William Wyler, 1961]); death (*Egymasra nezve/Another Way* [Karoly Makk, 1982]); family pressure (*Coup de foudre/At First Sight* [Diane Kurys, 1984]); fear of discovery or job loss (*Lianna* [John Sayles, 1983]); or internalized homophobia (*Desert Hearts* [Donna Deitch, 1985]), the story is still built around problems preventing the couple from uniting. One difficulty here is that many of these films reproduce negative social definitions of lesbianism – as neurotic, deviant, depressing, unhealthy, not to mention fatal – by associating the obstacle to romance with lesbian sexuality itself. In addition to this, broader ideological questions arise about reworking a popular genre in the context of a subcultural cinema. Is such a reworking really possible, or are the cultural meanings of romance so deeply embedded in heterosexuality that lesbian romance films merely reproduce heterosexual ideals and values?

Janice A Radway, *Reading the Romance: Women, Patriarchy and Popular Literature* (Chapel Hill, NC: University of North Carolina Press, 1984)   JcS

ROSEN, MARJORIE (193?–)

Marjorie Rosen, a journalist and film and television scriptwriter, has written FILM

> They wear suits, make jokes, take all the
> best lines and give men a hard time.
> These exemplary women feature in
> which Hollywood genre?

CRITICISM for popular magazines and film journals since the mid 1970s. Her reviews have appeared in such popular US magazines as *Ladies Home Journal* and *Ms*, as well as in film JOURNALS such as *Jump Cut* and *American Film*. Her book of feminist film criticism, *Popcorn Venus*, was first published in 1973, just before Molly HASKELL's *From Reverence to Rape*, though neither is said to have known of the other's work in progress. More sociological and less intellectual than Haskell's work, *Popcorn Venus* was an important and widely reviewed book. It points to, and proves the influence of, movies on the lives of women. It covers American movie history from SILENT CINEMA up to the date of the book's writing.

Rosen, like Haskell, sees a degeneration of roles for women in movies over this period, though she does tend to merge actress and role. This is particularly true of her section on Marilyn MONROE:

. . . almost entirely she played the delicious dumb blond with both head and heart as soft as a cotton ball. . . . For when she was in trouble, unsure of herself, she would return to the comfort of the image she obsessively wanted to wipe out.

Very much a pop sociologist in her approach to movies, Rosen defends this angle by calling herself a popular historian. She has also said that economic realities forced her to mix journalism and criticism for some of her magazine pieces, particularly those for *Ladies Home Journal*.

Marjorie Rosen, *Popcorn Venus: Women, Movies and the American Dream* (New York: Coward, McCann & Geoghegan, 1973)   MMc

A graduate of the University of Southern California Department of Cinema in the early 1960s, where she won the first Director's Guild of America fellowship ever awarded to a woman, Rothman started out doing second unit work on low-budget EXPLOITATION FILMS for Roger Corman at AIP and New World studios in Hollywood. Her first solo venture as director was the routine beach-party youth pic *It's a Bikini World* (1966), which, in spite of Rothman's and her collaborator/husband Charles Swartz's attempts to upgrade the GENRE's conventions, failed to transcend exploitation demands. Rothman's reputation as a stylish, politically aware filmmaker rests on the five films she directed subsequently – two for New World and three for her and Swartz's own company, Dimension Pictures. The first, *Student Nurses* (1970), coming at a time when there was growing public demand for more interesting women's roles, was a commercial success which inaugurated Corman's short-lived student-nurse cycle; into it Rothman was able to inject her own feminist interest in issues such as rape and abortion, while taking every opportunity to parody the basic principles of exploitation (in particular, its reliance on female nudity).

Her next film, *The Waking Hour/The Velvet Vampire* (1971), was less commercially successful, but has remained a cult art-house hit. An offbeat female VAMPIRE FILM set in southern California, it satirizes contemporary sexual mores while reversing the woman-as-victim expectations of vampire mythology. Comic reversals could be said to be the keynote of Rothman's films, combined with a playful approach to STEREOTYPES and genre clichés which enables her to turn back on audiences some of their voyeuristic and/or sadistic pleasures. This amalgam of satire and serious social comment is particularly marked in *Knuckle-Men/Terminal Island* (1973), a women-in-prison action movie containing a high level of violence. Clearly

347

uneasy about the violence, Rothman nevertheless refused to shirk it; instead, she made a film about the transition from a brutal patriarchal regime to a more cooperative, egalitarian alternative.

Despite her success in the exploitation field, and her obvious talent as a writer/director (she co-scripted *The Waking Hour*, *Group Marriage*, and *Knuckle-Men*, and wrote *The Working Girls*), Rothman has not moved into mainstream cinema as many of her contemporaries have done. Indeed, her career seems to have ground to a halt after *The Working Girls* (1974), when Dimension Pictures was dissolved. Her films remain a testament to the possibilities, and limitations, offered by exploitation film to women directors.

Blood Bath (co-d. Jack Hill, 1966); *It's a Bikini World* (1966); *Student Nurses* (1970); *The Waking Hour/The Velvet Vampire* (1971); *Group Marriage* (1972); *Knuckle-Men/Terminal Island* (1973); *The Working Girls* (1974)

Pam Cook, 'The Art of Exploitation, or How to Get into the Movies', *Monthly Film Bulletin*, vol. 52, no. 623 (1985)   PC

RUSSIA *see* SOVIET UNION

RUTLER, MONIQUE (1941–)

French-born Monique Rutler is PORTUGAL's most important woman filmmaker of the last two decades. Although she rejects the feminist label, her films show a clear concern for gender issues. *Velhos são os trapos* (1979), a fictionalized documentary, deals with the problems of senior citizens and their marginalization in society; and *Jogo de mão* (1983) looks behind the façade of machismo among the urban lumpenproletariat, seeing their passion for football not only as an expression of masculine cultural poverty, but also speaking a desire for a miracle that will bring about change. Women characters, however, are victims who do not try to break their bondage.

Velhos são os trapos/The Clothes Are Old (1979): *Jogo de mão/Sleight of Hand* (1983)
NT

RYSLINGE, HELLE (1944–)

Working in several areas of the Danish independent film sector – acting, script-writing, directing – Helle Ryslinge is a key figure in feminist cinema in DENMARK. As an actress, she can be seen in such films as *Kniven i hjertet* (1982), which was directed by FASSBINDER biographer Christian Braad Thomsen, for which, in collaboration with Johnny Bjørn, she also composed the music; and in *Koks i kulissen* (Christian Braad Thomsen, 1985), the story of two young women artists on tour. This film relies strongly upon Ryslinge's performance, and also on the improvised dialogue for which she was partly responsible. In 1986, Ryslinge turned to directing with the comedy *Flamberende hjerter*, in which her feminist concerns are combined with a burlesque sense of humor: the film was a great success. Ryslinge is currently making a new film, *Manden der ikke kunde lade vaere med at lyve* (*The Man Who Couldn't Give Up Lying*).

Flamberende hjerter/Coeurs flambés (1986); *Manden der ikke kunde lade vaere med at lyve* (in production)   ASW/AKo

SAGAN, LEONTINE (1899–1974)

Born in Vienna, Leontine Sagan spent her childhood in South Africa and returned to Austria in 1910. In Berlin she studied at the Max Reinhardt School and later became a highly successful actress and director in theaters in both Germany and Austria. Her first and only GERMAN feature film, *Maedchen in Uniform* (1931), was a great success. It caused a sensation abroad, too, but was soon forgotten; to be unearthed decades later under the aegis of the women's movement. Aside from the fascist works of Thea von HARBOU and Leni RIEFENSTAHL, *Maedchen in Uniform* remains the only well-known pre-1960s German film directed by a woman. The cast was exclusively female, and the script was based on the play *Gestern und Heute* by Christa Winsloe. The film is about a boarding school pupil (Hertha THIELE) and her love for her teacher (Dorothea Wieck). The homoerotic content of the film, quite obvious today, has made it a cult film for lesbians. However, the film's sexual politics went unremarked by contemporary critics, who saw it purely as a critique of the authoritarian Prussian educational ideal. The explicitly lesbian aspects of the play were already toned down by giving the film's 'artistic direction' to Carl Froehlich, who later played in numerous light entertainment films of the Nazi era: Froehlich diluted all of Sagan's more radical inputs to the film.

What is important about the history of this film is, first, that Nazism cut off this

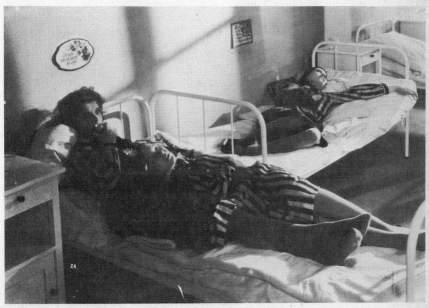

Maedchen in Uniform

beginning of feminist filmmaking to such a degree that women directors did not reemerge in Germany until the mid 1960s in the wake of NEW GERMAN CINEMA. Secondly, women's filmmaking was suppressed not only at the level of personnel but also at the level of content. If *Maedchen in Uniform* was praised for its formally aesthetic qualities when it was first released, its lesbian discourse was not acknowledged until about fifteen years ago.

In 1932, Sagan emigrated to England (*Maedchen in Uniform* was later banned by Goebbels), where she made only one film, for Alexander Korda: *Men of Tomorrow* (1932), which remains obscure. She later went to South Africa and devoted herself to building up the National Theater in Johannesburg. She died in Pretoria in 1974.

Maedchen in Uniform/Maidens in Uniform (1931); *Men of Tomorrow* (1932)

B Ruby Rich, 'From Repressive Tolerance to Erotic Liberation: *Maedchen in Uniform*', in *Re-vision: Essays in Feminist Film Criticism*, eds Mary Ann Doane, Patricia Mellencamp and Linda Williams (Los Angeles: American Film Institute, 1984)

See also: LESBIANISM AND CINEMA; NAZI CINEMA; WEIMAR CINEMA *AB*

SAMPER, GABRIELA (1918–74)

Born into a well-to-do family in Bogotá, COLOMBIA, Gabriela Samper traveled widely in Europe before attending Columbia University in New York. She lived briefly in Trinidad and intermittently in the United States. Always inclined toward the arts (dance, theater, literature, eventually children's theater and television) she turned to filmmaking only in 1963, ten years after the birth of her fifth and last child, upon her third marriage to the north American Ray Witlin, with whom she founded a film production company called Cinta Limited. The couple made a number of

DOCUMENTARIES in both Colombia and the United States, as well as publicity films to finance their Colombian projects. Samper is still most remembered in Colombia for her work with children's and puppet theater, but her last four audiovisual works – strikingly unconventional, independently produced ETHNOGRAPHIC shorts – have earned her a respected place as one of LATIN AMERICA's pioneering female documentarists. Samper was concerned that the concept of 'national development' so much touted since the 1960s should include the affirmation of Colombian cultural roots in all their variety, and the attempt to celebrate and conserve these elements of traditional culture became for her 'a genuine compulsion, . . . a battle against the clock.' That battle suffered a setback in 1970 with her failure to win a Guggenheim Fellowship that would have provided her with essential funding; and was seriously interrupted in 1972, when she was charged with being part of the urban branch of the National Liberation Army network, a leftwing guerrilla group. She spent five months in prison before the charges were dropped for lack of evidence. After her release she left the country to spend a year at Cornell University. Her battle against the clock was definitively halted by cancer in 1974.

Having worked intermittently as a teacher, Samper consistently enlisted young people's participation in her mission to record Colombia's rich cultural heritage. Jorge Silva, Marta RODRIGUEZ's collaborator, did photography for Samper on *El hombre de la sal* (1969). Inspired by Samper's example, the anthropologist Gloria Triana has subsequently produced *Yurupari*, a series of films on Colombian popular and regional traditions edited by Mady Samper, Gabriela's youngest child.

El páramo de Cumanday/The Heights of Cumanday (1965); *A Mask for You, A Mask for Me* (co-d., 1967); *Cities in Crisis: What's Happening?* (1967); *Festival folclórico de Fomeque/Fomeque Folk Festival*

(1969); *Los santísimos hermanos/The Brotherhood of the Most Holy* (1969); *El hombre de la sal/The Man of Salt/The Salt Maker* (1969)   JBu

SANDER, HELKE (1937–)

One of the first graduates of the Berlin Film and Television Academy, Helke Sander is a filmmaker working in WEST GERMANY, and a member of the movement known as the NEW GERMAN CINEMA. She came to film from a background in theater and television and has become known for her feminist views. Politically active during the student movement of the late sixties, Sander gave a major speech at the 1968 Socialist Students' Association conference which is generally considered to mark the beginning of the new German women's movement. Disillusioned at her experiences in leftwing circles, she became very active in the women's movement and helped found the Council for Women's Liberation.

Best known for her film *Die allseitig reduzierte Persoenlichkeit* (1977), about the experiences of a woman photographer at the hands of patriarchal capitalism, Sander has insisted on focusing her attention on women and how they see themselves. Much of her work stems from her close involvement with the women's movement: films such as *Kindergaertnerin, was nun?* (1969) and *Kinder sind keine Rinder* (1969) deal with daycare centers, while *Der subjektive Faktor* (1981) recalls the era

> The *boerevrou*, symbol of Afrikaner resilience, was introduced to the screen in 1931. What is she?

of the student movement and the development of the women's movement. Critical of the *ARBEITERFILM*, which deals only with problems at the workplace, Sander also made the first film to take up the discussion provoked by the women's movement about the rela-

tionship between the private and public spheres, *Eine Praemie fuer Irene* (1971). Throughout her career she has been concerned with the disadvantages working mothers such as herself have to overcome in order to compete with male colleagues. Her feminist stance has on occasions prevented her from getting funding for her film projects. Sander has also contributed extensively to the setting up of an institutional framework in West Germany to support and promote the work of women filmmakers. In 1973 she co-organized an international women's film seminar and in 1974 co-founded *FRAUEN UND FILM*, Europe's only feminist film JOURNAL.

Subjektituede/Subjectivity (1966); *Silvo* (1967); *Brecht die Macht der Manipulateure/ Crush the Power of the Manipulators* (1967–8); *Kindergaertnerin, was nun?/What Now, Nursery Workers?* (1969); *Kinder sind keine Rinder/Children are not Cattle* (1969); *Eine Praemie fuer Irene/A Bonus for Irene* (1971); *Macht die Pille frei?/Does the Pill Liberate?* (1972); *Maennerbuende/ Male Leagues* (1973); *Die allseitig reduzierte Persoenlichkeit/The All-round Reduced Personality* (1977); *Der subjektive Faktor/The Subjective Factor* (1981); *Der Beginn aller Schrecken ist Liebe/Love is the Beginning of all Terror* (1893); *Felix* (co-d., 1987)

Marc Silberman, 'Open Form – Interview with Helke Sander', *Jump Cut*, no. 29 (1984)   JK

SANDERS-BRAHMS, HELMA (1940–)

Born Helma Sanders, this WEST GERMAN filmmaker changed her name to Helma Sanders-Brahms in 1977 to avoid being confused with her NEW GERMAN CINEMA colleague Helke SANDER. After studying pedagogy, theater and acting, Sanders-Brahms worked as a television announcer before making the move into film. With production experience gained by working as assistant to directors Sergio Corbucci and Pier Paolo Pasolini, she made her first film in 1969,

Angelika Urban, Verkaeuferin, Verlobt: this brought her two prizes at the 1970 Oberhausen film festival. Sanders-Brahms has addressed a variety of issues in her work, ranging from an examination of her parents' generation's involvement in the Nazi era (*Deutschland, bleiche Mutter*, 1979); to a biography of the German writer Heinrich von Kleist, *Heinrich* (1976–7); and a film about a schizophrenic woman, *Die Beruehrte* (1981).

Although she is not closely involved with the women's movement, a substantial number of Sanders-Brahms's films do focus on women and their experiences. *Deutschland, bleiche Mutter* and *Fluegel und Fesseln* (1984), for instance, deal with mother–daughter relationships; and society's brutalization of women is a theme in such films as *Shirins Hochzeit* (1975), *Deutschland, bleiche Mutter*, and *Die Beruehrte*. Sanders-Brahms is also one of the few directors in West Germany to address the situation of the country's Turkish population, brought over to meet the labor shortage during the economic miracle of the 1950s. Her *ARBEITERFILM Die industrielle Reservearmee* (1970–71) is about Turkish students and workers living in West Germany, and *Shirins Hochzeit* examines the plight of a young Turkish woman who comes to Germany looking for her Turkish fiancé.

Whilst Sanders-Brahms's later work has tended toward a more mainstream art-house REALISM, her films are visually atmospheric and frequently comprise complex layers of meaning. She is also one of the few West German women filmmakers to have achieved international acclaim and success.

Angelika Urban Verkaeuferin, Verlobt/ Angelika Urban, Sales Assistant, Engaged (1970); *Gewalt/Power* (1970); *Die industrielle Reservearmee/The Industrial Reserve Army* (1970–71); *Der Angestellte/The White-Collar worker* (1971–2); *Die Maschine/The Machine* (1972–3); *Die letzten Tage von Gomorrha/The Last Days of Gomorrah* (1973–4); *Das Erdbeben in Chile/The Earthquake* (1974); *Unter dem Pflaster ist der Strand/The Beach under the Sidewalk* (1974); *Shirins Hochzeit/Shirin's Wedding* (1975); *Heinrich* (1976–7); *Deutschland, bleiche Mutter/Germany, Pale Mother* (1979); *Vringsveedeler Tryptichon/ The Vringsveedol Triptych* (1979); *Die Beruehrte/No Mercy No Future* (1981); *Luegenbotschaft* (episode in *Die Erbtoechter/The Daughters' Inheritance*, 1982); *Fluegel und Fesseln/The Future of Emily* (1984); *Laputa* (1985–6); *Felix* (co-d., 1987)

Julia Knight, *Women and the New German Cinema* (London: Verso, 1990)   JK

SANKOFA

A film workshop based in London, Sankofa is part of the dynamic 'new wave' of BLACK CINEMA in BRITAIN. Started in 1983 by a mixed group of five filmmakers, Sankofa was born at a time when the 1981 Brixton 'riots' were forcing institutions to recognize that a multicultural Britain is here to stay. Benefiting from the innovative cultural policies of the now-defunct Greater London Council and from other funding opportunities for small groups of filmmakers, Sankofa quickly established itself as a powerful voice in INDEPENDENT CINEMA and FEMINIST INDEPENDENT FILM. Sankofa describes itself as particularly concerned to replace existing racial STEREOTYPES with 'a range of images of the black subject . . . outside the realm of the Exotic, the Victim and the Threat.' They have, however, always rejected what has been described as 'the burden of representation' – the invisible demand to 'speak for the black community' always there behind the multiculturalism of public funding. Instead, Sankofa has chosen to speak *from*, but not *for*, black experience in Britain. Gender, desire, and homosexuality – subjects sometimes marginalized in black filmmaking – are placed at center stage in many of Sankofa's films, particularly *Territories*

(1985), *The Passion of Remembrance* (1986) and *Looking for Langston* (1989).

Named after a mythical Ghanaian bird, and signifying the act of looking back in order to prepare for the future, Sankofa has reinvigorated many of the formal techniques of COUNTER-CINEMA at a time when its former adherents were moving on (or back) to more straightforwardly narrative- and genre-based fiction. The resulting combination of densely evocative multilayered images, music and everyday scenes has been acclaimed as carrying feminist and independent work forward to a new, vital, stage. And while Sankofa's abstract and occasionally opaque approach has been controversial in some political forums, its work has been acknowledged as an important element in the growing body of black feminist independent film and video.

Kobena Mercer (ed.), *Black Film/British Cinema, ICA Documents 7* (London: Institute of Contemporary Arts/British Film Institute, 1988)

See also: BLACK WOMEN   JRo

SARMIENTO, VALERIA (1948–)

Born in Valparaiso, CHILE, where she participated in the cinema workshops set up at the University of Chile in Viña del Mar in the late sixties, Sarmiento belongs to a young generation of women filmmakers who began their filmmaking careers during the Popular Unity government of Salvador Allende but have been forced to pursue their work outside the country. This group also includes

....
: This feminist distributor has the world's :
: largest collection of films made by :
: women available for exhibition. What is :
: it called? :
....

Marilú MALLET and Angelina Vázquez. Sarmiento trained with Carlos Piaggio, an Argentinian editor at Chile Films, working on most of the features and documentaries produced in that period.

Since 1974 she has lived in Paris, where she has edited films for Guy Mollet, Robert Kramer, and her husband, Raul Ruiz. She has faced enormous difficulties in seeking financial support for her own films in France, due to her partnership with Ruiz, who has been recognized as a leading avant-garde filmmaker. Sarmiento sought production monies in Spain, Belgium, and Germany for the short features and documentaries on exile and immigration which she directed between 1976 and 1982. Meanwhile, she has secured the rights to adapt several novels by Corín Tellado, the best-known Spanish-language writer of women's romantic novels. *Mi boda contigo/Our Marriage* (1984) earned her critical notice in France through its ironic reworking of melodramatic conventions. Sarmiento's best-known film, *El hombre cuando es hombre* (1982), deals with myths of Latin American romanticism, and with the complexity of gender relations.

Un sueño como de colores (unfinished, 1972); *La femme au foyer* (1976); *La nostalgia/Le mal du pays* (1979); *Gens de toutes parts, gens de nulle part* (1980); *El hombre cuando es hombre/When a Man is a Man* (1982); *Mi boda contigo/Notre mariage* (1984)

Zuzana Pick, 'Chilean Cinema in Exile (1973–1986). The Notion of Exile: A Field of Investigation and its Conceptual Framework', *Framework* no. 34 (1987)   ZP

SASS, BARBARA (1936–)

Barbara Sass has a consistent record of work in the film industry in POLAND, and is one of the few Polish women directors to maintain such a consistency since her feature film debut in 1981 (others include Wanda JAKUBOWSKA and Ewa Petelska). Sass's career is typical of Polish film school graduates, beginning with a professional apprenticeship in television, where she worked with Andrzej Wajda's 'X' unit. However, all of her features have been made for Jerzy

Kawalerowicz's 'KADR' unit, the only survivor of the eight units established in 1956 when the Film Groups (Zespoly Filmowe) were introduced. Sass has always distanced herself from the notion of 'women's cinema'; but such a statement must be seen in the context of Polish film production and culture at large, in which feminist ideas are undeveloped and bear little relation to non-socialist countries' use of terms such as 'women's cinema.' In her 1987 production *W Klatce* she made an interesting alliance with the actress Katarzyna Figura, the Polish acting phenomenon of the late eighties, constructed and packaged as a STAR to embody the popular Polish ideal of female beauty and sexuality, who had previously appeared in a string of science fiction/sex comedies.

Bez Milosci/Without Love (1981); *Debiutantka/The Outsider* (1982); *Krzyk/The Scream* (1982); *Dziewczeta z Nowolipek/ The Girls From Nowolipek* (1985); *Rajska Jablon/The Apple Tree of Paradise* (1985); *W Klatce/Caged* (1987)

Frank Bren, *World Cinema 1: Poland* (London: Flick Books, 1986)   AG

SCANDINAVIA *see* DENMARK; FINLAND; ICELAND; NORWAY; SWEDEN

SCHNEEMANN, CAROLEE (1939–)

Carolee Schneemann has combined a career as an AVANT-GARDE filmmaker with being a painter, environmental and performance artist, and sculptor. She began working in the 1950s in the milieu of the abstract expressionist New York School of painting. Her work quickly took on the aesthetics of assemblage, using fragments of appropriated images, painted and placed in sculptural forms. Traces of this style of work can be seen in her highly edited, often hand-painted, films. Schneemann made her first film in 1963: *Carl Ruggles' Christmas Breakfast* signals the arena of the musical avant

garde into which she was cast through her marriage to composer James Tenney. Her best-known film, *Fuses* (1964), depicts their relationship as a rhythmic and visually varied sexual coupling. The intimate nature of the film material, its highly processed (painted, scratched, edited) look, and the fact that both the film and the sex acts were 'directed' by a woman set *Fuses* apart as an aesthetically radical and automatically politicized 'personal film.' Schneemann's two subsequent films, *Plumb Line* (1971) and *Kitch's Last Meal* (1978), trace differing relationships with different men. Each extends the limits of film form by manipulating little-used aspects of the medium to affect the content. Each creates simultaneous multiple images that repeat and emphasize each other or otherwise comment on each other. Sexual politics and artistic politics are consistently linked thematically. Since 1973, Schneemann has devoted her energies primarily to performance and the plastic arts, consistently developing themes evolved in and alongside her films.

Carl Ruggles' Christmas Breakfast (1963); *Fuses* (1964); *Viet-Flakes* (1965); *Plumb Line* (1971); *Kitch's Last Meal* (1978)

Ted Castle and Julia Ballerini, *Carolee Schneemann: Early and Recent Work* (New Paltz, NY: Documentext, 1982)   MKe

SCIENCE FICTION

In relation to cinema, science fiction has proven an immensely difficult GENRE to define. Given the obviousness of science fiction icons (bug-eyed monsters, robots, ray guns, time machines, future worlds, and so on), definition might seem easy enough. But the major problem centers on the relationship of science fiction to the HORROR film. Some critics attempt to separate the two genres, while others seek to draw connections. Certainly they share many characteristics: the mad scientist, monsters and creatures, bizarre experiments, terrified victims. Another view is that science

Sigourney Weaver in the sci-fi horror film *Alien*

fiction grew out of the horror genre, that it represents the horror 'technologized' in an attempt to satisfy an increasingly skeptical audience. Film theorist Vivian Sobchack argues convincingly that the major difference between them lies in their emphasis and area of exploration. While science fiction is primarily concerned with science and scientific method, the interests of the horror film are also often present – particularly in the shape of magic, religion, and the relationship of the human to the unknown. The difference is that whereas horror seeks to re-create the nightmare, science fiction is more interested in constructing a believable context for its nightmare. Sobchack argues that rather than separate the two genres, it is more useful and relevant to see them as different ends of a single spectrum.

Feminist critics have been interested in science fiction for several reasons. First, many science fiction films present a critique of science and technology. They examine the possibility that humanity may be destroyed through nuclear catastrophe or environmental devastation. This view intersects with the feminist critique of science and technology as institutions which, in the name of 'progress,' are determined to exploit the present regardless of future consequences. Science fiction also explores other underlying anxieties of contemporary society, such as moral concerns regarding current experiments in reproductive technology. In *Demon Seed* (Donald Cammell, 1977) the woman is raped by a computer; in *Xtro* (Harry Davenport, 1982) she is impregnated by an alien. In both films, she gives birth to the 'unknown.' In *Alien* (Ridley Scott, 1979) man gives birth through his stomach. In science fiction the body becomes a barometer for testing unconscious anxieties about the future. The importance of the primal scene in science fiction also raises questions for feminist research into FANTASY and its relationship to the female spectator.

Another area of interest concerns the depiction of SEXUALITY and sexual dif-

ference in science fiction. Like the horror film, science fiction also constructs woman as the 'creature' – the 'monstrous-feminine' whose image functions to establish notions about differences between human and nonhuman, male and female. The representation of androids also raises questions about the constructed nature of gender differences. In recent years, science fiction has also presented women in new roles; the Ripley character (Sigourney Weaver) in *Alien* and its sequel, *Aliens* (James Cameron, 1986) is a heroic, powerful figure whose representation cuts across conventional feminine roles. While it might be difficult to accept science fiction as 'progressive,' the genre is of interest to feminist critics because of its ability to address many contemporary issues relevant to a feminist critique of patriarchy.

Vivian Sobchack, *Screening Space: The American Science Fiction Film* (New York: Ungar 1987)   BC

SCOPOPHILIA

The concept of scopophilia, or the scopic drive, was developed by Sigmund Freud, in his 1915 essay 'Instincts and their Vicissitudes,' to refer to one of the infantile libido (or sexual) drives/instincts, the drive to pleasurable looking. The term has been adopted by PSYCHOANALYTIC FILM THEORY as a means of understanding the unconscious process brought into play in the spectator's looking at the image on the cinema screen, and in developing theories of the LOOK and its relation to PLEASURE, SEXUALITY, and sexual difference.   AKu

SCORSESE, MARTIN (1942–   )

A graduate of New York University's Film Department and one of the directors associated with NEW HOLLYWOOD CINEMA, Scorsese began his career working for Roger Corman, a successful independent producer of EXPLOITATION FILMS. *Mean Streets* (1973), based on a story by Scorsese and starring Robert de Niro, was the start of a long and continuing actor/director colla-boration, and also signaled Scorsese's preoccupation with Italian-American working-class subjects. *Alice Doesn't Live Here Anymore* (1974), starring Ellen Burstyn, is one of a group of films seen by feminists as part of a 'new women's cinema' emerging from Hollywood in the 1970s: films with narratives organized around the process of a woman's self-discovery and growing independence, with central characters who are not glamorous in the conventional Hollywood sense. *Alice Doesn't Live Here Anymore* opens with a fantasy sequence which is a blatant homage to the Hollywood MUSICAL – an example of how this new Hollywood director advertises and celebrates his 'second-generation' status with constant references – some affectionate, some cynical – to earlier film styles and forms.

Scorsese's reputation was established with *Taxi Driver* (1975), and controversy surrounding his work increased with the critical failure of *New York, New York* (1977). *Raging Bull* (1978), with de Niro as the brutal boxing champion Jake La Motta, is an obsessive study of working-class machismo (a recurrent theme in Scorsese's work). Some feminists saw this film as a radical critique of MASCULINITY, while others argued that violence and desire are depicted as inseparable and are, in fact, celebrated. Indeed, Scorsese's attitude toward masculinity and his portrayals of women have always been ambiguous.

Scorsese's reputation as one of Hollywood's major directors has increased with films like *King of Comedy* (1983), *After Hours* (1985), and *The Color of Money* (1986). *The Last Temptation of Christ* (1988), with its dream-sequence of Jesus making love to Mary Magdalene, resulted in calls from all over the world for a total ban on the film on grounds of blasphemy.

Pam Cook, 'Masculinity in Crisis? Tragedy and Identification in *Raging Bull*', *Screen*, vol. 23, no. 3/4 (1982). LF

SCREENWRITING

Screenwriting allows for films to be shot out of chronological order and still retain the continuity essential for NARRATIVE clarity. Around 1908, when film length became standardized at a thousand feet, the 'scenario' script provided for the complete telling of a story in ten minutes. When the multiple-reel film became the norm in the mid 1910s, the 'continuity' script, pioneered in the US film industry, numbered each shot and described the location, character action, and (eventually) dialogue. This script was the guideline for the pre-production planning necessary to feature-length films. The studio could organize its resources to ensure that each scene's cast, sets, costumes, crew, and equipment were ready when the scene was shot. Despite shooting out of order, continuous action was maintained by following the map of the script. In the HOLLYWOOD STUDIO SYSTEM, with many films in production at one time, studio script departments employed dozens of writers who could be assigned to write or revise any of the phases of a single script (treatments, temporary scripts, final script). Disputes about authorship were so common that the Screen Writers Guild arbitrated many decisions concerning which writers should receive screen credits. As a consequence of sexism in credits, women screenwriters like Catherine Turney and Lenore Coffee are little known. Both these writers developed WOMAN'S PICTURES for WARNER BROS. Turney's adaptation of *Mildred Pierce* (Michael Curtiz, 1945) had no flashback structure and retained Veda's interest in classical music. Coffee was called upon to write the scenes with Mrs Custer in *They Died With Their Boots On* (Raoul Walsh, 1942), a male action film. Better known, perhaps, are Elinor Glyn and Anita LOOS, who wrote scenarios for SILENT CINEMA and published screenwriting books (long out of print). Loos's comedy flair contributed greatly to Douglas Fairbanks's career in films like *Wild and Wool-*

ly (John Emerson, 1917), and she also authored the novel, stage play and film script for *Gentlemen Prefer Blondes* (Howard Hawks, Twentieth Century-Fox, 1953).

Jeanne Thomas Allen, *Now, Voyager* (Madison, WI: University of Wisconsin Press, 1984)

See also: CECCHI D'AMICO, SUSO; GUIDO, BEATRIZ; HARBOU, THEA VON; REVILLE, ALMA; SHIPMAN, NELL; SOVIET UNION   *MBH*

SEIDELMAN, SUSAN (1953–)

After graduating in design at Drexel University, Seidelman was accepted in 1974 by New York University Graduate School of Film and Television, where she made a satirical short (*And You Act Like One, Too* [1976]), whose plot about a bored suburban housewife prefigured *Desperately Seeking Susan* (1985). Another short, *Yours Truly, Andrea G Stern*, won several festival awards and earned enough for her to begin work on *Smithereens* (1982), the story of a street-

Making Mr Right

wise punkette's attempt to break into the East Village club scene. Shot in seven weeks on a miniscule budget, the film was an art-house success, paving the way for her next medium-budget picture, *Desperately Seeking Susan*. Directed, produced, and scripted (Leora Barish, who also co-wrote Chantal AKERMAN's *Golden Eighties* [1986]) by women, this updated screwball COMEDY featured Madonna just as she was about to become an international star. Madonna's presence certainly contributed to the film's unprecedented success; however, its audiences turned out to be less the traditional Madonna fans than cineliterate yuppies. Indeed, *Desperately Seeking Susan* heralded a new genre of oddball yuppie comedies (*Lost in America* [Albert Brooks, 1985]; *After Hours* [Martin Scorsese, 1985]; *Who's That Girl* [James Foley, 1987]; *Blind Date* [Blake Edwards, 1987]).

But Seidelman's characteristic combination of New York-independent style self-referential playfulness, and post-feminist wit were also significant factors. *Desperately Seeking Susan* emulated the classic WOMAN'S PICTURE in giving positive value to aspects of FEMININITY derided or ignored by other genres (style, glamor, friendship, FANTASY), creating an eighties female ambience at once heterogeneous and subversive (though its upbeat ending, in which its two heroines win the day, was a departure from the ambivalent resolutions of its classic precursors). Her next feature, *Making Mr Right* (1987), trailed as a SCIENCE FICTION fantasy full of special effects, follows a similar pattern, setting the tacky, wacky world of its image consultant heroine against the cool 'rationalism' of the male scientist's perspective to point up the latter's inadequacies. But though Seidelman's touch with zany comedy and visual gags does not falter, the serious subtheme about remaking MASCULINITY was not sufficiently developed at script level. Nevertheless, on the basis of her first three feature films Seidelman has already established herself as one of the sharpest feminist commentators on contemporary postmodern culture.

And You Act Like One, Too (short, 1976); *Deficit* (short, 19??); *Yours Truly, Andrea G Stern* (short, 19??); *Smithereens* (1982); *Desperately Seeking Susan* (1985); *Making Mr Right* (1987); *Cookie* (1989); *She-Devil* (1990)

Jackie Stacey, 'Desperately Seeking Difference', *Screen*, vol. 28, no. 1 (1987)   PC

SEMBENE, OUSMANE (1923–   )

One of AFRICA's first novelists and filmmakers, and certainly ranking amongst the greats of world cinema, Sembene was born in the Casamance region of Senegal. He has been a fisherman, has served with the French armed forces, and has worked on the Dakar –Niger railway construction, participating in the strike which was to form the basis of his novel *God's Bits of Wood* (1960). Sembene's writing career began when he joined the literary group Présence Africaine in Paris, but before long he realized that only a limited number of Africans were able to read his books – inevitably in French – and that cinema would be a more effective means of communication. After training in Moscow, his first film was *Borom Sarret* (1963). Through a look at one day in the life of a poor cart-driver, Sembene juxtaposes his shanty-town existence with the other Dakar, whose rich colonial-built housing is still protected by policemen, even after independence. The audience is invited to 'see between the scenes' that there are real causes of the characters' poverty – such as dishonest post-independence politicians hand in glove with neocolonialism – and that their misery is not inevitable.

The position of African women has formed a central theme in many of Sembene's films. *La noire de . . .* (1966) is about a young woman taken to France to look after her employers' children, and treated like a servant, or as some exotic object. Her only resistance is silence, which culminates in suicide. The women of *Emitai* (1972) also use silence as resistance when a French World War II army platoon demands a donation from the rice harvest. The women are forced to sit in the fierce sun but do not give in; the men, meanwhile, debate and make futile gestures. Both *Mandabi* (1968) and *Xala* (1974) are based on novels by Sembene, and both have as central characters devout Muslims. In *Xala*, El Hadji Abdou Kader Beye decides to take a third wife who is the same age as his daughter. The pampered bride's mother is pleased to find a rich, albeit aged, husband. El Hadji's first, traditional, wife accepts unwillingly but with grace; his second, uneducated, European-style wife is furious; his daughter, educated and politicized, defends her mother and denounces her hypocritical father. But none of the women is responsible for the xala (curse of impotence) El Hadji suffers on his wedding night – that would be too simple, and his self-aggrandizement is far-reaching. In the course of this film Sembene shows up self-seeking politicians, false religions, the power of money, and the plight of the dispossessed. In *Ceddo* (1977) the central female character, Princess Dior, is kidnapped and her rescue becomes the focus of a battle between religious beliefs, a battle which will determine whether leadership is inherited by the son or the nephew. If, at the end of the film, Dior is not actually shown enjoying power herself, such a possibility is certainly entertained.

Borom Sarret (1963); *Niaye* (1964); *La noire de . . . /Black Girl* (1966); *Mandabi/ The Money Order* (1968); *Emitai/God of Thunder* (1972); *Taaw* (1970); *Xala/The Curse* (1974); *Ceddo* (1977); *Thiarroye 44* (with Thierno Faty Sow, 1987)

Teshome H Gabriel, *Third Cinema in the Third World: The Aesthetics of Liberation* (Ann Arbor: UMI Research Press Studies in Cinema, 1982)   AM

SEMIOTICS

When Ferdinand de Saussure predicted, in his *Course in General Linguistics* (written up and published posthumously in 1915 by his students), that one day there would be a science of 'the life of signs within society,' he called it 'semiology' and said that it would be a part of 'social psychology.' Linguistics would be only part of semiology. While Saussure is by no means the 'father' of contemporary semiotics (a role often accorded equally to the American philosopher C S Peirce, from whom the term 'semiotic' most immediately derives), it gives a sense of the complexity of its history to begin from the image of a nonexistent science projected into the future by a text which its author didn't write, then practiced by disciples who ignored its predictions.

It is also appropriate to a study of signs in society that there have been as many kinds of semiotics as there are different societies, and different visions of life within them. One strand of 'scientific semiotics' today (associated with the work of A J Greimas) developed internationally from the critique of Saussure by linguists (Louis Hjelmslev, Roman Jakobson, Emile Benveniste). However, the western European semiotics associated with the movement of STRUCTURALISM in the late 1950s and the 1960s has had the strongest influence on feminists interested in the meanings invested in 'woman' as sign and as myth, how these meanings are socially produced, how they work in relation to political and economic structures, how they shape women's experiences, and how they can be changed.

In their early work, semioticians like Roland Barthes, Umberto Eco, and Christian Metz worked *from* Saussure's linguistics of natural language *to* other signifying systems (film, architecture, literature, fashion, painting . . .). This implied that semiotics was part of linguistics, and not the other way round. However, semiotics diversified rapidly in the 1970s by abandoning a 'linguistic' model, and by criticizing the premises of Saussure's theory (a process which, through the work of Jacques Derrida, laid a basis for POSTSTRUCTURALISM in philosophy). Others turned to Peirce for a theory of interpretation, reading Peirce quite differently from the conservative American school now associated with Thomas Sebeok.

As the description of 'systems' gave way to theorizing how people *make* meanings actively, the emphasis shifted from 'the sign' to the study of texts, codes, and discourses. Much of this work was influenced by Jacques Lacan's rethinking of psychoanalysis through terms borrowed from Saussure and Jakobson. Some writers soon rejected the whole idea of semiotics as a 'science,' preferring a politics and a poetics of criticism. (In this spirit Roland Barthes finally revived the old Saussurean term 'semiology' to distinguish his work from that of Saussure's 'scientific' heirs.) Others, like Julia Kristeva, imagined a new kind of analysis ('semanalysis') combining and displacing semiotics, marxism, and psychoanalysis. FEMINIST FILM THEORY has most strongly participated in this second phase of semiotics, drawing especially on work about the construction of FEMININITY and SEXUALITY.

Teresa de Lauretis, *Alice Doesn't: Feminism, Semiotics, Cinema* (Bloomington: Indiana University Press, 1984)   MMo

SEQUEYRO, ADELA ('PERLITA') (1901–)

Born in Veracruz, MEXICO, Sequeyro began her film career as an actress at the age of twenty-two. With the advent of the 'talkies,' her fame was secured when she starred in *El prisionero numero trece/The Prisoner Number Thirteen* (Fernando de Fuentes, 1933). Realizing the need to exercise control over her creative work, in 1935 she formed a film cooperative which produced the first film she wrote, *Más allá de la muerte/Beyond Death*, directed by Ramon Peon. After conflict ensued among the cooperative members, Sequeyro left to form another cooperative, CAROLA, with which she began her shortlived career as a film director. In 1937 she wrote, produced, directed, and acted in her first feature film, *La mujer de nadie*. Her second and last film, *Diablillos del arrabal* (1939), suffered devastating financial loss which left her insolvent. After numerous attempts to reinstate herself as a director failed, Sequeyro retired in 1943 and left the film industry permanently.

La mujer de nadie/No One's Woman (1937); *Diablillos del arrabal/Slum Devils* (1939)

CH-N

SEX GODDESSES

The term 'sex goddess' betrays both the legacy of the classical star system (in which STARS were traditionally compared to gods) and the basic relationship between male filmmakers/viewers and the image of woman: adulation of a commodity. Although there is no objective definition of who is or is not a 'sex goddess' (Gloria Swanson? the early Greta GARBO?), the category obviously designates female stars whose image is dominated by – and marketed as – overt SEXUALITY, in both the type of characters they portray and their physical appearance. To the latter is added a fetishistic panoply of make-up, jewelry, tight dresses, high-heeled shoes . . . with national variations: for instance, in some Italian films of the 1950s, Silvana Mangano, Gina Lollobrigida, and Sophia Loren sported muddy bare feet and clinging wet peasant dresses, evoking an 'earthy' sexuality for the American market. For despite the mythology of unfettered sexuality attached to sex goddesses, they are historically grounded, and in particular they relate to CENSORSHIP codes. Their portrayal or evocation of sex is thus more explicit in Hollywood cinema before the inception of the PRODUCTION CODE in 1934 (Theda BARA, Pola NEGRI, Louise BROOKS, Jean HARLOW) and internationally after its gradual weakening in the post-World War II

period (Marilyn MONROE, Brigitte BARDOT and their clones, Jane Russell, Sophia Loren, Diana DORS). During the heyday of the Hays Office in the 1930s and 1940s, the representation of sexuality in American cinema was rather allusive and stylized (Marlene DIETRICH, Rita HAYWORTH), while for example in French film of the same period, subject to less censorship, national stars like Ginette Leclerc and Viviane Romance gave blatant erotic portrayals. Although it has been argued that the post-1960s 'permissive' age has signed the death warrant of the sex goddess (and seen the rise of the porn star: Linda Lovelace, Marilyn Chambers), actresses such as Ursula Andress and Raquel Welch, and more recently Kim Basinger and Beatrice Dalle, have had their careers built principally on their 'sexy' star images.

In fact, the notion of the sex goddess depends on censorship and repression for its very existence and appeal, whether as object of reprobation for conservative legions of decency (Bara, Mae WEST, Dietrich, Bardot), or as 'subversive' idol for male intellectuals (MUSIDORA, Louise Brooks). Recent feminist-inspired work on stars has identified the sex goddess as a series of paradoxes: a male creation which equates women and sex, but simultaneously represses women's sexuality; an ambiguous source of pleasure for male viewers, arousing desire for the female body while evoking fear of female 'otherness' and power (or, psychoanalytically, of 'castration'). The paradox goes further for women spectators: although sex goddesses may be the ultimate male playthings, their roles are all-important to the narratives (and their erotic appeal is not confined to male viewers); as actresses and public figures, they were often fabulously rich and powerful. But perhaps a more important aspect of the sex goddess is excess, whether burlesque (Mae West, Jayne Mansfield) or not. The ways Monroe or Bardot pout, giggle, and walk, the poses of Dietrich or Harlow, often verge on self-parody. The intense fetishization of their figures, or of parts of their bodies (Bardot's behind, Monroe's, Russell's, and Mansfield's breasts, Dietrich's and Betty Grable's legs) by camera angles, LIGHTING, and accessories, also heightens the parodic effect and points to the fact that the sex goddess is part of an elaborate – and conscious – MASQUERADE of FEMININITY, rather than the expression of 'pure sex.'

Richard Dyer, *Stars* (London: British Film Institute, 1979)   GV

SEXUALITY

A general term covering sexual meanings, acts, identities, and pleasures, as well as the realms of desire and EROTICISM, sexuality in western cultures is seen as fundamental to gender identity. Whether defined as institution, as practice, or as IDEOLOGY, sexuality is regarded by feminists as one of the key sites of women's subordination. Sexuality is particularly significant to an understanding of how gender works in film, for popular cinema is characterized by obsessive sexual objectification of women on the screen. Typically, MASCULINITY is defined as active, initiating and powerful and FEMININITY as passive, receptive and compliant. Such definitions, however, obviously vary tremendously according to the RACE, class, nationality and social, cultural and historical context of filmmakers and audiences.

Sexuality, central to an understanding of the significance of women in all forms of cinema – from PORNOGRAPHY to popular fiction, has been analyzed from many different perspectives by feminists. Criticism of STEREOTYPES of female sexuality in film began with the work of FILM CRITICS like Molly HASKELL and Marjorie ROSEN, who argue that roles for women in Hollywood films define female characters in relation to their sexuality – either by its excessiveness (the VAMP, the FEMME FATALE, the SEX GODDESS) or by its absence (the spinster, the mother, the virgin). In this sense,

female roles can be seen as more limited, stereotyped, and demeaning than male ones, which are less rigidly defined in relation to sexuality. Furthermore, Hollywood female STARS have usually been defined in terms of their sexuality: the popularity and fame of many of the biggest stars of CLASSICAL HOLLYWOOD CINEMA, such as Mae WEST, Marlene DIETRICH and Marilyn MONROE, have rested on their glamorous looks and sex appeal.

> *This 1981 film from the Netherlands is 'a crime film turned upside-down.' What is this subversive film called? Who made it?*

Other feminists have looked at how the visual conventions of Hollywood cinema contribute to the sexualization and objectification of women. Aspects of MISE-EN-SCENE, such as LIGHTING, framing, composition, COSTUME, and setting, as well as the use of particular camera angles, shots, and EDITING conventions, contribute to the sexual objectification of the woman on the screen. The term 'sexual spectacle' is used in FEMINIST FILM THEORY to describe this construction of the female as passive object of desire, on display for male approval and erotic gratification. Analyzing such cinematic conventions, feminist film theorist Laura MULVEY has developed a critique of Hollywood's visual pleasures. Using PSYCHOANALYTIC theories, she argues that the PLEASURES of popular film appeal to masculine desires to possess, control, and punish feminine sexuality and propose a masculine spectator position which reproduces the patriarchal organization of sexuality around an active/masculine and passive/feminine divide. Other critics, however, see some displays of sexuality as signs of resistance (Rita HAYWORTH's over-the-top PERFORMANCE in *Gilda* [Charles Vidor, Columbia, 1946], for example), or raise the question of the erotic pleasures films may offer female spectators.

Not only has classical Hollywood cinema objectified women through specific visual conventions; sexuality has also been a central theme of popular films, especially in genres like the thriller, HORROR, FILM NOIR, and MELODRAMA. Popular NARRATIVEs, typically structured around the disruption of a fictional equilibrium by a threat or a problem, and the restoration of a new equilibrium in the story's resolution, often construct female sexuality as the threat or the problem that sets the story in motion. Narrative resolution is achieved through the punishment, the marriage, or both, of the heroine. For example, female sexuality is the site of both pleasure and danger in thrillers and films noirs like *Double Indemnity* (Billy Wilder, Paramount, 1944), where the resolution involves overcoming the threat posed by the heroine's transgressive or duplicitous sexuality. Similarly the horror film is often structured around the menace posed to 'normality' by sexuality, be this the threat of 'monstrous' female sexuality to the family or the community, as in *Fatal Attraction* (Adrian Lyne, 1987), or the heroine's vulnerability to male (or alien) sexual possession, as in the VAMPIRE film.

Whilst popular film is obsessively concerned with heterosexuality, lesbian and gay sexuality have been relatively absent from the screen. Until recently, representations of lesbian and gay sexuality typically functioned as the 'deviant other' defining the norm of heterosexuality. Very few depictions of lesbianism or homosexuality offered stories in which the outcome of 'indulgence' in this deviation was not loneliness, depression, ostracism, or suicide. However, in the 1970s and 1980s a considerable number of lesbian and gay films were made, largely within the independent sector, which challenge these depictions and explore the pleasures, as well as the dangers, of these sexual identities, lifestyles, and subcultures. Some films, such as those of Barbara HAMMER in the USA, have used experimental forms; whilst others have reworked popular genres such as the ROMANCE, two successful examples being *Desert Hearts* (Donna Deitch, 1985) and *My Beautiful Laundrette* (Stephen Frears, 1985).

See also: CROSSDRESSING; EXPLOITATION FILM; LESBIAN INDEPENDENT CINEMA; LESBIANISM AND CINEMA; LOOK, THE; PHALLIC WOMAN   JcS

SHANNON, KATHLEEN (1935–)

Entering CANADA's film industry as a woman in the 1950s was not easy, but Kathleen Shannon managed to forge a pioneering career, first as assistant to the music director of Crawley Studios in 1952, then progressively as music/sound editor and picture editor from the time she joined the NATIONAL FILM BOARD OF CANADA in 1956, as a director from 1970, and then Producer with 'Challenge for Change'. Her greatest significance is as founder (in 1974) and subsequently Executive Producer of the NFB's special women's unit, STUDIO D. She has encouraged the work of many women filmmakers and has generated the production of films on feminist, environmental, and peace issues, believing that films should be used as catalysts for change, and that they should appeal to a wide range of viewers. As a producer/ director, her films are characterized by traditional DOCUMENTARY techniques and an effective didactic humanism, with the exception of *Goldwood* (1975), a personal film about her childhood roots.

I Don't Think It's Meant for Us (1971); *Working Mothers* series (1974–5); *Goldwood* (1975); *Dream of a Free Country: A Message from Nicaraguan Women* (1983)

Chris Sherbarth, 'Why Not D? An Historical Look at the NFB's Woman's Studio', *Cinema Canada*, no. 139 (1987)   KA

SHEPITKO, LARISSA (1938–79)

SOVIET director Shepitko quickly made her presence felt in Soviet cinema after her film institute diploma movie, *Znoi* (1963), won several prizes. Her next film, *Krylia* (1966), is an insightful portrayal of a woman – a World War II pilot and local war hero – struggling to deal with the banality of postwar society and an unsatisfactory personal life. Despite the brilliance (and distinctive visual style) of these two early films, there is little doubt that Shepitko's greatest achievement is her 1977 movie *Voskhozhdenie*, a searing depiction of collaboration and betrayal during World War II. *The Ascent* was widely seen abroad – garnering numerous prizes and firmly establishing Shepitko as a major cinematic talent. Shepitko faced difficulties working as a filmmaker in the Soviet political climate of the sixties and seventies, and many (if not all) of her films, including *The Ascent*, suffered limited distribution in the USSR.

Shepitko was filming an adaptation of V G Rasputin's story 'Proshchanie s Materoi'/'Farewell to Matera' when she was killed in an automobile accident on 2 July 1979, along with several members of her film crew (including cinematographer Vladimir Chukhnov, who had shot *The Ascent*). *Proshchanie/Farewell* was completed in 1982 by Shepitko's husband, director Elem Klimov who also made a moving documentary tribute to her, *Larissa* (1980).

Znoi/Heat (1963); *Krylia/Wings* (1966); *V trinadtsatom chasu/At One O'clock* (1968); *Ty i ia/You and I* (1972); *Voskhozdenie/ The Ascent* (1977)

Barbara Quart, 'The Films of Larissa Shepitko', *Cineaste*, vol. 16, no. 3 (1988)
DJY

SHIPMAN, NELL (1892–1970)

Nell Shipman is the only woman in CANADA successfully to write, produce, direct, and star in her own feature films. She was born in Vancouver but as a young woman went to California, where she began to star in films at the age of fourteen. She wrote her first scripts in 1912, vehicles which used her own talents as star, and then in 1914 became one of the first women anywhere to direct her own films. In 1920 she established her own production company, specializing in outdoor adventure films making colorful use of her menagerie of tamed wild animals, including skunks, raccoons, wolves, and bears. As a historical figure, she remains surprisingly undocumented. Her husband, Ernest Shipman, entered the film industry only after meeting her, and after she had already starred in and probably directed (which she usually did under a male pseudonym) two highly successful films based on James Oliver Curwood's short stories, *God's Country and the Woman* and *Baree, Son of Kazan*. Curwood had agreed to give Nell Shipman exclusive rights to his stories while she contracted to star exclusively in his work. Shipman's new husband was co-signatory to the deal. At this point, it is Ernest Shipman who takes over as the figure for detailed historical investigation by Canadian scholars. Nevertheless, the next Curwood/Shipman vehicle – titled *Back to God's Country* (1919) to capitalize on the success of the previous film – gives every indication of Nell Shipman's talent and temperament. The film had the usual elements of a Curwood plot: a melodramatic triangle of heroine, hero, and villain, a setting in the 'wilds of Canada,' a dog as co-hero, plus many other animals and the omnipresent Northwest Mounted Police. As scriptwriter, Nell Shipman revised the plot significantly, enlarging the heroine's role and downplaying that of the dog. Actually shot in the frozen north, the climax involves a heroic chase by dogsled as Shipman/Dolores races to save the life of her sick husband and to defeat the lecherous villain. One scene had Shipman cavorting with wild animals and diving nude into a pool whilst being observed by the villain disguised as a Mountie.

Shipman is a striking heroine.

Although the conventions of melo-dramatic FEMININITY are rather at odds with her robust beauty, she is at her best in the action scenes, fending off the villain's attempted rape, rescuing her father and saving her husband's life. She is magnificent in the scenes with the animals. After *Back to God's Country*, the Shipmans separated. Nell formed her own production company and continued to write, direct, produce, and star in her own films throughout the silent period. Later she wrote scripts, usually featuring heroic animals, for films produced by other studios. She died in Los Angeles, 'broke to the wide,' as she put it, but refusing to accept welfare. She left behind a manuscript of memoirs which she called *The Silent Screen and My Talking Heart*.

Outwitted by Billy (scen., 1913); *Under the Crescent* (scen. and star, 1915); *God's Country and the Woman* (co-d., co-scen., star, 1915); *Baree, Son of Kazan* (co-d., co-scen., star, 1917); *Back to God's Country* (scen. and star, 1919); *Something New* (scen., co-d., star, 1920); *The Girl From God's Country* (prod./scen., co-d., star, 1921); *The Grub Stake* (prod., co-d., scen., star, 1923); *The Golden Yukon* (co-d., scen., star, 1927); *Wings in the Dark* (scen., Paramount, 1935)

Peter Morris, 'Ernest Shipman and *Back to God's Country*', in *Embattled Shadows: A History of the Canadian Cinema, 1895 –1939* (Montreal: McGill-Queen's University Press, 1978)   KA

SHUB, ESFIR (1894–1959)

A leading SOVIET documentarist and film editor, Shub began her film career in 1922 as an editor for Goskino. She edited numerous western feature films – making movies such as Fritz Lang's *Dr Mabuse* (1922) 'fit' for Soviet consumption – thereby teaching herself the art of film EDITING. In the early twenties, Shub also undertook the study of pre-revolutionary Russian documentary films that eventually led to her master-piece, the compilation documentary

Padenie dinastii romanovykh (1927). This film, which has exceptional historical importance as well as being a superb example of the compilation DOCUMENTARY, set the standard for all future such works. Shub's later documentaries, while not as visually dynamic as *Romanov Dynasty*, are nonetheless significant works: for example, *Velikii put* (1927) was commissioned by the Soviet government in honor of the tenth anniversary of the Russian Revolution. Shub worked steadily throughout the thirties, and in 1932 pioneered the Soviet sound documentary with *KShE (Komsomol – Shef elektrifikatsii)*. From 1943 to 1953 she worked mainly as an editor; after her retirement she devoted her time to writing her memoirs, *Krupnym planom/In Close-Up* (1959). A second volume was published posthumously: *Zhizn moia: kinematograf/My Life: Cinematography* (1972).

Padenie dinastii romanovykh/The Fall of the Romanov Dynasty (1927); *Velikii put/The Great Path* (1927); *Rossiia Nikolaia II i Lev Tolstoi/The Russia of Nicholas II and Lev Tolstoi* (1928); *Segodnik/Today* (1930); *KShE (Komsomol – Shef elektrifikatsii)/ KSE (The Komsomol – Sponsor of Electrification)* (1932); *Moskva stroit metro/ Moscow Builds the Metro* (1934); *Stranc Sovetov/The Country of the Soviets* (1937); *Turtsiia na podeme/Turkey at the Turning Point* (1937); *Ispaniia/Spain* (1939); *20 let sovetskogo kino/Twenty Years of Soviet Cinema* (1940); *Fashizm budet razbit/Fascism Will Be Defeated* (1942); *Strana rodnaia/Native Land* (1942); *Sud v Smolenske/ Court in Smolensk* (1946)

Vlada Petric, 'Esther Shub: Film as a Historical Discourse', in *'Show Us Life': Toward a History and Aesthetics of the Committed Documentary*, ed. Thomas Waugh (Metuchen, NJ: Scarecrow Press, 1984)
DJY

SILENT CINEMA

Technically, silent cinema refers to films without synchronous SOUND: the 'coming of sound' is usually dated to the

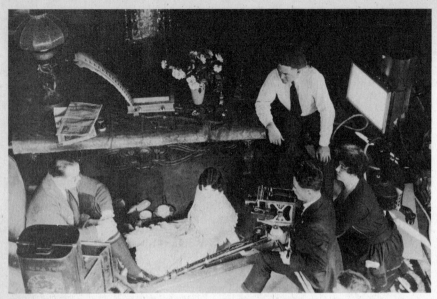

Silent movie set in the early 1920s, Lois Weber directing

late 1920s, though cinema was never, strictly speaking, 'silent' before that time. Film historians divide the pre-sound period into two or three phases: the 'primitive cinema' of the first few years after the earliest public showings of films in the mid 1890s is sometimes distinguished from 'early cinema', which predates and merges into the start of the silent era proper in the mid to late 1910s. These periods are associated with developments in the film industry worldwide, which culminated in the rise of the HOLLYWOOD STUDIO SYSTEM and US dominance of world film markets, of the narrative feature film, and of the aesthetic pattern set by CLASSICAL HOLLYWOOD CINEMA.

In the earliest days of cinema, when production was 'artisanal' and the medium's status low, opportunities for women filmmakers were relatively plentiful: for example, FRANCE's Alice GUY is recognized as one of the pioneers; in ITALY, Elvira NOTARI began directing films in 1906; and Anna HOFMAN-UDDGREN, SWEDEN's first woman

director, made several films in the early 1910s. Cinema's increasing respectability and the growing hierarchization of film production, in combination with the post-World War I eclipse of Europe's film industries, led to a decline in opportunities for women behind the camera; though this same period saw a rise in status and rewards for some women performers as the STAR system developed. Nevertheless, during the silent era proper a number of women directors worked successfully in the now-dominant Hollywood industry: the best known today is undoubtedly Lois WEBER; others, however, include Margery Wilson, Dorothy Davenport (Mrs Wallace Reid) and Ida May Park.

Films made in the heyday of US silent cinema during the 1910s and 1920s were very much part of the wider social changes taking place in that country at the time. This was an era of progressive reform, World War I, and the sexual revolution. With the standardization of feature film and the building of movie palaces in the mid 1910s, film became a democratic art as its appeal was expanded to include the middle class. Filmmakers were especially intent on courting middle-class women, since their attendance at the cinema was considered a sign of respectability. Consequently, the representation of woman in silent film was in part the result of industry strategy during a period when the status of women was affected by broad sociocultural changes. Among the latter was a reconceptualization of female SEXUALITY resulting from the use of contraception by middle-class women. Jazz Age youth were more sexually permissive than their parents' generation, and believed in companionate marriage, a heterosexual ideal that contrasted with sex segregation during the Victorian era. The 'new woman' became an economic, as well as a sexual, symbol in that the family had been transformed into the basic unit of consumption in a mass-consumer economy. Advertising encouraged self-definition through CONSUMERISM and the commodification of social relationships.

Within this context the representation of woman in silent film, especially archetypal female characters drawn from Victorian melodrama and sentimental literature, was significantly modified. Specifically, the bifurcation of woman into virgin and VAMP became less extreme – though such characterizations, as exemplified by Janet Gaynor and Margaret Livingston in F W Murnau's *Sunrise* (Fox, 1927), persisted late into the twenties. For the most part, the virginal heroine associated with the moral values of rural or small-town America, such as the Lillian GISH characters in D W GRIFFITH melodramas, symbolized a bygone era. As America's sweetheart, Mary PICKFORD had wielded enormous power in the industry during the 1910s, but she cut off her famous corkscrew curls in 1927. Similarly, the dark-haired, exotic and wicked vampire, portrayed by stars like Theda BARA, became outmoded. The Victorian drama of seduction and sexual aggression, which represented extreme danger for both sexes, gave way to a more playful approach to human sexuality in the postwar period.

During the Jazz Age, the 'new' eroticized woman, a product of the democratization of feminine ideals such as those promoted by the film industry through commercial tie-ins, became a commodity in a consumer culture. The star system played a significant role in mediating for the female audience images of FEMININITY associated with consumption. As evident in films like *It* (Clarence Badger, Famous Players-Lasky, 1927), starring Clara Bow, working girls who knew how to package themselves experienced upward mobility via marriage to well-heeled men. Socialites typified by the Gloria Swanson character in Cecil B DE MILLE spectacles titled *Don't Change Your Husband* (1919) and *Why Change Your Wife?* (1920) modeled the latest coiffures and gowns to illustrate the power of conspicuous consumption. Flappers like Colleen Moore, Leatrice Joy, Eleanor Boardman, Louise BROOKS, and Joan CRAWFORD represented the determination of American youth to be hedonistic and frivolous. With exceptions, such as the controversial Erich von Stroheim film *Foolish Wives* (1922), sexual encounters were no longer as compelling as the Victorian drama of seduction fraught with moral danger. Social preoccupation with female conduct remained inordinate, however. Sex had become more playful, but the 'new woman' had to walk a fine line. As a pal who sported boyish fashions and bobbed hair, she exerted sex appeal but was not quite as abandoned as she might appear. Several HEROINES of the silent screen, including Greta GARBO's vamp and the flapper, were prototypes of the 'good-bad girl' in forties FILM NOIR.

Paralleling changes in the representation of female sexuality in silent cinema was a sliding scale of MASCULINITY as embodied by actors whose images were often contradictory within a single text or across a series of texts. First of a number of well-publicized Latin lovers,

Rudolph Valentino portrayed a swashbuckling hero in *The Sheik* (George Melford, 1921) and *Son of the Sheik* (George Fitzmaurice, 1926), but appeared quite diffident in *The Conquering Power* (Rex Ingram, 1921). John Gilbert, one of the silent screen's great romantic idols, was reduced to a mama's boy by Jeanne Eagles in *Man, Woman and Sin* (Monta Bell, MGM, 1927). Douglas Fairbanks costume dramas provided the appropriate setting for male athleticism, however juvenile, but 'the little man' was engulfed by the inhuman scale of twentieth-century urban and bureaucratic life: King Vidor's *The Crowd* (MGM, 1928) was aptly titled. Furthermore, the contemporary male often found himself beleaguered during courtship and in marriage by the spirited 'new woman.'

> Set in New York, this 1983 first feature by a US feminist filmmaker is fiery and fabulous. What is its name? What is her name?

As silent films attest, masculinity became problematic in a mass-consumer economy in which human relations were reified and persons, like products, became standardized and interchangeable. Although the NARRATIVE conventions of romantic love in commercial features produced for female spectators mitigated the implications of consumerism, heterosexual relations were nevertheless informed by the forces of economic change.

Sumiko Higashi, *Virgins, Vamps, and Flappers: The American Silent Movie Heroine* (Montreal: Eden Press, 1978)

See also: DULAC, GERMAINE; LOOS, ANITA; LYELL, LOTTIE; McDONAGH SISTERS; MUSIDORA; NEGRI, POLA; NIELSEN, ASTA; SHIPMAN, NELL

SHi

SILVER, JOAN MICKLIN (1935–)

US director Silver's debut film *Hester Street* – the least commercial film thinkable in 1975, in black and white and in Yiddish – was also one of the earliest of recent feminist films, made in homage to the strong immigrant women in Silver's family. Silver shifts the Abraham Cahan tale of a man who came to America to a woman's story. Starting out a powerless and bewildered stranger in a strange land, the heroine Gitl increasingly shapes her own life – while (the other side of women's skill in handling the world) the least macho man in the film, gentle and bookish, is by far the most attractive one.

Silver's next two feature films show her range and her gains in technical skill. *Between the Lines* (1977) is a winning comedy about a late sixties counterculture Boston newspaper, *The Backbay Mainline*, its demise the demise of a time. A sharply observant feminist eye is also apparent in the film, especially when the subject is couples – as it frequently is in Silver's work. Her third feature, *Chilly Scenes of Winter* (1979), from an Ann Beattie novel, is a love drama, more commercial than her other work but still probably too quietly intelligent to satisfy the American mass-market management. During the hiatus that followed, Silver worked in theater and TV drama: directing F Scott Fitzgerald's 'Bernice Bobs Her Hair,' and 'Finnigan Begin Again,' about a middle-aged love affair; co-creating '"A" . . . My Name is Alice,' on Off-Broadway. Her two most recent films make a more obvious bid to navigate the currents of the commercial film box office world, while trying to hold on to serious adult levels underneath. *Crossing Delancey* (1988), made at Warner Bros., has achieved a quiet success with its nuanced depiction of the world of a young 'single' woman in New York and its return to the old ethnic world of the (uncomfortably sentimental) grandmother and the traditional values of marriage she embodies. *Lover Boy* (1989) takes a totally commercial idea, of a pizza delivery boy who sexually services a variety of older women. But while aiming for light entertainment,

Silver also notes the power and attractiveness of these older women, even though their husbands have turned to younger lovers; and she creates a young hero who is appealing because he really enjoys pleasing these women. Silver's tenacious struggle to maintain her own integrity, and yet remain viable as a director in the terms the American film industry allows, has been paradigmatic.

Hester Street (1975); *Between the Lines* (1977); *Chilly Scenes of Winter* (1979); *Crossing Delancey* (1988); *Lover Boy* (1989)

Barbara Koenig Quart, *Women Directors: The Emergence of a New Cinema* (New York: Praeger, 1988)   BKQ

SINGER, GAIL (1946–   )

One of the few women filmmakers in CANADA to be able to make a living in independent DOCUMENTARY production, Gail Singer has also been a consistently committed advocate of feminism and socially progressive issues. She began as a researcher and assistant in the late 1960s, and along the way worked as locations manager in the feature film industry, but she quickly established herself as a director of intelligence and clarity on social documentaries on mercury poisoning in Canada's waterways, native cultures, Arctic oil spills, battered women, breastfeeding, abortion, obstructive government bureaucracy, and children of divorce, as well as several films about artists. She has worked at various times with the Canadian Broadcasting Corporation and with the NATIONAL FILM BOARD OF CANADA in STUDIO D, but manages to maintain an independent profile in Canadian film culture. Her work tends toward an uninflected traditional documentary style, but she has experimented with somewhat formalist elements of voice, address, and MISE-EN-SCENE in *Loved, Honoured and Bruised* (1980). Particularly in co-productions with Studio D, she has often worked with women as principal crew members. She is currently in production with a large-budget documentary feature and television miniseries on women comedians, and is in the process of developing a feature drama.

Films as writer, director, producer or all three: *Labour History* (1973); *Northern Biology* (1974); *Riverain: Gift of Passage* (1976); *Time of the Cree* (1976); *We Don't Live Here Anymore* (1977); *Arctic Oil Spills* (1978); *Season of Plenty* (1978); *Fiddlers of Names Bay* (1979); *The World's Children* (1980); *Loved, Honoured and Bruised* (1980); *A Moveable Feast* (1981); *Portrait of an Artist as an Old Lady* (1982); *Abortion Stories North and South* (1984); *Trade Secrets* (1985); *Neighbourhoods* (1986); *Hayley's Home Movie* (1987); *Is Everybody Here Crazy?* (1988); *Wisecracks* (1989); *True Confections* (in development, 1989)   KA

SIRK, DOUGLAS (1900–87)

This Danish-born Hollywood director (born Claus Detlev Sierk, then known as Detlef Hans Sierck) worked in Germany in theater and film before emigrating to the USA in the late 1930s. Though he touched on several genres, such as the WESTERN (*Taza Son of Cochise* [Universal, 1953], *Take Me to Town* [Universal, 1952]), the MUSICAL (*Has Anybody Seen My Gal?* [Universal, 1951], *Meet Me at the Fair* [Universal, 1952]), the thriller (*Lured* [United Artists, 1946], *Schockproof* [Columbia, 1948]), and the historical epic (*Sign of the Pagan* [Universal, 1954]), Sirk is forever associated with MELODRAMA. It is in this GENRE that he made his first commercial successes in Germany (*Schlussakkord* [1936], *La Habañera* [1937]) and the films that constitute his American 'canon' – characterized by their baroque MISE-EN-SCENE and powerful emotional appeal: *Magnificent Obsession* (Universal, 1953), *All That Heaven Allows* (Universal, 1955), *There's Always Tomorrow* (Universal, 1955), *Written on the Wind* (Universal, 1956), *The Tarnished Angels* (Universal, 1957), *Imitation of Life* (Universal, 1958).

Dorothy Malone in Sirk's *Written on the Wind*

Sirk's films were central to the critical reappraisal of melodrama after its derogatory relegation to 'women's genres.' British critics in the 1970s analyzed their stylistic 'excess' as a critique of the conservative IDEOLOGY of their basic material, itself typical of 1950s Hollywood. Sirk's use of brash primary colors (*Written on the Wind*), stage-like decors (*Imitation of Life*), cliché characters and situations (*Magnificent Obsession*), as well as his often unconvincing 'happy' endings and use of undemonstrative actors such as Rock Hudson, became instances of distanciation, traced back to his early training in Brechtian theater; family relationships were seen as symbolic of larger class conflicts. Later, feminists also pinpointed the crucial place of women within these family plots, and the (ambiguous) PLEASUREs Sirk's films, often told from a woman's point of view, give their female audience. *All That Heaven Allows* may be an indictment of small-town America, but it is also (like *All I Desire* [Universal, 1953] and *Imitation of Life*) a dramatization of a woman's SEX-UALITY, severely limited by conventions but ultimately triumphant. In any case, distanciation or not, the compelling emotional power of Sirk's films – which were often huge popular successes – cannot be underestimated.

Laura Mulvey, 'Notes on Sirk and Melodrama', in *Home Is Where The Heart Studies in Melodrama and the Woman's Film*, ed. Christine Gledhill (London: British Film Institute, 1987)   *GV*

SLASHER FILM *see* HORROR

SOAP OPERA

A form of serial fiction pioneered in the late 1920s by American, mainly female, radio program makers, soap opera – characterized by an emphasis on human relations, domesticity, and daily life – rapidly developed into one of the most popular forms of entertainment on radio. The 'soaps' – so called because they were originally sponsored by soap manufacturers – built up a faithful following, especially among housewives. With the advent of TELEVISION, soap opera took on a new lease of life, and the GENRE continues to flourish in many parts of the world: in American daytime serials such as 'All My Children,' in British early-evening serials like 'Coronation Street' and 'EastEnders,' in the highly successful Australian 'Neighbours,' and in the Brazilian 'telenovelas.' It has also moved into prime-time television with more lavish productions such as 'Dallas' and 'Dynasty.' Soap opera now attracts serious critical attention within the fields of CULTURAL STUDIES and FEMINIST FILM THEORY, aimed at understanding the special appeal of the genre to female AUDIENCES. Feminists have pointed to the cultural significance of the unending quality – the 'infinitely expandable middle' – of soap opera NARRATIVE, which sets the genre apart from its film equivalents, MELODRAMA and the WOMAN'S PICTURE; to the 'cultural competences' required of audiences in order to read soap opera; and to the ways in which viewing soaps slots into women's work and social relations within home and family.

Ien Ang, *Watching Dallas: Soap Opera and the Melodramatic Imagination* (London: Methuen, 1985)   AKu

SOCIALIST CINEMA

A presupposition of socialist cinema is the belief that art has a role to play in challenging the economic and social relations engendered by capitalism, in identifying the interests of the exploited and oppressed, and in assisting in the process of transforming society in order to meet the needs of the majority of the population, including women. However, the history of socialist and marxist theories of art is full of disagreements about the methods to be adopted in order to realize these goals. The theory and practice of socialist cinema embodies a wide variety of aesthetic and political positions (from SOCIALIST REALISM to COUNTER-

CINEMA, from anti-imperialism to the critique of male chauvinism).

The socialist emphasis on representing class exploitation has often ignored, and sometimes actively suppressed, the issue of women's oppression in the sexual division of labor. In formal and aesthetic terms the open-minded pluralism of the 'let a thousand flowers bloom' approach, and Marx's own warnings that art should not be reduced to the tendentiousness of a political pamphlet, have often been rejected in favor of a censorious dogmatism. Only since the 1970s have the massive underrepresentation of women as cultural producers, and the suppression of women's voice, experience and point of view, begun to be adequately recognized within the socialist movements, and within socialist cinema.

Since the 1920s, socialist and feminist women have struggled to work and to be recognized as filmmakers in both socialist and capitalist countries. More recently, the issue of women's oppression and of our great contribution to movements for national liberation and social justice have been foregrounded in much Third World cinema – for example, in the work of Sarah MALDOROR, Ousmane SEMBENE, and Sara GOMEZ. Many contemporary CUBAN films highlight the struggle against male chauvinism and for women's emancipation; for example *De cierta manera/One Way or Another* (Sara Gómez, (1975–7), *Lucía* (Humberto Solás, 1969), *Hasta cierto punto/Up to a Point* (Tomás Gutiérrez Alea, 1984). The development of a new kind of lyrical and analytical cinema is signaled in the short film *Oracion (por Marilyn Monroe)/Prayer* (1985) by Cuban woman director Marisol Trujillo.

Interesting examples of work dealing with women's issues are to be found in the cinemas of the SOVIET UNION, CHINA, INDIA, and EASTERN EUROPE, as well as in western INDEPENDENT CINEMA. Examples of progressive representations of women in north American and European cinema include *Salt of the Earth* (Herbert

Biberman, 1953), *Norma Rae* (Martin Ritt, 1979), *La Fiancée du pirate* (Nelly Kaplan, 1969), *Doll's Eye* (Jan Worth, 1982), and *The Passion of Remembrance* (Maureen Blackwood and Isaac Julien, 1986).

Peter Steven (ed.), *Jump Cut: Hollywood, Politics and Counter Cinema* (Toronto: Behind the Lines, 1985)   SHa

SOCIALIST REALISM

Defined by Stalin as 'a true and historically concrete depiction of reality and its revolutionary development,' socialist realism had its origins in the Soviet Union in the 1930s. Since that time, it has become the officially endorsed (or at least preferred) method or approach for artists in all media, both in the SOVIET UNION and in other socialist countries. Its migration to other cultural contexts has often wrought changes in the method, and even in the Soviet Union itself socialist realism has sometimes been rather liberally interpreted. As a cross-media method, however, socialist realism retains several defining characteristics. As Stalin's dictum suggests, history and social development are meant to be central features; in socialist realism history always 'speaks' through characters. Historical and social changes are expressed centrally through developments in consciousness on the part of characters, so that history and character encapsulate one another. From this emerges 'typification' – characters are drawn as social types, as well as individuals with their own traits of personality: in terms of narrative cinema, this is the fundamental distinction between socialist realism and the REALISM of CLASSICAL HOLLYWOOD CINEMA, in which narratives are driven largely by characters' personal traits and motivations. The central characters of socialist realist texts often embody heroic qualities; this is a mark of the influence of 'revolutionary romanticism,' which aims to offer a vision of the future – but a vision always grounded rather than utopian, a sense that things could plausibly change in particular ways. This optimism is embodied in the positive hero (or, less often, perhaps, the positive HEROINE) of socialist realism, a character represented as having the usual complement of faults and good qualities, who is propelled by the narrative into changes of consciousness, eventually leading to action in the social-historical sphere. Characteristically, while the conflicts and obstacles overcome by the positive hero are simultaneously personal and social, the socialist realist NARRATIVE does resemble that of classical Hollywood cinema in its impetus toward closure. When translated to cinema, these cross-media characteristics are often – though not inevitably – organized in the 'invisible' style characteristic of Hollywood.

Socialist realist cinema has sometimes taken working-class women's struggles as a point of social-historical identification, placing a woman in the role of positive 'hero' and making her gender (as well as her class and sometimes her race) significant in terms of narrative development. The positive heroine in such cases represents not just one (fictional) woman but all women (of a certain social class and/or ethnic group), so that women are accorded the status of historical subjects. An important example of such 'socialist-feminist' realism in cinema comes not from a socialist country but from the USA: *Salt of the Earth* (Herbert Biberman, 1953) was made by leftwing filmmakers exiled from Hollywood by the McCarthyite witchhunts of the 1940s and 1950s. The film's heroine and narrator is Esperanza Quintero (Rosaura Revueltas), a Mexican-American mother whose miner husband becomes involved in a strike. The story follows the miners' wives' increasing politicization, Esperanza's concurrent struggles to be taken seriously by her husband as a person in her own right, her own politicization and triumph in both domestic and community spheres, and the victory of the miners and their families through community solidarity and collective action. While *Salt of the Earth* embodies all the qualities of classic socialist realism, films from some socialist countries have been freer in their interpretation of the method. From a feminist standpoint, *De cierta manera/One Way or Another* (1975–7), directed by CUBA's Sara GOMEZ, provides an interesting case of how socialist realism – essentially, perhaps, a western artistic method – seasoned in other contexts with elements of indigenous culture, can be productively revitalized.

Annette Kuhn, *Women's Pictures: Feminism and Cinema* (London: Routledge & Kegan Paul, 1982)

See also: ARBEITERFILM; REVOLUTIONARY MODEL FILM; SOCIALIST CINEMA   AKu

SOLAS, HUMBERTO (1942–)

A passionate student of architecture and history, and a seasoned anti-Batista fighter from the age of fourteen, Solás joined the CUBAN Film Institute (ICAIC) in the year of its founding, 1959. Working on his own or in collaboration with Octavio Cortázar or Oscar Valdés, Solás made seven short films in as many years, several of an experimental nature. He has subsequently made one medium-length and six major features, five of which position women as central to discourses on Cuban history and national identity. The most important of these, *Lucía* (1968), is a trilogy which depicts the precarious (im)balance between personal passions and sociopolitical forces in the lives of three fictional protagonists across seven decades. For many years ICAIC's most ambitious production (until it would be outstripped in cost many times over by his own epic *Cecilia* [1982]), *Lucía* is a brilliant tour de force, each of whose segments is made in a style appropriate to the historical period depicted. Neither the earlier *Manuela* (1966), a medium-length love story set during the guerrilla war to overthrow the Batista dictatorship, nor the subsequent *Cecilia* (an overblown effort based on Cuba's most famous novel, *Cecilia Valdez*, about the liaison between a *mulatta*

and an aristocrat) rivals the influence and accomplishment of the *Lucía* trilogy, arguably still LATIN AMERICA's most memorable woman-centered feature.

Of his tendency to position female characters at the center of his features, Solás has said:

> because women are traditionally assigned a submissive role, [they] have suffered more from society's contradictions and are thus . . . more hungry for change. From this perspective, I feel that the female character has a great deal of dramatic potential through which I can express the entire social phenomenon I want to portray. This . . . has nothing to do with feminism per se.

Solás's films include: *Manuela* (1966); *Lucía* (1968); *Un día de noviembre/A Day in November* (1972); *Simparele* (1974); *Amada* (1978); *Cecilia* (1982); *Un hombre de éxito/A Successful Man* (1987)

Tête Vasconcelos and Julianne Burton, 'Every Point of Arrival is a Point of Departure', in *Cinema and Social Change in Latin America: Conversations with Filmmakers*, ed. Julianne Burton (Austin: University of Texas Press, 1986)   JBu

SOLNTSEVA, IULIIA (1901–)

SOVIET actress and director Solntseva made her debut as the eponymous heroine of Yakov Protazanov's *Aelita* (1924), then starred in Yuri Zheliabuzhski's *The Cigarette Girl* (1924). Her meeting with and marriage to Aleksandr Dovzhenko in 1929 marked the end of her acting career (she played her last role in his *Zemlia/Earth* [1930]) and the beginning of their lifelong collaboration: from *Earth* onward Solntseva was first the assistant director, then associate and subsequently co-director of all Dovzhenko's films, including several outstanding World War II documentaries. After Dovzhenko's death in 1956, she directed the film he had scripted and planned – *Poema o morie* (1958) – stressing her intention to remain faithful to his style: 'I must complete this film in accordance with Dovzhenko's artistic conception, putting aside every trace of my own individual vision.' When the film was nominated for the Lenin Prize, Solntseva wrote to the director of Mosfilm Studio asking him to nominate Dovzhenko rather than herself as the film's major creator – and it was indeed Dovzhenko who was subsequently awarded the prize. She made three other films – *Povest plamennikh let* (1961), *Zacharovannaia Desna* (1964) and *Nazabivaiemoie* (1968) – based on Dovzhenko's writings and skillfully reproducing his cinematic and literary styles; and a film about him, *Zolotie vorota* (1971). Only her penultimate film, *Takiie vysokiie gory* (1974) – about the problems of modern education – had nothing of Dovzhenko in it.

In line with her declared intention, Solntseva continued Dovzhenko's romantic tradition. Her films eschew naturalistic causality and detail and create epic panoramas, poetic metaphors, and larger-than-life characters. Whilst undoubtedly influenced by her husband, Solntseva became an accomplished director in her own right: she has imaginatively transposed Dovzhenko's style into the medium of color CinemaScope and extended it into the genres of semidocumentary (*Zolotie vorota*) and the selfconsciously literature-based film (*Zacharovannaia Desna*). Solntseva has been awarded the Dovzhenko Medal for films on the subject of patriotism (1972), the medal Golden Lion of St Mark at the Book Exhibition in Venice (1975) for her contribution to the book *Earth*, and she took part in the preparation of Dovzhenko's *Collected Works*.

Bukovina – zemlia ukrainskaia/Bukovina – Ukrainian Land (1940); *Bitva na nashu Sovietskaiu Ukrainu/The Fight for our Soviet Ukraine* (1943); *Yegor Bulichov and Others* (1953); *Revizori ponevole/Unwilling Inspectors* (short, 1955); *Poema o morie/ Poem of a Sea* (1958); *Povest plamennikh let/Story of Flaming Years* (1961); *Zachar-* *ovannaia Desna/The Enchanted Desna* (1964); *Nazabivaiemoie/The Unforgettable* (1968); *Zolotie vorota/The Golden Gate* (1971); *Takiie vysokiie gory/Such High Mountains* (1974); *Mir v triokh izmereniiakh/The World in Three Dimensions* (1980)

Efim Levin, 'Lofty Calling', *Soviet Film*, no. 12 (1986)   ME

SONTAG, SUSAN (1933–)

The work of this intellectual, who came to prominence in the United States during the 1960s, is impossible to classify in terms of any one 'art' or 'profession,' and its consistency lies in her conception of modern art as an exploration of *problems*. Trained as a philosopher, she lectured until becoming a full-time writer after the publication of her first novel, *The Benefactor* (1963). A famous collection of essays, *Against Interpretation* (1966), was followed by another novel (*Death Kit*), a film (*Duet for Cannibals*), more essays (*Styles of Radical Will*), and in 1971 a second film, *Brother Carl*.

Many critics compare Sontag's novels and films unfavorably with her much-admired essays, but they are most interesting when read in relation to each

> She is Japan's first woman director. She was taken aback and taken down when Kenji Mizoguchi announced that women should not make films. Who is she?

other rather than as isolated forays into different media. In the films and novels, she was thinking through the questions raised in essays like 'Against Interpretation' and 'The Aesthetics of Silence', as well as by her studies of Bresson, Bergman, and Resnais: for example, the status of language for modern art ('the dilemmas of speaking, of being silent, of finding it hard . . . to speak at all'). In both films and essays, she explored the *forms* of emotional, spiritual, and aesthetic articulation in art (repetition, doubling, the figure of the couple), and related these concerns of high MODERNISM to the forms of mass culture, and contemporary social experience. This is the subject of a major essay from *Styles of Radical Will*, 'Godard' (1968). While 'Notes on Camp' may still be the best-known text by a critic noted for her ability to define new movements in culture, 'Godard' was much more complex and far-reaching – setting out most of the terms of the debate that emerged in the 1980s as POSTMODERNISM.

'Trip to Hanoi' (1968) marked a new phase of trying to integrate her political convictions with her aesthetic concerns. This was also the project of *Promised Lands*, a controversial film about the tragic and contradictory elements within the state of Israel. Sontag has since concentrated on specific cultural issues (*On Photography* and *Illness as Metaphor*), returning to cinema with a study of Syberberg's *Hitler*, and 'Fascinating Fascism' – on the relationship between sadomasochistic PORNOGRAPHY, fascist aesthetics, and the critical 'rehabilitation' of Leni RIEFENSTAHL.

Duet for Cannibals (1969); *Broder Carl/Brother Carl* (1971); *Promised Lands* (1974)

A Susan Sontag Reader, (New York: Hill & Wang: 1982)   MMo

SOUND

Sound has accompanied the visual image from the very beginnings of cinema. Through the 1920s, live and recorded music as well as sound effects played in theaters provided manually synchronized sound. Various film cultures, such as JAPAN's, have also employed individuals to speak lines of dialogue or to comment on screen action. During the 1920s, technology to reproduce voices improved, as did amplification systems, permitting mechanical synchronization of sound and image; and since the mid 1930s this has been the dominant practice worldwide.

Analysis of soundtracks calls for various distinctions: for example between sources of sound – such as onscreen and offscreen (that is, the sound source is or is not visible within the frame) and diegetic or nondiegetic (that is, the source does or does not belong to the story-world of the NARRATIVE); another distinction is the temporal relation between sound and image (synchronous or not). Additionally, some writers categorize sounds as MUSIC, speech, and sound effects (or noise), marking the varieties of subject matter potentially conveyed by each: of these, human speech or dialogue has received the greatest emphasis, particularly in CLASSICAL HOLLYWOOD CINEMA, due to the centrality of human characters to its stories. Even early sound films were known as 'talkies,' an idea which did not please formally innovative directors like René Clair, Sergei Eisenstein (Eisenstein registered his protests in a 1928 statement with two other Soviet directors). These filmmakers criticized the use of natural, synchronized sound that ran parallel to the image, advocating instead that sound be used in counterpoint to the image to break with classical notions of verisimilitude and unity.

The 'parallel' conception of sound has influenced theory as much as it has governed film production. Traditional critics as well as practitioners have considered it to be something that should follow, enhance, or otherwise serve the film image. The feminization of this subordinate function of sound is apparent in the sound editor's task of 'marrying' the soundtrack to the film print. Theory would seem to support the association of FEMININITY with sound, since the two are largely defined by their 'invisibility.' Using psychoanalysis, feminists like Luce Irigaray, Hélène Cixous and, in PSYCHOANALYTIC FILM THEORY, Laura MULVEY, Mary Ann Doane, and Kaja Silverman have noted how Freud's account of sexual difference stresses the visibility of the male sex organ, whereas woman is defined by her apparent anatomical 'lack,' her sex which remains hidden from sight. Consequently, many feminists have placed special weight on the idea of sound as an alternative form of expression, cinematic and otherwise (this has been the case especially for music, which has been insistently linked to the idea of female discourse).

Although there are problems in assigning gender to forms of representation, the connection remains important for feminists to explore; and the linking of woman and sound partially explains the innovative and important role awarded the soundtrack in feminist COUNTER-CINEMA – as in, for example, the films of Yvonne RAINER, Sally POTTER, and in Lizzie BORDEN's *Born in Flames* (1983).

Elisabeth Weis and John Belton (eds), *Film Sound: An Anthology* (New York: Columbia University Press, 1986)

See also: BUTE, MARY ELLEN; CHILD, ABIGAIL; DURAS, MARGUERITE; TRINH T MINH-HA   JaS/CF

SOUTH AFRICA

No history of a South African cultural industry, whether it be cinema, drama or music, can afford to skirt the issue of race. In a country where feminist issues have only recently come to the fore, the mass democratic movement has concentrated its effort on a more just dispensation for the majority of its disenfranchised citizens

Movie theaters were first erected in 1905, but the local feature film industry took off only in 1916, with fourteen films, all subtitled in English, except *De Voortrekkers/Winning a Continent* (Harold Shaw, 1916, English and Dutch). Like *Symbol of Sacrifice* (I W Schesinger, 1918), this film was produced in the epic style. Many films produced before 1924 were high adventure, jingoistic colonial stories: for example, *King Solomon's Mines* (Lisle Lucoque, 1918), *Alan Quartermain* (1919), *Prester John* (African Film Productions, 1920) and *Isban Israel* (Joseph Albrecht, 1920). This was a

'white' man's world: 'blacks' and women featured only as the prize of conquest.

The feature industry slumped during the 1920s. *Sarie Marie* (Joseph Albrecht, 1931) was South Africa's first sound film, ironically produced in Afrikaans at a time when the entertainment industry was dominated by English capital. A culturally important film, *Moedertjie/Little Mother* (Joseph Albrecht, 1931), introduced the *boerevrou* (farmwife) to the screen. The primary matriarchal force, source of folk wisdom, in her guise as *volkmoeder* (mother of the nation) the *boerevrou* is a symbol of Afrikaner resilience and nationalism. The surge of Afrikaner nationalism gained impetus in 1938 with the centenary reenactment of the Great Trek, filmed as docudramas in *Bou van 'n Nasie/They Built a Nation* (Joseph Albrecht, 1939) and *'n Nasie hou Koers/A Nation Goes Forward* (Joseph Albrecht, 1939). Other Afrikaner-nationalist films followed: *Ons Staan 'n Dag Oor/We Stand Another Day* (1942) and *Pinkie se Erfenis/Pinkie's Inheritance* (Pierre de Wet, 1946), which repeated the theme of the Afrikaner's close connection to the soil.

After a grim period of deprivation during World War II, the 1950s saw a glut of escapist films. Musical comedies were particularly popular: *Hier is ons Weer/Here We Are Again* (Pierre de Wet, 1950); *Altyd in my Drome/Always in My Dreams* (Pierre de Wet, 1952); *Nooi van my Hart/Girl of My Heart* (Pierre de Wet, 1958). Musicals continued to appear for another fifteen years: *Jy is my Liefling/You Are My Love* (Dirk de Villiers, 1968) and *Lied in my Hart/Song in My Heart* (1970). Jamie Uys, later to produce *The Gods Must Be Crazy* (1980), began his comic career with *Daar Doer in die Bosveld/Far Away in the Bushveld* (1951); *Geld soos Bossies/Money to Burn* (1955); and the bilingual *Fifty-vyftig/50:50* (1954).

For the next two decades, a series of love/hate films dominated cinema screens. Films in this *boeredogter* (daughter of the soil) GENRE are overlaid with the political/ideological dimension of the insider–outsider conflict. Calvinist ethics are romanticized, sex is repressed, and there is a deep suspicion of materialist values and urban lifestyles. In Pierre de Wet's *Die Oupa en die Plaasnooitjie/The Grandpa and the Farm Girl* (1960), the 'insider' – a pure, blonde, virginal, naive, pleasant, capable *boeredogter* – is contrasted with the outsider, a treacherous city sophisticate with an affected anglicized accent, who has turned her back on her true Afrikaner national identity. Another film in this genre is Jan Scholtz's *Die Winter van 14 Julie/The Winter of the 14 July* (1977), a hanky-wringing ROMANCE in which the intrepid airman braves all in his attempt to prevent his girlfriend's inevitable abortion. Particularly noticeable is the heavy use of soft focus, a characteristic ICONOGRAPHIC feature of the *boeredogter* genre.

In a second wave of the genre, the heroine is maimed, either physically or psychologically. This ritual maiming suggests a social trauma in the status of the *boeredogter*: in *MoMo/Tomorrow* (Elmo de Wet, 1973) she is paralyzed; in *Katrina* (Jans Rautenbach, 1969) she is rejected because of her color; in *Plekkie in Son/Place in the Sun* (Bill Faure, 1979) she is a leper. In *Ter Wille van Christine/For the Sake of Christine* (Elmo de Wet, 1975) she is a Roman Catholic in a Calvinist community. In *Debbie* (Elmo de Wet, 1965), the earliest of this cycle, the heroine, pregnant out of wedlock, is punished by ostracism – an unsubtle comment on the dangers of transgressing group norms. *Onwettige Huwelik/Unlawful Wedding* (Mario Schiess, 1970), a lighthearted comedy, is a variation on the same theme. Both *Debbie* and *Onwettige Huwelik* were fiercely attacked by the Publications Control (censorship) Board, which stated that Afrikaans girls do not get pregnant out of wedlock, and that in South Africa there was no such thing as an unlawful wedding.

Over the years, numerous films have been made for 'black' audiences in South Africa, but no 'black' directors or producers emerged. 'Black' women feature only as adjuncts in these films, none of which displays any feminist consciousness. Recently, however, 'black' women have cooperated closely in a number of ANTI-APARTHEID FILMS AND VIDEOS of resistance: these, however, have not enjoyed wide distribution in South Africa, usually being confined to festival-type screenings.

Women have been employed in the cinema industries in the traditional spheres of wardrobe, make-up, production secretaries, and so on, and have only recently undertaken more technical positions. A very few South African commercial films have been made by women: for example, Katinka HEYNS directed *Fiela se Kind/Fiela's Child* (1988), Helena NOGUEIRA directed *Quest for Love/Quest for Truth* (1988) and Lindi Wilson directed the 16mm anti-apartheid films *Crossroads* (1973) and *Last Supper at Hortsley Street* (1984).

Keyan Tomaselli, *The Cinema of Apartheid: Race and Class in South African Film* (London: Routledge/New York: Lake View Press/Johannesburg: Century Hutchinson, 1989)

See also: RAUTENBACH, JANS and NOFAL, EMIL   WJA/RET

SOVIET UNION

Perhaps no other national cinema has had so narrow a section of its canon so intensively and exclusively scrutinized. The literature devoted to the great avant-garde classics of Soviet cinema's 'golden age' aside, little is available in western languages on Soviet films, the Soviet industry, and Soviet film theory and criticism. At present, it is certainly the least studied of all major NATIONAL CINEMAs, though there are welcome signs that this is changing. The reasons for this idiosyncratic treatment of Soviet film history are in large part political. The Soviet film industry, nationalized in 1918, was until recently highly centralized and under the control of the state film trust Goskino and various censorship agencies. The Leningrad and

Moscow studios (currently known as Lenfilm and Mosfilm) are the two major centers for feature film production, but the union republics of the USSR all have their own studios as well. The productions of these studios tend to be of local rather than national or international interest, and for this reason some well-known directors from the Soviet ethnic minorities prefer to make Russian-language films for Lenfilm or Mosfilm. Nonetheless, fine work has come from all the republic studios; the Georgian studio Gruziafilm enjoys an international reputation, many considering it to be at the vanguard of Soviet film production.

Despite nationalization, the degree of state control and the extent of censorship have fluctuated throughout Soviet history. Except during the Civil War (1918–21), the Communist Party did not seek to use film as a propaganda tool until the 'Cultural Revolution' of 1928–32; hence the fabled 'flowering' of the twenties. From the thirties until the 'Thaw' of the late fifties that followed the death of Stalin and the rise of Khrushchev, Soviet films attempted to adhere to the ever-changing Party line and conformed, with varying degrees of success, to the tenets of SOCIALIST REALISM. Although some interesting, and even entertaining, films were produced in the USSR during Stalin's regime, they were little seen in the West (and western films were rarely shown in the USSR).

With the 'Thaw,' a select number of Soviet movies, like *Ballada soldata/Ballad of a Soldier* (Grigorii Chukhrai, 1959) and *Lezhat zhuravli/The Cranes Are Flying* (Mikhail Kalatozov, 1957) made it into western theaters, but after Khrushchev was ousted in 1964 the Soviet cultural establishment fairly quickly resumed its old habits and reverted to enforcing a more orthodox 'line' in the arts. But Soviet directors have managed historically to cope with censorship rather creatively, and the films of the seventies, though for the most part stylistically conservative, are solidly crafted. The melodrama of contemporary life, often infused with trenchant social criticism, is a genre popular with both the public and the better directors.

Soviet film GENREs actually differ little from their American and European counterparts, except that the pure romance does not exist, but the depiction of women in Soviet films has differed markedly from those STEREOTYPES which dominate western commercial films. From the twenties to the end of the Stalin era, women in Soviet films have been shown as strong and independent – valued contributors to the new society. 'Bourgeois' women – that is, beautiful women whose main concern is seducing men – existed, but only as villainesses or foils for true Soviet womanhood. Many of the best examples of the strong film HEROINE come, not surprisingly, from the exuberant twenties: *Katka bumazhnii ranet/Katka the Apple Seller* (Fridrikh Ermler, 1926); *Novyi Vavilon/New Babylon* (Grigorii Kozintsev and Leonid Trauberg, 1929); *Dom na Trubnoi/House on Trubnaia Square* (Boris Barnet, 1927). But there are countless more from the thirties and forties: for example, *Chlen pravitelstva/Member of the Government* (A G Zarkhi and Iosif Heifitz, 1939); *Ona zashchishchaet rodinu/She Defends Her Country* (Ermler, 1943). Interestingly, it

> 'This, like most conceptions of femininity, is associated with unsteadiness and duplicity since the effects it produces are emotional, irrational, and intensely pleasurable.' To what unsound element does this quote refer?

has been only recently (in the late sixties and early seventies) that an antifeminist backlash has been evident in Soviet cinema. This trend can be noted in numerous films, but is best illustrated by a picture widely seen both in and out of the Soviet Union, *Moskva slezam ne verit/Moscow Does Not Believe in Tears* (Vladimir Menshov, 1979).

Many talented women have worked in

Soviet cinema. From the silent days onward women scenarists worked across the entire spectrum, contributing to every genre and tackling a wide variety of subjects. Popular novelists such as Lidia Seifullina, Galina Nikolaieva, and Vera Panova adapted their own works. Other writers, such as Katerina Vinogradskaia, Maria Smirnova, Sima Roshal, and Natalia Riazantseva, specialized in scriptwriting *per se*. The third group are women directors, who often wrote their own scripts. Women's notable achievements include the script by children's poet Agniia Barto and actress Rina Zelionaia of the comedy *Podkidysh/ Foundling* (Tatiana Lukashevich, 1939); Vinogradskaia's *Oblomok imperii/Fragment of an Empire* (Fridrikh Ermler, 1929), a film about a veteran of World War I recovering from amnesia; and *Partiinyi bilet/Party Card* (Ivan Piriev, 1936), a film that tackled the sensitive subject of a political wrecker during Stalin's purges; Vera Stroeva's and Sima Roshal's *Pokoleniye pobeditelei/The Generation of Conquerors* (Stroeva, 1936), about Russia's revolutionary past; Maia Turovskaia's documentary *Obyknovennyi fashism/Ordinary Fascism* (Mikhail Romm, 1966); and Riazantseva's *Krylia/Wings* (Larissa Shepitko, 1966), *Dolgiye provody/Long Farewells* (Kira Muratova, 1972) and *Chuzhie pisma/ Someone Else's Letters* (Ilya Averbakh, 1976), a study of a triangle. Two outstanding films produced in the new climate of glasnost – *Malinkaia Vera/Little Vera* (Vasily Pichul, 1987), a portrait of a materialistic working-class family oblivious to all moral norms, and *Muzh i doch Tamari Aleksandrovni/The Husband and Daughter of Tamara Aleksandrovna* (Olga Narutskaia, 1988) – were scripted by women, Maria Khmelik and Olga Kozhushannaia respectively, two highly promising newcomers to the profession.

It is probably most fruitful, however, to look to directors to exemplify the importance of women in Soviet cinema. Since the heady early days, women directors have occupied a prominent place in

Soviet filmmaking, and the number of women who got their start in the twenties testifies to the artistic vitality of the 'Golden Age.' In fact, all the major women directors active from the twenties through the mid fifties had entered the studios by 1929: Aleksandra Khokhlova, Nadezhda Kosheverova, Olga PREOBRAZHENSKAIA, Esfir SHUB, Elizaveta SVILOVA, Iuliia SOLNTSEVA, and Vera STROEVA. These women came to cinema from different social and ethnic backgrounds, and along different paths, but some similarities may be noted. Preobrazhenskaia, Khokhlova, and Solntseva were well-known film actresses (though from very different schools) and Shub and Svilova were seasoned film editors (again, of differing experience). At least four of the seven were married to men who were also prominent in the film world – Khokhlova to Lev Kuleshov, Solntseva to Aleksandr Dovzhenko, Stroeva to Grigorii Roshal, Svilova to Dziga Vertov; but, significantly, it was never suggested that these women had gotten where they were by any means other than their own talents.

To date, there has been no comprehensive analysis of the contributions of these directors to the development of Soviet cinema, nor any study comparing their work in terms of thematic content or images. While it is certainly possible that some substantive similarities might emerge were such a study undertaken, it is perhaps more important to note that the films they made were as varied as the women who made them. Shub, Solntseva, and Svilova were primarily documentarists; Khokhlova made narrative fiction films; Stroeva favored literary adaptations and musicals; Kosheverova, comedies; and Preobrazhenskaia, certainly the most versatile of the group, made children's films, melodramas, and historical epics. Most of these directors began their independent work as filmmakers near the end of the silent era. The two most prominent in the twenties – and they were very well known indeed

– were Olga Preobrazhenskaia and Esfir Shub. Of the women who began directing in the thirties, Khokhlova, Solntseva, and Svilova never achieved the prominence of Preobrazhenskaia and Shub, though their contributions to Soviet cinema should not be underestimated. Aleksandra Khokhlova was a gifted silent film actress who turned to direction in 1929. She directed only four films in the fifteen years between 1929 and 1944, but was influential as a teacher at VGIK, the state film institute. Elizaveta Svilova worked primarily as an editor during the twenties, and then as an assistant director on Vertov's films.

The movies of Vera Stroeva and Nadezhda Kosheverova, if not the artistic successes of Preobrazhenskaia's and Shub's early works, were nonetheless popular. Stroeva started her film career in 1925 as a scenarist and directed her first feature in 1930. Of her pictures from the thirties, *Peterburgskaia noch/Petersburg Night* (1934) is the most highly regarded, but she came into her own in the fifties as the director of filmed concerts and operas, most notably *Boris Godunov* (1955) and *Khovanshchina* (1959). She continued to direct into the early eighties. Nadezhda Kosheverova was trained as a theater actress but joined the Leningrad film studio in 1929. She worked as an assistant director to Kozintsev and Trauberg in their famous 'Maksim Trilogy' (1935–9) and began making her own films in 1940, with the comedy *Arinka*. She directed steadily from the late forties, primarily comedies and fairytales, and made her last movie in 1982. Her work is unfortunately little known in the west.

This 'first generation' of women directors was unusually talented and exceptionally productive. Yet the 'second generation,' though slightly fewer in number, has carried on the traditions of the pioneering women filmmakers admirably. This generation, as varied as its forerunner, is represented by Dinara ASANOVA, Lana GOGOBERIDZE, Kira MURATOVA, Larissa SHEPITKO, and Aida Manasarova. The oldest of the group, Aida Manasarova, began her film work in newsreels and joined the Mosfilm studio in 1956. Between 1962 and 1984 she directed eight features on themes from contemporary Soviet life. Her best are considered to be: *Ishchu moiu sudby/I Am Looking for My Fate* (1975), *Vy mne pisali/You Wrote Me . . .* (1977), *Utrennyi obkhod/Morning Round* (1980), and *Oglianis/Look Back* (1984).

The next generation of Soviet film directors is only now emerging, and faces the challenges of the reform era. Given the richness of this heritage, one can be confident that young Soviet filmmakers, women and men alike, will make a significant impact on world cinema and will benefit from the contributions of their predecessors.

Lynne Alford and Sian Thomas (eds), *Women in Soviet Cinema* (London: Pandora Press, 1991)   DJY/ME

SPAIN

In looking at the history of women in Spanish cinema, one is faced with the dismaying reality that the number of films directed by women is still much below the average for most European countries. Recent statistics show that of 1155 feature films produced in Spain between 1973 and 1987, only eighteen were directed by women. With regard to financially more accessible short films, the situation is slightly better: of the national output of 1324 in the same period, fifty-nine were directed by women. 1988, however, was exceptional in yielding three films by women first-time directors. In this context any notion of a 'feminist voice' within mainstream Spanish cinema has no meaning. Many explanations might be offered for this absence of women behind the camera; but none really answers the question why, unlike other Mediterranean countries such as ITALY, with its very similar attitudes toward women, Spain has not produced women directors with the output of a Lina WERTMULLER or a Liliana CAVANI. The input of women to Spanish cinema remains largely in ancillary areas such as ART DIRECTION, hairdressing, COSTUMES, or at best SCREENWRITING.

In looking at the history of Spanish cinema, the work of a few male directors stands out, either because of their understanding of the female sensibility or because they refuse to portray women in the 'traditional manner.' These men are most notably Luis Buñuel, Carlos Saura and, in recent times, that Spanish phenomenon Pedro Almodóvar, whose films (for example, the internationally acclaimed *Women on the Verge of a Nervous Breakdown* [1988]) always include very complex and positive portrayals of women. Almodóvar is clearly unwilling to disregard the cinematic possibilities offered by half the human race.

The sparse history of Spanish women filmmakers begins with a Catalan pioneer, Rosario Pi, who, after working as a scriptwriter and producer, directed *El gato montes/The Wild Cat* (1935) and a second feature, *Molinos de viento*, in 1937, in the midst of the Civil War. Like many others she was forced into exile, and she died in 1968 without ever directing again. In the 1950s the actress Margarita Aleixandre co-directed (with Rafael Torrecilla) two films: *La ciudad perdida* and *La gata* (1955), the latter being the first CinemaScope film shot in Spain. Another well-known actress, Ana Mariscal, a woman of outstanding intellectual qualities with a very considerable body of directorial work to her credit (eleven features and many TV productions), sadly remains almost unknown, and her films are rarely seen outside Spain.

The development of cinema is never isolated from its surrounding political climate. The forty years of Franco's dictatorship – which gave male directors (such as Saura) a very clear target to aim at – did not produce a strong response from women. Perhaps this absence is due to the fact that women would have had to break down a double barrier: the personal as well as the political. Sadly, the atrocities of the Franco years and the isolation of exile destroyed the hopes and trust which the Spanish republic had placed in women. In the last two decades, only two women have succeeded in directing feature films: Pilar MIRO and Josefina MOLINA. This grim situation in regard to quantity – if not to quality – is, however, modified somewhat by an increase in recent years in women's contributions to the NATIONAL CINEMA of Spain: women now working behind the camera include Pilar Tavora, Cristina Andreu, Isabel Coixet, and Ana Diez. Their efforts, however, are somewhat uneven, the most interesting perhaps being Ana Diez's *Ander and Yul* (1988). Curiously, this increase in the number of women filmmakers coincides with Spanish cinema's currently very commercial orientation. But if Spain is producing a larger number of features each year, their quality is on the whole lower than in the Franco years. From a feminist point of view, it is sad to note that, with few exceptions, commercial cinema in Spain is full of meaningless plots, cobbled together with exploitive images of women.

While Spanish FILM FESTIVALS (such as those of San Sebastian and Valladolid) have consistently included women's films in their selections, the 'Ateneo Feminista' in Madrid organized the first 'Muestra de cine realizado por mujeres' in 1985. This WOMEN'S FILM FESTIVAL now takes place annually in November and has assumed a very important role, giving women a forum in which to show their own films, as well as putting onscreen 'forgotten' films by other Spanish women, and exhibiting films by women from outside Spain which might not otherwise be seen there. As the festival grows in size and quality, it could well become an effective vehicle for bringing women filmmakers to public attention. Ideally, too, the increasing numbers of shorts and videos being directed by women will help more of them to develop into major figures in Spanish cinema, perhaps allowing us in the future to hear the true, and as yet unheard, voice of Spanish women.

John Hopewell, *Out of the Past: Spanish Cinema after Franco* (London: British Film Institute, 1986)   RB

SPECIAL EFFECTS

From the earliest years of cinema, aspects of film technology have been used to produce images and shots which were never actually present before the camera lens. Special effects include masking (sections of the image are exposed and the film is then reexposed with the opposite areas masked); pixillation (shooting frame by frame and manipulating the MISE-EN-SCENE so that inanimate objects seem to move by themselves); glass shots, mirror shots, and miniatures (techniques to manipulate illusions in the mise-en-scène); and rear screen projection (projecting previously photographed material in the background of a scene). Special effects not only save money but also create spectacle and illusion; as such, they are associated with particular film GENREs, such as SCIENCE FICTION and HORROR. A number of women filmmakers, notably those working in ANIMATION and AVANT-GARDE FILM, have exploited the possibilities of special effects technology, often to visualize fantasy or subjective states. Maya DEREN's *Meshes of an Afternoon* (1943), for example, uses double exposures, split screens, and looping.   JaS

SPECTATORS *see* AUDIENCE AND SPECTATOR

SPHEERIS, PENELOPE (1946–)

Starting out in educational films, and then directing music videos as well as hour-long sales presentation films, US director Penelope Spheeris's first feature-length documentary, *The Decline of Western Civilization* (1981), about Los Angeles punk rockers, announces her fascination with the frustration, despair,

and violence of the marginal young. In the fiction feature films that followed, *Suburbia* (1984) and *The Boys Next Door* (1985), the latter about two teenagers who celebrate their high-school graduation by going on a vicious murder spree, Spheeris continued to deal with the violent disaffected young, though this time within the codes of EXPLOITATION FILM. While Spheeris herself calls *Hollywood Vice Squad* (1986) a bad film, with *The Decline of Western Civilization: Part II – The Metal Years* (1988) she returned to a feature-length documentary format, again combining interviews and music – to examine the heavy-metal music scene in Los Angeles, its young performers and its elder statesmen, British and American. A kind of detached anthropologist in the country of alienated adolescent white males – who are also often outrageously sexist – in her most recent film *Dudes* (1988) Spheeris returns to similar material: a pair of young men, punk rockers, on the road, traveling through the West, encountering violent attack.

The Decline of Western Civilization (1981); *Suburbia* (*The Wild Side*) (1984); *The Boys Next Door* (1985); *Hollywood Vice Squad* (1986); *The Decline of Western Civilization: Part II – The Metal Years* (1988); *Dudes* (1988)

Carol Caldwell, 'Rude Bitches' (Interview with Spheeris), *Sotto News*, 1 July 1981   BKQ

SROUR, HEINY (1945–)

Born in LEBANON and now based in London, Srour is an important figure in the new ARAB CINEMA. She studied Social Anthropology in Paris and, working as a journalist and film critic, became interested in the emerging Third World cinemas. With no film training, Srour made her debut in 1974 with a documentary, *Saat El Tahrir Dakkat*, the first Arab film made by a woman to be selected for the Cannes Film Festival. It features the guerrilla war in Oman, one

Heiny Srour's *Leila and the Wolves*

of the Arab world's most radical struggles, and is noted for its support of the women's cause. In making the film, Srour covered 400km on foot in a roadless, bombarded area. Praised by critics for its originality and talent, it was distributed worldwide but banned in most Arab countries.

Women are a central concern of Srour's films, and she is particularly interested in showing the interdependence of national liberation movements and the liberation of women. *Leila Wal Zi'ab* (1984) is implicitly critical of all political factions in the Middle East for their attitudes toward women. This film adopts an 'Arabian Nights' structure (story within story within story), taking the spectator across time and space to expose the hidden role of Arab women in the modern history of Palestine and Lebanon. Shot in often dangerous conditions and seven years in the making, this feature film has been described as a 'triumph of artistic ambition over seemingly insurmountable odds,' and an important contribution to Third World aesthetics.

Khoubz Biladian/Bread from Our Mountains (short, 1969); *Saat El Tahrir Dakkat/ The Hour of Liberation* (1974); *Leila Wal Zi'ab/Leila and the Wolves* (1984)

Heiny Srour, 'Femme, arabe et cinéaste', in *Paroles . . . Elles tournent*, eds Des femmes de Musidora (Paris: des femmes, 1975)   BR

STANTIC, LITA (1942–   )

Today a successful executive producer in ARGENTINA, Stantic began as a filmmaker in the years after the decline of the NUEVA OLA movement. After experimenting with short films in the mid1960s (a time of great cultural excitement in Argentina) she spent many years earning a living in advertising whilst maintaining her interest in cinema by participating in the activities of Cine Liberación (an alternative production and distribution collective responsible for the production and clandestine exhibition of *La Hora de los hornos/The Hour of the Furnaces* (1966–8)). In the 1970s, while continuing to work in advertising, she also began to gain experience as head of production. Although filmmaking declined in Argentina under the strict repression of the military dictatorship that assumed power in 1976, Stantic worked on over a dozen films in the 1970s, including Sergio Renán's *La tregua/The Truce* (1974), Lautaro Murúa's *La Raulito/Tomboy Paula* (1975), Adolfo Aristaraín's *La parte del león/The Lion's Share* (1978), and Alejandro Doria's *La isla/The Island* (1978), the first Argentine film to be a box office success during the military dictatorship. The weakening of the military's power in the 1980s coincided with Stantic's collaborative association with director María Luisa BEMBERG. As executive producer, Stantic has worked in all of Bemberg's productions and has established a company, GEA Cinematográfica, to produce and distribute films by Bemberg and others.   *ALo*

STANWYCK, BARBARA (1907–90)

Born Ruby Stevens in Brooklyn and orphaned at an early age, Stanwyck (who spelt her stage name BarBara) was a chorus girl in the Ziegfeld Follies before working her way up to straight lead acting parts. After her appearance in the silent *Broadway Nights* (Joseph C Boyle, First National, 1927), Hollywood beckoned and she went – making two mediocre movies, for which she received encouraging reviews but no further offers of work. Impressed by one of her screen tests, Frank Capra finally persuaded Harry Cohn, head of COLUMBIA, to sign her for *Ladies of Leisure* (Capra, Columbia, 1930). Stanwyck picked up nonexclusive contracts with COLUMBIA and Warner BROS., and, in an era dominated by the HOLLYWOOD STUDIO SYSTEM, managed to remain an independent. By the time she was fifty she had made eighty-one movies – not all good ones – leaving her at one point the highest-paid woman in the United States.

As an actress, Stanwyck was renowned for her discipline and hard work; as a screen presence, she endowed her roles with a strength of purpose and a strong dramatic sense. She rarely accepted parts in what she called 'a man's story,' taking instead a range of center-screen female roles. Although her STAR image is now the tough female, characterized by her cynical career woman in *Meet John Doe* (Frank Capra, Warner Bros., 1941), her characters are better defined as fighters in a world structured and dominated by men. That, together with her 'ordinary' attractiveness, made her a prime object of empathy and identification for the fantasies of a largely female cinema audience, whether she played a flashy, sacrificing mother in *Stella Dallas* (King Vidor, Goldwyn, 1937), a comedic stripper in *Ball of Fire*

WHY DO MEN WANT TO BE "DADDIES" TO BABY FACE GIRLS?

No use warning them! They'll have to find out for themselves that Baby Face is about as "innocent" as Cleopatra, and as "helpless" as a tiger cat!

BARBARA STANWYCK and THIRTEEN MEN in 'Baby Face'

A Warner Bros. Picture with GEORGE BRENT

STRAND

Publicity for a Stanwyck film

(Howard Hawks, RKO, 1942), a gun-slinger in *Annie Oakley* (George Stevens, RKO, 1935) or a murderous FEMME FATALE in *Double Indemnity* (Billy Wilder, Paramount, 1944).

In the 1960s, Stanwyck turned to television, bringing together her experience in WESTERNs to create the tough matriarch in 'The Big Valley.' When she joined the prime-time SOAP OPERA 'The Colbys,' television crystallized the most dominating of her screen persona qualities into an icon.

Linda Williams, 'Something Else Besides a Mother – *Stella Dallas* and the Maternal Melodrama', in *Home Is Where the Heart Is: Studies in Melodrama and the Woman's Picture*, ed. Christine Gledhill (London: British Film Institute, 1987)   ALi

STARS

In popular consciousness there are two ways of thinking about film stars: one, that stars are produced by the film industry in order to sell films – they have no particular qualities, anyone can be made into a star; two, that stars are actors who have some 'exceptional,' but usually unidentifiable, 'quality.' Neither view is entirely satisfactory. The first derives from an overly economistic or conspiratorial model, while the second reduces the complex phenomenon of stardom to an effect of unique and exceptional individuals. Film theorist Richard Dyer argues that rather than trying to define what a star is, we should ask why do we get stars and why do we get the particular stars we do? The first question concerns stardom as an aspect of production, while the second concerns stardom as an aspect of consumption. As production, stars do indeed represent a form of 'capital' and are indeed used as marketing devices for the selling of films; and this is true of most NATIONAL CINEMAS, even in socialist countries. The star system reached its height in the HOLLYWOOD STUDIO SYSTEM: but although the studios exerted considerable control over the production of a star's image,

complete control could never be guaranteed. For example, events in the star's life (such as Marilyn MONROE's posing for the *Golden Dreams* calendar, Jane Fonda's politics, or Ingrid Bergman's illegitimate child) may be beyond the studios' control: in each of these cases, the star herself refused to follow studios' orders on how to deal with the 'scandal,' and in each case these events in her life became part of her star image, despite the studios' wishes. The term star image emphasizes the distinction between a film star as a media text and as a 'real person.' Star images combine a number of elements which may be mutually reinforcing (John Wayne) or contradictory (Marilyn Monroe). Star images have multiple but finite meanings, and these change over time. Stars contribute importantly to the meanings available in films.

As a phenomenon of consumption, star images address specific contradictions within and between IDEOLOGIES, and seek to 'manage' or resolve them. There is disagreement about whether all stars ultimately embody culturally dominant values or whether some star images challenge such values (Jane Fonda, James Dean). Whatever the conclusion, it is worth pointing out that stardom in the West is both ethnocentric and heterosexist, in that film stars have been almost exclusively white and (publicly at least) heterosexual. It is significant in this context that the most intense star–audience identification seems to occur amongst adolescents, women, and in gay ghetto culture: this may reflect these groups' extreme role/identity conflict and their exclusion from adult, male, heterosexual cultures. A somewhat different approach to the function of stars, however, is taken by PSYCHOANALYTIC FILM THEORY, which emphasizes the importance of processes of identification with an ego-ideal in film spectatorship, and points to the ways in which castration anxiety is dealt with by turning the figure of woman into a fetish. This, it is argued, explains the extreme idealization of the female star image.

Richard Dyer, *Stars* (London: British Film Institute, 1979)

See also: ACTING; BACALL, LAUREN; BARA, THEDA; BARDOT, BRIGITTE; BROOKS, LOUISE; CONSUMERISM; CRAWFORD, JOAN; DANDRIDGE, DOROTHY; DAVIS, BETTE; DAY, DORIS; DIETRICH, MARLENE; DORS, DIANA; FANDOM; GARBO, GRETA; GISH, LILLIAN; GOSSIP COLUMNS; HARLOW, JEAN; HAYWORTH, RITA; HEPBURN, KATHARINE; LEIGH, VIVIEN; NEGRI, POLA; NIELSEN, ASTA; PERFORMANCE; PICKFORD, MARY; STANWYCK, BARBARA; WEST, MAE   TP

STEREOTYPES

This concept has been central in feminists' attempts to understand how films function in forming women's consciousness, and in feminist critiques of DOMINANT CINEMA. There is a tendency to think of stereotypes as simplistic, pejorative, false, and static ideas; but this is perhaps misleading. Stereotypes may appear simple and easily recognizable by members of a culture, but they actually rely on complex knowledge about the ordering of the social relations to which they refer. Even though we may 'reject' stereotypes in the sense of not believing, say, that BLONDES are 'dumb' or that BLACK WOMEN are 'happy-go-lucky,' we nonetheless understand the meaning system of which those stereotypes are part, and we use that system to make sense of – even to get pleasure from – stories or jokes about the stereotype. Stereotypes provide a lot of information very economically. They tell us what to expect. But our expectations may be proved wrong, and this can be the whole point of the story – as in the case of the 'dumb' blonde who turns out to be a brilliant economist. In films our understanding and appreciation of minor characters frequently presuppose knowledge of a stereotype: the spinster aunt, the gold-digger, the cleaning lady. Stereotypes in films draw on and feed into our 'knowledge' of stereotypes in

other areas. But films provide a particular experience of the stereotype, often individualizing it, weaving a story around it which involves us, giving it a character, feelings, a body – in short, an existence – which makes it seem real and true. Nor are stereotypes static: their meanings are partly determined by the particular historical moment of their use. Stereotypes fade away, new ones arise, and others are more or less subtly transformed. These changes are themselves significant, and films are an important cultural site where changes occur and new meanings circulate.

Art historian Erwin Panovsky argues that fixed ICONOGRAPHY and stereotyping in films developed in the early days of the medium to help audiences understand what was on the screen. Feminists have suggested that whereas male stereotypes were soon broken down and male characters in films became increasingly differentiated and individuated, female roles remained shallow stereotypes reflecting the IDEOLOGY of FEMININITY as eternal and unchanging. But perhaps the rigid stereotyping of women in CLASSICAL HOLLYWOOD CINEMA makes stereotypes more obvious and thus easier to challenge than the more 'subtle' or 'realistic' women characters of, say, ART CINEMA. Some Hollywood stars' PERFORMANCES have been cited as subverting female stereotypes simply by making them 'over-the-top,' as in MONROE's performance in *Gentlemen Prefer Blondes* (Howard Hawks, Twentieth Century-Fox, 1953).

Richard Dyer, 'Stereotyping,' in *Gays in Film* (London: British Film Institute, 1977)

See also: CAREER WOMAN; FEMME FATALE; TOMBOY; VAMP   TP

STERNBERG, JOSEF VON (1894–1969)

The Hollywood director who is widely believed to have discovered Marlene

DIETRICH, Austrian-born Sternberg acquired a reputation not only for an undisputed mastery of the American screen but also, during his peak years at PARAMOUNT, for a turbaned, high-booted, eccentric authoritarianism. Though his career was uneven, punctuated by abandoned projects such as *The Sea Gull* (1926) and *I, Claudius* (1937) and disputes with both Paramount and MGM, even his earliest work evidences the Sternberg feel for, and fore-grounding of, the visual play of light and shadow within the film frame: indeed, he once went so far as to say that he would welcome his films being projected up-side-down, so that story and character involvement would not get in the way of spectators' enjoyment of the image. Sternberg's insertion of scrims, veils, nets, fog, or smoke between subject and camera lends his films a certain surreal quality, but there is a parallel fascination – obsession, even – with the spectacle of woman, and – from *The Blue Angel* (1930) onward – more particularly with the image of Dietrich.

The compelling iconic power of Sternberg's Dietrich images raises pre-figurative questions concerning who was really in control in the Dietrih/Sternberg couple: these questions have opened into complex and far-reaching debates within feminist PSYCHOANALYTIC FILM THEORY concerning the nature of the unconscious fantasies addressed by these spectacular images. Theorists debate the degree to which Dietrich's image challenges patriarchy.

The thirty or so films directed by Sternberg include: *The Salvation Hunters* (Academy Photoplays, 1925); *Underworld* (Paramount, 1927); *The Last Command* (Paramount, 1928); *Der blaue Engel/The Blue Angel* (1930); *Morocco* (Paramount, 1930); *Shanghai Express* (Paramount, 1932); *Blonde Venus* (Paramount, 1932); *The Scarlet Empress* (Paramount, 1934); *The Devil Is a Woman* (Paramount, 1935); *The Shanghai Gesture* (Arnold Pressberger Prods, 1941).

Gaylyn Studlar, *In the Realm of Pleasure: Von Sternberg, Dietrich and the Masochistic Aesthetic* (Urbana and Chicago: University of Illinois Press, 1988)   EAK

STOECKL, ULA (1938–)

A filmmaker working in WEST GERMANY, Ula Stoeckl is associated with the movement known as NEW GERMAN CINEMA. She came to filmmaking through film school, attending the Ulm Film Academy, where she studied under Alexander Kluge and Edgar Reitz. One of the most prolific women filmmakers in West Germany, she has nevertheless had difficulty winning recognition for her work. Although she frequently writes and produces her own films, she has often been cited as a co-worker of Reitz's rather than as a filmmaker in her own right.

> Who is Irma Vep?

All Stoeckl's films, known for their episodic nature, focus on women and how they see themselves. They portray women's attempts to find their own language and consciousness, with women's relationship to patriarchal culture forming a recurrent theme. Her first feature-length film, *Neun Leben hat die Katze* (1968), explores the attempts of four women to break out of the positions of dependency imposed on them by a patriarchal culture. After two collaborative film projects and some short films for television, Stoeckl went on to make *Ein ganz perfektes Ehepaar* (1973), which deals with the emotional relationship between an apparently sexually emancipated married couple. A later film, *Erikas Leidenschaft* (1976), takes up and continues the relationship between two of the women in *Neun Leben*. Her next film, *Eine Frau mit Verantwortung* (1977), was co-scripted with Jutta BRUECKNER and is about a woman's mental decline as a result of repressing her own desires in an attempt

387

to conform to the social role forced on women.

Although she has been making films since the mid 1960s, Stoeckl has only recently been recognized as one of West Germany's first feminist filmmakers. Indeed, her work has been criticized by some feminists on the basis that her protagonists rarely break out of the roles society has imposed on them. Yet as American critic Marc Silberman has stressed, her films 'prefigure many of the concerns in the current women's movement, and as such they represent an important contribution to social enlightenment.'

Antigone (1964); *Haben Sie Abitur?/Did You Finish School?* (1965); *Sonnabend 17 Uhr/Saturday 5pm* (1966); *Neun Leben hat die Katze/A Cat Has Nine Lives* (1968); *Geschichten vom Kuebelkind/Stories of a Latch-key Kid* (1969); *Das goldene Ding/ The Golden Stuff* (1971); *Sontagemalerei/ Sunday Painting* (1971); *Hirnhexen/Goblins of the Mind* (1972); *Der kleine Loewe und die Grossen/The Lion Cub and the Grown-ups* (1973); *Ein ganz perfektes Ehepaar/A Very Perfect Couple* (1973); *Hase und Igel/Hare and Hedgehog* (1974); *Popp und Mingel/Popp and Mingel* (1975); *Erikas Leidenschaft/Erika's Passion* (1976); *Eine Frau mit Verantwortung/A Woman with Responsibility* (1977); *Den Vaetern vertrauen, gegen alle Erfahrung* (episode in *Die Erbtoechter/The Daughters' Inheritance* [1982]); *Der Schlaf der Venunft/The Sleep of Reason* (1984); *Peter und die Tauben/ Peter and the Doves* (1985)

Marc Silberman, 'Ula Stoeckl: How Women See Themselves', in *New German Filmmakers*, ed. Klaus Phillips (New York: Ungar, 1984)   *JK*

STRUCTURALISM

Structuralism is an approach to cultural phenomena that stresses underlying or recurring structures rather than surface or individual details. In postwar FILM THEORY, it first modified and then displaced theories of AUTHORSHIP, finally being itself displaced by POST-STRUCTURALISM.

Structuralism in film analysis drew on the writings of postwar French intellectuals such as Claude Lévi-Strauss, who adopted a structuralist approach to anthropology and myth; Roland Barthes, who adopted a structuralist approach to NARRATIVE; and Ferdinand de Saussure, the originator of SEMIOTICS, who took a structuralist approach to linguistics. The structuralist movement arose in France in opposition to both existentialism and deterministic marxism, the two other major postwar French intellectual movements. The structuralist position may be summarized as follows:

1. The system, rather than its individual elements, needs analysis; individual persons, actions, or objects are not self-sustaining and cannot be understood without examining the context of their underlying systems.

2. The individual element, given to observation, is not a reliable index of reality. What is given is the effect of other, latent relations. It cannot be taken as truthful or real, but is symptomatic of a deeper, non-observable system.

3. Structuralism is thus antihumanist, seeing consciousness and experience as the unrecognized effects of complex, unconscious relations of which individuals are unaware.

4. As an interdisciplinary method, structuralism shows the interconnections of all social phenomena and, above all, the crucial contribution of language to social and cultural life.

Early applications of structuralism in film theory tended to focus on CLASSICAL HOLLYWOOD CINEMA, locating recurring visual and thematic motifs across the films of a particular director (John Ford, for instance) or genre (the WESTERN, for example), rather than seeking deeper structures in the unconscious and the social order. Later, however, under the influence of philosopher Louis Althusser's theory of IDEOLOGY and Lacanian psychoanalytic theory, marxist and feminist critics began to locate larger formal and psychoanalytic structures, ones that served to fix the viewing subject in ideology, in film TEXTS. Theorists Peter Wollen and Raymond Bellour identified a male Oedipal trajectory in the narrative structure of classic Hollywood films. Closely analyzing a number of such films, Bellour found regularities in Hollywood codes of EDITING and framing that functioned to evade the problem of sexual difference and produce the ideology of the couple. In FEMINIST FILM THEORY, Pam Cook and Claire JOHNSTON studied the films of Hollywood director Raoul Walsh and found that woman functioned as a sign of exchange between men rather than as a subject in them. Others argued that, through centered frame composition, renaissance-style perspective, and the suturing or binding of the viewing subject into the film text through classical editing codes, mainstream film served to reproduce liberal capitalist ideology by producing a false sense of autonomy, unity and power in the viewer. Laura MULVEY argued that woman functions as an object to be looked at, rather than as a subject, in classical Hollywood film, through structures of the LOOK, which she equated with the male gaze and attributed to the operations of the patriarchal unconscious. Through voyeurism and fetishism, the male viewer can fend off the threat of castration and deny sexual difference. Thus, these analysts sought to relate the formal structures of film (visual and narrative codes) to larger structures in society and the unconscious.

The structuralist approach to film analysis has generated much useful work on the formal and ideological operations of film texts, but in the long run has been perceived as deterministic and reductive.

Pam Cook, 'Structuralism and Auteur Study', and Sheila Johnston, 'Film Narrative and the Structuralist Con-troversy', in *The Cinema Book*, ed. Pam Cook (London; British Film Institute, 1985)   *FF*

STUDIO D

Of all the films emerging from the NATIONAL FILM BOARD OF CANADA (NFB) in the 1980s, *Not a Love Story* (Bonnie Sher Klein, 1980) and *If You Love This Planet* (Terri Nash, 1981) have undoubtedly left the deepest impressions on a broad spectrum of viewers, in CANADA and around the world. Years after their release, they remain the most frequently booked films in the NFB catalogue. Both films are productions of Studio D, the NFB women's unit founded in 1974 by Kathleen SHANNON, the first woman executive producer at the Film Board. From a shoestring budget of $100,000 in 1974 to the present $1.5 million, Studio D has managed to support a permanent staff of women filmmakers, numerous independent projects and technical training programs, and to produce upward of one hundred documentaries. As the films have utilized an unquestioning DOCUMENTARY realism based in cinéma vérité techniques, they have been criticized for naivety in relation to film technique, cinematic language, and FEMINIST FILM THEORY. Nevertheless, with its series on working mothers, children, heroines from Canadian history, international feminism, women artists, ecology, and peace, the studio has been eminently successful in following through on producer Shannon's mandate to speak to 'a wide audience of garden-variety Canadian women.' Distributed free from NFB offices across the country, the films have been gratefully used by women's groups, and the anti-pornography *Not a Love Story* in particular awakened a new population of women to feminism in a period when the women's movement seemed to be flagging. Under new executive producer Rina Fraticelli, Studio D is currently undergoing major changes, becoming a predominantly freelance studio for training and production with disadvantaged, visible minority and young women filmmakers.

Chris Sherbarth, 'Why Not D? An Historical Look at the NFB's Woman's Studio', *Cinema Canada*, no. 130 (1987)

See also: SINGER, GAIL   KA

STUDIOS *see* EALING STUDIOS; GAINSBOROUGH STUDIOS; HOLLYWOOD STUDIO SYSTEM

SVILOVA, ELIZAVETA (1900–75)

SOVIET documentary editor and director Svilova began her career in 1914 with Pathé. In 1923, as an editor at Goskino, she joined the documentarist Dziga Vertov's 'Cine-eye' group and became his wife and collaborator. It was Vertov's *Kinopravda* (*Cinetruth*) newsreels that prompted her to renounce conventional fictional film in favor of his experiments – the montage of DOCUMENTARY footage designed not merely to record facts but to bring out their significance. Vertov's method required an editor who would share the director's approach to film form and its semantic potential. Svilova became editor and later assistant and co-director of all Vertov's films: together they evolved the genre of poetic documentary distinguished by such classics as *Cheloviek s kinoaparatom/Man with a Movie Camera* (1929), *Simfoniia Donbassa/Enthusiasm* (1930), and *Tri pesni o Leninie/Three Songs of Lenin* (1934).

In the mid thirties, Vertov's method came under attack as 'formalist' and he had difficulty in finding work. With her skills much in demand, Svilova managed to earn a living for the two of them, directing her own and editing other people's films. With the increased importance of documentaries during World War II, she and Vertov were again able to make several films together. In 1946, Svilova received the Stalin Prize as co-editor of Iuli Raizman's *Berlin*. Her own *Zverstva fashistov* (1946) was used as evidence at the Nuremberg Trials, and she was one of the directors (supervised by Roman Karmen) of *Sud narodov* (1946), the film shot at Nuremberg. After Vertov's death in 1954, she preserved his archive and was instrumental in publishing his theoretical legacy.

O transporte/About Transport, V kolkhozakh uchatsia/They Learn at the Collective Farms (1939); *Krisha mira/The Roof of the World, Reka Chusovaia/The Chusovaia River, Piatiletie metro/Five Years of the Metro* (1940); *V predgoriakh Alatau/Near the Alatau Mountains, Kliatva molodikh/The Oath of the Young* (1943); *Osventsim/Auschwitz, Burei rozhdionnie/Born by the Storm* (1945); *Parad molodosti/The Parade of the Youth, Zverstva fashistov/Fascist Atrocities, Sud narodov/Peoples' Trial* (1946); *Slavianski kongress v Belgrade/The Slavonic Congress in Belgrade* (1947)

Masha Enzensberger, 'Dziga Vertov', *Screen*, vol. 13, no. 4 (1972/3)   ME

SWEDEN

As is true of many NATIONAL CINEMAs belonging to small language groups, the cinema of Sweden has always been characterized by a strong ethnocentric streak – for instance, images of forests, fire and water are very common. Regarded as exotic by the outside world, these features are decisive reasons for the international success of Swedish SILENT CINEMA (as, for instance in the work of Victor Sjöström/Seastrom). However, when the coming of sound put an end to film as an international language, Swedish cinema entered a long period of isolation which promoted the production of narrowly defined nationalistic genres and stereotypes. These proved immensely popular with Swedish audiences, but contributed to a decrease in esteem for the art of film among the cultural elite – one consequence being that since 1911 cinema censorship has attempted to protect the young against the negative effects that cinematic

Swedish director Pauline Brunius

representations of sexuality, and especially of violence, are assumed to have. Until the founding of the Swedish Film Institute (SFI) in 1963, the film industry was dominated by three major companies, Svensk Filmindustri, Sandrews and Europa Film (the latter now no longer in existence), in control not only of production but of distribution and exhibition as well. In an attempt to curb growing criticism and raise the status of their productions in the decades following the silent film era, the major companies embarked on producing a number of ambitious and costly 'quality films,' most of which were adaptations of successful literary works. The very expression 'quality film' became a byword, especially during the 1960s, when it was somewhat of a *raison d'être* for the Swedish Film Institute.

As for the role of women in Swedish silent cinema, this field was dominated by Anna HOFMAN-UDDGREN, not only Sweden's first woman director but also one of the country's film pioneers, who managed to get Strindberg to agree to her filming his plays *Miss Julie* and *The Father*. Another woman director of silent films – in this case of short comedies and farces – was Pauline Brunius, later to be the first woman director of Sweden's national theater. With the coming of sound, however, cinema became a more complicated and costly business, the playful pioneering spirit was lost, and as a result opportunities for women to work behind the camera virtually disappeared. In the three decades between the 1930s and the 1950s an average of one woman per decade managed to make one film each. It was not until the 1960s that a woman director, Mai ZETTERLING, succeeded in making more than one feature film. Understandably, Zetterling's films were an enormous inspiration to the many women filmmakers who followed, but a more mundane reason for the rise of women in the industry was the establishment in the early 1960s of a film school under the auspices of the newly inaugurated Film Institute. This meant a definite break with the hitherto patriarchical system of apprenticeship within the film industry, and paved the way for women photographers and directors. By the end of the 1960s, the newly fledged – and politically radical – directors from the Film School found themselves in a much-publicized conflict with the SFI – which led to the foundation of the Film Centrum and Folkets Bio (the People's Cinema). These also functioned as alternative routes for women filmmakers to make their films known. Many of the noted documentaries of the late 1960s were made by women, among them Ingela Romare and Mai Wechselmann. In the mid to late 1970s, many of the now established women directors made their feature debuts: among them Gunnel Lindblom, actress in a number of Ingmar BERGMAN films; Marianne AHRNE, also a writer and documentary filmmaker; and Marie-Louise De Geer-Bergenstrahle, already a successful painter. In 1976 the Svenska Kvinnors Film Forbund (Swedish Women's Film Association) was established, and has since functioned as an increasingly important forum for the exchange of ideas, organizing filmmaking courses as well as more theoretically oriented seminars on film-related topics.

In the 1980s, increased specialization has allowed women interested in the medium of film to develop as artists in their own right and according to their own needs, without feeling they must produce 'gendered' work. Among this group are Ingrid Thulin, another well-known Bergman actress who in 1982 made a feature film based on her childhood memories; and Suzanne OSTEN, a well-established director and artistic leader of her own theater company, who in 1985 had a resounding success with a film comedy, *The Mozart Brothers*. This fairly happy state of affairs pertains not only to women making feature films but to documentarists and animators as well. Most probably it has been helped along by the fact that a large number of Sweden's most competent and successful film producers happen to be women: Anna-Lena Wibom and Lisbet Gabrielsson, for example, both at the SFI. And in 1989 Ingrid Edström, a former producer at Swedish national TV, was chosen as the new president of the SFI – the first woman ever to hold this post.

Brian McIlroy, *World Cinema 2: Sweden* (London: Flick Books, 1986)

See also: GARBO, GRETA   MKo/TS

SWORDPLAY

A Chinese martial arts film GENRE also called *wu xia pian* (films about combats and chivalry), swordplay films are adapted from pulp *wu xia* novels of wandering bandits. They first appeared in mainland CHINA in the late 1920s, but had their heyday in HONG KONG between the 1950s and the 1970s. This popular genre operated on transformations of a mythic narrative, in which vengeance for the death of a father (either of the natural family or of the martial arts family) occasions spectacular displays of destructive feats. The fictitious realm of pre-twentieth-century China provides a site for working-class men to play out antisocial fantasies and desires for power and ethical order, signified often by skillful combats among knight figures from feuding clans, or by martial arts schools representing the pluralistic values of Chinese religions and philosophies. 'Revisionist' swordplay films provide more spectacular and tragic violence, as in King Hu's Zen Buddhist *Xia Nu/A Touch of Zen* (1971), Hark Tsui's fantastic *Die Bian/Butterfly Murders* (1979) and Patrick Tam's anti-heroic *Ming Jian/The Sword* (1980).

Wu lin, an iconic world with wild terrain, temples, small coach stations, and tiled roofs, provides the MISE-EN-SCENE for demonstrations of an array of *wu gong*, or martial arts feats, that include weightless leaps, palm power, night prowling skills, and choreographed swordfights. A *xia* or swords(wo)man is defined by unquestioning loyalty to the patriarchal family (hierarchized according to age and gender and headed by a *sifu/master*) and its codes of honor. Swordfights, the genre's primary spectacles of pleasure, are sometimes supplemented by animation or hand-tinting of flying magical weapons made up of daggers, animals, gourds, or symbols signifying the school or the philosophical origin of the duellists. Women are usually subordinate, their position as symbol or image attributed to the logic of different philosophies: Confucian views are associated with cold and threatening swordswomen who stand out from the usual range of ageing matriarchs, helpless and submissive housewives, maids, and promiscuous prostitutes; Buddhist codes treat women as objects of sexual abstinence on the part of swordsmen who must maintain their (phallic) invincibility through celibacy; Taoist standards produce either fragile-appearing females who are very capable of self-defense, or avenging angels for whom domesticity is an aberration.

Fifth Hong Kong International Film Festival, *A Study of the Hong Kong Swordplay Film* (Hong Kong: The Urban Council, 1981)

See also: KUNG FU   EY

SYDNEY WOMEN'S FILM GROUP

Formed in AUSTRALIA in 1971 as an offshoot of the Women's Liberation Movement's media group, the SWFG's history is closely tied to the changing fortunes of the Sydney Filmmakers Co-op and the WOMEN'S FILM FUND. From the outset feminist film workers developed a two-pronged strategy. Training and funding were pursued on the basis of women's right to gain access to production. Filmmaking, DISTRIBUTION, and EXHIBITION practices were based on the principle of engaging audiences in the process of challenging dominant images of women in the monopoly-controlled mass media.

In 1974 two seminal events took place: the Womenvision conference and the first Women's Film Workshop. The combination of consciousness raising and hands-on, collectively organized, film workshops characterized the activities generated by the SWFG. Key films associated with the group were *Film For Discussion* (1974) and *Woman's Day 20 Cents* (1973). The 1977 Womenwaves Festival of thirty-five international films and videos made by women, and the Sydney and Melbourne training workshops, presaged a prolific production period which included *Size 10* (Sarah Gibson and Susan Lambert, 1978), *Maidens* (Jeni Thornley, 1978), *Woolloomooloo* (Pat Fiske, Peter Gailey and Denise White, 1978), *Behind Closed Doors* (Sarah Gibson and Susan Lambert, 1980), *On Guard* (Sarah Gibson and Susan Lambert, 1983) and *For Love or*

Money (Megan McMurchy and Jeni Thornley, 1983). A diversity of formal approaches is evident in these films, ranging from 'talking heads' REALISM to reprocessed images, from a 'girls' own' heist to archival DOCUMENTARY. Themes range from self-image and the genealogy of identity to inner-city redevelopment, domestic violence, *in vitro* research and the history of women's work.

The Sydney Filmmakers Co-op's monthly publication, *Filmnews*, was instrumental in promoting feminist films, interrogating the policies of training and funding bodies and providing a forum for feminist theoretical work. The Co-op is no longer in existence, but the last few years of its operation were marked by challenges to the orthodoxies of feminist filmmaking, especially in their circulation and promotion of *Serious Undertakings* (Helen Grace, 1982), *A Song of Ceylon* (Laleen Jayamanne, 1985), and *My Life Without Steve* (Gillian Leahy, 1986), and in the lambasting of the Women's Film Units set up as short-term employment programs in Sydney (1984) and Melbourne (1985). The responsibility for feminist initiatives was invested in a paid women's film worker, and the SWFG lapsed into an informal network of filmmakers involved in various film organizations.

Lesley Stern, 'Independent Feminist Filmmaking in Australia', in *An Australian Film Reader*, eds Albert Moran and Tom O'Regan (Sydney: Currency Press, 1985)   FC

> Supposedly God created her; and she inspired a new word in the French language. Who is she?

SYRIA

Syrian Cinema developed after the war of June 1967, when the government set up the Syrian Cinema Organization which, under the directorship of the dynamic Hamid Marei, fostered Syrian and Arab talents. Being traditionally 'the beating heart of Arab nationalism,' Syria became in this period a refuge for ARAB directors suffering political or economic censorship. The loss of the Golan Heights made Syria particularly militant on the question of Palestine after the defeat of June 1967. Praiseworthy films on Palestine were produced (*Al Makhdooun/The Cheated* by Egyptian Toufic Saleh [1972]); or co-produced (*Kfar-Kassem* by Lebanese Borhan Alaouie[1975]). Both were labeled 'marxist' by European and Arab film critics, despite their sexist and feudal images of women. The sexism of these films was presented as 'mere realism' by these directors. Socially aware films, such as the fine – and banned – documentary *Al Hayat Al Yawmiyya fi Oaria Souria/Daily Life in a Syrian Village* (Omar Amilralay, 1974), omit any reference to gender relations in an otherwise lucid analysis of social contradictions. The feature film *Al Sayyed Al Takadoumi/Mr Progressiste* (Nabil Maleh, 1973), a social critique of the Syrian ruling elite, was also banned. Film production has started up again in recent years with films ranging from the NEOREALISM of *Hadeth al Nousf Metr/ The Half Meter Incident* (Samir Zikra, 1981) to the lyrical REALISM of *Ahlam Al Madina/City Dreams* (Mohamed Malas, 1984). In both films, however, new forms serve old conventions regarding representations of women: the girl who falls pregnant by a cowardly seducer in the first; the mother as victim in the second. To date women directors work only in television in Syria.

See also: LEBANON; PALESTINE   HS

SYSTACH, MARYSE (1952–)

Born in MEXICO of a Catalan father and a French mother, Systach became a politicized feminist as a young woman. Her interest in film emerged out of her early studies as a social anthropologist and from the need to address the un-answered questions of poverty, alienation, and lack of communication among peoples. In 1977 she began her film training in the Centro De Capacitación Cinematografic (CCC), one of the two major film schools in Mexico City. Her thesis film, *Y si platicamos de Agosto* (1980), won critical acclaim, and an Ariel – equivalent to an Academy Award – for best short subject. The film addressed the sexual awakening of an adolescent male by a young woman who in the process transforms his consciousness. Here Systach critiques the values ascribed to sexual difference and how these values are clearly woven into the social fabric of the latin family.

In 1981 Systach began to write the script which would culminate in her most controversial and critically discussed feature film, *Conozco a las tres* (1983), starring Irene Martines, Chela Cervantes, and Laura Ruiz. Systach's intention was to depict three middle-class Mexican women who, following the aftermath of the 1968 student revolution, choose to break with tradition and the close supervision of their families. She was interested in exploring issues of rape, sexuality, and desire, and how times have changed for middle-class Mexican latinas since their portrayal in Mexican films of the 1940s and 1950s, in which women who dare to venture into the public sphere inevitably end up as prostitutes or dead.

In 1987, Systach won a grant to pursue studies in Cuba with Gabriel Garcia Marquez on the art of scriptwriting, a side profession she has pursued, writing extensively for television. Her most recently completed film, *Los pasos de Ana* (1988), explores single female parenthood, existential crisis, sexuality, and desire. *El peso del sol/The Weight of the Sun*, her latest project, will begin filming next year. Systach describes this film as a 'voyage toward death,' in which a young woman on the eve of her wedding flees with her former lover to the mountains of Guerrero. It will be based on a historical event which occurred in the 1970s in the region of Pinotepa, Guerrero, where the revolutionary Luis Cabánas became involved in a guerrilla uprising which led to his eventual death in 1974.

Y si platicamos de Agosto/And If We Speak of August? (1980); *Conozco a las tres/I Am Acquainted With The Three* (1983); *Los pasos de Ana/The Steps of Ana* (1988)

Jorge Ayala Blanco, 'Un punto de vista de autora, Maryse Systach', in *La Condición del cine mexicano, 1973–1985* (Mexico City: Editorial Posada, 1986)   CH-N

TAI'IDI, FARZANEH (1945–   )

A star of the new Iranian cinema, Tai'idi studied theater and acting in Los Angeles and made her screen debut in 1970 as the lead in one of the first films in IRAN to revolve around a woman: *Hashtoumine Rooze Haffteh*. This role won her an award – a Seppasse – as best actress at the Teheran International Film Festival. It also brought her a flood of offers from commercial producers, who saw in her blonde hair and fair complexion Iran's answer to Hollywood archetypes. After her long fight to become a serious actress she found the work offered offensive, and embarked on a public campaign against commercial cinema's portrayal of women as sex objects and its contribution to women's low status in society. While commercial producers responded by boycotting her, audiences chose her as best actress in 1972; and her fourth film, *Pardeh Bardory* (1972) – in which she plays a discontented wife – won a Seppasse for best 16mm feature.

Farzaneh Ta'idi

Tai'idi's most challenging role to date was in *Ghaire Aze Khoudo Hitch Kasse Naboud* (Tahmineh Mir Mirany, 1975), in which she plays a lesbian aristocrat who has to choose between social respectability and her natural desires. The film was never released in Iran because of its explicit lesbian sex scenes, and media coverage of it further distanced her from the commercial imitators of foreign movies. During the period of stagnation between 1977 and 1979, Tai'idi was one of the few who dared speak out against the relegation of women and the compulsory veil. She worked for the popular stage in Teheran's Laleh Zare between 1979 and 1981, before being placed on the banned persons list. She survived several years of humiliating harassment by the revolutionary guards before escaping in 1986 to exile in London, where she now lives and works.

Tai'idi's films include: *Jahanname Be'ezofeh Mann* (1971); *Hashtoumine Rooze Haffteh* (1970); *Khoake/The Earth* (1972); *Chaanghack* (1974); *Taalagh* (1974); *Ghaire Aze Khoudo Hitch Kasse Naboud* (1975); *Pardeh Bardory* (1972); *Salote Zouhre/The Moon* (1973); *Vosseteho/Middlemen* (1975); *Faryaod Zir Abbe* (1976); *Saafar Sang/Saffar Sang* (1976); *Myrase Mann Jounoun* (1978); *Bounghah Theatral* (1975)

Bahman Maghsoudlou, *Iranian Cinema* (New York: New York University Press, 1987)   BR

TAIWAN

Feature film production in Taiwan remained virtually nonexistent until the mid 1950s. In the first few years after the nationalist government moved from mainland CHINA to Taiwan, films were produced by the state-owned Agricultural Education Motion Picture Corporation, by China Film Studio, and by Taiwan Film Studio. Newsreels, documentaries, and educational films were supervised by the Kuomintang party, the military, and the provincial government. Feature films were invariably propagandistic in content – they cleaved faithfully to the themes of anti-Communism, agricultural reform, and elimination of racial conflicts. Poor attendance at these didactic films made way for imports from the West and from HONG KONG. In 1954, imports from Europe and the USA constituted 76 percent of the entire Taiwan market.

In 1955, the state-owned studios received American funds and began active collaboration with Hong Kong studios. This led to the rise of a new type of feature film in the late 1950s and early 1960s which adopted the themes of Hong Kong MELODRAMAs. Female roles started to gain importance as a vehicle of traditional values, and made way for the subsequent emergence of a star system. Meanwhile, the Agriculture Education Motion Picture Corporation and the independent Taiwan Motion Picture Corporation had merged to become the Central Motion Picture Corporation (CMPC), which was to be a major figure in the Taiwan New Wave movement in the 1980s.

The late 1950s also saw the rise of Amoy dialect (Taiwanese as distinct from Mandarin) films. With smaller budgets and genres that ran the gamut from OPERA, detective, horror, slapstick, to melodrama, Amoy films soon gained popularity among the working class, while Mandarin films appealed more to the middle class and the new mainland immigrants. In 1958, Amoy film production reached its peak with an annual output of seventy-six features. However, with the arrival of television and technical innovations (color and widescreen) in Mandarin films, Amoy dialect films soon faded into oblivion.

The domestic film market was monopolized by Mandarin films, and Cantonese films from Hong Kong were dubbed into Mandarin. But although their production ceased, Amoy films had bred creative talents – including actor Ou Wei, directors Li Hsin, Lin Fu-di, and Li Chia – who turned to Mandarin productions. The first woman director, Chen Wenmin, also made Amoy films.

The local film industry thrived during the 1960s with increasing cross-fertilization with Hong Kong cinema. In 1963 CMPC, led by its president Kung Hung, launched productions in the name of 'wholesome realism,' which modeled itself on SOCIALIST REALISM. This form, an odd combination of optimistic outlook, entertainment, and political simplicity, proved rather successful and became the main current in Taiwan cinema. Films like *Ke Niu/Oyster Girl* (Li Hsin and Li Chia, 1964), *Yang Ya Jen Chia/Beautiful Duckling* (Li Hsin, 1964), *Ya Niu Chin Shen/The Silent Wife* (Li Hsin, 1965), and *Wo Niu Jo Lan/Orchid and My Love* (Li Chia, 1966) gained an avid following in southeast Asia. Consequently, Taiwan also became one of the world's most prolific centers of film production: in 1968, 230 features were produced. Female roles became the controlling sensibility of 'wholesome realism.'

Concurrently, Hong Kong cinema resumed its popularity. The Shaw Brothers and Cathay Organization found their biggest outlet in Taiwan. By the end of the 1960s, macho genres from Hong Kong – SWORDPLAY and KUNG FU – replaced opera films, becoming a counterpoint to the local female 'weepies.' These women's films, mostly adapted from bestsellers written by Chiung Yao, led the mainstream to a more escapist ROMANCE fantasy in the 1970s. The missing female characters in Hong Kong macho genres, and the missing male characters in Taiwan female 'weepies,' became strange bedfellows. The dichotomy of audience appeal ('weepies' catering to women, swordplay and kung fu to men) gradually separated filmgoers into demographic subgroups. Formulaic repetitions of escapist content, however, soon became too clichéd for increasingly sophisticated audiences.

With the economic booms of the 1980s, new forms of entertainment have prevailed, and the film industry has been confronted with a crisis of dispersed audiences. The growing cultural consciousness of local intellectuals, together with a new and expanding bourgeoisie, have formed a public ready for a revolution in film. Partly inspired by Hong Kong's new cinema, and partly encouraged by the government, a group of young directors and critics, mostly in their thirties and educated in film schools in the West, have set out to turn films into an art form. *Kuan Yin De Gu Shih/In Our Time* (Tao De-chen, Edward Yang, Ko Yi-chen and Chang Yi, 1982) is a portmanteau film marking the directorial debuts of four young filmmakers. Its box office receipts, in addition to support from the critics, inspired another portmanteau film, *Er Ze De Da Wan Ou/The Sandwich Man* (Hou Hsiao-hsien, Roy Tsang and Wan Jen, 1983). In 1983, *Hsiao Bi De Gu Shih/Growing Up* (Chen Kenhou, 1983) won the Best Film title in the Golden Horse Awards. Thereafter, the Taiwan 'New Cinema' secured increasing interest from investors and growing international film festival attention. Between 1983 and 1985, fifteen directors made their debuts. Together, these filmmakers have cultivated a NATIONAL CINEMA that deals with the everyday, with distinctive authorial styles.

> More women have taken part in this national cinema than in any other, yet it is reputed for its misogyny. The cinema of which country?

Three women, Chu Tien-wen, Sylvia Chang, and Wang Hsiao-di, have made a significant contribution to this new

movement. Chu has collaborated on almost every screenplay of Hou Hsiao-hsien's; Chang was a driving force behind the TV series *Shi Yi Ge Niu Jen/ Eleven Women* (1982), which discovered talents like Edward Yang and Ko Yi-chen. Wang Hsiao-di, an energetic TV producer/director who collaborated with director Wang Tong on several of his screenplays, also worked closely with Sylvia Chang as producer/director of *Huang Se Gu Shih/Story of a Woman* (1987). Aside from these women filmmakers, many young male directors have focused attention on the dilemma of women's changing roles in a repressed patriarchal society moving toward a new urban culture. Chang Yi's *Yu Chin Sou/ Jade Women* (1983) and *Wo Ze Yang Ko Le Yi Shen/Kuei Mei, A Woman* (1985) are noteworthy for their sympathetic treatment of women's fate under the moral code and family ethics of a traditional society. A more overt and progressive feminist consciousness has yet to be developed in Taiwan cinema, however.

Hsiung-ping Chiao and others, Essays on Taiwan cinema in *Free China Review*, vol. 38, no. 2 (1988)   H-PC

TANAKA, KINUYO (1909–77)

JAPAN's first woman director started as an actress for Shochiku Studio in 1924 and was Japan's top female star in the early 1930s, ending her acting career in 1977 in Kei Kumai's *Sandakan 8*, a film which won her Japan's Best Actress Award. As an actress, Tanaka's repertoire includes ten films directed by Yasujiro Ozu, from *Daigaku wa Deta Keredo/I Graduated, but . . .* (1929) to *Higanbana/ Equinox Flower* (1958); fourteen with Kenji MIZOGUCHI, including *Saikaku Ichidai Onna/The Life of Oharu* (1952), which won the Venice Film Festival International Prize, and *Sansho Dayu/ Sansho the Bailiff* (1954). Tanaka's roles varied from a Japanese 1920s flapper to an ageing mother who has to be taken to the mountains to await her death in Keisuke Kinoshita's *Narayamabushi-ko/The Ballad of Narayama* (1958). Although her roles reflect the definition of woman from a male perspective, Tanaka's personal life did not conform with traditional expectations. Her dedication to her craft, for example, led her to remove her front teeth for the *Narayama* role; and her determination to support singlehanded her once wealthy provincial family – which had fallen on hard times – exemplify her sense of independence.

In 1953 Tanaka directed her first film, *Koibumi*, which reflects the concerns of the *shomen-geki*. Despite its melodramatic quality, *Koibumi* appropriately captured the atmosphere of the times. Tanaka's second film, *Tsuki ga Agarinu* (1955), is based on a script written by Yasujiro Ozu. Tanaka's feminist awareness is apparent in the role of the youngest of three sisters, whose innocent associations and humorous carefree behavior with her male friends is contrasted with that of her sisters. On the eve of her wedding, however, she is admonished to endure hardships because of the meager teacher's salary of her husband-to-be.

Despite the help she received from the traditionalist Ozu, Tanaka's directorial ambitions were shortlived because of the male-dominated studio system. Her personal liaison with Mizoguchi, who was then head of the directors' organization, did not help her when he decreed that women should not make films. The relationship, which had started in about 1947, ended shortly after this.

Koibumi/Love Letter (1953); *Tsuki ga Agarinu/The Moon Has Risen* (1955)

Audie Bock, *Japanese Film Directors*, rev. edn (Tokyo: Kodansha International Ltd, 1978)　　　　　JYY

TELEVISION

Although increasingly economically powerful, until recently television has been seen as something of a cultural poor relation to film. In the past few years, however, the lines between the two media have become increasingly blurred, with television providing the financing and major exhibition outlet for much work which would previously have been seen unambiguously as 'film.' And in many countries, a new generation of women filmmakers have got their start working in TV drama.

At the same time, the new feminist thinking has been applied to the small screens of the western world. Early discussions centered mainly on television's poor record with regard to the employment of women, and the marginalized or domesticated roles occupied by women in most prime-time television programs and almost all advertising. Head-counting surveys documented the lack of serious onscreen roles for women in news and current affairs, a situation officially justified by women's 'lack of authority.' This situation has improved somewhat since the mid 1970s, partly as a result of feminist campaigns. In BRITAIN a small, but growing, number of DOCUMENTARY programs have examined the position of women from a feminist standpoint, while existing programs began to address feminist agendas more seriously. And fiction aimed at women, with new, complex – and sometimes controversial – women characters began to be seen in mainstream television forms: 'Angels' and 'Tenko,' for example, built on a foundation of MELODRAMA; while 'Juliet Bravo,' 'Widows,' and the US series 'Cagney and Lacey' introduced women into the previously predominantly male TV genres of police and crime series.

Encouraged by desire on the part of feminists to understand and evaluate these new types of television, a reinvigorated brand of feminist television criticism has developed. Rather than simply criticizing images *of* women, this new writing investigates how ideas are constructed within television; for example, by examining how programs go about structuring FEMININITY and MASCULINITY. While some of this writing was clearly indebted to literary theory and FILM THEORY, an increasing amount of it deals with television in its own terms. Thus writings on SOAP OPERA stress the continuous and open-ended nature of this serial form, characteristics which clearly set it apart from mainstream fiction cinema. Marriage, for instance, is rarely an *ending* in soap opera: it is far more likely to signal the start of a series of storylines around marital relationships and, possibly, eventual divorce.

This kind of criticism inevitably raises questions about how television 'for women' is understood – and enjoyed – by its audience. Recent writing on television has been particularly interested in the ways audiences get pleasure from programs and bring their own cultural knowledge and personal interpretations to what they see. For example, soap opera may validate the idea of 'gossip' and women's role in social life; while television and video can play important social roles within the family. Some recent FEMINIST FILM THEORY has drawn on some of the insights of feminist television criticism, particularly its emphasis on AUDIENCES and PLEASURE. It now seems likely that feminist-influenced television work will in turn influence the film culture which gave birth to it.

Helen Baehr and Gillian Dyer (eds), *Boxed In: Women and Television* (London: Pandora Press, 1987)   *JRo*

TEXT

In FILM THEORY, this term refers to the internal structure and organization of any one film. Its usage usually implies that film is the object of a certain type of analysis, one based in the methods of STRUCTURALISM and/or SEMIOTICS, in which films – in terms of NARRATIVE and ICONOGRAPHY – are treated as shaped by underlying structures or codes. While these codes are not immediately apparent, they can be brought to light by textual analysis. Textual analysis involves deconstructing the text, or breaking it down into its constituent parts, then reconstructing it with its hidden meanings revealed. As a method, textual analysis has an important part to play in IDEOLOGICAL film criticism, in certain types of PSYCHOANALYTIC FILM THEORY, and in some FEMINIST FILM THEORY.

Roland Barthes, 'The Structuralist Activity', in *The Structuralists: From Marx to Lévi-Strauss*, eds R and F DeGeorge (New York: Anchor Books, 1972)   *AKu*

THIELE, HERTHA (1908–84)

Christa Winsloe's play *Gestern und Heute* played a key part in the professional career of GERMAN actress Hertha Thiele: in 1930 she was given the central role for the play's Leipzig premiere, for its run in Berlin, and also in the film version, *Maedchen in Uniform* (1931), directed by Leontine SAGAN. Thiele emanated a physical ambiguity between girlishness and womanliness, and her expressive PERFORMANCE contributed greatly to the success of Sagan's film. Thiele's role as the young Anni in *Kuehle Wampe* (Slatan Duedow, 1932) – for which Bertholt Brecht wrote the script and Hans Eisler composed the music – brought her to one of the 'proletarian films' of WEIMAR CINEMA. In this film, however, women's issues and questions around sexuality are subordinated to the main theme of class struggle.

> West German filmmaker Ulrike Ottinger made in 1988 a feature about four women traveling on the Trans-Siberian railway. It has an intriguingly odd title – what is it?

When the National Socialists came to power, Thiele's career was interrupted before it had really begun. She refused to work with the Nazis, though they admired the 'natural' type of woman she portrayed, and was excluded from the Reichsfilmkammer (Reich Film Organization). In 1937 she emigrated to Switzerland and made a living there in various jobs. In 1966 Hertha Thiele went to live in East Germany, where she worked in some television and film productions.

Hans Helmut Prinzler, 'Hertha Thiele', in *Exil: Sechs Schauspieler in Deutschland, vol. 3* (Berlin: Internationale Filmfestspiele/Stiftung Deutsche Kinemathek, 1983)   *VR*

TOMBOY

The tomboy is a cultural STEREOTYPE which describes girls who have what are conventionally thought of as boyish traits: such as the ability to climb trees, play football/baseball/cricket and get involved in fights, a dislike of pretty clothes and cleanliness. Tomboys are also usually marked off from conventional girls by the possession of some mental attribute: they may be notably intelligent and bookish (Jo in *Little Women* [Mervyn LeRoy, MGM, 1949]); streetwise (Annie in *Annie* [John Huston, 1982]); or mechanically minded (Marjorie in *By the Light of the Silvery Moon* [Butler, Warner Bros., 1953]). Somewhat contradictorily, tomboys are frequently also portrayed as sexually naive and innocent of the ways of the world (*Calamity Jane* [David Butler, Warner Bros., 1953]), *Cat Ballou* ([Eliot Silverstein, 1965]). This naivety undermines any authority which boyish attributes might otherwise confer on girls and makes them vulnerable, so revealing to the knowing audience that at heart tomboys are really girls. Films with tomboys as central characters generally deal with attempts to feminize them and with their (ultimately unsuccessful) resistance to these attempts. The love of a good man makes the tomboy recognize the error of her ways as she assumes a proper FEMININITY. The tomboy stereotype has provided countless girl cinemagoers with virtually the only strong and active HEROINE with whom they could identify, yet this heroine is invariably compromised and undermined by the film's resolution. Such a contradictory ego-ideal seems painfully appropriate for girls. While the tomboy is in many respects a positive stereotype, the parallel male stereotype – the sissy – is entirely negative. This reflects the fact that while it may be understandable for girls to want male attributes, it is inconceivable that boys could desire female ones. The adult equivalent of the tomboy is probably the CAREER WOMAN.

Marjorie Rosen, *Popcorn Venus* (New York: Avon, 1973)

See also: AMAZONS; CROSSDRESSING
                                                    TP

TORONTO INTERNATIONAL FESTIVAL OF WOMEN'S CINEMA

In late 1972 a dozen women in Toronto, CANADA, got together to put on a festival of women's cinema. WOMEN'S FILM FESTIVALS had been organized only twice before (in Edinburgh and New York), and never on the scale that these women planned. After six months of fundraising, research, and screening thousands of films, they mounted a ten-day festival in a major state cultural center, complete with daycare in the green room, video installations, and a health food concession in the chandeliered lobby. Over three hundred films by women were shown, including mint archival prints of Nell SHIPMAN's *Back to God's Country* (Canada, 1919), films by Lois WEBER, Mabel Normand, and Dorothy Gish and Lillian GISH, Olga PREOBRAZHENSKAIA's *Peasant Women of Riazan* (Soviet Union, 1923), and a wide selection of international contemporary films. Guest filmmakers included Joyce WIELAND, Beryl FOX, Joyce CHOPRA, Mai ZETTERLING, Agnes VARDA, Stephanie ROTHMAN, Freude Bartlett, Barbara Peeters, Shirley CLARKE, and Viva. After the event in Toronto, a selection of films, organizers, and guests traveled to eighteen cities in Canada in an unprecedented national outreach. This was the beginning of feminist film culture in Canada.   *KA*

TORRE-NILSSON, LEOPOLDO (1924–78)

The son of film director Leopoldo Torre Ríos, Torre-Nilsson grew up in the studios of the classic ARGENTINE cinema of the 1930s, worked on his father's films in the 1940s, and carefully studied the European ART CINEMA of the 1950s. Much influenced by this cinema, his films always stood apart from those of his Argentine contemporaries because of their cultural and intellectual ambitions. Although, as many have claimed, they were indeed 'Europeanized' and almost exclusively focused on the bourgeoisie, Torre-Nilsson's films did deal with national concerns and were usually adapted from the literary *oeuvre* of his wife and script collaborator, Beatríz GUIDO. His ninth film, *La casa del ángel*, was the first Argentine feature to receive widespread international recognition.

The success of his subsequent features allowed Torre-Nilsson to set up an independent production company (Producciones Angel) to produce his own films as well as those of some of the younger and less well-heeled filmmakers of the NUEVA OLA. With his own production company, Torre-Nilsson was able to retain complete control over his films and to become the first internationally recognized auteur of the Argentine cinema.

It was these features which gained Torre-Nilsson's cinema international recognition – its focus on easily recognizable bourgeois angst and its self-presentation as intellectualized personal expression – that eventually, in the late 1960s, led Argentine cineastes to reject his kind of filmmaking. Nevertheless, in the years between 1957 and 1962, before any other Latin American cinema had received international recognition, Torre-Nilsson's achievement was enormous and had a profound impact on all young filmmakers.

The thirty or so films directed by Torre-Nilsson include: *La casa del ángel/The House of the Angel* (1957); *La caída/The Fall* (1959); *Fin de fiesta/The Party's Over* (1960); *La mano en la trampa/The Hand in the Tramp* (1961); *Piel de verano/Summer Skin* (1961)

ALo

TOYE, WENDY (1917–)

One of the very few women in BRITAIN to have made a career as a film director in the 1950s and 1960s, Wendy Toye is equally well known for her work in theater and choreography. A 'child prodigy' in ballet, she appeared as a dancer in such films as *Dance Pretty Lady* (Anthony Asquith, 1931) and *Invitation to the Waltz* (Paul Herzbach, 1935), and formed her own company, Ballet-Hoo de Wendy Toye, in 1947. Her first venture into filmmaking was a short independent production, *The Stranger Left No Card* (1952), a surreal fantasy set to music which won her international critical acclaim. Subsequently, Toye was put under contract by Alexander Korda and went on to make feature films which, although popular, were never quite so enthusiastically received by the critical establishment.

Toye's work falls into two distinct categories: FANTASY and COMEDY. The fantasies (like *In the Picture* [1953] and *On the Twelfth Day* [1955]) are delicate and charming, but also have a darker, more subversive edge. It is her mainstream domestic comedies, however, that have the greatest feminist appeal. Working in a period when the British film industry was consciously promoting its male stars and a particularly 'British' vein of boisterous comedy (designed to appeal to American audiences), Toye makes the best of it by using role-reversal (*Raising a Riot* [1955]) or other comic devices to problematize, and make fun of, MASCULINITY. In *All For Mary* (1955), for example, male helplessness is enjoyably foregrounded in the shape of incompetent, sexless twit Humpy, who can become 'adult' only through a powerful mother-figure, in this case his old nanny. Since the 1960s

Wendy Toye with Sally Potter

Wendy Toye has worked mainly in theater, although she has made occasional programs for television, including a tame remake of *The Stranger Left No Card* for Anglia TV in 1981.

The Stranger Left No Card (1952); *Three Cases of Murder* (1953) (Toye directed one section, *In the Picture*); *The Teckman Mystery* (1954); *On the Twelfth Day* (1955); *Raising a Riot* (1955); *All For Mary* (1955); *True as a Turtle* (1956); *A Life to be Lived* (1961); *We Joined the Navy* (1962); *The King's Breakfast* (1963)

Sylvia Paskin, 'A Delicate but Insistent Trail of Confetti . . .', *Monthly Film Bulletin*, vol. 53, no. 632 (1986)   CM

TRINH T MINH-HA (1953–   )

Born in Vietnam, independent filmmaker, writer and composer Trinh T Minh-ha migrated to the USA in 1970 and pursued graduate studies in literature and music there and in France. A research expedition in Senegal and three years as a professor at the National Conservatory of Music in Dakar helped lay the groundwork for her first – influential, and somewhat controversial – film on women in Senegal, *Reassemblage* (1982). This forty-minute film outlines the problematic of Trinh's work in cinema to date: its 'subject' is not simply 'women in Senegal' but also ETHNOGRAPHIC method, DOCUMENTARY truth, and the filmmaker herself; and it explicitly challenges the traditional role of Third World women in anthropological discourse. Trinh's second film, *Naked Spaces: Living is Round* (1985), a two-hour-long poetic study of vernacular architecture in five West African countries, again positioned her as the observer of a foreign culture. Her most recent film, *Surname Viet Given Name Nam* (1989), looks at the role of women in Vietnamese culture, and is perhaps her most rigorously feminist work. Based on interviews with women in Vietnam and Vietnamese women in the USA, the film includes archival footage, folk poetry, printed texts, and documentary footage from refugee communities in the USA, writing a history of women's resistance.

Trinh T Minh-ha has invented a form of 'subjective documentary' – interrogating the voyeuristic gaze of the

Trinh T Minh-ha's *Reassemblage*

ethnographic filmmaker; undercutting the referentiality and continuity of the image-track; substituting a complex sound montage of music and women's voices for an authoritative male voice-over; foregrounding the difficulty of translation; and calling attention to her own presence – and absence – as the 'voice' behind her films. As a writer and lecturer as well as a filmmaker, Trinh also plays a prominent role in academic and theoretical debates on post-colonialism and feminism. She currently teaches in the Department of Cinema at San Francisco State University.

Reassemblage (1982); *Naked Spaces: Living is Round* (1985); *Surname Viet Given Name Nam* (1989)

Kathleen Hulser, 'Ways of Seeing Senegal: Interview with Trinh T Minh-ha', *The Independent*, vol. 6, no. 10 (1983)

PW

TROTTA, MARGARETHE VON (1942–)

The best-known and most successful of WEST GERMANY's women film directors, Margarethe von Trotta first became interested in cinema whilst working in Paris, where she became involved with various film collectives. On returning to Germany, she studied to become an actress, and in the late sixties and early seventies pursued an active film and television career, winning much critical acclaim.

After making her directorial debut in a collaboration with her filmmaker husband, Volker Schloendorff, on the film version of Heinrich Böll's controversial book *Die verlorene Ehre der Katherina Blum* (1975), von Trotta has gone on to become a prominent member of the NEW GERMAN CINEMA movement. Working at the mainstream end of the movement and using REALIST conventions, she has directed a number of feature films focusing on female protagonists. Based on the real-life story of a Munich kindergarten teacher who robbed a bank to obtain funds to maintain her alternative daycare center, her first full-length feature, *Das zweite Erwachen der Christa Klages* (1978), was one of the first New German Cinema films to make reference to the spate of terrorism that dominated West German life during the seventies, and was a great critical success. Her next film, *Schwestern, oder die Balance des Gluecks* (1979), about the relationship between two sisters, has been discussed in the context of feminine expression; while in *Die bleierne Zeit* (1981), von Trotta returns to the theme of terrorism, exploring the issue through – again – the relationship between two sisters. Von Trotta's interest in women, their lives and their relationships is evident in most of her films, but she has rejected a labelling of her work as 'women's films.' She has stated a preference for dealing with the private sphere, for looking at personal relationships rather than at public events. Her earlier critical success has, however, been followed by a more lukewarm reception of her most ambitious project to date – a film on the life of Communist revolutionary Rosa Luxemburg.

Die verlorene Ehre der Katharina Blum/The Lost Honour of Katherina Blum (1975); *Das zweite Erwachen der Christa Klages/The Second Awakening of Christa Klages* (1978); *Schwestern, oder die Balance des Gluecks/Sisters, or the Balance of Happiness* (1979); *Die bleierne Zeit/The German Sisters (GB)/Marianne and Julianne (USA)* (1981); *Heller Wahn/Sheer Madness* (1983); *Rosa Luxemburg* (1985); *Felix*

Von Trotta's *The Second Awakening of Christa Klages*

(co-d., 1987); *Fuerchten und Liebe/Love and Fear* (1987)

H B Moeller, 'West German Women's Cinema: The Case of Margarethe von Trotta', *Film Criticism*, vol. 9, no. 2 (1984–5)   *JK*

TUNISIA

In Tunisia the state runs film imports, leaving distribution to the private sector. The state film production body SAT-PEC coexists with the private sector and helps sponsor national talent – within the constraints of censorship. It took a long battle for Tunisia to be equipped with its now excellent film laboratory, in the course of which Tahar Cheria, father of ARAB CINEMA and founder of the Carthage Film Festival, was jailed for a year: difficulties arose because local labs clashed with French interests. Tunisia had a prolific amateur film movement which cut the teeth of a number of filmmakers: from this sector came the fine short film *Atabat Mamnoua/Forbidden Thresholds* (Rida El Behi, 1972), a critique of tourism, in which a young poor man rapes a German tourist in a mosque. His film banned, Behi had to go to MOROCCO to shoot, in more mainstream style, *Shams El Dibaa'/Hyena's Sun* (1976) – also on the issue of tourism – before choosing the 'international solution': Julie Christie and Ben Gazzara as European settlers in *Scarlet Memory* (1986), an English-language film about the alienation brought about by colonialism. Perhaps the best film on the depersonalization of Tunisia by fake independence and tourism is by painter Naceur Khemir, maker of the innovative *Hikayat Balad Min Melk Rabbi/The Story of the Country of God* (1976) and the brilliant *Al Ha'imoun/Searchers in the Desert* (1984), one of the best Arab films. The latter is a reflection on Arab culture, which is seen as a men-only problem: obsessed by the lost paradise of Andalusia and the 'Arabian Nights,' it is a parable of the Arab world

rushing stupidly after the mirage of gold while its best men, the political dissidents, wander the desert. The children are the most lucid elements of this society, while women, if not comforting grandmothers, are mere shadows. Women are more real, and indeed often the central characters, in Abdel-Latif Ben Ammar's films: *Une si simple histoire* represented Tunisia at Cannes in 1970; *Sejnane* (1973) and *Aziza* (1980) followed, both portraying women with sensitivity. Following his nationalist trilogy *Al Fajr/Dawn*, *Al Moutamarid/The Rebel* (1968), and *Al Fallaka/The Fellaghas* (1970), Omar Khlifi shot what is considered to be his best film, *Sourakh/Screaming* (1975), centered on women's predicament in a male society: a rape victim is killed by her family to 'wash away the dishonor'; while another is married against her will.

In 1975 Selma Baccar, the first woman filmmaker in Tunisia apart from TV director Fatma Skandarani, shot a documentary (*Fatma '75*) about the history of Tunisian women. The Tunisian government, which commissioned the film for UN women's year, banned it. Apparently, President Bourguiba, supporter of secularization and women's rights, did not like the fact that the film portrayed women's emancipation as coming from their own struggle rather than as a gift granted by himself. CINEMIEN, the Dutch distribution network, rescued the film from oblivion. Nejia Ben Mabrouk, another Tunisian woman, made her debut with a moving feature film, *Al Sama/The Trace* (1988), about a clever girl who leaves her village for the capital where, hindered by a society hostile to women – as well as by the drawbacks of her own education – she fails her exams, then decides to leave her beloved mother to go to France. Rarely has the relationship between an Arab mother and her daughter been described so accurately. MASCULINITY is no less problematic and repressive in *Rih El Sadd/Man of Ashes* (1986): the film's director Nouri Bouzid, who was once jailed for five years for belonging to a radical group, sympathetically and courageously portrays an old Jew who sings Tunisian songs but stereotypes women.

See also: AFRICA; EGYPT   HS

TWENTIETH CENTURY-FOX

Incorporated in 1915 out of William Fox's earlier holdings, the Fox Film Corporation became fully integrated in the mid 1920s with the purchases of a number of movie theater chains in the USA. One of the innovators of film SOUND, Fox found itself in financial difficulties as early as December 1929, partly as a result of over-extension in relation to the October stock market crisis; and reorganization forced William Fox out of the company. In 1934 Fox merged with a new independent company, Twentieth Century. Although the firm experienced difficulties in the 1960s and early 1970s, it diversified and several box office successes in the late 1970s made it an attractive takeover target. Between 1981 and 1984 Marvin Davis purchased one hundred percent of its stock, but then sold the firm to Rupert Murdoch.

During the HOLLYWOOD STUDIO SYSTEM years, Twentieth Century-Fox chose a strong central producer for managing its top-quality filmmaking, with Darryl F Zanuck running the production studio almost continuously from 1935 to 1970. Although Zanuck gave his directors control during the production of their films, he shaped the films as he desired during pre-production and post-production. Sol Wurtzel managed the B-level production. In the mid 1930s, the success of child star Shirley Temple's movies provided important revenues to the firm, with Temple ranked as the number one STAR from 1935 through 1938. Other valuable Fox actresses were Janet Gaynor, Sonja Henie, Betty Grable, and, in the 1950s, Marilyn MONROE. Having started her career as a story reader, Sherry Lansing in 1980 became Twentieth Century-Fox's studio head, the first woman to achieve such a position in a major US film company.

Aubrey Solomon, *Twentieth Century-Fox: A Corporate and Financial History* (Metuchen, NJ: Scarecrow Press, 1988)

                                        JaS

UNITED STATES OF AMERICA

see HOLLYWOOD

UNIVERSAL

Started by Carl Laemmle's DISTRIBU-TION and EXHIBITION interests in the USA, the film production company Universal was formed in 1912. By the mid 1920s and in the early years of the HOLLYWOOD STUDIO SYSTEM, Universal was a second-rung company with no significant film theater holdings. It sold those it owned when the Depression arrived. Continued losses resulted in receivership in 1933, and Laemmle sold his holdings in 1936. The company's fortunes improved during World War II, in good part due to the success of Deanna Durbin's films. In 1946 Universal acquired International Pictures; and in 1954 Decca Records purchased a majority share in the company, with the Music Corporation of America buying up both firms in 1959. A series of blockbusters in the 1970s allowed Universal to diversify extensively, acquiring, for example, a major interest in Cineplex Odeon Theaters, one of the top four US theatrical chains.

Universal had started using a unit production method by the mid 1930s, the heyday of the HOLLYWOOD STUDIO SYSTEM. Moving from second-run pictures into A-production after the 1936 change of ownership and new profits from its films, Universal also set up some independent production deals. After World War II, Universal became the studio home for a number of independent companies.

Clive Hirschhorn, *The Universal Story* (New York: Crown, 1983)   JaS

China's modern filmmakers Peng Xiaolian and Hu Mei are female members of which generation?

USSR *see* SOVIET UNION

VAMP

The figure of the vamp flourished in SILENT CINEMA. Although the vamp represents a feminine stereotype, different actresses brought their own personal touches to their versions of it – Irving Berlin even referred to Constance Talmadge as a 'virtuous vamp.' In general, however, the vamp represents woman as 'other,' the fatal woman who has the power to lure man to his doom through sexual excesses. With her smoldering look, hypnotic gaze, and wicked intentions, the vamp represents the opposite of the virgin. Where the virgin is virtuous and pure, the vamp is immoral and tainted. She is the virgin's alter ego or doppelganger. The word vamp also suggests 'female vampire' or bloodsucker – the woman who drains man of his vital fluids. In the films of the silent period, the vamp was defined by her clothing and appearance and other elements of ICONOGRAPHY: she wore revealing black dresses; she smoked cigarettes from long elaborate holders; her nails were long and pointed; her costume was often decorated with snake or spider patterns. In general, the American vamp was played by a European or supposedly 'foreign' actress – women such as Pola NEGRI and Theda BARA.

Feminists are interested in the figure of the vamp because it is a STEREOTYPE. Feminist theory argues that feminine stereotypes tell us very little about woman herself, but a great deal about male fears and desires about woman. The vamp represents woman-as-mystery; she is man's enigmatic opposite, a force which must be defeated or destroyed. Film theorist Claire JOHNSTON argues that unlike primitive stereotypes of man in the early cinema, those of woman were reduplicated with hardly any modification at all. This is because stereotypes of woman draw on myths which present the feminine as eternal and unchanging, in order to provide rationalization for the essentialist argument that women are dominated by their sexual appetites and as such must be kept under (male) control. Variations of the vamp's image can be found in all cultures at different historical times. The Sirens, who lured men to their death with their beautiful song, were an earlier form of the vamp. Eve and Lilith, the fallen women of Christianity, are also vamps or evil seductresses. In the cinema, the role and function of the vamp was later absorbed into the figure of the PHALLIC WOMAN or FEMME FATALE of FILM NOIR. Allowing for variations in style and fashion, woman as evil temptress continues to represent a powerful stereotype in contemporary cinema.

Claire Johnston, 'Myths of Women in the Cinema', in *Women and the Cinema*, eds Karyn Kay and Gerald Peary (New York: E P Dutton, 1977)

See also: MUSIDORA; NIELSEN, ASTA   BC

VAMPIRE FILM

The cult of the vampire has provided a rich source of material for the cinema, from the silent period to the present, and inspired some of the screen's greatest classics: Murnau's *Nosferatu* (1922); Dreyer's *Vampyr* (1932); and Browning's *Dracula* (1931). Actors like Bela Lugosi and Christopher Lee have acquired enormous fame for their chilling performances of the evil Count. Bram Stoker's novel *Dracula* (1897) has strongly influenced Hollywood's representation of the vampire: the dank gothic castle, unsuspecting guests, the dreaded hour of midnight. Other features include coffins; creaking lids; corpses of the un-dead; crucifixes and garlic. The vampire, however, is not always male. The legend of Countess Bathory and the heroine of Sheridan Le Fanu's novella *Carmilla* (1871) have inspired many film rep-resentations of Countess Dracula and introduced images of the LESBIAN VAMPIRE to the screen.

There have been many interpretations of the myth and reasons for its popular-ity. One is that the legend, because it is so materialistic (the body can live on with-out a soul), is perfectly suited to the values of the late twentieth century. Another view is that the legend appeals to our preoccupations with sex and death. Feminist critics are divided in their responses to the vampire film. Some argue that the dominant, male vampire film represents yet another misogynistic GENRE. Invariably, Dracula's victims are young girls, pale virginal figures who swoon at the approach of the dark Byronic figure. The female vampire, like her counterpart of the silent period, the VAMP, signifies yet another feminine STEREOTYPE – woman as 'blood-sucker.' Others argue that the female vampire film is interesting because it represents women in a powerful role, while introducing the question of lesbian desire.

One unusual and convincingly argued account comes from Penelope Shuttle and Peter Redgrove. In their book *The Wise Wound* (New York: Richard Marek, 1978), they see the vampire film as a modern reworking of myths and rituals surrounding menstruation. The vampire (female or male) symbolizes unconscious forces that bring on the blood flow. In many cultures, the notion of being bitten by a snake which lives in the moon is used to explain menstruation – womb, snake and moon all go through similar processes of shedding and renewal. These motifs are reworked in the vam-pire film. On the night of the full moon, the vampire glides into the bedrooms of young virgins who lie pale and listless. The vampire commences an erotic seduction, leaving two puncture marks in the neck. Interestingly, the two neat holes always appear closer together than the spread of the vampire's fangs would realistically allow; rather, these holes re-semble a snake bite. The vampire bites the 'neck' because it symbolizes the 'neck' of the womb. After bleeding, the girls become active and sexual. This view of the vampire film is of particular in-terest to feminists working in the areas of film and mythology.

James Donald (ed.), *Fantasy and the Cin-ema* (London and New York: Routledge, 1989)

See also: HORROR   BC

VAN BRAKEL, NOUCHKA (1940–)

Nouchka van Brakel was the first woman to study at the Dutch Film Academy. Her films, which are amongst the major public successes in the NETHERLANDS, include *Een Maand Later* (1987), which had already been bought by Warner Bros. for worldwide distribution in its pre-production stage. This comedy tells the half-comic, half-cynical story of a temporary exchange of identities between two young women with radically different lifestyles. Van Brakel's earlier films are also about women who break out of society's con-ventions and who want something 'controversial': in *Het Debuut* (1977) a fourteen-year-old girl falls in love with a much older man; in *Een Vrouw als Eva* (1979) a young mother demands a room of her own for the first time in her life, and falls in love with another woman; and with *Van de Koele Meren des Doods* (1982) van Brakel made a film of a popu-lar Dutch turn-of-the-century novel ab-out a young woman who rebels against the sexual constraints of the bourgeois milieu in which she lives. Van Brakel has also made documentary films and videos on various topics of feminist interest, such as children's education and the training of midwives. Her features are particularly successful with audiences, and despite their somewhat conventional style offer women some appealing characters with whom to identify.

Het Debuut/The Debut (1977); *Een Vrouw als Eva/A Woman Like Eve* (1979); *Van de Koele Meren des Doods/Hedwig, or the Cool Lakes of Death* (1982); *Een Maand Later/One Month Later* (1987)   AF

VARDA, AGNES (1928–   )

A film director based in FRANCE who trained in art and photography (her first career and still a strong interest), Varda – unlike so many women directors who have worked unrecognized – has received many prestigious prizes and has been called the 'mother of the NEW WAVE': her first feature, *La pointe courte* (1954), heralded this movement in terms of both production methods and aesthetics. World recognition came with her second feature, *Cléo de 5 à 7* (1961). From the start, her career has included shorts (which some consider her best work) and features. Among the latter, *Sans toit ni loi/Vagabonde* (1985) was a universal success.

Varda's work is in the classic auteur mold, with its central belief in film as personal expression: 'I make auteur films . . . I am always very precisely implicated in my films, not out of narcissism, but out of honesty.' However, in the spirit of the 'left bank' New Wave (with Chris Marker and Alain Resnais), she firmly places the inner world of her characters in a social context. Her leftwing politics inform her work, and are explicit in her DOCUMENTARY *Black Panthers* (1968) as well as in her participation in the anti-American *Loin du Vietnam/Far from Vietnam* (1967). At the core of her work is a dualism: inner subjectivity versus social objectivity, what she calls 'the pictures of one's inner life and the actual images of life as it is lived.' This thematic dichotomy is echoed stylistically in her dual

emphasis on REALISM on the one hand, and a symbolic impulse on the other – the latter complementing and simultaneously questioning the former. This is particularly evident in *Vagabonde*, which combines a statement on the disillusioned post-1968 generation with a reworking of Christian and pagan myths.

Varda's relationship to feminism is a complex matter. She claims to be a feminist, and her work in the 1970s is explicitly so. *L'Une chante l'autre pas* (1976) is a fictional rendering of the consciousness-raising phase of the women's movement in France. Although the film undoubtedly valorizes women's experience and survival spirit, its celebration of FEMININITY in its biological dimension is problematic. It comes close to what feminist critic Claire JOHNSTON saw, in her earlier film *Le Bonheur* (1965), as endorsing (male) bourgeois myths of women, a criticism that could also be directed at *Jane B par Agnès V* and *Kung Fu Master* (both 1987). Johnston also criticized Varda for her reliance on the cinematic style of the European ART CINEMA, arguing the need for a more radical film language for women. For others, though, Varda's search for a specific film expression ('*cinécriture*'), and questioning of cinema's 'impression of reality,' are in themselves radical. Notwithstanding these debates, Varda's avowed feminism marks her as unusual among contemporary French women directors, and – as she herself points out – despite her international reputation, she still has to struggle to produce and finance each of her films.

Shorts: *O saisons ô châteaux* (1957); *L'Opéra-Mouffe, Du côté de la côte* (1958); *Salut les Cubains* (1963); *Elsa la rose* (1966); *Uncle Yanco* (1967); *Black Panthers* (1968); *Réponse de femme* (1975); *Plaisir d'amour en Iran* (1976); *Ulysse* (1982); *Les dites cariatides, 7p., cuis., s. de b., à saisir* (1984); *T'as de beaux escaliers tu sais* (1986). Features: *La pointe courte* (1954); *Cléo de 5 à 7/Cleo From 5 to 7* (1961); *Le*

Bonheur/Happiness (1965); *Les Créatures/ The Creatures* (1966); *Lions Love* (1969); *Nausicaa* (1976); *Daguerréotypes* (1975); *L'Une chante l'autre pas/One Sings the Other Doesn't* (1976); *Mur murs* (1980); *Documenteur* (1981); *Une minute pour une image* (1983); *Sans toit ni loi/Vagabonde* (1985); *Jane B par Agnès V, Kung Fu Master* (1987)

Sandy Flitterman-Lewis, *To Desire Differently: Feminism and the French Cinema* (Urbana: University of Illinois Press, 1990)   GV

VEGA, PASTOR (1940–)

Like virtually all CUBAN filmmakers at the national film institute (ICAIC), Vega started out as a documentarist, working on a variety of assigned topics. Since 1979, even while serving for nearly a decade as ICAIC's Head of Foreign Relations and as director of Havana's annual International Festival of the New Latin American Cinema, he has scripted and directed three feature films, each starring his wife Daysi Granados, Cuba's best-known film actress, and each exploring

marital strains within a social context that professes to seek more equal relations between the sexes. His first, *Retrato de Teresa* (1979), the most internationally acclaimed, had the most profound impact on the Cuban public, generating unprecedented box office interest and passionate debates on the double standard and the double day.

Between 1961 and 1974, Vega made ten short and two feature-length documentaries on assorted topics: they include *La guerra/War* (1961); *La canción del turista/ The Song of the Tourist* (1967); *¡Viva la República!/Long Live the Republic* (1972). His features are: *Retrato de Teresa/Portrait of Teresa* (1979); *Habanera/Woman From Havana* (1984)

Julianne Burton, 'Being, Seeing, Being Seen in *Portrait of Teresa*: Contradictions of Sexual Politics in Contemporary Cuba', *Social Text*, no. 4 (1981)   JBu

VENEZUELA

During the first half-century of cinema's history, Venezuela's film production was

Daysi Granados in Pastor Vega's *Portrait of Teresa*

less sporadic than that of many Latin American countries, while never achieving the levels of the three major regional producers – MEXICO, BRAZIL, and ARGENTINA. In the 1960s, Venezuela began to emerge as a competitive site for commercial co-productions from ITALY, SPAIN, and especially Mexico. During this period, the country's rising oil revenues suggested to many that building a Venezuelan film industry might no longer be an idle dream. The acclaim earned by Margot BENACER-RAF's pair of documentaries made in the previous decade had become a sort of national legend which fanned the ashes of this long-smoldering dream. Between the mid 1970s and the early 1980s, the dream came tantalizingly close to realization.

The late 1960s saw the emergence of a socially aware and politically militant DOCUMENTARY movement resembling those emerging throughout the continent. The approach developed by Cine Urgente (1968–73), a particularly interesting group experiment in the education and mobilization of marginal sectors through cinematic intervention, was carried on by an all-female collective, Grupo Feminista Miércoles, which was founded in the late 1970s by Josefina Jordán, a co-founder of Cine Urgente, and the Italian-born Franca Donda. Their collaborations include *Sí podemos/Yes We Can* (1972), *María de la Cruz, una mujer venezolana/Maria de la Cruz, A Venezuelan Woman* (1974), and *Yo, tú, Ismaelina/You, Me, Ismaelina* (1981).

For a brief and stimulating period in the 1970s, Venezuela boasted a strong institutional infrastructure which included *Ojo al cine*, the most critically ambitious and handsomely produced film JOURNAL in LATIN AMERICA (under the editorship of Italian-born Ambretta Marrosu); Decimoveca and Palcine, distribution companies organized by nationals like Edmundo Aray in collaboration with exiled cinephiles from CHILE and Uruguay; the very active Escuela de Cine (Film School) at the Uni-versity of the Andes in Mérida, which hosted a historic documentary festival in 1968; as well as a national film archive and several active film societies. Between 1975 and 1980 the government provided partial financing (largely through the Ministry of Tourism) for twenty-nine feature films, boosting national production to twelve films a year, a very respectable average relative to other Latin American countries. This leap in national film production can be credited in large part to the efforts of a group of three young US-educated women who ran the Venezuelan National Film Office. Latin American film history holds no other example of women's participation in film production on such an ambitious and effective scale as that of this energetic and eminently capable trio, dubbed 'Las Amazonas del Cine.' Among the period's most active filmmakers were Roman Chalbaud, Mauricio Wallerstein, Carlos Rebolledo, Antonio Llerandi, Ivan Feo, Alfredo Anzola, and Clemente de la Cerda.

Most of this infrastructure did not survive the debt crisis of the 1980s. The number of features produced annually dropped markedly as funding became more scarce and government institutions failed to follow through on the exemplary programs they had launched. Despite high quality and impressive box office success, Venezuela has not succeeded in developing a successful export market for its films. Given the general bleakness of the current picture, it is encouraging to note that several women number among Venezuela's feature filmmakers. Scandinavian-born Solveig Hoogesteijn, raised from an early age in Venezuela, released her third and most successful feature to date, *Macu, la mujer del policía/Macu, the Policeman's Wife*, in 1987. Two debut features, Fina Torres's *Oriana* (1985) and Haydee Asacanio's *Unas son de amor/Some Are of Love* (1987), combine – as does Hoogesteijn's work – polished screenplays, impressive performances, and high production values with a commitment to exploring women's subjective experience in the context of a broad social composite which is both effectively localized and also regionally, culturally, or politically emblematic.

Finally, Venezuela's leadership in super-8mm film production and exhibition, under the inspiration of Julio Neri, and in anthropological film and video under the aegis of Carlos Azpúrrua, merit mention as indicators of a film culture which – despite daunting obstacles – remains lively, active, and diverse.

Joao Luiz Viera, 'Tropical Disease: Towards Development of an Alternative Cinema in Venezuela', *Millennium Film Journal*, nos 10–11 (1982)   JBu

VERBAND DER FILMARBEITERINNEN

Translatable as the Association of Women Film Workers, the Verband der Filmarbeiterinnen is a WEST GERMAN organization founded by a group of women during the 1979 Hamburg Film Festival. Its founding was a spontaneous reaction to the lack of representation of women's interests during discussions about the German film industry that took place at the festival. The choice of the words 'film workers' was deliberate, in recognition of the fact that it was not only women directors who needed their interests represented, but women working in all spheres of the industry, from directors and producers, through camerawomen, editors, make-up artists and scriptwriters to film students. The objective of the Association has been to achieve parity at all levels throughout the industry, so that women receive an equal share of subsidy monies and training places. Their stated aims also include the promotion of films by women that reflect a feminist commitment, cataloguing and archiving films made by women, contributing to publications about women working in the film sector, providing an information resource, and cooperating with other organizations pursuing similar goals.

In the past decade the Association has not only done much to promote the interests of women working in the film industry in West Germany, but has also published a women's film handbook, listing all the women who have made films in West Germany since 1945. However, whilst the Association has proved an important pressure group, it has as yet been unable to achieve all its goals: women filmmakers working in West Germany still experience institutional sexism and can still have difficulty getting their projects funded. In an attempt to rectify this, a group of Association members recently filed an action with the Federal Constitutional Court. They argued that film subsidy laws do not abide by West German basic law, which states that no one shall be discriminated against on the grounds of sex. According to the Association, the lack of female representation on film subsidy committees means that women are discriminated against. The action was, however, rejected and the Association now plans to take the matter to the European Court at Strasbourg.

Julia Knight, *Women and the New German Cinema* (London: Verso, 1990)   JK

VERE, ALISON DE *see* DE VERE, ALISON

VIDEO

Although experiments in recording and playing back television pictures go back to the 1930s, it was not until 1956 that CBS's Hollywood Studios used video over the air. The intention was to alleviate the pressure of broadcasting live, and to avoid expensive shooting on film. As video moved into the domestic market, it became more portable and simpler to use. Home video arrived in 1972 when the first cassette, as opposed to cumbersome reel-to-reel, systems were produced. VHS format, using half-inch tape, was the most commercially successful, and sales of video cassette recorders (VCRs) boomed. By the late 1970s many educational institutions and community centers were using video. Cheaper, portable cameras and recyclable videotapes meant that for the first time non-professionals could have hands-on experience of 'filmmaking,' and see the results immediately rather than wait and pay for film processing. The politics of 'access' developed: access to equipment, training, and a means of expression for those traditionally denied a voice in the media, especially women.

In BRITAIN, for example, feminism has informed most of the women-only video courses run in the 1980s, developing analyses of how images are produced and consumed. Community video provides women with the confidence and skills to make independent grant-aided work, go on to further training, or attempt to enter the television and film industries. Like independent women filmmakers freed from the restrictions of commercial production, some women working in video choose women-only, non-hierarchical crews, questioning traditional notions of AUTHORSHIP and extending technical skills. Some of their work has been broadcast on TELEVISION: Karen Alexander's *Ms Taken Identity* (Albany Video, 1986) and *Let Our Children Grow Tall* (Sheffield Film Co-op, 1986), for example. Exile, racism, identity, sexuality, health, sexual abuse, and self-defense are among the issues explored in the wealth of small independent video workshops throughout Britain. Elsewhere – in AUSTRALIA and CANADA, for example – video has proved an effective medium for native peoples seeking their own ways of documenting their cultures. Video's accessibility – in terms of consumption as well as production – can also enable it to bypass state CENSORSHIP, and it has become an important 'underground' means of communication in repressive milieus, as for example in CHILE.

Women videomakers are involved in all these areas.

While such uses of video tend to take a documentary approach to social issues and marginalized cultural perspectives, video art practices have also developed worldwide in fine art or AVANT-GARDE contexts. Women video artists have often pushed at the aesthetic, political, and formal boundaries of conventional film practice, through PERFORMANCE or manipulation of the medium, producing stimulating and provocative work in which the reconstruction of gender is central.

From having to fight to be screened at video festivals, often controlled by men, to being rejected by broadcast television due to ideological differences disguised as 'technical problems,' women's video culture has had to struggle hard to survive. Nonetheless, FEMINIST DISTRIBUTION groups such as CIRCLES and CINEMIEN have extended the visibility of this challenging work, and established alternative ways of viewing.

See also: ABORIGINAL FILM AND VIDEO; CINE-MUJER; GAVIOLA, TATIANA; GROUPE INTERVENTION VIDEO; HAMMER, BARBARA; IDEMITSU, MAKO; VIDEO FEMMES   CS

VIDEO FEMMES

Organized in Quebec City (Canada) as a development of the cross-Canada film festival 'Women and Film/La femme et le film' in 1974, the group originally called itself 'La femme et le film,' changing its name to Video Femmes in 1981. Video Femmes is an independent collective which concerns itself with feminist communication, both as a production unit and as a distributor of videos. (Infrequently, members of the collective have used film formats.) The group was attracted to the medium of VIDEO from its founding. QUEBEC in the 1970s was involved in social struggle: in this context video presented the ideal tool for popular expression and social action, because it permitted greater interaction and immediacy and was relatively economical and accessible as a technique. As part of this social trend, the members of Video Femmes took up the medium to become complicit documentors of women's struggles. The group adopted the social themes and filmmaking styles that had been developing as a result of the women's movement, then in full bloom.

> *Indian cinema has developed a genre all of its own – what is it?*

In their work, Video Femmes concentrated on popular education. Members of the collective researched archives in order to document visually the major events of the history and culture of women – including lesbians – in Quebec. In the 1980s, the work of Video Femmes became marked by a less collective style; members began to develop their own themes and artistic methods. Videos of this period rework the codes of fiction, documentary, and rock video, while searching for techniques and aesthetic approaches particular to the video medium. FEMINIST DISTRIBUTION maintained the group's collective strength and financial survival. To integrate themselves into the communities that used their videos, Video Femmes offered their services for group animation and consultation. Their distribution service is worldwide and is used by individuals, women's groups, institutions, labor unions, and so on. The collective also organized the QUEBEC WOMEN'S FILM AND VIDEO FESTIVAL/Festival des filles des vues de Quebec for eleven years.

Productions include: *Chaperons rouges/Red Riding Hood* (Helen Doyle and Hélène Bourgault, co-produced with GROUPE INTERVENTION VIDEO, 1979); *Six femmes à leur place/Yes, We Can* (Louise Giguère and Louise LeMay, 1981); *C'est pas le pays des merveilles/This Isn't Wonderland* (Helen Doyle and Nicole Giguère, 1981); *Tous les jours, tous les jours . . .* (Johane Fournier and Nicole Giguère, 1982); *Demain, la cinquantaine/Turning Fifty* (Hélène Roy, 1986); *SOS; MTS/SOS, STD* (Lise Bonefant and Marie Fortin, 1987) BF

VISUAL PLEASURE see LOOK, THE; SCOPOPHILIA

VON HARBOU, THEA see HARBOU, THEA VON

VON STERNBERG, JOSEF see STERNBERG, JOSEF VON

VON TROTTA, MARGARETHE see TROTTA, MARGARETHE VON

WALSH, AISLING (196?–)

Aisling Walsh, a graduate of the National Film and Television School in England, returned to her native IRELAND to make her first feature film. *Joyriders* (1988) is a contemporary ROMANCE revolving around Perky (Andrew Connolly) and Mary (Patricia Kerrigan), the joyriders of the title. While the film follows the growing closeness of these two – and hence can be seen as a universal love story – it is distinctly rooted in the post-abortion referendum Ireland of the late 1980s. Visually the film articulates, often ironically, the sober resonances of the Catholic church's and the Irish state's containment – and sometimes their crippling – of women in traditional roles. The title itself hints at Irish tabloid shorthand, with its connotations of both a young male subculture and a discourse of 'Law and Order.' Throughout the film there are scattered allusions to the confining male LOOK at the woman: Mary is accosted by two sailors, and she and her friend Tammy suffer the unwanted attentions of their male boss, as well as the uninvited confidences of some of the men who come to the hotel dances where she works as a hostess. While the film does suggest that both men and women are repressed, it is Mary and Tammy who appear to come off as the worst victims: Tammy falls from stardom into alcoholism, and Mary is forced from a violent marriage into abandoning her children, only to be rescued by 'the right man.'

Walsh's first feature demonstrates that however personal, even prosaic, a subject might seem, the politics of the Irish context can filter through and transform the conventional narrative's resolution of events.

Joyriders (1988)   SM

WARNER BROS.

Warner Bros. began as a producer of feature films in the USA, but in the mid 1920s the firm developed a long-range plan that included innovating mechanically synchronized SOUND. The success of *The Jazz Singer* (Alan Crosland, 1927) and wise investment strategies produced a firm that rapidly expanded into EXHIBITION and diversified into radio, music publishing, and related entertainments. When the Depression hit, Warners sold unprofitable theaters and reduced production costs. In the 1950s Warners moved into television production, but in the early 1960s the firm's profits were declining. In 1967 Seven Arts bought control of Warners, then in 1969 Kinney National Services took it over. Two years later, Kinney split off Warner Communications, which has proceeded to become a giant diversified firm in the leisure industry. In early 1989 Warners and Time, Inc. announced their merger.

Throughout the 1930s and into the 1940s, in the years of the HOLLYWOOD STUDIO SYSTEM, Warners pursued a cautious production policy, carefully calculating the best ways to keep costs in line with anticipated revenues. One or two prestige films per year headed a group of lower-cost program and second-bill pictures. One way to keep costs down was to use current events as the basis of stories, with production chief Jack Warner heading a set of associate producers who concentrated on GENRE filmmaking. Such a strategy used the stable of STARS under Warners' contract in a mix-and-match arrangement, with some players doing as many as six films per year. Among Warners' major contract stars were Bette DAVIS, Ida LUPINO, Ruby Keeler, Joan Blondell, and, in the late 1940s, Joan CRAWFORD (coming from MGM) and Lauren BACALL.

Nick Roddick, *A New Deal in Entertainment: Warner Brothers in the 1930s* (London: British Film Institute, 1983)   JaS

WEBER, LOIS (1881–1939)

Reputed in 1916 to be the highest-salaried director in the world, Lois Weber estimated that she made between two and four hundred films: of these, fewer than fifty remain. Born in Pennsylvania, Weber trained as a pianist and toured widely in the USA as a concert prodigy until she was seventeen. After joining a Salvation Army-style organization she became an actress, 'convinced the theatrical profession needed a missionary.' She went to Gaumont Talking Pictures, where she wrote, directed, and played in her first film, and became a director of talking sound-on-disk pictures. She was a leading director with Universal, and by 1915 was as well known as D W GRIFFITH or Cecil B DE MILLE, tackling in her films – which were promoted as 'quality' products – controversial social issues such as religious hypocrisy (*Hypocrites* [1914]), abortion (*Where Are My Children?* [1916]) and capital punishment (*The People vs John Doe* [1916]). In 1917 she formed Lois Weber Productions, and in 1920 reached the peak of her career with a five-picture contract, for $50,000 apiece, with Famous Players-Lasky. Whether her films seemed old-fashioned or too saccharine to postwar audiences, or the growth of big studios limited the material she could work with, after the early 1920s Weber became unpopular, lost her company, and suffered a breakdown. She was unable to find work as a director after 1934, and freelanced as a script supervisor and screen-tested new stars for Universal. When she died in 1939, her funeral expenses were paid by friends.

The importance of Lois Weber's contribution to SILENT CINEMA, downplayed in many of the standard film histories, was brought to light in the early 1970s with screenings of her films at various WOMEN'S FILM FESTIVALS; and some of them are now circulated by FEMINIST DISTRIBUTION organizations. While Weber's films offer nuanced evocations of character and setting, and

Lois Weber's *The Blot*

418

are sensitive in their treatment of moral dilemmas, latter-day feminists often find their moralism – obviously quite acceptable in their own time – hard to take; with the result that Weber's work has yet to be subjected to full scholarly treatment by feminist critics.

Weber's films include: *The Heiress* (1911); *On the Brink* (1911); *The Troubadour's Triumph* (1912); *Suspense* (1913); *The Eyes of God* (1913); *The Jew's Christmas* (1913); *His Brand* (1913); *The Female of the Species* (1913); *The Merchant of Venice* (1914); *Traitor* (1914); *Like Most Wives* (1914); *Hypocrites* (1914); *False Colors* (1914); *It's No Laughing Matter* (1914); *The Fool and His Money* (1914); *The Leper's Coat* (1914); *The Career of Waterloo Peterson* (1914); *Behind the Veil* (1914); *Jewel* (1915); *Sunshine Molly* (1915); *A Cigarette, That's All* (1915); *Scandal* (1915); *The Flirt* (1916); *Discontent* (1916); *Hop, the Devil's Brew* (1916); *Where Are My Children?* (1916); *The French Downstairs* (1916); *Alone in the World* (1916); *The People vs John Doe* (1916); *The Rock of Riches* (1916); *John Needham's Double* (1916); *Saving the Family Name* (1916); *Shoes* (1916); *The Dumb Girl of Portici* (1916); *Idle Wives* (1916); *Wanted – a Home* (1916); *The Hand that Rocks the Cradle* (1917); *Even As You and I* (1917); *The Mysterious Mrs Musselwhite* (1917); *The Price of a Good Time* (1917); *The Man Who Dared God* (1917); *There's No Place Like Home* (1917); *For Husbands Only* (1917); *The Doctor and the Woman* (1918); *Borrowed Clothes* (1918); *When a Girl Loves* (1919); *Mary Regan* (1919); *A Midnight Romance* (1919); *Scandal Managers* (1919); *Home* (1919); *Forbidden* (1919); *Too Wise Wives* (1921); *What's Worth While?* (1921); *To Please One Woman* (1921); *The Blot* (1921); *What Do Men Want?* (1921); *A Chapter in Her Life* (1923); *The Marriage Clause* (1926); *Sensation Seekers* (1927); *The Angel of Broadway* (1927); *White Heat* (1934)

Louise Heck-Rabi, *Women Filmmakers: A Critical Reception* (Metuchen, NJ; Scarecrow Press, 1984)   CS

WEILL, CLAUDIA (1947–   )

After a decade as a camerawoman and director of DOCUMENTARIES (among them *The Other Half of the Sky* (1974) on China, made for Shirley MacLaine; and *Joyce at 34* (1972, with Joyce CHOPRA), Claudia Weill began *Girlfriends* (1978) as a documentary about growing up Jewish in New York City, and then as a ten-minute fictional short. In the end distributed by Warner Bros., yet with all the integrity of the independent film it was, *Girlfriends* made a mainstream impact partly because of its fresh and engaging quality, and partly because it appeared at exactly the right moment as one of the earliest of recent American films addressing feminist issues. It decisively subordinates the love interest to the young heroine's struggle to shape her professional life as a photographer and to her relationship with her woman friend. Weill also bestows on her heroine an unusual individuality in the American context, rooted in New York ethnicity. *It's My Turn* (1980), the big-budget Columbia film the success of *Girlfriends* won for Weill, features a glossier heroine in Jill Clayburgh and addresses over-professionalism as a problem, the heroine's neglect of lover commitments for work involvement. Since this film Weill has directed theater and television productions, and has been at work on various film projects.

Joyce at 34 (1972); *The Other Half of the Sky: A China Memoir* (1974); *Girlfriends* (1978); *It's My Turn* (1980)

Barbara Koenig Quart, *Women Directors: The Emergence of a New Cinema* (New York: Praeger, 1988)   BKQ

WEIMAR CINEMA

The term Weimar Cinema encompasses films made in GERMANY during the Weimar Republic (1918–33): this is still considered the heyday of German cinema. The period was preceded by an era of stability for the film industry during

World War I; while after the Weimar period, film was appropriated by the National Socialists as a propaganda tool. During the Weimar period of social liberalism and explosive aesthetic diversity – facilitated by a temporary slackening of censorship – various film styles and genres emerged: the historical *Ausstattungsfilm* (costume film), the *Aufklaerungsfilm* (sex education film), German Expressionism, the *Kammerspielfilm* (chamber film), the *Strassenfilm* (street film), *Neue Sachlichkeit* (New Sobriety), and the *Proletarische Film* (proletarian film). The AVANT GARDE and the ANIMATION films of Lotte REINIGER established themselves outside the confines of the commercial film industry. Weimar produced such directors as Ernst Lubitsch, F W Murnau, G W Pabst, Fritz Lang, to name only the best known.

Consolidation of capital and the economic crisis that followed in its wake, combined with women's increasing influence on and presence within the public sphere, produced striking ambivalences; among them on the one hand a tension between female desire along with women's liberation, and on the other a crisis of masculine identity along with male desire for domination. MELODRAMA served to express on the aesthetic level the ambivalent struggle between liberation and conservatism: it found its strongest expression in the *Kammerspielfilm* and the *Strassenfilm*. These films take up early cinema's fascination with unstaged reality and public places, but situate them in stories about the loss of petty-bourgeois male identity. Film theorist Patrice Petro discusses the extent to which Weimar melodramas specifically addressed a female audience: the representation of the economic, as well as the social and sexual, mobility of women, the erotic representation of passive men, and the transgression of bourgeois norms, are cinematic expressions of the female desire for emancipation. On a formal level, melodrama confronts the legibility of filmic expression, its heterogeneity and the 'depiction of endless repetition,' with a cinematic language enforced by male voyeurism. In her analysis, Petro challenges the received view – advanced, for example, by earlier critics, including Lotte EISNER and Siegfried Kracauer – that Weimar Cinema portrays a crisis of the subject: for Petro the subject in crisis is specifically masculine.

Other Weimar genres are more intensely preoccupied with staging male identity: Expressionism, for example – which enables the soul to 'speak' through its flatness of decor, LIGHTING, CAMERA MOVEMENT, gesture and mime. The domination of this interiority, which connotes maleness, brings about the negation of exteriority, which early film had been interested in: representations of female SEXUALITY give way to demonizations of the sexual. This tendency is also demonstrated in a number of 'ornamental' films directed by Fritz Lang and scripted by Thea von HARBOU, which take up – often in melodramatic form – a female variant of the expressionistic *Doppelgaenger* motif, playing with the split between consciousness and the subconscious. Here, the sexually and socially mobile woman gives way to her desexualized likeness, who is destined for pathetic renunciation. In contrast to the *Kammerspielfilm* and the *Strassenfilm*, which portray as unfulfillable male/conservative desires as well as female/emancipatory desires, the films of Lang/Harbou assert the potential fulfillment of those desires within the framework of patriarchal hierarchies. These hierarchies are not only introduced through the narrative, but may be found in the ornamentally rigid structures of the set, which, in situating the human body amidst monumentality, violates that body. The New Sobriety attempts to avoid psychologizing and melodramatic moments: in its reproduction of surfaces, it no longer evokes a naive SCOPOPHILIA, but rather the power of the cinematic apparatus. Here, scopophilia is associated with sadistic structures, while the female body – and with it the female gaze – is associated with masochistic structures.

Only a few films made toward the end of the Weimar Republic manage to break free of this uniformity of cinematic language and inscription of gender difference – the latter having been perfected further with the rise of the 'talkie.' Commercial cinema increasingly mirrored repressive tendencies in society, before dedicating itself wholly to its propagandist tasks under National Socialism.

Patrice Petro, *Joyless Streets: Women and Melodramatic Representation in Weimar Germany* (Princeton: Princeton University Press, 1989)

See also: BROOKS, LOUISE; SAGAN, LEONTINE; THIELE, HERTHA   *VR*

WERTMULLER, LINA (1928–   )

A film director working in ITALY, Lina Wertmuller was born into an aristocratic family of Swiss descent. She began her career in puppet shows and theater. Before turning to film directing in the early sixties, and throughout the sixties, she wrote shows, musicals, and comedies for television. Her first job in film was as assistant director to Federico Fellini in *8 e mezzo/8½* (1963). In the same year she made her first feature, *I basilischi*, a portrait of '*vitelloni*' (young men). Her films are sociosexual parables, constructed in the framework of 'comedy Italian style.' The 1972 film *Mimi metallurgico ferito nell'onore* launched the actors' team Giancarlo Giannini and Mariangela Melato. Wertmuller's commercial successes include *Travolti da un insolito destino nell'azzurro mare d'agosto* (1974) and *Pasqualino settebellezze* (1976). Wertmuller has been most successful in the USA; in 1977 Warner Bros. offered her an exclusive contract to make films in the English language.

Although claiming to be sympathetic toward some feminist issues, Wertmuller does not define herself as a feminist. A number of feminist critics have challenged in particular the views expressed in Wertmuller's sociosexual parables. Feminist critics have objected to her use of violence and vulgarity, claiming that her cinema reinforces cultural and sexist stereotypes.

I basilischi/The Lizards (1963); *Questa volta parliamo di uomini/Let's Talk about Men* (1965); *Mimi metallurgico ferito nell'onore/The Seduction of Mimi* (1972); *Film d'amore e d'anarchia,* or *Stamattina alle dieci in via dei fiori nella nota casa di tolleranza/Love and Anarchy* (1973); *Tutto a posto e niente in ordine/All Screwed Up* (1974); *Travolti da un insolito destino nell'azzurro mare d'agosto/Swept Away* (1974); *Pasqualino settebellezze/Seven Beauties* (1976); *The End of the World in Our Usual Bed in a Night Full of Rain* (1977); *Fatto di sangue tra due uomini per causa di una vedova: si sospettano motivi politici/Blood Feud* (1978); *Una domenica sera di novembre* (1981); *A Joke of Destiny Lying in Wait Round The Corner Like A Street Bandit* (1983); *Sotto Sotto* (1983); *Complicato intrigo di donne vicoli e delitti* (1985); *Summer Night with Greek Profiles Almond Eyes and Scent of Basil* (1986); *Up to Date* (1988)

Tania Modleski, 'Wertmuller's Women: Swept Away by the Usual Destiny', *Jump Cut*, no. 10–11 (1976)   *GB*

WEST, MAE (1893–1980)

Hollywood's queen of sexual satire and innuendo, and the author of some of its most famous lines, was brought up in Brooklyn, took to the stage at the age of five, and started writing her own comic material at fifteen. In 1926 her play *Sex*, a smash hit on Broadway, caused her to be charged with obscenity and sent to the workhouse for ten days. As a result of her success in vaudeville, where her good time, loudmouth persona had its origins in vehicles including *Drag* (a sympathetic look at homosexuality) and *Diamond Lil* (later filmed as *She Done Him Wrong* [Lowell Sherman, Paramount, 1933]),

West was offered a contract with PARA-MOUNT. There she wrote most of her films herself, demanded complete control over all of them, and with the likes of *Night After Night* (Archie Mayo, 1932), *She Done Him Wrong, I'm No Angel* (Wesley Ruggles, 1933), *Belle of the Nineties* (Leo McCarey, 1934), and *Goin' To Town* (Alexander Hall, 1935), rescued the studio from the brink of financial disaster.

Typically, West played an independent adventuress, usually an entertainer, pursued by a wealthy older man, who chooses instead a young buck and metes out her own brand of natural justice

::
What is technologized horror?
::

on whatever situation she encounters in a world divided between crooks and hustlers and snobbish upper classes. The message, in accord with the Depressed American Dream, was that anyone with guts could succeed: the difference was that West, who was consistently ordered by the censorious PRODUCTION CODE administration to tone down her scripts, was not just a woman but predatory to boot.

With her BLONDE marcelled wig, tight corset, and exaggerated sashay, West's STAR image appeared to be the ultimate sexual STEREOTYPE; but her ribald humor turned that into parody. Although she never consciously espoused new sets of values for women, West was, in effect, the PHALLIC WOMAN who reversed male/female roles: male characters were exploited by her, she belittled monogamy and acted on her own good-humored initiative. Instead of subservience to a man, her HEROINES sought power over their own lives: sexual pleasure rather than romantic love was the issue at stake. In her hands, female sexual enticement and prowess represented autonomy and liberation for women which, together with her brand of comedy, exploded the

hypocrisies and inhibitions of accepted notions.

By the end of the thirties West, along with HEPBURN, CRAWFORD, DIETRICH, and others, was labeled 'box office poison' by a leading exhibitor. Her retaliation, in 1940, was the flawed but extremely popular *My Little Chickadee* (Edward Cline, Universal) with W C Fields. After the unsatisfying *The Heat's On* (Gregory Ratoff, Columbia, 1943), West eschewed movies in favor of her stage shows, including a revue backed by scantily clad musclemen, before going into retirement in the late 1950s. Although she wrote her own lines for her two next and final films, the infamous *Myra Breckinridge* (Michael Sarne, 1970) and *Sextette* (Ken Hughes, 1978), they had few of the qualities of her earlier films. While she had modeled the shaky plots of those to best advantage around her screen persona, these last efforts, made in the wake of the women's movement, showed her sex-obsessed character to little advantage: the only satisfaction to be derived from them being that of the appearance of an unabashedly remorseless camp cult figure from another era.

Joan Mellen, 'The Mae West Nobody Knows', in *Women and their Sexuality in the New Film* (London: Davis Poynter, 1974)   ALi

WESTERN

It is usually assumed that the Western, with its concern with MASCULINITY, is not a film GENRE that interests women. Film theorist John Cawelti, for example, claims that it appeals mainly to an immature audience or to a rural, predominantly male, working-class audience. He explains that through the Western the youngster escapes the helplessness and limitations of childhood, while adolescent Oedipal identity problems are worked out through symbolic narratives exposing the 'bad father' and supporting the 'good father.' In the case of the working-class male, Cawelti maintains that the Western allows male aggressions that are rooted in a modern industrial society to be assuaged through identification with the hero's legitimized killing of opponents. Conversely, the Western's traditional female roles have had little appeal for women.

When women admit identifying with the Western, it is by crossing sexual lines to identify with the active male hero. If women characters (the farmer's daughter, Indian or Mexican woman, or schoolmarm and frontier woman) had little appeal, it was because they were generally no more than passive symbols in the active hero's dilemma of choice. A man with a horse, this hero is linked to the freedom of the wilderness. He is a man with a gun which he employs with reluctance, control and elegance; and he is a wanderer, a man who rejects the ethic of success but who, for the time span of the narrative, is called upon to act. Through his actions the hero confronts a system of opposing values aligned on the poles of wilderness versus civilization. Women characters typically play opposing symbols in this configuration. Through the years, a few Westerns have featured a female hero. Yet even in these exceptional Westerns, the role never allows the woman to experience the tension of acting on the frontier of opposing ideologies that marks the best Westerns. The most memorable Western with a female hero, *Johnny Guitar* (Nicholas Ray, Republic, 1954), although commendable for giving voice to women's frustrations with their sideline roles, makes camp of the Western's stylizations, leaving no room to question seriously the possibility of replacing the male with a female hero.

The history of the American West offers many models of heroines and many stories of the empowerment that moving to the West gave to women – if film producers were interested in those stories. Their refusal to bring these stories to the screen in a realistic fashion can be attributed to a reluctance to present role images, even historically accurate images, that do not fit the current period's definition of women's roles or which threaten accepted notions of history. More recently, Westerns have begun to admit strong women HEROINES, but only by moving the Western out of its traditional setting. The physical/ideological frontier is still present, but the historical West is abandoned for a modern setting where the horse, for example, is transformed into a motorcycle, or for a fantasy or futuristic setting when the Western is combined with other genres (SCIENCE FICTION in particular). Though the Western has declined significantly in importance in the last few decades, and attempts to revive it have been shortlived, the appeal to women spectators of the strong heroines of the transformed Westerns offer new possibilities for the genre's survival. The stories depicted in these films – such as WOMEN'S REVENGE against rape in *Shame* (1987), by Australian director Steve Jodrell – allow female audiences for the first time to identify as women with a NARRATIVE structure that once seemed to have appeal only for the male spectator.

Jacqueline Levitin, 'The Western: Any Good Roles for Feminists?', *Film Reader*, no. 5 (1982)   JL

WEST GERMANY

At the end of World War II the four Allied powers took over control of the film industry in GERMANY. While indigenous film production in the Russian zone was allowed to get under way relatively quickly, in the western zones licenses authorizing film production were granted only gradually. With Germans eager to see films the Nazis had banned and the Americans stipulating that the West Germans were not allowed to impose an import quota on American films, dubbed Hollywood films soon began, and have largely continued, to dominate the West German market.

The early postwar film production that was allowed gave rise to a series of critically acclaimed *Truemmerfilme* (rubble films) such as *Die Moerder sind unter uns/The Murderers are Among Us* (Wolfgang Staudte, 1946) and *In jenen Tagen/In Former Days* (Helmut Kaeutner, 1947), which tried to reflect on the events of recent history. By the 1950s, however, production in West Germany had become more commercially oriented, costume epics, literary adaptations, romantic comedies, and *Heimat* (or homeland) films predominating. One of the most popular, yet most critically despised, GENREs in German cinema, the *Heimat* film presents idealized images of rural life among the landscapes of the 'German Fatherland.' Whilst the West German film industry experienced something of a boom during the 1950s, by the early 1960s box office receipts had started to decline, and feature film production dropped back to its 1952 level. In 1961 no West German film was considered worthy of the Federal Film Prize, and as the 1960s progressed, PORNOGRAPHY started to dominate commercial feature film production.

In West Germany, however, the state is considered 'responsible for the maintenance and perpetuation of national heritage and culture.' As a result, the state proved responsive to the demands made by a small group of would-be feature film directors, who drew up the Oberhausen Manifesto in 1962 demanding the opportunity to create a new German cinema: in 1965 an innovative form of state film subsidy was set up. Administered by the *Kuratorium junger deutscher Film* (Board for New German Film), it offered the necessary financial assistance to enable filmmakers to make their first feature-length films. Since then, a whole film subsidy network has developed, providing five major sources of funding: the *Kuratorium*, the Film Promotion Board, Federal Film Awards, regional film funding and, most importantly, television. The subsidy system has also put money into exhibition,

distribution, and script and project development. This has enabled a wide range of filmmaking to develop in West Germany. Not only has it given rise to the critically acclaimed NEW GERMAN CINEMA, it has also enabled West German film to achieve commercial successes both at home and abroad. *Otto – der Film/Otto – the Film* (Otto Waalkes/Xaver Schwarzenberger, 1985) and its 1987 sequel have broken all box office records on the domestic market; *Maenner/Men* (Doris Doerrie, 1985) has received rave reviews in Britain and America; Wolfgang Petersen has been described as a German Steven Spielberg; and the films of R W FASSBINDER, Wim Wenders, and Werner Herzog are readily available on the home video market. West German cinema's dependence on public funding has, however, also made it subject to censorship, with both filmmakers and funding bodies avoiding politically sensitive subjects (such as terrorism during the seventies).

Over the years women's contribution to West German cinema has been considerable. Although there were only a small number of women making films during the 1950s, during the 1960s an increasing number were starting to work as directors, among them Claudia von Alemann, Danièle HUILLET, Erika Runge, Helke SANDER, May Spils, and Ula STOECKL. With the advent of the new women's movement during the late sixties and early seventies, this number rose considerably. Whilst many of these women were working on the periphery of mainstream cinema and often closely connected with the women's movement, a number of developments during the 1960s and 1970s have gradually enabled women to move into all areas of the film industry. In 1973 Claudia von Alemann and Helke Sander organized an International Seminar on Women's Film in West Berlin, providing West German women filmmakers for the first time with a forum in which to discuss their work. In the mid to late 1960s a number of film and television schools were established. While these initially had a low intake of women students, during the 1970s the ratio of women to men improved, equipping more women with the necessary technical skills to enter the industry. Television has also offered women filmmakers a variety of openings, and proved to be a major source of funding for their work.

Women are now working in practically all branches of the West German film industry. Women such as Jeanine Meerapfel and Doris DOERRIE are working as feature film directors; Cristina PERINCIOLI and Helga Reidemeister are highly acclaimed DOCUMENTARY filmmakers; and women such as Birgit HEIN and Dore O are working in the area of AVANT-GARDE filmmaking. In fact, West Germany has now become well known for its women filmmakers, especially those associated with the New German Cinema such as Margarethe von TROTTA, Helma SANDERS-BRAHMS, Helke Sander, Ula Stoeckl, Jutta BRUECKNER, and Ulrike OTTINGER. However, women have not gained ground only in the field of directing: Clara Burckner, Renee Gundelach and Ursula Ludwig have made names for themselves as producers; Heidi Genee and Beate Mainka-Jellinghaus as editors; Elfi MIKESCH and Gisela Tuchtenhagen as camerawomen; and Hanna Schygulla, Barbara Sukowa, and Katherina Thalbach as actresses. The diversity of activity notwithstanding, recurring themes in their work are evident: a concern with the Nazi era, women's rights and emancipation, lesbian sexuality and female eroticism, and mythology.

Despite this apparent success story, institutional sexism and censorship have proved recurring problems for West German women filmmakers. In an attempt to improve their situation within the industry, a pressure group, the VERBAND DER FILMARBEITERINNEN (Association of Women Film Workers), was set up in 1979. Other initiatives – some more successful than others – have included the setting up of a feminist film JOURNAL, *FRAUEN UND FILM*, women's media centers, a women's film distributor, and WOMEN'S FILM FESTIVALS.

Julia Knight, *Women and the New German Cinema* (London: Verso, 1990)

See also: *ARBEITERFILM*; EAST GERMANY; FEMINALE   JK

WFTVN see WOMEN'S FILM, TELEVISION AND VIDEO NETWORK

WIELAND, JOYCE (1931–)

One of CANADA's best-known AVANT-GARDE filmmakers, Joyce Wieland has also carved out a thirty-year career as a multi-media artist, working at various periods in plastic, cloth, assemblages, bronze, watercolors, and oils, as well as film in all gauges. She made her first film in 1958, and in 1962 moved with her then husband Michael Snow to New York, where they became founding members of the structural film movement. Wieland's films investigated the film apparatus, playing with light, reflections, masking, and lenses, using leader, piercing the emulsion, and other similar devices of the material or structural film.

Daniela Eltit and Tatiana Gaviola have contributed to this vital 'oppositional practice.' What is it?

They were also precisely formal in structure, many of them single-image films, or based on a single formal premise such as an editing technique (repetition or looping, for example) or a specific kind of shot. Unlike some of the other films from that group, Wieland's were also always personal and sensual, often lyrical, meditative, or ritualistic, and whimsically humorous. Her use of text on the screen in combination with particular images or editing techniques, as well as her investigation of forms of NARRATIVE, anticipate many of the issues of the deconstructivist, semiotic, or oppositional avant garde, and her erotic self-reflexivity, using her own body as part of the work, anticipates what would later be called *l'écriture féminine*. In 1975 Wieland made a large-budget 35mm feature narrative, realizing her dream of bringing her patriotic, aesthetic, environmentalist, and feminist concerns to a broad general audience. *The Far Shore*, based on the quintessential Canadian painter Tom Thomson and a fictional French-Canadian woman, was structured as a semi-parodic but unabashedly romantic MELODRAMA utilizing narrative conventions of the SILENT CINEMA. The film received a disappointing response from mainstream audiences, and hostility from champions of the avant garde, who saw as incorrect her excursions into melodramatic narrative (in which she was again anticipating a movement that would be active in the avant garde a decade later): as a result Wieland gave up filmmaking of any kind for almost ten years. In the past five years she has revived some interest in the medium, bringing to completion some films which had been shot in the early 1970s; but her principal interest is in making large oil paintings which combine abstraction, expressionism, narrative, and self-reflexivity with her abiding themes of nature and landscape, eroticism, politics, and the female experience.

Tea in the Garden (1958); *Larry's Recent Behaviour* (1963); *Peggy's Blue Skylight* (1964); *Patriotism, Part One* (1964); *Patriotism, Part Two* (1964); *Water Sark* (1966); *Bill's Hat* (1967); *Barbara's Blindness* (with Betty Ferguson, 1967); *Sailboat* (1967); *1933* (1967); *Handtinting* (1967); *Catfood* (1967); *Rat Life and Diet in North America* (1968); *Dripping Water* (with Michael Snow, 1969); *Reason Over Passion/La raison avant la passion* (1969); *Pierre Vallières* (1972); *Solidarity* (1973); *The Far Shore* (1976); *A & B in Ontario* (with Hollis Frampton, 1972–83); *Birds at Sunrise* (1972–84); *Wendy and Joyce* (in progress)

Lauren Rabinowitz, 'The Development of Feminist Strategies in the Experimental Films of Joyce Wieland', *Film Reader* no. 5 (1982)   KA

WOMAN'S PICTURE

The woman's picture is defined as a GENRE by the way it privileges a female perspective. It offers the viewpoint of a female character and specifically addresses a female spectator through concerns coded as 'feminine,' such as domestic relationships and ROMANCE. Some examples of the Hollywood woman's picture would be *Stella Dallas* (King Vidor, Goldwyn, 1937), *Mildred Pierce* (Michael Curtiz, Warner Bros., 1945), or *Dark Victory* (Edmund Goulding, Warner Bros., 1939), and more recently, *Alice Doesn't Live Here Anymore* (Martin Scorsese, 1974) and *Terms of Endearment* (James L Brooks, 1983). The NARRATIVE conflicts characteristic of the woman's picture are largely those of MELODRAMA, with an emphasis on psychological tensions based on conflicts between female desire and socially endorsed FEMININITY – whose high point in the woman's picture is embodied in the figure of the mother. While such stories allow female characters space to exercise independence, ambition, or sexuality in pursuit of their own desires, all these must be sacrificed in favor of the positive virtues of MOTHERHOOD. Female desire may take many forms, but in all cases it is a desire that surfaces outside its conventional channels and is therefore shown as transgressive. The resolution of feminine dilemmas can be achieved only at inescapable cost.

Attention to the woman's picture within FEMINIST FILM THEORY has been central in developing theories of reception and consumption of films. A central female perspective has been seen as offering female spectators the PLEASURE of identifying with active and transgressive feminine desire, while from the masculine point of view this identification appears dangerous and threatening. It has been suggested that the woman's picture addresses an instability at the heart of feminine identity, where women are forced to repress irreconcilable conflicts. The emotional effect of the loss experienced in the films' endings thus replays the cost of the repression required of women within patriarchal culture.

While recognition of female desire, of the contradictions of women's experience, and of women as agents acting on their behalf in the narrative have united feminist critics in support of the woman's picture, the endings of the films elicit diverse responses. While some see the sacrifice or punishment of the female character as subjugating her to the patriarchal order, others suggest that the gaps and incoherences of the untidy ending challenge the notion that women can ever be adequately contained by patriarchy, proposing that the film's memorable moments remain despite their masochistic resolutions. These arguments extend to television SOAP OPERAs, which contain many features of the woman's picture, with the characteristic – and crucial – difference that there is no ending, so that the dilemmas and irresolutions of FEMININITY persist.

Thus while the woman's picture has attracted much critical derision as mushy romance and escapism, feminist criticism has retrieved the genre, arguing that we can understand narratives of women torn between conflicting paths as showing social tensions over women's actual social and domestic roles. The coincidence of World War II with the height of the genre has also encouraged historical analysis, using the social context to investigate the nature of these tensions and also what such films, with plots concerning the changes brought to women's lives by their entry into the workforce, meant to contemporary women audiences.

Mary Ann Doane, '"The Woman's Film": Possession and Address', in *Home is Where the Heart Is: Studies in Melodrama and the Woman's Film*, ed. Christine

Gledhill (London: British Film Institute, 1987)

See also: ALTMAN, ROBERT; ARZNER, DOROTHY; AUDIENCE AND SPECTATOR; CUKOR, GEORGE; DE MILLE, CECIL B; LUPINO, IDA; OPHULS, MAX   GS

WOMAN WARRIORS *see* AMAZONS

WOMEN AND FILM

A US JOURNAL published between 1972 and 1975, *Women and Film* provides an example of early western feminist approaches to representations of women in cinema. Its aims were to rediscover the work of forgotten women filmmakers, to analyze images of women in popular cinema, and to report on contemporary feminist film activities. While the journal incorporated broad political interests and exercised an open editorial policy, a perspective emerged around a sociological critique of CLASSICAL HOLLYWOOD CINEMA – which was seen to represent a restricted and distorted image of women's lives. Criticism focused on female characters in mainstream cinema, who were seen as passive, denying opportunities for positive identifications for women filmgoers. The journal's writing on women filmmakers' work particularly favored cinéma vérité forms of DOCUMENTARY for new feminist cinema. These were seen as holding the potential to counter STEREOTYPES with images drawn from the reality of women's experience, so providing material for consciousness-raising within the woman's movement.

In 1974, four of the journal's editorial group left because of what they saw as *Women and Film*'s lack of attention to the specific textual operations of film and uncritical espousal of REALIST conventions for feminist cinema. The breakaway collective produced the journal *CAMERA OBSCURA*; but articles in later issues of *Women and Film* do show the beginnings of an engagement with the

Janet Leigh in peril in Hitchcock's *Psycho*

SEMIOTIC criticism that formed the impetus of *Camera Obscura*'s work.　GS

WOMEN IN PERIL

From the era of SILENT CINEMA until today, the woman in peril has endured as a central motif in western cinema. In the silent days of Hollywood, for example, Pearl White, STAR of the adventure film serial *The Perils of Pauline* (Pathé, 1914), was the woman in peril at the crisis moment of each episode. Her woman in peril was of the 'being-tied-to-the-railway-line-by-the-villain-and-rescued-at-the-last-moment-by-the-hero' variety. And the silent adventure serial demonstrates the NARRATIVE function of the woman in peril: she is presented to the audience as passive, vulnerable to danger; as 'spectacle,' object of the LOOK – whilst providing the male lead with the opportunity to assume the active narrative role, taking control of events and moving the story along. With the development of film GENREs – notably thriller, HORROR and disaster films – the woman in peril has shifted her meanings, to be renamed woman as victim in such films as Brian DE PALMA's *Dressed to Kill* (1980) and Sam Peckinpah's *Straw Dogs* (1971). In Alfred HITCHCOCK's films, the woman in peril is used selfconsciously (as in *Shadow of a Doubt* [Universal, 1943] or *Psycho* [Shamley, 1960]) to bring in the audience as collaborators with the privileged – and in these cases highly voyeuristic – point of view of the storyteller: we know the nature of the threat to the unknowing woman in peril, and we look at her. In *Rear Window* (Paramount, 1954) and *Vertigo* (Paramount, 1958), Hitchcock also places his male characters in the position conventionally occupied by the woman in peril, reducing the male to woman's place in the narrative by disabling him.

Like Hitchcock, and perhaps most evidently in western cinema of the 1980s, filmmakers have consciously exploited the audience's familiarity with the narrative place of the woman in peril in ways which arguably allow the woman herself to take up the challenge to her safety and assume control of narrative events. The roles played by Sigourney Weaver in both *Alien* (Ridley Scott, 1979) and *Aliens* (James Cameron, 1986), and by Gena Rowlands in *Gloria* (John Cassavetes, 1980), exemplify this phenomenon. Such a shift, however, does not allow feminist theorists or audiences to reclaim and celebrate the woman in peril in DOMINANT CINEMA. During the late 1980s, the man in peril resurfaced in such Hollywood films as *Jagged Edge* (Richard Marquand, 1985) or *Fatal Attraction* (Adrian Lyne, 1987). However, rather than taking up the male narrative role and springing, a Superwoman, to the rescue and to the resolution of the narrative, in these films Glenn Close's independent women characters are deftly repositioned and re-presented as other derogatory STEREOTYPES: woman as monster in *Fatal Attraction*, and woman as victim – this time of her own sexual weakness and professional misjudgement – in *Jagged Edge*. For feminists, the history of the women in peril in mainstream cinema gives ample reason to suspect that women cannot win.

Linda Williams, 'When the Woman Looks', in *Re-Vision: Essays in Feminist Film Criticism*, eds Patricia Mellencamp, Mary Ann Doane and Linda Williams (Los Angeles: American Film Institute, 1984)   *PB*

WOMEN MAKE MOVIES

A New York City-based nonprofit media arts organization and distributor of films and videos by and about women, Women Make Movies was founded in 1972 as a production collective. It began its FEMINIST DISTRIBUTION service with one of its own productions, *Healthcaring: From Our End of the Speculum* (Denise Bostrom and Jane Warrenbrand, 1977). Recognizing the need for a national organization advocating feminist film and video production and exhibition as well as promoting the diversity of women's film culture, Women Make Movies has expanded its distribution activities since the early 1970s. The current catalogue of more than one hundred and fifty films and videos includes feature films by Sally POTTER, TRINH T Minhha, Michelle CITRON, and Julie DASH as well as documentaries, video art, and animated and experimental films produced by women from all around the world. The organization has also sponsored WOMEN'S FILM FESTIVALS, conferences, and workshops, provides technical assistance to women filmmakers and videomakers, and publishes a newsletter. Since 1984, Women Make Movies has been the only women's film distributor in the USA, maintaining a commitment to increasing access for all women to the means of media production as well as making available feminist media to ever larger audiences.

Felicity Oppé, 'Distribution and Exhibition: The Practices of the Women's Movement', in *The New Social Function of Cinema*, eds Rod Stoneman and Hilary Thompson (London: British Film Institute, 1981)   *PW*

WOMEN'S FILM FESTIVALS

Since 1972–3, when Edinburgh mounted its first special women's cinema event and the FILM FESTIVALS of New York, Paris and Toronto followed quickly with larger events, festivals devoted exclusively to women's films have contributed immeasurably to feminist film culture. In 1972 none of the major women's film JOURNALS yet existed, and there was in print only one pathetically incomplete filmography of 150 women film directors (in *Film*

Comment). Much of the early scholarly research into the history of women filmmakers was thus carried out not in the academy but by organizers and activists. Since then, the women's film festivals which have taken permanent root in many international centers have, at their best, continued to carry out a three-pronged mandate: recovery of lost women filmmakers throughout the history of cinema, exhibition of current films by women and especially of feminist cinema, and fostering of critical and theoretical work on women's films. Otherwise, the flavor and emphasis of women's film festivals varies widely. Los Angeles Women In Film and Video is commercially oriented, with sliding definitions of women's cinema, while the MONTREAL INTERNATIONAL FESTIVAL OF FILMS AND VIDEOS BY WOMEN is rigorously feminist, and CRETEIL (now in its eleventh year) does invaluable archival work in its 'Enthousiasmes et découvertes' section.

See also: COCINA DE IMAGENES; FEMINALE; INCONTRI INTERNAZIONALI DI CINEMA E DONNE; QUEBEC WOMEN'S FILM AND VIDEO FESTIVAL; TORONTO INTERNATIONAL FESTIVAL OF WOMEN'S CINEMA   KA

WOMEN'S FILM FUND

The Women's Film Fund was established in AUSTRALIA as a result of the reallocation of $100,000 originally earmarked for Germaine Greer to make a TV series on reproduction as part of the Gough Whitlam Labor government's contribution to International Women's Year. Three key factors have determined the fund's activities: its relatively minuscule budget in the face of escalating production costs; its administration by the Australian Film Commission (AFC); and its cooption of personnel from the independent sector. Its major initiatives have included surveys into women's position in the industry, and the 1984–5 Women's Film Units. Both initiatives served two

government objectives: the voluntary implementation of affirmative action programs, and the creation of short-term jobs for the long-term unemployed. The fund has been the target for feminist lobbying since its initial allocations of funds to two feature films directed by men: *Caddie* (Donald Crombie, 1976) and *The Picture Show Man* (John Power, 1977). The involvement of Joan Long as scriptwriter on the former and scriptwriter/ producer on the latter provided the only rationale for the fund's substantial contribution to these films. As a result of intensive lobbying by the SYDNEY WOMEN'S FILM GROUP, a full-time administrator was appointed in 1980, and the fund concentrated on putting money into short films likely to return their investment or win awards and/or critical acclaim: *Serious Undertakings* (Helen Grace, 1982), *Ned Wethered* (Lee Whitmore, 1983). The biggest conflict emerged around the fund's conception of INDEPENDENT CINEMA as an apprenticeship for feature filmmaking. This aim was incompatible with feminist criticism of commercial narrative cinema, with the result that terms like 'innovative' and 'experimental' were introduced into the fund's rhetoric; so that, for example, Jane Campion's quirky films (*Peel* [1982], *A Girl's Own Story* [1983], *After Hours* [1984], *Two Friends* [1986]) have been promoted as the cutting edge of experimentation. The success of the Women's Film Units in producing fifteen films under stringent conditions in 1984–5 coincided with the fund's policy review which decided to abolish the fund in 1990.

Annette Blonski, Barbara Creed and Freda Freiberg (eds), *Don't Shoot Darling!* (Melbourne: Greenhouse, 1987)   FC

WOMEN'S FILM, TELEVISION AND VIDEO NETWORK

The Women's Film, Television and Video Network (WFTVN) was set up in BRITAIN in 1983 to campaign for better representions *of* women in the visual media, and better representation *for* women in the media industry as a whole, particularly in technical grades. After initial well-attended London meetings, a London office was set up, followed in 1984 by a network of regional offices thoughout Britain. Funding from various sources, including the Greater London Council (GLC) and CHANNEL FOUR TELEVISION, followed. Much of WFTVN's work was grounded in the immediate and practical – day-schools for girls on working in film and television, 'familiarization' sessions on hitherto male-dominated occupations such as sound recordist, and a 'networking' directory of women working in the industry. But unlike some 'professional feminist' organizations, WFTVN was not concerned simply with career advancement: their approach has always been to link job-based issues to questions of representation.

In 1986, however, when the GLC was closed down by the Conservative government, WFTVN found that the disappearance of a central backer placed its funding in jeopardy. In 1988, London-based arts funding was terminated entirely. Since Channel Four's short-term commitment was not renewed, funded workers and a string of regional offices became a thing of the past for WFTVN. Unlike many GLC-funded projects, however, the organization did not disappear, and continues to be active on a smaller scale, mainly on a regional basis outside London.

The period of WFTVN's greatest activity coincided with a shift in the status of women inside the British film and television industries. Increased numbers of women can now be found in technical grades; most large broadcasting organizations now have a commitment, however token, to equal opportunities; and many more women can be found in the smaller independent television companies formed after the creation of Channel Four. While WFTVN has not been solely responsible for these changes, its importance as the pressure-group arm of FEMINIST INDEPENDENT FILM cannot be underestimated. As well as popularizing the link between images and working practices, WFTVN has played an important role as an industrial irritant, chivvying, persuading, and campaigning for a new attitude toward women in the media.

JRo

WOMEN'S REVENGE FILM

This is a relatively new popular film GENRE, which appears to have emerged in response to a more open public acknowledgement of the problem of rape within the family and society. Like the WESTERN, its concern is with justice and the failure of the law to protect the individual from lawbreakers. Stories typically revolve around male violence, male–female relationships, and the position of women within the law. The resolution of these issues always involves the heroine taking the law into her own hands. The genre is of particular interest to female audiences because the NARRATIVE is organized by the viewpoint of a female protagonist – a figure whose actions transgress socially acceptable notions of appropriate behavior for women. In contrast with, say, the WOMAN'S PICTURE, the heroine of the revenge film is never punished for her deviant behavior.

A look at this genre reveals differences in relation to the representation of rape. In some films, violence enacted against the female victim is depicted in graphic and sometimes voyeuristic detail, as in *I Spit On Your Grave* (Meir Zarchi, 1980), *Lipstick* (Lamont Johnson, 1976), and *Savage Streets* (Danny Steinmann, 1984). Although these films depict the heroine as a strong figure who ultimately takes revenge, it can be argued that the significance of this is undercut by the film's initial voyeuristic and exploitive interest in the plight of the female victim(s).

In other versions, the rape/violence is not filmed voyeuristically – if at all.

Emphasis is primarily on the effects of rape and the problem of male violence against women. In these films (*Violated* [A K Allen, 1984], *Naked Vengeance* [Cirio Santiago, 1985], *Shame* [Steve Jodrell, 1987]), the heroine's revenge is usually violent and deadly. Female AUDIENCES tend to respond very positively to these narratives, which extoll the actions of independent, strong HEROINES. In relation to this cycle, it is interesting to note that women are often involved in the film's making – either at the production or the pre-production stage.

As women's revenge films are usually located in video shops alongside 'male' action and adventure films, it is not clear at what audience they are aimed. It could be argued that this genre is designed to appeal to masochistic desires in the male spectator, and that the avenging heroine is actually another version of the monstrous-feminine in the role of castrating mother – a figure central to the HORROR film. Indeed, castration is often literally carried out on the male victims. If these films are designed to appeal to masochistic desires in the male spectator, then they offer an interesting field for research into theories about male spectatorship and MASCULINITY. In this context, these films may also relate to figures such as the PHALLIC WOMAN found in some types of PORNOGRAPHY. More importantly for female viewers, they raise questions about the representation of women, particularly the strong heroine, and the response of female audiences to her.

Barbara Creed, *The Monstrous-Feminine: Women in the Horror Film* (London and New York: Routledge, forthcoming)

See also: AMAZONS; INDIA; SEXUALITY; WOMEN IN PERIL   BC

WORKING-CLASS WOMEN *see* *ARBEITERFILM*; SOCIALIST REALISM

XIE JIN (1923–)

This director working in the People's Republic of CHINA is renowned for his handling of intricate political themes in tearjerking melodramatic form. Born in eastern Zhejiang, Xie Jin was steeped from his youth in Zhejiang opera and classical Chinese literature. He started acting in patriotic plays in Shanghai in 1938, and later became a student of the dramatists Cao Yu and Hong Shen in the State Theater Institute, where he also read European and Russian literature. In 1950, he attended the Political Research Institute in the Northeastern Revolutionary University to study marxist literary theory. Since 1953, he has been living in Shanghai and directing at the Shanghai Film Studio. Xie Jin's unique synthesis and transformation of Italian NEOREALIST, Hollywood and Russian styles in Chinese MELODRAMA to convey clear political messages was tested in *Wutai Jiemei* (1965), a heartrending story of two women Zhejiang opera singers which earned him the epithet 'bourgeois humanist' and several years' imprisonment during the early years of the Cultural Revolution. Since 1981, Xie Jin's popular melodramas have combined patriotism, sentimentality, and pleas for change, again using women as simultaneously powerful rhetorical figures and subordinate objects of exchange. His local and international fame was quickly

Xie Jin's *Hibiscus Town*

established after *Tianyunshan Chuanqi* (1981) won the first national Golden Rooster Award in China in 1981, and *Wutai Jiemei* won the British Film Institute Award at the 1980 London Film Festival.

The contradictions with regard to women's position in Xie Jin's films are symptomatic of China's ambivalence in this area: there is a strong and persistent advocacy of woman's emancipation and rights, defined mostly in progressive political terms, but the ideal woman who possesses a combination of beauty and virtue is defined in very conservative terms. For this reason, Xie Jin was called a neoConfucianist in a critical controversy in the mid 1980s, and his transparent narrative REALISM has also been challenged by the 'FIFTH GENERATION' of younger filmmakers. Yet the continuing popular appeal of his films to massive rural and urban Chinese audiences does call attention to the inter-related issues of gender, melodrama, revolution and popular reception in Chinese cinema.

Yichang Fengbo/An Incident (co-d. Lin Nong, 1954); *Nulan Wuhao/Woman Basketball Player No. 5* (1957); *Hongse Niangzhijun/The Red Detachment of Women* (1960); *Da Li, Lao Li he Shao Li/Big Li, Old Li, and Small Li* (1962); *Wutai Jiemei/ Two Stage Sisters* (1965); *Haigang/On the Docks* (co-d. Xie Tieli 1972); *Cun Miao/ Cun Miao* (co-d. Yan Bili, Leong Tinfeng, 1975); *Tianyunshan Chuanqi/Legend of Tianyun Mountain* (1981); *Mumaren/ The Herdsman* (1982); *Qiu Jin/Qiu Jin, a Revolutionary* (1983); *Gaoshansha De Huawan/Wreaths At the Foot of the Mountain* (1984); *Furong Zhen/Hibiscus Town* (1987)

Paul Clark, *Chinese Cinema: Culture and Politics Since 1949* (Cambridge: Cambridge University Press, 1987)   EY

YAMASAKI, TIZUKA (1948–)

Tizuka Yamasaki, a BRAZILIAN of Japanese origins, began her career in film as an assistant to Nelson Pereira dos Santos, the 'father' of CINEMA NOVO. Her first film, *Gaijín, caminhos de liberdade* (1980), was an intimate fresco of Japanese immigration to Brazil in the early twentieth century. Yamasaki chooses the private story of one family to point to the general situation. In *Parahyba, mulher macho* (1983), women's sexual freedom becomes a central concern. *Patriamada* (1985) uses documentary footage of the election of Tancredo Neves in 1984, an opening to democracy, as setting for a traditional love triangle between a woman filmmaker, an intellectual, and a politician, with the objective of reflecting the state of the country at large.

Gaijín, caminhos de liberdade/Gaijín, Roads to Freedom (1980); *A embaixada do cinema/ The Cinema's Embassy* (1982); *Parahyba, mulher macho/Parahyba, a Macho Woman* (1983); *Patriamada/Beloved Motherland* (1985)   NT

YANCOVIC, NIEVES (1916–85)

The only woman director in CHILE during the fifties and sixties, Yancovic was previously known as an actress under the name of Nieves Yanco. Born in Antofagasta, she lived in Europe between 1928 and 1942. She was co-founder in 1943 of the Experimental Theater of the University of Chile. Her debut as an actress, in *Romance de medio siglo* (Luis Moglia Barth, 1944), coincided with one of the most active periods of Chilean feature filmmaking. Yancovic also performed in *La amarga verdad* (Carlos Borcosque, 1945), *El padre Pitillo* (Roberto del Ribón, 1946), *El paso maldito* (Fred Matter, 1946), *La dama de la muerte* (Carlos Hugo Christensen, 1946), *El idolo* (Pierre Chenal, 1952) and *Confesión al amanecer* (Pierre Chenal, 1954). She worked behind the camera as an assistant director in the films of Carlos Hugo Christensen and Pierre Chenal. In 1946 she married Jorge di Lauro, an Argentinian sound technician, and directed documentaries with him from 1958 onward. Most of her work was sponsored by state agencies, but Yancovic and di Lauro used documentary as an art form. *Andacollo* (1958), particularly, made an impact on the development of socially committed documentary in Chile. Their last film was made for Chile Films in 1972, but was never released. After the military coup that overthrew the socialist government of Salvador Allende in 1973, they worked as teachers. Her expansive personality made her the leading member of the Yancovic–di Lauro team, and she was much admired by her contemporaries and by the younger filmmakers who sought her advice.

Andacollo (1958); *Los artistas chilenos plásticos* (1959–60); *Isla de Pascua* (1961); *Verano en invierno* (1962); *San Pedro de Atacama* (1963–4); *Cuando el pueblo avanza* (1966); *Operación Sitio* (1970); *Obreros campesinos* (1972). All co-directed with Jorge di Lauro

Alicia Vega, *Re-visión del cine chileno* (Santiago: Editorial Aconcagua, 1979)
                                  ZP

ZETTERLING, MAI (1925–)

Born in SWEDEN, Mai Zetterling began her career as a stage actress, and was offered her first screen role in 1941. She turned to filmmaking in the 1960s. Her film acting career includes *Frenzy* (Alf Sjöberg, 1944) and *Musik i mörker/Night Is My Future* (Ingmar Bergman, 1948), as well as a number of roles in British films, such as *The Ringer* (Guy Hamilton, 1952), *Desperate Moments* (Compton Bennett, 1953), *Faces in the Dark* (David Eady, 1961). Zetterling's career as a filmmaker began with a series of documentaries for the BBC and an allegorical

short film, *The War Game* (1963), which received a prize in Venice. In the 1970s she returned to documentary filmmaking for several years. Her first full-length feature, *Alskande par*, appeared in 1964. It is a very personal adaptation of several novels by Agnes von Krusenstjerna, a Swedish writer of the first half of the twentieth century famous for her treatment of lesbianism, which Zetterling has also chosen to portray in her latest film, *Amarosa* (1986). Zetterling, particularly in these two films, concentrates on themes such as women's sexuality, problems in reaching maturity, and madness. In 1966 Zetterling brought her own

Mai Zetterling (with cinematographer Sven Nykvist) directing *Loving Couples*

novel, *Natt lek*, to the screen; and in 1982 made a fiction film in semi-documentary style, *Scrubbers*, about young women prisoners. Feminist concerns and an often polemical tone have marked all of Zetterling's work.

The full-length features directed by Zetterling are: *Alskande par/Loving Couples* (1964); *Natt lek/Night Games* (1966); *Doktor Glas/Doctor Glas* (1968); *Flickorna/The Girls* (1969); *Scrubbers* (1982); *Amarosa/Amorosa* (1986)

Louise Heck–Rabi, *Women Filmmakers: A Critical Reception* (Metuchen, NJ: Scarecrow Press, 1984)   *ASW*

TRIVIA
ANSWERS

Page
6   A beautiful sixteenth-century Hungarian noblewoman, primary historical source for the female vampire film
16   'The putting into discourse of "woman" as . . . intrinsic to the conditions of modernity' is discussed by Alice Jardine in her book *Gynesis: Configurations of Woman and Modernity*
21   Pauline Kael
24   Cultural critic Susan Sontag
37   Film criticism
40   Semanalysis
51   Feminist documentary
52   Women's revenge
54   'Visual Pleasure and Narrative Cinema', by Laura Mulvey, published in *Screen* in 1975
56   For the silhouette animations she had devised
58   A cartoon spy-pigeon in Fred Tashlin's World War II propaganda cartoons
62   Sadomasochism
67   *Frauen und Film*
71   *Maenner/Men*
81   Asta Nielsen
88   Australian
90   The US avant-garde
94   Yvonne Rainer
107 Judy Holliday
113 Opera
116 The 'Carry On' series of films
123 Jean Harlow
128 Doris Day
131 Sarah Maldoror
135 The Big Five Hollywood studios used this system to reserve first distribution of their films to deluxe theaters, the majority of which were owned by the Big Five
137 To the Roxy Picture Palace, New York

146 *Gold Diggers of 1933*
150 Greta Garbo
158 Alice Guy
160 Femininity as masquerade
163 Dance
175 Irish filmmaker Pat Murphy
182 The film critic Bryher
199 Soviet director Dinara Asanova
203 Olga Preobrazhenskaia
205 The film journal *Camera Obscura*
211 South African
216 It is the first full-length commercial feature film in South Africa to be scripted and directed by a woman
222 The vamp
229 Celia Johnson in *Brief Encounter*
231 Mexican
233 Simple-minded Maria
240 Lois Weber
244 Claire Johnston
253 C A Lejeune
258 Nature documentaries
265 Vivien Leigh
271 *Uncle Tom's Cabin*, by Harriet Beecher Stowe
276 *Imitation of Life*, its heroine a black domestic servant
283 Nina Fonoroff
292 Nell Shipman
300 *Maedchen in Uniform*
309 Elvira Notari
315 *Thriller* by Sally Potter
317 She gave birth onscreen to her own baby
321 Lillian Gish
329 Carmen Miranda
338 Colette
342 Brazilian
347 Screwball comedy
351 The 'woman of the land' of South African cinema
353 *Cinemien*, in the Netherlands
362 *De Stilte Rond Christine M/A Question of Silence*, Marleen Gorris

368 *Born in Flames*, Lizzie Borden
374 Kinuyo Tanaka
378 Music
387 French silent star Musidora in
     Louis Feuillade's popular adven-
     ture serial *Les Vampires* (1915–16)
393 Brigitte Bardot, who inspired
     'bardolâtrie'

398 France
400 *Johanna d'Arc of Mongolia*
408 The 'Fifth Generation' group
416 The mythological genre
422 Science fiction film
425 Video

INDEX of films directed, written or produced by women

Page numbers in *italic* refer to the illustrations

A & B in Ontario, 426
A corps perdu, 318
A.E.I., 254
A hjara veraldar, 211, 227
A holdudvar, 262
'A Legge, 299
'A mala nova, 299
A Marechiaro ce sta 'na fenesta, 299
A Piedigrotta, 299
A primera vista, 83
'A Santanotte, 299
AAA Offresi, 223
Die Abenteuer des Prinzen Achmed, 337, 338
Abortion Problems in France, 8
Abortion Stories North and South, 369
Abortproblem i Frankrike, 8
About Overtime and Voluntary Labor, 179
About Something Else, 81, 107
About the Verb to Love, 39
About Transport, 390
Abschenputtel, 338
Abstract film No. 11, 141
Abstonic, 60
Acaso irreparable, 265
L'accalappiacani, 299
Acting Out, 86
Acuarela, 170
Addio mia bella addio . . . l'armata se ne va . . ., 299
Ademloos, 287
Adjungkierte Dislokationen, 142
Adolescent Sweet Love, 239
Adoption, 209, 262
The Adventurer, 185
The Adventures of Prince Achmed, 337, 338

Affair in Berlin, 68
L'Affiche, 137
After Hours, 430
After the Verdict, 339
After Twenty Years, 136
Afwan Ayouha Al Kanoun, 134
Ahava Rishona, 37
Aimé Césaire, le masque des mots, 253
Ajolanto, 297
Aktorzy prowincjonalni, 201
Al di la' del bene e del male, 68
An Algorithm, 179
All For Mary, 402, 403
All Lit Up, 38
All my Girls, 183, 184
The All-round Reduced Personality, 351
All Screwed Up, 421
All the Way Up There, 326
Alla Luigi XIV, 299
Alle meine Maedchen, 183, 184
Álljon meg a menet!, 186
Die allseitig reduzierte Persoenlichkeit, 351
Den allvarsamma leken, 52
Alone in the World, 419
Alskande par, 437
Alternative Information in Italy, 313
Altitude 3200, 136–7
Am I Normal, 289
The Amazing Equal Pay Show, 246
Ame d'artiste, 127
Amensuensis, 341
American Aristocracy, 248
American Graffiti, 195
The Americano, 248

Amerika Klassenverhaeltnisse, 208
Ames d'enfants, 137
Ames de fous, 126, 127
Les Âmes du soleil, 146
Le amiche, 17, 69
Amisk, 302
Among Grey Stones, 274
Among Noisy Sheep, 125
Amorosa, 436, 437
Amuhuelai-Mi, 254
Amy, 273
Ana, 96
Anastasie oh ma chérie, 329
Anatomy of Love, 69
And If We Speak of August, 395
And We've Got 'Sabor', 178
And What Does Your Mommy Do?, 83
And You Act Like One, Too, 358, 359
Andacollo, 435
Ander and Yul, 381
The Angel of Broadway, 419
Angel Of the Junk Heap, 326
Angelan sota, 40, 41
Angela's War, 41
Angeles, 172
Angelika Urban, Sales Assistant, Engaged, 352
Angelika Urban, Verkaeuferin, Verlobt, 352
Angels of Light, 87
Der Angestellte, 19, 352
Angry Harvest, 202
Ania, 325
Animal Farm, 37, 38

The Animals and the Lawn
  Mower, 326
Animation for Live
  Action, 288
Animus, Parts I and
  II, 213
Anna, 40, 262
Anna Christie, 270
Anne Devlin, 274, 275,
Anne Trister, 83, 318
Annie Mae, Brave Hearted
  Woman, 282
Ansikter, 52
Ansprache Ausprache, 141
Antigone, 388
Antonia's Life, 180
Anybody's Woman, 25
Anything You Want To
  Be, 289
The Apple Game, 81
The Apple Tree of
  Paradise, 354
April 3, 1973, 87
April, April I Love
  You, 184
Aqui Espana, 270
Arabesque for Kenneth
  Anger, 260, 261
Araya, 40
The Arch 206
Arctic Oil Spills, 369
Arequipa, 188
Arinka, 380
Army Nurse, 78, 157
Arne Bendik Sjur, 52
Gli arrivederci, 299
Ars Lucis, 141
Arthur et Rosa, 227
Artie Shaw: Time Is All
  You've Got, 63
Artificial Paradise, 83
Los artistas chilenos
  plásticos, 435
Arven, 52
The Ascent, 364
Asemie, 142
L'aspirant, 85
The Ass and the Stick, 38
At Eltham, 64
At the End of Summer,
  315
At First Glance, 83

At First Sight, 37, 166,
  346
At Land 117, 117, 118
At One Hundred and Fifty
  Km an Hour, 224
At One O'clock, 364
At the Roads End, 248
At Uluru, 64
L'atelier du diable, 308
Atención pre-natal año
  uno, 179
Atlantic Story, 224
Audience, 188
Auf + Zu + Ab +
  An, 141
Gli augurali, 299
Aurélia Steiner, 128
Auschwitz, 390
Ausdatiertes Material, 195
Australian Dream, 30
Automat 'Svět', 81
Avskedet, 297

Baara, 85
Bab Ala Al Sama, 272
Baby riazanskie, 325
Bachelor Girl, 30, 337
Back to God's Country, 62,
  364, 365, 401
The Backbay Mainline, 368
Backwards Somersault, 184
The Bad Sister, 273
Bagatelle for Willard
  Maas, 261
A Bagful of Fleas, 81
Bakh, 188
Balance of Terror, 163
The Ballad of Therese, 8
Balladen om Therese, 8
Ballerina e buffoncello, 299
Ballettens boern, 196
Ballo delle farfalle, 299
La Banque Némo, 164
Barbara's Blindness, 426
Il barcaioulo d'Amalfi, 299
Baree, Son of Kazan, 364,
  365
Barndommens gade, 196
Baryshnia-krestianka, 325
I basilischi, 421
Bastion Point, 268
Baxter, Vera Baxter, 128

Be a Man – Sell Out!, 163
The Beach under the
  Sidewalk, 352
The Beachcomber, 49
Bebé in giardino, 299
Bebé in salotto, 299
Bebé va a letto, 299
Bebé vi saluta, 299
The Bed, 188
Beda, 25
Bedtime Stories I, II &
  III, 188
Before the Time
  Comes, 316
Der Beginn aller Schrecken
  ist Liebe, 351
Behind Closed Doors, 393
Behind the Mask, 185
Behind the Veil, 419
Behind the Windows, 130
Beirut My Town, 239
La Belle dame sans
  merci, 127
Bellissima, 69
Beloved Motherland, 178,
  435
Beneath the Czar, 185
Bent Time, 188
Beresford Street Primary
  School, 326
Berlin, 390
The Berlin Apartment, 64
Die Beruehrte, 352
Besetzung und
  Selbstverwaltung eines
  Studentenwohneheims,
  313
Die Betoenung der blauen
  Matrosen, 306
Better Than Cure, 196
Betteshanger, Kent, 246
Between the Lines, 368,
  369
Das Bewaffnete Auge, 142
The Bewitchment of
  Drunken Sailors, 306
Beyond Death, 360
Beyond Good and Evil, 68
Beyond the Door, 68
Beyrouth ma ville, 239
Bez Milosci, 354
Bez znieczulenia, 202

Bialy Mazur, 224
The Bicycle, 130
Bicycle Thieves, 69
Big, 256
The Big Bath Night, 132
Big City Vampires, 8
Big Story, 163
The Bigamist, 249
Bihar El Atache, 134
Bildnis einer Trinkerin –
  aller jamais retour, 306
Bill's Hat, 426
Bimbo, 96
Binding Sentiments, 262
Bingo, Bridesmaids and
  Braces, 22
Birds at Sunrise, 426
Bita, 218
Bittere Ernte, 201
Bitva na nashu Sovietskaiu
  Ukrainu, 374
De blå undulater, 196
The Black Angustias, 233
The Black Dog, 119
The Black Hills Are Not
  For Sale, 282
Black Panthers, 411
Black Shack Alley, 83, 308
A Blade of Grass in Kunlun
  Mountains, 78
Een blandt mange, 196
Die blaue Distanz, 267
Das blaue Licht, 184, 341
Die bleierne Zeit, 405
Ein Blick – und die Liebe
  bricht aus, 58
Blind Endeavour, 186
Blonde of the Follies, 248
Blood and Sand, 24
Blood Bath, 348
Blood Feud, 421
Blood of the Walsungs, 297
Blossoms in the Dust, 248
The Blot, 418, 419
Blott en dröm, 201
The Blue Distance, 267
The Blue Light, 184, 341
The Blue Mountains
  Mystery, 250
Blue Scar, 99
The Boat People, 206
Body Politics, 142

Bolly, 38
Le Bonheur, 411–12
A Bonus for Irene, 351
Boom Babies, 220
Borderline (HD, Bryher
  and Macpherson), 193
Borderlines (Gogoberidze),
  177
Les Borges, 254
Boris Godunov, 380
Born by the Storm, 390
Born in Flames, 47, 49, 82,
  178, 243
Borrowed Clothes, 419
Both 1 & 2, 74
Both Sides of the Law, 49
Bouddi, 64
Boy from the Taiga, 325
The Boy Who Saw
  Through, 60
The Boys Next Door, 140,
  382
Der Braeutigam, die
  Komoediantin und der
  Zuhalter, 207
Bread and Honey, 221
Bread from Our
  Mountains, 383
Breathless, 287
Brecht die Macht der
  Manipulateure, 351
Brickmakers 92, 344
The Bride Wore Red, 25
The Bridegroom, the
  Comedienne and the
  Pimp, 207
The Bridge: A Story Of
  Men In Dispute, 269
Bridges Go Round, 87
Bright City, 325
Broder Carl, 374, 375
Bröderna Mozart, 305, 305
Broken Mirrors, 180, 180
Brother Carl, 374, 375
The Brotherhood of the
  Most Holy, 351
The Brothers, 49
Bruxelles 'Loops', 87
Budujemy, 224
Budujemy nowe Wsie, 224
Los Buenromero, 265
Bufera d'anime, 299

Bukovina – Ukrainian
  Land, 374
Bukovina – zemlia
  ukrainskaia, 374
Bullfight, 87
Buona sera piccante, 299
Buone feste, 299
Burei rozhdionnie, 390
The Burning Wolf, 40
Buscando caminos, 84
The Bushwackers, 250
But No One, 168
By Design, 163
By the Steep Ravine, 274
Bygones, 287

The Cabbage Fairy, 184
Cadavres en vacances, 27
Caddie, 430
Café Bar, 119
The Cages, 354
Calamity, 81
Caliph Stork, 338
Calling the Shots, 91
Camargue, det forlorade
  landet, 8
Camargue – the Lost
  Country, 8
Camila, 39, 40
Camille without
  Camellias, 17, 69
Le Camion, 128
La campagnola, 299
I campagnuoli, 299
Campesinos, 344
Cananea, 155
The Candidate, 85
The Candlemaker, 38
Cani, 207
I cannibali, 68
The Cannibals, 68
Cannon Fodder, 288
Capri incantevole, 299
La Caraque blonde, 27
The Career of Waterloo
  Peterson, 419
Carl Ruggles' Christmas
  Breakfast, 354
Carmela la pazza, 299
Carmela la sartina di
  Montesanto, 299
Carmen, 338

Carmen Carrascal, 83–4, 83
Carnival in the Clothes Cupboard, 38
Carry Greenham Home, 198
Carry on Milkmaids, 38
La carta de deberes y derechos, 265
Čas je neúprosný, 81
La casa del ángel, 183
La casa in Italia, 68
Cash on Delivery, 49
Castles of Sand, 67
A Cat Has Nine Lives, 388
Catfood, 426
Cattura di un pazzo a Bagnoli, 299
Ceiling, 81
Celia, 30, 337
The Central Character, 182, 183
Central Times and Noyes 179
C'est la faute d'Adam, 27
C'est pas le pays des merveilles, 416
The Challenge, 69
Change of Fortune, 274
Chaperons rouges, 182, 416
A Chapter in Her Life, 419
Charley series, 38
The Chasm, 297
The Cheap One and the Good One, 136
The Cheaters, 258
Cheloviek s kinoaparatom, 390
Chéri, 91
Il cherubino, 299
Les Chevaux du Vercors, 27
Chiarina la modista, 299
The Chief, 163
A Child's Sacrifice, 185
Children are not Cattle, 351
Children of Desired Sex, 278
Chilly Scenes of Winter, 368, 369
China – The Arts – Everyday Life, 307

China – Die Kuenste – Der Alltag, 306, 307
A China Memoir, 419
Chircales, 92, 344
Christmas at Moose Factory, 302
Christopher Strong, 13, 24, 25, 65, 70
Chronick der Anna Magdalena Bach, 207, 208
The Chronicle of Anna Magdalena Bach 207, 208
Chto ty vybral, 25
The Church and the Woman, 250
The Chusovaia River, 390
Chuzhie pisma, 379
Ciccio, il pizzaioulo del Carmine, 299
Cielo celeste, 299
Cielo 'e Napule, 299
La Cigarette, 127
A Cigarette, That's All, 419
Cinderella, 338
The Cinema's Embassy, 435
Cinetruth, 390
Cinq jours d'une vie, 85
Cities in Crisis: What's Happening, 350
The City Girl, 96
La ciudad perdida, 381
La ciudad, positivo y negativo, 170
Class Relations, 208
Classic Fairy Tales series, 38
Classified People, 138
Cléo de 5 à 7, 411
Cleo From 5 to 7, 411
The Clothes Are Old, 348
Co-existence, 186
Le Cœur de Paris, 136, 137
Cœur Fidèle, 136, 137
Cœurs flambés, 348
A Cold Draft, 341
Coleçao de marfil, 13
Colombi e birichino, 299
Colombi viaggiatori, 299
Colombo Plan, 38

The Color Purple, 45
Colossal Love, 58
Colours of Love, 224
Comment ça va, 177
Committed, 72, 82, 83
A Commonplace Story, 135, 136
The Commonwealth, 38
The Company of Wolves, 53
Complicato intrigo di donne vicoli e delitti, 421
Comptines, 182
Confusion, 177
Conmigo las pasaras muy bien, 300
The Connection, 87
Conozco a las tres, 394
The Constant Nymph, 339
Contact, 38
Conversation Piece, 69
Conversations with Eugene Ionesco, 113
Cookie, 359
Cool Hands Warm Heart, 168
The Cool World, 87
La Coquille et le clergyman, 127
Coração de madre, 2
Core é frate, 299
Coś za coś, 201
Cosa de mujeres, 265
Coscritto, 299
Cosi piange Pierrot, 299
Council Matters, 240
The Country of the Soviets, 365
Coup de foudre, 166, 346
Cours de bonheur conjugal, 27
Court in Smolensk, 365
Covert Action, 74
Craig's Wife, 25
Cream Soda, 90, 91
Les Créatures, 412
The Creatures, 412
Creeps on the Crescent, 326
El crimen de Cuenca, 267
The Criminal Woman, 162
Crónica de una señora, 39
Cronica del olvido, 265

Crops and Robbers, 240
Crossing Delancey, 368, 369
Crossroads, 377
The Cruel Embrace, 188
Crush the Power of the Manipulators, 351
The Cruz Brothers and Mrs Malloy, 44
Crystal Gazing, 273
Cuando el pueblo avanza, 435
Cuando una mujer no duerme, 104
Cucú setté, 299
The Cuenca Crime, 267
Cuentos eróticos, 270
La cuisine rouge, 330
Cuoco Sansone, 299
A Cure for Suffragettes, 248
Cutting, 140, 141
Cykledrengene i torvegraven, 196

Dagbork van een Oude Dwaas, 287
Daguerréotypes, 412
Daisies, 81
Dalla Nube alla Resistenza, 207
Dam the Delta, 38
Damned If You Don't, 168
Dance, Girl, Dance, 13, 24, 25, 110, 312
Dance In Chains, 224
Dance in the Sun, 87
Dansk politi i Sverige, 196
De danske sydhavsoer, 196
Danton, 202
Dat's Show Biz, 326
Daughter Rite, 80, 86, 86, 153
The Daughters' Inheritance, 58, 352, 388
Daughters of the Dust, 112
David: Off and On, 96
Day 507, 268
Day Longer than Night, 177
Day of Freedom: Our Armed Forces, 341

Daylight Test Section, 74
Days in the Trees, 128
Dazwischen, 125
De cierta manera, 153, 178, 178, 179, 371, 373
De encaje y azucar, 300
De mère en fille, 315
De pokkers unger, 196
De todos modos Juan te llámas, 155
Dear Address!, 186
Dear, Dearest, Beloved, Only One, 25
Debiutantka, 354
The Debut, 410, 411
Het Debuut, 410, 411
The Decision, 288
The Decline of Western Civilization, 382
The Decline of Western Civilization: Part II – The Metal Years, 382
Deficit, 359
Délibábok országa, 262
Delta: Ein Stueck, 142
Demain, la cinquantaine, 416
Den dlinnee nochi, 177
Denmark Grows Up, 196
Departed Love in the Evening, 156
Department of the Interior, 163
Depraved, 300
Depth of Filmed, 295
Derry Video News, 118
Des fusils pour Banta, 253
Des journées entières dans les arbres, 128
Desde el cristal con que se mira, 265
Desert Hearts, 83, 114, 122, 243, 346, 363
Desperately Seeking Susan, 358, 359
A Dessert for Constance, 253
Un dessert pour Constance, 253
Destroy, She Said, 128
Détective, 177
Détruire, dit-elle, 128
De Deur va het Huis, 287

Deutschland, bleiche Mutter, 290, 352
The Devil's Workshop, 308
Diablillos del arrabal, 361
Diary for My Children, 209, 261, 261, 262
Diary for My Loves, 131, 262
Diary of an African Nun, 111, 112
Diary of a Maasai Village, 138
The Diary of an Old Fool, 287
Did You Finish School?, 388
Diez años después, 84
A Different Image, 44
Digging for Victory, 38
The Dinkum Bloke, 250
Discontent, 419
Discussion Club, 136
Les dites cariatides, 7p., cuis., s. de b., à saisir, 411
Ditte, Child of Man, 196
Ditte Menneskebarn, 196
Divine, 91
Divine Horsemen, 117–18
Divorce Problems in Italy, 8
Do Right and Fear Nobody, 58
Do You Know 'Sunday–Monday'?, 186
The Doctor and the Woman, 419
Dr Elizabeth, 163
Doctor Glas, 437
Dr Holl, 189
Doctor, Lawyer, Indian Chief, 283
Document, 163
Un documental a propósito del transito, 179
A Documentary About Mass Transit, 179
Documenteur, 412
Does the Pill Liberate?, 351
Doktor Glas, 437
Dokumentation, 195

Dokumente zum
  Internationalen
  Aktionismus, 142
Dolgiie proshchaniia, 274
Dolgiye provody, 379
Doll House (Hammer),
  188
Doll's Eye, 56, 372
A Doll's House (Molina),
  270
The Doll's House
  (Niskanen), 297
Dolly Put the Kettle
  On, 38
Una domenica sera di
  novembre, 421
Donde voy a encontrar otra
  Violeta, 254
Dong Furen, 206
The Donna, 297
La donna nella Resistenza,
  68
Don't Call Me Girlie, 22
Don't Cry, Pretty
  Girls, 262
A Door on the Sky, 272
Doppelprojektion I, 195
Doppelprojektion
  II–IV, 195
Dorian Gray im Spiegel der
  Boulevardpresse, 306–7,
  306
Dorian Gray in the Mirror
  of the Popular
  Press, 306–7, 306
Le Double amour, 137
Double Strength, 188
The Dove on the Roof, 184
Down to Earth, 248
Dragons, Dreams – and a
  Girl from Reality, 8
Drakar, drümmar och en
  flicka från verkligheten, 8
Draw Me a Circle, 326
Dream of a Free Country:
  A Message from
  Nicaraguan Women, 363
Dreaming Rivers, 44, 67
Dresden Dynamo, 341
The Drip, 221
Dripping Water, 426
Drips and Strips, 261

The Drover's Wife, 31
The Drunkard, 2
A Dry White Season, 308
Du Côté de la Côte, 411
Du Verbe Aimer, 39
Dudes, 382
Duet for Cannibals, 374,
  375
Duie Paravise, 299
The Dumb Girl of
  Portici, 419
The Durability of
  Memory, 136
Dust, 187, 188
Dustbin Parade, 37, 38
Dwightiana, 261
Dyketactics, 188
Dziewczeta z
  Nowolipek, 354

E' piccerella, 299
Each Other, 37
Earth, 373
Earth Message, 64
The Earthquake, 352
L'École des cocottes, 27
Eel History Is A
  Mystery, 255
Eelemani: The Story of Leo
  and Leva, 1
Egami, 337
Eggs, 188
Egy kicsit én . . . egy kicsit
  te . . ., 186
Egyszerú történet, 135, 136
Együttélés, 186
8½, 421
Eikon, 64
Einer muss die Leiche
  sein, 184
Einleitung zu Arnold
  Schoenbergs Begleitmusik
  zu einer
  Lichtspielszene, 207
Eleonora, 270
Eleven Women, 398
Elsa la rose, 411
Eltávozott nap, 262
A embaixada do
  cinema, 435
The Ember, 271
Emergence, 45

Az emlékezet
  tartóssága, 136
Empathy, 163
Employment
  Discriminations: The
  Troubleshooters, 96
The Empress, 185
Empty Suitcases, 179
En el pais de los pies ligeros
  o el Niño Raramuri, 155
En la otra isla, 178
Én nem is láttam ilyet, de
  nem is csináltam, 136
¿En que estamos?, 84
En rachachant, 208
The Enchanted Arts:
  Pablita Velarde, 282
The Enchanted Desna, 374
Encounter, 135
El Encuentro, 265
The End of Our
  World, 224
The End of the World in
  Our Usual Bed in a
  Night Full of Rain, 421
Endangered, 188
Enemy Paths, 325
L'enfant aimé, 10
The Engagement Party, 267
Ensemble for
  Sonnambulists, 118
Enthusiasm, 390
Entre nous, 5
An Equal Opportunity, 239
Equilibre, 188
Der er noget i luften, 196
Die Erbtoechter, 58, 352,
  388
Das Erdbeben in Chile, 352
Erikas Leidenschaft, 387,
  388
Erika's Passion, 388
L'eroismo di un aviatore a
  Tripoli, 299
Das erste Recht des
  Kindes, 189
Der erste Walzer, 124–5
Es premera vez, 300
Escapade, 130
Escape, 60
Eshteghal-e-Mohojereen
  Roustai, 34, 35

Espontanea belleza, 265
Esquilache, 270
Et brev til en son, 196
Et minde om to
   mandage, 196
L'eta' di Stalin, 68
L'evangile à
   Solentiname, 254
Even As You and I, 419
Evening at Abdon's, 201
Evening Performance, 270
Evening Star, 60
Every Revolution is a
   Throw of Dice, 207
Every Wednesday, 186
Except the People, 74
Excursion, 261
Excursion a
   Vueltabajo, 178
Execution – A Study of
   Mary, 267
Eye Music in Red
   Major, 261
The Eyes of God, 419
The Eyes of the Soul, 319
Eyewitness, 49

Få mig att skratta, 8
Facing a Family, 142
Fad Jal, 146
Fagyöngyök, 136
Das Fahrrad, 130
The Fall of the Romanov
   Dynasty, 365
False Colors, 419
False Friends, 119
Faludy György Költo, 186
Eine Familie Braun, 337
Ein Familienfilm von
   Waltraut Lehner, 141
Familienglueck, 19
Family Business, 10
Fantasia 'e surdato, 299
I fantasmi del fallo, 223
Far from Vietnam, 411
The Far Paradise, 258, 259
The Far Road, 226
The Far Shore, 63, 426
Farahang-e-Massraffi, 35
The Farewell (Niskanen),
   297
Farewell (Shepitko), 364

Farewell to Africa, 297,
   298
Farewell to Charms, 337
Farewell to the Devil, 224
Farewell to Winter, 130
Fascism Will Be
   Defeated, 365
Fascist Atrocities, 390
Fashions for Women, 24
Fashizm budet razbit, 365
Fast Times, 140
La fata di Borgo
   Loreto, 299
The Fatal Wedding, 250
Fate, 288
The Father, 200, 201,
   391
Fatma '75, 83, 406
Fatto di sangue tra due
   uomini per causa di una
   vedova, 421
Faunovo příliš pozdní
   odpolende, 81
La Fée aux choux, 184
Felix, 352, 405–6
Fem dagar in Falköping, 8
The Female of the
   Species, 419
The Feminists Have
   Arrived, 83
La femme au foyer, 353
La femme de l'hôtel, 318
La Femme du Gange, 128
Les femmes de l'Amérique
   latine, 254
Femmes de rêves . . ., 182
Fenesta ca lucive, 299
Feng Jie, 206
Ferai, 8
Festival folclórico de
   Fomeque, 350–1
La Fête espagnole, 126, 127
Le Feu de paille, 137
Fever, 201
La Fiancée du pirate, 372
Fiddlers of Names Bay, 369
Fiela se Kind, 198, 199,
   377
Fiela's Child, 198, 199,
   377
Fields of Endless Days, 163
Fiesta, 270

The Fifth Chair, 339
58 Seconds, 186
Fifty-Fifty, 337
Fight for our Soviet
   Ukraine, 374
La figlia del vesuvio, 299
Figlio del reggimento, 299
The Figurehead, 38
Une fille de ma gang, 182
Les filles du roy, 315–16,
   329
Filling the Gap, 38
Film About a Woman Who
   . . ., 172, 334
Film d'amore e
   d'anarchia, 421
Film for Discussion, 393
Filmraum:
   Reproduktionsimmanente
   Aesthetik, 195
La fin des Étés, 315
Finding Our Own Faces,
   66
Finye, 85
Fire in a Concrete
   Box, 275
Fire Film, 295
First Comes Courage, 24,
   25
First Line of Defence, 38
First Love, 37
The First 99, 38
The First Waltz, 125
Fisher's Ghost, 250
The Five, 38
Five Days in a Life, 85
Five Days in Falköping, 8
5 Out of 5, 74
Five Years of the
   Metro, 390
Flamberende hjerter, 348
Flamenco at 5.15, 330
La Flamme cachée, 277
Flavia, 295
Flickorna, 437
The Flirt, 419
Las flores, 344
Floterian – Hand Paintings
   From A Film History, 64
Flowers, 344
Fluegel und Fesseln, 352
Fly About the House, 38

Flyktningar finnar en
 hamm, 196
Folletto di fiamma, 299
Fomeque Folk Festival
 350–1
The Fool and His
 Money, 419
Foothills, 193
For Better For Worse, 38
For Husbands Only, 419
For Love or Money, 31,
 393
For the First Time, 300
For Women – Chapter
 1, 313
Forbidden, 419
Forfolgelsen, 52
Forraederiet, 196
Fortini, 207
40,000 Horsemen, 29–30,
 73
Foto-Film, 195
Fotografia a sorspresa, 299
Foundling, 379
Four Journeys Into Mystic
 Time, 87
4000 Frames, An
 Eye-Opener Film, 64
Four Women, 84,
 109, 111, 112
14's Good, 18's Better, 22
Fra le stelle, 299
Fragment of an Empire, 379
Fran, 29
France/tour/détour/
 deux/enfants, 177
Francesco d'Assisi, 68
Fratelli, 223
Eine Frau mit
 Verantwortung, 387–8
Frauen hinter der
 Kamera, 312, 313
Die Frauen von
 Harrisburg, 313
Freak Orlando. Kleines
 Welttheater in fuenf
 Episoden, 306, 312
Freak Orlando: Small
 Theatre of the World in
 Five Episodes, 306, 312
Free Stone, 183
The French Downstairs, 419

Frida and Tina, 273
Frihetens murar, 8
Fröken Julie, 201
From the Cloud to the
 Resistance, 207
From the Cradle Endlessly
 Rocking, 60
Das Fruehstueck der
 Hyaene, 266, 267
Fruits amers, 27
Fuer Frauen – 1.
 Kapitel, 312, 313
Fuerchten und Liebe, 406
Fuga del gatto, 299
Fugard's People, 297, 298
Funcion de noche, 270
Fuses, 354
Fussball, 195
Fusswaschung, 195
The Future of Emily, 352
The Future of Saint Denis,
 253

Gabriel Goes to the
 City, 302
Gabriele il lampionaio del
 porto, 299
Gaijín, caminhos de
 liberdade, 435
Gaijín, Roads to
 Freedom, 435
Galathea, 338
Galileo, 68
La gallinita ciega, 170
Game, 74
Games of Love and
 Loneliness, 52
Gamle, 52
Ein ganz perfektes
 Ehepaar, 387, 388
Ein ganz und gar
 verwahrlostes
 Maedchen, 58
La Garçonne, 27
Gary Cooper que estas en
 los cielos, 267
Gary Cooper Who Art in
 Heaven, 267
La gata, 381
El gato montes, 381
Il gattopardo, 69
Gebrokene Spiegels, 180

Gelati, 177
The Generation of
 Conquerors, 379
Genetics, Animation
 Allegation, 287
Gengeninformation in
 Italien, 313
Gennariello il figlio del
 galeotto, 299
Gennariello
 polizziotto, 299
Gens de toutes parts, gens de
 nulle part, 353
Gentili signore, 223
Gentlemen Prefer
 Blondes, 248, 386
Gently Down the Stream,
 167, 167, 168, 242–3
The German Sisters, 405
Germany, Pale
 Mother, 290, 352
Germination d'un
 haricot, 127
Geschichten von
 Kuebelkind, 388
Geschichtsunterricht, 207
Gesichtsgrimassen, 141
Gesu' mio fratello, 68
Get Your Man, 24
Getting Ready, 242
Getting to Know the Wide
 World, 274
Getulio Vargas, 67
Gewalt, 352
Gezocht: Lieve Vader en
 Moeder, 286
Ghafferi An
 Khataouki, 133
Ghaire aze Khoudo Hitch
 Kasse Naboud, 218
Ghazi El Banat, 239
Gigi, 27, 91, 248
Ginger Mick, 250
Giocare d'azzardo, 223
Il giorno della pace, 68
Giovanni, 287
The Girl, 85, 261, 262
The Girl Friends, 17, 69
The Girl From God's
 Country, 365
Girl In Red, 78
Girlfriends, 96, 419

The Girls, 437
Girls at 12, 80
The Girls From
  Nowolipek, 354
Girls' Night Out, 15
A Girl's Own Story, 430
Give Us a Smile, 240
Glimpse of the
  Garden, 260, 261
Glooscap Country, 63, 281
Gloria ai caduti, 299
Gnesella, 299
Go! Go! Go!, 261
Goblins of the Mind, 388
God Bless America, 195
God's Country and the
  Woman, 364, 365
The Gold Diggers, 56,
  260, 322, 323, 323
The Golden Calf, 162
A Golden Couple, 104
The Golden Eighties, 10,
  277, 358
The Golden Gate, 374
The Golden Stuff, 388
The Golden Yukon, 365
Das goldene Dig, 388
Goldwood, 363
Golven, 287
Golyamoto Noshtno
  Kupane, 132
Gongola, 188
Goob na nu, 146
Good-for-Nothing, 25
Goraça Linia, 224
Goraczka, 201
Gossette, 126, 127
Gotta Run!, 297
Gracias a la vida, 75
Grain of the Voice series,
  64
Un grand Amour de
  Balzac, 27
The Grand Illusion, 297
Le grand remue-ménage, 330
La Grande espérance, 137
The Great Adventure, 185
The Great Goddess, 188
Great Mother Series, 213
The Great Path, 365
The Great Wall of Los
  Angeles, 114

Greater Love Hath No
  Man, 185
Greed, 179
Greenhide, 73
Greetings From
  Wollongong, 31
Greta's Girls, 242
Gretel, 22
Group Marriage, 348
Growing Up, 298
Growing Up Female, 124,
  289
The Grub Stake, 365
Gruen, 195
Gruppo di famiglia in un
  interno, 69
Guerra italo-turca tra
  scugnizzi napoletani, 299
The Guest, 68
Guns for Banta, 253

Haben Sie Arbitur?, 388
Habitat 2000, 163
Hablamos esta noche, 267
Haettest was Gscheits
  gelernt, 125
Haiku Film Project, 118
Hail Mary!, 177
Haircut, 188
Hairpiece: A Film for
  Nappy-Headed
  People, 44, 73-4, 84
Hame'ahev, 37
The Hammer And The
  Anvil, 268
Hand Movie, 334
The Hand That Rocks the
  Cradle, 419
Handtinting, 426
The Handyman, 233
Hang On A Minute, 341
Hanging out-Yonkers, 10
Happiness, 412
The Happy Family, 49
Hard, Fast and
  Beautiful, 250
Hare and Hedgehog, 388
Hareje aze
  Mahdoudeh, 219
Harlan County,
  USA, 229, 230
Harlequin, 338

Harry Hooton, 64
Harumi, 213
The Harvest is Over, 146
Hase und Igel, 388
A Határozat, 136
Hauchtext:
  Liebesgedicht, 141
Hayley's Home Movie, 369
Healthcaring: From Our
  End of the Speculum, 429
The Heart of a Painted
  Woman, 185
Heartbreak Kid, 258
Heat, 364
Heave Away My
  Johnny, 38
Hedda Gabler, 270
Hedwig or the Cool Lakes
  of Death, 411
The Heights of
  Cumanday, 330
Heinrich, 352
The Heiress (Weber), 419
The Heiresses (Meszaros),
  262
Hélène, 137
Heller Wahn, 405
Herbergisterne, 52
Here And There With My
  Octoscope, 261
Here Come the Seventies
  series, 163
Heritage, 73
A Hero's Life, 233
Hersenschinnen, 287
Hesan El Tin, 134
Hest på sommerferie, 196
Hester Street, 368, 369
Hideo-chan,
  Mama-Yo, 212-13
Hideo Dear, It's Me,
  Mama, 213
High Tide, 22, 30
Highbrow Love, 248
Hinter den Fenstern, 130
Hirnhexen, 388
Hiroshima mon amour, 128
His Brand, 419
Une histoire de femmes, 330
L'histoire de Noël, 63
Histoires d'A, 166
Historia de vida, 265

La historia official, 234
History Lessons, 207
History of the World According to a Lesbian, 188
The Hitchhiker, 250
Hodja fra Pjort, 196
Hold Your Man, 248
Holdup, 326
Hollywood Vice Squad, 382
El hombre cuando es hombre, 353
El hombre de la sal, 350, 351
Home, 419
Home and Dry, 240
Home Movie – A Day in the Bush, 64
L'homme à la valise, 10
L'homme à tout faire, 232, 233
Un homme amoureux, 166
Homo Meter, 142
Hongyi Shaonu, 78
Honor Among Lovers, 25
The Honourable René Levesque, 163
Hookers on Davie, 90–1
Hooks and Feelers, 336
Hop, the Devil's Brew, 419
A hora dele estrela, 13, 83
La hora de los hornos, 384
Horse on Holiday, 196
Horse of Mud, 134
Hot Flash, 188
The Hot Line, 224
Hot Water, 168
Hot Wheels, 163
Hotel Colonial, 223
Hotel Monterey, La chambre, 10
The Hour of Liberation, 383
The Hour of the Furnaces, 384
The Hour of the Star, 13, 83
A House Divided, 184, 185
The House Door, 287
House of Cards, 185
The House of the Angel, 183

Housing Problems, 55
How I Threw Art Out of the Window, 326
How Long does Man Matter?, 135
How the Loon Got Its Necklace, 63
How to Fight with Your Wife, 163
Hra o jablko, 81
Huaishu Zhuang, 78
Huang Se Gu Shih, 398
Huis-clos, 27
A Hungarian Village, 135, 136
Hungerjahre, 58, 290
Hurry! Hurry!, 261
The Husband and Daughter of Tamara Aleksandrovna, 379
Hush-a-Bye Baby, 118
Hustruer, 52, 298
Hustruer ti år etter, 52
The Hyaena's Breakfast, 267
Hydraulip II, 188
Hyperbolie, 142
Hypocrites, 418, 419

I Am Acquainted With The Three, 395
I Am Looking for My Fate, 380
I am Somebody, 44
I (Beat [It]), 140, 142
I Can See the Sun, 177
I Don't Think It's Meant for Us, 363
I Often Think of Hawaii, 267
I Shall Go to Santiago, 178
I Suggest Mine, 168
I, the Worst of All, 39
I Will Choose Courage, 297
I, Your Mother, 146
Ia vizhu solntse, 177
The Icelandic Shock Station, 212
Ich denke oft an Hawaii, 266, 267

Ich heisse Erwin und bin 17 Jahre, 19
Ich liebe dich April, April, 184
Ici et ailleurs, 177
Idle Wives, 419
If the Earth Wasn't Round, 184
If Ya'd Only Learned Something Practical, 125
If You Love This Planet, 330, 389
Illuminacja, 201
Illumination, 201
Illusionernas Natt, 8
Illusions (Dash), 44, 111–12, 111
Illusions (Honigmann), 287
Im Innern des Wals, 125
Images of the Wild, 163
L'impot de tout . . . de tout, 315
Improvviso, 223
In Again Out Again, 248
In Between, 125
In Paris Parks, 87
In Search of the Pale Blue Horizon, 300
In the Belly of the Whale, 125
In the Best Interest of the Children, 242
In the Land of Light Feet, 155
In the Picture, 402
In This Life's Body, 64
Inauguration of Officers, 136
Incident at Restigouche, 302
India Cabaret, 278
India Song, 128
Gli indifferenti, 69
Industria, 67
The Industrial Reserve Army, 352
Die industrielle Reservearmee, 352
Inexorable Time 81
The Inhabitants of Manor Houses, 135
The Innocent, 69

L'innocente, 69
Instant film, 141
Instructive Story, 136
Integration, 87
Interno berlinese, 68
Interrupted Line, 142
Interview, 239
Intolerance, 248
Introduction to Arnold
    Schoenberg's
    Accompaniment to a
    Cinematographic
    Scene, 207
Invisible Adversaries, 141,
    141, 142
Invitation, 224
Io sono mia, 223
Iré a Santiago, 178
Iris, 287
Is Everybody Here
    Crazy?, 369
Is This What You
    Were Born
    For?, 74
Ishchu moiu sudby, 380
Ishtar, 258
La isla, 384
Isla de Pascua, 435
Isla del tesoro, 178
Una isla rodeada de
    agua, 300
The Island, 384
An Island Surrounded by
    Water, 300
Ismeri a
    szandi-mandit?, 186
Isolde Pakolainen, 40–1
isolde the Refugee, 41
Ispaniia, 365
Istenmezején
    1972–73, 135, 136
It Happens To Us, 289
L'Italia s'é desta, 299
It's a Bikini World, 347,
    348
It's In the Bag, 339
It's My Turn, 419
It's No Laughing
    Matter, 419
Itto, 137
I've Heard the Mermaids
    Singing, 63

I've Never Seen or Done
    Anything Like It, 136
Ivory Collection, 13

Jade Women, 398
Jaded Vision, 295
J'ai faim, j'ai soif, 9, 10
Jama Masjid, 278
Jamaica Inn, 339
Al Jamra, 271
Jane B par Agnès V, 411,
    412
Janie's Janie, 124
Jaune le soleil, 128
Je tu il elle, 9, 242
Je vous salute Marie, 177
Jeanne Dielman, 23 Quai
    du Commerce, 1080
    Bruxelles, 8, 10, 153,
    260
Jedda, 30, 73
Jerusalem, 163
The Jester and the
    Queen, 81
Jesusfilm, 195
The Jew's Christmas, 419
Jewel, 419
The Job, 69
Jogo de mão, 348
Johanna d'Arc of
    Mongolia, 306, 307
Johanna Went 'The
    Box', 87
Johanna Went
    'Performance', 87
John Needham's
    Double, 419
Johnny Dangerously, 140
A Joke of Destiny Lying in
    Wait Round The Corner
    Like A Street
    Bandit, 421
José Balmes y Gracia
    Barrios, 170
Jostedalsrypa, 52
Un jour Pina a demandé, 9,
    10
Journal inachevé, 254, 330
Joy of Sex, 96
Joyce at 34, 78–80, 124,
    289, 419
Joyriders, 417

Julie de Carneilhan, 91
Jungle Warfare, 38
Juno and the Paycok, 339
Juquetes, 40
Just Like at Home, 262
Juvenile Court, 233

Kaddu Beykat, 146
Kaerlighed på kredit, 196
Kai Purakau, 326
Kalamita, 81
Kali, 195
Karanga Hokianga, 268
Kashtanka, 325
Kaskade rueckwaerts, 184
Kastélyók lakoi, 135
Kate and Anna
    McGarrigle, 239
Kavaró, 136
Keeping On, 230
Keskidee – Aroha, 268–9
Keys to Happiness, 324
Khareje Aze
    Mahdoudeh, 35
Khatwa, Khatwa, 239
Khoubz Biladian, 383
Khovanshchina, 380
Kilenc hónap, 262
Kilencedik emelet, 186
Kinder sind keine
    Rinder, 351
Kindergaertnerin, was
    nun?, 351
King Mat, 224
The King's Breakfast, 338,
    403
Kinopravda, 390
Kitch's Last Meal, 354
Kitchen Sink, 251, 294
Kiyoko no
    Kurushimeru, 213, 226
Kiyoko's Situation, 213,
    226
W Klatce, 354
Der kleine Loewe und die
    Grossen, 388
Das Kleine
    Schornsteinfeger, 338
Kliatva molodikh, 390
Kliuch bez prava
    peredachi, 25
Kliuchakh schastia , 324

Klyftan, 297
Knuckle-Men, 347–8
Kobieta samotna, 201
Kogda zatsvel mindal, 177
Koibumi, 226, 399
Koks i kulissen, 348
Kolme sisarta, 297
Kolory Kochania, 224
Kolossale Liebe, 58
Koniec Naszegoswiata, 224
Ein Konsumerlebnis, 141
Koportos, 186
Kopytem sem, kopytem
  tam, 81
Korotkie vstrechi, 274
Kranes konditori, 196
Kreuzberg Belongs to
  Us, 313
Kreuzberg gehoert uns, 313
Krisha mira, 390
Kristina Talking
  Pictures, 334
Kristinihald undir jokli, 212
Kristinus Bergman, 196
Krol Macius, 224
Krugovorot, 177
Krylia, 364, 379
Krzyk, 354
KSE (The Komsomol –
  Sponsor of
  Electrification), 365
KShE (Komsomol – Shef
  elektrifikatsii), 365
Kuei Mei, A Woman, 398
Kultainen vasikka, 162
Kumak the Sleepy
  Hunter, 63
Kung Fu Master, 411, 412
Kunlun Shangshang Yike
  Cao, 78
Kurt Schwitters I, II, III,
  195
Der Kuss, 140, 141
Kvinden og soldaten, 196

Labour History, 369
Lac aux dames, 91
Ladri di biciclette, 69
The Lady from
  Constantinople, 135
The Lady Peasant, 325
The Lady Vanishes, 339

The Land, 286
The Land of Mirages, 262
The Land That Does Not
  Exist, 297
Het Land van Mijn
  Ouders, 286
Landet som icke är, 297
Långt borta och nära, 8
Laocoon and Sons, 306
Laokoon und Soehne, 305,
  306
Laputa, 352
Larry's Recent
  Behaviour, 426
The Last Attraction, 325
The Last Days of
  Gomorrah, 352
Last Grave at Dimbasa, 16
The Last Knight
  Vampire, 8
The Last Letter to
  Children, 177
Last Reflections on a
  War, 163
The Last Step, 224
Last Supper in Hortsley
  Street, 16, 377
Last Tango in Paris, 23
Látogatóban, 136
Laufen Lernen, 58
Laundry Shed, 300
Laurent Lamerre
  Portier, 317, 318
Lavaderos: Sobre las
  olas, 300
Il lavoro, 69
Learning Fast, 326
Learning to Run, 58
Lebanon in Turmoil, 239
Legend of the Raven, 63
La leggenda di Napoli, 299
Leila, 133
Leila al Badawiyya, 133
Leila and the Wolves, 383,
  383
Leila, bint el Sahra, 133
Leila, Daughter of the
  Desert, 133
Leila the Beduin, 133
Leila Wal Zi'ab, 383, 383
The Lemon Sisters, 80
Lendemains moroses, 227

Lengue, 8
Lentement, 254
The Leopard, 69
The Leper's Cat, 419
Let Our Children Grow
  Tall, 415
Lethal Film, 305
Let's Talk about Men, 421
Let's Talk Tonight, 267
Letters Home, 9
Une lettre de cinéaste, 10
Die letzten Tage von
  Gomorrha, 352
Le Liban dans la
  tourmente, 239
Lif til Einhvers, 227
A Life to be Lived, 403
The Light, 85
Light Music, 341
Light Reading, 341
Lights, 261
Like Most Wives, 419
Line, 334
The Lion Cub and the
  Grown-ups, 388
Lions Love, 412
The Lion's Share, 384
Le lit, 187, 188
Liten Ida, 298
Little Bird of
  Happiness, 219
Little Red Riding Hood, 40
Little Red Riding Hood –
  Year 2000, 262
Little Vera, 379
Liubao De Gushi, 78
Lives of Performers, 260,
  312, 333, 334
Livsfarlig film, 305
The Lizards, 421
Llegaron las feministas, 83
Local Power, People's
  Power, 179
Locust Tree Village, 78
The Lodger, 339
Lohn und Liebe, 19
Loin du Vietnam, 411
Lokki, 297
Lola, 300
Lola Casanova, 233
London, 195
London on Parade, 55

The London Story, 323
The Lonely Persons'
Club, 186
Long Farewells, 274, 379
Look Back, 380
Looking for Langston, 352
Loperjenten, 298
The Lorry, 128
Losing Ground, 44
The Lost Honour of
Katharina Blum, 405
Louisiana Story, 286
Love, 87
Love and Anarchy, 421
Love and Fear, 406
Love is the Beginning of all
Terror, 351
Love Letter (Tanaka), 226,
399
Love Letters
(Jones), 140
Love Stinks – Bilder des
taeglichen
Wahnsinns, 195
Loved, Honoured and
Bruised, 369
The Lover, 37
Lover Boy, 368-9
Love's Half, 39
Loving Couples, 436,
436, 437
Low Visibility, 183
Lowlands, 341
Loyalties, 63
Luciella, 299
Lucky Stroke, 162
Ludwig, 69
Luegenbotschaft, 352
Luftwurzeln, 58
Lugares comunes, 265
Lulu, 40
The Lure, 185
The Lure and The
Lore, 74
Le Lys de mer, 27

Een Maand Later, 286,
410, 411
Machalí, fragmentos de una
historia, 170
The Machine, 352
Machorka-Muff, 207

Die Macht der Maenner ist
die Geduld der
Frauen, 312, 313
Macht die Pille frei?, 351
Macu, La mujer del
policiía, 413
Macu, the Policeman's Wife
413
Macumba, 83, 266, 267
Madame X – Eine absolute
Herrscherin, 290, 306
Madame X – an Absolute
Ruler, 290, 306
Madeleine Is . . ., 63
Madison, 195
La madonnina del
pescatore, 299
Maedchen in Uniform, 148,
149, 245, 349-50, 349,
400
Maenner 124, 125, 424
Maennerbuende, 351
Maeve, 274
Magányosok klubja, 186
Das Magische Auge, 141
I magliari, 69
The Maiden Has a Red
Ribbon, 40
Maidens, 393
Maidens in Uniform, 149,
349-50, 349
Maids and Madams, 72
Mais Qu'est-ce qu'elles
veulent, 166
Une maison de
naissances, 182
Majd holnap, 136
Make a wish, 182
Make Me laugh, 8
Making Mr Right, 358,
358, 359
Making Utu, 326
Le mal du pays, 353
Malcolm, 30, 337
Male Leagues, 351
Les Malheurs de Sophie, 27
Malinkaia Vera, 379
Malli, 297
Mamma, 305
A Man and the
Woman, 185
A Man in Love, 166

Man in the Polar
Regions, 87
Man Into Superman, 163
Man nennt mich jetz Mimi
. . ., 184
The Man of Salt, 351
Man sa yay, 146
Man with a Movie
Camera, 390
The Man with the
Suitcase, 10
The Man Who Couldn't
Give Up Lying, 348
The Man Who Dared
God, 419
The Man Who Envied
Women, 333, 334
Manden der ikke kunde
lade vaere med at
lyve, 348
Mandolinata a mare, 299
Manhattan Cocktail, 25
Mann & Frau &
Animal, 142
Mar de rosas, 67
Maria de la Cruz,
A Venezuelan
Woman, 413
María de la Cruz, una
mujer venezolana, 413
Mária-Nap, 136
Maria Rose di Santa
Flavia, 299
Maria's Day, 136
Le Mariage du hibou, 63
Marianne and Julianne, 405
Marja Pieni, 40
The Marriage, 133
The Marriage Clause, 419
The Marriage of
Yasushi, 213
Martha Clark Light and
Dark: A Dancer's
Journal, 80
Martinovics, 136
Marusa no Onna, 226
Mary Regan, 419
Maryam va Monny, 218
Más allá de la muerte, 360
La Maschera, 223
La maschera del vizio, 299
Die Maschine, 352

Maschinenkoerper – Koerpermaschinen – Koerperraum, 142
A Mask for You, A Mask for Me, 350
Materialfilme I, 195
Materialfilme II, 195
Maternale, 223
La Maternelle, 136, 137
Maternité, 137
A Matter of Life and Death, 8
Mauri, 255, 268, 269, 294
Maybe Tomorrow, 136
Mayhem, 74
The Meal Ticket, 248
Meddig él az ember, 135
Medea di Portamedina, 299
The Media Hysteria of Aids, 188
Meditation on Violence, 117, 118
Medusa, 118
Meeting at Dusk, 224
Mej och dej, 196
Mémoires d'une enfant des Andes, 254
Memorial to Martin Luther King, 163
Memorias de un mexicano, 264
Memories of a Mexican, 264
Men, 125, 424
Men of Tomorrow, 350
Menschenfrauen, 142
Menses, Sisters!, 188
Menstruationsfilm, 141
Mental Images oder der Zugang zur Welt, 142
Menuet, 38, 287
The Merchant of Venice, 419
Mercy, 74
Merrily We Go To Hell, 25
Meshes of the Afternoon, 117, 118, 382
Message, 186
Message to Sandra, 212
La messagère, 308

The Messenger, 308
Metamorphosis of M. Samsa, 63
The Metamorphosis of Mr Samsa, 239
Metropolitan Avenue, 138
Mettete l'avvocato, 299
Mexico, istoria de su poblacion, 265
Mi boga contigo, 353
Mi lupe y mi caballo, 263
Michigan Avenue, 179
Midair, 288
A Midnight Romance, 419
Mig og Dig, 196
Mignon e partita, 223
Mignon Has Come to Stay, 223
Mikey and Nicky, 258
Milarepa, 68
The Million Dollar Robbery, 185
The Mills of the Gods: Viet Nam, 163
Milyi, dorogoi, liubimyi, edinstvennyi, 25
Mimi metallurgico ferito nell'onore, 421
Min bedstefar er en stok, 196
Minden szerdán, 186
The Minders, 336
Mindout, 326
Mine soskend Goddad, 52
Minimum Charge No Cover, 90, 91
Minne, 27, 277
Minne ou l'ingénue libertine, 27
Minuet, 287
Une minute pour une image, 412
Mir v triokh izmereniiakh, 374
Miracle in Milan, 69
Miracolo a Milano, 69
Il miracolo della Madonna di Pompeii, 299
La mirada de Myriam, 84
The Miraflores Housing Project, 177–8
Miriam's Stare, 84

Misery Index, 163
Misfortune, 25
La misma vieja historia, 265
Miss Julie, 200–1, 391
Miss Mary, 21, 39, 40
Miss/Mrs, 246
Mr Frog Went A-Courting, 63
Mr Lord Says No!, 49
Mr Pascal, 119
Mr Wrong, 326
Misterio, 155
Mistletoes, 136, 208
Mrs Soffel, 22
Mit den Waffen einer Frau, 313
Mitsou, 27
Mitten ins Herz, 125
Mixer, 136
The Model, 297
Modern Guide to Health, 38
La Moitié de l'amour, 39
Mojak Kojak, 326
Molinos de Viento, 381
Moment in Love, 87
Momentos, 40
Momentos de un domingo, 84
Moments, 37, 40
Monangambee, 8, 253
Monse, 265
The Monster and the Girl, 185
A Month Later, 286
Mood Contrasts, 60
Mood Mondrian, 261
The Moon Has Risen, 226, 399
Moonplay, 261
More Than a School, 96
Morning Round, 380
La Mort du soleil, 127
La Morte du cygne, 137
Moscow Builds the Metro, 365
Moses und Aaron, 207
Moskva stroit metro, 365
The Moth of Moonbi, 73
Mother and Daughter, 262
Mother Ireland, 118, 275

Mother of Many
  Children, 302
Mother Right, 87
Mother-to-be, 315
A Mother's Heart, 2
The Mountain Wolf, 40
Mourir à tue-tête, 315, 316,
  329
A Moveable Feast, 369
The Mozart Brothers, 305,
  305, 392
Ms Taken Identity, 44, 67,
  415
Muerte en Santa Maria de
  Iquique, 170
Mujer ante el espejo, 104
La mujer de nadie, 361
Multiple Orgasm, 188
The Mummy's Curse, 288
El mundo de la mujer, 40
Mur murs, 412
Murder!, 339
Muren rundt fengslet, 52
La Musica, 128
Musica a ballo, 299
Musique d'Amérique
  latine, 254
Den Muso, 85, 85
Mutiny, 74
The Mutiny on the
  Bounty, 250
Muzh i doch Tamari
  Aleksandrovni, 379
My American Cousin, 63
My Brilliant Career, 22,
  30, 259
My Life Without
  Steve, 393
My Madonna, 185
My Name is Erwin and I'm
  17, 19
My Parents' Country, 286
My Survival as an
  Aboriginal, 1, 2, 31
My Twentieth
  Century, 209
My Wife Has Left, 25
The Mysterious Mrs
  Musselwhite, 419
Mystery, 155

Nacer de nuevo, 344

Nad Niemnem, 224
Naked Spaces: Living is
  Round, 403, 404
Nana, 25
Nano rosso, 299
Napló gyermekeimnek,
  262
Napló Szerelmeimnek, 131,
  262
Napoli sirena della
  canzone, 299
Napoli terra d'amore, 299
Når man kun er ung, 196
Nash chestnyi khleb, 274
Nathalie Granger, 128
Native Land, 365
Natt lek, 437
Naturaleza muerta, 265
nausicaa, 412
Le Navire Night, 128
Nazabivaiemoie, 374
Ne bolit golova u
  diatla, 25
Near and Far Away, 8
Near the Alatau
  Mountains, 390
'Neath Austral Skies, 250
Ned Wethered, 430
La negra Angustias, 233
Neighbourhoods, 369
Nelson Pereira dos
  Santos, 67
Neskolko interviu po
  lichnym voprosam, 177
Neun Leben hat die
  Katze, 387, 388
Never Fear, 250
New Grounds, 286
A New Leaf, 258
The New York Hat, 248
News from Home, 9, 10,
  10, 172
News From My
  Village, 146
News Review, 286
Next of Kin, 52
'Nfama, 299
Ni con el pétalo de una
  rosa, 84
Ni de aqui ni del alla, 265
Nicaragua: los que haran la
  libertad, 265

Nice Coloured Girls, 1,
  30, 31
Nicht Versoehnt, oder es
  Hilft nur Gewalt, wo
  Gewalt herrscht, 207
Niedzielne dzieci, 201
Nieuwe Gronden, 286
Night Games, 437
The Night Porter, 23, 68
The Nightcleaners, 153,
  269-70
Nihongdeng Sha De
  Shaobing, 78
Nikudyshnaia, 25
Nille, 196
Nine Months, 262
1933, 426
Ninth Floor, 186
Nixon's Visit and the
  University Struggle, 313
Nixonbesuch und
  Hochschulkampf, 313
No es por gusto, 265
No le pedimos un viaje a la
  luna, 265
No le tengo miedo a
  nada, 170
No Mercy No Future, 352
No Myth, 337
No No Nooky TV, 188
No Nukes, 230
No One's Woman, 361
No Trace of Romance:
  Martina (19) Becomes a
  Shepherdess, 125
No Virginity, No
  Nationality, 66
Nobody's Wife, 40
Les noces barbares, 187-8,
  187
Nocturno amor que te
  vas, 156
I nomadi, 299
North with the Spring, 163
Northern Biology, 369
La nostalgie, 353
Not a Love Story, 148,
  319, 389
Not a Pretty Picture, 95, 96
Not Even with a Rose
  Petal, 84
Not Just a Pretty Face, 22

Not Reconciled, 207
Not Wanted, 249
Note on Berlin, the Divided
    City, 64
Notebook, 32, 260–1
Notre mariage, 353
Le notti bianche, 69
The Nouba of the Women of
    Mount Chenoua, 122
Noubat Nissa Djebel
    Chenoua, 122
A Novel Affair, 49
November Moon, 290
Novembermond, 290
Now it's My Turn, Now
    it's Yours, 186
Nowhere To Run, 91
Nuer Lou, 78, 157
Nuestra voz de tierra,
    memoria y futuro, 344
Nukkekoti, 297
Numéro deux, 176, 177
Nuren De Gushi, 78, 157

'O cuppe' d'a morte, 299
O ebrio, 2
'O munaciello, 299
O něčem jiném, 80, 107
O saisons ô châteaux, 411
Ó transporte, 390
The Oath of the Young, 390
Oblomok imperii, 379
Obreros campesinos, 435
Obyknovennyi fashism, 379
Occupation and
    Self-Administration of a
    Student Halls of
    Residence, 313
The Ocean Waif, 185
Of Human Rights, 286
Of Lace and Sugar, 300
Off the Limits 35, 35, 219
The Official Story, 234
Oglianis, 380
Ohne Titel 1, 141
Ohne Titel XR, 141
Ojeblikket, 196
Ök ketten, 262
Az olcsóját és a jóját, 136
Old Crow, 302
An Old-fashioned
    Woman, 96

Old Wives' Tales, 38
Os olhos da alma, 319
Olivia, 27, 27
Oltre la porta, 68
Olyan mint otthon, 262
Olympia, 341
Omega Rising: Women of
    Rastafari, 66
On Earth as it is in
    Heaven, 227
On the Brink, 419
On Guard, 393
On neidolla punapaula, 40
On the Move, 262
On the Other Island, 178
On the River Niemen, 224
On the Twelfth Day, 402,
    403
On voulait pas de
    miracles, 182
One Glance – and Love
    Breaks Out, 58
One Hundred a Day, 22
One Month Later, 411
One More River, 163
One Sings the Other
    Doesn't, 166, 412
One, Two, That's It, 104
One Way or Another, 104,
    153, 178, 178, 179, 371,
    373
The Only One You
    Need, 326
Onnenpotku, 162
L'Opéra-Mouffe, 411
Opéración Sitio, 435
Opowiesc Atlantycka, 224
Optic Nerve, 188
Oracion (por Marilyn
    Monroé), 371
Ordinary Fascism, 379
Orfeo, 239
The Ornament of the
    Loving Heart, 337
Ornamentals, 74
Ornette – Made in
    America, 87
Ornette Coleman – A Jazz
    Video Game, 87
Örökbefogadás, 262
Örökség, 262
L'Ospite, 68

Ostatni Etapo, 224
Osventsim, 390
The Other Half of the
    Sky, 289, 419
Othon, 207
Our Honest Bread, 274
Our Life is Now, 305
Our Marriage, 353
Our São Paolo, 13
Our Trip, 188
Our Voice Made of
    Earth, Memory and
    Future, 344
Out of Chaos, 99
Outing to Vueltabajo, 178
Outrage, 249
The Outsider, 354
Outwitted by Billy, 365
Over the Waves, 300
Ovoce stromů rajských
    jíme, 80
The Owl and the
    Pussycat, 239
The Owl Who Married a
    Goose, 239
Oxo Parade, 38

P4W Prison for
    Women, 90–1
På liv och död, 8
Pacific Far East Line, 74
Padenie dinastii
    romanovykh, 365
Palace of Illusions, 8
Palava Susi, 40
Palle Allene i Verden, 196
Panelstory, 81
Papagenus, 338
Paper Bird, 52
Papirfuglen, 52
Parabola, 60
Parad molodosti, 390
The Parade of the
    Youth, 390
Paradies, 125
The Paradine Case, 339
Paradise, 125
Parahyba, a Macho
    Woman, 435
Parahyba, mulher
    macho, 435
Paraíso artificial, 83

El páramo de
Cumanday, 350
Paramount on Parade, 25
Una pareja de oro, 104
Paren iz taigi, 325
Parendeh Kouchake
Khoushbakhty, 219
Paris 1900, 165
La parte del león, 384
Parthenogenesis, 87
Partiinyi bilet, 379
Party Card, 379
Los paso de Ana, 394
Pasqualino Settebellezze,
421
Passa a bandiera, 299
Passages from Finnegans
Wake, 60
La passante 146
The Passer-by, 146
Passing On, 288
Passion, 177
The Passion of
Remembrance, 44, 67,
172, 352, 372
The Passionate Industry, 22
The Passionate Stranger, 49
Passionless Moments, 31
Patriamada, 178, 435
Patricia's Moving
Picture, 329
Patriotism, Part One, 426
Patsany, 25
Patu!, 255, 268, 269
Paula aus Portugal, 125
Paula from Portugal, 125
Pauses, 337
Pay For Your Mistake, 133
Pearls in the Abyss, 107
Peasant Women of
Riazan, 325, 325, 401
Peasants, 344
Peau de pêche, 136, 137
Peccato che sia una
canaglia, 69
Peel, 430
Peggy's Blue
Skylight, 426
La pelle, 68
Pense à ton désir, 182
Penthesilea, Queen of the
Amazons, 273

The People vs John
Doe, 418, 419
Peoples of the Potlatch, 63,
281
Peoples' Trial, 390
Peppermint Freedom, 290
Peppermint Frieden, 290
Peremena uchasti, 274
Perepolokh, 177
Ein Perfectes Paar oder die
Unzucht Wechselt Ihre
Haut, 142
Perils, 74
Peripeteia I, 74
Peripeteia II, 74
La Perle rare, 182
Perlicky na dně, 107
Permissible Dreams, 134
Pervertida, 300
El peso del sol, 394
Peter and the Doves, 388
Peter und die Tauben, 388
Peterburgskaia noch, 380
Petersburg Night, 380
La peticion, 267
La p'tite violence, 329
Les Petits Matins, 27
Philippe Pétain: processo a
Vichy, 68
Photoplay, 95–6
Piange Pierrot, 299
Piano Bar, 39
Piano Film, 295
Pianoforte, 223
Piatiletie metro, 390
The Picture Show
Men, 430
Pictures for Barbara, 188
Pictures on Pink Paper, 341
The Pictures That
Moved, 22
Piedra libre, 183
Pierre Vallières, 426
Pieta, 30, 337
Ping Pong, 141
The Pioneeers, 250
Pip and Bessie, 288
The Piper's Tune, 49
Piping Hot, 38
Pit of Loneliness, 27
A Place of Goodness, 16
Place Mattes, 188

Le Plaisir, 182
Plaisir d'amour en Iran, 411
Planas: testimonio de un
etnicidio, 344
Planas: Testimony of an Act
of Ethnocide, 344
Planeta Venere, 223
Planning, 118
Plumb Line, 354
Pocspetri, 136
Pod odnim nebom, 177
Poder local, poder
popular, 179
Podkidysh, 379
Poem of a Sea, 373–4
Poema o Morie, 374
The Poet George
Faludy, 186
La pointe courte, 292, 411
Pokoleniye pobeditelei, 379
Political Realities for the
Peasant Woman, 84
Polka Graph, 60
Pools, 188
Poor Maria, 40
Popp und Mingel, 388
Popsicles, 75
Porter, 85
Il portiere di notte, 23, 68
Portraets I, 195
Portraets II, 195
Portraets III, 195
Portrait of an Artist as an
Old Lady, 369
Portrait of a Female
Alcoholic – Ticket of No
Return, 306
Portrait of Jason, 87
Posillipo da Napoli, 299
Poslednii attraktsion, 325
Poslednoe pismo
detiam, 177
Possum Paddock, 250
Poundmaker's Lodge: A
Healing Place, 302
Pour qui tourne la roue, 182
La poursuite de
bonheur, 232–3
Povera Tisa, povera
madre, 299
Povest plamennikh let, 374
Power, 352

The Power of the
Camera, 248
The Power of Men Is the
Patience of
Women, 312, 313
Pozegnanie z Diablem, 224
Poznavaia belyi svet, 274
The Practice of Love, 142
Eine Praemie fuer
Irene, 351
Prague, the Restless Heart
of Europe, 81
Praha, neklidné srdce
Europy, 81
Die Praxis der Liebe, 142
Prayer, 371
Precarious Vision, 295
Prefab Story, 81
Prefaces, 74
La preghiera di bebé, 299
Preludio, 265
Prenatal Care in the First
Year, 179
Prénom Carmen, 177
Pretend You'll Survive, 240
The Price of a Good
Time, 419
A Prince for Cynthia, 49
La Princesse Mandane, 127
Processo a Caterina
Ross, 223
Il processo Cuocolo, 299
Processo per stupro, 223
A Project for Thought and
Speech, 13
Projected Light, 64
Projeto pensamiento e
linguajen, 13
Prolematica de la mujer, 84
Promenad i de gamlas
land, 8
Promenade in the Land of
the Aged, 8
Promised Lands, 375
Proposición para (entre)
cruzar espacious
limites, 75
Proschanie, 364
proselyt, 141
Provincial Actors, 201
Pulqueria 'La Rosita', 264
Punahilkka, 40

Punainen Ruukku, 41
Pupatella, 299
A Purpose in Life, 227
The Pursuit of
Happiness, 30, 233
Pusilleco Addiruso, 299
Pytel blech, 80

Qing Chun Ji, 78
La quarantaine, 315, 316
La que quiere azul
celeste, 300
Querida Carmen, 300
Quest for Love, 297,
297, 298, 377
Quest for Truth, 297,
297, 298, 377
Questa volta parliamo di
uomini, 421
A Question of Silence, 13,
26, 82, 180, 286
The Quiet Don, 325
The Quiet Ocean, 287

Rain, 286
Rainbow's End, 211, 227
A Raisin in the Sun, 45
Raising a Riot, 402, 403
La raison avant la
passion, 426
Rajska Jablon, 354
Rape, 52
Rat Life and Diet in North
America, 426
The Rats of Tobruk, 30, 73
Rattle of a Simple Man, 49
La Raulito, 384
Raumsehen und
Raumhoeren, 142
Reaching for the Moon, 248
Real Genius, 96
Realidades políticas para la
mujer campesina, 84
Reason Over Passion, 426
Reassemblage, 403, 404,
404
Recsz 1950–53, 186
Red-Headed Woman, 248
The Red Pot, 41
Red Riding Hood, 182, 416
Reefer and the Model, 221
Reel Time, 295

Reflections on Three Images
by Baldwin Spencer,
64
Regen, 286
Reginella, 299
Regrouping, 49
Eine Reise ist eine Reise
Wert, 141
Reka Chusovaia, 390
Remote . . . Remote, 140,
142
Ren Guai Qing, 78
Les rendezvous d'Anna, 9,
10
Replay, 195
Réponse de femme, 411
Report Number One, 224
Reportage Brésil: 1, 182
Reportaz nr 1, 224
Reproductions 3, 195
The Resolution, 136
The Restricted Key, 25
Restringierter Code, 142
Return to Kansas
City, 163
Reverón, 40
Revizori ponevole, 374
Revolutionary Watch, 264
Rezar, 265
Rhode Island Red, 334
Rhythm in Light, 60
The Ribbon, 16
Rich and Strange, 339
Richard Cardinal: Cry from
a Diary of a Metis
Child, 302
Riddance, 262
Riddles of the Sphinx, 273
Right in the Heart, 125
Rikky and Pete, 337
Rikollinen nainen, 162
Rimpianto, 299
The Ring, 339
Risky Business, 240
Ritorna all'onda, 299
Ritratto di donna
distesa, 223
Ritual in Transfigured
Time, 110, 118
Rituals of Memory, 274
Riverain, Gift of
Passage, 369

Robert Frost: A Lover's Quarrel With The World, 87
Rocco and His Brothers, 69
Rocco e i suoi fratelli, 69
The Rock of Riches, 419
Rock Wallaby and Blackbird, 64
Rohfilm, 195
The Romantic Story of Margaret Catchpole, 250
Rompiendo el silencio, 265
Ronda revolucionaria, 264
The Roof Needs Mowing, 22
The Roof of the World, 390
Roots of Grief, 8
Rooze Jahoni Koreghar, 35
Rosa de areira, 96
Rosa Luxemburg, 405
Rose's House, 163
Rossiia Nikolaia II i Lev Tolstoi, 365
Rough Treatment, 202
Rubezhi, 177
Ruby and Rata, 326
Rud's Wife, 251
Rudd's New Selection, 250
Ruddigore, 38
Rudolfino, 25
Rue cases nègres, 66, 83, 308
The Russia of Nicholas II and Lev Tolstoi, 365
Russians at War, 286

S&W, 195
Saat El Tahrir Dakkat, 382–3
Sabotage, 339
Sachiko, 213
Sacrificed Youth, 78
Saigon: Portrait of a City, 163
Sailboat, 426
Salaam Bombay!, 278
The Salt Maker, 351
Salut les Cubains, 411
Salut Victor!, 315, 316
Salvatore Giuliano, 69
Al Sama, 406

Sambizanga, 7, 8, 66, 252, 253
San Francisco, 248
La San Giorgio, 299
San Pedro de Atacama, 435
Sand, or Peter and the Wolf, 239
A Sand Rose, 96
Sandra, 69
Sandwich, 134
Sannu Bature, 188
Sans toit ni loi, 411, 412
Los santísmos hermanos, 351
São Paolo de todos nos, 13
Sappho, 188
Sarah and Son, 25
Sarah Bernhardt, 170
Šašek a královna, 81
Satdee Night, 22
Satisfaction, 344
Saturday 5pm, 388
Saute ma ville, 10
Sauve qui peut (la vie), 176
Savage, 87
Saving the Family Name, 419
Le savoir-faire s'impsoe, 315
Sazemonhayi Moli Yahoud, 35
Scandal, 419
Scandal Managers, 419
Scar Tissue, 168
A Scary Time, 87
Der Schlaf der Vernunft, 388
Schnitte, 142
Schwester, oder die Balance des Glucks, 405
The Scream, 354
A Scream from Silence, 316
Screen Test, 201
Scrubbers, 437
Scugnizza, 299
Scugnizzo napoletano, 299
Scuola senza fine, 223
A Sea of Roses, 67
The Seagull, 297
The Sealed Soil, 218
Searching for Pathways, 84

The Seashell and the Clergyman, 127
Season of Plenty, 369
The Second Awakening of Christa Klages, 290, 405, 405
Second Class Mail, 15
The Second Journey (To Uluru), 64
The Secret, 206
The Secret Agent, 339
Le Secret du chevalier d'Éon, 27
Secret Sounds Screaming: The Sexual Abuse of Children, 44, 74
La secreta obcenidad de cada día, 170
Secrets of Life series, 156
Secrets of Nature series, 156
Sedmikrásky, 80
Seduction: The Cruel Woman, 83, 267
The Seduction of Mimi, 421
Segodnik, 365
Sehtext: Fingerdicht, 141
Ein Seitensprung, 130
Self-Defense, 87
Semana de 22, 13
Sempre avanti, Savoia, 299
Send a Gorilla, 294, 335, 336
Señora de nadie, 40
Sensation Seekers, 419
Senso, 69
The Sentimental Bloke, 250
Sentinels Under the Neon Lights, 78
A sereia de pedra, 319
Serious Undertakings, 28, 31, 393, 430
Servant of All, 163
Seth Mattsonin tarina, 297
Seven Beauties, 421
Seven Sisters, 64
Seven Women, Seven Sins, 179
The Seventh Veil, 49

Several Interviews on Personal Questions, 177
La sfida, 69
Shadow of A Doubt, 339
Shadows of the Moulin Rouge, 185
Shadows, Parts I and II, 213
She Must Be Seeing Things, 137
Sheer Madness, 405
Shi Yi Ge Niu Jen, 398
Shirins Hochzeit, 19, 352
Shirin's Wedding, 19, 352
The Shoemaker and the Hatter, 38
Shoes, 419
Short Encounters, 274
Shub Vivah, 16
Si dice donna, 223
Sí podemos, 413
Siamo donne, 69
Sidewalks, 261
Sie Susse Nummer, 141
Sieben Frauen und Sieben Sünden, 142
Sieg des Glaubens, 341
Sifted Evidence, 183
Sigmund Freud's Dora, 151
La signora senza camelie, 17, 69
Silas Marner, 119
The Silence of Dean Maitland, 250
The Silent One, 294
Silver City, 30
Silvo, 351
Simfoniia Donbassa, 390
Simon and Laura, 49
The Singer and the Dancer, 22
The Single Woman and the Double Standard, 163
Den sista riddarvampyren, 8
Sisters, or the Balance of Happiness, 405
Six et demi onze, 137
Six femmes à leur place, 416
Six fois deux, 177
Size 10, 393
Skibet er ladet med, 196

Skilabod til Söndru, 211–12
Skilsmässoproblem i italien, 8
The Skin, 68
The Skin Game, 339
The Skin of our Teeth, 60
Skin of Your Eye, 64
Skyscraper, 87
Slavianski kongress v Belgrade, 390
The Slavonic Congress in Belgrade, 390
The Sleep of Reason, 388
Sleight of Hand, 348
Slides, 295
Slow Motion, 176
Slowly, 254
Slum Devils, 361
Slumber Party Massacre, 140
Small Happiness, 289
The Smiling Madame Beudet, 126, 127, 127, 148
Smithereens, 358, 359
Smokes and Lollies, 22
Smooth Talk, 79, 80
Snack-Bar 'World', 81
Snow Job, 188
The Snowman, 14
So Far from India, 278
So This is London, 55
Sobre horas extras y trabajo voluntar io, 179
Sobre la olas, 300
The Social Secretary, 248
Les Sœurs ennemies, 127
Sohno de valsa, 67
Soigne ta droite, 177
Soldier of Victory, 224
Solidarity, 426
Solstik, 196
Sombre dimanche, 27
Some American Feminists, 329
Some Are of Love, 413
Some Exterior Presence, 74
Some Phases of an Empire, 163
Someone Else's Letters, 379
Someone Has to be the Corpse, 184

Something for Something, 201
Something New, 365
Son nom de Venise dans Calcutta désert, 128
Sonatine, 232, 233
A Song of Ceylon, 393
The Song of The Shirt, 56, 153
Sonnabend 17 Uhr, 388
Sons of Matthew, 30, 73
Sontagemalerei, 388
Sorry, It's the Law, 134
SOS Kindtand, 196
SOS; MTS, 416
SOS, STD, 416
Sotto il carcere di San Francisco, 299
Sotto San Francisco, 299
Sotto Sotto, 421
Souls of the Sun, 146
Sources d'inspiration, 85
Sources of Inspiration, 85
La Souriante Madame Beudet, 126, 127, 127, 148
Spaanse Aarde, 286
Spain, 365
Spanish Earth, 286
The Spider's Web, 146
Split Reality, 140, 141
Splitscreen – Solipsismus, 141
Spook Sport, 60
Spotkania w mroku, 224
Ein Sprachfest, 141
Sredi serikh kamney, 274
The Stage, 136
Stage Fright, 339
Stamattina alle dieci in via dei fiori nella nota casa di tolleranza, 421
Starstruck, 22
Stella i orlofi, 212
Stemning i April, 196
Step by Step, 239
Stepan Razin, 325
The Steps of Ana, 395
De Stille Oceaan, 287
Stills, 195
De Stilte Rond Christine M, 179–80, 286

Stockholmsdamernas
    älskling, 201
Stockholmsfrestelser, 200,
    201
Stone Circle, 188
The Stone Mermaid, 319
Storia del terzo Reich, 68
Stories of a Latch-key
    Kid, 388
Stories of Three
    Women, 157
Storstadsvampyrer, 8
The Story of Adèle H., 113
The Story of Camilla, 298
Story of Flaming
    Years, 374
Story of a Lady, 39
Story of Liubao, 78
The Story of a Secret
    Forced Labour
    Camp, 186
The Story of Seth
    Mattson, 297
Story of Three Women, 78
Story of a Woman, 398
Strana rodnaia, 365
Strana Sovetov, 365
The Stranger, 69
The Stranger Left No
    Card, 402, 403
Lo straniero, 69
Strass Café, 317–18
Strawberries and Gold, 96
The Street, 63, 238, 239
Street Corner, 49
Strreet Journal, 278
Street of Mirrors, 83
Street of My
    Childhood, 196
Streetwalker, 233
Striking My Eyes, 313
Strip Searching – Security
    or Subjugation, 118
Strop, 80
Strukturelle Studien, 195
Student Nurses, 347, 348
A Study in Choreography
    for Camera, 117, 118
The Subjective Factor, 351
Subjectivity, 351
Subjekituede, 351
Der subjektive Faktor, 351

The Substance of Things
    Hoped For, 163
Suburbia (The Wild
    Side), 140, 382
Subway in the Sky, 49
Such High Mountains, 374
Sud narodov, 390
Sud v Smolenske, 365
Un sueño como de
    colores, 353
Sui fili telefonici, 299
Summer in Mississippi, 163
Summer Night with Greek
    Prophiles Almond Eyes
    and Scent of Basil, 421
Sunday Children, 201
Sunday Moments, 84
Sunday Painting, 388
Sunshine Molly, 419
Superdyke Meets Madame
    X, 188
Supergirl, 149
Superman und
    Superwoman, 195
Surfacing, 163, 336
Surname Viet Given
    Name Nam, 403,
    404
Suspense, 419
Suspicion, 339
Suuri Illuusio, 297
Svetlii gorod, 325
Svo a jördu sem a
    himni, 227
Sweet Sugar Rage, 66
Swept Away, 421
Sydney Eastbound, 55
Sync Touch, 188
Synchronization, 60
Synchrony No. 2, 60
Syntagma, 142
Systrarna, 201
Syvilla: They Dance to Her
    Drum, 73
Szabad lélegzet, 262
Szép lányok, ne
    sírjatok, 262
Sziget a szárazföldön, 135
Színpad, 136

Ta'Dabir Eghtessadi-y-
    Janghi, 34–5

Tag der Freiheit: Unsere
    Wehrmacht, 341
Tahta Al Ankad, 309
A Tainted Horseplay, 81
Take My Hand, 163
Take the Plunge, 337
Takiie vysokiie gory, 374
Taking a Look, 337
Taking Over, 326
Találkozás, 135
Találkozunk 1972-ben, 136
Talkback, 251
Tam-tam à Paris, 5
Tamarkoze, 35
Tantas vidas, una
    historia, 170
Tantörténet, 136
Tapp und Tast Kino, 140,
    141
Tar People, 74
Tarantella (Bute), 60
La tarantella(Notari), 299
Tarnished Reputations, 185
T'as de beaux escaliers tu
    sais, 411
Die Taube auf dem Dach,
    184
A Taxing Woman, I and
    II, 226
Tbilisi 1500 let, 177
Tbilisi, 1,500 Years
    Old, 177
Tea in the Garden, 426
The Teckman Mystery, 403
Tempi nostri, 69
Le temps de l'avant, 316
The Temptations of
    Stockholm, 200
Ten Modern
    Commandments, 24
Ten Years After . . . Ten
    Years Older, 31
Ten Years Later, 84
Tenderhooks, 30
Teresa de Jesús, 270
Terminal Island, 347–8
Terre de Nos Aieux, 63,
    281
Territories, 352
Thèmes et variations, 127
There's a Bag of Fleas on
    the Ceiling, 80

There's No Place Like
   Home, 419
They Call me Mimi Now
   . . ., 184
They called us 'Les Filles du
   Roy', 316
They Learn at the
   Collective farms, 390
The Thin Blue Line, 90
The Thin Line, 37
Thirsty Sea, 134
30 Minutes Mr Plummer,
   315
The Thirty-Nine Steps, 339
This Hour Has Seven
   Days, 163
This is the Air Force, 38
This Isn't Wonderland, 416
This Other Eden, 49
A Thoroughly Neglected
   Girl, 58
Those Who Love, 258, 259
Three Cases of Murder, 403
Three Colour Separation
   Studies – Landscapes, 64
Three Lives, 267
Three Men and a
   Cradle, 166
Three on a Match, 163
The Three Sisters, 297
Three Songs of Lenin, 390
Thriller, 82, 151,
   152, 153, 172, 280, 303,
   322, 323
The Tide of Death, 250
Tiefland, 341
El tiempo del desprecio, 265
Tiempo para un líder, 170
The Ties That
   Bind, 167–8, 242
La tigresa, 262
The Tigress, 185
Tikhii Don, 325
Time of Indifference, 69
Time of the Cree, 369
Tischbemerkungen –
   November 1985, 142
Tisztavatás, 136
Tisztelt Cím!, 186
Tita Wong, 133
Tivoli-garden spiller, 196
To Be a Woman, 99

To Be Born Anew, 344
To Dorothy, a Son, 49
To Kill a Priest, 202
To Please One
   Woman, 419
To the Diary, 295
The Tocher, 338
Today, 365
Today We Live, 55
Toheroamania, 326
Toi Ippon no Michi, 226
La toile d'arraignée, 146
A Token Gesture, 232, 233
Tomboy Paula, 384
Tonfilm, 141
Tongues, 87
Too Bad She Is Bad, 69
Too Early Too Late, 208
Too Wise Wives, 419
Too Young to Love, 49
Tou Bin Nuhai, 206
Touching, 141
Touching the Earth series,
   64
Tourist, 188
Tous les jours, tous les
   jours, 416
Toute Révolution est un
   coup de dés, 207
Toute une nuit, 9–10, 251
Toys, 40
The Trace, 406
Trade Secrets, 369
Trailer, 233
Train Trouble, 38
Traitor, 419
Trás-os-Montes, 96
Travel and Leisure, 163
Travolti da un insolito
   destino nell'azzurro mare
   d'agosto, 421
Treasure Island, 179
La tregua, 384
Trente Minutes Mr
   Plummer, 315
Tri pesni o Leninie, 390
The Trial of Caterina
   Ross, 223
Trial for Rape, 223
Trial Run, 294, 335, 336
Tribunal para menores, 233
La Triche, 166

Tricolore, 299
Trio Film, 334
Trionfo cristiano, 299
Das tripas coração, 67
Triumph des Willens, 341
Triumph of the Will, 341
Trois hommes et un
   couffin, 166
Trop tôt trop tard, 208
Trotacalles, 233, 264
The Troubadour's
   Triumph, 419
The Trouble With
   Angels, 250
The Truce, 384
True as a Turtel, 403
True Confections, 369
The Truth About
   Women, 49
Tsiamelo, 16
Tsuki ga Agarinu, 226,
   399
Tue Recht und scheue
   Niemand, 58
Tunturisusi, 40
Turkey at the Turning
   Point, 365
Turning Fifty, 416
Turning Forty, 316
Turnover, 177
Turtsiia na podeme, 365
Tutto a posto e niente in
   ordine, 421
TV Tart, 188
24 Frames Per Second, 87
Twenty Years of Soviet
   Cinema, 365
Two Bad Daughters, 188
Two Faces, 119
Two Friends, 30, 430
Two Laws, 1, 31, 138
Two Minutes' Silence 258,
   259
The Two of Them
   (Women), 262
Two Women, 64
Ty i ia, 364

U krutogo yara, 274
U stropu je pytel blech, 80
Ukjent man, 196
Ultima tango a Parigi, 23

Ulysse, 411
Unas son de amor, 413
Uncivilised, 73
Uncle Yanco, 411
Und Sie, 195
Under One Sky, 177
Under the Crescent, 365
Under the Rubble, 309
L'Une chante l'autre
    pas, 166, 411, 412
Unfinished Diary, 254
The Unforgettable, 374
The Unhappy Hat, 209
Unica, 142
Union Maids, 289
United States of
    America, 179
Uno, Dos, Eso Es, 104
Unsichtbare Gegner, 141,
    142
Unter dem Pflaster ist der
    Strand, 352
Unter lauter Schafen, 125
Unwilling Inspectors 374
Up to Date, 421
Útközben, 262
Utrennyi obkhod, 380
Üzenet, 186

V kilkhozakh uchatsia, 390
V predgoriakh Alatau, 390
V trinadtsatom chasu, 364
Den Vaertern vertrauen,
    gegen alle Erfahrung, 388
La Vagabonde (Bussi), 164
La Vagabonde (Musidora),
    277
Vagabonde (Varda), 411,
    412
Vaghe stelle dell'Orsa, 69
Vakvilágban, 186
Valie Export, 141
Valitsen rohkeuden, 297
Valkoinen Peura, 162
Valley Girl, 96
Il valore della donna e il suo
    silenzio, 83
Valzer d'amore, 299
The Vampire, 185
Van de Koele Meren des
    Doods, 410, 411
The Vanquished, 17, 69

Variety, 179, 319
Velhos são os trapos, 348
Velikii put, 365
The Velvet Vampire, 347,
    348
Vend dig ikke om, 196
Vénus victrix, 127
Vera . . . a Cruel
    Story, 270
Vera . . . un cuento
    cruel, 270
Verano en invierno, 435
Verbotene Bilder, 195
Verdammt in alle
    Ewigkeit, 195
Verfuehrung: die grausame
    Frau, 83, 266, 267
Die verlorene Ehre der
    Katharina Blum, 404
Veronica 4 Rose, 72
The Very Eye of
    Night, 118
The Very Late Afternoon of
    a Faun, 81
A Very Perfect Couple, 388
Vesterhavsdrenge, 196
Via degli specchi, 83
Vicios de cocina, 265
Victory of Faith, 341
La vida toda, 265
Videotape I, 195
Videotapes: Series no. 1, 87
Videotapes: Series no. 2, 87
La vie revée, 63, 329
Viet-lakes, 354
A View From the 21st
    Century, 163
Viktoriia, 325
Vinterboern, 196
I vinti, 17, 69
Virgin Machine, 243
Visages, 297
The Visible Woman, 163
Visiting, 136
A Visual Diary, 87
Visual Variations on
    Noguchi, 260, 261
Vitaklub, 136
Vive la vie, 137
Vlčí bouda, 81
Voglio a tte, 299
Voldtekt, 52

Volleyball, 334
Von Romantik keine Spur,
    Martina (19) wird
    Schaeferin, 125
Voskhozhdenie, 364
Vrazhi tropi, 325
Vringsveedeler
    Tryptichon, 352
The Vringsveedol
    Triptych, 352
Vroeger is Dood, 287
Een Vrouw als Eva, 410,
    411
Vy mne pisali, 380

Waere die Erde nicht rund
    . . ., 184
Wages and Love, 19
Wait a Sec!, 186
The Wake of the
    Bounty, 73
The Waking Hour, 347,
    348
Walking Track, 64
A Waltz-like Dream, 67
Waltzes From Vienna, 339
Wanda, 83
Wanted – a Home, 419
Wanted: Loving Father and
    Mother, 286
The War Game, 436
Warum ist Frau B.
    Gluecklich?, 19
Was halten Sie von Leuten,
    die malen?, 184
Was soll'n wir denn machen
    ohne den Tod, 266, 267
Water Sark, 426
Water the Way You Want
    It, 326
Waterfall, 64
Watts with Eggs, 261
The Waves, 287
The Way We Live, 99
We Are Mothers Too Early
    . . ., 112
We Don't Live Here
    Anymore, 369
We Eat the Fruit of the
    Trees of Paradise, 81
We Joined the Navy, 403
We the Women, 69

Weather Forecast, 55
A Weave of Time, 282
Wedded Bliss, 19
The Week of 1922, 13
The Weight of the Sun, 394
We'll Meet in 1972, 136
Wendy and Joyce, 426
Wendy Clarke's Whitney
    Show, 87
We're Building, 224
We're Building New
    Villages, 224
Werther, 267
Wet Dot, 38
What Do Men Want?, 419
What Do They Want?, 166
What Do You Think
    of People Who
    Paint?, 184
What Now, Nursery
    Workers?, 351
What Will People
    Say?, 185
What Would We Do
    Without Death, 267
What You Take For
    Granted, 86
Whatever You Do You
    Lose, 155
What's Cooking?, 38
What's Worth While?, 419
When a Girl Leaves, 419
When a Man is a Man, 353
When a Woman Doesn't
    Sleep, 104
When Almond Trees Were
    in Blossom, 177
When Ladies Meet, 248
When We Were
    Young?, 132
When You and I Were
    Young, 185
Where Are My
    Children?, 418, 419
Where Are We At?, 84
Which Would You
    Choose?, 25
The White-Collar
    Worker, 19, 352
White Heat, 419
White Nights, 69
The White Reindeer, 162

Who Needs Nurseries? We
    Do!, 240
Whose Choice?, 246
Why is Mrs B. Happy?, 19
Wieczór u Abdona, 201
Wild and Woolly, 248
The Wild Cat, 381
The Wild Party, 25
Wild Refuge series, 163
The Wind, 85
Wing Beat, 193
Wings, 364, 379
Wings in the Dark, 365
Winter Ade, 130
A Winter Tan, 59–60
Winterborn, 196
Wis, 195
Wisecracks, 369
The Witch Hunt, 52
Witch's Cradle, 118
With Babies and Banners,
    289
With Me You Will Enjoy
    Yourself, 300
With Our Own Hands, 66
With the Heart in the
    Hands, 67
With the Weapons of a
    Woman, 313
Without Love, 354
Wives, 52, 298
Wives – Ten Years
    After, 52
Wo Ze Yang Ko Le Yi
    Shen, 398
Wolf's Hole, 81
The Wolland Family, 19
Die Wollands, 19
Woman, 146
A Woman Alone, 201
Woman Demon Human, 78
Woman in Front of the
    Mirror, 104
A Woman in Transit, 318
A Woman Like Eve, 411
The Woman of
    Mystery, 185
The Woman Suffers, 250
Woman to Woman, 114,
    124
A Woman with
    Responsibility, 388

Woman's Day 20
    Cents, 393
Woman's Greatest Value is
    her Silence, 83
The Women, 248
Women Behind the
    Camera, 313
Women from South
    Lebanon, 309
Women I Love, 188
The Women of Brewster
    Place, 114
The Women of
    Harrisburg, 313
Women of the
    Rhondda, 246, 246
Women Seen, 337
The Women's Olamal, 138
Women's Problematic, 84
Women's Rites, 188
Woodpeckers Don't Get
    Headaches, 25
Woolloomooloo, 393
Work in Progress Part
    A, 195
Working Girls (Arzner), 25
Working Girls (Borden),
    47, 49
The Working Girls
    (Rothman), 348
Working Models of
    Success, 112
Working Mothers series,
    330, 363
Working Title: Journeys
    from Berlin/1971, 334
The World in Three
    Dimensions, 374
The World of Children, 288
World of Light: A Portrait
    of May Sarton, 242
The World of Women, 40
The World's Children, 369

'X', 188

Y si platicamos de
    Agosto, 394, 395
¿Y su mamá que hace?, 83
Y tenemos sabor, 178
Yaltecas, 265
Yangba-Bola, 8

Yasushi no Keikon, 213
Years of Hunger, 58, 290
Yeelen, 85
Yegor Bulichov and
    Others, 374
The Yellow Car, 35
Yellow Submarine, 119
The Yellow Traffic, 185
Yentl, 103
Yes, We Can (Giguère and
    LeMay), 416
Yes We Can (Grupo
    Feminista Miércoles),
    413
Les Yeux ne veulent pas en
    tout temps se fermer, 207
Yksinäinen nainen, 297
Yo, la más pobre de
    todas, 39
Yo me comprometo, 170
Yo, tú, Ismaelina, 413
Yoji,
    Do-Shita-no?, 212–13
Yoji, What's Wrong With
    You?, 213
You and I, 364
You Have Struck a
    Rock, 16
You, Me, Ismaelina, 413

You Wrote Me . . ., 380
Young and Innocent, 339
Young Toughs, 25
Your Children Come Back
    to You, 44
Yours Truly, Andrea G.
    Stern 358, 359
Youth: In Search of
    Morality, 163
Yu Chin Sou, 398
Yudie, 289
Yukon Quest, 142
Yumiko, 213
Yurupari, 350

Zacharovannaia Desna, 374
Zahrat al Koundoul, 309
Zajota and the Boogie
    Spirit, 73, 74
Zap, 64
Zaporoszenie, 224
Zarede Ghaneri, 35
Zatrap, 66
Al Zawag, 133
Zdjęcia próbne, 201
Al Zerda, 122
The Zerda, 122
Zhena ushla, 25
Znoi, 364

Zolnierz Zwyciestwa, 224
Zolotie vorota, 374
Zonar de dolor IV, 75
Zverstva fashistov, 390
Die Zweiheit der
    Natur, 142
Das zweite Erwachen der
    Christa Klages 290, 405,
    405

The following films have
foreign language titles
which begin with
numbers.

7 AM, 300
8 e 90, 299
8 e mezzo, 421
17. maj – en film on
    ritualer, 52
20 év múltán, 136
20 let sovetskogo kino, 365
58 másodperc, 186
150 na Godzine, 224
333, 141
625, 195
3000 mujeres cuatro, 172

GENERAL INDEX

Page numbers in *italic* refer to the illustrations

A bout de souffle, 22, 176, 292
A Jihua, 231
De Aanslag, 286
Aaron, Jane, 15
ABC (Australian Broadcasting Corporation), 1, 64
The ABC of Love, 296
Abdelkhalek, Ali, 133
Abdelsalam, Shadi, 18, 134
Abdelwahab, Fatine, 133 134
Abnoudi, Attiat El, 18, 134
El Abocato Madiha, 134
Abusuan, 7
The Abyss, 296
The Accidental Tourist, 254
Achard, Marcel, 164
Acht Stunden sind kein Tag, 145
Acker, Kathy, 179
ACPAY (Association Coopérative de Productions Audio-Visuelles), 329
O acto da primavera, 303
Actors' Studio, 3, 270
The Actress, 105
Adam's Rib, 13, 106, 197
Adler, Renata, 157, 158, 229
Adler, Stella, 95
Adolescent Sweet Love, 240
Adrian, 144, *144*
The Adventure, 17
The Adventures of Jon and Gvendur, 211
Advertising Advisory Council, 3
Aelita, 373

Affair in Trinidad, 193
Afgrunden, 296
Afram, Silvana, 235
African Film Productions, 376
The African Queen, 197
Afrikaner nationalism, 376
After Hours, 357, 358
After the Rehearsal, 42
Afterimage (journal), 228
Afzien, 287
L'Age d'or, 164
The Age of the Earth, 343
Agee, James, 229
Ager, Cecilia, 158
Agricultural Education Motion Picture Corporation, 397
Ahlam Al Madina, 394
Akhtar, Javed, 33
Akomfrah, John, 44
Al Zoubeidi, Kais, 308
Alan Quartermain, 376
Alaouie, Borhan, 239, 309, 394
Alassane, Mustapha, 5, 7
Alazraki, Benito, 264
Albania, 131
Albrecht, Joseph, 376
Aldrich, Robert, 101, 112, 160, 245
Alea, Tomás Gutiérrez, 104, 371
Aleixandre, Margarita, 381
Alemann, Claudia von, 424
Alexander, Karen, 44, 67, 415
Alexandria Why?, 134
Alfonsín, Raúl, 21
Ali, 145
Alice Doesn't Live Here

Anymore, 198, 291, 357, 426
'Alice Guy Collective', 223
Alien, 355, 356, 429
Aliens, 198, 207, 356, 429
All About Eve, 112, 194, 270
All I Desire, 64, 370
'All My Children', 371
All of Us and Aids, 289
All That Heaven Allows, 24, 369, 370
All These Women, 41
Alla en el rancho grande, 263
Allégret, Marc, 91
Allégret, Yves, 165
Allen, A. K., 432
Allen, Robert C., 296
Allende, Salvador, 75, 254, 353, 435
Allio, René, 165
Allouache, Merzak, 11
Almeida, Virginia Castro e, 319
Almodóvar, Pedro, 381
Alphaville, 177
Alternative Cinema (journal), 295
Althusser, Louis, 214, 321, 389
Altyd in my Drome, 376
Alvarez, María José, 71
Alvarez, Santiago, 104
Alvin Purple, 29
Always in My Dreams, 376
Aly Khan, Prince, 191
Alyam, Alyam, 271
Amada, 373
La amarga verdad, 435
Amator, 317
American (journal), 310

American Film (journal), 347

American Indian Film Festival, 282

American International Pictures, 291

L'Ami de mon amie, 345

Le amiche, 17

Amiens Film Festival, 283

Amilralay, Omar, 394

Amir, Aziza, 133

AMLAE, 71, 72

Ammar, Abdel-Latif Ben, 406

Amok, 272

Amor de la calle, 263

Amor de perdiceo, 303

L'Amore, 285

Amou Sibilou, 42

L'Amour fou, 342

L'Amour l'après-midi, 345

L'Amour par terre, 342

L'Amour violé, 166

Amoy films, 397

Ana Hourra, 134

And God Created Woman, 23, 36, 292

De andere Cinema, 38

Anderson, Lindsay, 53, 57

Anderson, Madeline, 44

Andrade, Joaquim Pedro de, 81

Andress, Ursula, 361

Andreu, Christina, 381

Andrews, Dana, 23–4

Andrews, Julie, *103*

Angel, 121

El angel exterminador, 264

'Angels', 399

Angels Hard As They Come, 115

Angola, 7, 8

Angry Arts Group, 53

Angst Essen Seele Auf, 145

Ani Ohev Otach Rosa, 37

Aniki-Bóbó, 303

Ankur, 33

Anna and Edith, 313

Anna Christie, 170

Anna Karenina, 170

Anna und Edith, 313

Annie, 401

Annie Oakley, 385

The Anniversary, 112

Another Time Perhaps, 42

Another Way, 346

Ansah, Kwaw, 5, 7

Ansara, Martha, 1, 30

Ansikte mot ansikte, 41

Ansiktet, 41

Antin, Manuel, 21, 301

Anton, Karl, 284

António das mortes, 343

Anzola, Alfredo, 413

Apon, Annette, 287

Applause, 276

The Apprenticeship of Duddy Kravitz, 232

Arabian Nights, 337

Aravidan, G., 311

Aray, Edmundo, 413

Arayiss Min Kasab, 272

The Archers, 324

Archibugi, Francesca, 223

Arden, Eve, 13

Ardh Satya, 311

Aria, 276

Arias, Imanol, 39

Aristaraín, Adolfo, 384

Arliss, Leslie, 169, 346

Armatage, Kay, 63, 159

Armendariz, Pedro, 263

Armstrong, Mary, 330

Arnadottir, Nina Bjork, 227

ARRFQ (Association des réalisateurs et réalisatrices de films du Quebec), 331

Art of Love, 121

Artaud, Antonin, 127

Arts Council (Great Britain), 84, 275, 295, 340–1

Arts Council (Ireland), 220

Arvelo, Ritva, 162

Aryety, Sam, 5

Asacanio, Haydee, 413

Ashur, Geri, 124

The Asphalt Jungle, 270

L'aspirant, 85

Asquith, Anthony, 402

The Assassination of the Duke of Guise, 303

Associated Realist Film Producers, 55

Associated Talking Pictures (ATP), 129

Association of Independent Video and Film-makers, 95

Astaire, Fred, 191, 276, 342

Astruc, Alexandre, 292

At Middle Age, 78

Atabat Mamnoua, 46

The Attack, 286

Attille, Martina, 44, 46, 67

L'aube des Damnés, 10

Audé, Françoise, 128

Audran, Stéphane, 293

Aufklaerungsfilm, 174

Die Augen der Mumie Mâ, 284

August First studios, 78, 157

Aus dem Leben des Marionetten, 41–2

Austin, Chris, 16

Australasian Films, 28–9

The Australian (journal), 238

Australian Film Commission (AFC), 29, 430

Australian Film Development Corporation, 29

Australian Film and Television School, 22

The Australian Journal of Screen Theory, 228

Austria, 146

Autant-Lara, Claude, 165, 292

Autumn Sonata, 41

Averbakh, Ilya, 379

Avery, Tex, 15

The Aviator's Wife, 345

Avintyri Jons og Gvendar, 211

L'avventura, 16

Awaara, 278

Awake from Mourning, 16
Al Ayyam Al Tawila, 219
Aziza, 406
Azpúrra, Carlos, 414
Azteca Film company, 262

Baara, 85
Baard, Frances, 16
Babai Zhuangshi, 77
Baccar, Selma, 18, 83, 406
Bacon, Lloyd, 112
Badger, Clarence, 367
Badrakhan, Ahmad, 133
Baghdadi, Maroun, 239–40
Baillargeon, Paule, 329, 330
Baimaonu, 340
Baisler, Marianne, 187
Baker, Roy Ward, 112, 243
Bakri, Asma Al, 134
Balaban, Barney, 309
A balada da Praia dos Caes, 97
Balázs, Béla, 161
Balcon, Michael, 129, 169
Les baliseurs du désert, 18
Ball, Lucille, 194
Ball of Fire, 384–5
Ballad of Crowfoot, 282–3
The Ballad of Dog's Beach, 97
The Ballad of Narayama, 398–9
Ballad of a Soldier, 378
Ballad of Tara, 42
Ballada soldata, 378
Ballade aux sources, 205
Balogun, Ola, 5, 6
Balsaitis, Jonas, 30
Band of Outsiders, 177
La banda del automovil gris, 262
Bande à part, 177
The Bandit, 50
Bank, Mirra, 289
Baqianli Lu Yun He Yue, 77
Barba, Meche, 233

Barbados, 65
Barberousse, 11
Barberousse Akhawati, 11
Barberousse, My Sisters, 11
Barclay, Barry, 255
Al Baree, 133
Barish, Leora, 358
Barnard, Chris, 198
Barnet, Boris, 378
Barr, Charles, 129
Barrandov studios, 80
Barravento, 343
Barren Lives, 81
Barreto, Lima, 50
Barrett, Franklyn, 28
Barrett, Lezli-An, 53
Barrios, Gita de, 50, 234
Barstow, Stan, 53
Barth, Luis Moglia, 435
Barthes, Roland, 315, 360, 388
Bartlett, Freude, 401
Barto, Agniia, 379
Barton, Nathalie, 330
Bartosch, Berthold, 337
Baryshnikov, Mikhail, 109–10
Les Bas-fonds, 339
Bas Ya Bahr, 231
Basaglia, Maria, 50
Basinger, Kim, 361
Bateson, Gregory, 138, 259
Bathily, Moussa Yoro, 7
Bathory, countess Elisabeth, 243, 410
The Battle of Chile, 75
Baudrillard, Jean, 320–1
Bausch, Pina, 9
Baxter, Anne, 194
Bazin, André, 161, 165, 292, 336
Beatles, 343
Beattie, Anne, 368
Beatty, Warren, 229
Le Beau mariage, 345
Le Beau Serge, 292
Beaudine, William, 314
Beaudry, Diane, 330
Beaumont, Harry, 99
The Beautiful Days of Sheherazade, 272

Beautiful Duckling, 397
Beautiful Sixteen, 77
Beauvoir, Simone de, 8, 36, 165
Les beaux jours de Sheherazade, 272
Becht, Ruth, 146
Becker, German, 74
Becker, Jacques, 165
Beggars of Life, 58
Bei Aiqing Yiwang de Jiaoluo, 78
Beijing Film Academy, 156
Beijing studios, 78
Beineix, Jean-Jacques, 166, 303
Beirut, O Beirut, 239, 240
Béla Balázs Studio (BBS), 135, 136, 210
Bell, Monta, 368
La belle et la bête, 143
Belle of the Nineties, 422
The Belles of St Trinians, 238
Bellissima, 285
Bellocchio, Marco, 222, 291
Bellon, Yannick, 91, 165, 166, 292
Bellour, Raymond, 389
Belmont, Charles, 166
Belo, Jane, 259
Belyazid, Farida, 272
Ben Mabrouk, Nejia, 18
Benani, Hamid, 271
Benbarka, Souheil, 271, 272
Benegal, Shyam, 33, 217, 311
Benilde ou a Virgem Mãe, 303
Benilde, the Virgin Mother, 303
Bennett, Compton, 436
Bennett, Enid, 250
Bennett, Joan, 154, 159
Benning, James, 179
Benoît-Lévy, Jean, 136, 137
Bensusan, Tony, 16
Benton, Robert, 65, 256

Benveniste, Emile, 360
Beresford, Bruce, 21
Berg, Marina de, 27
Berg-Ejvind ock hans
    hustru, 211
Bergholm, Timo, 40
Bergman, Ingrid, 285,
    385
Berkeley, Busby, 24, 139,
    235, 237, 276
Berlin, Irving, 409
Berlin Film Festival, 159
Berman, Brigette, 63
Bernhardt, Curtis, 101,
    225
Berõringen, 41
Bertini, Francesca, 222
Berto, Juliet, 166
Bertolucci, Bernardo, 23,
    222, 291
Bertsch, Marguerite, 203
Berwick Street Film
    Collective, 53, 153,
    269–70
Besos brujos, 232
Besson, Luc, 166
The Best Years of Our
    Lives, 23
La Bête humaine, 338,
    339
Between Mountain and
    Shore, 211
Bewitched Kisses, 232
Beye, Ben Diogaye, 7
Bhumika, 310, 311
Die Bian, 392
Biberman, Herbert, 237,
    371–2
Les Bicots-nègres, vos
    voisins, 7, 205
Bicycle Thieves, 285
The Big Boss, 231
The Big Chill, 276
The Big Doll House, 140
Big Li, Old Li, and Small
    Li, 434
The Big Sky, 191
The Big Sleep, 34, 191,
    280
A Bill of Divorcement, 196
Billon, Pierre, 91
The Birds, 200

Birkin, Jane, 187
Birmingham University,
    Centre for
    Contemporary Cultural
    Studies, 106
The Birth of A Nation, 44,
    47, 175, 181, 332
The Birth of a Race, 44
Bissonnette, Sophie, 330
Bitter Rice, 22, 285
The Bitter Tea of General
    Yen, 333
The Bitter Tears of Petra
    von Kant, 145
Die bitteren Traenen der
    Petra von Kant, 145
Bjerring-Parker, Gudrun,
    62
Bjørn, Johnny, 348
Blaché, Herbert, 185
Blaché, Features Inc, 185
Black, Cathal, 220
Black, Edward, 169
Black Audio Film
    Collective, 44
The Black Box (video
    magazine), 210
The Black Cannon Incident,
    157
Black Girl, 359
Black God, White Devil,
    343
Black Narcissus, 324
Black Sweat, 11
Blackburn, Marthe, 315
Blackmail, 199
Blackwood, Maureen, 44,
    46, 67, 172, 372
Blasetti, Alessandro, 69
Der blaue Engel, 119, 121,
    387
Blier, Bertrand, 166
Blind Date, 358
Bloen Marion, 286
Blonde Venus, 121, 346,
    387
Blondell, Joan, 417
Blood and Guts, 232
Blood and Roses, 243
Blood and Sand, 191
Blood Simple, 160
Blood Wedding, 272

Blow-up, 257
The Blue Angel, 119, 121,
    387
Blue Movie, 286
Blue Murder at St Trinians,
    238
Blumenschein, Tabea,
    305–6
Blystone, John G., 237
Boardman, Eleanor, 367
Bob le flambeur, 165
Body and Soul, 44
Body Double, 116
Body Heat, 160
Bogarde, Dirk, 122–3
Bogart, Humphrey, 34,
    280
Bogdanovich, Peter, 96,
    115, 290
La Bohème, 176
Bohr, José, 263
Böll, Heinrich, 404
Bond, Ralph, 55
Les bonnes femmes, 293
Bonnie and Clyde, 229
Booth, Herbert, 28
Booth, Margaret, 266
Boothe, Claudine, 66
Borcosque, Carlos, 435
Borelli, Lyda, 222
Born Yesterday, 47, 94, 106
Borom Sarret, 5, 359
Borroloola Aboriginal
    Community, 31
Bortnik, Aída, 234
Borzage, Frank, 101
El Bostagui, 134
Bostan, Elisabeta, 132
Bostrom, Denise, 429
Böszörményi, Géza, 185
Bou van 'n Nasie, 376
Bouabdallah, Hassan, 11
Bouamari, Mohamed, 11
Boubou-cravate, 7
Boudu sauvé des eaux, 338
Boudu Saved From
    Drowning, 338–9
Boulton, Laura, 63, 281,
    329
Bounghah Theatral, 396
Bourgault, Hélène, 182
Bourguiba, President, 406

Bourquia, Farida, 271
Bouzid, Nouri, 406–7
Bow, Clara, 367
Box, Betty, 53
Box, Sydney, 49, 169
Boyd, Millie, 1
Boyer, Charles, 14
Boyle, Joseph C., 384
Boytler, Arcady, 263
Brabant, Sylvie van, 330
Brabin, Charles J., 35
Bracho, Carlos, 155
Bracho, Julio, 233, 263
Brakel, Nouchka van, 286
Brakhage, Stan, 32, 257, 260
Brambila, Rocio, 155
Brandauer, Klaus Maria, 209
Brando, Marlon, 3, 237
Brandon, Henry, 332
Brandon, Lianne, 289
Bravo, Estela, 105
Bravo, Sergio, 75
Brazil Vita Filme, 50
Breathless, 22, 176, 293
Brecht, Bertolt, 98, 130, 135, 217, 227, 400
Breen Office, 326
Breer, Robert, 288
Bremer, Sylvia, 250
Brenon, Herbert, 35
Bressan, Arthur, 256
Bresslaw, Bernard, 67
Bresson, Robert, 165, 292, 374
Brewster McCloud, 12
Bridget Productions, 249
Brief Encounter, 345, 346
Bright, Sara, 83
Bright Road, 111
Bringing Up Baby, 191, 196
Brink, André, 308
Brink of Life, 41
British Broadcasting Corporation (BBC), 99, 297, 436
British Council, 5, 99
British Instructional Films, 49, 156

British Sounds, 177
Brittain, Vera, 49
Broadway Nights, 384
Broken Barrier, 255, 293
Broken Blossoms, 176, 181
Brooks, Albert, 358
Brooks, James L., 426
Brooks, Sue, 31
Brophy, Philip, 31
Brossard, Nicole, 329
The Brothers, 169
Brown, Clarence, 101, 144, 170
Browning, 409
Bruck, Edith, 223
Brunel, Adrian, 339
Brunius, Pauline, 391, 391
Brussels Royal Film Archives, 38–9
Bruxelles-Transit, 38
Bruyn, Dirk de, 30
Budapest studios, 210
Budawanny, 220
Buddies, 256
Budow, Slatan, 400
Die Buechse der Pandora, 58
Buenos dias, Buenos Aires, 43
Buesst, Nigel, 30
Buffalo Bill and the Indians, 12
Bugajski, Ryszard, 225
Bulgaria, 131–2
Buñuel, Luis, 138, 164, 264, 381
Burckner, Clara, 425
Burgess, Marilyn, 182
Burkina Faso, 5, 7
The Burning of the Red Lotus Temple, 77
Burstall, Tim, 29
Burstyn, Ellen, 357
Burton, Richard, 244
Bus Stop, 270
Bussi, Simone, 91
Bussi, Solange, 164
Buta to Gunkan, 226
Butler, David, 102, 113, 198, 401
Butterfly Murders, 392

By the Light of the Silvery Moon, 113, 401
Bye Bye Brasil, 51

Cabanas, Luis, 395
Cabezas cortadas, 343
CADA, 75
Caesar and Cleopatra, 241
Caged Heat, 115
'Cagney and Lacey', 399
Cahan, Abraham, 368
Cahiers du cinéma, 135, 161, 165, 200, 228, 292, 320
Cai Chusheng, 77
La caída, 402
Caiozzi, Silvio, 75
Calamity Jane, 102, 113–4, 198, 401
Caliche sangriento, 74
Callaghan, Mary, 30
Calmos, 166
Calvert, Phyllis, 129–30, 169
Calzada, Maripi Saenz de la, 265
Camacho, Avila, 263
Camera Buff, 317
Camera Women, 223
Camerini, Mario, 69
Cameron, James, 198, 207, 356, 429
Cameroon, 7
Camille, 105, 170, 345, 346
Camille without Camellias, 17
Camiragua, Patricia, 75, 170
Cammell, Donald, 356
Campbell, Barbara, 30
Campion, Jane, 30, 430
Canada Council, 63
Canadian Broadcasting Corporation (CBC), 163, 282, 283, 302, 369
Canaille, Caro, 165
La canción del turista, 412
The Candidate, 85, 335
O cangaceiro, 50
Os canibais, 303

Cannes Film Festival, 42, 159, 382
The Cannibals, 303
Canoa, 264
A Canterbury Tale, 324
Cantiflas, 263
Cantrills Filmnotes, 64
Canyon Cinema Cooperative, 74
Cao Yu, 433
Capomazza, Tilde, 223
Le Caporal épinglé, 339
Capra, Frank, 93, 237, 333, 384
Captain Khourshid, 218
Les Carabiniers, 176–7
Carax, Leos, 166
Cardenal, Ernesto, 254
Cardens, Lazaro, 263
Carl, Renée, 164
Carle, Gilles, 232
Carlsen, Henning, 116
Carmen, 284
Carmen Jones, 45, 110, 111
Carné, Marcel, 164, 165, 292
CAROLA, 361
Le Carosse d'or, 338, 339
Carré, Louise, 330–1
Carrie, 116
Carrioza, Eulalia, 83
The Cars That Ate Paris, 29
Carter, Angela, 53
Carthage Film Festival, 406
La casa del ángel, 402
Casque d'Or, 165
Cassavetes, John, 51, 429
Casta Diva, 287
Castillo, Inés, 51
Castro, Fidel, 103–4
Cat Ballou, 401
Cat People, 206
Cathay Organization, 397
Catholic Church, 220, 316, 319, 417
Catholic Legion for Decency, 326
Caught, 304, 305
Cavadini, Alessandro, 31, 138

Cawelti, John, 422–3
Cazals, Felipe, 264
CBS, 414
Cecilia, 373
Ceddo, 7, 359
Celestina, María V. de, 234
Céline and Julie Go Boating, 32
Céline et Julie vont en bateau, 342
Central African Republic, 8
Central Australian Aboriginal Media Association (CAAMA), 1
Central Motion Picture Corporation (CMPC), 397
Central Office for Polish Cinematography, 316
Centre Bruxellois de l'Audiovisuel (CBA), 39
Centre Simone de Beauvoir, 166
Centro De Capacitación Cinematografica (CCC), 265, 394
Centro de Estudios Cinematograficos (CUEC), 264
Centro Portugues de Cinema, 320
Centro Sperimentale di Cinematografia, 68
Centro Sperimentale di Roma, 42
Černy Petr, 107
Cervantes, Chela, 394
Césaire, Aimé, 253
Chaanghack, 396
Chabrol, Claude, 232, 293
El Chacal de Nahueltoro, 74
Chahal, Randa, 239
Chahine, Youssef, 133, 134
Chait, Melanie, 72
Chalbaud, Roman, 413
Chambers, Marilyn, 361

Chamoun, Jean, 239, 308, 309
Chang Sylvia, 398
Chang Yi, 398
Changchun studios, 78
The Chapel, 7
Charlie, Bob, 282
Charlotte, 286
Chase, Doris, 109
Chaskel, Pedro, 75
Chávez, Rebeca, 104
The Cheat, 114
The Cheated, 18, 309, 394
Chen Boer, 77–8
Chen Kaige, 157
Chen Ken-hou, 398
Chen Shouzhi, 76
Chen Wenmin, 397
Chenal, Pierre, 164, 435
Cheng Bugao, 77
Cheng Yin, 340
El Chergui, 271, 272
Cheria, Tahar, 406
The Chess Players, 33
Cheyenne Autumn, 332
Chicago Film Festival, 159
Chidambaram, 311
La Chienne, 338
Children's Film Foundation, 156
The Children's Hour, 245, 346
Chile Films, 74, 75, 435
China Central Film Studio, 77
China Film Distribution Corporation 78
China Film Studio, 77, 397
China Seas, 189
Chinatown, 160
La Chinoise, 176, 177
Chiung Yao, 397
Chlen pravitelstva, 378
The Choice, 7
Chouik, Mohamed, 11
Christensen, Benjamin, 115
Christensen, Carlos Hugo, 435

The Christian Science Monitor, 158
Christie, Agatha, 34
Christie, Julie, 39, 323, 406
Chronicle of the Years of Embers, 10
Chu Tien-wen, 398
Chuangye, 340
Chukhnov, Vladimir, 364
Chukhrai, Grigorii, 378
Chuncan, 77
The Churning, 311
Churubusco film studios, 264, 265
Le Ciel est à vous, 165
The Cigarette Girl, 373
Cimino, Michael, 290
Cinco Vezes Favela, 81
'Cine-eye' group, 390
Cine Liberación, 383
Ciné Libre, 38
Cine-mujer, 83, *83*
Cine-Ojo, 75
Cine Urgente, 413
Cineaste, 227
Cinema Action, 53
Cinema City (Hong Kong), 205
Cinema Djidid, 11
'Cinema of Moral Anxiety', 224, 225, 317
Cinema Novo (Portugal), 320
Cinema Papers, 113
Cinémathèque Française, 135, 137, 185, 277
Cinémathèque Québécoise, 331
Cinematografía Latino Americana Sociedad Anonima (CLASA), 263
Cineplex Odeon Theaters, 408
Cinesisters, 82
Cinesound, 29
Cineteca, 90
Cinq jours d'une vie, 85
Cinta Limited, 350
The Citadel, 11
Citizen Kane, 310

Citizen's Band, 115
La città delle donne, 285
City Dreams, 394
City of Women, 285
Civelli, Carla, 50
Cixous, Hélène, 322, 375
Claes, Ernest, 38
Clair, René, 121, 164, 375
Claire's Knee, 345
Clash of the Ash, 220
Clavell, James, 343
Clayburgh, Jill, 419
Clayton, Jack, 57
Clayton, Susan, 56, 153
Clément, Catherine, 303
Clément, René, 165, 292
Cleopatra, 194
Clifton, Elmer, 249
Cline, Edward, 422
Close, Glenn, 429
Close Up (Journal), 59, 193
Clouzot, Henri-Georges, 36, 165
The Coalburner, 11
Coalface, 55
The Cobweb, 34
Cocteau, Jean, 32, 143
Coen, Joel, 160
Coetzee, J. M., 187
Coffee, Lenore, 357
Coffey, Essie, 1, 2, 31
Cohl, Emile, 185, 288
Cohn, Harry, 191, 193, 384
Le Coiffeur des quartiers pauvres, 272
Coixet, Isabel, 381
Colbert, Claudette, 194
'The Colbys', 385
Coles, Tom, 80
Colette, 91
La Collectionneuse, 345
Collins, Kathleen, 44
Collins, Richard, 19
Colonel Redl, 209
Colonial Film Unit, 5
The Color of Money, 357
Colson-Malleville, Marie-Anne, 165
Coma, 256
Come and Get It, 191

Come Back to the Five and Dime, Jimmy Dean, Jimmy Dean, 12
Comencini, Francesca, 223
Comencini, Luigi, 69
Comerford, Joe, 220
Committee for the Fifth Amendment, 34
Commonwealth Film Unit, 28
The Communicants, 41
Communist Party (Soviet Union), 378
Companeez, Nina, 165
Con las mujeres cubanas, 104
Concerns of American Indian Women, 282
Concerto pour un exil, 7
Confesión al amanecer, 435
Congo, 7
Conlon, Evelyn, 275
Connolly, Andrew, 417
Connor, Kenneth, 67
The Conquering Power, 368
Conrad, Patrick, 38
Consortium Inter-africain de Distribution Cinématographique (CIDC), 6
Contempt, 36, 176, 177
Contreras, Adriana, 265
Controversia, 104
Conway, Jack, 190, 326
Cook, Pam, 24, 153, 389
Cooper, 47
Copland, Aaron, 60
Coppola, Francis Ford, 95, 115, 116, 239, 290
Le Corbeau, 165
Corbucci, Sergio, 351
Cordova, Arturo de, 263
Corfixen, Lizzie, 116
Corman, Roger, 115, 140, 206, 291, 347, 356
Corner Forsaken by Love, 78
Corona, Ernest, 233
Corona, Isabela, 233
'Coronation Street', 371

Corporacion Nacional Cinematografica (CONACINE), 265
Corporacion Nacional Cinematografica de Trabajadores y Estado (CONACITE I & II), 265
Cortazar, Ernesto, 263
Cortázar, Octavio, 104, 373
Cortes, Bussi, 90, 265
Cortines, Adolfo Ruiz, 264
Costa Rica, 71
Counterattack, 340
Le Coup du Berger, 342
Couselo, Jorge Miguel, 21
Les Cousins, 292
Cover Girl, 191
Cowan, Tom, 29
Coward, Noël, 52
Cox, Alex, 344
Cox, Paul, 254
Crabtree, Arthur, 169
Craczyk, Ed, 12
The Cranes Are Flying, 378
Crawford, Anne, 237
Crawford, Anne Marie, 30
Crawley, Judith, 62, 63
Crawley Studios, 363
Crazy Love, 38
Creative Film Foundation, 116
Crepeau, Jeanne, 330
Crichton, Michael, 256
Cries and Whispers, 41
Le Crime de Monsieur Lange, 338, 339
Os crimes de Diogo Alves, 319
The Crimes of Diogo Alves, 319
Criminal Conversation, 220
Crisis, 41
Crocodile Dundee, 29
Crombie, Donald, 430
Cronaca di un amore, 16
Crosby, Bing, 258, 309

Crosland, Alan, 417
The Crossroads, 77
Crouillère, Monique, 330
The Crow, 42
The Crowd, 368
Crown Film Unit, 55, 338
The Cruel Sea, 231
Cruikshank, Sally, 15
The Cry, 107
Cry Freedom, 6
Cuba si!, 292
CUEC (University Center for Cinematographic Studies), 154, 156
Cultural Revolution (China), 339
Cultural Studies (journal), 228
Cun Miao, 434
Cunningham, Merce, 333
The Curse, 7, 359
Curtiz, Michael, 13, 65, 70, 101, 113, 272, 357, 426
Curwood, James Oliver, 364
Cutts, Graham, 339
Czechoslovakia, 5, 6
Czinkóczi, Zsuzsa, 262
Czlowiek z Marmaru, 224, 317
Czlowiek z Zelaza, 317

Da Li, Lao Li he Shao Li, 434
Da Lu, 77
Daar Doer in die Bosveld, 376
Dadaists, 269
Dagher, Assia, 133
Daghidi, Ines, 134
Dahr, Eva, 298
Daigaku wa Deta Keredo, 398
Daily Life in a Syrian Village, 394
Daily Mail, 36
Dale, Jim, 67
Dali, Salvador, 164
'Dallas', 371

Dalle, Beatrice, 361
La dama de la muerte, 435
Dan Duyu, 77
Dance Pretty Lady, 402
Dancers, 109
Danis, Aimée, 329
Dansereau, Mireille, 63, 329, 330
Dante, Joe, 140
Daopoulo, Roni, 223
D'Arcangelo, Maresa, 214
Dark Passage, 34
Dark Victory, 112, 426
Dassonville, Hélène, 165
Dastfouroush, 218
Daughters of Darkness, 38, 243
Davandeh, 42
Davenport, Dorothy, 366
Davenport, Harry, 356
Daves, Delmer, 34
David, Tissa, 14
Davidson, Paul, 174
Davies, Marion, 310
Davis, David, 289
Davis, Denis Elmina, 66
Davis, Joanna, 341
Davis, Marvin, 407
Davison, Tito, 263
Dawn, 406
A Day in November, 373
De Mayerling à Sarajevo, 305
Dead by Dark Injustice, 76
Dean, James, 3, 12, 385
Deasy, Frank, 220
Death Be Your Santa Claus, 44
Debbie, 377
Decary, Marie, 330
Decca Records, 408
Decimoveca, 413
Dédée d'Anvers, 165
DEFA film studios, 130, 183, 184
Deghidi, Ines, 18
De Havilland, Olivia, 194
Le Déjeuner sur l'herbe, 338, 339
Del Rio, Dolores, 235, 263, 343

Delaney, Shelagh, 53
Delannoy, Jean, 26
Deleuze, Gilles, 321
Delgado, Miguel, 264
Delia Film, 126
Deling, Bert, 29
Delluc, Louis, 126, 164, 277
Delvaux, André, 38
Demcauk, Irène, 182
Demon Seed, 356
Os demónios de Alcácer-Kibir, 97
De Niro, Robert, 356, 357
Denning, Lord, 54
Depke, Irene-Aimee, 282
Derain, Lucie, 164
Derakhshandeh, Pouran, 219
Derba, Mimi, 262–3
Dermondy, Susan, 22
Derrida, Jacques, 321, 322, 360
Deruddere, Dominique, 38
Desai, Arunaraje, 217
De Santis, Giuseppe, 22, 222, 285
Il deserto rosso, 16
De Sica Vittorio, 69, 222, 238, 285, 336
Desire (Borzage), 121
Desire (Jasný), 107
Desperate Moments, 436
Destry Rides Again, 121
Deus e o diablo na terra do sol, 343
Deutsche Lichtspiel Gesellschaft, 174
Deux ou trois choses que je sais d'elle, 176, 177
The Devil is a Woman, 119, 121, 387
The Devil's Eye, 41
The Devils of Alcácer-Kibir, 97
The Devil's Wanton, 41
La devoradora, 263
Devoyod, Suzanne, 164
Di Lauro, Jorge, 75, 435
Un día de noviembre, 373

Dialog studios, 210
The Diary of a Chambermaid, 339
Diary of a Lost Girl, 58
Díaz, Rolando, 104
Dickens, Charles, 52
Dickinson, Thorold, 221
Didden, Marc, 38
Diegues, Carlos, 51, 81
Dienar, Baruch, 221
Dieterle, William, 121
Diez, Ana, 381
Dikongue-Pipa, Jean-Pierre, 7
DiMaggio, Joe, 270
Dimanche à Pékin, 292
Dimension Pictures, 347, 348
Ding Jun Mountain, 76
Ding Jun Shan, 76
Dinner at Eight, 105, 190
Diop, Djibril Mambety, 7
Diop, Mustapha, 7
La diosa arrodillada, 263
Director's Guild of America, 347
A Dirty Western, 318
Dishonored, 121
Disney, Walt, 14, 288, 337, 338
Dittborn, Eugenio, 75
Diva, 303
Divine, 304
Djamila the Algerian, 133
Djävulens öga, 41
Djeli, 7
Do Ma Dan, 206
Doane, Mary Anne, 257, 304, 312, 375
Dr Mabuse, der Spieler, 189, 365
The Doctor of Gafiré, 7
Dom na Trubnoi, 378
Dona diabla, 263
Donaldson, Mona, 73
Donaldson, Roger, 294
Donan, Stanley, 276
Donda, Franca, 413
Donen, Stanley, 114
Dong Kena, 78
Dongen, Helen van, 286
Dongfang Yetan, 77

Donner, Jorn, 40
Donner, Richard, 206
Don't Change Your Husband, 367
Don't Let It Get You, 293
De Dood van Elmien Alder, 198
Doolan, Leila, 221
Dora Film, 298–9
Dordi, Loredana, 223
Doria, Alejandro, 384
Dos Santos, Nelson Pereira, 51, 81, 435
Double Indemnity, 154, 159, 313, 363, 385
Douro, faina fluvial, 302
Douro, River Work, 302
Dovzhenko, Aleksandr, 373–4, 379
Doyle, Hélène, 182, 330
Doyle, Stuart, 29
Dracula, 409
A Dream Walking, 15
Dreams, 41
Dressed To Kill, 116, 207, 428
Dressier, Marie, 266
Dreyer, 409
Dreyer, Carl, 115
Dreyfuss, Richard, 232
A Drunkard's Reformation, 181
Dual, Denise, 165
Dudding, Kathy, 294
Duelle, 342
Duigan, John, 29
Duncan, Alma, 63
Dunham, Katherine, 117
Dunkley-Smith, John, 30
Dunn, Willy, 282–3
Dunning, George, 119, 343
Duparc, Henri, 7
Durbin, Deanna, 408
Dutch Film Academy, 286
Dutt, Guru, 217
Dutt, Sunil, 279
Duvivier, Julien, 164, 292
Dwoskin, Steve, 257
Dyer, Richard, 270, 385

Dymon, Frankie Jr, 44
'Dynasty', 371

Eady, David, 436
Eagles, Jeanne, 368
Early Spring, 226
The Earrings of Madame de
. . . , 305
The Earth, 396
'EastEnders', 371
Ecaré, Désiré, 7–8
Echeveria, Luis, 264
The Eclipse, 16
L'ellisse, 16
Eco, Umberto, 360
Ecstasy, 107
Edelman, Heinz, 119
Edinburgh Film Festival,
159, 227, 273
Edison, Thomas, 138,
173
Edström, Ingrid, 392
Edwards, Blake, 102,
113, 358
Edwards, J. Gordon, 35
Effi Briest, 145
Efter repetitionen, 42
Egymasra nezve, 346
Die Ehe der Maria Braun,
145
Eight Hours Don't Make a
Day, 145
Eight Thousand Miles of
Clouds and the Moon, 77
Eisenstein, Sergei, 59,
117, 132, 135, 193, 263,
269, 343, 375
Eisler, Hans, 400
El Ani, Youssef, 219
El Behi, Rida, 406
El Chahhal, Randa, 308
El Derkaoui, Mustapha,
271–2
El Tazi, Abdel Rahmane,
272
El Zoubaidi, Kais, 219
Eldad, Ilan, 221
Eléna et les hommes, 339
Eliot, George, 119
Elles, 11
Ellis, John, 143
Ellis, Ruth, 126

Eltit, Diamela, 75, 170
Emei Studios, 78
Emerald, Connie, 248
Emerald Productions, 249
Emerson, John, 248, 357
Emitai, 6, 359
Empire Marketing Board
Film Unit, 55
Endless Night, 238
Les Enfants du paradis, 165
Engström, Ingemo, 162,
290
Enoch Arden, 181
Enter the Dragon, 231
Enter the Fat Dragon, 231
L'Entraîneuse, 164
Enyedi, Ildiko, 209
Epstein, Jean, 136, 137
Epstein, Mitch, 278
Equinox Flower, 398
Er Ze De Da Wan Ou,
398
Erba Jiaren, 77
Ermler, Fridrikh, 378,
379
Der ewige Jude: Ein
Dokumentarfilm ueber das
Weltjudentum, 284
Escuela de Cine
(Uruguay), 413
Escuela Internacional de
Cine, Television and
Video, 235
The Eskimo Baby, 296
Das Eskimobaby, 296
Espinosa, Julio García, 104
La estacion del retorno, 75
'Estudios America', 264
Et Dieu créa la femme,
22–3, 36, 292
Etemaad, Rakhshan Bani,
219
The Eternal Jew, 284
Ethiopia, 6, 7
Eulogy of the Dragon
River, 340
Europa Film, 391
European Court, 414
Eustache, Jean, 166
The Ever Free, 334
Everywhere or Perhaps
Nowhere, 205

L'Exile, 7
The Exile, 7, 305
The Exorcist, 207
Experimental Film Fund
(EFF), 29–30
Experimental Group of
the University of
Chile, 75
Expiation, 59
Exposure, 220
Expressionism, 174, 206,
336, 420
Extase, 107
The Exterminating Angel,
264
The Eye Above the Well,
286
The Eyes of the Mummy,
284
Eyre, Richard, 53

The Face, 41
Face to Face, 41
Faces in the Dark, 436
Faces of Women, 7–8
The Facts of Life, 194
Fad Jal, 7
Fadika, Kramo Lancine,
7
Al Fahham, 11
Fairbanks, Douglas, 314,
357–8, 368
Fairy Showering Flowers,
76
Al Fajr, 406
Falastine, Zakirat Shaab,
308
The Fall, 402
Al Fallaka, 406
Famous Players and
Plays, 185
Famous Players-Lasky
Studios, 115, 339, 418
Fängelse, 41
Fanji, 340
Fanny and Alexander, 41,
42
Fanny och Alexander, 41,
42
Fanshel, Susan, 282
Far Away in the Bushveld,
376

Faraah, Empress of Iran, 218
Farahang, Dariush, 218
Farhati, Jilali, 272
Farias, Roberto, 136
Farmer's Weekly, 241
The Faro Document, 41
The Faro Document 1979, 41
Färödokument, 41
Färödokument 1979, 41
Farrar, Geraldine, 115
Faryaod Zir Abbe, 396
Fatal Attraction, 149, 363, 429
Father and Son, 206
Faulkner, William, 190
Faure, Bill, 377
Faustrecht der Freiheit, 145
Favela Five Times, 81
Fear Eats the Soul, 145
Feature Play Company, 114
Federal Women's Film Program (Quebec), 330
Fédération Panafricain des Cinéastes (FEPACI), 5, 6
Fei Long Guo Jiang, 231
Fei Mu, 77
Feijoo, Beda Docampo, 39
Feix, Andrée, 165
Felag Kvikmyndagerdar-manna (Icelandic Filmmakers' Association), 211
Feldman, Simon, 301
Felix, Marian, 263
The Fellaghas, 406
Fellini, Federico, 222, 280, 285, 421
Female on the Beach, 101
Feminist Review, 228
Feministo, 270
La Femme de l'aviateur, 345
Une Femme est une femme, 22, 176
Une Femme mariée, 23, 176, 177
Feo, Ivan, 413
Ferguson, Betty, 426

Fernández, Carolina, 265
Fernández, Emilio 'El Indio', 233, 263
Fernández, Rosa Marta, 90, 265
Ferrara, Juan, 155
Ferreri, Marco, 222, 291
Ferreyra, Agustin 'El Negro', 232
Fertile Memory, 309
Festival Panafricain du Cinéma de Ouagadougou (FESPACO), 5
Feuillade, Louis, 185, 277
Feuillère, Edwige, 27
Feyder, Jacques, 164
Fields, W. C., 422
50:50, 376
Fifty-vyftig, 376
Fight to the Last, 77
Figura, Katarzyna, 225, 354
La Fille de l'eau, 338
La Fille du puisatier, 165
Film and History Project, 153
Film and Theater Censorship Committee (China), 77
Film Australia, 28
Film Centrum, 391
Film Comment (journal), 113, 190, 227, 429–30
Film Daily, 115
Film d'Art company, 164
Film Finance Corporation (Australia), 30
Film Finance Corporation (India), 216
Film Heritage (journal), 190
Film International, 286–7
Film Korrespondenz, 113
Film-Kurier, 135
Film Makers Ireland, 221
Film Polski, 224, 316
Film Workshop, 205
FilmBase, 221
Filmkultura (journal), 210

Filmliga, 285–6
Film-makers' Distribution Center (USA), 85
Filmmakers Cooperative (New York), 74, 85
Filmmakers Inc., 249
Filmnews (journal), 393
Films and Filming (journal), 227
Les Films Soleil Ô, 204
Filmstudio 70, 223
Fin de fiesta, 402
Fink, Margaret, 21
Finnane, Kieran, 31
Finnish Television Broadcasting Company, 296
Finye, 85
Fire Festival, 226
The First Foundation of Buenos Aires, 43
First Steps, 11
The Fisherman's Song, 77
Fiske, Pat, 393
Fists of Fury, 231
Fitzgerald, F. Scott, 368
Fitzmaurice, George, 235–7, 368
Five Days in a Life, 85
Flaherty, Robert, 138, 286, 336
Flajano, Ennio, 69
The Flame of New Orleans, 121
Flamingo Road, 101
Flashdance, 276
Fleetwood, David, 318
Fleischer, Max, 15
Fleming, Victor, 45, 189, 276
Le Fleuve, 338, 339
Flitterman, Sandy, 127
Floating Clouds, 226
Flodder, 286
Flooded Out, 43
Flor Sylvestre, 263
Flowing, 226
Flying Down to Rio, 235
FOCINE, 91
Foley, James, 358
Folkets Bio, 391

Les folles années du twist, 11

Fonda, Jane, 13, 385

Fong, Allen, 205, 206

Fontaine, Jean, *304*

Fontaine Effi Briest, 145

A Fool There Was, 35

Foolish Wives, 367

Foot, Michael, 99

För att inte tala om alla dessa kvinnor, 41

For the Sake of Christine, 377

For Sentimental Reasons, 14

Forbidden Paradise, 284

Forbidden Thresholds, 406

Forch, Juan, 75

Ford, Alexander, 221

Ford, Glenn, 191

Ford, John, 194, 256, 290, 332, 343, 388

Ford, Sue, 337

Ford-Smith, Honor, 66

A Foreign Affair, 121

Formalism, 161

Forman, Miloš, 107, 132, 276

Formations (journal), 228

Forst, Willy, 284

Forster, E. M., 52

Fortuna Films, 319

44, or The Tales of the Night, 271

Foster, William, 43

Foucault, Michel, 334

Four Adventures of Reinette and Mirabelle, 345

The 400 Blows, 292

Fox, William, 407

Fox and His Friends, 145

Fox Film Corporation, 407

Fraga, Jorge, 177

Framework (journal), 228

Frampton, Hollis, 334, 426

La Française, 126

Francia, Aldo, 74

Francis, Sam, 213

Francisca, 303

Franck, Arnold, 341

Franco, Debra, 289

Franco, General, 381

Frank, Melvin, 194

Franken, Mannus, 285

Frankfurt School, 161

Franklin, Miles, 21

Frapié, Léon, 136

Fraticelli, Rina, 389–90

Frauen in New York, 145

Frears, Stephen, 53, 363

'Free Cinema' movement, 53, 57

Freeland, Thornton, 235

Freeman, Joan, 344

French Cancan, 338, 339

Frenzy, 436

Freud, Sigmund, 144, 247, 313–14, 327, 356, 375

Frey, Peter, 221

Friedkin, William, 207

Frisch, Larry, 221

Frith, Simon, 344

Fritz, Sonia, 265, 300

Froehlich, Carl, 349

From the Life of the Marionettes, 41–2

La Fronde, 126

Frost, Willi, 283

Fuentes, Fernando de, 263, 360

La fuerza del deseo, 264

Fugitive Cinema Holland, 286–7

A Full Life, 226

Full Moon in Paris, 345

Furlong, Hilary, 22

Furong Zhen, 78, 434

Futemma, Olga, 51

Futurists, 222

Fuzi Qing, 206

Os fuzis, 81

FVVA, 7

Gabin, Jean, 165

Gable, Clark, 189

Gabrielsson, Lisbet, 392

Gad, Urban, 115

Gagliardo, Giovanna, 83, 223

Gagne, Jeanine, 330

Le Gai savoir, 177

Gailey, Peter, 393

Galal, Ahmed, 133

'Galal Studios', 133

Galen, Henry, 339

Gallehr, Theo, 19

Galvez, Esther Morales, 264

Gamaat Al Cinema al Guedida, 133

Gamila Al Gazaeria, 133

Gance, Abel, 121, 126, 137, 164, 165

Ganda, Oumarou, 7

Gandhi, Indira, 279

Ganga Zumba, 81

The Gang's All Here, 237

Gaoshansha De Huawan, 434

García Márquez, Gabriel, 40, 92, 394

Gardel, Carlos, 19

Gardin, Vladimir, 325

Gardinal, Gil, 283

Gardner, Ava, 244

Garland, Judy, 266

Garnett, Tay, 189

Garota de Ipanema, 81

Garson, Greer, 266

Gaslight, 105

Gaudard, Lucette, 164

Gaumont, Léon, 184

Gaumont newsreels, 127

Gauntier, Gene, 203

Gavaldon, Roberto, 233, 263

Gavin, John, 28

Gavshon, Harriet, 16

Gay, Ramón, 233

Gaynor, Janet, 367, 407

Gazzara, Ben, 406

GB Instructional Films (GBI), 156

GECU (Experimental Universtiy Film Group), 71

Geer-Bergenstrahle, Marie-Louise de, 392

Geisel, President, 136

Geld soos Bossies, 376

Gendron, Louise, 182

Genee, Heidi, 425

The General Line, 59

Le Genou de Claire, 345
Gentlemen Prefer Blondes, 24, 191, 270, 358, 386
Genu Hong Mudan, 77
Gerasimov, Sergei, 274
Gerima, Haile, 5, 7
Gerstein, Evelyn, 158
Gervaise, 165
Get To Know Your Rabbit, 116
Geti Tey, 7
Getino, Octavio, 21
Ghaire aze Khoudo Hitch Kasse Naboud, 396
Ghana, 5, 6, 7
Gharibeh va Maah, 42
Ghatak, Ritwik, 217
Giannini, Giancarlo, 421
Gibson, Sarah, 393
Giddes, Carol, 283
Gift of God, 7
Giguère, Nicole, 330
Gilbert, Brian, 256
Gilbert, Craig, 259
Gilbert, John, 368
Gilda, 154, 160, 191, 192, 193, 312, 362
Gill, Seema, 44
Gilliatt, Penelope, 57, 158, 229
Gillis, Don, 60
Gimme Shelter, 343
Girard, Hélène, 329, 330
Girardot, Annie, 166
The Girl, 85
The Girl Can't Help It, 343
The Girl Friends, 17
The Girl from Ipanema, 81
A Girl in Every Port, 58
Girl of My Heart, 376
A Girl of the Bush, 28
Les Girls, 105
The Girls He Left Behind, 237
Gish, Dorothy, 176, 401
Gislason, Oskar, 211
Give Me Back My Country, 77
Gledhill, Christine, 246
Glen, John, 45
Gloria, 429

Glyn, Elinor, 357
God is With Us, 133
God of Thunder, 359
Goddard, Paulette, 309
The Goddess, 77
The Gods Must Be Crazy, 376
Goebbels, Joseph, 284, 350
Goèmons, 165
Goethe, Johann wolfgang von, 267
Gogan, Jane, 221
Goin' To Town, 422
Gold Diggers of 1933, 4, 24, 139
The Golden Coach, 339
Golden Harvest studio, 205, 231
Gone to Earth, 324
Gone With the Wind, 45, 241
Gonzalez, Francisco Rojas, 233
Good Housekeeping (journal), 241
Good Morning Buenos Aires, 43
Good-time Girl, 169
Goodbye Pork Pie, 294, 295
Gordon, Michael, 114, 345
Gordon, Richard, 289
Gosho, Heinosuke, 225
Goskino, 365, 377, 390
Goulding, Edmund, 101, 112, 426
GPO Film Unit, 55, 293, 338
Grable, Betty, 362, 407
Grace, Helen, 28, 31, 393, 430
Graham, Martha, 333
Granados, Daysi, 412
Grand Hotel, 101
Grand Illusion, 339
Le grand voyage, 272
La Grande illusion, 338, 339
Grandin, Ethel, 203
The Grandpa and the Farm Girl, 377

Grau, Jorge, 243
Gray, Lorraine, 289
Grease, 276
The Great St Trinians Train Robbery, 238
Great Seclusion, 107
Great Spirit Within the Hole, 282
The Great Voyage, 272
Greater London Council (GLC), 431
Green, Alfred E., 314
Green, Maj, 30
Green for Danger, 238
The Green Ray, 345
Greene, Graham, 52
Greenhide, 72
Greer, Germaine, 430
Greer, Jane, 313
Greimas, A. J., 360
Grémillon, Jean, 164, 165
Grierson, John, 55, 123, 156, 281
Grierson, Marion, 55
Grierson, Ruby, 55
Griffith, Melanie, 115
'Les Griots', 253
Grønlykke, Lene, 116
Grønlykke, Sven, 116
Grote, Alexandra von, 289, 290
Groulx, Sylvie, 330
The Group of the New Cinema, 133
Growing Up, 398
Gruber, Bettina, 146
Grupo Cine Liberación, 21
Grupo Feminista Miércoles, 413
Grupo Tercer Año, 75
Gruziafilm, 378
Guadeloupe, 65, 66
Guan Haifeng, 77
Guangxi studios, 78
Guatemala, 71
Gudmundsson, August, 211
Gudmundsson, Loftur, 211
La guerra, 412

Guerra, Dorotea, 265
Guerra, Ruy, 40, 81
La guerre du pétrole n'aura pas lieu, 272
Guess Who's Coming to Dinner, 197, 256, 333, 345
Guilbault, Luce, 329, 330
Guinea-Conakry, 6
Guitry, Sacha, 164
Gulbenkian Foundation, 320
Gulf & Western, 309
Gundelach, Renee, 425
The Guns, 81
Gutiérrez Alea, Tomás, 177, 178
Guyana, 65
Guzmán, Patricio, 75
Gycklarnas afton, 41
Gypsy Blood, 284

Haas, Elsie, 45, 66
La Habanera (Sirk), 369
Habanera (Vega), 104, 412
Hackford, Taylor, 109
Hadeth al Nousf Metr, 394
Der Haendler der vier Jahreszeiten, 145
Hafez, Bahiga, 133
Haigang, 340, 434
Al Ha'imoun, 406
Hair, 276
Hair Piece, 43
The Hairdresser of the Poor Neighbourhoods, 272
Hajjar, Rafic, 308
Halas, John, 37–8
Halas and Batchelor, 14, 37–8, 119
The Half Meter Incident, 394
Half Truths, 311
Hall, Alexander, 422
Hall, Grayson, 244
Hall, Ken G., 28, 29
Hall, Stuart, 106
Halldorsdottir, Gudny, 212
Halleck, DeeDee, 72
Hallelujah, 45, 276
Halliwell, Leslie, 189

Hambly, Glenda, 29
Hamburg Film Festival, 414
Hamer, Robert, 129
Hamilton, Guy, 436
Hammer Horror, 53
Hammer Studios, 206
Hammermesh, Mira, 72
Hammid, Alexander (Sasha), 117, 118
Hamnstad, 41
Hamza, Nadia, 18, 134
The Hand in the Tramp, 402
Handsworth Songs, 44
Hani, Susumu, 199, 226
Hanig, Josh, 289
Hansberry, Lorraine, 45
Hansen, Rudolf, 189
The Happiest Days of Your Life, 238
The Hard Way, 248
The Harder They Come, 65
Harlan, Veit, 283, 284
Harper's Bazaar, 34
Harriet Craig, 101
Hart, Robbe de, 39
Hartman, Rivka, 30, 337
Harvest 3000 Years, 7
Harvey, Anthony, 197
Has Anybody Seen My Gal?, 369
Hashmi, Safdar, 33
Hashtoumine rooze Haffteh, 396
Hassani, Kameran, 219
Hasta cierto punto, 178, 371
Hathaway, Henry, 270
Havana Film Festival, 235
Hawal, Qasim, 219, 308
Hawtrey, Charles, 67
Al Hayat Al Yawmiyya fi Oaria Souria, 394
Hays Office, 326, 361
Hayward, Ramai, 254–5
Hayward, Rudall, 254, 293
Hearst, William Randolph, 310

Hearts of the World, 176, 181
The Heat's On, 422
Hecht, Ben, 190
Heckerling, Amy, 140
Hei Ji Yuanhun, 76
Hei Pao Shi Jian, 157
Heifitz, Iosif, 378
Heimat, 424
Hein, Wilhelm, 194–5
Heinz Stiehlke, Fifteen Years Old, 130–1
The Heiress, 194
Helge, Ladislav, 107
Heller in Pink Tights, 105
Hellman, Lillian, 244–5
Help Me to Live, 232
Hemert, Ruud van, 286
Hemingway, Ernest, 190
Hemmings, David, 121
Henderson, Anne, 330
Henie, Sonja, 407
Henning-Jensen, Bjarne, 196
Henzell, Perry, 65
Hepburn, Audrey, 194
Her First Biscuits, 314
Herbstsonat, 41
The Herdsmen, 434
Here We Are Again, 376
The Heritage, 11
Hermosillo, Humberto, 265
Hernández, Germinal, 178
Hernandez, Rosario, 265
The Hero's Wife, 221
Hert, Robbe de, 38
Herz, Juraj, 107
Herzbach, Paul, 402
Herzog, Werner, 289, 424
Hessling, Catherine, 338
Heym Hayu Asara, 221
Heynowski, 130
Hibiscus Town, 78, *433*, 434
Hickey, Kieran, 220
Hier is ons Weer, 376
Higanbana, 398
Higgins, Arthur, 250
Higgins, Colin, 13
High Sierra, 248
High Tension, 41

The Highway, 77
Los hijos de la guerra fria, 75
Hikayat Balad Min Melk Rabbi, 406
Hill, George Roy, 194
Hill, Jack, 140
Hill 24 Doesn't Answer, 221
Hiller, Arthur, 345
Hilyard, Virginia, 30
Himatsuri, 226
Hinemoa, 254, 293
Hinton, Carma, 289
Hippler, Fritz, 284
Hiroshima mon armour, 292
Hirszman, Leon, 51, 81
His Girl Friday, 13, 191
La historia oficial, 21
Hitler, Adolf, 168, 175, 341
Hithergunge Quex, 283
Hjelmslev, Louis, 360
Hoass, Solrun, 337
Hoffman, Dustin, 102
Hogan, Paul, 29
Hoggart, Richard, 106
Holiday, 105
Holliday, Judy, 47, 94, 106
Holt, Seth, 112
Un hombre de éxito, 373
Home from the Hill, 253, 256
L'homme voilé, 240
Honduras, 71
Hong Gaoliang, 78
Hong Shen, 433
Hongdeng Ji, 340
Hongfen Kulou, 77
Hongse Niangzhijun, 340, 434
Honingmann, Hedy, 287
Hoogesteijn, Solveig, 413
Hooper, Tobe, 206
Hope, Bob, 258, 309
Hopper, Hedda, 181
La hora de los hornos, 21
Horne, Lena, 110
Horne, Tina, 330
Horrocks, Roger, 295
Horthy, Admiral, 209

The Hot Box, 115, 140
Hot Pepper, 237
Hou Hsiao-hsien, 398
The Hour of the Furnaces, 21
The Hour of Liberation, 239
Hour of the Wolf. 41
Houria, 11
Houroub Saghira, 239–40
The House of the Angel, 402
House of Pleasure, 305
House on Trubnaia Square, 378
Houston, Spud, 14
Hovmand, Annelise, 116
Howard, Trevor, 187
Howarde, Kate, 250
Howarth, Jocelyn, 250
Hoyts, 28
Hsiao Bi De Gu Shih, 398
Hu Mei, 78, 157
Huan Wo Guxiang, 77
Huang Jianxin, 157
Huang Shuqian, 78
Huang tudi, 157
Hubley, Faith, 15
Hudson, Rock, 24, 332, 370
Hugenberg, 175
Hughes, Howard, 342, 343
Hughes, Ken, 422
Hui, Anne, 205, 206
Hulme, Keri, 326
The Human Beast, 339
Human Desire, 338
Humoresque, 101
Hundred Flowers movement, 78
The Hunger, 207, 244
Hunnia studios, 210
Hinnicutt, Wade, 256
Hunting Flies, 224
Huoshao Hongliansi, 77
Huppert, Isabelle, 166
Las Hurdes, 138
Hurrell, George, 3
Husák, Gustav, 81, 107–8
El húsar de la muerte, 74
Husbands, 51

Hush . . .Hush Sweet Charlotte, 112
Hussein, Saddam, 133
Huston, John, 34, 197, 244, 270, 401
Hyena's Sun, 406

I Accuse, 284
I Am Free, 134
I, Claudius, 387
I Don't Want To Be a Man, 102
I Graduated, but . . ., 398
I Just Want You to Love Me, 145
I Know Where I'm Going, 324
I Live for Love, 235
I Love You, Rosa, 37
I See a Dark Stranger, 238
I Spit On Your Grave, 431
I Walked With A Zombie, 206
I Want a Solution, 134
I Was a Male War Bride, 191
Ibsen, Henrik, 20
ICAIC (Cuban Institute of Cinematic Art and Industry), 75, 104, 105, 177, 373, 412
Iceland in Moving Pictures, 211
Ich klage an, 284
Ich will doch nur, dass ihr mich liebt, 145
Ichikawa, 225
A idade da terra, 343
Identification of a Woman, 17, 17
Identificzione di una donna, 17, 17
Idestam-Almquist, Bengt, 200
El idolo, 435
Ikiru, 226
Ikonen, Ansa, 162
Ill-Fated Love, 303
Illicit Interlude, 41
Illusions (journal), 295
I'm No Angel, 422
Imagen Latente, 75

Imamura, Shohei, 199
Imitation of Life, 149, 198, 369, 370
Immamura, Shohei, 226
Imparja, 1
Impossible Love, 296
In Former Days, 424
In jenen Tagen, 424
In Our Time, 398
In the Name of the Father, 291
An Incident, 434
INCINE, 71
The Independent (journal), 227
Independent Video, 227
India Song, 128
Indians, American, 281–2
Industrail Britian, 55
Infante, Pedro, 263
Infascelli, Fiorella, 223
Ingram, Rex, 368
Inner Mongolia studios, 78
The Innocent, 133
The Insect Woman, 199, 226
Inspiration Pictures, 176
Institut des Hautes Etudes Cinématographiques, 40
Institut du cinema québécois, 330
International Association of Women Filmmakers, 177
International Centre for Films for Children, Brussels, 156
International Festival of the New Latin American Cinema, Havana, 105, 412
International Film School, Havana, 43
International Photographer (journal), 3–4
International Pictures, 408
Intolerance, 175, 181
Inuit, 281
Los inundados, 42–3
Invitation to the Waltz, 402

Iribe, Marie-Louise, 164
Irigaray, Luce, 322, 375
Iris Films, 242
Irish Film Board, 220
Irish Film Institute, 220, 221
Irvine, Louisa, 267
Isaksen, Eva, 298
Isban Israel, 376
Ishtar Films, 242
Iskindiria . . . Leh?, 134
Island i lifandi myndum, 211
Island in the Sun, 111
Isn't Life Wonderful, 181
Issartel, Marielle, 166
Isserman, Aline, 166
Istanbul, 38
It, 367
It Always Rains on Sunday, 129
It Happened One Night, 93
It Rains on Our Love, 41
It Should Happen to You, 106
Itami, Juzo, 226
It's My Life, 176
Itsmo Films, 71
Ivens, Joris, 39, 285–6
Ivory Coast, 7, 8
Izcue, Nora de, 234

Jabor, Arnaldo, 51
Jacka, Elizabeth, 22
Jackie Chan, 231
Jackson, Diane, 14
Jacobs, Lewis, 60
Jacques, Hattie, 67
Jade Pear Death, 77
Jager, Claire, 337
Jagged Edge, 429
Jaguar, 138
Jahanname Be'ezofeh Mann, 396
Jakobson, Roman, 360
Jamaica, 65, 66
James, Sidney, 67
Jameson, Frederic, 321, 334
Jancsó, Miklós, 223
Janitzio, 263
Jankel, Annabel, 14

Jannie Totsiens, 334, 335
Jardine, Alice, 321
Jasný, Vojtěch, 107
Jasset, Victorin, 185
Jayamanne, Laleen, 393
Jazz Age, 367
The Jazz Singer, 417
Jean Renoir, le Patron, 342
Jedda, 2
Jeha, Regina, 51
Jemima and Johnnie, 44
Jenny, 164
Jensen, Ingrid Oustrup, 116
Jesus Christ Superstar, 343
Jewison, Norman, 343
Jezebel, 93, 112, 346
Jiang Qing, 339–40
Jimenez, Mary, 39
Jing Wu Men, 231
Jireš, Jaromíl, 107
Jochukko, 199
Jodrell, Steve, 423, 432
Johnny Guitar, 13, 101, 198, 245, 256, 423
Johnson, Amy, 24
Johnson, Avril, 44
Johnson, George, 44
Johnson, Lamont, 431
Johnson, Nobel, 44
Jones, Allen, 273
Jones, Amy, 140
Jones, Chuck, 14
Jones, Grace, 45
Joplin, Janis, 344
Jordán, Josefina, 413
Jordan, Marion, 67
Jordan, Neil, 53
Joritz, Cathy, 146
Joseph, Helen, 16
Le Jour se lève, 164
Journées Cinématographique de Carthage (JCC), 5
Journey Among Women, 29
Journey into Autumn, 41
Joy, Leatrice, 367
Joyce, James, 60
Juana Imes de la Cruz, Sor, 39
Jud Suess, 283–4
Judex, 277

Judgement at Nuremberg, 121
Judith of Bethulia, 181
Jules et Jim, 22, 190
Julia, 13
Julian, Rupert, 206
Julien, Isaac, 44, 372
'Juliet Bravo', 399
Julio Comienza en Julio, 75
Jump Cut (journal), 347
Junco, Victor, 155
Jungfrukällan, 41
The Jungle Princess, 145, 194
Junoon, 33
Just a Gigolo, 121
Justiniano, Gonzalo, 75
Juventud desenfrenada, 264
Jy is my Liefling, 376

Kabore, Gaston, 7
Kaeutner, Helmut, 424
Kahlo, Frida, 155
Al Kalaat, 11
Kalatozov, Mikhail, 378
Kamal, Hussein, 133, 134
Kamba, Sebastian, 7
Kamwa, Daniel, 7
Die Kandidaat, 334, 335
Kane, Carol, 80
Kann, Michael, 130
Kannava, Anna, 31
Kanojo to Kare, 199, 226
Kaplan, E. Ann, 230, 269
Kaplan, Nelly, 23, 165, 372
Kapoor, Raj, 217, 278–9
Karanth, Prema, 217
Karina, Anna, 166, 293
Karlovy Vary film festival, 40
Karmen, Roman, 390
Karu, Erkki, 162
Karvells, Georgina, 16
Kasdan, Lawrence, 160, 254, 276
Kast, Pierre, 292
Kathleen Mavourneen, 35
Katka bumazhnii ranet, 378
Katka the Apple Seller, 378
Katon, Roseann, 112

Katrina, 198, 334, 335, 377
Katzelmacher, 145
Kaul, Mani, 217
Kaulen, Patricio, 74
Kawalerowicz, Jerzy, 353–4
Kay, Karyn, 24
Kazan, Elia, 237, 241
Ke Niu, 397
Keaton, Diane, 80
Keel, Howard, 114
Keeler, Ruby, 417
Kellerman, Annette, 250
Kelly, Gene, 191
Kelly, Grace, 47, 194
Kelly, Mary, 269
Kent, Jean, 169
Kerkovian, Kirk, 266
Kerrigan, Patricia, 417
Keuken, Johan van der, 286
The Key, 308
Key Largo, 34
Kfar-Kassem, 239, 240, 309, 394
Khalaagh, 42
Khan, Mehboob, 217, 278
Khandhar, 33
Khemir, Naceur, 18, 406
Khleifi, Michel, 39, 309
Khlifi, Omar, 406
Khmelik, Maria, 379
Khoake, 396
Khokhlova, Aleksandra, 379, 380
Khrushchev, Nikita, 107, 378
Kidder, Margot, 116
Kidron, Beeban, 53, 198
Kieslowski, Krzysztof, 317
Kilas, o mau da fita, 97
Kilas, the Film's Baddie, 97
The Killing of Sister George, 245
A Kind of Loving, 57
King, Donna Conway, 62
King, Henry, 176
King, Noel, 230
King, Stephen, 116

King of Comedy, 357
The King of Kings, 115
King Hu, 392
King Kong, 47
King Solomon's Mines, 376
Kinney National Services, 417
Kinoshita, Keisuke, 398
Kirkwood, James, 314
Kismet, 121
Kiss Me Deadly, 160
Kissat Lika, 11
Klein, Bonnie Sher, 148, 319, 329, 389
Klein, Jim, 124, 289
Kleiser, Randal, 276
Kleist, Heinrich von, 273, 352
Klimov, Elem, 364
Klodawski, Hélène, 330
Kluge, Alexander, 113, 387
Klute, 13, 160
Kniven i hjertet, 348
Ko Yi-chen, 398
Koch, Carl, 337
Kocking, Leo, 75
Kohlberg, 284
Kohon, David José, 301
Komoedie vom Geld, 304
Korda, Alexander, 121, 209, 241, 324, 350, 402
Kosheverova, Nadezhda, 379, 380
Kotcheff, Ted, 232
Kozhushannaia, Olga, 379
Kozintzev, Grigorii, 378, 380
Kracauer, Siegfried, 229, 420
Kramer, Robert, 353
Kramer, Stanley, 121, 197, 256, 333, 345
Kramer vs Kramer, 65, 256
Kratisch, Ingo, 19
Křik, 107
Kris, 41
Kristeva, Julia, 207, 334, 360
Krumbachová, Ester, 80

Krusenstjerna, Agnes von, 436
Kuan Yin De Gu Shih, 398
Kubelka, Peter, 32
Kuehle Wampe, 400
Kuemel, Harry, 38, 243
Kuhn, Rodolfo, 301
Kuleshov, Lev, 59, 132, 379
Kumai, Kei, 398
Kumari, Meena, 217
Kumo no Sujo, 226
Kung Hung, 397
Kuomintang party (China), 397
Kuosmanen, Mirjam, 162
Kuratorium junger deutscher Film, 424
Kurosawa, Akira, 225, 226
Kurys, Diane, 37, 166, 346
Kuyper, Eric de, 287
Kuzwayo, Ellen, 16
Kvinnodröm, 41
Kvinnors väntan, 41

La Cava, Gregory, 196
La Cerda, Clemente de, 413
La Parra, Pim de, 65
La Torre, Raúl de, 39
Labrune, Jeanne, 166
Lacan, Jacques, 161, 214, 247, 321, 322, 327, 360
Lacau-Pansini, Rose, 164
LaCava, Gregory, 144
Lacayo, Rossana, 71
Lacreta, Rosa, 51
Ladd, Alan Jr, 12
Ladies Home Journal, 347
Ladies of Leisure, 384
Ladri di biciclette, 285
The Lady from Shanghai, 154, 191
Lady Hamilton, 241
The Lady Vanishes, 169, 200
Laemmle, Carl, 408
Laffont, Bernadette, 293
Lah, Vlasta, 234

Lakhdar-Hamina, Mohamed, 10
Lallem, Ahmed, 11
Lamarr, Hedy, 194, 309
Lambart, Evelyn, 63
Lambert, Susan, 393
Lamour, Dorothy, 145, 194, 309
Lamprecht, Gerhard, 284
Land, Robert, 121
Land and Sons, 211
Land in Anguish, 343
The Land of Desire, 41
Land og Synir, 211
Lander, 2
Landow, George, 334
Lanfield, Sidney, 191
Lang, Fritz, 121, 135, 154, 158, 159, 174, 189, 338, 365, 420
Langlois, Henri, 135
Lansing, Sherry, 204, 407
Lao Jing, 78
Lara, Mari Carmen de, 90, 265
Largo viaje, 74
Larissa, 364
Larkin, Alile Sharon, 44
Larocque, Monique, 315
Larraz, Joseph, 243
Lasky, Jesse L., 114
The Last Command, 387
The Last Embrace, 115
The Last Temptation of Christ, 357
Laura, 154, 159
The Law They Forgot, 232
Lawrenson, Helen, 158
Le Chang Zhasa, 157
Le Fanu, Sheridan, 243, 410
Le Roy, Mervyn, 163
League of Leftist Writers (China), 77
Leahy, Gillian, 393
Lean, David, 197, 345
Lebanese National Movement, 239
Leclerc, Ginette, 361
Ledoux, Jacques, 39
Lee, Bruce, 231
Lee, Christopher, 409

Lee, Joe, 220
Lee, Michael, 30
Lee-Thompson, J., 126
Lefèvre, Geneviève, 166
Left Right and Centre, 238
Legend of Tianyun Mountain, 434
Lehman, Ernest, 221
Leigh, Janet, *428*
Leila and the Others, 11
Leila and the Wolves, 240
Leila Wal Zi'ab, 240
En lektion i kärlek, 41
Leñero, Vicente, 155
Lenfilm, 24, 378
Lennox, Annie, 344
Lenoir, Claudine, 164
Lenya, Lotte, 193
Leonard, Marion, 203
Leonard, Robert Z., 143
Leone, Lu, 223
Der leone had sept cabecas, 343
Leong Tinfeng, 434
Leppänen, Glory, 162
LeRoy, Mervyn, 254, 401
Lesage, Julia, 72, 124, 230, 267
A Lesson in Love, 41
Let's Make Love, 105
Letter from an Unknown Woman, 260, 304, *304*, 305
Letter to Jane, 177
Letty Lynton, 101, 144
Lévi-Strauss, Claude, 161, 388
Levitin, Jacqueline, 330
Lewton, Val, 206
La ley que olvidaron, 232
Lezhat zhuravli, 378
L'Herbier, Marcel, 126, 164, 277
Li Chia, 397
Li Hsin, 397
Li Minwei, 76
Li Wenhua, 340
Li Yalin, 78
Lianna, 346
Libeled Lady, 190
Liberman, Lilian, 265
Liebelei, 304

Liebeneier, Wolfgang, 284
Lieberman, Liliane, 90
Das Liebes-ABC, 296
Lied in my Hart, 376
The Life and Death of Colonel Blimp, 324
Life magazine, 110
The Life of Oharu, 226, 269, 398
De Lift, 286
The Lift, 286
The Light, 7, 85
The Light That Failed, 248
Lili Marlene, 145
Lilith Video Collective, 83, 235
Liminana, Eva, 263
Limit, 50
Límite, 50
Lin Fu-di, 397
Lin Nong, 434
Lincoln Motion Picture Company, 44
Lindblom, Gunnel, 391
Linder, Max, 164
Linnanheimo, Regina, 162
The Lion Has Seven Heads, 343
Lion's Gate Films, 12
Lip: A Feminist Arts Journal, 337
Lipstick, 431
Lispector, Clarice, 13
The Listener (journal), 113, 295
Littin, Miguel, 74, 75
Little Annie Rooney, 314
Little by Little, 146
Little Dorrit, 53
The Little Foxes, 112
Little Lord Fauntleroy, 314
Little Mother, 376
The Little Princess, 190
Little Wars, 239–40
Little Women, 196, 401
Liu Jialiang, 231
Liu Zhonglun, 76
Livingston, Margaret, 367
Llerandi, Antonio, 413

Llewellyn-Davies, Melissa, 138
Lloyd Webber, Andrew, 343
Lo Wei, 231
Loach, Ken, 57
Loasiaga, Miriam, 71
Lockwood, Margaret, 169
Loden, Barbara, 83
Loebner, Vera, 130
Loew's, 266
Logan, Joshua, 270
Løkkeberg, Vibeke, 298
Lola, 145
Lola Montès, 304, 305
Lollobrigida, Gina, 285, 361
London Evening Standard, 99
London Film Festival, 42, 159, 434
London Film-Makers' Co-operative, 295, 340
Long, Joan, 22, 430
The Long Days, 133, 219
The Long Goodbye, 12
Long Jiang Sung, 340
Long Live the Republic, 412
Longfellow, Brenda, 63
Longford, Raymond, 28, 238, 250
Lopez Portillo, José, 265
Lopez Portillo, Margarita, 265
Lorca, Federigo García, 272
Loren, Sophia, 285, 361
Los Angeles Film Festival, 159
Los Angeles Women In Film and Video, 430
Losey, Joseph, 126
Lost in America, 358
Loufti, Nabiha, 134, 308
Love, 285
Love Brewed in the African Pot, 7–8
Love in the Afternoon, 345
Love on the Ground, 342
Love Me or Leave Me, 113

Love Me Tender, 343
Love Story, 169, 345
Lovelace, Linda, 361
Lowe, Gloria, 45, 66
Lowing, Catherine, 30
Loy, Myrna, 143
Lu Xiaoya, 78
Luan Hua, 77
Lubbert, Orlando, 75
Lubitsch, Ernst, 121, 170, 284, 420
Lucas, George, 116
Lucía, 104, 104, 371, 373
Lucoque, Lisle, 376
Ludendorff, Erich, 174
Ludwig, Ursula, 425
Luedcke, Marianne, 19
Lugosi, Bela, 409
Lukashevich, Tatiana, 379
Lulu, 343
Lumière brothers, 50, 138, 173, 215–16, 225
Lumiton, 20
Luna, Amina, 71
Lupino, Stanley, 248
Lured, 369
Luttes en Italie, 177
Luxemburg, Rosa, 227, 405
Lye, Len, 293
Lyne, Adrian, 149, 276, 363, 429
Lyotard, Jean-François, 321

Ma nuit chez Maud, 345
Maanouni, Ahmed, 271
Maas, Dick, 286
Maas, Willard, 260
Mabrouk, Nejia Ben, 406
McAdam, Trish, 221
MacCabe, Colin, 176
McCall, 151
McCalls (journal), 229
McCarey, Leo, 422
McDaniel, Hattie, 45
MacDonald, David, 169
McDougall, David, 138
Mace, Nicole, 298
McGlone, Carmel, 335
Machatý, Gustav, 107
McIntyre, Hercules, 29

Mackássy, Gyula, 251
Mackay, Yvonne, 294
McKee, Lonette, 112
Mackendrick, Alexander, 129
McKimmie, Jackie, 30
McKinney, Nina Mae, 45, 110
MacLaine, Shirley, 419
McLaren, Norman, 60, 63
McLaughlin, Sheila, 72, 82, 83, 137
McMurchy, Megan, 31, 393
McNally, Raymond, 243
Macpherson, Jeannie, 203
Macpherson, Kenneth, 193
MacQuitty, William, 99
McRobbie, Angela, 344
Macy's, 144
Mad Max, 29
Mad Max: Beyond Thunderdome, 45
The Mad Years of the Twist, 11
Madagascar, 7
Madame Bovary, 284, 339
Madame de . . ., 304, 305
Madame Dubarry, 284
Madame Sousatzka, 33
Madame Wants No Children, 121
Madame wuenscht keine Kinder, 121
Madamu to Nyobo, 225
Made in USA, 177
Madhubala, 217
Madiha the Lawyer, 134
Madonna, 344, 358
Madonna of the Seven Moons, 169
Mafi-Williams, Lorraine, 1
Mafilm, 210
Maggie Magaba Trust, 16
The Magic Flute, 41, 303
The Magician, 41
Magnani, Anna, 69, 285, 338

Magnificent Obsession, 369, 370
Magny, Claude-Edmonde, 158
Mahomo, Nana, 16
The Maid's Kid, 199
Mainfilm, 330
Mainka-Jellinghaus, Beate, 425
La maison des quatre Inc, 331
Major Sommer, 198
Al Makhdooun, 18, 394
Makhmalbaffe, Mohsen, 218
Makk, Karoly, 346
Malas, Mohamed, 394
Male and Female, 115
Maleh, Nabil, 394
Mali, 7
Malle, Louis, 36, 165
Maloney, Shereen, 294
Malu Tienshi, 77
La Maman et la putain, 166
Mamma Roma, 285
Mamoulian, Rouben, 13, 121, 170, 191, 245, 276
The Man in Grey, 169
Man of Ashes, 406
Man of Flowers, 254
Man of Iron, 317
Man of Marble, 224, 317
Man with a Movie Camera, 257
The Man with an Umbrella, 41
The Man Who Knew Too Much, 199
The Man Who Shot Liberty Valence, 194
Man, Woman and Sin, 368
Manasarova, Aida, 380
Manchester Guardian, 241
Mandabi, 359
Mandi, 33
Mandy, 129–30
Mangano, Silvana, 22, 285, 361
Mangiacapre, Lina, 214, 223
Mankiewicz, Joseph L., 112, 194, 197, 270

Mannequin, 101
Manning, Mary, 60
La mano en la trampa, 402
Mansfield, Jayne, 361
Manthan, 311
Manuel, Jacques, 91
Manuela, 373
Mao Zedong, 339–40
Maona, 138
Maraini, Dacia, 223
Marcel, Gabriel, 183
Marchiani, Georgina, 234
Marcotte, Nancy, 182
Marei, Hamid, 394
Marguerite, Victor, 27
Maria Candelaria, 263
Marijnissen, Sarah, 286
Mariscal, Ana, 381
Marked Woman, 112, 144–5
Marker, Chris, 292, 411
Marnie, 93, 200
Marquand, Richard, 429
Marquez, Maria Elena, 233
Marriage in Galilee, 309
The Marriage of Maria Braun, 145
Married to the Mob, 115
A Married Woman, 23, 177
Marrosu, Ambretta, 413
The Marrying Kind, 106
Le Marseillaise, 338, 339
Marsh, Jane, 62, 63, 281, 329
Marshall, George, 121
Marshall, Penny, 256
Martin, Helen, 294–5
Martines, Irene, 394
Martínez Suárez, José A., 301
Martinique, 65, 66, 308
Marx, Karl, 213, 371
Marzouk, Said, 134
Mascara, 38
Masculin-féminin, 177
Masculine-Feminine, 177
Maselli, Francesco, 69, 222, 291
M*A*S*H, 12
The Masher, 45
Maskell, Virginia, 238

Mason, James, 169
Masri, May, 309
Le Matin (newspaper), 166
Matrocinque, Camillo, 243
Matter, Fred, 435
A Matter of Life and Death, 324
Mature, Victor, 194
Maunder, Paul, 255
Mauritania, 7
Mauro, Humberto, 50, 234
Max Factor, 252
May, Debora, 16
May, Joe, 121
Mayer, Gerald, 111
Mayerling to Sarajevo, 305
Mayfair, 16
Mayo, Archie, 422
Mayo, Virginia, 24
Maysles, David, 344
Maysles brothers, 230
Mazif, Sid Ali, 11
Mazurka, 283, 284
Mazursky, Paul, 291
Mazzetti, Lorenza, 223
Mean Streets, 356–7
Le médecin de Gafiré, 7
Meerapfel, Jeanine, 425
Meet John Doe, 384
Meet Me at the Fair, 369
Meet Me in St Louis, 276
Mehrejouyie, Dariush, 218
Meilanfang, 76
Meireles, Marcia, 235
Het Meisje met het Rode Haar, 286
Mejía, Lylliam, 71
Mekas, Jonas, 32, 260
Melato, Mariangela, 421
Melbourne, 337, 393
Melbourne Film Festival, 159
Melbourne Filmmakers' Co-op, 337
Melford, George, 368
Méliès, Gaston, 293
Méliès, Georges, 164
Mellen, Joan, 41, 190

Melo, Jacira, 235
Melville, Jean-Pierre, 165
Melvin and Howard, 115
Member of the Government, 378
The Mender of Nets, 181
Meng Long Guo Jiang, 231
Menotti, Gian Carlo, 163
Menshov, Vladimir, 378
Mentasti, Angel, 20
Menzel, Jiří, 107
Mephisto, 224
Le Mépris, 36, 176, 177
The Merchant of Four Seasons, 145
Merry go round, 342
Mes voisins, 205
The Message, 97, 320
Messter, Oskar, 173
Messter-Film, 174
Mészáros, László, 131, 261
'Method' acting, 3
Metz, Christian, 161, 327, 360
O meu caso, 303
Meyers, Janet, 242
m/f (journal), 228
Mi hijo el Che, 43
Micheaux, Oscar, 44
Michel, Samora, 297
Michelson, Annette, 32
Middlemen, 396
MIDINRA, 71
Midler, Bette, 94
Miéville, Anne-Marie, 166, 176
Al Miftah, 308
Mikkelsen, Laila, 298
Mildred Pierce, 13, 65, 70, 89, 101, 272, 357, 426
Miles, Vera, 194
Milestone, Lewis, 225
Mille et une mains, 271
Miller, Arthur, 116, 270
Miller, David, 101
Miller, George, 21, 45
Miller, Kennedy, 29
Milli fjalls og fjöru, 211
Millions Like Us, 237
Ming Jian, 206, 392
Ming Xing, 77

Minnelli, Vincente, 34, 91, 253, 256, 260, 276
Miou-Miou, 166
Mira, Beatriz, 265, 300
Miranda, Carmen, 50, 110, 234, 237, 343
Mirany, Tahmineh Mir, 218, 396
Miret, Pedro, 155
Miroslava, 233
Mirt Sost Shi Amit, 7
Miscuglio, Annabella, 223
Misère au Borinage, 39
The Misfits, 270
Misselwitz, Helke, 130
Mr 420, 278
Mr Hawarden, 38
Mr. Progressiste, 394
Mr. Said, 219
Mitasareta Seikatsu, 226
Mitchell, Mike, 282
Mitchell, Yvonne, 126
Mizrahi, Moshe, 37
M'Mbugu-Schelling, Flora, 8
Modleski, Tania, 200
Moedertjie, 376
Die Moerder sind unter uns, 424
Moffatt, Tracey, 1, 30, 31
Mogulescu, Miles, 289
Mohamed, Amina, 133
Mollet, Guy, 353
MoMo, 377
The Money Order, 359
Money Power, 7
Money to Burn, 376
Monicelli, Mario, 69
Monika, 41
Monkey Business, 191
Monthly Film Bulletin, 227
Monti, Adriana, 223
The Moon, 396
Moore, Colleen, 367
Moore, Juanita, 198
Moore, Marianne, 193
Morales, Jose Diaz, 264
Morazin, Jeanne, 315
Moreau, Jeanne, 22, 166, 293
Moreno, Antonio, 263

Morgan, Michèle, 164
Morin, Albanie, 271
Morning Glory, 196
Moroccan Cinema Center
    (CCM), 272
Morocco, 25, 102, 119,
    121, 245, 268, 387
Morris, Meaghan, 334
Morton Rocky, 14
Moscow Does Not Believe
    in Tears, 378
Mosfilm, 374, 378, 380
Moskva slezam ne verit,
    378
Moth of Moonbi, 72
The Mother and the Whore,
    166
Mother India, 278, 279
Mother Kuesters Goes to
    Heaven, 145
Motion Picture Export
    Association of America
    (MPEAA), 5
Motion Picture Producers
    and Distributors
    Association (MPPDA),
    70, 326, 327
Al Moumia, 134
Al Moutamarid, 406
Mouth to Mouth, 29
Mouzaoui, Ali, 11
Movie (journal), 228
Mozafarrull Din Shah,
    King, 218
Mozart, Wolfgang
    Amadeus, 305
Mozgokep Innovacios
    Tarsulas, 210
Ms (journal), 228, 347
Mucret, Veronique, 45
Muehl, Christa, 130
Mugica, Francisco, 20
La mujer de todos, 263
La mujer del puerto, 263
La mujer gue yo ame, 263
A mulher do próximo, 97
Mumaren, 434
El Mumia, 18
Muna Moto, 7
Munerato, Elice, 234
Muratov, Aleksandr,
    274

Murder!, 199
The Murder Case, 76
The Murderers are Among
    Us, 424
Murdoch, Rupert, 407
Muriel, 292
Muriel, Emilio Gomez,
    263
Murnau, F. W., 135, 158,
    206, 336, 367, 409, 420
Murphy, Geoff, 255, 294
Murúa, Lautaro, 301, 384
Muscogee Creek Nation,
    282
Museum of Modern Art
    (MOMA), 36, 37
Music Corporation of
    America, 408
Música, mocambique!, 97
Musik i mörker, 41, 436
Den Muso, 85, 85
The Mustachioed Uncle, 42
Mutter Kuesters' Fahrt zum
    Himmel, 145
My Beautiful Laundrette,
    53, 363
My Best Friend's Boyfriend,
    345
My Case, 303
My Fair Lady, 105, 276
My First Wife, 254
My Life to Live, 176
My Little Chickadee, 422
My Love Burns, 269
My Neighbours, 205
My Night with Maud, 345
My Son Che, 43
My Survival as an
    Aboriginal, 31
My Wife is
    Director-General, 134
Myles, Lynda, 273
Myra Breckinridge, 422
Myrase Mann Jounoun, 396

'n Nasie hou Koers, 376
Nabili, Marva, 218
Nagareru, 226
Nainen on valttia, 162
The Naked Night, 41
Naked Vengeance, 432
Nakhouda Khourshid, 218

Nan Fu Nan Qi, 76
Nana, 338
Naniwa Ereji, 269
The Nanny, 112
Nanook of the North, 138
Naples, 222
Napoléon, 121, 137
Nära livet, 41
Narayamabushi-ko, 398
Naruse, 225, 226
Narutskaia, Olga, 379
Nash, Terri, 330, 389
Nashville, 12, 276
Nasser, Gamal Abdul, 17,
    133, 134
Nation (periodical), 238
A Nation Goes Forward,
    376
National
    Cinematographic Bank
    (Mexico), 263–4, 265
National Film
    Development
    Corporation (India),
    216
National Film Unit (New
    Zealand), 293–4
Native American Film
    and Video Festival, 282
Native American Public
    Broadcasting
    Consortium (NAPBC),
    281–2
Nattvardsgästerna, 41
Navarro, Berta, 72, 90
Navarro, Carlos, 263
The Navigator: A Medieval
    Odyssey, 294
Naylor, Gloria, 114
Nazarin, 264
Ndiaye, Samba Felix, 7
Neale, Steve, 207
Necoechea, Angeles, 300
Negrete, Jorge, 263
Negulesco, Jean, 101
The Neighbor's Wife and
    Mine, 225
'Neighbours', 371
Neilan, Marshall, 314
Nel nome del padre, 291
Nelson, Ricky, 343
Némec, Jan, 107

'Nemesiache', 223
Nemeskürty, István, 210
Neri, Julio, 414
Neussbaum, Raphael, 221
Neves, Tancredo, 435
New Babylon, 378
New Formations (journal),
228
New Republic (journal),
229
New Women, 77
New World Productions,
115, 291
New York Film Festival,
159
New York Herald
Tribune, 36
New York magazine, 190
New York, New York, 357
The New York Review of
Books, 229
New York Times, 241
New Yorker, 229
New Zealand Film
Commission, 294
Newman, Paul, 194
Newsreel Collective, 152
Newton-John, Olivia,
277
Ngakane, Lionel, 5, 44
Ngati, 255
Ngoyi, Lilian, 16
Niagara, 270
Niaye, 359
Niblo, Fred, 24
Nicaragua, 71–2
Nichols, Mike, 257
Nickel, Gitta, 130
Nietzsche, Friedrich
Wilhelm, 68
Niger, 5, 7
Nigeria, 5, 7
The Night, 17
Night and Fog, 292
Night After Night, 422
Night Is My Future, 41,
436
Night Mail, 55
The Night of Counting the
Years, 18, 134
Night of the Iguana, 244
Night's End, 33

Nihalani, Govind, 311
Nikolaieva, Galina, 379
Nine to Five, 13
Ninotchka, 170
Nippon Konchuki, 199,
226
Nishant, 33
Nixon, Richard M., 230
No Tears for Ananse, 5
No Trace of Sin, 97
Noces de sang, 272
Noguchi, 260
La Noire de . . ., 359
Nooi van my Hart, 376
Norden, Isidora de, 91–2
Nordisk, 174
Norma Rae, 372
Normand, Mabel, 401
Noroît, 342
Norsk Film A/S, 298
North by North-West, 200
Nor'west, 342
Noschese, Christine, 138
Nosferatu, 206, 409
Notari, Edoardo, 298
Notari, Nicola, 298
Notes on Women's Cinema,
149–50
Notorious, 200
La notte, 16
Noua, 11
Nous aurons toute la mort
pour dormir, 204, 205
Novarro, Berta, 265
Novyi Vavilon, 378
Now About These Women,
41
Now Voyager, 112, 260,
346
Now We Have no Land, 16
Nugent, Elliott, 237
Nuit et brouillard, 292
Les Nuits de la pleine lune,
345
Nulan Wuhao, 434
Numéro Deux, 176
The Nun, 342

O, Dore, 425
O the Days, 271
Al Oadissiya, 219
Oates, Joyce Carol, 80

Oberhausen Manifesto,
289, 424
Oberon, Merle, 24
Objektiv studios, 210
Observer (newspaper),
158, 241, 323
Occupe-toi d'Amélie, 165
Ocean Ocean, 31
Office of Arts and
Libraries (Britain), 56
The Official Story, 21
The Official Version, 21
Ogilvie, George, 45
O'Hara, Maureen, 13, 24
The Oil War Won't
Happen, 272
Ojo al cine (journal), 413
Oklahoma, 276
An Old Man With Great
Wings, 43
Old Well, 78
Old Wives for New, 115
Olive for President, 15
Oliveira, Maria Helena
Darcy de, 234
Olivier, Laurence, 241
Omar Gatlato, 11
The Omen, 206
On a volé un homme, 304
On Golden Pond, 197
On Moonlight Bay, 113
On Our Selection, 29
On the Docks, 340, 434
On the Hunting Ground, 157
Ona zashchishchaet rodinu,
378
ONCIC, 10
One Arabian Night, 284
One Man, Several Women,
7
One Night of Love, 93
One People, 65
One Plus One, 177
One Thousand and One
Hands, 271
O'Neill, Martha, 221
Ongewenste Vreemdeling,
334, 335
Only Angels Have Wings,
191
Only Two Can Play, 238
Ons Staan 'n Dag Oor, 376

Onwettige Huwelik, 377
Het Oog Boven de Put, 286
The Opening of the
    Auckland Exhibition,
    293
Orchid and My Love, 397
Ordaz, Gustavo Diaz, 264
Ordinary People, 256
Ordoqui, Teresa, 105
The Oriental Nights, 77
Orphans of the Storm, 176,
    181
Orphée, 143
Osaka Elegy, 269
Osawa, Sandra Sunrising,
    282
Osborne, John, 53
O'Shea, John, 255
Osten, Gerd, 305
Ostrer, Maurice, 169
Oswalda, Ossi, 102
The Other Man's Child, 7
Otto - der Film, 424
Otto - the Film, 424
Ou Wei, 397
Ouedraogo, Idrissa, 7
Oughnia Ala Al Mamar,
    133
Die Oupa en die
    Plaasnooitjie, 377
Our Dancing Daughters, 99
Ouridou Hall, 134
Al Ousfour, 134
El Oustaza Fatma, 134
Out 1: Noli Me Tangere,
    342
Out 1: spectre, 342
Out of the Past, 159, 313
The Outlaw, 211
Outlaw: The Saga of Gisli,
    211
Outlook, 99
Oxenberg, Jan, 242
Oyster Girl, 397
Ozu, Yasujiro, 225, 226,
    398, 399

Pabst, G. W., 58, 135,
    193, 420
Pacific Films Ltd, 293
El padre Pitillo, 435
Pagnol, Marcel, 164, 165

Paid, 101
Pajaczkowska, 151
Pajama Game, 114
Pakula, Alan J., 13, 65,
    160, 291
Pal Joey, 193
Palacios, Beatriz, 234
Palcine, 413
Palestine, Chronicle of a
    People, 308
Palestine Cinema Unit,
    308
Palestinian Resistance
    Movement, 17, 239,
    240
Palsdottir, Kristin,
    211–12
Palsson, Sigurdur, 227
Pan Si Dong, 77
Panama, 71
Pandora's Box, 58
Pannonia studios, 210
Panova, Vera, 379
Panovsky, Erwin, 386
Paoli, Paola, 214
Pape, Lygia, 50, 51
Pappa Lap, 334
Paradis perdu, 164
Paranjpee, Sai, 217
Pardeh Bardory, 396
Paris Belongs to Us, 342
Paris nous appartient, 342
Paris, Texas, 254
Park, Ida May, 366
Parker, Alan, 53
Parker, Claire, 15
Parker, Gudrun, 329
Parmar, Pratibha, 44, 45
Parra, Catalina, 75
Parra, Pim de la, 286
Une Partie de campagne,
    338, 339
Parting Glances, 256
Partout ou peut-être nulle
    part, 205
The Party and the Guests,
    107
The Party's Over, 402
El paso maldito, 435
Pasolini, Pier Paolo, 17,
    222, 285, 291, 351
O passado e o presente, 303

A Passage To India, 53
The Passenger, 17
Passer, Ivan, 107
A Passion (Bergman), 41
Passion (Lubitsch), 284
The Passion of Anna, 41
A Passion Play, 303
The Past and the Present,
    303
Pat and Mike, 65, 106
Patel, Jabbar, 311
Patewabano, Buckley,
    282
Pathé studios, 342, 390
Pather Panchali, 216
Patton, Alan, 308
Pauline à la plage, 345
Pauline at the Beach, 345
Pavese, Cesare, 69
Paweogo, 7
Paxton, Steve, 333
Pearl River studios, 78
Peary, Gerald, 24
Pec-Slesicka, Barbara,
    316
Peckinpah, Sam, 428
Pecoraro, Susú, 39
The Peddlar, 218
Peeping Tom, 206, 257,
    324
Peers, Lynda, 182
Peeters, Barbara, 401
Peirce, C. S., 360
Peixote, Mario, 50
Peking Opera, 339–40
Peking Opera Blues, 206
Peluffo, Ana Luisa, 264
Peng Xiaolian, 76, 78,
    157
Peon, Ramon, 360
People of the First Light
    Series, 282
Perdida, 263
Perelman, Pable, 75
The Perils of Pauline, 428
La perla, 263
Perneke, 38
Perón, Isabel, 21
Perón Juan, 20, 21
Perry, Joseph, 28
Perry, Margaret, 63, 281
Persona, 41

Personal Best, 346
Perusse, Michelle, 330
Pesti Mozi (journal), 209
Petelska, Ewa, 316, 353
Peter and Paula, 107
Petersen, Wolfgang, 424
Petit à petit, 146
Le petit soldat, 176
Le Petit théâtre de Jean
    Renoir, 339
La Petite marchande
    d'allumettes, 338
Petrie, Daniel, 45
Petro, Patrice, 420
Pettery, Margaret, 329
Pevney, Joseph, 101
The Phantom of the Opera,
    206
The Philadelphia Story,
    105, 197
Photoplay Company, 43
Pi, Rosario, 381
Piaggio, Carlos, 353
Pialat, Maurice, 165
Pichul, Vasily, 379
Pickford, Jack, 314
Picnic at Hanging Rock, 29
Pictorial Parade, 293
Picturegoer, 248
Piel de verano, 402
Pierrot le fou, 176, 177
Pigs and Battleships, 226
Pilcher, Velma, 158
Pillar of Fire, 221
Pillow Talk, 114, 345
Pillsbury, Sam, 294
Pincher Creek Festival,
    283
Pinewood Studios, 169
The Pink Skeleton, 77
Pinkie se Erfenis, 376
Pinkie's Inheritance, 376
Pinkus, Gertrud, 83
The Pioneers, 340
Piriev, Ivan, 379
Pitt, Susan, 15
Place in the Sun (Faure),
    377
A Place in the Sun
    (Stevens), 194
Le Plaisir, 305
Plath, Sylvia, 9

The Pleasure Garden, 199,
    339
Plekkie in Son, 377
The Ploughman's Lunch,
    53
Poe, Edgar Allan, 206
Poitier, Sidney, 256
Poitras, Diane, 182
Poland, 5
Polanski, Roman, 132,
    160, 317
Polisario, a People in Arms,
    205
Polisario, un peuple en
    armes, 205
'The Polish School', 317
Pollack, Sydney, 102
Pollak, Mimi, 170
Pollard, Harry, 45
Polowanie na Muchy, 224
Le Pont du Nord, 342
Pontecorvo, Gillo, 222,
    291
Poor Cow, 57
The Poor Little Rich Girl,
    314
Popeye, 12
Porfirio Diaz and William
    Taft in El Paso Texas,
    1908, 262
Porgy and Bess, 45, 110
Porky's Romance, 14
Port of Call, 41
Port of Shadows, 164
Porter, 85
Porter, Edwin S., 314,
    332
Porter, Vincent, 19
Portman, Eric, 237
Portnoy's Complaint, 221
Portrait of Teresa, 104,
    412
Portugalia Films, 319
Possessed (Bernhardt—,
    101
Possessed (Brown), 101
The Postman, 134
Pound, Ezra, 193
Powell, Frank, 35
Power, John, 430
Prague Film School
    (FAMU), 80

Praunheim, Rosa von,
    266
Pravda, 176, 177
Pravov, Ivan, 325
Preminger, Otto, 45, 110,
    154, 159
Présence Africaine, 359
Presley, Elvis, 343
Prester John, 376
The Price of Alliance, 7
La primera fundación de
    Buenos Aires, 43
Primrose Path, 144
Les princes noirs de St
    Germain-des-Prés, 7
Prinzessin Olla, 121
El prisionero numero trece,
    360
Prisioneros de la tierra, 20
Prison, 41
The Prisoner Number
    Thirteen, 360
The Prisoner of Zenda, 339
Prisoners of the Land, 20
Le prix de la liberté, 7
Pro Arte, 2
Produciones Angel, 402
Production Fund
    (Netherlands), 286
Professione: reporter, 17
Progrès film 38
Project A, 231
Projektion-AG Union,
    174
Proletarische Film, 174
The Promised Woman, 29
Protazanov, Yakov, 373
Psycho, 200, 206, 322,
    323, 428, 428
The Public Enemy, 326
Publications Control
    Board (South Africa),
    377
Puccini, Giacomo, 172,
    280
Pudovkin, 59
Puenzo, Luis, 21
Puerto Rico, 65
Punch (magazine), 323
The Pure Hell of St
    Trinians, 238
Pure S, 29

Qija Baihutuan, 340
Qiu Jin, 434
Quai des Brumes, 164
44, ou les récits de la nuit,
271
Quarterly Review of Film
Studies, 228
Quatre aventures de Reinette
et Mirabelle, 345
Les 400 coups, 293
Queen Christina, 13, 170,
171, 245
Queen Elizabeth the
Second Arts Council,
294
Queeny, Mary, 133
Queffelec, Yann, 187
Querschnittsfilm, 174
Qui Jin, A Revolutionary,
434
The Quiet Earth, 294
Quinn, Bob, 220
Quinn, Edel, 221
Quinn, Joanna, 15
Quintero, Jose, 241
Quo Vadis, 163

Rached, Tahani, 330
Rachedi, Ahmed, 10
Rademakers, Fons, 286
Rademakers, Lili, 38, 287
Radio Venceremos, 71
Radziwillowicz, Jerzy,
225
Rafael Alberti, Portrait of
the Poet, 43
Rafel Alberti, un retrato del
poeta, 43
Rafman-Lisser, Carolynn,
271
Ragbar, 42
Raging Bull, 357
Rags, 314
Rahim, Hadji, 11
Rahnama, Feraidoun, 218
RAI, 68, 223
Raices, 264
Raid on White Tiger
Regiment, 340
The Railroad Porter, 43
Raizman, Iuli, 390
Ramati, Alexander, 221

Ramírez, Dora Cecilia, 83
Ramster, P. J., 258
Rancho Notorious, 121
La rancon d'une alliance, 7
Random Harvest, 254
Randrasana,
Ignace-Solko, 7
Rank, J. Arthur, 156
Rank Organization, 129
Rape of Love, 166
Rapf, Harry, 99
Rapper, Irving, 112, 260,
346
Rasputin, V. G., 364
Rastafarianism, 66
Ratoff, Gregory, 422
Ray, Man, 164
Ray, Nicholas, 13, 101,
198, 245, 256, 260, 423
Ray, Satyajit, 33, 216,
217, 311
Raynaud, Bérénice, 345
Le Rayon vert, 345
Rear Window, 194, 200,
428
Rebecca, 154, 200, 245,
345
Rebecca of Sunnybrook
Farm, 314
The Rebel, 406
Rebels Against the Light,
221
Rebolledo, Carlos, 413
O recado, 97, 320
The Reckless Moment, 304,
305
Reckord, Lloyd, 44
Red Desert, 16
The Red Detachment of
Women, 340, 434
Red Dust, 189
Red Flags Can Be Seen
Better, 19
The Red-headed Girl, 286
Red Headed Woman, 190,
326
Red Hot Riding Hood, 15
The Red Lantern, 340
Red River, 191
The Red Shoes, 324
Red Sorghum, 78
Redes, 263

Redford, Robert, 194,
256
Redgrove, Peter, 410
Reed, Carol, 169
Reefer and the Model, 220
Reggab, Mohmed, 272
La Règle du jeu, 388, 339
Det regnar pa var kärlek, 41
Regnault, Félix-Louis,
138
Rehman, Waheeda, 217
Rei, Aurelio da Paz dos,
319
Reichert, Julia, 124, 289
Reichsfilmkammer (Reich
Film Organization),
175, 400
Reid, Beryl, 245
Reidemeister, Helga, 290,
425,
Reiner, Rob, 344
Reinhardt, Max, 119,
158, 162, 337, 349
Reisz, Karel, 53, 57
Reiter, Jackie, 72
Reitz, Edgar, 387
Rekanati, Mira, 222
La Religieuse, 342
The Reluctant Dragon, 14
Remodelling Her Husband,
176
Ren Dao Zhongnian, 78
Renán, Sergio, 384
Renault, Monique, 15
Resnais, Alain, 128, 165,
292, 374, 411
Restrepo, Patricia, 83
Retake Film Collective,
44
Le retour, 7
Retrato de Teresa, 412
The Return, 7
Return to the Nest, 20
Reverón, Armando, 40
The Revolt of Mamie
Stover, 247
Revue du cinéma, 135
Revueltas, Rosaura, 236,
237, 372
Reyjkavik Film Festival,
211
Rhodesia, 5

Rhone, Trevor, D., 65
Riad, Slim 10
Riah Al Janoub, 11
Riascos, Clara, 83
Riazantseva, Natalia, 379
Ribe, Gloria, 265
Ribón, Roberto del, 435
Rice, Tim, 343
Richards, Shirley Ann, 250
Richardson, Amanda, 198
Richardson, Dorothy, 193
Richardson, Tony, 53, 57
Richler, Mordecai, 239
Richter, Hans, 337
Rih El Sadd, 406
Rik El Awras, 10
Rimbaud, Arthur, 227
Rimpinen, Marjut, 162
The Ringer, 436
Rio Bravo, 191, 343
Rio Lobo, 191
Rip van Wyk, 334
Riso amaro, 22, 285
The Rite, 41
Ritt, Martin, 45, 372
Ritten, 41
The Ritual, 41
Ritual of Blood, 243
Ritz, Lan Brooke, 282
The River, 339
Rivera, Pedro, 71
Rivero, Fernando, 263
Rivero, Panchita, 104
Riviere, Joan, 257
Rivière, Marie, 345
The Road, 10
The Road to Glory, 190
Roazantseva, 379
Robeson, Eslanda, 193
Robeson, Paul, 44, 193
Roboh, Caroline, 166
Robyns, Pat, 294
Roc, Patricia, 169
Rock Around the Clock, 343
Rockefeller family, 342
Rodríguez Silva, Luis, 344
Rogers, Ginger, 144, 276, 277, 342

Rogers, Peter, 67
Rojo, Helena, 155
The Role, 311
Rolin, Dominique, 187
Rolling Stones, 344
Rollover, 65
Roma città aperta, 285
Roman Holiday, 194
The Roman Spring of Mrs Stone, 241
Romance, Viviane, 361
Romance de medio siglo, 435
A Romance of Happy Valley, 181
Romance on the High Seas, 113
Romania, 131–2
Romare, Ingela, 391
Rome Open City, 285
Romm, Mikhail, 379
Romola, 176
La Ronde, 304, 305
Room at the Top, 57
A Room with a View, 53
The Root of All Evil, 169
Roots Ballad, 205
Rosaleva, Gabriella, 223
Rosas, Enrique, 262
The Rose, 344
Rosebaum, Marianne, 290
Rosenfeld, Lotty, 75, 170
Roshal, Grigorii, 379
Roshal, Sima, 379
Rosi, Francesco, 69, 222, 291
Ross, Elizabeth, 109
Ross, Herbert, 109
Rossellini, Roberto, 222, 280, 285, 336
Rossen, Robert, 111
Rossignol, Iolande, 330
Rostamy, Abbasse Kia, 218
Rote Fahnen sieht man besser, 19
Roth, Philip, 221
Rothschild, Amalie, 289
Die Rothschilds, 284
Rotterdam Film Festival, 286

Rouch, Jean, 138, 146, 292
Rouchdi, Fatma, 133
Roussopoulos, Carole, 166
Rowlands, Gene, 429
Roy, Bimal, 217
Roy, Helene, 330
Rozema, Patricia, 63
RTA, 10, 122
Ruan Lingyu, 77
Rudolph, Agna, 286
Ruggles, Wesley, 422
The Ruins, 33
Ruiz, Laura, 394
Ruiz, Raúl, 74, 75, 353
Rule, Jane, 114
Rules of the Game, 339
Runaway, 293
Runge, Erika, 19, 290, 424
The Runner, 42
Russek, Jorge, 155
Russell, Jane, 247, 343, 361
Russell, Ken, 343
Russell, Rosalind, 13, 65, 191
Ruth, Roy del, 113
Ruttman, Walter, 337
Rydell, Mark, 197, 344
Rye, Stellan, 174
Rygard, Elisabeth, 116

SA Mann Brand, 283
Saab, Joceline, 18, 239
Saafar Sang Saffar Sang, 396
Saat El Tahrir Dakkat, 239
Sabnani, Nina, 15
Sabra, 221
Sabrina, 194
Sacher-Masoch, 266
Sachs, Hans, 193
Sade, Marquis de, 266
Safar, 42
Sahar, Abdel Hamid Gawda, 134
Said Effendi, 219
Sai'idy, Kobra, 218
Saikaku Ichidai Onna, 226, 269, 398

Saint-Saëns, Camille, 303
Saks, Mady, 287
Salazar, António de
    Oliviera, 320
Saleh, Al Tayyeb, 231
Saleh, Toufic, 18, 133,
    219, 309, 394
Salem, Nadia, 18, 134
Saleny, Emilia, 234
Sallesse, Sohrabe Shahid,
    218
Salomé, Lou Andreas, 68
Salote Zouhre, 396
Salt, Saliva, Sperm, Sweat,
    31
Salt of the Earth, 236, 237,
    371–3
El Salvador, 71
Salvation Army, 28
The Salvation Hunters, 387
Samba le grand, 7
Samo Hung, 231
Samper, Mady, 350
Samson and Delilah, 194,
    194
San Sebastian Film
    Festival, 381
Sancho, the Bailiff, 226
Sand Winds, 11
Sandakan 8, 398
Sandino, Augusto César,
    71
Sandrews, 391
Sandrich, Mark, 65, 196,
    276
The Sandwich Man, 398
Sang Hu, 340
La sangre manda, 263
Sanjinés, Jorge, 234
Sanou, Kollo, 7
Sans lendemain, 305
Sansho Dayu, 226, 269,
    398
Sansho the Bailiff, 269, 398
Sant händer inte här, 41
Santa, 263
Santiago, Cirio, 432
Santos, Carmen, 50, 234
Sapiain, Claudio, 75
Sarie Marie, 376
Sarne, Michael, 422
Sarraounia, 6, 204–5

Sarris, Andrew, 190, 229
Sartre, Jean-Paul, 253
Säsom i en spegel, 41
The Satin Shoe, 303
Saturday Night and Sunday
    Morning, 57
Saura, Carlos, 303, 381
Sauriol, Brigitte, 330
Saussure, Ferdinand de,
    322, 359–60, 388
Sautet, Claude, 165
Savage Streets, 431
Sawdust and Tinsel, 41
Sayles, John, 346
Al Sayyed Al Takadoumi,
    394
Sbaire, Harmel, 45
SBS, 1
Scandurra, Sofia, 223
The Scarecrow, 294
Scarface, 191
The Scarlet Empress, 387
The Scarlet Letter, 176
Scarlet Memory, 406
Scarlet Street, 154, 338
Scener ur ett äktenskap, 41
Scenes From a Marriage, 41
Schankkan, Ine, 287
Schepisi, Fred, 21
Schertzinger, Victor, 93
Schesinger, I. W., 376
Scheumann, 130
Schiess, Mario, 377
Schiffman, Suzanne, 166
Schiller, Greta, 242
Schillinger, Joseph, 60
Das Schlangenei, 41
Schlesinger, John, 33, 53,
    57
Schloendorff, Volker, 58,
    289, 404
Schlussakkord, 369
Schmitt, Evelyn, 130
Schoedsack, 47
Schoener Gigolo - armer
    Gigolo, 121
Scholtz, Jan, 377
Schorm, Evald, 107
Schuebel, Rolf, 19
Schwarz, Lillian, 14
Schwarz, Monique, 30,
    337

Schwarz-Bart, Simone,
    253
Schwarzenberger, Xaver,
    424
Schwegman, Wendy, 16
Schygulla, Hanna, 425
Scola, Ettore, 291
Scott, Cynthia, 330
Scott, Emmett, 44
Scott, Jill, 30
Scott, Ridley, 53, 356,
    429
Scott, Tony, 207, 244
Screaming, 406
Screen (journal), 228, 336
Screen Writers Guild,
    357
The Sea Gull, 387
The Searchers, 332
Searchers in the Desert, 18
Sears, Fred, 343
Seasons of a Navajo, 282
Seastrom, Victor see
    Sjöstrom, Victor
Seban, Paul, 128
Sebeok, Thomas, 360
Seberg, Jean, 22
Secrets of Women, 41
The Seedling, 33
Segreto, Alfonso, 50
Die Sehnsucht Veronika
    Voss, 145
Seif, Leila Abu, 134
Seif, Salah Abu, 133, 134,
    219
Seifullina, Lidia, 379
Seiter, William A., 191
Sejnane, 406
Sellers, Peter, 238
Seltz, Franz, 283
Selznick, David, 200,
    241, 245
Sem sombra de pecado, 97
Sen, Aparna, 217
Sen, Mrinal, 33, 217, 311
Senegal, 5, 7, 403
Sequence, 57
Serena, Suzana, 51
Serfontein, Hennie, 16
The Serpent's Egg, 41
Serrano, Marcela, 75
Serreau, Coline, 166

Seven and Five Group, 293
Seven Arts, 417
Seven Days (journal), 273
Seven women, 256
The Seven-Year Itch, 270
The Seventh Seal, 41
Severed Heads, 343
Sextette, 422
Seye Seyeti, 7
Seyrig, Delphine, 8, 166, 306
Shaas, Ghaleb, 308
Shadow of a Doubt, 428
Shaffer, Beverly, 330
Shahani, Kumar, 217, 311
Shahin, 231
Shajiabang, 340
Shakespeare, William, 52
Shame, 41, 423, 432
Shams El Dibaa', 406
Shanghai, 205
Shanghai Express, 121, 387
The Shanghai Gesture, 387
Shanghai Studios, 157, 433
Shanghai Yi Furen, 77
Shantaram, V., 216
Shaolin Sanshiliu Fang, 231
Sharman, Jim, 29
Shatranj ke Khilari, 33
Shaw, George Bernard, 52, 241
Shaw, Harold, 376
Shaw Brothers, 205, 397
Shchory, Edit, 222
She and He, 199, 226
She Defends Her Country, 378
The She-Devil, 35
She Done Him Wrong, 421
Shearer, Norma, 143, 266
Sheffield Film Co-op, 415
The Sheik, 368
Shen Nu, 77
Shen Xilin, 77
Shepard, David, 289
Sheridan, Ann, 191
Sherman, Lowell, 196, 421

Sherman, Vincent, 101, 193
Sherwood, Bill, 256
Shi Dongshan, 77
A Ship to India, 41
Shipman, Ernest, 364–5
Shipyard, 55
Shirley Thompson versus the Aliens, 29
Shizi Jietou, 77
Shochiku Studio, 398
Shockproof, 369
Short Film Fund, 294
Show Boat, 45
Shoyad Vaghty Dighar, 42
Shree 420, 278
Shuen, Shu, 206
Shuttle, Penelope, 410
Une si simple histoire, 406
Siamo donne, 285
Sid and Nancy, 344
Siddiki, Tayyeb, 272
Al Siddiq, Khaled, 231
Sidney, George, 193
Siegal, Lois, 330
Sienna, Pedro, 74
Sight and Sound, 59, 113, 227, 241
Sign of the Pagan, 332, 369
La signora di tutti, 304
La signora senza camelie, 17
Signoret, Simone, 166
Sigurjonsson, Johann, 211
Silberman, Marc, 388
The Silence, 41
The Silent Wife, 397
Silva, Jorge, 92, 92, 344, 350
Silvera, Charlotte, 166
Silverman, Kaja, 175, 375
Silverstein, Eliot, 401
Silvestre, Armando, 233
Simone, Nina, 111
Simparele, 373
Sims, Joan, 67
Sin, 35
Sinaia, 221
Singin' in the Rain, 276
Singsong Girl Peony, 77
Sinin El Jamr, 10
Sinke, Digna, 287

The Siren's Song, 35
Sistema Sandinista de Televisión, 71
Sisters, 116
Sistren, 66
Sita-Bella, Thérèse, 5
Sitney, P. Adams, 32
Sjöberg, Alf, 436
Sjöstom (Seastrom), Victor, 176, 211, 390
Det sjunde inseqlet, 41
Skammen, 41
Skandarani, Fatma, 406
Skepp till Indialand, 41
Sketch (newspaper), 241
Skladanowski brothers, 173
Sklan, Carole, 337
Skolimowski, Jerzy, 132, 317
O slavnosti a hostech, 107
Slingerbaum, Szamy, 38
Slnko v sieti, 107
Small, Edward, 121
The Small Back Room, 324
Smash Palace, 294
Smihi, Moumen, 271
Smile Orange, 65
Smiles of a Summer Night, 41
Smirnova, Maria, 379
Smith, Beaumont, 28
Smothers, Tommy, 116
Smultronstället, 41
Snow, Michael, 32, 333, 425, 426
Snow White, 337
Snowden, Alison, 15
So Close to Life, 41
Sobchak, Vivian, 356
Södergran, Edith, 296
Soffici, Mario, 20
SOGIC (Société générale des industries culturelles de Quebec), 330
Solanas, Fernando, 21
Solax film company, 185
Soldiers of the Cross, 28
Soleil Ô, 204, 205
Solicitor Fatma, 134
Somarlek, 41

Some Like It Hot, 102,
113, 270
Something Wild, 115
Sometime City, 220
Sommaren med Monika, 41
Sommarnattens leende, 41
Son of the Sheik, 368
Song in My Heart, 376
Song of Songs, 121
Song of the Canary, 289
The Song of the Tourist,
412
Song of the Track, 133
Sonneblom Films, 198
Sono Films, 20
Sons For The Return
Home, 255
Sos, Maria, 209
Soshun, 226
Soto, Helvio, 74
Soul, Veronica, 239
Le soulier de satin, 303
The Sound of Music, 229
Sounder, 45
Sourakh, 406
Sources d'inspiration, 85
Sources of Inspiration, 85
South African
Broadcasting
Corporation, 297
South Wind, 11
The Southerner, 339
Sow, Thierno Faty, 359
Spacek, Sissy, 116
Spare Rib (journal), 228,
273
The Sparrow, 134
The Spectator (journal), 36
The spell, 218
Spence, Louise, 332
Spencer, Charles Cozens,
250
Spencer, Walter Baldwin,
28
Spice, Evelyn, 55, 62, 329
The Spider's Cave, 77
Spielberg, Steven, 45, 116
Spils, May, 424
Spotted Eagle, Chris, 282
Sprague, Bronwen, 293
Spring, Sylivia, 63
Spring in a Small City, 77

Spring River Flows East,
77
Spring Silkworms, 77
The Squatter's Daughter,
28
The Squaw Man, 114
Stage Door, 196
Stage Fright, 121, 200
Stagnaro, Juan Bautista,
39
Stalin, Joseph, 107, 372,
378, 379
Stam, Robert, 332
A Star is Born, 105
START, 224
Starting Over, 291
Staudte, Wolfgang, 424
STCYQ (Syndicat des
techniciennes et
techniciens du cinéma
et de video de Quebec),
331
Steaming, 126
Stein, Gertrude, 193, 297
Steinhoff, Hans, 283
Steinmann, Danny, 431
Stella Dallas, 260, 272,
384, 426
Stelli, Jean, 165
Stern, Lesley, 227
Stern, Monika Funke, 146
Stevens, George, 64, 194,
197, 385
Stevenson, Jayne, 30
Stewart, James, 194
Stiehlke, Heinz,
Fuenfzehn, 130–1
Stiller, Mauritz, 170
The Sting, 194
Stockholm Film School,
8
Stoker, Bram, 243,
409–10
Stop Making Sense, 115,
344
Storck, Henri, 39
Storey, David, 53
Story of a Love Affair, 17
The Story of an Encounter,
11
The Story of the Country of
God, 406

The Story of the Kelly
Gang, 27
Story of Three Women, 76
Strachan, Carolyn, 1, 31,
138
Strange Interlude, 143
A Strange Love Affair, 287
The Stranger and the Fog,
42
Strasberg, Lee, 3, 95, 270
Straub, Jean-Marie, 207
Straw Dogs, 428
Straw Dolls, 272
Street Angel, 77
A Streetcar Named Desire,
241
Streisand, Barbra, 103
Strictly Dynamite, 237
Strindberg, August, 20,
200, 391
Stroeva, Vera, 379, 380
Stroheim, Erich von, 367
Struggle in Italy, 177
Studlar, Gaylyn, 119
Su Li, 340
Subah, 311
A Successful Man, 373
Sudden Fear, 101
Suddenly last Summer, 197
Sueur noire, 11
The Suffering Couple, 76
Sukowa, Barbara, 425
Summer Interlude, 41
Summer Skin, 402
Summer with Monika, 41
Summertime, 197
Sumurun, 284
Sun Yu, 77, 78
The Sunday Times, 323,
341
Sunrise, 367
Sunset Boulevard, 154, 313
Sunshine in a Net, 107
Superfly, 12
Surrealism, 137, 164, 206,
215, 260, 269, 277
Suspended, 225
Suzán, Margarita, 72, 265
Svensk Filmindustri, 391
Svenska Kvinnors Film
Forbund, 392
Swamp Water, 339

Swanson, Gloria, 115,
  313, 361, 367
Swartz, Charles, 347
Swedish Film Institute,
  391
Swimming to Cambodia, 115
Swing Shift, 115
Switzer, Phyllis, 63
Switzerland, 146
The Sword, 206, 392
Syberberg, 303, 375
Sydney, 337, 393
Sydney Film Festival, 159
Sydney Film-makers
  Co-operative, 1, 29,
  393
Sylvia Scarlett, 102, 105,
  196, 197
Symbol of Sacrifice, 376
Sympathy for the Devil,
  177
Szabo, István, 135, 209,
  210, 224
Szalai, Györgyi, 209
Szwarc, Jeannot, 149

Taalagh, 396
Taaw, 359
Tagebuch einer Yerlorenen,
  58
Taghvayie, Nasser, 218
Tait, Charles, 27
Taiwan Film Studio, 397
Take Me to Town, 369
Take One, 113
Taki no Shirato, 269
*Taking Tiger Mountain by
  Strategy*, 340
Talavera, Miriam, 104
Talero, María Elvira, 92
The Tales of Hoffmann,
  324
Talking Heads, 115
Tallents, Stephen, 55
Taller Popular de Video,
  71
Talmadge, Constance,
  409
Talmadge, Norma, 203
Tam, Patrick, 205, 206,
  392
Tamana, Dora, 16

Tames, Maria Eugenia,
  265
Tang Shan Da Xing, 231
Tango!, 20, 232
Tangos: Exile of Gardel, 21
Tangos: El exilio de gardel,
  21
Tanzania, 6, 8
Tao De-chen, 398
Tar, 272
Tarang, 311
Taraporevala, Sooni, 278
Target Tiran, 221
Al Tariq, 10
The Tarnished Angels, 369
Tarr, George, 293
Tarragy, Goly, 218
Tasaka, Tomotaka, 199
Tashlin, Frank, 14, 15,
  227, 343
Tass, Nadia, 30, 337
A Taste of Honey, 57
Tati, Jacques, 165
Tatoli, Elda, 223
Tatters, 286
Tavares, Joao, 319
Tavernier, Bertrand, 165
Taviani, Paolo, 222, 291
Taviani, Vittorio, 222,
  291
Tavora, Pilar, 381
Taxi Driver, 357
Tayar, Elyane, 164
Taylor, Clyde, 111
Taylor, Elizabeth, 111,
  194
Al Tayyeb, Atef, 133
Taza Son of Cochise, 369
Tcherike-Ye-Tara, 42
Tchissoukou,
  Jean-Michel, 7
Tecnicos Y Actores
  Cinematograficos
  Asociados (TACMA),
  233
Teheran International
  Film Festival, 218, 396
Tekwan, 198
Teleanálisis, 75
Telesm, 218
Televisa (Mexico), 155
Tellado, Corín, 353

Temple, Shirley, 407
Ten Bob in Winter, 44
The Ten Commandments,
  115
The Tender Enemy, 304
La Tendre ennemie, 304
'Tenko', 399
Tenney, James, 354
Ter Wille van Christine,
  377
Terms of Endearment, 426
Terra em transe, 343
Terror in the Crypt, 243
Terry, Phillip, 89
Tess of the Storm Country,
  314
*Das Testament des Dr
  Mabuse*, 189
*Le Testament du docteur
  Cordelier*, 339
*The Texas Chainsaw
  Massacre*, 206
*The Texas Chainsaw
  Massacre II*, 54
Thalbach, Katherina, 125,
  425
That Cold Day in the Park,
  12
Theremin, Leon, 60
There's Always Tomorrow,
  369
These Three, 245
They Built a Nation, 376
*They Died Wtih their Boots
  On*, 357
They Drive By Night, 248
They Were Sisters, 169
They Were Ten, 221
Thiarroye 44, 359
Thiele, William, 145, 194
Things Are Looking Up,
  241
*The Third Part of the
  Night*, 317
Thirst, 41
*The 36th Chamber of
  Shaolin*, 231
The Thirty-nine Steps, 200
This Can't Happen Here,
  41
This is Spinal Tap, 344
This Land is Mine, 339

Thomas, Dylan, 116
Thomas, Gerald, 67
Thomas, Ralph, 122, 123
Thompson, Lotus, 250
Thomsen, Christian Braad, 348
Thomson, Tom 426
Thorleifsdottir, Thorhildur, 212
Thorndike, Annelie, 130
Thornley, Jeni, 31, 393
Three Strange Loves, 41
Three Women, 12
The Threshold, 311
Throne of Blood, 226
Through a Glass Darkly, 41
Thulin, Ingrid, 392
Thy Neighbour's Wife, 97
Tiainen, Arja, 40
Tian Shan studios, 78
Tian Zhuangzhuang, 157
Tianyunshan Chuanqi, 434
Tien Yi, 77
Tiennu Sanhua, 76
Tiger Rose, 235–7
Tighe, Fergus, 220
Till glädje, 41
Tilley, Brian, 16
Tillman, Lynne, 72, 82, 83
Tire dié, 42, 43
Tiyabu Biru, 7
To Have and Have Not, 34, 191
To Joy, 41
To Live, 226
To Sir With Love, 343
Tobón de Romero, Fanny, 83
Todorov, Tzvetan, 143–4
Toivonen, Ester, 162
Tokyo Monogatari, 226
Tokyo Story, 225–6
Tolby, Abdelaziz, 11
Tolstoy, Lev, 20
Tommy, 343
Tomorrow, 377
Toni, 339
Tootsie, 102, 103
Top Hat, 276

Torre Ríos, Leopoldo, 402
Torrecilla, Rafael, 381
Torres, Camilo, 344
Torres, Fina, 413
Torres Rios, Leopoldo, 20
Torrini, Cinzia, 223
Törst, 41
Toscano, Carmen, 234, 264
Toscano, Salvador, 262, 264
Toss Me a Dime, 43
The Touch, 41
Tough of Evil, 121
A Touch of Zen, 392
Touchez pas au grisbi, 165
Touha, 107
Touki-Bouki, 7
Tourneur, Jacques, 159, 227, 313
Tourneur, Maurice, 314
Tours Festival, 5
Tout va bien, 177
Town and Country, 36
Towne, Robert, 346
Toys, 77
Traba, Marta, 91
Traces, 271
Tracy, Spencer, 105–6, 197
Tragoedie der Liebe, 121
The Traitress, 296
Trances, 271
Transes, 271
Trauberg, Leonid, 378, 380
Trautman, Tereza, 51, 235
Treczia Czesc Nocy, 317
Tree, Tanya, 330
Treilhou, Marie-Claude, 166
Tres tristes tigres, 74
Treut, Monika, 83, 243, 266
Triana, Gloria, 92, 350
Triana, Jorge Ali, 92
Trinidad, 65, 66
Trintignant, Nadine, 165
Trollflöjten, 41, 303

True Heart Susie, 176, 181
Truffaut, François, 22, 53, 113, 165, 190, 293
Trujillo, Marisol, 104, 105, 371
The Truth, 36
Tsaki, Ibrahim, 11
Tsang, Roy, 398
Tschoertner, Petra, 130
Tsimatisima, Blanche, 16
Tsui, Hark, 205, 206, 392
Tuchtenhagen, Gisela, 425
Tulio, Teuvo, 162
Turim, Maureen, 207
Turkiewicz, Sophia, 30
Turkish Delight, 286
Turks Fruit, 286
Turner, Ann, 30, 337
Turner, Lana, 198
Turner, Tina, 45
Turney, Catherine, 357
The Turning Point, 109
Turovskaia, Maia, 379
Tweedie, Merlyn, 293
Twentieth Century, 191
Twickenham Film Studios, 339
Twilight, 342
Two Cities Films, 99
Two or Three Things I know about Her, 176, 177, 312
Two Stage Sisters, 434
Two Thousand Women, 238
Twomey, Siobhan, 220
Tyler, Parker, 116
Tyndall, 151
Týrlová, Hermína, 108
Tyson, Cicely, 45
Tystnaden, 41

Ibu Film Group, 29
Udigrudi (Underground), 51
Ufa (Universum Film AG), 174, 175
Ufi (Ufa Film GmbH), 175
Ugetsu, 269
Ugetsu Monogatari, 269

Uher, Štefan, 107
Uhlan Winning the
    Auckland Cup, 293
Ukigumo, 226
The Ultimate Solution of
    Grace Quigley, 197
Umbartha, 311
Uncle Tom's Cabin, 332
Undercut (journal), 228
Underworld, 387
Unexpected Stranger, 335
Union Pacific, 194
United Artists, 266, 314
United States Congress,
    326
Unlawful Wedding, 377
An Unmarried Woman, 291
Unmoegliche Liebe, 296
The Untouchables, 116
Up to a Point, 104, 178,
    371
Upper Volta, 5, 6
Urs Al Zein, 231
Urs fil Jalil, 309
Utamaro and His Five
    Women, 269
Utamaro o Meguru no
    Onna, 269
Ute Indians, 282
Utlaginn, 211
Utu, 255, 294
Uys, Jamie, 376

Vadim, Roger, 23, 36,
    243, 292
The Vagabond, 278
Valdés, Oscar, 373
Valentin, Albert, 164
Valentino, Rudolph, 24,
    368
Vallodolid Film Festival,
    381
Vallejo, Gerardo, 21
Valparaiso, mi amor, 74
Vamp, 45
The Vampire Lovers,
    243-4
Les Vampires (Feuillade),
    277
Vampyr (Dreyer), 409
Vampyres (Larraz), 243,
    244

Vanina, 296
Vanity Fair (journal),
    158
The Vanquished, 17
Varga, Maribel, 265
Vargtimmen, 41
Vayre, Gabriel, 262
Vázquez, Angelina, 75,
    353
Vedder, Maria, 146
Védrès, Nicole, 165
Vega, Belkis, 105
Velasco, Maria, Elena,
    265
Velez, Lupe, 235-7, 343
Velká samota, 107
Ven, Monique van de,
    287
Venezuelan National Film
    Office, 413
Venice Film Festival, 125
Vent de sables, 11
Vent d'Est, 176, 177
La Vénus aveugle, 165
Vera Cruz studios, 50
Verberena, Cleo de, 50,
    234
Verbitskaia, Anastasiia,
    324
Verbong, Ben, 286
Verhage, Gerrard, 287
Verhoeven, Paul, 286
La Vérité, 36
Verity Films, 49
Verneuil, Henri, 292
Veronika Voss, 145
Die Verraeterin, 296
Verstappen, Wim, 286
Vertigo, 25, 200, 428
Vertov, Dziga, 176,
    256-7, 379, 380, 390
A Very Private Affair, 36
VGIK (Soviet state film
    institute), 380
Vibrations, 311
Vice Versa, 256
Vickers, Martha, 280
Victor/Victoria, 102, 103,
    113
Victorian Women's Film
    Unit, 337
Vidas secas, 81

Videonic, 71
Vidor, Charles, 113, 154,
    160, 191, 312, 362
Vidor, King, 45, 176,
    260, 272, 276, 368, 384,
    426
La Vie est à nous, 338,
    339
Vie privée, 36
Un viejo con alas enormes,
    43
Viel, Marguerite, 164
Vietnam, 291, 403
A View to Kill, 45
Vigil, 294
Vigilance Record, 327
Vijayantimala, 217
Vilasís, Mayra, 104
Village Theatres, 28
The Village Voice
    (journal), 229
Villiers, Dirk de, 376
Vinogradskaia, Katerina,
    379
I vinti, 17
Viola, Joe, 140
Violante, Marcela
    Fernández, 264
Violated, 432
Virgin Mary, 316
The Virgin Spring, 41
Viridiana, 264
Visages de femmes, 7-8
Visconti, Luchino, 69,
    222, 285
Viskningar och rop, 41
Visnews, 5
Vitti, Monica, 16-17
Viva, 401
Viva la República!, 412
Viva Zapata, 237
Vivre sa vie, 176
Vladimir et Rosa, 177
Vogue (journal), 36, 158,
    190
Voice (journal), 190
Le Voile bleu, 165
Voluspa Film, 227
Volver, 74
De Voortrekkers, 376
Vosseteho, 396
The Voyage, 42

La vraie nature de Bernadette, 232
La vuelta al nido, 20

Waalkes, Otto, 424
Waga Koi wa Moenu 269
Wagner, Jane, 204
Wagner, Ray, 12
Wagner, Richard, 275, 303
Wahba, Saad, 134
Wahba, Youssef, 134
Waiting Women, 41
Wajda, Andrzej, 201, 224–5, 317, 353
Walker, Alice, 45, 111
Wallace, Richard, 339
Wallerstein, Mauricio, 413
Wallner, Martha, 72
Walsh, Raoul, 227, 248, 357, 389
Waltari, Mika, 296
Wan brothers, 77
Wan Jen, 398
Wan Pipel, 65
Wang Hsiao-di, 398
Wang Ping, 78
Wang Qimin, 78
Wang Tong, 398
War, 412
Ward, Vincent, 294
Warhol, Andy, 269
Warner, Jack, 417
Warrenbrand, Jane, 429
The Warrior Husband, 196
Warum laeuft Herr R. Amok?, 145
Waschneck, Erich, 284
Washington, Booker T., 44
Washington, Fredi, 110
Washington Film Festival, 159
The Water Magician, 269
Waterloo road, 237
Way Down East, 176, 181
Wayne, John, 194, 332, 385
Le Wazzou polygame, 7
We Dance Around the World, 284

We Stand Another Day, 376
We the Women, 285
Weaver, Sigourney, 355, 356, 429
Webb, Robert, 343
Wechma, 271
Wechselmann, Mai, 391
A Wedding, 12
The Wedding of Zein, 231
Wedekind, Frank, 40
Weekend, 23, 177
Weekly Review, 293
Wegener, Paul, 337
Weibel, Peter, 140, 141
Weider, Ioana, 166
Weinberg, Paul, 16
Weinstein, Paula, 308
Weinstock, 151
Weir, Peter, 21, 29
Weisz, Frans, 286
Welch, Raquel, 361
We'll Have the Whole of Eternity for Sleeping, 205
Welles, Orson, 121, 154, 191, 310, 336, 343
Wellman, William, 58, 248, 326
Wend Kuni, 7
Wenders, Wim, 113, 254, 289, 424
Wendhausen, Fritz, 189
Wenk, Richard, 45
Werker, Alfred L., 14
Werther, 305
West Indies, ou les nègres marrons de la liberté, 204, 205
West Indies Story, 205
Westdeutscher Rundfunk (WDR), 19
Wet, Elmo de, 377
Wet, Pierre de, 376, 377
Wexler, Haskell, 230
Whale, James, 45
The Whales of August, 176
Whannel, Paddy, 106
Wharton, Edith, 248
Whatever Happened to Baby Jane?, 101, 112
What's Opera Doc?, 15
Wheeler, Anne, 63

White, Denise, 393
White, Pearl, 428
The White-Haired Girl, 340
White Nights, 109
The White Sister, 176
Whitehouse, A. H., 293
Whitey, 38
Whitlam, Gough, 430
Whitman, Walt, 60, 177
Whitmore, Lee, 430
The Who, 343
Who Framed Roger Rabbit?, 15
Who's That Girl, 358
Why Change Your Wife?, 115, 367
Why Does Mr. R. Run Amuck?, 145
Wibom, Anna-Lena, 392
The Wicked Lady, 169, 346
'Widows', 399
Wieck, Dorothea, 349
Wielopolska, Brita, 116
Wind and Woolly, 357–8
Wild Season, 335
Wild Strawberries, 41
Wilde Seison, 334, 335
Wilder, Billy, 102, 113, 121, 154, 159, 194, 270, 313, 363, 385
Wilder, Thornton, 60
Wilder, William, 346
Wilensky, Steve, 155
Wilkins, Madelon, 337
Williams, Brock, 169
Williams, Kenneth, 67
Williams, Raymond, 106
Williamson, Wendy, 67
Wilson, Barbara, 283
Wilson, Lindi, 16, 377
Wilson, Margery, 366
Wilson, Sandy, 63
The Wind, 85, 176
The Wind of the Aures, 10
Windsor, Barbara, 67
Winfrey, Oprah, 114
Winkler, Paul, 30
Winning a Continent, 376
Winsloe, Christa, 349, 400

Winter Light, 41
The Winter of the 14 July, 377
Die Winter van 14 Julie, 377
Winters, Shelley, 194
Wir tanzen um die Welt, 284
Witcombe, Eleanor, 21
With the Cuban Women, 104
Withers, Googie, 129
Witlin, Ray, 350
Witness for the Prosecution, 121
De witte van Sichen, 38
The Wizard of Oz, 276
Wo Niu Jo Lan, 397
Wollen, Peter, 161, 273, 389
Wolpert, Betty, 16
Woman From Havana, 412
A Woman in Shanghai, 77
The Woman in the Window, 154
A Woman is a Woman, 22, 176
Woman of the Year, 64, 197
The Woman on the beach, 339
A Woman Rebels, 65, 196
The Woman Suffers, 250
Woman, Villa, Car, Money, 7
A Woman's Face, 105
The Women (Cukor), 101, 105
The Women (Lallem), 11
Women Against Violence Against Women, 240
The Women are Trumps, 162
Women Basketball Player No.5, 434
Women in New York, 145
Women on the Verge of a Nervous Breakdown, 381
Women's Labor History Project, 152
Womenvision Film Festival, 337

Womenwaves Festival, 393
Wood, Robin, 206
Wood, Sam, 101
The Wooing and Wedding of a Coon, 45
Woolfe, Bruce, 156
Worth, Jan, 56, 372
Wreaths At the Foot of the Mountain, 434
Wright, Teresa, 24
Written on the Wind, 34, 93, 253, 369, 370, 370
Wrong Side of the Road, 2
Wu Tianming, 78, 157
Wu Yonggang, 77
Wu Zhaodi, 340
Wu Ziniu, 157
Wurtzel, Sol, 407
Wutai Jiemei, 433, 434
Wuthering Heights, 342
Wyatt Cattaneo Productions, 119
Wyler, William, 23, 93, 112, 194, 245, 336, 346
Wyman, Jane, 24

Xala, 7, 359
Xia Nu, 392
Xian studios, 78
Xiao Cheng Ji Chun, 77
Xiao Wanyi, 77
Xiaoxiang studios, 78
Xie Tieli, 340, 434
Xin Nuxing, 77
Xtro, 356

Ya Niu Chin Shen, 397
Yam Daabo, 7
Yan Bili, 434
Yan Shanshan, 76
Yanagimachi, Mitsuo, 226
Yang, Edward, 398
Yang Ya Jen Chia, 397
Yanruisheng, 76
Yeelen, 7, 85
Yehoshua, A. B., 37
Yellow Earth, 157
Yellow Submarine, 343
Yichang Fengbo, 434
Yield to the Night, 126

Yijiang Chunshui Xiang Dongliu, 77
Ying Yunwei, 77
Yorkshire Arts, 240
Yoshiwara, 304
Yoshizawa company, 225
You Are My Love, 376
You Were Never Lovelier, 191
You'll Never Get Rich, 191
Young, Linda, 109
Young and Innocent, 169
'Young Cinema' (Portugal), 97
Your Neighbours the Niggers, 7, 205
Yu Guang Qu, 77
Yu Li Hun, 77
Yu Yanfu, 340
Yuan Muzhi, 77
Yugoslavia, 131

Zafra, 90, 235
Al Zakira A Khasiba, 309
Zalionaia, Rina, 379
Zampa, Luigi, 69
Zanuck, Darryl F., 407
Zanussi, Krzysztof, 201
Zarchi, Meir, 431
Zarkhi, A. G., 378
Zauberman, Volande, 138
Zavattini, Cesare, 69, 222, 285
Zawgati, Mudir Am, 134
W Zawieszeniy, 225
ZDF, 6
Zecca, Ferdinand, 164, 185
Zeffirelli, Franco, 69
Zeft, 272
Zemeckis, Robert, 15
Zemlia, 373
Zemmouri, Mahmoud, 11
Zespoly Filmowe, 316, 354
Zhang Nuanxin, 78
Zhang Qi, 78
Zhang Shichuan, 76, 77
Zhang Yimou, 78, 157

Zheliabuzhski, Yuri, 373
Zhelyazkova, Binka,
131–2
Zheng Junli, 77
Zheng Zhengqiu, 76, 77
Zhigu Weihushan, 340
Zhuangzi Shi Qi, 76

Zhuangzi Tests His Wife,
76
Ziewer, Christian, 19
Zikra, Samir, 394
Zimbabwe, 5
Zinnemann, Fred, 13,
263, 276

Zlin studios, 108
Zobel, Josef, 66, 308
Zoetrope Studios, 95–6
Zowe, Leonie Yangba,
8
Zukor, Adolph, 114–15
Zulawski, Andrzej, 317

The Women's Companion to International Film is the first comprehensive feminist guide to cinema. Compiled and written by an authoritative panel of eighty contributors from many countries, it provides new information and a fresh perspective on the women – and significant men – who have contributed to world cinema, through directors and producers to gossip columnists and critics. It covers the history of filmmaking from Hollywood and the main-stream to the avant garde, from Hitchcock to Agnes Varda, and explains an impressive range of concepts and critical and technical terms – a pleasurable and provocative exploration for inquisitive cinemagoers worldwide.

Annette Kuhn, known internationally for her work on film theory and criticism, is the author of *Women's Pictures: Feminism and Cinema* (1982), *The Power of the Image* (1985) and *Cinema, Censorship and Sexuality 1909–1925* (1988); co-editor of *Feminism and Materialism* (1978) and *Ideology and Cultural Production* (1979) and editor of *Alien Zone: Cultural Theory and Contemporary Science Fiction Cinema* (1990). She teaches Film and TV Studies at the University of Glasgow. **Susannah Radstone**, editor of *Sweet Dreams: Sexuality, Gender and Popular Fiction* (1988), lectures in English, Film and Cultural Studies at Keele University.